Get the eBooks FREE!

(PDF, ePub, Kindle, and liveBook all included)

We believe that once you buy a book from us, you should be able to read it in any format we have available. To get electronic versions of this book at no additional cost to you, purchase and then register this book at the Manning website.

Go to https://www.manning.com/freebook and follow the instructions to complete your pBook registration.

That's it!
Thanks from Manning!

Dependency
Injection in .NET

MARK SEEMANN

MANNING

SHELTER ISLAND

For online information and ordering of this and other Manning books, please visit
www.manning.com. The publisher offers discounts on this book when ordered in quantity.
For more information, please contact

    Special Sales Department
    Manning Publications Co.
    20 Baldwin Road
    PO Box 261
    Shelter Island, NY 11964
    Email: orders@manning.com

Manning Publications Co.   Development editor: Cynthia Kane
20 Baldwin Road   Copyeditors: June Eding, Tiffany Taylor
PO Box 261   Proofreader: Katie Tennant
Shelter Island, NY 11964   Typesetter: Dennis Dalinnik
    Cover designer: Marija Tudor

ISBN: 9781935182504
Printed in the United States of America
13 14 15 16 – SP – 22 21 20 19 18

To Cecilie
I couldn't have done it without you

brief contents

contents

foreword

My first experience with Dependency Injection was almost 10 years ago. I was working at an ISV (independent software vendor) as an architect on an enterprise framework building LOB (line-of-business) applications. In those days, it seemed like all my friends in the industry were building similar frameworks. The framework supported various layers across *n*-tier applications addressing data access, business, and UI concerns. The product-supported business objects could be persisted across multiple databases and represented in multiple UIs; the challenge was finding a way to build the system to make it extensible and maintainable. We found our answer by wading into the waters of Dependency Injection. Using a DI approach, we clearly defined contracts for the layers, allowing us to more easily test the layers as well as to swap their implementations without breaking the code.

Mark talks quite a bit in this book about "poor man's DI" and this is exactly what we were doing. In those days, we didn't have DI containers at our disposal. We also didn't have the type of guidance you'll find in this book. As a result, we made a lot of mistakes—mistakes you won't have to make.

In the past four years, I've personally worked with hundreds of customers and I'm aware of thousands that have found success using the techniques described in this book.

It all starts with patterns.

DI containers are just tools. The tools are only useful if you're building systems that incorporate the patterns that the tools are addressing. They aren't the solution to every problem. Ideally, you need to first learn what Dependency Injection is, what kinds of problems it solves, and what the patterns are for using it. Then you can look at the various tools as aids in applying those patterns.

This book will help you with all of the above. The early chapters present an overview of the general problems that occur when software is tightly coupled. The book then discusses ways we can apply various techniques, both simple and advanced, to address those problems. Along the way, the book classifies various patterns and identifies when they are most appropriate for specific situations. In the second half, the book presents a comprehensive overview of the most common DI containers/frameworks in .NET and explains how to use them to apply different techniques.

With this book, you will benefit from the knowledge of someone who has many years of real-world experience in applying these techniques. This is a real treat; often, those who start using DI quickly find themselves lost in a sea of confusion. This book addresses any potential misunderstanding, starting with basic questions like, "Where should I put my IoC?" or "Should I expose my container?" Mark covers these questions and many more.

Throughout the book, Mark not only describes the techniques but really goes into depth explaining when you should—and, more importantly—*shouldn't* use them. When he describes a problem, he uses realistic examples to keep the big picture in focus.

If you are new to IoC, I believe you'll find *Dependency Injection in .NET* to be a great resource for learning. Even if you have extensive experience with IoC, you'll still benefit from the painstaking work Mark has done to classify various patterns and create a taxonomy for IoC. I also think that you will find his comparisons with other IoC containers beneficial.

Regardless of your level of experience, I wish you success with this book.

GLENN BLOCK
SENIOR PROGRAM MANAGER
MICROSOFT

preface

There's a peculiar phenomenon related to Microsoft called the *Microsoft Echo Chamber*. Microsoft is a huge organization and the surrounding ecosystem of Microsoft Certified Partners multiplies that size by orders of magnitude. If you're sufficiently embedded in this ecosystem, it can be hard to see past its boundaries. Whenever you look for a solution to a problem with a Microsoft product or technology, you're likely to find an answer that involves throwing even more Microsoft products at it. No matter what you yell within the echo chamber, the answer is *Microsoft!*

When Microsoft hired me in 2003, I was already firmly embedded in the echo chamber, having worked for Microsoft Certified Partners for years—and I loved it! They soon shipped me off to an internal tech conference in New Orleans to learn about the latest and greatest Microsoft technology.

Today, I can't recall any of the Microsoft product sessions I attended—but I do remember the last day. On that day, having failed to experience any sessions that could satisfy my hunger for cool tech, I was mostly looking forward to flying home to Denmark. My top priority was to find a place to sit so I could attend to my email, so I chose a session that seemed marginally relevant for me and fired up my laptop.

The session was loosely structured and featured several presenters. One was a bearded guy named Martin Fowler, who talked about Test-Driven Development (TDD) and dynamic mocks. I had never heard of him and I didn't listen very closely, but, nonetheless, something must have stuck in my mind.

Soon after returning to Denmark, I was tasked with rewriting a big ETL (extract, transform, load) system from scratch, and I decided to give TDD a try (it turned out to be a *very* good decision). The use of dynamic mocks followed naturally, but also introduced a need to manage dependencies. I found that to be a very difficult but very captivating problem, and I couldn't stop thinking about it.

What started as a side effect of my interest in TDD became a passion in itself. I did a lot of research, read lots of blog posts about the matter, wrote quite a few blogs myself, experimented with code, and discussed the topic with anyone who cared to listen. Increasingly, I had to look outside the Microsoft Echo Chamber for inspiration and guidance. Along the way, people associated me with the ALT.NET movement even though I was never very active in it.

I made all the mistakes it was possible to make, but I was gradually able to develop a coherent understanding of Dependency Injection (DI).

When Manning approached me with the idea for a book about Dependency Injection in .NET my first reaction was, *Is this even necessary?* I felt that all the concepts you need to understand DI were already described in numerous blog posts. Was there anything to add? Honestly, I thought DI in .NET was a topic that had been done to death already.

Upon reflection, however, it dawned on me that while the *knowledge* is definitely out there, it's *very* scattered and uses a lot of conflicting terminology. Before this book, there were no titles about DI that attempted to present a coherent description of it. After thinking about it further, I realized that Manning was offering me a tremendous challenge and a great opportunity to collect and systematize all that I knew about DI.

The result is this book. It uses .NET and C# to introduce and describe a comprehensive terminology and guidance for DI, but I hope that the value of the book will reach well beyond the platform. I think that the pattern language articulated here is universal. Whether you are a .NET developer or use another object-oriented platform, I hope that this book will help you be a better software engineer.

acknowledgments

Gratitude may seem like a cliché, but this is only because it's such a fundamental part of human nature. While I was writing the book, many people gave me good reasons to be grateful, and I would like to thank them all.

First of all, writing a book in my spare time has given me a new understanding of just how taxing such a project is on marriage and family life. My wife Cecilie stayed with me and actively supported me during the whole process. Most importantly, she understood just how important this project was to me. We are still together and I look forward to being able to spend more time with her and our kids Linea and Jarl (who miss me, although I've been right here all the time).

Both my parents and in-laws have also been a huge help in keeping the family running during those times when I needed to direct my efforts towards the book. I couldn't have done it without them.

On a more professional level, I wish to thank Manning for giving me this opportunity. Karen Tegtmeyer originally "discovered" me and helped me establish a relationship with Manning. Michael Stephens initiated the project and believed in me when things looked bleak. There were times when it looked like I'd never be able to finish the book by myself, but Michael took a chance with me, and I'm immensely grateful that I was allowed to complete the book as the consistent work of a single person. Cynthia Kane served as my development editor and kept a keen eye on the quality of the text. She helped me identify weak spots in the manuscript and provided extensive constructive criticism. Despite all the frustration along the way, I'm particularly grateful that she convinced me to rework chapters 1 through 3. *Kill your darlings,* as the saying goes. I'm much happier with the final result, and I have Cynthia to thank for that.

Although writing the book was an unpaid side project, I never had any doubt that it would impact my work performance. When I started the project, my manager at the time, Peter Haastrup, was very supportive. I want to thank both him and our CEO, Niels Flensted-Jensen, for providing an inspiring and supportive work environment. Unfortunately, the company went out of business, but my new employer, Jørn Floor Andersen, has been exceptionally patient with me.

Karsten Strøbæk and Brian Rasmussen read through numerous early drafts and provided much helpful feedback. Karsten also served as the technical proofreader during production.

The following reviewers read the manuscript at various stages of development and I am grateful for their comments and insight: Christian Siegers, Amos Bannister, Rama Krishna Vavilala, Doug Ferguson, Darren Neimke, Chuck Durfee, Paul Grebenc, Lester Lobo, Jonas Bandi, Braj Panda, Alan Ruth, Timothy Binkley-Jones, Andrew Siemer, Javier Lozano, David Barkol, and Patrick Steger.

Many of the participants in the Manning Early Access Program (MEAP) also provided feedback and asked difficult questions that exposed the weak parts of the text.

I was so fortunate that the existing .NET DI CONTAINER community received the book project with a very positive attitude. Several of the specific DI CONTAINERS' creators offered to review the chapters on "their" container. Krzysztof Koźmic reviewed the Castle Windsor chapter, Stephen Bohlen the Spring.NET chapter, Nicholas Blumhardt the Autofac chapter, Chris Tavares the Unity chapter, and Glenn Block looked over the MEF chapter while Jeremy Miller answered my stupid questions via Twitter and the StructureMap forum. I'm grateful for their participation, for it provided confirmation that my way of presenting their work could be aligned with their own. I would also like to thank Glenn Block for contributing the foreword.

Mogens Heller Grabe courteously allowed me to use his picture of a hairdryer wired directly into a wall outlet, and Patrick Smacchia provided me with a copy of *NDepend* and reviewed the related section.

In many ways, Martin Gildenpfennig sowed more seeds for this book than he may realize. Even before I was (lightly) exposed to Martin Fowler's presentation of TDD back in 2003, Martin Gildenpfennig had already introduced me to the concept of unit testing, although we never got around using it at that time. Much later, I was stuck with the false conviction that SERVICE LOCATOR was a blessing, and, with a few simple sentences, he made me realize that there's a better alternative.

My former colleague, Mikkel Christensen, was a pleasure to work with while I wrote great portions of the book. We had many good discussions about API design and patterns, and I could bounce even my craziest ideas off of him and always get an open and qualified discussion out of it.

Finally, I wish to thank Thomas Jaskula for all the support and inspiration along the way. We've never had the pleasure of meeting each other, but Thomas has time and again exhibited an almost overwhelming delight with my work. He may not realize it, but there were times when this was the only thing that kept me going.

about this book

This is a book about Dependency Injection first and foremost. It's also a book about .NET, but that's much less important. C# is used for code examples, but much of the discussion in this book can be easily applied to other languages and platforms. In fact, I learned a lot of the underlying principles and patterns from reading books where Java or C++ was used in examples.

Dependency Injection (DI) is a set of related patterns and principles. It's a way to think about and design code more than it's a specific technology. The ultimate purpose of using DI is to create maintainable software within the object-oriented paradigm.

The concepts used throughout this book all relate to object-oriented programming. The problem that DI addresses (code maintainability) is universal, but the proposed solution is given within the scope of object-oriented programming in statically typed languages: C#, Java, Visual Basic .NET, C++, and so on. You can't apply DI to procedural programming, and it may not be the best solution in functional or dynamic languages.

DI in isolation is just a small thing, but it's closely interconnected with a large complex of principles and patterns for object-oriented software design. Whereas the book focuses consistently on DI from start to finish, it also discusses many of these other topics in the light of the specific perspective that DI can give. The goal of the book is more than just teaching you about DI specifics: it's to make you a better object-oriented programmer.

Who should read this book?

It would be tempting to state that this is a book for all .NET developers. However, the .NET community today is vast and spans developers working with web applications, desktop applications, smartphones, RIA, integration, office automation, content management systems, and even games. Although .NET is object-oriented, not all of those developers write object-oriented code.

This is a book about object-oriented programming, so at minimum readers should be interested in object orientation and understand what an interface is. A few years of professional experience and knowledge of design patterns or SOLID will certainly be a benefit as well. In fact, I don't expect beginners to get much out of the book; it's mostly targeted towards experienced developers and software architects.

The examples are all written in C#, so readers working with other .NET languages must be able to read and understand C#. Readers familiar with non-.NET object-oriented languages such as Java and C++ may also find the book valuable, because the .NET platform-specific content is relatively light. Personally, I read a lot of pattern books with examples in Java and still get a lot out of them, so I hope the converse is true as well.

Roadmap

The contents of this book are divided into four parts. Ideally, I'd like you to first read it from cover to cover and then subsequently use it as a reference, but I understand if you have other priorities. For that reason, a majority of the chapters are written so that you can dive right in and start reading from that point.

The first part is the major exception. It contains a general introduction to DI and is probably best read sequentially. The second part is a catalog of patterns and the like, whereas the third part is an examination of DI from three different angles. The fourth and largest part of the book is a big catalog of six DI CONTAINER libraries.

There are a lot of interconnected concepts and because I introduce them the first time it feels natural, this means that I often mention concepts before I've formally introduced them. To distinguish these universal concepts from more local terms, I consistently use SMALL CAPS to make them stand out. All these terms are briefly defined in the glossary, which also contains references to a more extensive description.

- Part 1 is a general introduction to DI. If you don't know what DI is, this is the place to start; but even if you do, you may want to familiarize yourself with the contents of part 1, as it establishes a lot of the context and terminology used in the rest of the book. Chapter 1 discusses the purpose and benefits of DI and provides a general outline. Chapter 2 contains a big and rather comprehensive example, and chapter 3 explains how DI CONTAINER libraries fit into the overall picture. Compared to the other parts, part 1 has a much more linear progression of its content. You'll need to read each chapter from the beginning to gain the most from it.

- Part 2 is a catalog of patterns, anti-patterns, and refactorings. This is where you'll find prescriptive guidance on how to implement DI, and the dangers to look out for. Chapter 4 is a catalog of DI design patterns, and, conversely, chapter 5 is a catalog of anti-patterns. Chapter 6 contains generalized solutions to commonly occurring issues. As a catalog, each chapter contains a set of loosely related sections that are designed to be read in isolation as well as in sequence.

- Part 3 examines DI from three different angles: OBJECT COMPOSITION, LIFETIME MANAGEMENT, and INTERCEPTION. In chapter 7, I discuss how to implement DI on top of existing application frameworks such as WCF, ASP.NET MVC, WPF, and others. In many ways, you can use chapter 7 as a catalog of how to implement DI on a set of frameworks. Chapter 8 describes how to manage dependency lifetimes to avoid resources leaks. Whereas the structure is a little less stringent than previous chapters, a large part of the chapter can be used as a catalog of well-known lifetime styles. Chapter 9 finally describes how to compose applications with CROSS-CUTTING CONCERNS. This is where we harvest the benefits of all the work that came before, so, in many ways, I consider this to be the climax of the book.

- Part 4 is a catalog of DI CONTAINER libraries. Six chapters each cover a specific container in a fair amount of detail: Castle Windsor, StructureMap, Spring.NET, Autofac, Unity, and MEF. Each chapter covers its container in a rather condensed form to save space, so you may want to read about only the two or three containers that interest you the most. In many ways, I regard part 4 as a very big set of appendixes.

To keep the discussion of the DI principles and patterns free of any specific container APIs, most of the book, with the exception of part 4, is written without referencing a particular container. This is also why the containers appear with such force in part 4. It's my hope that by keeping the discussion general, the book will be useful for a longer period of time.

You can also take the concepts from parts 1 through 3 and apply them to container libraries not covered in part 4. There are good containers available that, unfortunately, I couldn't cover, but even for users of these libraries, I hope that this book has a lot to offer.

Code conventions and downloads

There are many code examples in this book. Most of it is C#, but there's also a bit of XML here and there. Source code in listings and text is in a fixed-width font to separate it from ordinary text.

All the source code for the book is written in C# and Visual Studio 2010. The ASP.NET MVC applications are written against ASP.NET MVC 3.

Only a few of the techniques described in this book hinge on modern language features. I started writing loosely coupled code in .NET 1.1 and I could have written most of the book's code examples on that platform without having to change my conclusions. As it were, I wanted to strike a reasonable balance between conservative and modern coding styles. When I write code professionally I use the modern language features to a much greater degree, but here the most advanced features are generics and LINQ. The last thing I want is for you to get the idea that DI can only be applied with ultra-modern languages.

Writing code examples for a book presents its own set of challenges. Compared to a modern computer monitor, a book only allows for very short lines of code. It was very tempting to write code in a terse style with short but cryptic names for methods and variables. Such code is already difficult to understand as real code when you still have an IDE and a debugger nearby, but it becomes really difficult to follow in a book. I found it very important to keep names as readable as possible. To make it all fit, I've often had to resort to some unorthodox line breaks. All the code compiles, but sometimes the formatting looks a bit funny.

The code also makes extensive use of the var keyword. In my professional code I use this almost exclusively, but for written text I often find it helpful when paired with explicit declarations because the IDE isn't around to help. Still, to save space, I use var wherever I judge that an explicit declaration is unnecessary.

The word *class* is often used as a synonym for a *type*. In .NET, classes, structs, interfaces, enums, and so on are all *types*, but because the word *type* is also a word with a lot of overloaded meaning in ordinary language, it would often make the text less clear if used.

Most of the code in this book relates to an overarching example running through the book: an online store complete with supporting internal management applications. This is about the least exciting example you can expect to see in any software text, but I chose it for a few reasons:

- It's a well-known problem domain for most readers. Although it may seem boring, I think this is an advantage because it doesn't steal focus from DI.
- I also have to admit that I couldn't really think of any other domain that was rich enough to support all the different scenarios I had in mind.

I wrote a lot of code to support the code examples, and most of that code is not even in the book. In fact, I wrote almost all of it using Test-Driven Development (TDD), but as this isn't a TDD book, I generally don't show the unit tests in the book.

The source code for all examples in this book is available from Manning's website: http://manning.com/DependencyInjectionin.NET. The ReadMe.txt in the root of the download contains instructions for compiling and running the code.

Author Online

The purchase of *Dependency Injection in .NET* includes free access to a private web forum run by Manning Publications, where you can make comments about the book, ask technical questions, and receive help from the author and from other users. To access the forum and subscribe to it, point your web browser to http://manning.com/Dependency-Injectionin.NET. This page provides information on how to get on the forum once you're registered, what kind of help is available, and the rules of conduct on the forum.

Manning's commitment to our readers is to provide a venue where a meaningful dialogue between individual readers and between readers and the author can take place. It isn't a commitment to any specific amount of participation on the part of the author, whose contribution to the forum remains voluntary (and unpaid). We suggest you try asking the author some challenging questions lest his interest stray! The Author Online forum and the archives of previous discussions will be accessible from the publisher's website as long as the book is in print.

About the author

Mark Seemann is a programmer, software architect, and speaker living in Copenhagen, Denmark. He has been working with software since 1995 and TDD since 2003, including six years with Microsoft as a consultant, developer, and architect. Mark is currently professionally engaged with software development, and is working out of Copenhagen. He enjoys reading, painting, playing the guitar, good wine, and gourmet food.

about the cover illustration

On the cover of *Dependency Injection in .NET* is "A woman from Vodnjan," a small town in the interior of the peninsula of Istria in the Adriatic Sea, off Croatia. The illustration is taken from a reproduction of an album of Croatian traditional costumes from the mid-nineteenth century by Nikola Arsenovic, published by the Ethnographic Museum in Split, Croatia, in 2003. The illustrations were obtained from a helpful librarian at the Ethnographic Museum in Split, itself situated in the Roman core of the medieval center of the town: the ruins of Emperor Diocletian's retirement palace from around AD 304. The book includes finely colored illustrations of figures from different regions of Croatia, accompanied by descriptions of the costumes and of everyday life.

Vodnjan is a culturally and historically significant town, situated on a hilltop with a beautiful view of the Adriatic and known for its many churches and treasures of sacral art. The woman on the cover wears a long black linen skirt and a short black jacket over a white linen shirt. The jacket is trimmed with blue embroidery and a blue linen apron completes the costume. The woman is also wearing a large-brimmed black hat, a flowered scarf, and big hoop earrings. Her elegant costume indicates that she is an inhabitant of the town, rather than a village. Folk costumes in the surrounding countryside are more colorful, made of wool, and decorated with rich embroidery.

Dress codes and lifestyles have changed over the last 200 years, and the diversity by region, so rich at the time, has faded away. It is now hard to tell apart the inhabitants of different continents, let alone of different hamlets or towns separated by only a few miles. Perhaps we have traded cultural diversity for a more varied personal life—certainly for a more varied and fast-paced technological life.

Manning celebrates the inventiveness and initiative of the computer business with book covers based on the rich diversity of regional life of two centuries ago, brought back to life by illustrations from old books and collections like this one.

Part 1

Putting Dependency Injection on the map

Dependency Injection (DI) is one of the most misunderstood concepts of object-oriented programming. The confusion is abundant and spans terminology, purpose, and mechanics. Should it be called *Dependency Injection, Inversion of Control,* or even *Third-Party Connect?* Is the purpose of DI only to support unit testing or is there a broader purpose? Is DI the same as Service Location? Is a DI CONTAINER required?

There are plenty of blog posts, magazine articles, conference presentations, and so on that discuss DI, but, unfortunately, many of them use conflicting terminology or give bad advice. This is true across the board, and even big and influential actors like Microsoft add to the confusion.

It doesn't have to be this way. In this book I present and use a consistent terminology that I hope others will adopt. For the most part, I've adopted and clarified existing terminology defined by others, but occasionally I add a bit of terminology where none existed previously. This has helped me tremendously in evolving a specification of the scope or boundaries of DI.

One of the underlying reasons behind all the inconsistency and bad advice is that the boundaries of DI are quite blurry. Where does DI end and other object-oriented concepts begin? I think that it's impossible to draw a distinct line between DI and other aspects of writing good object-oriented code. To talk about DI we have to draw in other concepts such as SOLID and Clean Code. I don't feel that I can credibly write about DI without also touching on some of these other topics.

The first part of the book helps you understand the place of DI in relation to other facets of software engineering—putting it on the map, so to speak.

The first chapter gives you a quick tour of DI, covering its purpose, principles, and benefits, as well as providing an outline of the scope for the rest of the book. If you want to learn what DI is, and why you should be interested in it, this is the place to start. The chapter assumes you have no prior knowledge of DI, but even if you already know about it you may still want to read it—it may turn out to be something other than what you expected.

Chapter 1 is focused on the big picture and doesn't go into a lot of details. Chapter 2, on the other hand, is completely reserved for a big example. This example is intended to give you a much more concrete feel for DI. It's divided into two parts and almost shaped like a narrative. To contrast DI with a more "traditional" style of programming, the chapter first showcases a typical, tightly coupled implementation of a sample application, and then subsequently re-implements it with DI.

The third and final chapter of part 1 introduces the concept of a DI CONTAINER and explains how it fits into the overall picture of DI. I discuss DI in general terms and, although I provide code examples that demonstrate how a typical DI CONTAINER works, the purpose of the chapter isn't to explain specific API details. The main point of chapter 3 is to show that a DI CONTAINER is a (very helpful) optional tool. It's entirely possible to utilize DI without using a DI CONTAINER, so parts 2 and 3 more or less ignore DI CONTAINERS and instead discuss DI in a container-agnostic way. Then, in part 4, we return to DI CONTAINERS to dissect six specific containers.

Part 1 establishes the context for the rest of the book. It's aimed at readers who don't have any prior knowledge of DI, but experienced DI practitioners may also benefit from skimming the chapters to get a feeling for the terminology used throughout the book. By the end of part 1, you should have a firm grasp of the vocabulary and overall concepts, even if some of the concrete details are still a little fuzzy. That's okay—the book becomes more concrete as you read on, so parts 2, 3, and 4 should answer the questions you're likely to have after reading part 1.

A Dependency Injection tasting menu

Menu

- Misconceptions about Dependency Injection
- Purpose of Dependency Injection
- Benefits of Dependency Injection
- When to apply Dependency Injection

You may have heard that making a *sauce béarnaise* is difficult. Even many people who cook regularly have never attempted to make one. This is a shame, because the sauce is delicious (it's traditionally paired with steak, but it's also an excellent accompaniment with white asparagus, poached eggs, and other dishes). Some resort to substitutes like ready-made sauces or instant mixes, but these aren't nearly as satisfying as the real thing.

> **DEFINITION**   A sauce béarnaise is an emulsified sauce made from egg yolk and butter that's flavored with tarragon, chervil, shallots, and vinegar. It contains no water.

The biggest challenge to making a sauce béarnaise is that preparation can fail—the sauce may curdle or separate, and if that happens, you can't resurrect it. It takes about 45 minutes to prepare, so a failed attempt means that you'll have no time for a second try.

On the other hand, any chef can prepare a sauce béarnaise. It's part of their training and, as they will tell you, it's not difficult. You don't have to be a professional cook to make it. Anyone learning to make it will fail at least once, but once you get the hang of it, you'll succeed every time.

I think *Dependency Injection (DI)* is like sauce béarnaise. It's assumed to be difficult and so few employ it. If you try to use it and fail, it's likely there won't be time for a second attempt.

> **DEFINITION**   *Dependency Injection* is a set of software design principles and patterns that enable us to develop loosely coupled code.

Despite the Fear, Uncertainty, and Doubt (FUD) surrounding DI, it's as easy to learn as making a sauce béarnaise. You may make mistakes while you learn, but once you've mastered the technique, you'll never again fail to apply it successfully.

The software development Q&A website Stack Overflow features an answer to the question *How to explain Dependency Injection to a 5-year old.* The most highly rated answer, provided by John Munsch,[1] provides a surprisingly accurate analogy targeted at the (imaginary) five-year-old inquisitor:

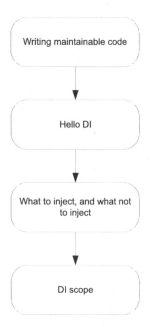

Writing maintainable code

Hello DI

What to inject, and what not to inject

DI scope

> *When you go and get things out of the refrigerator for yourself, you can cause problems. You might leave the door open, you might get something Mommy or Daddy doesn't want you to have. You might even be looking for something we don't even have or which has expired.*
>
> *What you should be doing is stating a need, "I need something to drink with lunch," and then we will make sure you have something when you sit down to eat.*

What this means in terms of object-oriented software development is this: collaborating classes (the five-year-olds) should rely on the infrastructure (the parents) to provide the necessary services.

As figure 1.1 shows, this chapter is fairly linear in structure. First, I introduce DI, including its purpose and benefits. Although I include examples, overall, this chapter has less code than any other chapter in the book.

Before I introduce DI, I'll discuss the basic purpose of DI: maintainability. This is important because it's easy to misunderstand DI if you aren't properly prepared. Next, after an example (Hello DI), I'll discuss benefits and scope,

Figure 1.1 The structure of the chapter is fairly linear. You should read the first section before the next, and so on. This may seem obvious, but some of the later chapters in the book are less linear in nature.

---

[1] John Munsch et al., "How to explain Dependency Injection to a 5-year old," 2009, http://stackoverflow.com/questions/ 1638919/how-to-explain-dependency-injection-to-a-5-year-old

essentially laying out a road map for the book. When you're done with this chapter, you should be prepared for the more advanced concepts in the rest of the book.

To most developers, DI may seem like a rather backward way of creating source code, and, like sauce béarnaise, there's much FUD involved. To learn about DI, you must first understand its purpose.

1.1 *Writing maintainable code*

What purpose does DI serve? DI isn't a goal in itself; rather, it's a means to an end. Ultimately, the purpose of most programming techniques is to deliver working software as efficiently as possible. One aspect of that is to write maintainable code.

Unless you write prototypes or applications that never make it past release 1, you'll soon find yourself maintaining and extending existing code bases. To be able to work effectively with such a code base, it must be as maintainable as possible.

One of many ways to make code maintainable is through *loose coupling*. As far back as 1995, when the Gang of Four wrote *Design Patterns*,[2] this was already common knowledge:

> *Program to an interface, not an implementation.*

This important piece of advice isn't the conclusion, but, rather, the premise, of *Design Patterns*; to wit: it appears on page 18. Loose coupling makes code extensible, and extensibility makes it maintainable.

DI is nothing more than a technique that enables loose coupling. However, there are many misconceptions about DI, and sometimes they get in the way of proper understanding. Before you can learn, you must unlearn what (you think) you already know.

1.1.1 *Unlearning DI*

Like a Hollywood martial arts cliché, you must unlearn before you can learn. There are many misconceptions about DI, and if you carry those around, you'll misinterpret what you read in this book. You must clear your mind to understand DI.

There are at least four common myths about DI:

- DI is only relevant for late binding.
- DI is only relevant for unit testing.
- DI is a sort of Abstract Factory on steroids.
- DI requires a DI CONTAINER.

Although none of these myths are true, they're prevalent nonetheless. We need to dispel them before we can start to learn about DI.

---

[2] Erich Gamma et al., *Design Patterns: Elements of Reusable Object-Oriented Software* (New York, Addison-Wesley, 1994), 18.

Late binding

Figure 1.2   Late binding is enabled by DI, but to assume it's only applicable in late binding scenarios is to adopt a narrow view of a much broader vista.

LATE BINDING

In this context, *late binding* refers to the ability to replace parts of an application without recompiling the code. An application that enables third-party add-ins (such as Visual Studio) is one example.

Another example is standard software that supports different runtime environments. You may have an application that can run on more than one database engine: for example, one that supports both Oracle and SQL Server. To support this feature, the rest of the application can talk to the database through an interface. The code base can provide different implementations of this interface to provide access to Oracle and SQL Server, respectively. A configuration option can be used to control which implementation should be used for a given installation.

It's a common misconception that DI is only relevant for this sort of scenario. That's understandable, because DI *does* enable this scenario, but the fallacy is to think that the relationship is symmetric. Just because DI enables late binding doesn't mean it's only relevant in late binding scenarios. As figure 1.2 illustrates, late binding is only one of the many aspects of DI.

If you thought DI was only relevant for late binding scenarios, this is something you need to unlearn. DI does much more than enable late binding.

UNIT TESTING

Some people think that DI is only relevant to support unit testing. This isn't true, either—although DI is certainly an important part of supporting unit testing.

To tell you the truth, my original introduction to DI came from struggling with certain aspects of Test-Driven Development (TDD). During that time I discovered DI and learned that other people had used it to support some of the same scenarios I was addressing.

Even if you don't write unit tests (if you don't, you should start now), DI is still relevant because of all the other benefits it offers. Claiming that DI is only relevant to support unit testing is like claiming that it's only relevant for supporting late binding. Figure 1.3 shows that although this is a different view, it's a view as narrow as figure 1.2. In this book, I'll do my best to show you the whole picture.

If you thought DI was only relevant for unit testing, unlearn this assumption. DI does much more than enable unit testing.

Late binding   Unit testing

Figure 1.3   Although the assumption that unit testing is the sole purpose of DI is a different view than late binding, it's also a narrow view of a much broader vista.

AN ABSTRACT FACTORY ON STEROIDS

Perhaps the most dangerous fallacy is that DI involves some sort of general-purpose Abstract Factory[3] that we can use to create instances of the DEPENDENCIES that we need.

In the introduction to this chapter, I wrote that "collaborating classes…should rely on the infrastructure…to provide the necessary services."

What were your initial thoughts about this sentence? Did you think about the *infrastructure* as some sort of service you could query to get the DEPENDENCIES you need? If so, you aren't alone. Many developers and architects think about DI as a service that can be used to locate other services; this is called a SERVICE LOCATOR, but it's the exact opposite of DI.

If you thought of DI as a SERVICE LOCATOR—that is, a general-purpose Factory—this is something you need to unlearn. DI is the opposite of a SERVICE LOCATOR; it's a way to structure code so that we never have to imperatively ask for DEPENDENCIES. Rather, we *force* consumers to supply them.

DI CONTAINERS

Closely associated with the previous misconception is the notion that DI *requires* a DI CONTAINER. If you held the previous, mistaken belief that DI involves a SERVICE LOCATOR, then it's easy to conclude that a DI CONTAINER can take on the responsibility of the SERVICE LOCATOR. This might be the case, but it's not at all how we should use a DI CONTAINER.

A DI CONTAINER is an optional library that can make it easier for us to compose components when we wire up an application, but it's in no way required. When we compose applications without a DI CONTAINER we call it POOR MAN'S DI; it takes a little more work, but other than that we don't have to compromise on any DI principles.

If you thought that DI *requires* a DI CONTAINER, this is another notion you need to unlearn. DI is a set of principles and patterns, and a DI CONTAINER is a useful, but *optional* tool.

You may think that, although I've exposed four myths about DI, I have yet to make a compelling case against any of them. That's true. In a sense, this whole book is one big argument against these common misconceptions.

In my experience, unlearning is vital because people tend to try to retrofit what I tell them about DI and align it with what they think they already know. When this happens, it takes a lot of time before it finally dawns on them that some of their most basic

---

[3] Ibid., 87.

premises are wrong. I want to spare you that experience. So, if you can, try to read this book as though you know nothing about DI.

Let's assume that you don't know anything about DI or its purpose and begin by reviewing what DI does.

1.1.2   *Understanding the purpose of DI*

DI isn't an end-goal—it's a means to an end. DI enables loose coupling, and loose coupling makes code more maintainable. That's quite a claim, and although I could refer you to well-established authorities like the Gang of Four for details, I find it only fair to explain why this is true.

Software development is still a rather new profession, so in many ways we're still figuring out how to implement good architecture. However, individuals with expertise in more traditional professions (such as construction) figured it out a long time ago.

CHECKING INTO A CHEAP HOTEL

If you're staying at a cheap hotel, you might encounter a sight like the one in figure 1.4. Here, the hotel has kindly provided a hair dryer for your convenience, but apparently they don't trust you to leave the hair dryer for the next guest: the appliance is directly attached into the wall outlet. Although the cord's long enough to give you a certain degree of movement, you can't take the dryer with you. Apparently, the hotel management has decided that the cost of replacing stolen hair dryers is high enough to justify what's otherwise an obviously inferior implementation.

What happens when the hair dryer stops working? The hotel has to call in a skilled professional who can deal with the issue. To fix the hardwired hair dryer, they will have to cut the power to the room, rendering it temporarily useless. Then, the technician will use special tools to painstakingly disconnect the hair dryer and replace it with a new one. If you're lucky, the technician will remember to turn the power to the room back on and go back to test whether the new hair dryer works…if you're lucky.

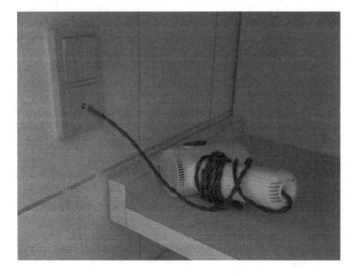

Figure 1.4   In a cheap hotel room, you might find the hair dryer wired directly into the wall outlet. This is equivalent to using the common practice of writing *tightly coupled* code.

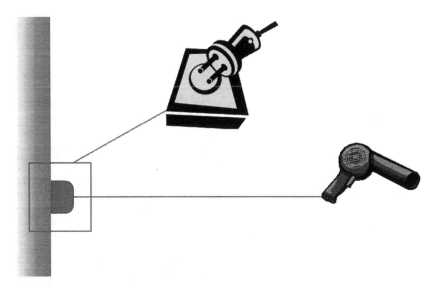

Figure 1.5 Through the use of sockets and plugs, a hair dryer can be *loosely coupled* to the wall outlet.

Does this procedure sound at all familiar?

This is how you would approach working with *tightly coupled* code. In this scenario, the hair dryer is tightly coupled to the wall and you can't easily modify one without impacting the other.

COMPARING ELECTRICAL WIRING TO DESIGN PATTERNS

Usually, we don't wire electrical appliances together by attaching the cable directly to the wall. Instead, as in figure 1.5, we use plugs and sockets. A socket defines a shape that the plug must match. In an analogy to software design, the socket is an *interface*.

In contrast to the hardwired hair dryer, plugs and sockets define a *loosely coupled* model for connecting electrical appliances. As long as the plug fits into the socket, we can combine appliances in a variety of ways. What's particularly interesting is that many of these common combinations can be compared to well-known software design principles and patterns.

First, we're no longer constrained to hair dryers. If you're an average reader, I would guess that you need power for a computer much more than you do for a hair dryer. That's not a problem: we unplug the hair dryer and plug a computer into the same socket, as shown in figure 1.6.

It's amazing that the concept of a socket predates computers by decades, and yet it provides an essential service to computers, too. The original designers of sockets couldn't possibly have foreseen personal computers, but because the design is so versatile, needs that were originally unanticipated can be met. The ability to replace one end without changing the other is similar to a central software design principle called the LISKOV SUBSTITUTION PRINCIPLE. This principle states that we should be able to

Figure 1.6   Using sockets and plugs, we can replace the original hair dryer from figure 1.5 with a computer. This corresponds to the LISKOV SUBSTITUTION PRINCIPLE.

replace one implementation of an interface with another without breaking either client or implementation.

When it comes to DI, the LISKOV SUBSTITUTION PRINCIPLE is one of the most important software design principles. It's this principle that enables us to address requirements that occur in the future, even if we can't foresee them today.

As figure 1.7 illustrates, we can unplug the computer if we don't need to use it at the moment. Even though nothing is plugged in, the wall doesn't explode.

If we unplug the computer from the wall, neither the wall outlet nor the computer breaks down (in fact, if it's a laptop computer, it can even run on its batteries for a period of time). With software, however, a client often expects a service to be available. If the service was removed, we get a `NullReferenceException`. To deal with this type of situation, we can create an implementation of an interface that does "nothing." This is a design pattern known as *Null Object*,[4] and it corresponds roughly to unplugging the

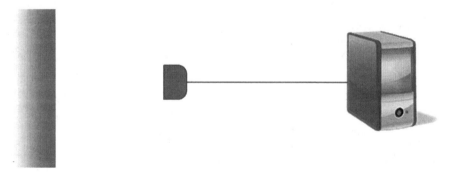

Figure 1.7   Unplugging the computer causes neither wall nor computer to explode. This can be roughly likened to the Null Object pattern.

---

[4]   Robert C. Martin et al., *Pattern Languages of Program Design* 3 (New York, Addison-Wesley, 1998), 5.

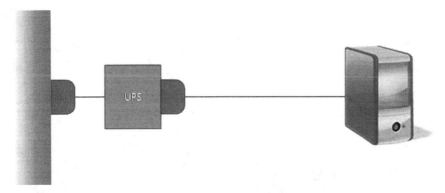

Figure 1.8 An Uninterrupted Power Supply can be introduced to keep the computer running in case of power failures. This corresponds to the Decorator design pattern.

computer from the wall. Because we're using loose coupling, we can replace a real implementation with something that does nothing without causing trouble.

There are many other things we can do. If we live in a neighborhood with intermittent power failures, we may wish to keep the computer running by plugging in into an Uninterrupted Power Supply (UPS), as shown in figure 1.8: we connect the UPS to the wall outlet and the computer to the UPS.

The computer and the UPS serve separate purposes. Each has a SINGLE RESPONSIBILITY that doesn't infringe on the other appliance. The UPS and computer are likely to be produced by two different manufacturers, bought at different times, and plugged in at different times. As figure 1.6 demonstrates, we can run the computer without a UPS, but we could also conceivably use the hair dryer during blackouts by plugging it into the UPS.

In software design, this way of INTERCEPTING one implementation with another implementation of the same interface is known as the *Decorator*[5] design pattern. It gives us the ability to incrementally introduce new features and CROSS-CUTTING CONCERNS without having to rewrite or change a lot of our existing code.

Another way to add new functionality to an existing code base is to compose an existing implementation of an interface with a new implementation. When we aggregate several implementations into one, we use the *Composite*[6] design pattern. Figure 1.9 illustrates how this corresponds to plugging diverse appliances into a power strip.

The power strip has a single plug that we can insert into a single socket, while the power strip itself provides several sockets for a variety of appliances. This enables us to add and remove the hair dryer while the computer is running. In the same way, the Composite pattern makes it easy to add or remove functionality by modifying the set of composed interface implementations.

---

[5] Gamma, *Design Patterns*, 175.
[6] Ibid., 163.

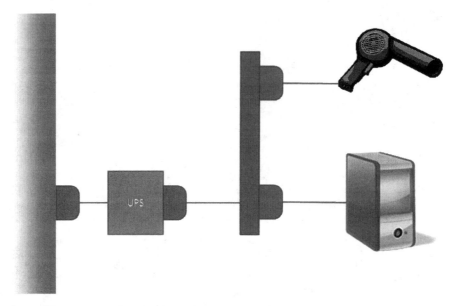

Figure 1.9   A power strip makes it possible to plug several appliances into a single wall outlet. This corresponds to the Composite design pattern.

Here's a final example. We sometimes find ourselves in situations where a plug doesn't fit into a particular socket. If you've traveled to another country, you've likely noticed that sockets differ across the world. If you bring something, like the camera in figure 1.10, along when traveling, you need an adapter to charge it. Appropriately, there's a design pattern with the same name.

The *Adapter*[7] design pattern works like its physical namesake. It can be used to match two related, yet separate, interfaces to each other. This is particularly useful

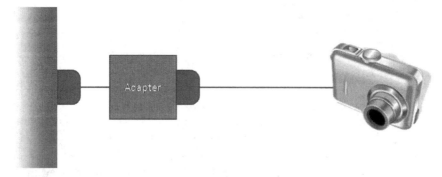

Figure 1.10   When traveling, we often need to use an adapter to plug an appliance into a foreign socket (for example, to recharge a camera). This corresponds to the Adapter design pattern.

---

[7] Ibid., 139.

when you have an existing third-party API that you wish to expose as an instance of an interface your application consumes.

What's amazing about the socket and plug model is that, over decades, it's proven to be an easy and versatile model. Once the infrastructure is in place, it can be used by anyone and adapted to changing needs and unpredicted requirements. What's even more interesting is that, when we relate this model to software development, all the building blocks are already in place in the form of design principles and patterns.

Loose coupling can make a code base much more maintainable.

That's the easy part. Programming to an interface instead of an implementation is easy. The question is, where do the instances come from? In a sense, this is what this entire book is about.

You can't create a new instance of an interface the same way that you create a new instance of a concrete type. Code like this doesn't compile:

```
IMessageWriter writer = new IMessageWriter();
```

Program to an interface   Does not compile

An interface has no constructor, so this isn't possible. The `writer` instance must be created using a different mechanism. DI solves this problem.

With this outline of the purpose of DI, I think you're ready for an example.

1.2 Hello DI

In the tradition of innumerable programming textbooks, let's take a look at a simple console application that writes "Hello DI!" to the screen. In this section, I'll show you what the code looks like and briefly outline some key benefits without going into details—in the rest of the book, I'll get more specific.

1.2.1 Hello DI code

You're probably used to seeing Hello World examples that are written in a single line of code. Here, we'll take something that's extremely simple and make it more complicated. Why? We'll get to that shortly, but let's first see what Hello World would look like with DI.

COLLABORATORS

To get a sense of the structure of the program, we'll start by looking at the `Main` method of the console application, and then I'll show you the collaborating classes:

```
private static void Main()
{
    IMessageWriter writer = new ConsoleMessageWriter();
    var salutation = new Salutation(writer);
    salutation.Exclaim();
}
```

Figure 1.11   The `Main` **method creates new instances of both the** `ConsoleMessageWriter` **and** `Salutation` **classes.** `ConsoleMessageWriter` **implements the** `IMessageWriter` **interface, which** `Salutation` **uses. In effect, Salutation uses** `ConsoleMessageWriter`, **although this indirect usage isn't shown.**

The program needs to write to the console, so it creates a new instance of `Console-MessageWriter` that encapsulates exactly that functionality. It passes that message writer to the `Salutation` class so that the `salutation` instance knows where to write its messages. Because everything is now wired up properly, you can execute the logic, which results in the message being written to the screen.

Figure 1.11 shows the relationship between the collaborators.

The main logic of the application is encapsulated in the `Salutation` class, shown in the following listing.

Listing 1.1   `Salutation` **class**

```
public class Salutation
{
    private readonly IMessageWriter writer;                        ❶ Inject
                                                                      Dependency
    public Salutation(IMessageWriter writer)
    {
        if (writer == null)
        {
            throw new ArgumentNullException("writer");
        }

        this.writer = writer;
    }

    public void Exclaim()
    {                                                              ❷ Use
        this.writer.Write("Hello DI!");                              Dependency
    }
}
```

The `Salutation` class depends on a custom interface called `IMessageWriter`, and it requests an instance of it through its constructor ❶. This is called CONSTRUCTOR INJECTION and is described in detail in chapter 4, which also contains a more detailed walkthrough of a similar code example.

The `IMessageWriter` instance is later used in the implementation of the `Exclaim` method ❷, which writes the proper message to the DEPENDENCY.

`IMessageWriter` is a simple interface defined for the occasion:

```
public interface IMessageWriter
{
    void Write(string message);
}
```

It could have had other members, but in this simple example you only need the `Write` method. It's implemented by the `ConsoleMessageWriter` class that the `Main` method passes to the `Salutation` class:

```
public class ConsoleMessageWriter : IMessageWriter
{
    public void Write(string message)
    {
        Console.WriteLine(message);
    }
}
```

The `ConsoleMessageWriter` class implements `IMessageWriter` by wrapping the Base Class Library's `Console` class. This is a simple application of the Adapter design pattern that we talked about in section 1.1.2.

You may be wondering about the benefit of replacing a single line of code with two classes and an interface with a total line count of 11, and rightly so. There are several benefits to be harvested from doing this.

1.2.2   *Benefits of DI*

How is the previous example better than the usual single line of code we normally use to implement Hello World in C#? In this example, DI adds an overhead of 1,100%, but, as complexity increases from one line of code to tens of thousands, this overhead diminishes and all but disappears. Chapter 2 provides a more complex example of applied DI, and although that example is still overly simplistic compared to real-life applications, you should notice that DI is far less intrusive.

I don't blame you if you find the previous DI example to be over-engineered, but consider this: by its nature, the classic Hello World example is a *simple* problem with well-specified and constrained requirements. In the real world, software development is never like this. Requirements change and are often fuzzy. The features you must implement also tend to be much more complex. DI helps address such issues by enabling loose coupling. Specifically, we gain the benefits listed in table 1.1.

In table 1.1, I listed the *late binding* benefit first because, in my experience, this is the one that's foremost in most people's minds. When architects and developers fail to understand the benefits of loose coupling, this is most likely because they never consider the other benefits.

LATE BINDING

When I explain the benefits of *programming to interfaces* and DI, the ability to swap out one service with another is the most prevalent benefit for most people, so they tend to weigh the advantages against the disadvantages with only this benefit in mind.

Table 1.1 Benefits gained from loose coupling. Each benefit is always available but will be valued differently depending on circumstances.

Benefit	Description	When is it valuable?
Late binding	Services can be swapped with other services.	Valuable in standard software, but perhaps less so in enterprise applications where the runtime environment tends to be well-defined
Extensibility	Code can be extended and reused in ways not explicitly planned for.	Always valuable
Parallel development	Code can be developed in parallel.	Valuable in large, complex applications; not so much in small, simple applications
Maintainability	Classes with clearly defined responsibilities are easier to maintain.	Always valuable
TESTABILITY	Classes can be unit tested.	Only valuable if you unit test (which you really, really should)

Remember when I asked you to unlearn before you can learn? You may say that you know your requirements so well that you *know* you'll never have to replace, say, your SQL Server database with anything else. However, requirements change.

NoSQL, Windows Azure, and the argument for composability

Years ago, I was often met with a blank expression when I tried to convince developers and architects of the benefits of DI.

"Okay, so you can swap out your relational data access component for something else. For what? Is there any alternative to relational databases?"

XML files never seemed like a convincing alternative in highly scalable enterprise scenarios. This has changed significantly in the last couple of years.

Windows Azure was announced at PDC 2008 and has done much to convince even die-hard Microsoft-only organizations to reevaluate their position when it comes to data storage. There's now a real alternative to relational databases, and I only have to ask if people want their application to be "cloud-ready." The replacement argument has now become much stronger.

A related movement can be found in the whole NoSQL concept that models applications around denormalized data—often document databases, but concepts such as Event Sourcing[8] are also becoming increasingly important.

In section 1.2.1, you didn't use late binding because you explicitly created a new instance of IMessageWriter by hard-coding creation of a new ConsoleMessageWriter

---

[8] Martin Fowler, "Event Sourcing," 2005, www.martinfowler.com/eaaDev/EventSourcing.htmls

instance. However, you can introduce late binding by changing only a single piece of the code. You only need to change this line of code:

```
IMessageWriter writer = new ConsoleMessageWriter();
```

To enable late binding, you might replace that line of code with something like this:

```
var typeName =
    ConfigurationManager.AppSettings["messageWriter"];
var type = Type.GetType(typeName, true);
IMessageWriter writer =
    (IMessageWriter)Activator.CreateInstance(type);
```

By pulling the type name from the application configuration file and creating a Type instance from it, you can use Reflection to create an instance of IMessageWriter without knowing the concrete type at compile time.

To make this work, you specify the type name in the messageWriter application setting in the application configuration file:

```
<appSettings>
  <add key="messageWriter"
       value="Ploeh.Samples.HelloDI.CommandLine.ConsoleMessageWriter,
       ➡HelloDI" />
</appSettings>
```

> **WARNING** This example takes some shortcuts to make a point. In fact, it suffers from the CONSTRAINED CONSTRUCTION anti-pattern, covered in detail in chapter 5.

Loose coupling enables late binding because there's only a single place where you create the instance of the IMessageWriter. Because the Salutation class works exclusively against the IMessageWriter interface, it never notices the difference.

In the Hello DI example, late binding would enable you to write the message to a different destination than the console—for example, a database or a file. It's possible to add such features even though you didn't explicitly plan ahead for them.

EXTENSIBILITY

Successful software must be able to change. You'll need to add new features and extend existing features. Loose coupling enables us to efficiently recompose the application, similar to the way that we can rewire electrical appliances using plugs and sockets.

Let's say that you want to make the Hello DI example more secure by only allowing authenticated users to write the message. The next listing shows how you can add that feature without changing any of the existing features: you add a new implementation of the IMessageWriter interface.

Listing 1.2 Extending the Hello DI application with a security feature

```
public class SecureMessageWriter : IMessageWriter
{
    private readonly IMessageWriter writer;
```

```
public SecureMessageWriter(IMessageWriter writer)
{
    if (writer == null)
    {
        throw new ArgumentNullException("writer");
    }

    this.writer = writer;
}

public void Write(string message)
{
    if (Thread.CurrentPrincipal.Identity       ❶ Check
        .IsAuthenticated)                          authentication
    {
        this.writer.Write(message);             ◁── Write
    }                                            ❷  message
}
}
```

The SecureMessageWriter class implements the IMessageWriter interface while also consuming it: it uses CONSTRUCTOR INJECTION to request an instance of IMessageWriter. This is a standard application of the Decorator design pattern that I mentioned in section 1.1.2. We'll talk much more about Decorators in chapter 9.

The Write method is implemented by first checking whether the current user is authenticated ❶. Only if this is the case does it allow the decorated writer field to Write ❷ the message.

> **NOTE**   The Write method in listing 1.2 accesses the current user via an AMBIENT CONTEXT. A more flexible, but slightly more complex, option would've been to also supply the user via CONSTRUCTOR INJECTION.

The only place where you need to change existing code is in the Main method, because you need to compose the available classes differently than before:

```
IMessageWriter writer =
    new SecureMessageWriter(
        new ConsoleMessageWriter());
```

Notice that you decorate the old ConsoleMessageWriter instance with the new SecureMessageWriter class. Once more, the Salutation class is unmodified because it only consumes the IMessageWriter interface.

Loose coupling enables you to write code which is *open for extensibility, but closed for modification*. This is called the OPEN/CLOSED PRINCIPLE. The only place where you need to modify the code is at the application's entry point; we call this the COMPOSITION ROOT.

The SecureMessageWriter implements the security features of the application, whereas the ConsoleMessageWriter addresses the user interface. This enables us to vary these aspects independently of each other and compose them as needed.

PARALLEL DEVELOPMENT

Separation of concerns makes it possible to develop code in parallel teams. When a software development project grows to a certain size, it becomes necessary to separate the development team into multiple teams of manageable sizes. Each team is assigned responsibility for an area of the overall application.

To demarcate responsibilities, each team will develop one or more modules that will need to be integrated into the finished application. Unless the areas of each team are truly independent, some teams are likely to depend on the functionality developed by other teams.

In the above example, because the `SecureMessageWriter` and `ConsoleMessageWriter` classes don't depend directly on each other, they could've been developed by parallel teams. All they would've needed to agree upon was the shared interface `IMessageWriter`.

MAINTAINABILITY

As the responsibility of each class becomes clearly defined and constrained, maintenance of the overall application becomes easier. This is a known benefit of the SINGLE RESPONSIBILITY PRINCIPLE, which states that each class should have only a single responsibility.

Adding new features to an application becomes simpler because it's clear where changes should be applied. More often than not, we don't even need to change existing code, but can instead add new classes and recompose the application. This is the OPEN/CLOSED PRINCIPLE in action again.

Troubleshooting also tends to become less grueling, because the scope of likely culprits narrows. With clearly defined responsibilities, you'll often have a good idea of where to start looking for the root cause of a problem.

TESTABILITY

For some, TESTABILITY is the least of their worries; for others, it's an absolute requirement. Personally, I belong in the latter category: in my career, I've declined several job offers because they involved working with certain products that aren't TESTABLE.

DEFINITION   An application is considered *TESTABLE* when it can be unit tested.

The benefit of TESTABILITY is perhaps the most controversial of the benefits I've listed. Many developers and architects don't practice unit testing, so they consider this benefit irrelevant at best. Others, like me, consider it essential. Michael Feathers even defines the term *Legacy Application* as any application that isn't covered by unit tests.[9]

Almost by accident, loose coupling enables unit testing because consumers follow the LISKOV SUBSTITUTION PRINCIPLE: they don't care about the concrete types of their DEPENDENCIES. This means that we can inject *Test Doubles* into the *System Under Test* (SUT), as we shall see in listing 1.3.

The ability to replace the intended DEPENDENCIES with test-specific replacements is a by-product of loose coupling, but I chose to list it as a separate benefit because the derived value is different.

---

[9]   Michael Feathers, *Working Effectively with Legacy Code* (New York, Prentice Hall, 2004), xvi.

TESTABILITY

The term *TESTABLE* is horribly imprecise, yet it's widely used in the software development community, chiefly by those who practice unit testing.

In principle, any application can be tested by trying it out. Tests can be performed by people using the application via its user interface or whatever other interface it provides. Such manual tests are time consuming and expensive to perform, so automated testing is much preferred.

There are different types of automated testing, such as unit testing, integration testing, performance testing, stress testing, and so on. Because unit testing has few requirements on runtime environments, it tends to be the most efficient and robust type of test; it's often in this context that *TESTABILITY* is evaluated.

Unit tests provide rapid feedback on the state of an application, but it's only possible to write unit tests when the unit in question can be properly isolated from its DEPENDENCIES. There's some ambiguity about how granular a *unit* really is, but everyone agrees that it's certainly not something that spans multiple modules. The ability to test modules in isolation is very important in unit testing.

It's only when an application is susceptible to unit testing that it's considered *TESTABLE*. The safest way to ensure TESTABILITY is to develop it using Test-Driven Development (TDD).

It should be noted that unit tests alone don't ensure a working application. Full system tests or other in-between types of tests are still necessary to validate whether an application works as intended.

Depending on the type of application I'm developing, I may or may not care about the ability to do late binding, but I always care about TESTABILITY. Some developers don't care about TESTABILITY, but find late binding important for the application they're developing.

Test Doubles

It's a common technique to create implementations of DEPENDENCIES that act as stand-ins for the real or intended implementations. Such implementations are called *Test Doubles*, and they will never be used in the final application. Instead, they serve as placeholders for the real DEPENDENCIES, when these are unavailable or undesirable to use.

There's a complete pattern language around Test Doubles, and many subtypes, such as *Stubs, Mocks,* and *Fakes.*[10]

---

[10] Gerard Meszaros, *xUnit Test Patterns: Refactoring Test Code* (New York, Addison-Wesley, 2007), 522.

EXAMPLE: UNIT TESTING THE "HELLO" LOGIC

In section 1.21, you saw a Hello DI example. Although I showed you the final code first, I actually developed it using TDD. Listing 1.3 shows the most important unit test.

> **NOTE** Don't worry if you don't have experience with unit testing or dynamic mocks. They will occasionally pop up throughout this book, but are in no way a prerequisite for reading it.[11]

Listing 1.3 Unit testing the Salutation class

```
[Fact]
public void ExclaimWillWriteCorrectMessageToMessageWriter()
{
    var writerMock = new Mock<IMessageWriter>();
    var sut = new Salutation(writerMock.Object);

    sut.Exclaim();

    writerMock.Verify(w => w.Write("Hello DI!"));
}
```

The Salutation class needs an instance of the IMessageWriter interface, so you need to create one. You could use any implementation, but in unit tests a dynamic mock can be very useful—in this case, you use Moq,[12] but you could've used other libraries or rolled your own instead. The important part is to supply a test-specific implementation of IMessageWriter to ensure that you test only one thing at a time; right now you're testing the Exclaim method of the Salutation class, so you don't want any production implementation of IMessageWriter to pollute the test.

To create the Salutation class, you pass in the Mock instance of IMessageWriter. Because writerMock is an instance of Mock<IMessageWriter>, the Object property is a dynamically created instance of IMessageWriter. Injecting the required DEPENDENCY through the constructor is called CONSTRUCTOR INJECTION.

After exercising the System Under Test (SUT), you can use the Mock to verify that the Write method was invoked with the correct text. With Moq, you do this by calling the Verify method with an expression that defines what you expected. If the IMessage-Writer.Write method was invoked with the "Hello DI!" string, the Verify method call completes, but if the Write method wasn't called, or called with a different parameter, the Verify method would throw an exception and the test would fail.

Loose coupling provides many benefits: code becomes easier to develop, maintain, and extend, and it becomes more TESTABLE. It's not even particularly difficult. We program against interfaces, not concrete implementations. The only major obstacle is to figure out how to get hold of instances of those interfaces. DI answers this question by injecting the DEPENDENCIES from the outside. CONSTRUCTOR INJECTION is the preferred method of doing that.

---

[11] You may, however, want to read *The Art of Unit Testing* followed by *xUnit Test Patterns*. See the bibliography for more details.

[12] code.google.com/p/moq/

1.3   *What to inject and what not to inject*

In the previous section, I described the motivational forces that make us think about DI in the first place. If you're convinced that loose coupling is a good idea, you may want to make everything loosely coupled. Overall, this is a good idea. When you must decide how to package modules, loose coupling provides especially useful guidance. You don't have to abstract everything away and make everything pluggable. In this section, I'll provide you with some decision tools that can help you decide how to model your DEPENDENCIES.

The .NET Base Class Library (BCL) consists of many assemblies. Every time you write code that uses a type from a BCL assembly, you add a dependency to your module. In the previous section, I discussed how loose coupling is important, and how *programming to an interface* is the cornerstone.

Does this imply that you can't reference any BCL assemblies and use their types directly in your application? What if you would like to use an XmlWriter, which is defined in the System.Xml assembly?

You don't have to treat all DEPENDENCIES equally. Many types in the BCL can be used without jeopardizing an application's degree of coupling—but not all of them. It's important to know how to distinguish between types that pose no danger and types that may tighten an application's degree of coupling. Focus mainly on the latter.

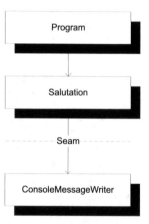

1.3.1   *Seams*

Everywhere we decide to program against an interface instead of a concrete type, we introduce a SEAM into the application. A SEAM is a place where an application is assembled from its constituent parts,[13] similar to the way a piece of clothing is sewn together at its seams. It's also a place where we can disassemble the application and work with the modules in isolation.

The Hello DI sample I built in section 1.2 contains a SEAM between Salutation and ConsoleMessageWriter, as illustrated in figure 1.12. The Salutation class doesn't directly depend on the ConsoleMessageWriter class; rather, it uses the IMessageWriter interface to write messages. You can take the application apart at this SEAM and reassemble it with a different message writer.

Figure 1.12   The Hello DI application from section 1.2 contains a SEAM between the Salutation and ConsoleMessageWriter classes because the Salutation class only writes through the ABSTRACTION of the IMessageWriter interface.

As you learn DI, it can be helpful to categorize your dependencies into STABLE DEPENDENCIES and VOLATILE DEPENDENCIES, but deciding where to put your SEAMS will soon become second nature to you. The next sections discuss these concepts in more detail.

---

[13] Feathers, *Working Effectively with Legacy Code*, 29-44.

1.3.2   *Stable Dependencies*

Many of the modules in the BCL and beyond pose no threat to an application's degree of modularity. They contain reusable functionality that you can leverage to make your own code more succinct.

The BCL modules are always available to your application, because it needs the .NET Framework to run. The concern about *parallel development* doesn't apply to these modules because they already exist, and you can always reuse a BCL library in another application.

By default, you can consider most (but not all) types defined in the BCL as safe, or STABLE DEPENDENCIES—I call them *stable* because they're already there, tend to be backwards compatible, and invoking them has deterministic outcomes.

Most STABLE DEPENDENCIES are BCL types, but other dependencies can be stable as well. The important criteria for STABLE DEPENDENCIES are

- The class or module already exists.
- You expect that new versions won't contain breaking changes.
- The types in question contain deterministic algorithms.
- You never expect to have to replace the class or module with another.

Ironically, DI CONTAINERS themselves will tend to be STABLE DEPENDENCIES, because they fit all the criteria. When you decide to base your application on a particular DI CONTAINER, you risk being stuck with this choice for the entire lifetime of the application; that's yet another reason why you should limit the use of the container to the application's COMPOSITION ROOT.

Other examples may include specialized libraries that encapsulate algorithms relevant to your application. If you're developing an application that deals with chemistry, you may reference a third-party library that contains chemistry-specific functionality.

In general, DEPENDENCIES can be considered stable by exclusion: they're stable if they aren't *volatile*.

1.3.3   *VOLATILE DEPENDENCIES*

Introducing SEAMS into an application is extra work, so you should only do it when it's necessary. There may be more than one reason it's necessary to isolate a DEPENDENCY behind a SEAM, but they're closely related to the benefits of loose coupling, discussed in section 1.2.2.

Such DEPENDENCIES can be recognized by their tendency to interfere with one or more of these benefits. They aren't stable because they don't provide a sufficient foundation for applications, and I call them VOLATILE DEPENDENCIES for that reason. A DEPENDENCY should be considered *Volatile* if any of the following criteria is true:

- The DEPENDENCY introduces a requirement to set up and configure a runtime environment for the application. A relational database is the archetypical example: if we don't hide the relational database behind a SEAM, we can never replace it by any other technology. It also makes it hard to set up and run automated unit tests.

Databases are a good example of BCL types that are VOLATILE DEPENDENCIES: even though LINQ to Entities is a technology contained in the BCL, its usage implies a relational database.

Other out-of-process resources such as message queues, web services, and even the file system fall into this category. Please note that it isn't so much the concrete .NET types that are *Volatile*, but rather what they imply about the run-time environment.

The symptoms of this type of DEPENDENCY are lack of *late binding* and *extensibility*, as well as disabled TESTABILITY.

- The DEPENDENCY doesn't yet exist, but is still in development. The obvious symptom of such dependencies is the inability to do *parallel development.*
- The DEPENDENCY isn't installed on all machines in the development organization. This may be the case for expensive third-party libraries, or dependencies that can't be installed on all operating systems. The most common symptom is disabled TESTABILITY.
- The dependency contains nondeterministic behavior. This is particularly important in unit tests, because all tests should be deterministic. Typical sources of nondeterminism are random numbers and algorithms that depend on the current date or time.

Note that common sources of nondeterminism, such as `System.Random`, `System.Security.Cryptography.RandomNumberGenerator`, or `System.Date-Time.Now` are defined in mscorlib, so you can't avoid having a reference to the assembly in which they're defined. Nevertheless, you should treat them as VOLATILE DEPENDENCIES, because they tend to destroy TESTABILITY.

VOLATILE DEPENDENCIES are the focal point of DI. It's for VOLATILE DEPENDENCIES, rather than STABLE DEPENDENCIES, that we introduce SEAMS into our application. Again, this obliges us to compose them using DI.

Now that you understand the differences between STABLE and VOLATILE DEPENDENCIES, you may begin to see the contours of the scope of DI. Loose coupling is a pervasive design principle, so DI (as an enabler) should be everywhere in your code base. There's no hard line between the topic of DI and good software design, but to define the scope of the rest of the book, I'll quickly describe what it covers.

1.4   *DI scope*

As we saw in section 1.2, an important element of DI is to break up various responsibilities into separate classes. One responsibility that we take away from classes is the task of creating instances of DEPENDENCIES.

As a class relinquishes control of DEPENDENCIES, it gives up more than the decision to select particular implementations. However, as developers, we gain some advantages.

NOTE   As developers, we gain control by removing that control from the classes that consume DEPENDENCIES. This is an application of the SINGLE RESPONSIBILITY

PRINCIPLE: these classes should only deal with their given area of responsibility, without concerning themselves with how DEPENDENCIES are created.

At first, it may seem like a disadvantage to let a class surrender control over which objects are created, but, as developers, we don't lose that control—we only move it to another place.

However, OBJECT COMPOSITION isn't the only dimension of control that we remove, because a class also loses the ability to control the *lifetime* of the object. When a DEPENDENCY instance is injected into a class, the consumer doesn't know when it was created, or when it will go out of scope. Many times, this is of no concern to the consumer, but in other cases, it may be.

DI gives us an opportunity to manage DEPENDENCIES in a uniform way. When consumers directly create and set up instances of DEPENDENCIES, each may do so in its own way, which may be inconsistent with how other consumers do it. We have no way to centrally manage DEPENDENCIES, and no easy way to address CROSS-CUTTING CONCERNS. With DI, we gain the ability to *intercept* each DEPENDENCY instance and act upon it before it's passed to the consumer.

With DI, we can *compose* applications while *intercepting* dependencies and controlling their *lifetimes*. OBJECT COMPOSITION, INTERCEPTION, and LIFETIME MANAGEMENT are three dimensions of DI. Next I'll cover them briefly; a more detailed treatment follows in part 3 of the book.

1.4.1 Object Composition

To harvest the benefits of *extensibility, late binding,* and *parallel development,* we must be able to compose classes into applications (see figure 1.13). Such OBJECT COMPOSITION is often the foremost motivation for introducing DI into an application. Initially, DI was synonymous with OBJECT COMPOSITION; it's the only aspect discussed in Martin Fowler's original article on the subject.[14]

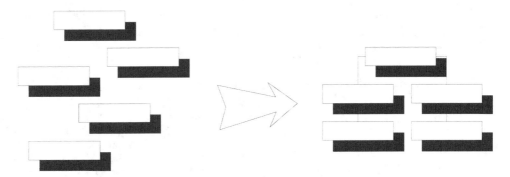

Figure 1.13 OBJECT COMPOSITION signifies that modules can be composed into applications.

---

[14] Martin Fowler, "Inversion of Control Containers and the Dependency Injection pattern," 2004, http://martinfowler.com/articles/injection.html

There are several ways we can compose classes into an application. When I discussed *late binding* I used a configuration file and a bit of dynamic object instantiation to manually compose the application from the available modules, but I could also have used CODE AS CONFIGURATION or a DI CONTAINER. We'll return to these in chapter 7.

Although the original meaning of DI was closely tied to OBJECT COMPOSITION, other aspects have also turned out to be relevant.

1.4.2 *Object Lifetime*

A class that has surrendered control of its DEPENDENCIES gives up more than the power to select particular implementations of an ABSTRACTION. It also gives up the power to control when instances are created, and when they go out of scope.

In .NET, the garbage collector takes care of a lot of these things for us. A consumer can have its DEPENDENCIES injected into it and use them for as long as it wants. When it's done, the DEPENDENCIES go out of scope. If no other classes reference them, they're eligible for garbage collection.

What if two consumers share the same type of DEPENDENCY? Figure 1.14 illustrates that we can choose to inject a separate instance into each consumer, whereas figure 1.15 shows that we may alternatively choose to share a single instance across several consumers. However, from the perspective of the con-

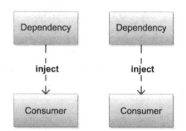

Figure 1.14   Each consumer sharing the same type of DEPENDENCY is injected with its own private instance.

sumer, there's no difference. According to the LISKOV SUBSTITUTION PRINCIPLE, the consumer must treat all instances of a given interface equally.

Because DEPENDENCIES may be shared, a single consumer can't possibly control its lifetime. As long as a managed object can go out of scope and be garbage collected, this isn't much of an issue, but when DEPENDENCIES implement the `IDisposable` interface, things become much more complicated.

As a whole, LIFETIME MANAGEMENT is a separate dimension of DI and important enough that I've set aside all of chapter 8 for it.

Giving up control of a DEPENDENCY also means giving up control of its lifetime; something else higher up in the call stack must manage the lifetime of the DEPENDENCY.

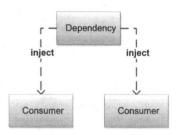

Figure 1.15   Separate consumers sharing the same type of DEPENDENCY are injected with a shared instance.

1.4.3 *Interception*

When we delegate control over DEPENDENCIES to a third party, as figure 1.16 shows, we also gain the power to modify them before we pass them on to the classes consuming them.

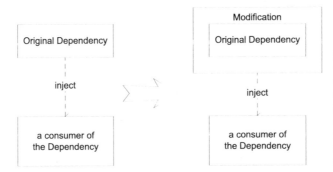

Figure 1.16 **Instead of injecting the originally intended** DEPENDENCY, **we can modify it by wrapping another class around it before we pass it on to its consumer. The dotted arrows indicate the direction of the action—the direction of** DEPENDENCY **goes the opposite way.**

In the Hello DI example, I initially injected a `ConsoleMessageWriter` instance into a `Salutation` instance. Then, modifying the example, I added a security feature by creating a new `SecureMessageWriter` that only delegates further work to the `Console-MessageWriter` when the user is authenticated. This allows us to maintain the SINGLE RESPONSIBILITY PRINCIPLE.

This is possible to do because we always *program to interfaces*; recall that DEPENDENCIES must always be ABSTRACTIONS. In the case of the `Salutation`, it doesn't care whether the supplied `IMessageWriter` is a `ConsoleMessageWriter` or a `SecureMessage-Writer`. The `SecureMessageWriter` can wrap a `ConsoleMessageWriter` that still performs the real work.

> **NOTE** INTERCEPTION is an application of the *Decorator* design pattern. Don't worry if you aren't familiar with the Decorator design pattern—I'll provide a refresher in chapter 9, which is entirely devoted to INTERCEPTION.

Such abilities of INTERCEPTION move us along the path towards *Aspect-Oriented Programming*—a closely related topic that, nonetheless, is outside the scope of this book. With INTERCEPTION, we can apply CROSS-CUTTING CONCERNS such as logging, auditing, access control, validation, and so forth in a well-structured manner that lets us maintain *Separation of Concerns*.

1.4.4 *DI in three dimensions*

Although DI started out as a series of patterns aimed at solving the problem of OBJECT COMPOSITION, the term has subsequently expanded to also cover OBJECT LIFETIME and INTERCEPTION. Today, I think of DI as encompassing all three in a consistent way.

OBJECT COMPOSITION tends to dominate the picture because, without flexible OBJECT COMPOSITION, there would be no INTERCEPTION and no need to manage OBJECT LIFETIME. OBJECT COMPOSITION has dominated most of this chapter, and will continue to dominate the book, but we shouldn't forget the other aspects. OBJECT COMPOSITION provides the foundation and LIFETIME MANAGEMENT addresses some important side effects, but it's mainly when it comes to INTERCEPTION that we start to reap the benefits.

In part 3, I've devoted a chapter to each dimension, but I provided an overview here because it's important to know that, in practice, DI is more than OBJECT COMPOSITION.

1.5   *Summary*

Dependency Injection is a means to an end, not a goal in itself. It's the best way to enable *loose coupling*, an important part of maintainable code. The benefits we can reap from loose coupling aren't always immediately apparent, but they become visible over time, as the complexity of a code base grows. A tightly coupled code base will eventually deteriorate into Spaghetti Code,[15] whereas a well-designed, loosely coupled code base can stay maintainable. It takes more than loose coupling to reach a truly Supple Design,[16] but *programming to interfaces* is a prerequisite.

DI is nothing more than a collection of design principles and patterns. It's more about a way of thinking and designing code than it is about tools and techniques—an important point about loose coupling and DI is that, in order to be effective, it should be everywhere in your code base.

> **TIP**   DI must be pervasive. You can't easily retrofit loose coupling onto an existing code base.[17]

There are many misconceptions about DI. Some people think that it only addresses narrow problems, such as *late binding* or unit testing; although these aspects of software design certainly benefit from DI, the scope is much broader. The overall purpose is maintainability.

In the beginning of the chapter, I stated that you must unlearn to learn DI. This will remain true for the rest of the book: you must free your mind. In an excellent blog post, Nicholas Blumhardt writes:

> *The dictionary or associative array is one of the first constructs we learn about in software engineering. It's easy to see the analogy between a dictionary and an IoC container that composes objects using dependency injection[.]*[18]

The idea of DI as a service modeled along the lines of a dictionary leads directly to the SERVICE LOCATOR anti-pattern. This is why I put so much emphasis on the need to clear your mind of even the most basic assumptions. After all, when we're talking about dictionaries, we're talking about stuff that belongs in the "reptile brain of programming."

The purpose of DI is to make code maintainable. Small code bases, like a classic Hello World example, are inherently maintainable because of their size; this is why DI tends to look like over-engineering in simple examples. The larger the code base becomes, the more visible the benefits. I've dedicated the next chapter to a larger and more complex example to showcase these benefits.

---

[15] William J. Brown et al., *AntiPatterns: Refactoring Software, Architectures, and Projects in Crisis* (New York, Wiley Computer Publishing, 1998), 119.

[16] Eric Evans, *Domain-Driven Design: Tackling Complexity in the Heart of Software* (New York, Addison-Wesley, 2004), 243.

[17] However, see Feathers, Michael, *Working Effectively with Legacy Code* (New York, Prentice Hall, 2004).

[18] Blumhardt, Nicholas, "Container-Managed Application Design, Prelude: Where does the Container Belong?" 2008, http://blogs.msdn.com/b/nblumhardt/archive/2008/12/27/container-managed-application-design-prelude-where-does-the-container-belong.aspx

A comprehensive example 2

Telling you that a sauce béarnaise is "an emulsified sauce made from egg yolk and butter" doesn't magically instill in you the ability to make one. The best way to learn is to practice; an example can often bridge the gap between theory and practice. Watching a professional cook making a sauce béarnaise is helpful before you try it out yourself.

When I introduced Dependency Injection in the last chapter, I presented a high-level tour to help you understand its purpose and general principles. However, this simple example didn't do justice to DI. DI is a way to enable loose coupling, and loose coupling is first and foremost an efficient way to deal with complexity.

Most software is complex in the sense that it must address many concerns at the same time. Besides the business concerns (which may be complex in their own right), software must also address concerns related to security, diagnostics, operations, and extensibility. Instead of addressing all of these concerns in one big ball of mud, loose coupling encourages us to address each concern separately. It's easier

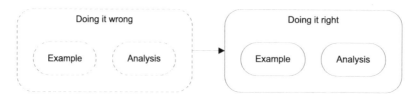

Figure 2.1   This chapter contains two variations of the same example. First, you'll see how easy it is to write tightly coupled code. Then, you'll see how to write the same application in a loosely coupled fashion. Both examples contain the example itself as well as an analysis. If you want to see loosely coupled code right away, you may want to skip the first section.

to address each concern in isolation—but ultimately we must still compose this complex set of concerns. Let's take a look at a complex example to better showcase DI.

> **WARNING**   The whole point of loosely coupled code is to deal with complexity in an efficient manner, and we need complex examples to illustrate complex concepts. You should expect most examples in this book to be complex and involve multiple classes from multiple libraries. Complexity is part of the game.

I have devoted this entire chapter to a complex example. I think it's important to contrast the loosely coupled code with a more "traditional," tightly coupled example, so in this chapter you'll find the same feature implemented in both ways. First, I set the stage by showcasing how easy it is to write tightly coupled code. Second, I implement the same functionality using DI. You can skip the tightly coupled example if you want to see some loosely coupled code right away. When you're done with this chapter, you should begin to understand how you can use DI to compose loosely coupled code.

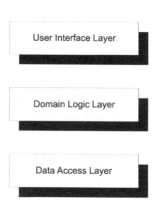

Figure 2.2   Standard three-layer application architecture. This is the simplest common variation of the *n*-layer application architecture, where an application is composed of *n* layers, each consisting of one or more modules. Some variants of *n*-layer diagrams will have vertical boxes that span multiple application layers. These are often used to represent CROSS-CUTTING CONCERNS, such as security or logging.

2.1   *Doing it wrong*

The idea of building loosely coupled code isn't particularly controversial, but there's a huge gap between intent and practice. Before I show you how to use DI to build a loosely coupled application, I want to show you how easily it can go wrong.

A common attempt at loosely coupled code is building a layered application. Anyone can draw a three-layer application diagram, and figure 2.2 proves that I can, too.

Drawing a three-layer diagram is deceptively simple, but the act of drawing the diagram is akin to stating that you'll have sauce béarnaise with your steak: it's a declaration of intent that carries no guarantee with regard to the final result. You may end up with something else, as you shall soon see.

2.1.1 Building a tightly coupled application

There's more than one way to view and design a flexible and maintainable complex application,[1] but the *n*-layer application architecture constitutes a well-known, tried-and-true approach. The challenge is to implement it correctly.

Armed with a three-layer diagram like the one in figure 2.2, you can now start building an application.

MEET MARY ROWAN

Mary Rowan is a professional .NET developer working for a local Certified Microsoft Partner that mainly develops web applications. She's 34-years old and has been working with software for 11 years. This makes her one of the more experienced developers in the company, and she often acts as a mentor for junior developers in addition to performing her regular duties as a senior developer.

In general, Mary is happy about the work that she's doing, but it frustrates her that milestones are often being missed, forcing her and her colleagues to work long hours and weekends to meet deadlines. She suspects that there must be more efficient ways to build software. In an effort to learn about efficiency, she buys a lot of programming books—but she rarely has time to read them.

Much of her spare time is spent with her husband and two girls. Mary likes to go hiking in the mountains. She's also an enthusiastic cook, and she definitely knows how to make a real sauce béarnaise.

Mary has been asked to create a new e-commerce application on ASP.NET MVC and the Entity Framework with SQL Server as the data store. To maximize modularity, it must be a three-layer application.

The first feature to be implemented should be a simple list of featured products, pulled from a database table and displayed on a web page; an example is shown in figure 2.3. If the user viewing the list is a preferred customer, the price on all products should be discounted by five percent.

Let's look over Mary's shoulder as she implements the application's first feature.

Figure 2.3 Screen shot of the e-commerce web application Mary has been asked to develop. It features a simple list of featured products and their prices ("kr." is the currency symbol for Danish Kroner).

---

[1] Currently, the most promising alternative to *n*-layer applications is an architectural style related to the Command-Query Responsibility Segregation (CQRS) pattern. For more information, see Rinat Abdullin, "CQRS Starting Page," http://abdullin.com/cqrs

DATA LAYER

Because she'll need to pull data from a database table, Mary has decided to begin by implementing the data layer. The first step is to define the database table itself. Mary uses SQL Server Management Studio to create the table shown in figure 2.4.

To implement the Data Access Layer, Mary adds a new library to her solution. From Visual Studio, she uses the Entity Data Model Wizard to generate an entity model from the database she just created. She changes a few names to finalize the model, as shown in figure 2.5.

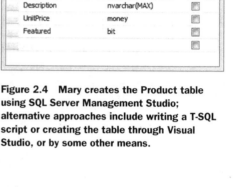

Figure 2.4 Mary creates the Product table using SQL Server Management Studio; alternative approaches include writing a T-SQL script or creating the table through Visual Studio, or by some other means.

> **NOTE** Don't worry if you aren't familiar with the Microsoft Entity Framework. The details of the data access implementation aren't *that* important in this context, so you should be able to follow the example even if you're more familiar with a different data access technology.

Figure 2.5 The `Product` entity generated from the Product database table shown in figure 2.4. Mary has changed the name of the Featured column to IsFeatured, as well as changed a few names in the generated `ObjectContext` (not shown).

The generated `ObjectContext` and the `Product` entity are public types contained within the same assembly. Mary knows that she'll later need to add more features to her application, but the data access component needed to implement the first feature is now completed.

Figure 2.6 shows how far Mary has come in implementing the layered architecture envisioned in figure 2.2.

Now that the Data Access Layer has been implemented, the next logical step is the Domain Logic Layer.

DOMAIN LAYER

In the absence of any domain logic, the list of Products exposed by the generated `ObjectContext` could technically have been used directly from the User Interface Layer.

> **WARNING** With the exception of pure data-reporting applications, there's always domain logic. You may not realize it at first, but as you get to know the domain, its embedded and implicit rules and assumptions will

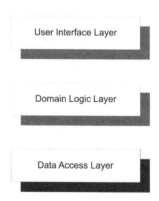

Figure 2.6 So far Mary has implemented the Data Access Layer of her application. The Domain Logic Layer and User Interface Layer are still left before the feature is complete.

gradually emerge. Implementing such logic in either the User Interface or Data Access Layers will lead to pain and suffering. Do yourself a favor and create a Domain Logic Layer from the beginning.

The requirements for Mary's application state that preferred customers should be shown the list prices with a five percent discount. Mary has yet to figure out how to identify a preferred customer, so she asks her coworker Jens for advice:

MARY: *I need to implement this business logic so that a preferred customer gets a five percent discount.*

JENS: *Sounds easy. Just multiply by .95.*

MARY: *Thanks, but that's not what I wanted to ask you about. What I wanted to ask you is, how should I identify a preferred customer?*

JENS: *I see. Is this a web application or a desktop application?*

MARY: *It's a web app.*

JENS: *Okay, then you can define a user profile and have an* IsPreferredCustomer *property. You can get the profile through the* HttpContext.

MARY: *Slow down, Jens. This code must be in the Domain Logic Layer. It's a library. There's no* HttpContext.

JENS: *Oh. [Thinks for a while] I still think you should use the Profile feature of ASP.NET to look up the value on the user. You can then pass the value to your domain logic as a Boolean.*

MARY: *I don't know...*

JENS: *That will also ensure that you have good separation of concerns, because your domain logic doesn't have to deal with security. You know: The SINGLE RESPONSIBILITY PRINCIPLE! It's the Agile way to do it!*

MARY: *I guess you've got a point.*

WARNING Jens is basing his advice on his technical knowledge of ASP.NET. As the discussion takes him away from his comfort zone, he steamrolls Mary with a triple combo of buzzwords. Be aware that he doesn't know what he is talking about: he misuses the concept of separation of concerns, completely misses the point with the SINGLE RESPONSIBILITY PRINCIPLE, and he only mentions Agile because he recently heard someone else talk enthusiastically about it.

Armed with Jens' advice, Mary creates a new C# library project and adds a class called ProductService, shown in the following listing. To make the ProductService class compile, she must add a reference to her Data Access library, because the CommerceObjectContext class is defined there.

Listing 2.1 Mary's ProductService class

```
public partial class ProductService
{
    private readonly CommerceObjectContext objectContext;
```

```
public ProductService()
{
    this.objectContext = new CommerceObjectContext();
}

public IEnumerable<Product> GetFeaturedProducts(
    bool isCustomerPreferred)
{
    var discount = isCustomerPreferred ? .95m : 1;
    var products = (from p in this.objectContext
                            .Products
                    where p.IsFeatured
                    select p).AsEnumerable();
    return from p in products
        select new Product
        {
            ProductId = p.ProductId,
            Name = p.Name,
            Description = p.Description,
            IsFeatured = p.IsFeatured,
            UnitPrice = p.UnitPrice * discount
        };
    }
}
```

Mary is happy that she has encapsulated data access technology (LINQ to Entities), configuration, and domain logic in the ProductService class. She has delegated the knowledge of the user to the caller by passing in the isCustomerPreferred parameter, and she uses this value to calculate the discount for all the products.

Further refinement could include replacing the hard-coded discount value (.95) with a configurable number, but, for now, this implementation will suffice. Mary is almost done—the only thing still left is the User Interface. Mary decides that can wait until the next day.

Figure 2.7 shows how far Mary has come with implementing the architecture envisioned in figure 2.2.

With the Data Access and Domain Logic Layers implemented, the only remaining layer to implement is the User Interface Layer.

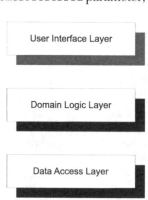

Figure 2.7   At this point, Mary has implemented the Data Access Layer and the Domain Logic Layer. Compared to figure 2.6, the Domain Logic Layer has been added. The User Interface Layer still remains to be implemented.

USER INTERFACE LAYER

The next day, Mary resumes her work with the e-commerce application, adding a new ASP.NET MVC application to her solution.

NOTE   Don't worry if you aren't familiar with the ASP.NET MVC framework. The intricate details of how the MVC framework operates aren't the focus of this discussion. The important part is how DEPENDENCIES are consumed, and that's a relatively platform-neutral subject.

ASP.NET MVC crash course

ASP.NET MVC takes its name from the Model View Controller[2] design pattern. In this context, the most important thing to understand is that when a web request arrives, a Controller handles the request, potentially using a (Domain) Model to deal with it and form a response that's finally rendered by a View.

A Controller is normally a class that derives from the abstract `Controller` class. It has one or more *action methods* that handle requests; for example, a `HomeController` class has an `Index` method that handles the request for the default page.

When an action method returns, it passes on the resulting Model to the View through a `ViewResult` instance.

The next listing shows how she implements an `Index` method on her `HomeController` class to extract the featured products from the database and pass them to the View. To make this code compile, she must add references to both the Data Access library and the Domain library because the `ProductService` class is defined in the Domain library, but the `Product` class is defined in the Data Access library.

Listing 2.2 Index method on the default controller class

```
public ViewResult Index()
{
    bool isPreferredCustomer =
        this.User.IsInRole("PreferredCustomer");

    var service = new ProductService();
    var products =
        service.GetFeaturedProducts(isPreferredCustomer);
    this.ViewData["Products"] = products;

    return this.View();
}
```

As part of the ASP.NET MVC lifecycle, the User property on the `HomeController` class is automatically populated with the correct user object, so Mary uses it to determine if the current user is a preferred customer. Armed with this information, she can invoke the Domain Logic to get the list of featured products. In a moment, I'll return to this, because it contains a trap, but for now, I'll let Mary discover it for herself.

---

[2] Martin Fowler et al., *Patterns of Enterprise Application Architecture* (New York: Addison-Wesley, 2003), 330.

The list of products must be rendered by the Index View. The following listing shows the markup for the View.

Listing 2.3   Index View markup

```
<h2>Featured Products</h2>
<div>
<% var products =                                    Get products populated
        (IEnumerable<Product>)this.ViewData["Products"];    by Controller
    foreach (var product in products)
    { %>
    <div>
    <%= this.Html.Encode(product.Name) %>
    (<%= this.Html.Encode(product.UnitPrice.ToString("C")) %>)
    </div>
<% } %>
</div>
```

ASP.NET MVC enables you to write standard HTML with bits of imperative code embedded to access objects created and assigned by the Controller that created the View. In this case, the HomeController's Index method assigned the list of featured products to a key called Products that Mary uses in the View to render the list of products.

Figure 2.8 shows how Mary has now implemented the architecture envisioned in figure 2.2.

With all three layers in place the applications should theoretically work, but only a test can verify whether that's the case.

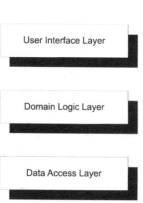

Figure 2.8   Mary has now implemented all three layers in the application. This figure is identical to figure 2.2, but repeated here to illustrate the current state of Mary's application.

2.1.2   Smoke test

Mary has now implemented all three layers, so it's time to see if the application works. She presses F5 and soon receives this message:

The specified named connection is either not found in the configuration, not intended to be used with the EntityClient provider, or not valid.

Because Mary used the default constructor of CommerceObjectContext (shown in listing 2.1), it *implicitly* expects that a connection string named CommerceObjectContext is present in the web.config file. As I alluded to when I discussed listing 2.2, this implicitness contains a trap. During the night, Mary forgot the implementation details of her Domain Layer. The code compiles, but the site doesn't work.

In this case, fixing the error is straightforward. Mary inserts the correct connection string in the web.config file. When she runs the application, the web page shown in figure 2.3 appears.

The *Featured Products* feature is now done, and Mary feels confident and ready to implement the next feature in the application. After all, she has followed established best practices and created a three-layer application.

2.1.3 *Evaluation*

Did Mary succeed in developing a proper, layered application? No, she did not—although she certainly had the best of intentions. She created three Visual Studio projects that correspond to the three layers in the planned architecture, as shown in figure 2.9. To the casual observer, this looks like the coveted layered architecture, but, as you'll see, the code is tightly coupled.

Figure 2.9 Mary's e-commerce web application has a Visual Studio project for each layer in the planned architecture—but is it a three-layer application?

Visual Studio makes it easy and natural to work with solutions and projects in this way. If we need functionality from a different library, we can easily add a reference to it and write code that creates new instances of the types defined in these other libraries. Every time we add a reference, we take on a DEPENDENCY.

DEPENDENCY GRAPH

When working with solutions in Visual Studio, it's easy to lose track of the important DEPENDENCIES, because Visual Studio displays them together with all the other project references that may point to assemblies in the .NET Base Class Library (BCL).

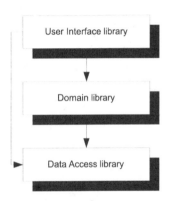

To understand how the modules in Mary's application relate to each other, we can draw a graph of the dependencies (see figure 2.10).

Figure 2.10 Dependency graph for Mary's application showing how the modules depend on each other. The arrows point towards a module's DEPENDENCY.

The most remarkable insight to be gained from figure 2.10 is that the User Interface library is dependent on both Domain and Data Access libraries. It seems as though the User Interface may bypass the Domain Layer in certain cases. This bears further investigation.

EVALUATING COMPOSABILITY

A major goal of building a three-layer application is to separate concerns. We'd like to separate our Domain Model from the Data Access Layer and the User Interface Layer so that none of these concerns pollute the Domain Model. In large applications, it's essential for it to be possible to work with one area of the application in isolation.

To evaluate Mary's implementation, we can ask a simple question:

TEST   Is it possible to use each module in isolation?

In theory, we should be able to compose modules in any way we like. We may need to write new modules to bind existing modules together in new and unanticipated ways, but, ideally, we should be able to do so without having to modify the existing modules.

> **NOTE** The following analysis discusses whether modules can be replaced, but be aware that this is a technique we use to evaluate composability. Even if we never want to swap modules, this sort of analysis uncovers potential issues regarding coupling. If we find that the code is tightly coupled, *all* the benefits of loose coupling are lost.

Can we use the modules in Mary's application in new and exciting ways? Let's look at some likely scenarios.

NEW USER INTERFACE

If Mary's application becomes a success, the project's stakeholders would like her to develop a rich client version in Windows Presentation Foundation (WPF). Is this possible to do while reusing the Domain Layer and the Data Access Layer?

When we examine the dependency graph in figure 2.10, we can quickly ascertain that no modules are depending on the Web User Interface, so it's possible to remove it and replace it with a WPF User Interface.

Creating a rich client based on WPF is a new application that shares most of its implementation with the original web application. Figure 2.11 illustrates how a WPF application would need to take the same dependencies as the web application. The original web application can remain unchanged.

Replacing the User Interface Layer is certainly possible with Mary's implementation, so let's examine another interesting decomposition.

NEW DATA ACCESS LAYER

Imagine that market analysts figure out that, to optimize profits, Mary's application should be available as a cloud application hosted on Windows Azure. In Windows Azure, data can be stored in the highly scalable Azure Table Storage Service. This storage mechanism is based on flexible data containers that contain unconstrained data. The service enforces no particular database schema, and there's no referential integrity.

The protocol used to communicate with the Table Storage Service is HTTP, and the most obvious data access technology on .NET is based on ADO.NET Data Services.

This type of database is sometimes known as a *key-value database*, and it's a different beast than a relational database accessed through the Entity Framework.

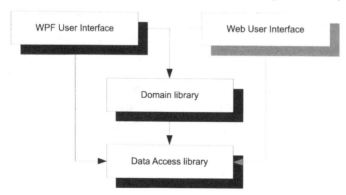

Figure 2.11 Replacing the Web User Interface with a WPF User Interface is possible because no module depends on the Web User Interface. The original Web User Interface remains in the figure in grayscale to illustrate the point that adding a new user interface doesn't preclude the original.

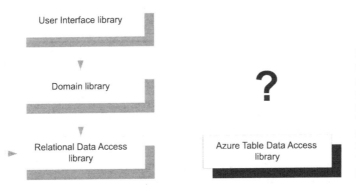

Figure 2.12 **Attempting to remove the relational Data Access library leaves nothing left, because all other modules depend on it. There's no place where we can instruct the Domain library to use the new Azure Table Data Access library instead of the original.**

To enable the e-commerce application as a cloud application, the Data Access library must be replaced with a module that uses the Table Storage Service. Is this possible?

From the dependency graph in figure 2.10, we already know that both User Interface and Domain libraries depend on the Entity Framework-based Data Access library. If we try to remove the Data Access library, the solution will no longer compile, because a required DEPENDENCY is missing.

In a big application with dozens of modules, we could also try to remove those modules that don't compile to see what would be left. In the case of Mary's application, it's evident that we'd have to remove all modules, leaving nothing behind.

Although it would be possible to develop an Azure Table Data Access library that mimics the API exposed by the original Data Access library, there's no way we could inject it into the application.

The application isn't nearly as composable as the project stakeholders would have liked. Enabling the profit-maximizing cloud abilities requires a major rewrite of the application, because none of the existing modules can be reused.

OTHER COMBINATIONS

We could analyze the application for other combinations of modules, but it would be a moot point because we already know that it fails to support an important scenario.

Besides, not all combinations make sense. We could ask whether it would be possible to replace the Domain Model with a different implementation. In most cases, this would be an odd question to ask, because the Domain Model encapsulates the heart of the application. Without the Domain Model, most applications have no raison d'être (reason for being).

2.1.4 *Analysis*

Why did Mary's implementation fail to achieve the desired degree of composability? Is it because the User Interface has a direct dependency on the Data Access library? Let's examine this possibility in greater detail.

DEPENDENCY GRAPH ANALYSIS

Why is the User Interface dependent on the Data Access library? The culprit is this Domain Model method signature:

```
public IEnumerable<Product> GetFeaturedProducts(bool isCustomerPreferred)
```

`Exposes Data Access type to clients`

The `GetFeaturedProducts` method returns a sequence of products, but the `Product` class is defined in the Data Access library. Any client consuming the `GetFeatured-Products` method must reference the Data Access library to be able to compile.

It's possible to change the signature of the method to return a sequence of a type defined within the Domain Model. It would also be more correct, but it doesn't solve the problem.

Let's assume that we break the dependency between the User Interface and Data Access libraries. The modified dependency graph would now look like figure 2.13.

Would such a change enable Mary to replace the relational Data Access library with one that encapsulates access to the Azure Table service? Unfortunately, no, because the Domain library still depends on the Data Access library. The User Interface, in turn, still depends on the Domain Model, so if we try to remove the original Data Access library, there would be nothing left of the application.

The root cause of the problem lies somewhere else.

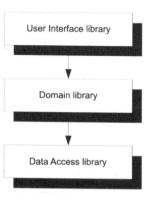

Figure 2.13 Dependency graph of the hypothetical situation where the dependency of the User Interface on the Data Access library has been severed.

DATA ACCESS INTERFACE ANALYSIS

The Domain Model depends on the Data Access library because the entire data model is defined there. The `Product` class was generated when Mary ran the LINQ to Entities wizard. Using the Entity Framework to implement a Data Access Layer may be a reasonable decision.

However, consuming it directly in the Domain Model isn't.

The offending code can be found spread out in the `ProductService` class. The constructor creates a new instance of the `CommerceObjectContext` class and assigns it to a private member variable:

```
this.objectContext = new CommerceObjectContext();
```

This tightly couples the `ProductService` class to the Data Access library. There's no reasonable way we can intercept this piece of code and replace it with something else. The reference to the Data Access library is hard-coded into the `ProductService` class.

The implementation of the `GetFeaturedProducts` method uses the `Commerce-ObjectContext` to pull `Product` objects from the database:

```
var products = (from p in this.objectContext
                    .Products
                where p.IsFeatured
                select p).AsEnumerable();
```

This only reinforces the hard-coded dependency, but, at this point, the damage is already done. What we need is a better way to compose modules without such tight coupling.

MISCELLANEOUS OTHER ISSUES

Before I show you the better alternative, I'd like to point out a few other issues with Mary's code that ought to be addressed.

- Most of the Domain Model seems to be implemented in the Data Access library. Whereas it's a *technical* problem that the Domain Model library references the Data Access library, it's a *conceptual* problem that the Data Access library defines such a class as the Product class. A public Product class belongs in the Domain Model.

- Under the influence of Jens, Mary decided to implement the code that determines whether or not a user is a preferred customer in the User Interface. However, how a customer is identified as a preferred customer is a piece of Business Logic, so it ought to be implemented in the Domain Model.

    Jens' argument about separations of concern and the SINGLE RESPONSIBILITY PRINCIPLE is no excuse for putting code in the wrong place. Following the SINGLE RESPONSIBILITY PRINCIPLE within a single library is entirely possible—that's the expected approach.

- The ProductService class relies on XML configuration. As you saw when we followed Mary's efforts, she forgot that she had to put a particular piece of configuration code in her web.config file. Although the ability to configure a compiled application is important, only the finished application should rely on configuration files. It's much more flexible for reusable libraries to be imperatively configurable by their callers.

    In the end, the ultimate caller is the application itself. At that point, all relevant configuration data can be read from a .config file and fed to the underlying libraries, as needed.

- The View (as shown in listing 2.3) seems to contain too much functionality. It performs casts and specific string formatting. Such functionality should be moved to the underlying model.

In the next section, I'll show you a more composable way of building an application with the same features as the one Mary built. I'll also address these minor issues at the same time.

2.2 *Doing it right*

Dependency Injection (DI) can be used to solve the issues that we discovered. Because DI is a radical departure from the way Mary created her application, I'm not going to modify it. Rather, I'm going to re-create it from scratch.

You shouldn't infer from this decision that it's impossible to refactor an existing application towards DI; it can be done, but it's hard. In my experience, it takes a lot of refactorings to get there.[3]

NOTE   As I walk you through this example, don't worry if you get lost along the way. DI *is* complex, and there are many elements in play. I chose this example because it resembles a realistic scenario, but the disadvantage is that it's more complex than a toy example. Later in the book, I'm going to delve deeper into the concepts and techniques that are being introduced here. After you've read more, you can always come back and reread this section.

Many people refer to DI as INVERSION OF CONTROL (IoC). These two terms are sometimes used interchangeably, but DI is a subset of IoC. Throughout the book, I'll consistently use the most specific term: *DI*. If I mean IoC, I'll refer to it specifically.

Dependency Injection or Inversion of Control?

The term *Inversion of Control (IoC)* originally meant any sort of programming style where an overall framework or runtime controlled the program flow.[4] According to that definition, most software developed on the .NET Framework uses IoC.

When you write an ASP.NET application, you hook into the ASP.NET page life cycle, but you aren't in control—ASP.NET is.

When you write a WCF service, you implement interfaces decorated with attributes. You may be writing the service code, but ultimately, you aren't in control—WCF is.

These days, we're so used to working with frameworks that we don't consider this to be special, but it's a different model from being in full control of your code. This can still happen for a .NET application—most notably for command-line executables. As soon as Main is invoked, your code is in full control. It controls program flow, lifetime, everything. No special events are being raised and no overridden members are being invoked.

Before DI had a name, people started to refer to frameworks that manage DEPENDENCIES as *Inversion of Control Containers,* and soon, the meaning of IoC gradually drifted towards that particular meaning: Inversion of Control over DEPENDENCIES. Always the taxonomist, Martin Fowler introduced the term *Dependency Injection* to specifically refer to IoC in the context of dependency management.[5] *Dependency Injection* has since been widely accepted as the most correct terminology.

In short, IoC is a much broader term that includes, but isn't limited to, DI.

---

[3]   There's a whole book about this subject. See Michael Feathers, *Working Effectively with Legacy Code* (New York: Prentice Hall, 2004).

[4]   Martin Fowler, "InversionOfControl," 2005, http://martinfowler.com/bliki/InversionOfControl.html

[5]   Martin Fowler, "Inversion of Control Containers and the Dependency Injection pattern," 2004, http://martinfowler.com/articles/injection.html

In the context of managing dependencies, Inversion of Control accurately describes what we're trying to accomplish. In Mary's application, the code directly controls its dependencies: when the `ProductService` needs a new instance of the `Commerce-ObjectContext` class, it simply creates an instance using the `new` keyword. When the `HomeController` needs a new instance of the `ProductService` class, it, too, news up an instance. The application is in total control. That may sound powerful, but it's actually limiting. I call this the Control Freak anti-pattern. Inversion of Control instructs us to let go of that control and let something else manage the dependencies.

2.2.1 *Rebuilding the commerce application*

When I write software, I prefer to start in the most significant place. This is often the user interface. From there, I work my way in, adding more functionality until the feature is done and I can move on to the next. This *outside-in* technique helps me to focus on the requested functionality without over-engineering the solution.

> **NOTE** The *outside-in* technique is closely related to the YAGNI principle ("You Aren't Gonna Need It"). This principle emphasizes that only required features should be implemented, and that the implementation should be as simple as possible.

Because I always practice Test-Driven Development (TDD), I start by writing unit tests as soon as my outside-in approach prompts me to create a new class. Although I wrote a lot of unit tests to create this example, TDD isn't required to implement and use DI, so I'm not going to show these tests in the book. If you're interested, they're available in the source code that accompanies the book.

User interface

The specification for the list of featured products is to write an application that extracts the featured products from the database and displays them in a list, as shown in figure 2.3. Because I know that the project's stakeholders will mainly be interested in the visual result, the User Interface sounds like a good place to start.

The first thing I do after opening Visual Studio is to add a new ASP.NET MVC application to my solution. Because the list of featured products needs to go on the front page, I start by modifying the `Index.aspx` to include the markup shown in the following listing.

Listing 2.4 Index `View` markup

```
<h2>Featured Products</h2>
<div>
<% foreach (var product in this.Model.Products)
   { %>
   <div><%= this.Html.Encode(product.SummaryText) %></div>
<% } %>
</div>
```

Notice how much cleaner listing 2.4 is compared to listing 2.3. The first improvement is that it's no longer necessary to cast a dictionary item to a sequence of products before iteration is possible. I accomplished this easily by letting the `Index.aspx` page inherit from `System.Web.Mvc.ViewPage<FeaturedProductsViewModel>` instead of `System.Web.Mvc.ViewPage`. This means that the Model property of the page is of the `FeaturedProductsView-Model` type.

The entire product display string is pulled directly from the `SummaryText` property of the product.

Both improvements are related to the introduction of View-specific Models that encapsulate the behavior of the View. These Models are Plain Old CLR[6] Objects (POCOs). Figure 2.14 provides an outline of their structure.

The `HomeController` must return a View with an instance of `FeaturedProductsViewModel` for the code in listing 2.4 to work. As a first step, this can be implemented inside the `HomeController` like this:

```
public ViewResult Index()
{
    var vm = new FeaturedProductsViewModel();
    return View(vm);
}
```

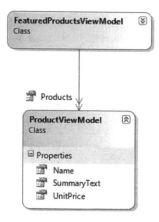

Figure 2.14   The `FeaturedProductsView-Model` **contains a list of** `ProductViewModels`**. Both are POCOs, which makes them eminently susceptible to unit testing. The** `SummaryText` **property is derived from the** `Name` **and** `UnitPrice` **properties to encapsulate rendering logic.**

This will enable the web application to execute without error, but the list of featured products will always be empty. Providing the list of featured products is a task for the Domain Model.

Figure 2.15 shows the current state of implementing the architecture envisioned in figure 2.2.

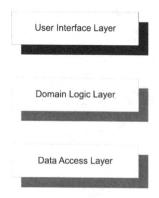

Figure 2.15   At this stage, only the User Interface Layer has been implemented, and the Domain Logic and Data Access Layers still remain. Contrast this figure with figure 2.6, which shows Mary's progress at a comparable stage. One advantage of starting with the user interface is that we already have software we can run and test. Only at a much later stage, shown in figure 2.8, does Mary arrive at a point where she can run the application.

---

[6]   Common Language Runtime

Although a user interface exists, it doesn't do much of interest. The list of featured products is always empty, so I need to implement some Domain Logic that can supply a proper list of products.

DOMAIN MODEL

The Domain Model is a plain vanilla C# library that I add to the solution. This library will contain POCOs and abstract types. The POCOs will model the Domain while the abstract types provide abstractions that will serve as my main external entry point into the Domain Model.

The principle of programming to interfaces instead of concrete classes is a cornerstone of DI. It's this principle that allows us to replace one concrete implementation with another.

> ### Interfaces or abstract classes?
>
> Many guides to object-oriented design focus on interfaces as the main abstraction mechanism, whereas the .NET Framework Design Guidelines endorse abstract classes over interfaces.[7] Should you use interfaces or abstract classes?
>
> With relation to DI, the reassuring answer is that it doesn't matter. The important part is that you program against some sort of abstraction.
>
> Choosing between interfaces and abstract classes is important in other contexts, but not here. You'll notice that I use the words interchangeably; I often use the term ABSTRACTION to encompass both interfaces and abstract classes.

I'm still following the outside-in approach, so I'll be adding code to the User Interface Layer for a while yet. Some of the code I'll add will now use types from the Domain Model. This means that I'll add a reference to the Domain Model from the User Interface, like Mary did. That will turn out okay, but I'll postpone doing a dependency graph analysis until section 2.2.2, so that I can provide you with the full picture.

A common abstraction over data access is provided by the Repository pattern,[8] so I'll define a `ProductRepository` abstract class in the Domain Model library:

```
public abstract class ProductRepository
{
    public abstract IEnumerable<Product> GetFeaturedProducts();
}
```

A full-blown Repository would have more methods to find and modify products, but, following the outside-in principle, I only define the classes and members I need for the task at hand. It's easier to add functionality to code than it is to remove anything.

---

[7] Krzysztof Cwalina and Brad Abrams, *Framework Design Guidelines: Conventions, Idioms, and Patterns for Reusable .NET Libraries* (New York, Addison-Wesley, 2006), 77-83.

[8] Fowler, *Patterns of Enterprise Application Architecture*, 322-327.

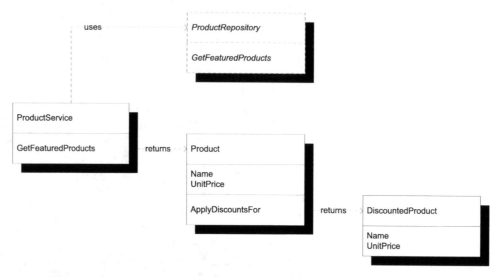

Figure 2.16 The `Product` class only contains the `Name` and `UnitPrice` properties, because these are the only properties needed to implement the desired application feature. The `ApplyDiscountFor` applies the discount (if any) for a user and returns an instance of the `DiscountedProduct` class. The abstract `GetFeaturedProducts` returns a sequence of Products.

The `Product` class is also implemented with the bare minimum of members, as illustrated in figure 2.16.

The `Index` method on `HomeController` should use a `ProductService` instance to retrieve the list of featured products, apply any discounts, convert the `Product` instances to `ProductViewModel` instances, and add them to the `FeaturedProducts-ViewModel`. Because the `ProductService` class takes an instance of `ProductRepository` in its constructor, the tricky part is to provide it with a proper instance. Recall from the analysis of Mary's implementation that newing up dependencies is a cardinal sin. As soon as I do that, I'm tightly coupled with the type I just used.

I'm going to relinquish control of the `ProductRepository` dependency. As shown in the next listing, I'd rather be relying on something else to provide me with an instance through the `HomeController`'s constructor. This pattern is called CONSTRUCTOR INJECTION—how the instance is created, and by whom, is of no concern to the `HomeController`.

Listing 2.5 `HomeController` with CONSTRUCTOR INJECTION

```
public partial class HomeController : Controller
{
    private readonly ProductRepository repository;

    public HomeController(ProductRepository repository)      ❶ Constructor
    {                                                            Injection
        if (repository == null)
        {
```

```
            throw new ArgumentNullException("repository");
        }
        this.repository = repository;                          Save injected
    }                                                          dependency for later

    public ViewResult Index()
    {
        var productService =                                   Pass injected
            new ProductService(this.repository);               dependency on

        var vm = new FeaturedProductsViewModel();

        var products =
            productService.GetFeaturedProducts(this.User);
        foreach (var product in products)
        {
            var productVM = new ProductViewModel(product);
            vm.Products.Add(productVM);
        }

        return View(vm);
    }
}
```

The `HomeController` constructor ❶ specifies that anyone wishing to use the class must provide an instance of `ProductRepository` (which, as you may remember, is an abstract class). A Guard Clause[9] guarantees this precondition by throwing an exception if the supplied instance is null. The injected dependency can be saved for later and safely used by other members of the `HomeController` class.

The first time I heard about CONSTRUCTOR INJECTION, I had a hard time understanding the real benefit. Doesn't it push the burden of controlling the DEPENDENCY onto some other class?

Yes, it does—and that's the whole point. In an *n*-layer application, we can push that burden all the way to the top of the application, into a COMPOSITION ROOT. This is a centralized place where the different modules of an application can be composed. This can be done manually or delegated to a DI CONTAINER.

The `HomeController` delegates most of its work to the `ProductService` class, shown in the following listing. The `ProductService` class corresponds to Mary's class of the same name, but is now a pure Domain Model class.

Listing 2.6 ProductService class

```
public class ProductService
{
    private readonly ProductRepository repository;            Constructor
                                                              Injection again
    public ProductService(ProductRepository repository)
    {
        if (repository == null)
        {
```

---

[9] Martin Fowler et al., *Refactoring: Improving the Design of Existing Code* (New York: Addison-Wesley, 1999), 250.

```
            throw new ArgumentNullException("repository");
        }

        this.repository = repository;
    }

    public IEnumerable<DiscountedProduct>                    ❶ Method
        GetFeaturedProducts(IPrincipal user)                    Injection
    {
        if (user == null)
        {
            throw new ArgumentNullException("user");
        }

        return from p in                                     Use both injected
                this.repository.GetFeaturedProducts()         dependencies to
                select p.ApplyDiscountFor(user);             implement behavior
    }
}
```

The GetFeaturedProducts method ❶ now takes an instance of IPrincipal that represents the current user. This is another departure from Mary's implementation in listing 2.1, which only took a Boolean value, indicating whether the user is a preferred customer. However, because deciding whether a user is a preferred customer is a piece of Domain Logic, it's more correct to explicitly model the current user as a DEPENDENCY. We must always adhere to the principle of *programming to an interface*, but in this case I don't need to invent one (as I did with ProductRepository) because the .NET Base Class Library (BCL) already includes the IPrincipal interface, which represents a standard way of modeling application users.

Passing a DEPENDENCY as a parameter in a method is known as METHOD INJECTION. Once again, control is delegated to the caller, similar to CONSTRUCTOR INJECTION. Although the details vary, the main technique remains the same.

At this stage, the application doesn't work at all. There are two problems left:

- There are no concrete implementations of ProductRepository. This is easily solved. In the next section, I'll implement a concrete ProductRepository that reads the featured products from the database.
- By default, ASP.NET MVC expects Controllers to have default constructors. Because I introduced a parameter to HomeController's constructor, the MVC framework doesn't know how to create an instance of HomeController. This issue can be solved by developing a custom IControllerFactory. How this is done is outside the scope of this chapter, but it's a subject that will be discussed in chapter 7. Suffice it to say that this custom factory will create an instance of the concrete ProductRepository and supply it to Home-Controller's constructor.

In the Domain Model, I work only with types defined within the Domain Model (and the .NET Base Class Library). The concepts of the Domain Model are implemented as POCOs. At this stage, there's only a single concept represented, namely, a Product. The

Domain Model must be able to communicate with the outside world (such as databases). This need is modeled as abstract classes (such as Repositories) that we must replace with concrete implementations before the Domain Model becomes useful.

Figure 2.17 shows the current state of implementing the architecture envisioned in figure 2.2.

The application's Domain Model isn't yet particularly object-oriented;[10] there's only the single abstract `Product-Repository` that I need to implement to close the loop.

DATA ACCESS

Like Mary, I'd like to implement my Data Access library using LINQ to Entities, so I follow the same steps as she did in section 2.1.1 to create the Entity Model. The main difference is that the Entity Model and the `Commerce-ObjectContext` are now only implementation details; but, with them, I can create an implementation of `Product-Repository`, as shown in the following listing.

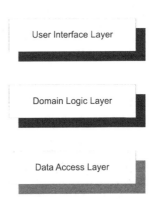

Figure 2.17 The User Interface and Domain Logic Layers are now both in place, while the Data Access Layer remains to be implemented. Contrast this figure with figure 2.7, which shows Mary's progress at a similar stage.

Listing 2.7 Implementing `ProductRepository` using LINQ to Entities

```
public class SqlProductRepository : Domain.ProductRepository
{
    private readonly CommerceObjectContext context;

    public SqlProductRepository(string connString)
    {
        this.context =
            new CommerceObjectContext(connString);
    }

    public override IEnumerable<Domain.Product> GetFeaturedProducts()
    {
        var products = (from p in this.context.Products
                        where p.IsFeatured
                        select p).AsEnumerable();
        return from p in products                          ❶ Convert to Domain
            select p.ToDomainProduct();                        Product
    }
}
```

In Mary's application, the generated `Product` entity was used as a Domain object, although it was defined in the database. This is no longer the case, because I already defined the `Product` class in the Domain Model. When I generated the Entity Model, the wizard created *another* `Product` class for me and I need to convert between the two ❶. Figure 2.18 illustrates how they're defined in two different modules. The

---

[10] We call this an Anemic model. Martin Fowler, "AnemicDomainModel," 2003, http://www.martinfowler.com/bliki/AnemicDomainModel.html

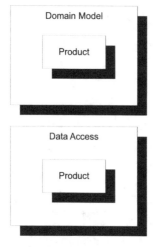

Figure 2.18   **The Domain Model and Data Access libraries both define a class named** `Product`**. The Domain** `Product` **is the important class that encapsulates the Domain concept of a** `Product`**. The Data Access** `Product` **class is only an artifact of the Entity Framework wizard. It can easily be renamed or made internal.**

`Product` entity class is merely an implementation detail, and I could easily have made it internal to express that more explicitly.

> **NOTE** You could argue that it's a specific shortcoming of the Entity Framework that it doesn't support persistence-ignorant entities[11] (at least not in the .NET 3.5 SP1 version). However, this is the sort of constraint you must deal with in real software projects.

The Entity `Product` defines a conversion to the Domain `Product` type. This conversion is a trivial mapping of property values. Although not particularly related to DI, I include it here for good measure:

```
Domain.Product p = new Domain.Product();
p.Name = this.Name;
p.UnitPrice = this.UnitPrice;
return p;
```

With `SqlProductRepository` implemented, I can now set up ASP.NET MVC to inject an instance of it into instances of `HomeController`. Because I discuss this in greater detail in chapter 7, I don't show that here.

Figure 2.19 shows the current state of the application architecture as envisioned in figure 2.2.

Now that everything is correctly wired together, I can browse to the application's homepage and get the same page as shown in figure 2.3.

---

[11] For a good introduction to persistence ignorance, see Jeremy Miller, "Patterns in Practice: The Unit Of Work Pattern And Persistence Ignorance," (MSDN Magazine, June 2009). Also available online at http://msdn.microsoft.com/en-us/magazine/dd882510.aspx

2.2.2 *Analyzing the loosely coupled implementation*

The previous section contained lots of details, so it's hardly surprising if you lost sight of the big picture along the way. In this section, I'll try to explain what happened in broader terms.

INTERACTION

The classes in each layer interact with each other in either direct or abstract form. They do so across module boundaries, so it can be difficult to follow how they interact. Figure 2.20 illustrates how dependencies are being connected.

When the application starts, the code in `Global.asax` creates a new custom Controller factory. The application keeps a reference to the Controller factory, so when a page request comes in, the application invokes `CreateController` on the factory. The factory looks up the connection string from `web.config` and supplies it

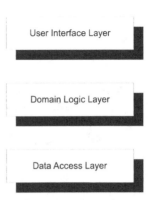

Figure 2.19 All three layers in the application are now implemented as envisioned in figure 2.2. This figure is identical, but is repeated here to illustrate the current state of the application. The figure is also identical to figure 2.8, which shows Mary's completed application.

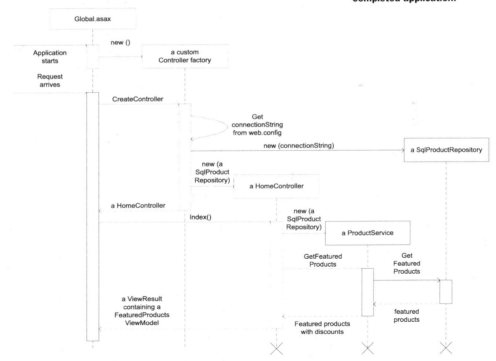

Figure 2.20 Interaction between elements involved in Dependency Injection in the Commerce application. Notice how the `SqlProductRepository` instance is injected into the `HomeController`, and then again later, through the `HomeController` into a `ProductService` that ultimately uses it.

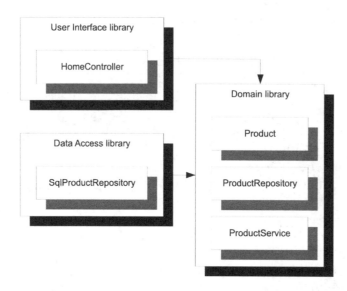

Figure 2.21 Dependency graph showing the example commerce application when Dependency Injection is applied. The most notable difference is that the Domain library no longer has any dependencies. The grey boxes within the black boxes show sample classes in each library to give you an idea which classes go where. There are more classes in each library than the ones shown.

to a new instance of SqlProductRepository. It injects the SqlProductRepository instance into a new instance of HomeController and returns that instance.

The application then invokes the Index method on the HomeController instance, causing it to create a new instance of ProductService, passing the SqlProduct-Repository instance to it in its constructor. The ProductService invokes the Get-FeaturedProducts method on the SqlProductRepository instance.

Finally, the ViewResult with the populated FeaturedProductsViewModel is returned, and the ASP.NET MVC framework finds and renders the correct page.

DEPENDENCY GRAPH

In section 2.1.3, we saw how a dependency graph can help us analyze and understand the degree of flexibility provided by the architectural implementation. Has DI changed the dependency graph for the application?

Figure 2.21 shows that the dependency graph has indeed changed. The Domain Model no longer has any dependencies and can act as a stand-alone module. On the other hand, the Data Access library now has a dependency; in Mary's application, it had none.

This should raise our hopes that we can answer the original questions about composability more favorably this time:

- Can we replace the web-based user interface with a WPF-based user interface? That was possible before, and is still possible with the new design. Neither the Domain Model nor the Data Access libraries depend on the web-based user interface, so we can easily put something else in its place.
- Can we replace the relational Data Access library with one that works with the Azure Table Service? In chapter 3 I'll describe how the application locates and instantiates the correct ProductRepository, so for now take the following at

face value: the Data Access library is being loaded by late binding, and the type name is defined as an application setting in web.config. It's possible to throw the current Data Access library away and inject a new one, as long as it also provides an implementation of `ProductRepository`.

It's no longer possible to use the current Data Access library in isolation, as it now depends on the Domain Model. In many types of applications, that's not an issue, but if the stakeholders want that feature, I can solve the problem by adding another layer of indirection: by extracting an interface from `Product` (say, `IProduct`) and changing `ProductRepository` to work with `IProduct` instead of `Product`. These abstractions can then be moved to a separate library that's shared by both the Data Access library and the Domain Model. It would require more work, because I'd need to write code to map between `Product` and `IProduct`, but it's certainly possible.

With the DI-based design, the original web application can be gradually transformed to a Software + Services application with a rich WPF interface and a cloud-based storage engine. The only thing remaining from the initial effort is the Domain Model, but that's only appropriate because it encapsulates all the important business rules and, as such, we should expect that to be the most essential module.

When we develop applications, we can't possibly foresee every future direction we may need to take the product, but that's no problem as long as we can keep our options open. DI helps us build loosely coupled applications so that we can reuse or replace different modules as needed.

2.3 Expanding the sample application

To support the rest of the book and fully demonstrate different aspects of DI, I'll need to expand the sample commerce application. Until now, I have kept the application as simple and small as possible to gently introduce some core concepts and principles. Because one of the main purposes of DI is to manage complexity, we need a complex application to fully appreciate its power.

I'll expand the application along two axes: an architectural refactoring and an added feature.

2.3.1 Architecture

So far, the sample application has been a three-layer application, but now I want to slide a *Presentation Model* layer in between the UI and the Domain Model, as shown in figure 2.22.

I move all the Controllers and ViewModels from the User Interface Layer to the Presentation Model layer, leaving only the Views (the .aspx and .ascx files) and the COMPOSITION ROOT in the User Interface Layer.

The main reason for this move is to separate the COMPOSITION ROOT from the presentation logic; this way, I can show you different variations of configuration styles while keeping invariant as much of the application as possible.

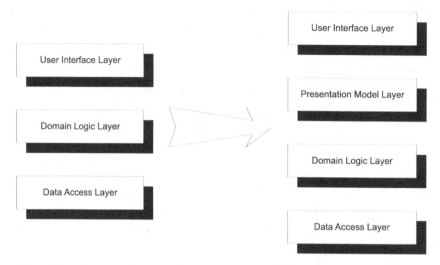

Figure 2.22   A Presentation Model layer is inserted into the sample application to separate the presentation logic from the application root.

Humble Object

It isn't only for educational purposes that I split up the application into a User Interface Layer and a Presentation Model layer; I routinely do this for all applications I write if they have a user interface at all.

This split provides clear separation of concerns between presentation logic (how user interfaces *behave*) and rendering (how user interfaces *look*). It puts all logic into a layer where it can be unit tested, and puts all markup in a layer where a graphic designer can work without fear of breaking things too easily.

The goal is to have as little imperative code as possible in the User Interface Layer, because I'm not going to write any unit tests for this layer.

An application root that contains only the bare minimum of code to bootstrap itself, after which it delegates all other work to TESTABLE modules, is called a *Humble Object*.[12] In this case, it contains only Views and bootstrap code: the COMPOSITION ROOT.

Apart from this architectural change, I also want to add a richer feature than what we've been looking at so far.

2.3.2   *Basket feature*

The list of featured products only presents us with a limited level of complexity: there's only a single Repository involved in a read-only scenario.

---

[12] Gerard Meszaros, *xUnit Test Patterns: Refactoring Test Code* (New York: Addison-Wesley, 2007), 695-708.

The logical next step is to introduce a shopping basket feature. Figure 2.23 shows a screenshot of the shopping basket in use.

To support a shopping basket for each user, I need a Basket, a BasketRepository, and a host of supporting classes. If you're like me, you want to see the Basket class first: figure 2.24 shows the basket and its list of items.

From a DI perspective, the Basket and Extent classes aren't particularly interesting: they're both Plain Old CLR Object (POCO) classes with no DEPENDENCIES. Of much more interest is the BasketService and supporting classes, shown in figure 2.25.

Figure 2.23 The spectacularly feature-poor shopping basket in the refactored commerce sample application.

A BasketService can be used to retrieve a user's Basket and apply discounts. It uses the abstract BasketRepository to get the contents of the Basket, and the abstract BasketDiscountPolicy to apply discounts. Both of these ABSTRACTIONS are injected into the BasketService via CONSTRUCTOR INJECTION:

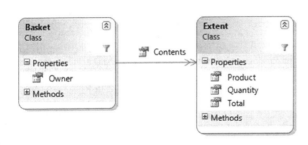

Figure 2.24 Basket and its Contents, which is a list of Extent<Evaluated-Product>. An Extent represents a quantity of a given product.

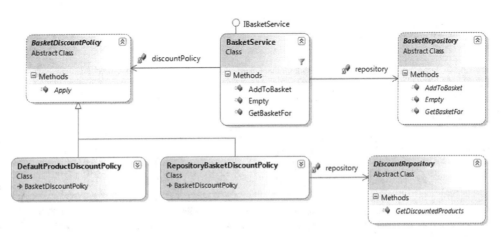

Figure 2.25 BasketService and supporting classes. A BasketService can retrieve and evaluate a Basket for a given user. It uses a BasketRepository to retrieve the Basket and a BasketDiscountPolicy to apply discounts (if any).

```
public BasketService(BasketRepository repository,
    BasketDiscountPolicy discountPolicy)
```

A `BasketDiscountPolicy` can be a simple implementation with a hard-coded policy, such as giving preferred customers a five percent discount, as we saw earlier in this chapter. This policy is implemented by the `DefaultProductDiscountPolicy`, while a more complex, data-driven implementation is provided by `RepositoryBasketDiscountPolicy`, that itself uses the abstract `DiscountRepository` to get a list of discounted products. This ABSTRACTION is once again injected into the `RepositoryBasketDiscountPolicy` via CONSTRUCTOR INJECTION:

```
public RepositoryBasketDiscountPolicy(DiscountRepository repository)
```

To manage all this, I can use the `BasketService` to orchestrate the operations on the `Basket`: adding items, as well as displaying and emptying the `Basket`. To do this, it needs both a `BasketRepository` and a `BasketDiscountPolicy` that (you guessed it) is supplied to it via its constructor:

```
public BasketService(BasketRepository repository,
    BasketDiscountPolicy discountPolicy)
```

To further complicate matters, I need an ASP.NET MVC controller called `Basket-Controller` that wraps around the `IBasketService` interface that I again inject into it via its constructor:

```
public BasketController(IBasketService basketService)
```

As figure 2.25 shows, the `BasketService` class implements `IBasketService`, so that's the implementation we use.

The `BasketController` is ultimately created by a custom `IControllerFactory`, so it will need these ABSTRACTIONS as well.

If you lost track along the way, figure 2.26 shows a diagram that illustrates how the DEPENDENCIES are to be composed in the final application.

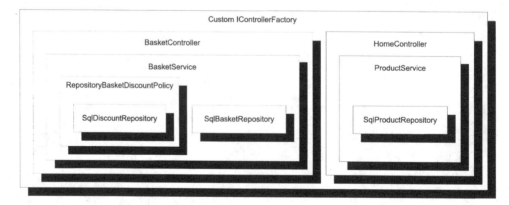

Figure 2.26 **Composition of the sample commerce application with the added Basket feature, as well as the original list of featured products on the front page. Each class encapsulates its contents, and only the COMPOSITION ROOT has knowledge of all DEPENDENCIES.**

The custom `IControllerFactory` creates instances of `BasketController` and `Home-Controller` by providing them with their respective Dependencies. The `Basket-Service`, for instance, uses the supplied `BasketDiscountPolicy` instance to apply a discount policy to the basket:

```
var discountedBasket = this.discountPolicy.Apply(b);
```

It has no inkling that *in this case*, the supplied `BasketDiscountPolicy` is an instance of `RepositoryBasketDiscountPolicy` that itself is a container of a `DiscountRepository`.

This expanded sample application serves as the basis for many of the code samples in the rest of the book.

2.4 Summary

It's surprisingly easy to write tightly coupled code. Even when Mary set out with the express intent of writing a three-layer application, it turned into a largely monolithic piece of Spaghetti Code[13] (when we're talking about layering, we call this Lasagna).

One of the many reasons that it's so easy to write tightly coupled code is that both the language features and our tools already pull us in that direction. If we need a new instance of an object, we can use the new keyword, and if we don't have a reference to the required assembly, Visual Studio makes it easy to add it.

However, every time we use the new keyword, we introduce a tight coupling.

The best way to minimize the use of new is to use the Constructor Injection design pattern whenever we need an instance of a Dependency. The second example in the chapter demonstrated how to re-implement Mary's application by programming to Abstractions instead of concrete classes.

Constructor Injection is an example of Inversion of Control because we invert the control over Dependencies. Instead of creating instances with the new keyword, we delegate that responsibility to a third party. As we shall see in the next chapter, we call this place the Composition Root. This is where we compose all the loosely coupled classes into an application.

---

[13] William J. Brown et al., *AntiPatterns: Refactoring Software, Architectures, and Projects in Crisis* (New York: Wiley Computer Publishing, 1998), 119.

DI Containers 3

When I was a kid, my mother and I would occasionally make ice cream. This didn't happen too often, because it required a lot of work and it was hard to get right. In case you've never tried making ice cream, figure 3.1 illustrates the process.

Real ice cream is based on a crème anglaise, which is a light custard made from sugar, egg yolks, and milk or cream. If heated too much, this mixture will curdle. Even if you manage to avoid this, the next phase presents more problems. Left alone in the freezer, the cream mixture will crystallize, so you have to stir it at regular intervals until it becomes so stiff that this is no longer possible. Only then will you have a good, homemade ice cream.

Although this is a slow and labor-intensive process, if you want to and you have the necessary ingredients and equipment, you can use the *technique* I've outlined to make ice cream.

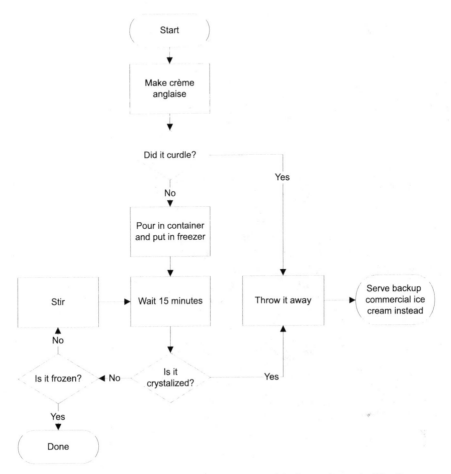

Figure 3.1 Making ice cream is an arduous process, with plenty of opportunities for error.

Today, some 30 years later, my mother-in-law makes ice cream with a frequency unmatched by my mother and me at much younger ages—not because she loves *making* ice cream, but because she uses *technology* to help her. The *technique* is still the same, but instead of regularly taking out the ice cream from the freezer and stirring it, she uses an electric ice cream maker to do the work for her (see figure 3.2).

DI is first and foremost a *technique*, but you can use *technology* to make things easier. In part 3, I'll describe DI as a technique. Then, in part 4, we'll take a look at the technology that can be used to support the DI technique. We call this technology DI CONTAINERS.

In this chapter, we'll look at DI CONTAINERS as a concept: how they fit into the overall topic of DI, some patterns and practices concerning their usage, and some history about .NET DI CONTAINERS. We'll also look at some examples along the way.

The general outline of the chapter is illustrated by figure 3.3. It begins with a general introduction to DI CONTAINERS, including a description of a concept called AUTO-WIRING, followed by a section on various configuration options. You can read

Figure 3.2 My mother-in-law's Italian ice cream maker.

about each of these configuration options in isolation, but I think it would be beneficial to at least read about CODE AS CONFIGURATION before you read about AUTO-REGISTRATION.

The central section in the chapter is a mini-catalog of design patterns related to DI CONTAINERS. Although it follows the catalog format, the REGISTER RESOLVE RELEASE (RRR) pattern description relies on the COMPOSITION ROOT pattern, so it makes sense to read both in sequence. You *can* skip the section about configuration options to go directly to the patterns, but those sections are best read in order.

The last section is different. It's much less technical and focuses on how DI CONTAINERS fit into the .NET ecosystem. You can skip reading this section if you don't care about that aspect.

The purpose of the chapter is to give you a good understanding of what a DI CONTAINER is and how it fits in with all the rest of the patterns and principles in this book; in a sense, you can view this chapter as an introduction to part 4 of the book. Here, we'll talk about DI CONTAINERS in general, whereas in part 4, we'll talk about specific containers and their APIs.

It may seem a bit strange that we talk about DI CONTAINERS here in chapter 3 and then more or less forget about them again in the next six chapters, but there's a

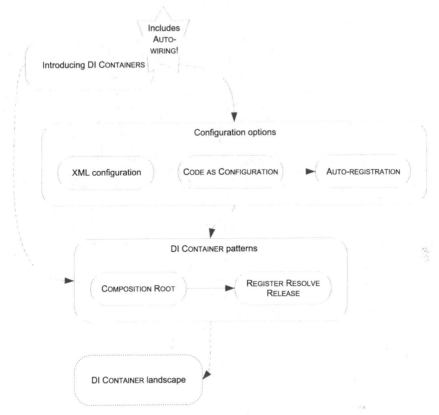

Figure 3.3   The structure of this chapter. The *DI Container landscape* section is optional.

reason for that. In this part of the book, I want to draw the big picture of DI, and it's essential that you understand how DI CONTAINERS fit into the scheme of things. In parts 2 and 3, I'll occasionally show you some examples that involve a DI CONTAINER, but for the most part I'll keep the discussion general. The principles and patterns described in the middle of the book can be applied to all DI CONTAINERS.

3.1   *Introducing DI Containers*

A DI CONTAINER is a software library that can automate many of the tasks involved in composing objects and managing their lifetimes. Although it's possible to write all the required infrastructure code with POOR MAN'S DI, it doesn't add much value to an application. On the other hand, the task of composing objects is of a general nature and can be resolved once and for all; this is what's known as a *Generic Subdomain.*[1]

> **DEFINITION**   A DI CONTAINER is a library that provides DI functionality.

---

[1]   Eric Evans, *Domain-Driven Design: Tackling Complexity in the Heart of Software* (New York: Addison-Wesley, 2004), 406.

NOTE DI CONTAINERS are also known as *Inversion of Control (IoC) Containers* or (more rarely) *Lightweight Containers*.

Although you need to address the application infrastructure, doing so doesn't in itself add business value, so using a general-purpose library makes the most sense. It's no different than implementing logging or data access. Logging application data is the kind of problem that's best addressed by a general-purpose logging library. The same is true for composing object graphs.

WARNING Don't expect a DI CONTAINER to magically make tightly coupled code loosely coupled. A DI CONTAINER can make the use of DI more efficient, but an application must first and foremost be designed with the DI patterns and techniques in mind.

In this section, I'll discuss how DI CONTAINERS compose object graphs, and I'll show you some examples to give you a general sense of what using a container might look like.

3.1.1 *Hello container*

A DI CONTAINER is a software library like any other software library. It exposes an API that you can use to compose objects. Composing an object graph is a single method call. All DI CONTAINERS also require you to configure them before you use them to compose objects, but I'll revisit that in section 3.2.

Here, I'll show you some examples of how DI CONTAINERS may resolve object graphs for the expanded sample application from section 2.3. For each request, the ASP.NET MVC framework will ask for an instance of the appropriate type of IController, so you must implement a method that uses a DI CONTAINER to compose the corresponding object graph.

TIP Section 7.2 contains detailed information about how to compose ASP.NET MVC applications.

The MVC framework will invoke the method with a Type instance that identifies the type of IController (for example, HomeController or BasketController) that it needs, and you must return an instance of that type.

This functionality can be implemented with all the DI CONTAINERS covered in part 4, but I'll show only a few examples here.

RESOLVING CONTROLLERS WITH VARIOUS DI CONTAINERS

Unity is a DI CONTAINER with a fairly pattern-conforming API. Assuming you already have an instance of Unity's UnityContainer class, you can resolve an IController instance from a controllerType Type argument:

```
var controller = (IController)this.container.Resolve(controllerType);
```

You'll pass the controllerType parameter to the Resolve method and get back an instance of the requested type, fully populated with all appropriate DEPENDENCIES.

Because the weakly-typed `Resolve` method returns an instance of `System.Object`, it must be cast to `IController`.

For those cases where you know the requested type at design time, there's also a generic version of the `Resolve` method.

Many of the DI CONTAINERS have APIs that are similar to Unity's. The corresponding code for Castle Windsor looks identical to Unity's, although the `container` instance would instead be an instance of the `WindsorContainer` class. Other containers have slightly varying names—with StructureMap, for example, the previous code would look like this:

```
var controller = (IController)this.container.GetInstance(controllerType);
```

The only real difference is that the `Resolve` method is called `GetInstance`. You can extract a general shape of a DI CONTAINER from these examples.

RESOLVING OBJECT GRAPHS WITH DI CONTAINERS

A DI CONTAINER is an engine that resolves and manages object graphs. Although there's more to a DI CONTAINER than resolving objects, this is a central part of any container's API. The previous examples show that containers have a weakly-typed method for that purpose. With variations in names and signature, it looks like this:

```
object Resolve(Type service);
```

As the previous examples demonstrate, because the returned instance is typed as `System.Object`, you often need to cast the return value to the expected type before using it.

Many DI CONTAINERS also offer a generic version for those cases where we know which type to request at compile time. They often look like this:

```
T Resolve<T>();
```

Instead of supplying a `Type` method argument, such an overload takes a type parameter (`T`) that indicates the requested type. The method returns an instance of `T`.

Most containers throw an exception if they can't resolve the requested type.

> **WARNING**   The signature of the `Resolve` method is extremely powerful and versatile. You can request an instance of *any* type and your code will still compile. In fact, the `Resolve` method fits the signature of a SERVICE LOCATOR,[2] and you'll need to exercise care not to use your DI CONTAINER as a SERVICE LOCATOR.

If we view the `Resolve` method in isolation, it looks almost like magic. From a compiler perspective, it's possible to ask it to resolve instances of arbitrary types. How does the container know how to compose the requested type, including all DEPENDENCIES?

It doesn't know this, and you'll have to tell it first. You do so using *registration* or *configuration* and this is where you map ABSTRACTIONS to concrete types—I'll return to

---

[2] Mark Seemann, "Pattern Recognition: Abstract Factory or Service Locator?" http://blog.ploeh.dk/2010/11/01/PatternRecognitionAbstractFactoryOrServiceLocator.aspx

this topic in section 3.2. If a container has insufficient configuration to fully compose a requested type, it will normally throw a descriptive exception. As an example, Castle Windsor has exemplary exceptions messages like this one:

> *Can't create component 'Ploeh.Samples.MenuModel.Mayonnaise' as it has dependencies to be satisfied.*
>
> *Ploeh.Samples.MenuModel.Mayonnaise is waiting for the following dependencies:*
>
> *Services:*
>
> *- Ploeh.Samples.MenuModel.EggYolk which was not registered.*

In this example, you can see that Castle Windsor can't resolve `Mayonnaise` because it wasn't configured to deal with the `EggYolk` class.

If the container is correctly configured, it can resolve even complex object graphs from the requested type. If something is missing from the configuration, the container can provide detailed information about what's missing. In the next section, we'll take a closer look at how this is done.

3.1.2 *Auto-wiring*

DI CONTAINERS thrive on the static information compiled into all classes that use CONSTRUCTOR INJECTION. Using Reflection, they can analyze the requested class and figure out which DEPENDENCIES are needed.

Some DI CONTAINERS also understand the PROPERTY INJECTION pattern, but all of them inherently understand CONSTRUCTOR INJECTION and compose object graphs by combining their own configuration with the information extracted from the classes' constructors. This is called AUTO-WIRING.

> **DEFINITION**   AUTO-WIRING is the ability to automatically compose an object graph from maps between ABSTRACTIONS and concrete types.

Figure 3.4 describes the general algorithm most DI CONTAINERS follow to AUTO-WIRE an object graph. A DI CONTAINER will use its configuration to find the appropriate concrete class that matches the requested type. It then uses Reflection to examine the class's constructor. If there's a default constructor, it will invoke the constructor and return the created instance.

If the constructor requires arguments, a recursive process starts where the DI CONTAINER will repeat the process for each argument type until all constructors can be satisfied.

In section 3.2, we'll take a closer look at how containers can be configured, but for now the most important thing to understand is that at the core of the configuration is a map of how various ABSTRACTIONS map to concrete classes. That sounds a bit theoretical (I'm sure that the word *abstraction* doesn't help), so I think an example will be helpful.

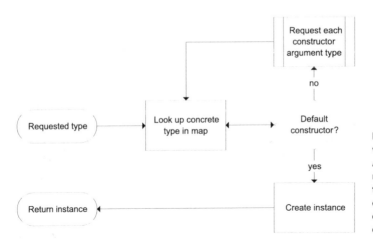

Figure 3.4 Simplified workflow for AUTO-WIRING. A DI CONTAINER will recursively find concrete types and examine their constructors until it can create the entire object tree.

EXAMPLE: AUTO-WIRING A BASKETCONTROLLER

In this example, I'll explain how AUTO-WIRING works in principle. The example doesn't rely on any particular DI CONTAINER but instead provides an outline of how containers compose object graphs.

Imagine that you want to resolve an instance of the BasketController class. You do this by invoking the Resolve method with typeof(BasketController). In the end, you'd like to end up with an instance of BasketController, composed as shown in figure 2.26. In order to achieve this, you must first make sure that the container has the correct configuration. Table 3.1 shows how this configuration maps ABSTRACTIONS to concrete types. I also added a column that shows whether the ABSTRACTION is an interface or abstract base class—from a DI CONTAINER's perspective this isn't important, but I thought it would help to clarify what's going on.

Table 3.1   Mapping types to support AUTO-WIRING of BasketController

ABSTRACTION type	ABSTRACTION	Concrete type
Concrete	BasketController	BasketController
Interface	IBasketService	BasketService
Abstract class	BasketRepository	SqlBasketRepository
Abstract class	BasketDiscountPolicy	RepositoryBasketDiscountPolicy
Abstract class	DiscountRepository	SqlDiscountRepository
String	connString	"metadata=res://*/CommerceModel.csdl| [...]"

When a DI CONTAINER receives a request for a BasketController, the first thing it will do is look up the type in its configuration. BasketController is a concrete class, so it maps to itself. The container then uses Reflection to inspect BasketController's constructor. From section 2.3.2 you may recall that `BasketController` has a single constructor with this signature:

```
public BasketController(IBasketService basketService)
```

Because this constructor isn't a default constructor, we need to repeat the process for the `IBasketService` constructor argument when following the general flowchart from figure 3.4.

The container looks up `IBasketService` in its configuration and finds that it maps to the concrete `BasketService` class. The single public constructor for `BasketService` has this signature:

```
public BasketService(BasketRepository repository,
    BasketDiscountPolicy discountPolicy)
```

That's still not a default constructor, and now you have two constructor arguments to deal with. The container takes care of each in order so it starts with the abstract `Basket-Repository` class that, according to the configuration, maps to `SqlBasketRepository`.

`SqlBasketRepository` has a public constructor with this signature:

```
public SqlBasketRepository(string connString)
```

The single constructor argument is a string parameter with the name `connString` which is configured to have a particular value. Now that the container has the appropriate value, it can invoke the `SqlBasketRepository` constructor. It has now successfully handled the `repository` parameter for the `BasketService` constructor, but it will need to hold on to that value for a while longer because it also needs to take care of the `discountPolicy` parameter.

According to the configuration, `BasketDiscountPolicy` maps to the concrete `RepositoryBasketDiscountPolicy` class, which has this public constructor:

```
public RepositoryBasketDiscountPolicy(DiscountRepository repository)
```

Looking up `DiscountRepository` in its configuration, the container finds that it maps to `SqlDiscountRepository`, which has this constructor:

```
public SqlDiscountRepository(string connString)
```

This situation is the same as what you encountered with the `SqlBasketRepository`. The `connString` argument is mapped to a particular connection string that the container can supply to the constructor.

It can now pass the new `SqlDiscountRepository` instance to the `Repository-BasketDiscountPolicy` constructor. Together with the `SqlBasketRepository` from before, it can now fulfill the `BasketService` constructor and invoke it via Reflection. Finally, it passes the newly created `BasketService` instance to the `BasketController` constructor and returns the `BasketController` instance.

Essentially, this is how AUTO-WIRING works, although it's more complicated than that. DI CONTAINERS also need to take care of LIFETIME MANAGEMENT and perhaps address PROPERTY INJECTION as well as other, more special creational requirements. The salient point is that CONSTRUCTOR INJECTION statically advertises the DEPENDENCY requirements of a class, and DI CONTAINERS use that information to AUTO-WIRE complex object graphs.

As the example shows, the container must be configured before it can compose object graphs. Registration of components can be done in various ways.

3.2   *Configuring DI Containers*

Although the `Resolve` method is where all the action happens, you should expect to spend more time with a DI CONTAINER'S configuration API. Resolving object graphs is, after all, a single method call.

DI CONTAINERS tend to support two or three of the common configuration options shown in figure 3.5. A few don't support AUTO-REGISTRATION and a single one also lacks support for CODE AS CONFIGURATION, whereas XML configuration is ubiquitous. Most allow you to mix several approaches in the same application.

These three configuration options have different characteristics that make them useful in different situations. Both XML and CODE AS CONFIGURATION tend to be explicit because they require us to register each component individually. AUTO-REGISTRATION, on the other hand, is much more implicit because it uses conventions to register a set of components by a single rule.

When we use CODE AS CONFIGURATION, we compile the container configuration into an assembly, whereas XML configuration enables us to support late binding where we can change the configuration without recompiling the application. In that dimension, AUTO-REGISTRATION falls somewhere in the middle, because we can ask it to scan a single assembly known at compile time, or alternatively to scan all assemblies in a predefined folder.

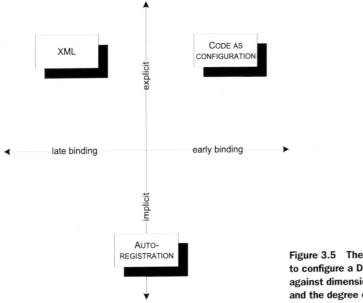

Figure 3.5   The most common ways to configure a DI CONTAINER shown against dimensions of explicitness and the degree of binding

Table 3.2 Configuration options

Style	Description	Advantages	Disadvantages
XML	Configuration settings (often in .config files) specify the mappings.	Supports replacement without recompilation High degree of control	No compile-time checks Verbose
CODE AS CONFIGURATION	Code explicitly determines mappings.	Compile-time checks High degree of control	No support for replacement without recompilation
AUTO-REGISTRATION	Rules are used to locate suitable components and build the mappings.	Supports replacement without recompilation Less effort required Helps enforce conventions to make a code base more consistent	Partial compile-time checks Less control

Table 3.2 lists the advantages and disadvantages of each option.

Historically, DI CONTAINERS started out with XML configuration, which also explains why all of them support this option. However, the current trend is that this feature is being downplayed in favor of more convention-based approaches.[3] Although AUTO-REGISTRATION is the most modern option, it's not the most obvious place to start. Because of its implicitness it may seem more abstract than the more explicit options, so instead I'll cover each option in historical order, starting with XML configuration.

3.2.1 *Configuring containers with XML*

When DI CONTAINERS first appeared back in the early 2000s, they all used XML as a configuration mechanism—most things did back then. Much experience with XML as a configuration mechanism has later revealed that this is rarely the best option.

XML tends to be verbose and brittle. When you configure a DI CONTAINER in XML, you identify various classes and interfaces, but you have no compiler support to warn you if you misspell something. Even if the class names are correct, there's no guarantee that the required assembly is going to be in the application's probing path.

The advantage of XML configuration is that you can change the behavior of the application without recompilation. This is valuable if you develop software that ships to thousands of customers because it gives them a way to customize the application. However, if you write an internal application or a website where you control the deployment environment, it's often easier to just recompile and redeploy the application when you need to change the behavior.

---

[3] For a good overview article on *Convention over Configuration*, see Jeremy Miller, "Patterns in Practice: Convention Over Configuration," (MSDN Magazine, February 2009). Also available online at http://msdn.microsoft .com/en-us/magazine/dd419655.aspx

TIP   Use XML configuration only in those cases where you *actively* wish to support late binding. Prefer CODE AS CONFIGURATION or AUTO-REGISTRATION in all other cases.

A DI CONTAINER is often configured with XML by pointing it at a particular XML file, but sometimes it can also pick up the configuration from the application configuration file. The following example uses the latter option.

EXAMPLE: CONFIGURING THE SAMPLE COMMERCE APPLICATION WITH XML
Because the Unity container is one of the more XML-centric of the DI CONTAINERS covered in this book, it makes sense to use it for an example of XML configuration.

In this example, you'll configure the sample commerce application from section 2.3. A large part of the task is to apply the configuration outlined in table 3.1, but you must also supply a similar configuration to support composition of the Home-Controller class. The following listing shows the configuration necessary to get the application up and running.

> **Listing 3.1   Configuring Unity with XML**

```
<register type="IBasketService"                                    ❶ Simple mapping
          mapTo="BasketService" />
<register type="BasketDiscountPolicy"
          mapTo="RepositoryBasketDiscountPolicy" />
<register type="BasketRepository"
          mapTo="SqlBasketRepository">
  <constructor>
    <param name="connString">                                      ❷ Specify
      <value value="CommerceObjectContext"                           connection
             typeConverter="ConnectionStringConverter" />             string
    </param>
  </constructor>
</register>
<register type="DiscountRepository"
          mapTo="SqlDiscountRepository">
  <constructor>
    <param name="connString">
      <value value="CommerceObjectContext"
             typeConverter="ConnectionStringConverter" />
    </param>
  </constructor>
</register>
<register type="ProductRepository"
          mapTo="SqlProductRepository">
  <constructor>
    <param name="connString">
      <value value="CommerceObjectContext"
             typeConverter="ConnectionStringConverter" />
    </param>
  </constructor>
</register>
<register type="CurrencyProvider"
          mapTo="SqlCurrencyProvider">
```

```
<constructor>
  <param name="connString">
    <value value="CommerceObjectContext"
           typeConverter="ConnectionStringConverter" />
  </param>
</constructor>
</register>
```

As you can see from even this simple code listing, XML configuration tends to be quite verbose. Simple mappings like the one from the `IBasketService` interface to the `BasketService` class ❶ are easily expressed with a simple `register` element.

However, as you may recall, some of the concrete classes take a connection string as input, so you need to specify how the value of this string is found ❷. With Unity, you can do that by indicating that you use a custom type converter called `Connection-StringConverter`. This converter will look up the value `CommerceObjectContext` among the standard `web.config` connection strings and return the connection string with that name.

The rest of the elements repeat these two patterns.

Because Unity can automatically resolve requests for concrete types even if there are no explicit registrations, you don't need to supply XML elements for `Home-Controller` and `BasketController`.

Loading the configuration into the container is done with a single method call:

```
container.LoadConfiguration();
```

The `LoadConfiguration` method loads the XML configuration from listing 3.1 into the container. With the configuration in place, the container can now resolve requests for `HomeController,` and so on.

Other DI CONTAINERS also support XML configuration. The exact XML schema is different for each container, but the overall structure tends to be similar.

> **WARNING** As your application grows in size and complexity, so will your configuration file if you use configuration-based composition. It can grow to become a real stumbling block because it models coding concepts such as classes, parameters, and such, but without the benefits of the compiler, debugging options, and so forth. Configuration files will tend to become brittle and opaque to errors, so only use this approach when you *need* late binding.

Because of the disadvantages of verbosity and brittleness, you should prefer the other alternatives for configuring containers. CODE AS CONFIGURATION is similar to XML configuration in granularity and concept, but obviously uses code instead of XML.

3.2.2 *Configuring containers with code*

Perhaps the easiest way to compose an application is to write code that does it. This may seem to go against the whole spirit of DI, because it hard-codes which concrete implementations should be used for all ABSTRACTIONS. However, if done in a COMPOSI-TION ROOT, it only violates a single of the benefits listed in table 1.1.

The benefit of *late binding* is lost if DEPENDENCIES are hard-coded, but, as I mentioned in chapter 1, this may not be relevant for all types of applications. If your application is deployed in a limited number of instances in a controlled environment, it may be easier to recompile and redeploy the application if you need to replace modules.

> *I often think that people are over-eager to define configuration files. Often a programming language makes a straightforward and powerful configuration mechanism.*
>
>   – Martin Fowler[4]

When we use CODE AS CONFIGURATION, we explicitly state the same discrete mappings as we do when we use XML configuration—only, we use code instead of XML.

With the single exception of Spring.NET, all DI CONTAINERS fully support CODE AS CONFIGURATION as an alternative to XML configuration—in fact, most of them present this as the default mechanism with XML configuration as an optional feature.

The API exposed to support CODE AS CONFIGURATION differs from DI CONTAINER to DI CONTAINER, but the overall goal is still to define discrete mappings between ABSTRACTIONS and concrete types.

> **TIP**   Prefer CODE AS CONFIGURATION over XML configuration unless you need *late binding*. The compiler can be helpful and the Visual Studio build system will automatically copy all required DEPENDENCIES to the output folder.

Many configuration APIs use generics and Fluent Builders to register components; StructureMap is no exception.

EXAMPLE: CONFIGURING THE SAMPLE COMMERCE APPLICATION WITH CODE

In section 3.2.1, you saw how to configure the sample commerce application with XML, using Unity. I could also demonstrate CODE AS CONFIGURATION with Unity, but in this example I'll instead use StructureMap; because it has a terser API, it fits better on the pages of the book.

Using StructureMap's configuration API, you can express the configuration from listing 3.1 more compactly, as shown in the following listing.

Listing 3.2   Configuring StructureMap with code

```
c.For<IBasketService>().Use<BasketService>();
c.For<BasketDiscountPolicy>()
    .Use<RepositoryBasketDiscountPolicy>();

string connectionString =
    ConfigurationManager.ConnectionStrings
    ["CommerceObjectContext"].ConnectionString;
c.For<BasketRepository>().Use<SqlBasketRepository>()
    .Ctor<string>().Is(connectionString);
c.For<DiscountRepository>().Use<SqlDiscountRepository>()
    .Ctor<string>().Is(connectionString);
```

---

[4] Martin Fowler, "Inversion of Control Containers and the Dependency Injection pattern," 2004, http://martinfowler.com/articles/injection.html

```
c.For<ProductRepository>().Use<SqlProductRepository>()
    .Ctor<string>().Is(connectionString);
c.For<CurrencyProvider>().Use<SqlCurrencyProvider>()
    .Ctor<string>().Is(connectionString);
```

Compare this code with listing 3.1 and notice how much more compact it is—even though it does the same thing. A simple mapping like the one from IBasketService to BasketService is expressed with the generic For and Use methods. The c variable is actually something called a ConfigurationExpression, but think about it as the container itself.

To support those classes that require a connection string, you continue the For/Use sequence with invoking the Ctor method and supplying the connection string. This Ctor method looks for a string parameter in the concrete class's constructor and uses the supplied value for that parameter.

The rest of the code repeats these two patterns.

Not only is CODE AS CONFIGURATION much more compact than XML configuration, it also enjoys compiler support. The type arguments used in listing 3.2 represent real types that the compiler checks. StructureMap's fluent API even comes with some generic constraints that tell the compiler to check whether the type identified by the Use method matches the ABSTRACTIONS indicated by the For method. If a conversion isn't possible, the code will not compile.

Although CODE AS CONFIGURATION is safe and easy to use, it still requires more maintenance than you might like. Every time you add a new type to an application, you must also remember to register it—and many registrations end up being similar. AUTO-REGISTRATION addresses this issue.

3.2.3   *Configuring containers by convention*

In listing 3.2, did you notice how similar many of the registrations are? Particularly all the SQL Server–based data access components follow a common pattern wherein you configure the component with the appropriate connection string.

Repeatedly writing registration code like that violates the DRY[5] principle. It also seems like an unproductive piece of infrastructure code that doesn't add much value to the application. You can save time and make fewer errors if you can automate the registration of components.

An increasingly popular architectural model is the concept of *Convention over Configuration.* Instead of writing and maintaining a lot of configuration code, you can agree on conventions that affect the code base.

The way ASP.NET MVC finds Controllers based on controller names is a great example of a simple convention:

---

[5] Don't Repeat Yourself

1 A request comes in for a Controller named *Home*.

2 The default Controller Factory searches through a list of well-known namespaces for a class named *HomeController*. If it finds such a class and it implements `IController`, it's a match.

3 The default Controller Factory uses the default constructor of the matched class to create an instance of the Controller.

At least two conventions are in play here: a controller must be named `[Controller-Name]Controller` and it must have a default constructor.

You can deviate from these conventions by implementing your own `IController-Factory`, and that's what I have done so far to support CONSTRUCTOR INJECTION—I discuss this in more detail in chapter 7.

It would be nice if you could use some conventions to get rid of all that error-prone and time-consuming container configuration. With the `DefaultController-Factory`, adding a new Controller is as simple as adding an appropriately named class in the correct namespace. We'd like to keep that convenience even when we use CONSTRUCTOR INJECTION.

Many DI CONTAINERS provide AUTO-REGISTRATION capabilities that allow us to introduce our own conventions.

> **DEFINITION** AUTO-REGISTRATION is the ability to automatically register components in a container by scanning one or more assemblies for implementations of desired ABSTRACTIONS.

Conventions can be applied to more than ASP.NET MVC Controllers. The more conventions you add, the more you can automate the various parts of the container configuration.

> **TIP** *Convention over Configuration* has more advantages than supporting DI configuration. It makes your code more consistent because your code will automatically work as long as you follow your conventions.

In reality, you may need to combine AUTO-REGISTRATION with CODE AS CONFIGURATION or XML configuration because you may not be able to fit every single component into a meaningful convention. However, the more you can move your code base towards conventions, the more maintainable it will be.

EXAMPLE: CONFIGURING THE SAMPLE COMMERCE APPLICATION WITH AUTO-REGISTRATION
StructureMap supports AUTO-REGISTRATION, but I thought it would be more interesting to use yet another DI CONTAINER to configure the sample commerce application using conventions. I chose Autofac because it has a fairly readable AUTO-REGISTRATION API.

If you consider listings 3.1 and 3.2, I hope you'll agree that the registrations of the various data access components are the most repetitive. Can we express some sort of convention around them?

All four concrete types share some characteristics:

- They are all defined in the same assembly.
- Each is a concrete class inheriting from an abstract base class.
- Each has a name that starts with *Sql*.
- Each has a single public constructor that takes a string parameter called *connString*.

It seems as though an appropriate convention would express these similarities by scanning the assembly in question and register all classes that match the convention. With Autofac it would look like this:

```
string connectionString =
    ConfigurationManager.ConnectionStrings
    ["CommerceObjectContext"].ConnectionString;
var a = typeof(SqlProductRepository).Assembly;
builder.RegisterAssemblyTypes(a)
    .Where(t => t.Name.StartsWith("Sql"))
    .As(t => t.BaseType)
    .WithParameter("connString", connectionString);
```

This particular convention should scan the assembly that contains the data access components. There are many ways you could get a reference to that assembly, but the easiest way is to pick a representative type, such as `SqlProductRepository`, and get the assembly from that. You could also have chosen a different class or found the assembly by name.

Now that you have the assembly, you can tell the container that you want to scan it. The `RegisterAssemblyTypes` method indicates an intention to register all types in the assembly that fit the criterion that the class name must start with *Sql*. The `builder` variable is an instance of the `ContainerBuilder` class, but you can think about it as representing the container.

Each of the classes that make it through the `Where` filter should be registered against their base class. For example, because `SqlProductRepository`'s base class is `ProductRepository`, it will end up as a mapping from `ProductRepository` to `SqlProductRepository`.

Finally, you state that you expect each constructor to have a *connString* parameter and that its value should be assigned from the connection string read from the configuration file.

Comparing this convention against the four registrations in listing 3.2 may not be entirely fair, because we're also holding two different DI CONTAINERS up against each other. Still, you may think that the benefit looks negligible. However, the convention scales much better.

Because there are only four data access components in the current example, you only save a few code statements with the convention. However, once the convention is written, it handles hundreds of components without extra effort.

You can also address the other mappings from listings 3.1 and 3.2 by conventions, but currently there wouldn't be much value from doing it. As an example, you can register all services by this convention:

```
builder.RegisterAssemblyTypes(typeof(BasketService).Assembly)
    .Where(t => t.Name.EndsWith("Service"))
    .AsImplementedInterfaces();
```

This convention scans the identified assembly for all types where the name ends with *Service* and registers each type against the interfaces it implements. This effectively registers BasketService against the IBasketService interface, but because you currently don't have any other matches for this convention, nothing much is gained. Still, it may make sense to formulate a convention up front in order to encourage developers to follow it.

AUTO-REGISTRATION is a powerful technique that has the potential to make the DI CONTAINER invisible. Once appropriate conventions are in place, you may only have to modify the container configuration on rare occasions.

So far, you've seen three different approaches to configuring a DI CONTAINER:

- XML
- CODE AS CONFIGURATION
- AUTO-REGISTRATION

None of these are mutually exclusive. You can choose to mix AUTO-REGISTRATION with specific mappings of abstract to concrete types, and even mix all three approaches to have some AUTO-REGISTRATION, some CODE AS CONFIGURATION, and some of the configuration in XML for late binding purposes.

As a rule of thumb, you should prefer AUTO-REGISTRATION as a starting point, complemented by CODE AS CONFIGURATION to handle more special cases. You should reserve XML for cases where you need to be able to vary an implementation without recompiling the application (which is rarer than you may think).

Now that we have covered how to configure a DI CONTAINER and how to resolve object graphs with it, you should have a good idea about how to use it. Using a DI CONTAINER is one thing, but using it *correctly* is another.

3.3   DI Container patterns

DI CONTAINERS are great tools, but, as with all tools, there are correct and incorrect ways of using them. In the same way that cooks know to treat their knives with respect, so should you learn to properly wield your DI CONTAINER—it doesn't have the potential to lop off your fingers, but you may not harvest the benefits it can provide.

The most important thing to understand is *where* in the application architecture a DI CONTAINER should be used. Once you understand that, you must also learn *how* to use it. The following two mini-patterns provide the answers.

3.3.1   Composition Root

Where should we compose object graphs?
AS CLOSE AS POSSIBLE TO THE APPLICATION'S ENTRY POINT.

A DI CONTAINER is a library that you can potentially use from wherever you would like—but that doesn't mean that you should. Although you *can* spread out the use of

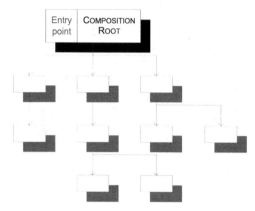

Figure 3.6   **When composing an application from many loosely coupled classes, the composition should take place as close to the application's entry point as possible. The COMPOSITION ROOT composes the object graph, which subsequently performs the actual work of the application.**

the container so that it permeates a large percentage of your classes, you should instead concentrate it into a single area of your application. This place is called the COMPOSITION ROOT and you should only use a DI CONTAINER from within that place.

The COMPOSITION ROOT concept isn't particularly tied to DI CONTAINERS. It also applies if you use POOR MAN'S DI, but I find it important to discuss it in this context because understanding this pattern enables you to use your DI CONTAINER correctly and effectively. Before I discuss the implications of COMPOSITION ROOT on the use of DI CONTAINERS, I'll briefly talk about it in general.

COMPOSITION ROOT AS A GENERAL CONCEPT

When you write loosely coupled code, you create many classes that you must compose to create an application. It can be tempting to compose these classes a little at a time in order to create small subsystems, but that limits your ability to INTERCEPT those systems to modify their behavior. Instead, you should compose classes all at once.

> **DEFINITION**   A COMPOSITION ROOT is a (preferably) unique location in an application where modules are composed together.

> **TIP**   The COMPOSITION ROOT can be spread out across multiple classes as long as they all reside in a single module.

When you look at CONSTRUCTOR INJECTION in isolation you may wonder, *doesn't it just defer the decision about selecting a dependency to another place?* Yes, it does, and that's a good thing; this means that you get a central place where you can connect collaborating classes. The COMPOSITION ROOT acts as a third party that connects consumers with their services. In fact, Nat Pryce prefers the term *Third-party Connect* over DI[6] for exactly that reason.

---

[6] Nat Pryce, "'Dependency Injection' Considered Harmful," 2011, http://www.natpryce.com/articles/000783.html

The longer you defer the decision on how to connect classes together, the more you keep your options open. Thus, the Composition Root should be placed as close to the application's entry point as possible.

> **NOTE** I like to think about Composition Roots as the architectural equivalent to a concept from Lean Software Development:[7] the *Last Responsible Moment*. The idea is to defer all decisions as long as *responsibly* possible (but no longer), because we'd like to keep our options open and base our decisions upon as much information as possible. When it comes to composing applications, we can similarly defer the decision about wiring Dependencies to the application root.

Even a modular application that uses loose coupling and late binding to compose itself has a root that contains the entry point into the application. Examples are

- A console application is an executable (.exe) with a `Main` method.
- An ASP.NET web application is a library (.dll) with an `Application_Start` event handler in its `Global.asax`.
- A WPF application is an executable (.exe) with an `App.xaml` file.
- A WCF service is a library (.dll) with a class that derives from a service interface, although you can hook into a more low-level entry point by creating a custom `ServiceHostFactory`.

Many other technologies exist, but common to them all is that one module contains the entry point of the application: this is the *root* of the application, as illustrated in figure 3.7. The Composition Root of the application should be located in the application's root so that it can properly compose the application.

You shouldn't attempt to compose classes in any of the modules because that approach limits your options. All classes in application modules should use Constructor Injection (or, in rare cases, one of the other patterns from chapter 4) and leave it up to the Composition Root to compose the application's object graph. Any DI Container in use should be limited to the Composition Root.

Using a DI Container in a Composition Root

A DI Container can be misused as a Service Locator, but it should only be used as an engine that composes object graphs. When you consider a DI Container in that perspective, it only makes sense to constrain it to the Composition Root. This also has the great benefit of removing any coupling between the DI Container and the rest of the application code base.

> **TIP** A DI Container should only be referenced from the Composition Root. All other modules should have no reference to the container.

---

[7] See, for example, Mary Poppendieck and Tom Poppendieck, *Implementing Lean Software Development: From Concept to Cash* (New York: Addison-Wesley, 2007).

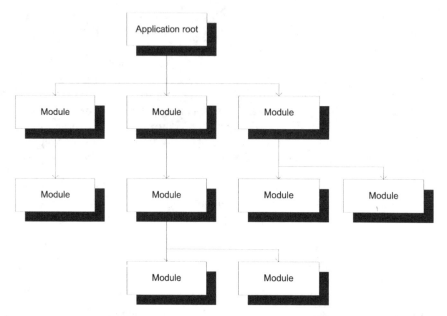

Figure 3.7   The entry point of an application is the root of a modular application. Either directly or indirectly, the root consumes the other modules. A COMPOSITION ROOT should be placed in the application's root—as close to the entry point as possible.

In figure 3.8 you can see that only the COMPOSITION ROOT has a reference to the DI CONTAINER. The rest of the application has no reference to the container and instead relies on the patterns described in chapter 4. DI CONTAINERS understand those patterns and use them to compose the application's object graph.

A COMPOSITION ROOT can be implemented with a DI CONTAINER. This means that you use the container to compose the *entire* application's object graph in a single call to the Resolve method. Whenever I talk to developers about doing it like this, I can always tell that it makes them uncomfortable because they're afraid that it's terribly inefficient and bad for performance. You don't have to worry about that because it's almost never the case, and in the very few situations where it is, there are ways to address the issue.[8]

> **TIP**   Don't worry about the performance overhead of using a DI CONTAINER to compose large object graphs. It's almost never an issue.

When it comes to request-based applications, such as websites and services, you configure the container only once, but resolve an object graph for each incoming request. The sample commerce application is an example of that.

---

[8]   Mark Seemann, "Compose object graphs with confidence," 2011, http://blog.ploeh.dk/2011/03/04/ComposeObjectGraphsWithConfidence.aspx

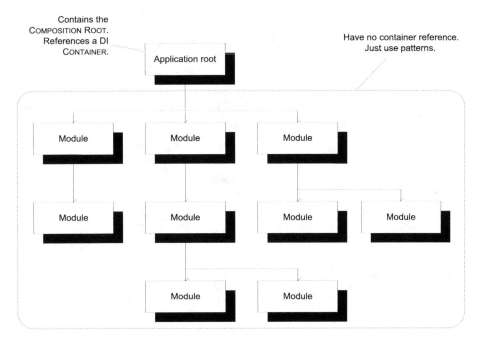

Figure 3.8 Only the COMPOSITION ROOT contained in the application root should have a reference to a DI CONTAINER. All other modules in the application should rely entirely on DI patterns and have no reference to the container.

EXAMPLE: IMPLEMENTING A COMPOSITION ROOT

The sample commerce application from section 2.3 must have a COMPOSITION ROOT to compose object graphs for incoming HTTP requests. As with all other .NET web applications, the entry point is in the `Application_Start` method in the `Global.asax` file.

In this example, I use the Castle Windsor DI CONTAINER, but the code would be similar with any other container. With Castle Windsor the `Application_Start` method could look like this:

```
protected void Application_Start()
{
    MvcApplication.RegisterRoutes(RouteTable.Routes);

    var container = new WindsorContainer();
    container.Install(new CommerceWindsorInstaller());

    var controllerFactory =
        new WindsorControllerFactory(container);

    ControllerBuilder.Current.SetControllerFactory(
        controllerFactory);
}
```

Before you can configure the container, you must create a new instance. Because the entire setup for the application is encapsulated in a class called `Commerce-WindsorInstaller`, you install that into the container to configure it. The code in

CommerceWindsorInstaller is obviously implemented with Castle Windsor's API, but, conceptually, it's identical to the examples in section 3.2.

To enable the container to wire up Controllers in the application, you must employ the appropriate SEAM in ASP.NET MVC, called an IControllerFactory (discussed in detail in section 7.2). For now, it's enough to understand that to integrate with ASP.NET MVC, you must create an Adapter[9] around the container and tell the framework about it.

Because the Application_Start method only runs once, the container is a single instance which is only initialized a single time. When requests come in, this container instance must handle each concurrently—but because all containers are implemented with thread-safe Resolve methods, that's not an issue.

Because you set up ASP.NET MVC with the custom WindsorControllerFactory, it will invoke its GetControllerInstance method for each incoming HTTP request (you can read about the details in section 7.2). The implementation delegates the work to the container:

```
protected override IController GetControllerInstance(
    RequestContext requestContext, Type controllerType)
{
    return (IController)this.container.Resolve(controllerType);
}
```

Notice that you're more or less back to the introductory examples from section 3.1.1. The Resolve method composes the complete graph that should be used to serve this particular request and returns it. This is the only place in the application where you invoke the Resolve method.

TIP An application's code base should only contain a *single* call to the Resolve method.

The COMPOSITION ROOT in this example is spread out across a few classes, as shown in figure 3.9. This is expected—the important thing is that all classes are contained in the same module, which in this case is the application root.

The most important thing to notice here is that these three classes are the only classes in the entire sample application that reference the DI CONTAINER. All the rest of the application code

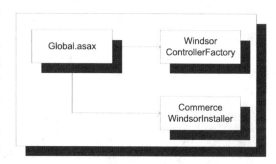

Figure 3.9 The COMPOSITION ROOT is spread across three classes, but they're all defined within the same module.

[9] Erich Gamma et al., *Design Patterns: Elements of Reusable Object-Oriented Software* (New York: Addison-Wesley, 1994), 139.

only uses the CONSTRUCTOR INJECTION pattern; go back and reread chapter 2 if you don't believe me.

> **TIP** I like to summarize all the guidance contained in this section by paraphrasing the Hollywood Principle: *don't call the container; it'll call you.*

Common Service Locator

There's an open source project called the Common Service Locator (http://common-servicelocator.codeplex.com/) that aims to decouple application code from specific DI CONTAINERS by hiding each container behind a common `IServiceLocator` interface.

I hope that this explanation of how a COMPOSITION ROOT effectively decouples the rest of the application code from DI CONTAINERS enables you now to understand why you don't need the Common Service Locator. As I explain in section 5.4, because SERVICE LOCATOR is an anti-pattern, it's best to stay away from it—and with a COMPOSITION ROOT, you don't need it, either.

You can read specific details on how to implement COMPOSITION ROOTS in various frameworks (including ASP.NET MVC) in chapter 7. In the current context, *how* you do it is much less important than *where* you do it. As the name implies, the COMPOSITION ROOT is that part of the application root where you compose all the loosely coupled classes. This is true whether you use a DI CONTAINER or POOR MAN'S DI. However, when you use a DI CONTAINER, you should follow the REGISTER RESOLVE RELEASE pattern.

3.3.2 *Register Resolve Release*

How should we use a DI Container?

BY FOLLOWING THE STRICT REGISTER RESOLVE RELEASE METHOD CALL SEQUENCE.

The COMPOSITION ROOT pattern describes *where* you should use a DI CONTAINER. However, it doesn't state *how* to use it. The REGISTER RESOLVE RELEASE pattern addresses this question.

A DI CONTAINER should be used in three successive phases called *Register, Resolve,* and *Release.* Table 3.3 describes each of the phases in more detail.

> **DEFINITION** The REGISTER RESOLVE RELEASE pattern states that a DI CONTAINER'S methods must be invoked in this strict sequence: *Register, Resolve,* and *Release* (see figure 3.10).

You must use the three phases in the correct order and you're not allowed to move back and forth willy-nilly. As an example, you shouldn't go back and reconfigure the container once you have started resolving object graphs. Sometimes people ask about how to add

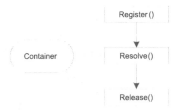

Figure 3.10 Container methods should be invoked in the strict sequence shown: first, the `Register` method, followed by the `Resolve` method, and terminated by the `Release` method.

Table 3.3   Container phases

Phase	What happens in this phase?	Further reading
Register	Register components with the container. You configure the container by informing it about which classes it can use, how it should map ABSTRACTIONS to concrete types, and, optionally, how certain classes should be wired together.	In section 3.2, I already discussed how to configure a DI CONTAINER. In part 4, I discuss configuration of six individual DI CONTAINERS in detail.
Resolve	Resolve root components. A single object graph is resolved from a request for a single type.	In section 3.1, we saw how to resolve object graphs with a DI CONTAINER. In part 4, you can read more about container-specific APIs.
Release	Release components from the container. All object graphs resolved in the previous phase should be released when they're no longer needed. This signals to the container that it can clean up the object graph, which is particularly important if some of the components are disposable.	In chapter 8, I discuss LIFETIME MANAGEMENT, including the importance of cleaning up. Additionally, in part 4, I look at LIFETIME MANAGEMENT APIs for individual DI CONTAINERS.

more components to a container after they have started resolving components. Don't do that—it will only give you grief.

> **NOTE** Some DI CONTAINERS don't support explicit `Release` of object graphs and instead rely on the .NET garbage collector. When using such containers, you must use a modified *Register Resolve* pattern instead and address the potential resource leaks in your object implementations. See chapter 8 for more details.

In the following section I talk about Register, Resolve, and Release *methods* as well as phases. Castle Windsor actually has three methods with these exact names, and the phases are named after these methods. Other DI CONTAINERS may use different names, but the underlying concept is identical. I only use the Castle Windsor names because they provide a consistent terminology—as well as a nice alliteration.

STATIC STRUCTURE

In its pure form, the REGISTER RESOLVE RELEASE pattern states that you should only make a *single* method call in each phase. Krzysztof Koźmic calls this the *Three Calls Pattern*[10]—you're only allowed to make three method calls to the container.

The `Resolve` and `Release` methods make this easy. In section 3.3.1 I already stated that an application should only contain a *single* call to the `Resolve` method. As a corollary, you should always Release what you Resolve.

---

[10] Krzysztof Koźmic, "How I use Inversion of Control containers," 2010, http://kozmic.pl/2010/06/20/how-i-use-inversion-of-control-containers

TIP Any object graph composed with the Resolve method should be decommissioned with the Release method.

Configuring a DI CONTAINER in a single method call requires more explanation. The reason that registration of components should happen in a single method call is because you should regard configuration of a DI CONTAINER as a single, atomic action. Once configuration is completed, the container should be regarded as read-only.

Autofac even makes this notion explicit by separating configuration of the container out into a distinct ContainerBuilder: you Register components with the ContainerBuilder and when you're done you ask it to build a container instance from the configuration. In Autofac, you don't directly configure the container.

By regarding configuration as a single atomic action, it becomes easier to manage the configuration code because it's evident where it should go. Many DI CONTAINERS also use this concept to freeze the configuration once you start resolving object graphs from it. This makes them perform better.

If you recall listing 3.2, you may argue that it contains more than a single method call. Registration is always going to involve many statements, but most DI CONTAINERS have a packaging mechanism that allows you to encapsulate all those configuration statements into a single class (perhaps composed of other classes). Autofac calls them *Modules,* StructureMap calls them *Registries,* and Castle Windsor calls them *Installers.* Common to them all is that they can be used to configure the container with a single method call. In section 3.3.1, you already saw Castle Windsor using an Installer:

```
container.Install(new CommerceWindsorInstaller());
```

For DI CONTAINERS that don't have a packaging mechanism, you can always create a custom class that encapsulates the configuration in a single method.

The advice that there must only be a single line of code each for Resolve and Release should be taken seriously—but for the Register phase, it should be understood more conceptually. The important point is that registration should be completed before the Resolve method is called. Figure 3.11 illustrates how the sequence looks, including the encapsulation of many Register method calls.

A common source of confusion is that the Three Calls Pattern makes an adamant statement about how often each method must appear in your code base, but it says nothing about how many times they must be invoked.

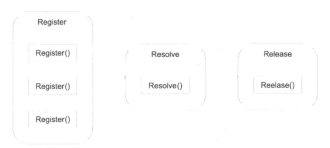

Figure 3.11 Any number of calls to the Register method can take place in the Register phase, but you should still regard it as an atomic action. In the Resolve and Release phase, you literally should have only one invocation of each method.

Figure 3.12 In a single-threaded application, each method will tend to be invoked only once. Configuration of the container is immediately followed by composing the application's object graph that performs the actual work. When the work is completed, the `Release` method is invoked before the application exits.

DYNAMIC INTERACTION

The name of the Three Calls Pattern may lead you to believe that each method must only be *called* once. The source of this confusion lies in the name itself, and this is one of several reasons I prefer the name REGISTER RESOLVE RELEASE.

The Three Calls Pattern states that there must only be a *single line of code* that invokes each method. However, depending on circumstances, some of the methods may be *invoked* more than once.

In a single-threaded application such as a desktop application, command-line utility, or batch job, each method will normally only be invoked once, as figure 3.12 illustrates.

In a request-based application such as a website, web service, or asynchronous message consumer, the COMPOSITION ROOT composes an object graph for each incoming request. In this type of application, as illustrated in figure 3.13, the `Register` method is still only invoked once, whereas the `Resolve` and `Release` methods are invoked in a pair for each request—a potentially huge number of times.

It's important to note that you must only configure the container once. The container is a shared instance that's used to resolve multiple requests, but the configuration must remain stable and complete.

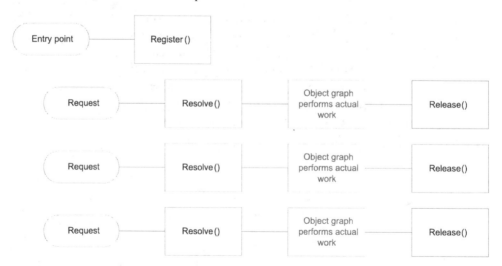

Figure 3.13 In a request-based application, the `Register` method is invoked only once, whereas the `Resolve` and `Release` methods are invoked many times—once per request.

The dynamic picture of REGISTER RESOLVE RELEASE is almost the inverse of the static view—contrast figure 3.11 with figure 3.13. In the static view, we tolerate multiple lines of code that invoke the Register method, but in the dynamic view, this block of code must be invoked exactly once. On the other hand, the static rule is that you must only have one line of code invoking Resolve and Release, but at runtime, these may be called multiple times.

This may sound complicated and difficult, but as the following example demonstrates, it's only three method calls.

EXAMPLE: USING REGISTER RESOLVE RELEASE

In this example you'll implement the COMPOSITION ROOT of the sample application from section 2.3 with the Castle Windsor DI CONTAINER. This is the same container you used in the example in section 3.3.1, so this example can be read as a continuation of the previous.

The entry point of the application is the Application_Start method, and because this is a website, the Register phase is isolated from the Resolve and Release phases because you must only configure the container once. The code is the same as in the previous example, but I want to change the focus a bit:

```
protected void Application_Start()
{
    MvcApplication.RegisterRoutes(RouteTable.Routes);

    var container = new WindsorContainer();
    container.Install(new CommerceWindsorInstaller());

    var controllerFactory =
        new WindsorControllerFactory(container);

    ControllerBuilder.Current.SetControllerFactory(
        controllerFactory);
}
```

According to the REGISTER RESOLVE RELEASE pattern, the first method call you make on the container instance should be an atomic Register call. In this case, the method is called Install and the CommerceWindsorInstaller encapsulates the individual registrations in a single class. The following listing shows the implementation of the CommerceWindsorInstaller.

Listing 3.3 Encapsulating multiple registrations

```
public class CommerceWindsorInstaller : IWindsorInstaller
{
    public void Install(IWindsorContainer container,
        IConfigurationStore store)
    {
        container.Register(AllTypes                          ❶ Register
            .FromAssemblyContaining<HomeController>()            calls
            .BasedOn<IController>()
            .Configure(r => r.LifeStyle.PerWebRequest));
```

```
        container.Register(AllTypes
            .FromAssemblyContaining<BasketService>()
            .Where(t => t.Name.EndsWith("Service"))
            .WithService
            .FirstInterface());
        container.Register(AllTypes
            .FromAssemblyContaining<BasketDiscountPolicy>()
            .Where(t => t.Name.EndsWith("Policy"))
            .WithService
            .Select((t, b) => new[] { t.BaseType }));

        string connectionString =
            ConfigurationManager.ConnectionStrings
            ["CommerceObjectContext"].ConnectionString;
        container.Register(AllTypes
            .FromAssemblyContaining<SqlProductRepository>()
            .Where(t => t.Name.StartsWith("Sql"))
            .WithService
            .Select((t, b) => new[] { t.BaseType })
            .Configure(r => r.LifeStyle.PerWebRequest
                .DependsOn((new
                {
                    connString = connectionString
                }))));
    }
}
```

➊ Register calls

The `CommerceWindsorInstaller` looks complicated, but the important thing to notice is that it encapsulates four calls to the `Register` method ➊ and that's the only way it interacts with the container. The rest of the code isn't important right now. It uses conventions to configure the container. You can read more about Castle Windsor's AUTO-REGISTRATION API in section 10.1.2.

Because the sample application is a website, Resolve and Release should be implemented as a single pair. For each HTTP request, you must Resolve an object graph that will handle that request, and when it's completed you must Release it again. You do this from a class called `WindsorControllerFactory` that derives from ASP.NET MVC's `DefaultControllerFactory`—you can read more about the details of the ASP.NET MVC SEAM in section 7.2.

The ASP.NET MVC framework invokes the `GetControllerInstance` method to resolve `IController`s and the `ReleaseController` method when the request has been handled. These are the appropriate methods for us to invoke the `Resolve` and `Release` methods:

```
protected override IController GetControllerInstance(
    RequestContext requestContext, Type controllerType)
{
    var controller =
        this.container.Resolve(controllerType);
    return (IController)controller;
}

public override void ReleaseController(IController controller)
{
```

```
    this.container.Release(controller);
}
```

In the `GetControllerInstance` method, you pass the `controllerType` argument to the Resolve method and return the resulting object graph. When the request has been handled, the ASP.NET MVC framework invokes the `ReleaseController` method with the `IController` instance previously created by the `GetControllerInstance` method, and you can pass that `controller` instance to the `Release` method.

Notice that these are the only appearances of the `Resolve` and `Release` methods in the entire code base of the application.

This example dug a little deeper than the previous example that demonstrated the COMPOSITION ROOT pattern, but it's essentially the same code. The COMPOSITION ROOT pattern addresses *where* you should compose object graphs, whereas REGISTER RESOLVE RELEASE deals with *how* to use a DI CONTAINER within a COMPOSITION ROOT.

In the next chapter I'll review more DI patterns, but before I do that I want to take a little detour and discuss how DI CONTAINERS fit into the overall .NET ecosystem.

3.4   DI Container landscape

Now that I have described what a DI CONTAINER is and how to apply it in a COMPOSITION ROOT, I want to change the pace a bit and provide an overview of the current state of DI CONTAINERS in the .NET ecosystem. These are the softer aspects of DI CONTAINERS, such as historical background and why there are so many open source containers available.

Because there's a plethora of DI CONTAINERS to choose from, I also want to provide a little bit of guidance on how to select a container.

3.4.1   Selecting a DI Container

The decision to use DI as a technique shouldn't hinge on the choice of a particular DI CONTAINER. DI is first and foremost a technique, and I'll use POOR MAN'S DI throughout most of parts 2 and 3 to emphasize this point.

Still, a DI CONTAINER will make your life easier, so use one whenever you can. Used according to the patterns outlined in this book, there are few disadvantages to using a container, but there are still things to consider.

DECISION PROCESS

A DI CONTAINER is a STABLE DEPENDENCY, so from a DI perspective, using one isn't an issue, but there are other, minor concerns to consider:

- Adding another library always adds a bit to the complexity of an application— not in terms of maintainability, but in terms of the learning curve. New developers will not only need to learn to understand the application's code, but also understand the API of the selected DI CONTAINER. In this chapter I hope that I managed to give you the impression that by isolating container usage to a COMPOSITION ROOT you can shield the container from beginners. If you use AUTO-REGISTRATION the container may even take care of the infrastructure for you without calling much attention to itself.

- With the exception of the Managed Extensibility Framework (MEF), you need to deploy the DI CONTAINER assemblies with your application. This could potentially have legal implications, although this isn't likely. All common open source DI CONTAINERS have permissive licenses, but I'm not a lawyer, so don't go and bet your business on my word: consult your own legal advisers.

- Once more with the exception of MEF, all other DI CONTAINERS are open source libraries. For each you have to assess how much you trust the people or organization behind it.

- There are technical differences between the various DI CONTAINERS. In the introduction to part 4 I've provided a table that lists the advantages and disadvantages of each container covered in this book. You can use this table as a starting point and then read the chapter on each of the containers you find interesting.

Selecting a DI CONTAINER need not be a big deal. Take one for a spin and see if it fits your need—if it doesn't, then replace it with another. When you constrain the DI CONTAINER to a COMPOSITION ROOT you can replace containers with relative ease.

SELECTED DI CONTAINERS

I won't tell you which DI CONTAINER to choose. Selecting a DI CONTAINER involves more than technical evaluation. You must also evaluate whether the license model is acceptable, whether you trust the people or organization that develops and maintains the DI CONTAINER, how it fits in to your organization's IT strategy, and so on.

Most .NET DI CONTAINERS are open source projects—also something to keep in mind, because there may be no official support and often limited documentation.

Table 3.4 lists the DI CONTAINERS covered in part 4 of the book. The selection is based on criteria such as relevance, market share, and distinguishing features, but can never be anything but a subjective and incomplete list. Several popular containers (such as Ninject) aren't included, mostly due to time and space constraints.

Table 3.4   Selected DI CONTAINERS. More are available, but these are selected either because they're in widespread usage, because they offer an interesting angle on DI, or because they're poised to become important in the future.

Name	Organization	Comments
Castle Windsor	Open source	Mature and widely used
StructureMap	Open source	Mature and widely used
Spring.NET	SpringSource	Mature and widely used port of the Java Spring DI CONTAINER
Autofac	Open source	More recent DI CONTAINER designed around C# 3.0 language features
Unity	Microsoft patterns & practices	Microsoft's first play in the DI space, but not a product per se
Managed Extensibility Framework (MEF)	Microsoft	Ships with .NET 4, but not really a DI CONTAINER

Part 4 is dedicated to these DI CONTAINERS, where each is covered by an entire chapter.

Note how this field is dominated by open source and other non-commercial projects, with Microsoft relegated to a minor role.

3.4.2 *Microsoft and DI*

Even though the .NET platform is a product of Microsoft, other organizations (often single individuals) are much more prominent when it comes to DI in .NET. In short, this can be attributed to the fact that Microsoft doesn't offer any DI CONTAINER in the Base Class Library (BCL). Even as a separate offering, Microsoft's only DI CONTAINER is the relatively recent Unity.

I think it's fair to say that for the first many years of the .NET Framework's life, Microsoft blissfully ignored the very concept of DI. It's not easy to explain exactly why, and I doubt that it was ever an explicit strategy.

A BRIEF HISTORY OF DI IN .NET

Here's my subjective attempt to outline the history of DI in .NET to explain why Microsoft ignored DI for so long (see figure 3.14). As far as I'm aware, there's no authoritative answer to that question.[11]

Before it hit .NET, DI seems to have grown out of the Java open source community. Martin Fowler published his DI article[12] in early 2004 as a *reaction* to ongoing work. At that time, .NET 1.1 was the current version, and Microsoft was working on .NET 2.0, while Java was rapidly approaching its decennary. It's my belief that Microsoft simply

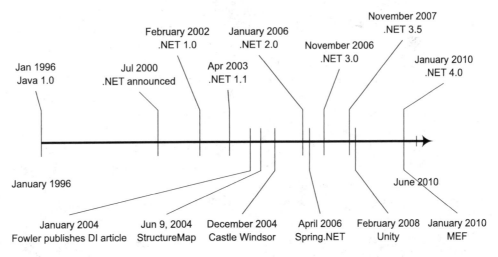

Figure 3.14   Timeline of selected platform and DI CONTAINER releases. Notice how mature Java appeared in 2004 compared to .NET.

---

[11] Although it doesn't deal with DI in particular, a good overview of the history of .NET in general can be found in Jon Skeet, *C# in Depth*, Manning, 2008.

[12] Martin Fowler, "Inversion of Control Containers and the Dependency Injection pattern," 2004, http://martinfowler.com/articles/injection.html

had their efforts directed elsewhere. Even if they'd been widely aware of DI at the time, I think they would still have prioritized other features, such as Generics, first.

In June 2004, the StructureMap DI CONTAINER was released, beating Castle Windsor by approximately half a year.

In late 2005, Microsoft released .NET 2.0 with Generics as the major new feature, and then decided to focus on WCF, WPF, and, later, LINQ for their next big release (Visual Studio 2008).

In the meantime, DI slowly gained in popularity. Spring.NET appeared in 2006.

It wasn't until early 2008, when *Microsoft patterns & practices* released Unity, that the mainstream Microsoft school of thought seemed to approach DI. That four-year time span gave skilled individuals a good head start, and DI CONTAINERS like StructureMap and Castle Windsor grew in popularity.

DI GRASSROOTS

An interesting observation about figure 3.14 is how quickly members of the .NET development community picked up the idea of DI. According to the Castle Windsor homepage, the concepts had been germinating even before Fowler's article:

> *Castle was born from the Apache Avalon project, in mid 2003, as an attempt to build a very simple inversion of control container.*
>
> – Castle web page at 2008.08.01[13]

For a long time, DI CONTAINERS for .NET remained a grassroots movement, and many leading members were sympathetic to Agile development. In fact, even if modular application architecture has a number of different benefits, it was first and foremost the question of TESTABILITY that seemed to motivate people to develop and use DI CONTAINERS (that was also true in my case).

At that time, the official development methodology at Microsoft was the Microsoft Solutions Framework (MSF) 3.0—a waterfall-style process that leaves little room for Agile development practices such as Test-Driven Development (TDD). In short, it was a completely different mindset.

Over time, Agile development, TDD, and DI have proven effective and gained in popularity, and Microsoft slowly seems to be moving to support that development style as well. In contrast to the situation in 2004, product teams now openly discuss DI, TDD, and other matters related to Agile development.

MICROSOFT DI CONTAINERS

Over the years, the *patterns & practices* (p&p) team in Microsoft has been developing a lot of proof of concepts for various .NET-related areas. Much of the experience harvested from these projects has been used to define and scope further development of the .NET Framework itself. As an example, the Updater Application Block provided a wealth of experience that was later used when ClickOnce was developed.

---

[13] http://www.castleproject.org/castle/history.html

In early 2008, p&p released their first Community Technical Preview (CTP) of Unity, their new DI CONTAINER, and release 1.0 followed in April 2008. Unity is a full-fledged DI CONTAINER that supports OBJECT COMPOSITION, LIFETIME MANAGEMENT, and INTERCEPTION. It's not a Microsoft *product*, but rather a *disclosed source*[14] project that just happens to be developed by Microsoft.

Object Builder

There seems to be some confusion as to exactly when p&p introduced a DI CONTAINER to the world. When the p&p Enterprise Library for .NET 2.0 was introduced in early 2006 it contained a module called *Object Builder* that was used to build complex objects from constituent elements.

It was attribute-driven and only worked for classes that integrated tightly with Object Builder itself. It was never introduced as a DI CONTAINER, although it was acknowledged that it might be possible to build a DI CONTAINER on top of it.

Many people mistakenly believe that Object Builder was Microsoft's first DI CONTAINER, but this isn't true: Unity has that title.

With .NET 4.0, Microsoft delivered the Managed Extensibility Framework (MEF) that marks the first time DI concerns are explicitly being addressed within .NET itself. In its first installment, MEF isn't a full-fledged DI CONTAINER that supports all three aspects of DI, but rather an engine focused on OBJECT COMPOSITION.

The MEF team is well aware of such aspects as LIFETIME MANAGEMENT and INTERCEPTION, so it's not unlikely that we'll see MEF evolve into a fully featured DI CONTAINER over the next few years (as I'm writing this, technical previews indicate that this is indeed the case).

3.5   Summary

A DI CONTAINER can be a tremendously helpful tool if you use it correctly. The most important thing to understand about it is that the use of DI in no way hinges on the use of a DI CONTAINER. An application can be made from many loosely coupled classes and modules, and none of these modules must know anything about a container. The most effective way to make sure that application code is unaware of any DI CONTAINER is to rigidly implement the REGISTER RESOLVE RELEASE pattern in a COMPOSITION ROOT. This effectively prevents you from inadvertently applying the SERVICE LOCATOR anti-pattern because it constrains the container to a small isolated area of the code.

Used in this way, a DI CONTAINER becomes an engine that takes care of a lot of the application's infrastructure. It composes object graphs based on its configuration.

---

[14] While the Unity source code is freely available, Microsoft doesn't accept patches. You can review the source, but not contribute. For that reason I find the term *disclosed source* more appropriate, as *open source* normally indicates that contributions can go both ways. However, to be fair the license is permissive, so you can use, modify, and redistribute the source.

This can be particularly beneficial if you employ CONVENTION-BASED CONFIGURATION—if suitably implemented, it can take care of composing object graphs and you can concentrate your efforts on adding new classes implementing new features. The container will automatically discover new classes that follow the established conventions and make them available to consumers.

In some cases, you need more explicit control over the configuration of the container. It's most efficient to use CODE AS CONFIGURATION, but if you need to support *late binding* you can also use XML to configure DI CONTAINERS.

This chapter concludes the first part of the book. The purpose of part 1 was to "put DI on the map." The previous chapters introduced DI in general, whereas this chapter explained how DI CONTAINERS relate to DI and application design in general. I found it only fitting to round off the chapter with a historical overview of DI CONTAINERS in the .NET ecosystem to really put the various containers on the map.

The chapter introduced COMPOSITION ROOT and REGISTER RESOLVE RELEASE as two mini-patterns that relate to DI CONTAINERS. In the next chapter, we'll focus on design patterns.

Part 2

DI catalog

Part 1 provided an overview of DI, discussing the purpose and benefits of DI and explaining how DI CONTAINERS fit into the overall picture. Even though chapter 2 contained an extensive example, I'm sure the first chapters still left you with some unresolved questions. In part 2, we dig a little deeper to answer some of those questions.

As the title of part 2 implies, this is a catalog of patterns, anti-patterns, and refactorings. Some people dislike design patterns because they find them dry or too abstract. Personally, I love patterns because they provide us with a high-level language that makes us more efficient and concise when we discuss software design. It's my intent to use this catalog to provide a pattern language for DI. Although a pattern description must contain some generalizations, I've attempted to make each pattern concrete, using examples.

You can read all three chapters in sequence, but each item in the catalog is also written so that you can read it by itself.

Chapter 4 contains a mini-catalog of DI design patterns. In a sense, these patterns constitute prescriptive guidance on how to implement DI, but you should be aware that I don't consider them to be of equal importance. CONSTRUCTOR INJECTION is by far the most important design pattern, whereas all the other patterns should be treated as fringe cases that can be applied in specialized circumstances. The AMBIENT CONTEXT pattern, in particular, should be so rarely employed that I seriously considered not including it in the book (I only left it in because those who read the book before publication asked me to keep it).

Whereas chapter 4 gives you a set of generalized solutions, chapter 5 contains a catalog of situations to avoid. These anti-patterns (or code smells) describe common, but incorrect ways to address typical DI challenges. In each case, the anti-pattern describes how to identify occurrences and how to resolve the issue. It's important to know and understand these anti-patterns to avoid the traps that they represent, and, just as chapter 4 presents one dominatingly important pattern, the most important anti-pattern is SERVICE LOCATOR, the antithesis of DI.

As you apply DI to real-life programming tasks, you will run into some challenges. I think we've all had moments of doubt where we feel that we understand a tool or technique, and yet we think, *"In theory, this may work, but my case is special..."* Whenever I find myself thinking like this, it's clear to me that I have more to learn.

During my career, I've seen a particular set of problems appear again and again. Each of these problems has a general solution you can apply to move your code towards one of the DI patterns from chapter 4. In the spirit of *refactoring to patterns* I chose to call this chapter *DI refactorings*, because it contains a catalog of issues and corresponding solutions.

Part 2 presents a complete catalog of patterns, anti-patterns, and refactorings. I expect this to be the most useful part of the book, because it's the most enduring. Hopefully, you'll return to these chapters months and even years after you first read them.

DI patterns

Like all professionals, cooks have their own jargon that allow them to communicate about complex food preparation in a language that often sounds esoteric to the rest of us. It doesn't help that most of the terms they use are based on French (unless you already speak French, that is).

Sauces are a great example of the way cooks use their professional terminology. In chapter 1, I briefly discussed sauce béarnaise, but I didn't elaborate on the taxonomy that surrounds it (see figure 4.1).

A sauce béarnaise is really a *sauce hollandaise* where the lemon juice is replaced by a *reduction* of vinegar, shallots, chervil, and tarragon. Other sauces are based on sauce hollandaise—including my favorite, *sauce mousseline*, which is made by *folding* whipped cream into the hollandaise.

Did you notice all the jargon? Instead of saying, "carefully mixing the whipped cream into the sauce, taking care not to collapse it," I used the term *folding*. When you know what it means, it's a lot easier to say and understand.

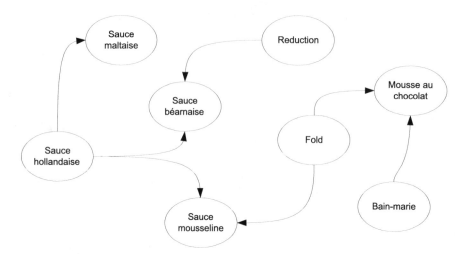

Figure 4.1   Several sauces are based on *sauce hollandaise*. In a *sauce béarnaise* the lemon is replaced with a *reduction* of vinegar and certain herbs, whereas the distinguishing feature of *sauce mousseline* is that whipped cream is *folded* into it—a technique also used to make *mousse au chocolat*.

The term *folding* isn't limited to sauces—it's a general way to combine something that's whipped with other ingredients. When making a classic *mousse au chocolat,* for example, I *fold* whipped egg whites into a mixture of whipped egg yolks and melted chocolate.

In software development, we have a complex and impenetrable jargon of our own. Although you may not know what the cooking term *bain-marie* refers to, I'm pretty sure most cooks would be utterly lost if you told them that "strings are immutable classes that represent sequences of Unicode characters."

When it comes to talking about how to structure code to solve particular types of problems, we have *Design Patterns* that give names to common solutions. In the same way that the terms *sauce hollandaise* and *fold* help us succinctly communicate how to make *sauce mousseline,* patterns help us talk about how code is structured. The eventing system in .NET is based on a design pattern called *Observer,* and foreach loops on *Iterator.*[1]

In this chapter, I'll describe the four basic DI patterns listed in figure 4.2. Because the chapter is structured to provide a catalog of patterns, each pattern is written so that it can be read independently. However, CONSTRUCTOR INJECTION is by far the most important of the four patterns.

Don't worry if you have only limited knowledge of design patterns in general. The main purpose of a design pattern is to provide a detailed and self-contained description of a particular way of attaining a goal—a recipe, if you will.

---

[1] Erich Gamma et al., *Design Patterns: Elements of Reusable Object-Oriented Software* (New York: Addison-Wesley, 1994), 293, 257.

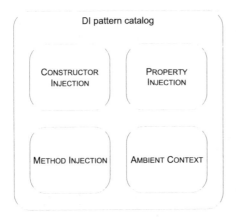

Figure 4.2   The structure of this chapter takes the form of a pattern catalog. Each pattern is written so it can be read independently of the other patterns.

For each pattern, I'll provide a short description, a code example, advantages and disadvantages, and so on. You can read about all four patterns in sequence or only read the ones that interest you. The most important pattern is CONSTRUCTOR INJECTION, which you should use in most situations; the other patterns become more specialized as the chapter progresses.

4.1   *Constructor Injection*

How do we guarantee that a necessary Dependency is always available to the class we're currently developing?

BY REQUIRING ALL CALLERS TO SUPPLY THE DEPENDENCY AS A PARAMETER TO THE CLASS'S CONSTRUCTOR.

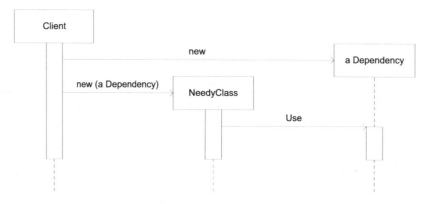

Figure 4.3   `NeedyClass` **needs an instance of Dependency to work, so it requires any Client to supply an instance via its constructor. This guarantees that the instance is available to** `NeedyClass` **whenever it's needed.**

When a class requires an instance of a DEPENDENCY to work at all, we can supply that DEPENDENCY through the class's constructor, enabling it to store the reference for future (or immediate) use.

4.1.1   *How it works*

The class that needs the DEPENDENCY must expose a public constructor that takes an instance of the required DEPENDENCY as a constructor argument. In most cases, this should be the only available constructor. If more than one DEPENDENCY is needed, additional constructor arguments can be used.

Listing 4.1   CONSTRUCTOR INJECTION

```
private readonly DiscountRepository repository;
public RepositoryBasketDiscountPolicy(            ❶ Inject Dependency          Dependency
    DiscountRepository repository)                    as constructor             field is
{                                                     argument                ❹ read-only
    if (repository == null)
    {
        throw new ArgumentNullException("repository");    ❷ Guard
    }                                                        Clause
                                     ❸ Save the Dependency
    this.repository = repository;        for later
}
```

The DEPENDENCY (in the previous listing that would be the abstract `DiscountRepository` class) is a required constructor argument ❶. Any client code that doesn't supply an instance of the DEPENDENCY can't compile. However, because both interfaces and abstract classes are reference types, a caller can pass in null as an argument to make the calling code compile; we need to protect the class against such misuse with a Guard Clause[2] ❷.

Because the combined efforts of the compiler and the Guard Clause guarantee that the constructor argument is valid if no exception is thrown, at this point, the constructor can save the DEPENDENCY for future use without knowing anything about the real implementation ❸.

It's good practice to mark the field holding the DEPENDENCY as readonly–this guarantees that once the initialization logic of the constructor has executed: the field can't be modified ❹. This isn't strictly required from a DI point of view, but it protects you from accidentally modifying the field (such as setting it to null) somewhere else in the depending class's code.

> **TIP** Keep the constructor free of any other logic. The SINGLE RESPONSIBILITY PRINCIPLE implies that members should do only one thing, and now that we use the constructor to inject DEPENDENCIES, we should prefer to keep it free of other concerns.

> **TIP** Think about CONSTRUCTOR INJECTION as *statically declaring a class's Dependencies*. The constructor signature is compiled with the type and is available for all to see. It clearly documents that the class requires the DEPENDENCIES it requests through its constructor.

When the constructor has returned, the new instance of the depending class is in a consistent state with a proper instance of its DEPENDENCY injected into it. Because it holds a reference to this DEPENDENCY, it can use it as often as necessary from any of its other members. It doesn't need to test for null, because the instance is guaranteed to be present.

4.1.2 When to use it

CONSTRUCTOR INJECTION should be your default choice for DI. It addresses the most common scenario where a class *requires* one or more DEPENDENCIES, and no reasonable LOCAL DEFAULTS are available.

CONSTRUCTOR INJECTION addresses that scenario well because it *guarantees* that the DEPENDENCY is present. If the depending class absolutely can't function without the DEPENDENCY, that guarantee is valuable.

> **TIP** If at all possible, constrain the design to a single constructor. Overloaded constructors lead to ambiguity: which constructor should a DI CONTAINER use?

In cases where the local library can supply a good default implementation, PROPERTY INJECTION may be a better fit—but this is often not the case. In the earlier chapters, I

---

[2] Martin Fowler et al., *Refactoring: Improving the Design of Existing Code* (New York: Addison-Wesley, 1999), 50.

showed many examples of Repositories as DEPENDENCIES. These are good examples of DEPENDENCIES where the local library can supply no good default implementation, because the proper implementations belong in specialized Data Access libraries.

Table 4.1 CONSTRUCTOR INJECTION advantages and disadvantages

Advantages	Disadvantages
Injection guaranteed Easy to implement	Some frameworks make using CONSTRUCTOR INJECTION difficult.

Apart from the guaranteed injection already discussed, this pattern is also easy to implement using the four steps implied by listing 4.1.

The main disadvantage to CONSTRUCTOR INJECTION is that you need to modify your current application framework to support it. Most frameworks assume that your classes will have a default constructor and may need special help to create instances when the default constructor is missing. In chapter 7, I explain how to enable CONSTRUCTOR INJECTION for common application frameworks.

An apparent disadvantage of CONSTRUCTOR INJECTION is that it requires that the entire dependency graph is initialized immediately—often at application startup. However, although this sounds inefficient, it's rarely an issue. After all, even for a complex object graph, we're typically talking about creating a dozen new object instances, and creating an object instance is something the .NET Framework does extremely fast. Any performance bottleneck your application may have will appear in other places, so don't worry about it.

In extremely rare cases this may be a real issue, but in chapter 8, I'll describe the *Delayed* lifetime option that offers one possible remedy to this issue. For now, I'll merely observe that there may (in fringe cases) be a potential issue with initial load and move on.

4.1.3   *Known use*

Although CONSTRUCTOR INJECTION tends to be ubiquitous in applications employing DI, it's not very present in the .NET Base Class Library (BCL). This is mainly because the BCL is a set of libraries and not a full-fledged application.

Two related examples where we can see a sort of CONSTRUCTOR INJECTION in the BCL is with System.IO.StreamReader and System.IO.StreamWriter. Both take a System.IO.Stream instance in their constructors. They also have a lot of overloaded constructors that take a file path instead of a Stream instance, but these are convenience methods that internally create a FileStream based on the specified file path—here are all the StreamWriter constructors, but the StreamReader constructors are similar:

```
public StreamWriter(Stream stream);
public StreamWriter(string path);
public StreamWriter(Stream stream, Encoding encoding);
public StreamWriter(string path, bool append);
```

```
public StreamWriter(Stream stream, Encoding encoding,
    int bufferSize);
public StreamWriter(string path, bool append, Encoding encoding);
public StreamWriter(string path, bool append, Encoding encoding,
    int bufferSize);
```

The `Stream` class is an abstract class that serves as an ABSTRACTION upon which `Stream-Writer` and `StreamReader` operate to perform their duties. You can supply any `Stream` implementation in their constructors and they will use it, but they will throw `ArgumentNullExceptions` if you try to slip them a null `Stream`.

Although the BCL can provide us with examples where we can see CONSTRUCTOR INJECTION in use, it's always more instructive to see an example. The next section walks you through a full implementation example.

4.1.4 *Example: Adding a currency provider to the shopping basket*

I'd like to add a new feature to the sample commerce application I expanded upon in chapter 2—namely, the ability to perform currency conversions. I'll spread the example throughout this chapter to demonstrate the different DI patterns in play, but when I'm done, the homepage should look like figure 4.4.

One of the first things you need is a `CurrencyProvider`—a DEPENDENCY that can provide you with the currencies you request. You define it like this:

Figure 4.4   The sample commerce application with currency conversion implemented. The user can now select among three different currencies, and both product prices and basket totals (on the basket page) will be displayed in that currency.

```
public abstract class CurrencyProvider
{
    public abstract Currency GetCurrency(string currencyCode);
}
```

The `Currency` class is another abstract class that provides conversion rates between itself and other currencies:

```
public abstract class Currency
{
    public abstract string Code { get; }

    public abstract decimal GetExchangeRateFor(
        string currencyCode);
}
```

You want the currency conversion feature on all pages that display prices, so you need it in both the `HomeController` and the `BasketController`. Because both implementations are quite similar, I'll only show you the `BasketController`.

A `CurrencyProvider` is likely to represent an out-of-process resource, such as a web service or a database that can supply conversion rates. This means that it would be most fitting to implement a concrete `CurrencyProvider` in a separate project (such as a Data Access library). Hence, there's no reasonable LOCAL DEFAULT. At the same time, the `BasketController` class will need a `CurrencyProvider` to be present; CONSTRUCTOR INJECTION is a good fit. The following listing shows how the `CurrencyProvider` DEPENDENCY is injected into the `BasketController`.

Listing 4.2   Injecting a `CurrencyProvider` into the `BasketController`

```
private readonly IBasketService basketService;          ❹ Dependency fields
private readonly CurrencyProvider currencyProvider;        are read-only

public BasketController(IBasketService basketService,   ❶ Inject Dependencies as
    CurrencyProvider currencyProvider)                      constructor arguments
{
    if (basketService == null)
    {
        throw new
            ArgumentNullException("basketService");
    }                                                   ❷ Guard
    if (currencyProvider == null)                          Clauses
    {
        throw new
            ArgumentNullException("currencyProvider");
    }

    this.basketService = basketService;                 ❸ Save Dependencies
    this.currencyProvider = currencyProvider;              for later
}
```

Because the `BasketController` class already had a DEPENDENCY on `IBasketService`, you add the new `CurrencyProvider` DEPENDENCY as a second constructor argument ❶ and then follow the same sequence outlined in listing 4.1: Guard Clauses guarantee that the DEPENDENCIES aren't null ❷, which means it's safe to store them for later use ❸ in read-only fields ❹.

Now that the `CurrencyProvider` is guaranteed to be present in the `BasketController`, it can be used from anywhere—for example, in the `Index` method:

```
public ViewResult Index()
{
    var currencyCode =
        this.CurrencyProfileService.GetCurrencyCode();
    var currency =
        this.currencyProvider.GetCurrency(currencyCode);

    // …
}
```

I haven't yet discussed the `CurrencyProfileService`, so for now, know that it provides the current user's preferred currency code. In section 4.2.4, I'll discuss the `CurrencyProfileService` in greater detail.

Given a currency code, the `CurrencyProvider` can be invoked to provide a `Currency` that represents that code. Notice that you can use the `currencyProvider` field without needing to check it in advance, because it's guaranteed to be present.

Now that you have the `Currency`, you can then proceed to perform the rest of the work in the `Index` method; note that I haven't yet shown that implementation. As we progress through this chapter, I'll build on this method and add more currency conversion functionality along the way.

4.1.5   *Related patterns*

CONSTRUCTOR INJECTION is the most generally applicable DI pattern available, and also the easiest to implement correctly. It applies when the DEPENDENCY is *required*.

If we need to make the DEPENDENCY optional, we can change to PROPERTY INJECTION if we have a proper LOCAL DEFAULT.

When the DEPENDENCY represents a CROSS-CUTTING CONCERN that should be potentially available to any module in the application, we can use an AMBIENT CONTEXT, instead.

The next pattern in this chapter is PROPERTY INJECTION, which is closely related to CONSTRUCTOR INJECTION; the only deciding parameter is whether the DEPENDENCY is optional or not.

4.2   *Property Injection*

> *How do we enable DI as an option in a class when we have a good Local Default?*

BY EXPOSING A WRITABLE PROPERTY THAT LETS CALLERS SUPPLY A DEPENDENCY IF THEY WISH TO OVERRIDE THE DEFAULT BEHAVIOR.

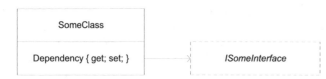

Figure 4.5 `SomeClass` has an optional DEPENDENCY on `ISomeInterface`; instead of requiring callers to supply an instance, it's giving callers an option to define it via a property.

When a class has a good LOCAL DEFAULT, but we still want to leave it open for extensibility, we can expose a writable property that allows a client to supply a different implementation of the class's DEPENDENCY than the default.

> **NOTE**   PROPERTY INJECTION is also known as SETTER INJECTION.

Referring to figure 4.5, clients wishing to use the `SomeClass` as-is can `new` up an instance of the class and use it without giving it a second thought, whereas clients wishing to modify the behavior of the class can do so by setting the `Dependency` property to a different implementation of `ISomeInterface`.

4.2.1   *How it works*

The class that uses the DEPENDENCY must expose a public writable property of the DEPENDENCY's type. In a bare-bones implementation, this may be as simple as the following listing.

Listing 4.3   PROPERTY INJECTION

```
public partial class SomeClass
{
    public ISomeInterface Dependency { get; set; }
}
```

`SomeClass` depends on `ISomeInterface`. Clients can supply implementations of `ISomeInterface` by setting the `Dependency` property. Notice that in contrast to CONSTRUCTOR INJECTION, you can't mark the `Dependency` property's backing field as `readonly` because you allow callers to modify the property at any given time of `Some-Class`'s lifetime.

Other members of the depending class can use the injected DEPENDENCY to perform their duties, like this:

```
public string DoSomething(string message)
{
    return this.Dependency.DoStuff(message);
}
```

However, such an implementation is fragile because the `Dependency` property isn't guaranteed to return an instance of `ISomeInterface`. Code like this would throw a `NullReferenceException` because the value of the `Dependency` property is null:

```
var mc = new SomeClass();
mc.DoSomething("Ploeh");
```

This issue can be solved by letting the constructor set a default instance on the property, combined with a proper Guard Clause in the property's setter.

Another complication arises if you allow clients to switch the Dependency in the middle of the class's lifetime. This can be addressed by introducing an internal flag that only allows a client to set the Dependency once.[3]

The example in section 4.2.4 shows how you can deal with these complications, but before I get to that, I'd like to explain when it's appropriate to use Property Injection.

4.2.2 *When to use it*

Property Injection should only be used when the class you're developing has a good Local Default and you still want to enable callers to provide different implementations of the class's Dependency.

Property Injection is best used when the Dependency is *optional.*

> **NOTE** There's some controversy around the issue of whether Property Injection indicates an optional Dependency. As a general API design principle, I consider properties to be optional because you can easily forget to assign them and the compiler doesn't complain. If you accept this principle in the general case, you must also accept it in the special case of DI.

Local Default

When you're developing a class that has a Dependency, you probably have a particular implementation of that Dependency in mind. If you're writing a Domain Service that accesses a Repository, you're most likely planning to develop an implementation of that Repository that uses a relational database.

It would be tempting to make that implementation the default used by the class under development. However, when such a prospective default is implemented in a different assembly, using it as a default would mean creating a hard reference to that other assembly, effectively violating many of the benefits of loose coupling described in chapter 1.

Conversely, if the intended default implementation is defined in the same library as the consuming class, you don't have that problem. This is unlikely to be the case with Repositories, but such Local Defaults are more likely as Strategies.[4]

The example in this section contains an example of a Local Default.

---

[3] Eric Lippert calls this *popsicle immutability.* Eric Lippert, "Immutability in C# Part One: Kinds of Immutability," 2007, http://blogs.msdn.com/ericlippert/archive/2007/11/13/immutability-in-c-part-one-kinds-of-immutability.aspx

[4] Gamma, *Design Patterns*, 315.

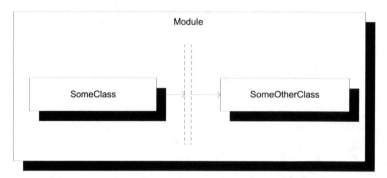

Figure 4.6   Even within a single module, we can introduce ABSTRACTIONS (represented by the vertical rectangle) that help reduce class coupling within that module. The main motivation for doing this is to enhance maintainability of the module by enabling classes to vary independently of each other.

In chapter 1, I discussed many good reasons for writing code with loose coupling, isolating modules from each other. However, loose coupling can also be applied to classes within a single module with great success. This is often done by introducing ABSTRACTIONS within a single module and letting classes communicate via ABSTRACTIONS, instead of being tightly coupled to each other.

Figure 4.6 illustrates that ABSTRACTIONS can be defined, implemented, and consumed within a single module with the main purpose of opening classes for extensibility.

NOTE   The concept of opening a class for extensibility is captured by the OPEN/CLOSED PRINCIPLE[5] that, briefly put, states that a class should be open for extensibility, but closed for modification.

When we implement classes following the OPEN/CLOSED PRINCIPLE, we may have a LOCAL DEFAULT in mind, but we still provide clients with a way to extend the class by replacing the DEPENDENCY with something else.

NOTE   PROPERTY INJECTION is only one among many different ways of applying the OPEN/CLOSED PRINCIPLE.

TIP   Sometimes you only wish to provide an extensibility point, but leave the LOCAL DEFAULT as a no-op. In such cases, you can use the `Null Object`[6] pattern to implement the LOCAL DEFAULT.

TIP   Sometimes you wish to leave the LOCAL DEFAULT in place, but have the ability to *add* more implementations. You can achieve this by modeling the DEPENDENCY around either the `Observer` or the `Composite` patterns.[7]

---

[5]   A good .NET-related introduction to the OPEN/CLOSED PRINCIPLE can be found in Jeremy Miller, "Patterns in Practice: The Open Closed Principle," (MSDN Magazine, June 2008). Also available online at http://msdn.microsoft.com/en-us/magazine/cc546578.aspx

[6]   Robert C. Martin et al., *Pattern Languages of Program Design 3* (New York: Addison-Wesley, 1998), 5.

[7]   Gamma, *Design Patterns*, 293, 163.

So far, I haven't shown you any examples of Property Injection, because the applicability of this pattern is more limited.

Table 4.2 Property Injection **advantages and disadvantages**

Advantages	Disadvantages
Easy to understand	Limited applicability Not entirely simple to implement robustly

The main advantage of Property Injection is that it's so easy to understand. I have often seen this pattern used as a first attempt when people decide to adopt DI.

Appearances can be deceptive, and Property Injection is fraught with difficulties. It's challenging to implement it in a robust manner. Clients may forget (or not want) to supply the Dependency, or mistakenly supply null as a value. Additionally: what should happen if a client tries to *change* the Dependency in the middle of the class's lifetime? This could lead to inconsistent or unexpected behavior, so you may want to protect yourself against that event.

With Constructor Injection, you could protect the class against such incidents by applying the `readonly` keyword to the backing field, but this isn't possible when you expose the Dependency as a writable property. In many cases, Constructor Injection is much simpler and more robust, but there are situations where Property Injection is the correct choice. This is the case when supplying a Dependency is optional, because you have a good Local Default.

The existence of a good Local Default depends in part on the granularity of modules. The .NET Base Class Library (BCL) ships as a rather large package; as long as the default stays within the BCL, it could be argued that it's also local. In the next section, I'll briefly touch upon that subject.

4.2.3 *Known use*

In the .NET BCL, Property Injection is a bit more common than Constructor Injection—probably because good Local Defaults are defined in many places.

`System.ComponentModel.IComponent` has a writable `Site` property that allows you to define an `ISite` instance. This is mostly used in design time scenarios (for example, by Visual Studio) to alter or enhance a component when it's hosted in a designer.

Another example that seems closer to how we're used to think about DI can be found in Windows Workflow Foundation (WF). The `WorkflowRuntime` class gives you the ability to add, get, and remove services. This isn't true Property Injection, because the API allows you to add zero or many untyped services through the same general-purpose API:

```
public void AddService(object service)
public T GetService<T>()
```

```
public object GetService(Type serviceType)
public void RemoveService(object service)
```

Although `AddService` will throw an `ArgumentNullException` if the service is null, there's no guarantee that you can retrieve a service with a given type because it may never have been added to the current `WorkflowRuntime` instance (in fact, this is because the `GetService` method is a SERVICE LOCATOR).

On the other hand, `WorkflowRuntime` comes with a lot of LOCAL DEFAULTS for each of the required services that it needs, and these are even named with the prefix *Default*, such as `DefaultWorkflowSchedulerService` and `DefaultWorkflowLoader-Service`. If, for example, no alternative `WorkflowSchedulerService` is added either via the `AddService` method or the application configuration file, the `DefaultWork-flowSchedulerService` class is used.

With these BCL examples as hors d'œuvres, let's move on to a more substantial example of using and implementing PROPERTY INJECTION.

4.2.4   *Example: Defining a currency profile service for the BasketController*

In section 4.1.4, I started adding currency conversion functionality to the sample commerce application, and I briefly showed you some of the implementation of the `BasketController`'s Index method—but glossed over the appearance of a `Currency-ProfileService`. Here's the deal:

The application needs to know which currency the user wishes to see. If you refer back to the screen shot in figure 4.4, you'll notice some currency links at the bottom of the screen. When the user clicks one of these links, you need to save the selected currency somewhere and associate that selection with the user. The `Currency-ProfileService` facilitates saving and retrieving the user's selected currency:

```
public abstract class CurrencyProfileService
{
    public abstract string GetCurrencyCode();

    public abstract void UpdateCurrencyCode(string currencyCode);
}
```

It's an ABSTRACTION that encodes the actions of applying and retrieving the current user's currency selection.

In ASP.NET MVC (and ASP.NET in general), you have a well-known piece of infrastructure that deals with such a scenario: the `Profile` service. An excellent LOCAL DEFAULT implementation of `CurrencyProfileService` is one that wraps around the ASP.NET `Profile` service and provides the necessary functionality defined by the `Get-CurrencyCode` and `UpdateCurrencyCode` methods. The `BasketController` will use this `DefaultCurrencyProfileService` as the default while exposing a property that will allow the caller to substitute it by something else.

Listing 4.4 Exposing a `CurrencyProfileService` property

```
private CurrencyProfileService currencyProfileService;

public CurrencyProfileService CurrencyProfileService
{
    get
    {
        if (this.currencyProfileService == null)
        {
            this.CurrencyProfileService =
                new DefaultCurrencyProfileService(
                    this.HttpContext);
        }
        return this.currencyProfileService;
    }
    set
    {
        if (value == null)
        {
            throw new ArgumentNullException("value");
        }
        if (this.currencyProfileService != null)
        {
            throw new InvalidOperationException();
        }
        this.currencyProfileService = value;
    }
}
```

❶ Lazy initialization of Local Default

❷ Only allow Dependency to be defined once

The DefaultCurrencyProfileService itself uses CONSTRUCTOR INJECTION because it requires access to the HttpContext, and because the HttpContext isn't available to the BasketController at creation time, it has to defer creation of the DefaultCurrency-ProfileService until the property is requested for the first time. In this case, lazy initialization ❶ is required, but in other cases, the LOCAL DEFAULT could have been assigned in the constructor. Notice that the LOCAL DEFAULT is assigned through the public setter, which ensures that all the Guard Clauses get evaluated.

The first Guard Clause guarantees that the DEPENDENCY isn't null. The next Guard Clause ❷ ensures that the DEPENDENCY can only be assigned once. In this case, I prefer that the CurrencyProfileService can't be changed once it's assigned, because otherwise it could lead to inconsistent behavior where a user's currency selection is first stored using one CurrencyProfileService and then subsequently retrieved from a different place, most likely yielding a different value.

You may also notice that, because you use the setter for lazy initialization ❶, the DEPENDENCY will also be locked once the property has been read. Once again, this is to protect clients from the case where the DEPENDENCY is subsequently changed without notification.

If you can get past all the Guard Clauses, you can save the instance for future use.

Compared to CONSTRUCTOR INJECTION, this is much more involved. PROPERTY INJECTION may look simple in its raw form as shown in listing 4.3, but properly implemented, it tends to be much more complex—and, in this example, I have even elected to ignore the issue of thread safety.

With the `CurrencyProfileService` in place, the start of the `BasketController`'s `Index` method can now use it to retrieve the user's preferred currency:

```
public ViewResult Index()
{
    var currencyCode =
        this.CurrencyProfileService.GetCurrencyCode();
    var currency =
        this.currencyProvider.GetCurrency(currencyCode);

    // …
}
```

This is the same code fragment shown in section 4.1.4. The `CurrencyProfileService` is used to get the user's selected currency, and the `CurrencyProvider` is subsequently used to retrieve that `Currency`.

In section 4.3.4, I'll return to the `Index` method to show what happens next.

4.2.5 *Related patterns*

You use PROPERTY INJECTION when the DEPENDENCY is optional because you have a good LOCAL DEFAULT. If you don't have a LOCAL DEFAULT, you should change the implementation to CONSTRUCTOR INJECTION.

When the DEPENDENCY represents a CROSS-CUTTING CONCERN that should be available to all modules in an application, you can implement it as an AMBIENT CONTEXT.

But before we get to that, METHOD INJECTION, in the next section, takes a slightly different approach, because it tends to apply more to the situation where we already have a DEPENDENCY that we wish to pass on to the collaborators we invoke.

4.3 Method Injection

How can we inject a Dependency into a class when it's different for each operation?
BY SUPPLYING IT AS A METHOD PARAMETER.

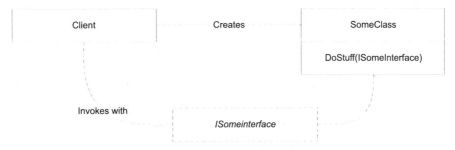

Figure 4.7 A Client creates an instance of SomeClass, **but first injects an instance of the**
DEPENDENCY ISomeInterface **with each method call.**

When a DEPENDENCY can vary with each method call, you can supply it via a method
parameter.

4.3.1 How it works

The caller supplies the DEPENDENCY as a method parameter in each method call. It can
be as simple as this method signature:

```
public void DoStuff(ISomeInterface dependency)
```

Often, the DEPENDENCY will represent some sort of context for an operation that's supplied alongside a "proper" value:

```
public string DoStuff(SomeValue value, ISomeContext context)
```

In this case, the value parameter represents the value on which the method is supposed to operate, whereas the context contains information about the current context of the operation. The caller supplies the DEPENDENCY to the method, and the
method uses or ignores the DEPENDENCY as it best suits it.

   If the service uses the DEPENDENCY, it should be sure to test for null references first,
as shown in the following listing.

Listing 4.5 Checking a method parameter for null before using it

```
public string DoStuff(SomeValue value, ISomeContext context)
{
    if (context == null)
    {
        throw new ArgumentNullException("context");
    }

    return context.Name;
}
```

The Guard Clause guarantees that the context is available to the rest of the method body. In this example, the method uses the context's name to return a value, so ensuring that the context is available is important.

If a method doesn't use the supplied DEPENDENCY, it doesn't need to contain a Guard Clause. This sounds like a strange situation because, if the parameter isn't used, then why have it at all? However, you may need to keep it if the method is part of an interface implementation.

4.3.2   *When to use it*

METHOD INJECTION is best used when the DEPENDENCY can vary with each method call. This can be the case when the DEPENDENCY itself represents a value, but is often seen when the caller wishes to provide the consumer with information about the context in which the operation is being invoked.

This is often the case in add-in scenarios where an add-in is provided with information about the runtime context via a method parameter. In such cases, the add-in is required to implement an interface that defines the injecting method(s).

Imagine an add-in interface with this structure:

```
public interface IAddIn
{
    string DoStuff(SomeValue value, ISomeContext context);
}
```

Any class implementing this interface can be used as an add-in. Some classes may not care about the context at all, whereas other implementations will. A client may use a list of add-ins by calling each with a value and a context to return an aggregated result. This is shown in the following listing.

Listing 4.6   A sample add-in client

```
public SomeValue DoStuff(SomeValue value)
{
    if (value == null)
    {
        throw new ArgumentNullException("value");
    }

    var returnValue = new SomeValue();
    returnValue.Message = value.Message;

    foreach (var addIn in this.addIns)
    {
        returnValue.Message =
            addIn.DoStuff(returnValue, this.context);       ① Pass context
    }                                                          to add-in

    return returnValue;
}
```

The private `addIns` field is a list of `IAddIn` instances, which allows the client to loop through the list to invoke each add-in's `DoStuff` method. Each time the `DoStuff` method is invoked on an add-in, the operation's context represented by the context field is passed as a method parameter ❶.

> **NOTE** METHOD INJECTION is closely related to the use of Abstract Factories described in section 6.1. Any Abstract Factory that takes an ABSTRACTION as input can be viewed as a variation of METHOD INJECTION.

At times, the value and the operational context are encapsulated in a single ABSTRACTION that works as a combination of both.

Table 4.3 METHOD INJECTION advantages and disadvantages

Advantages	Disadvantages
Allows the caller to provide operation-specific context	Limited applicability

METHOD INJECTION is different from other types of DI patterns we've seen so far in that the injection doesn't happen in a COMPOSITION ROOT, but, rather, dynamically at invocation time. This allows the caller to provide operation-specific context, which is a common extensibility mechanism used in the .NET BCL.

4.3.3 *Known use*

The .NET BCL provides many examples of METHOD INJECTION, particularly in the System .ComponentModel namespace.

System.ComponentModel.Design.IDesigner is used for implementing custom design-time functionality for components. It has an Initialize method that takes an IComponent instance so that it knows which component it's currently helping to design. Designers are created by IDesignerHost implementations that also take IComponent instances as parameters to create designers:

```
IDesigner GetDesigner(IComponent component);
```

This is a good example of a scenario where the parameter itself carries information: the component may carry information about which IDesigner to create, but at the same time, it's also the component upon which the designer must subsequently operate.

Another example in the System.ComponentModel namespace is provided by the TypeConverter class. Several of its methods take an instance of ITypeDescriptor-Context that, as the name says, conveys information about the context of the current operation. Because there are many such methods, I don't want to list them all, but here is a representative example:

```
public virtual object ConvertTo(ITypeDescriptorContext context,
    CultureInfo culture, object value, Type destinationType)
```

In this method, the context of the operation is communicated explicitly by the context parameter while the value to be converted and the destination type are sent as separate parameters. Implementers can use or ignore the context parameter as they see fit.

ASP.NET MVC also contains several examples of METHOD INJECTION. The IModel-Binder interface can be used to convert HTTP GET or POST data into strongly typed objects. Its only method is

```
object BindModel(ControllerContext controllerContext,
    ModelBindingContext bindingContext);
```

In the BindModel method, the controllerContext parameter contains information about the operation's context (among other things the HttpContext), whereas the bindingContext carries more explicit information about the values received from the browser.

When I recommend that CONSTRUCTOR INJECTION should be your preferred DI pattern, I'm assuming that you generally build applications based on frameworks. On the other hand, if you're building a framework, METHOD INJECTION can often be useful, because it allows you to pass information about the context to add-ins to the framework. That's one reason why we see METHOD INJECTION used so prolifically in the BCL.

4.3.4   *Example: Converting baskets*

In previous examples, we've seen how the BasketController in the sample commerce application retrieves the user's preferred currency (see sections 4.1.4 and 4.2.4). I'll now complete the currency conversion example by converting a Basket to the user's currency.

Currency is an ABSTRACTION that models a currency.

Listing 4.7   Currency

```
public abstract class Currency
{
    public abstract string Code { get; }

    public abstract decimal GetExchangeRateFor(
        string currencyCode);
}
```

The Code property returns the currency code for the Currency instance. Currency codes are expected to be international currency codes. For example, the currency code for Danish Kroner is DKK, whereas it's USD for US Dollars.

The GetExchangeRateFor method returns the exchange rate between the Currency instance and some other currency. Notice that this is an abstract method, which means that I'm making no assumptions about *how* that exchange rate is going to be found by the implementer.

In the next section, we'll examine how Currency instances are used to convert prices, and how this ABSTRACTION can be implemented and wired up so that you can convert some prices into such exotic currencies as US Dollars or Euros.

INJECTING CURRENCY

You'll use the Currency ABSTRACTION as an information-carrying DEPENDENCY to perform currency conversions of Baskets, so you'll add a ConvertTo method to the Basket class:

```
public Basket ConvertTo(Currency currency)
```

This will loop through all the items in the basket and convert their calculated prices to the provided currency, returning a new Basket instance with the converted items. Through a series of delegated method calls, the implementation is finally provided by the Money class, as shown in the following listing.

Listing 4.8   Converting Money to another currency

```
public Money ConvertTo(Currency currency)                    Inject Currency
{                                                            as method
    if (currency == null)                               ❶   parameter
    {
        throw new ArgumentNullException("currency");
    }
    var exchangeRate =
        currency.GetExchangeRateFor(this.CurrencyCode);
    return new Money(this.Amount * exchangeRate,
        currency.Code);
}
```

The Currency is injected into the ConvertTo method via the currency parameter ❶ and checked by the ubiquitous Guard Clause that guarantees that the currency instance is available to the rest of the method body.

The exchange rate to the current currency (represented by this.CurrencyCode) is retrieved from the supplied currency and used to calculate and return the new Money instance.

With the implementation of the ConvertTo methods, you can finally implement the Index method on the BasketController, as shown in the following listing.

Listing 4.9   Converting a Basket's currency

```
public ViewResult Index()
{
    var currencyCode =
        this.CurrencyProfileService.GetCurrencyCode();
    var currency =
        this.currencyProvider.GetCurrency(currencyCode);

    var basket = this.basketService          ❶  Convert the user's
        .GetBasketFor(this.User)                 basket to the
        .ConvertTo(currency);                    selected currency
    if (basket.Contents.Count == 0)
    {
        return this.View("Empty");
    }

    var vm = new BasketViewModel(basket);
    return this.View(vm);
}
```

The `BasketController` uses an `IBasketService` instance to retrieve the user's Basket. You may recall from chapter 2 that the `IBasketService` DEPENDENCY is provided to the `BasketController` via CONSTRUCTOR INJECTION. Once you have the `Basket` instance, you can convert it to the desired currency by using the `ConvertTo` method, passing in the currency instance ❶.

In this case, you're using METHOD INJECTION because the `Currency` ABSTRACTION is information-carrying, but will vary by context (depending on the user's selection). You could've implemented the `Currency` type as a concrete class, but that would've constrained your ability to define how exchange rates are retrieved.

Now that we've seen how the `Currency` class is used, it's time to change our viewpoint and examine how it might be implemented.

IMPLEMENTING CURRENCY

I haven't yet talked about how the `Currency` class is implemented because it's not that important from the point of view of METHOD INJECTION. As you may recall from section 4.1.4, and as you can see in listing 4.9, the `Currency` instance is served by the `CurrencyProvider` instance that was injected into the `BasketController` class by CONSTRUCTOR INJECTION.

To keep the example simple, I've shown what would happen if you decided to implement `CurrencyProvider` and `Currency` using a SQL Server database and LINQ to Entities. This assumes that the database has a table with exchange rates that has been populated in advance by some external mechanism. You could also have used a web service to request exchange rates from an external source.

The `CurrencyProvider` implementation passes a connection string on to the `Currency` implementation that uses this information to create an `ObjectContext`. The heart of the matter is the implementation of the `GetExchangeRateFor` method, shown in the following listing.

Listing 4.10 SQL Server–backed `Currency` implementation

```
public override decimal GetExchangeRateFor(string currencyCode)
{
    var rates = (from r in this.context.ExchangeRates
                 where r.CurrencyCode == currencyCode
                 || r.CurrencyCode == this.code
                 select r)
                 .ToDictionary(r => r.CurrencyCode);

    return rates[currencyCode].Rate
        / rates[this.code].Rate;
}
```

The first thing to do is get the rates from the database. The table contains rates as defined against a single, common currency (DKK), so you need both rates to be able to perform a proper conversion between two arbitrary currencies. You will index the retrieved currencies by currency code so that you can easily look them up in the final step of the calculation.

This implementation potentially performs a lot of out-of-process communication with the database. The ConvertTo method of Basket eventually calls this method in a tight loop, and hitting the database for each call is likely to be detrimental to performance. I'll return to this challenge in the next section.

4.3.5 *Related patterns*

Unlike the other DI patterns in this chapter, we mainly use METHOD INJECTION when we already have an instance of the DEPENDENCY we want to pass on to collaborators, but where we don't know the concrete types of the collaborators at design time (such as is the case with add-ins).

With METHOD INJECTION, we're on the other side of the fence compared to the other DI patterns: we don't consume the DEPENDENCY, but rather supply it. The types to which we supply the DEPENDENCY have no choice in how to model DI or whether they need the DEPENDENCY at all. They can consume it or ignore it as they see fit.

4.4   *Ambient Context*

How can we make a Dependency available to every module without polluting every API with
Cross-Cutting Concerns?

BY MAKING IT AVAILABLE VIA A STATIC ACCESSOR.

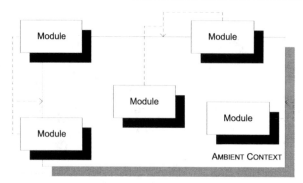

Figure 4.8   Every module can access
an AMBIENT CONTEXT if it needs to.

A truly universal CROSS-CUTTING CONCERN can potentially pollute a large part of the API
for an application if you have to pass an instance around to every collaborator. An
alternative is to define a context that's available to anyone who needs it and that can
be ignored by everyone else.

4.4.1   *How it works*

The AMBIENT CONTEXT is available to any consumer via a static property or method. A
consuming class might use it like this:

```
public string GetMessage()
{
    return SomeContext.Current.SomeValue;
}
```

In this case, the context has a static `Current` property that a consumer can access. This
property may be truly static, or may be associated with the currently executing thread.

To be useful in DI scenarios, the context itself must be an ABSTRACTION and it must
be possible to modify the context from the outside—in the previous example, this
means that the `Current` property must be writable. The context itself might be implemented as shown in the following listing.

Listing 4.11   AMBIENT CONTEXT

```
public abstract class SomeContext
{
    public static SomeContext Current
    {
        get
        {
            var ctx =
                Thread.GetData(
                Thread.GetNamedDataSlot("SomeContext"))
                as SomeContext;
```

❶ Get current
context
from TLS

```
            if (ctx == null)
            {
                ctx = SomeContext.Default;
                Thread.SetData(
                    Thread.GetNamedDataSlot("SomeContext"),
                    ctx);
            }
            return ctx;
        }
        set
        {
            Thread.SetData(
                Thread.GetNamedDataSlot("SomeContext"),
                value);
        }
    }
    public static SomeContext Default =
        new DefaultContext();

    public abstract string SomeValue { get; }
}
```

❷ **Save current context in TLS**

❸ **Value carried by the context**

The context is an abstract class, which allows us to replace one context with another implementation at runtime.

In this example, the `Current` property stores the current context in Thread Local Storage (TLS) ❶, which means that every thread has its own context that's independent from the context of any other thread. In cases where no one has already assigned a context to TLS, a default implementation is returned. It's important to be able to guarantee that no consumer will ever get a `NullReferenceException` when they try to access the `Current` property, so there must be a good LOCAL DEFAULT. Note that in this case, the `Default` property is shared across all threads. This works because, in this example, `DefaultContext` (a class that derives from `SomeContext`) is immutable. If the default context was mutable, you would need to assign a separate instance to each thread to prevent cross-thread pollution.

External clients can assign a new context to TLS ❷. Notice that it's possible to assign null, but if this happens, the next read will automatically reassign the default context.

The whole point of having an AMBIENT CONTEXT is to interact with it. In this example, this interaction is represented by a solitary abstract string property ❸, but the context class can be as simple or complex as is necessary.

WARNING For simplicity's sake, I've skipped lightly over the thread-safety of the code in listing 4.11. If you decide to implement a TLS-based AMBIENT CONTEXT, be sure that you know what you're doing.

TIP The example in listing 4.11 uses TLS, but you can also use `CallContext` to similar effect.[8]

---

[8] See Mark Seemann, "Ambient Context," 2007, http://blogs.msdn.com/ploeh/archive/2007/07/23/AmbientContext.aspx for more information.

NOTE An AMBIENT CONTEXT doesn't need to be associated with a thread or call context. Sometimes, it makes more sense to make it apply to the entire App-Domain by making it `static`.

When you want to replace the default context with a custom context, you can create a custom implementation that derives from the context and assign it at the correct time:

```
SomeContext.Current = new MyContext();
```

For TLS-based contexts, you should assign the custom instance when you spawn the new thread, whereas for truly universal contexts, you can assign it in a COMPOSITION ROOT.

4.4.2   *When to use it*

AMBIENT CONTEXT should only be used in the rarest of cases. In most cases, CONSTRUCTOR INJECTION or PROPERTY INJECTION is far more suitable, but you may have a true CROSS-CUTTING CONCERN that would pollute every API in your application if you had to pass it along to all services.

WARNING AMBIENT CONTEXT is similar in structure to the SERVICE LOCATOR anti-pattern that I'll describe in chapter 5. The difference is that an AMBIENT CONTEXT only provides an instance of a single, strongly-typed DEPENDENCY, whereas a SERVICE LOCATOR is supposed to provide instances for every DEPENDENCY you might request. The differences are subtle, so be sure to fully understand when to apply AMBIENT CONTEXT before you do so. When in doubt, pick one of the other DI patterns.

In section 4.4.4, I'll implement a `TimeProvider` that can be used get the current time, and I'll also discuss why I prefer that to the static `DateTime` members. The current time is a true CROSS-CUTTING CONCERN because you can't predict which classes in which layers may need it. Most classes could conceivably use the current time, but only a small fraction are going to do so.

This could potentially force you to write a lot of code with an extra `TimeProvider` parameter, because you never know when you're going to need it:

```
public string GetSomething(SomeService service,
    TimeProvider timeProvider)
{
    return service.GetStuff("Foo", timeProvider);
}
```

The previous method passes the `TimeProvider` parameter on to the service. That may look innocuous, but when we then review the `GetStuff` method, we discover that it's never being used:

```
public string GetStuff(string s, TimeProvider timeProvider)
{
    return this.Stuff(s);
}
```

In this case, the `TimeProvider` parameter is being passed along as extra baggage only because it might be needed some day. This is polluting the API with irrelevant concerns and a big code smell.

AMBIENT CONTEXT *can* be the solution to this challenge, provided the conditions listed in table 4.4 are met.

Table 4.4   Conditions for implementing AMBIENT CONTEXT

Condition	Description
You need the context to be queryable.	If you only need to write some data (all methods on the context would return void), INTERCEPTION is a better solution. This may seem like a rare case to you, but it's quite common: log that something happened, record performance metrics, assert that the security context is uncompromised—all such actions are pure *Assertions*[9] that are better modeled with INTERCEPTION. You should only consider using an AMBIENT CONTEXT if you need to query it for some value (like the current time).
A proper LOCAL DEFAULT exists.	The existence of an AMBIENT CONTEXT is implicit (more on this to follow), so it's important that the context *just works*—even in the cases where it was never explicitly assigned.
It must be guaranteed available.	Even with a proper LOCAL DEFAULT, it's still important to ensure that it's impossible to assign null, which would make the context unavailable and all clients throw `NullReferenceExceptions`. Listing 4.11 shows some of the steps you can take to ensure this.

In most cases, the advantages of AMBIENT CONTEXT don't justify the disadvantages, so make sure that you can satisfy all of these conditions, and if you can't, consider other alternatives.

Table 4.5   AMBIENT CONTEXT advantages and disadvantages

Advantages	Disadvantages
Doesn't pollute APIs Is always available	Implicit Hard to implement correctly May not work well in certain runtimes

By far the greatest disadvantage of AMBIENT CONTEXT is its implicitness, but, as listing 4.11 suggests, it can also be hard to implement correctly, and there may even be issues with certain runtime environments (ASP.NET).

In the next sections, we'll take a more detailed look at each of the disadvantages in table 4.5.

---

[9]   Eric Evans, *Domain-Driven Design: Tackling Complexity in the Heart of Software* (New York: Addison-Wesley, 2004), 255.

IMPLICITNESS

When an AMBIENT CONTEXT is in play, it's impossible to tell whether a given class uses it just by looking at its interface.

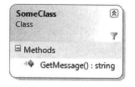

Consider the class shown in figure 4.9: it shows no outward sign of using an AMBIENT CONTEXT, yet the GetMessage method is implemented like this:

```
public string GetMessage()
{
    return SomeContext.Current.SomeValue;
}
```

Figure 4.9   The class and its GetMessage method show no outward sign of using an AMBIENT CONTEXT, yet this may very well be the case.

When the AMBIENT CONTEXT is correctly implemented, you can at least expect that no exceptions will be thrown, but in this example, the context impacts the behavior of the method because it determines the return value. If the context changes, the behavior may change, and you may not initially understand why this is the case.

> **NOTE**   In *Domain-Driven Design*, Eric Evans discusses *Intention-Revealing Interfaces*,[10] which captures the notion that an API should communicate what it does by its public interface alone. When a class uses an AMBIENT CONTEXT it does exactly the opposite: your only chances of knowing that this is the case are by reading the documentation or perusing the code itself.

Apart from the potential for subtle bugs, this implicitness also makes it hard to discover a class's extensibility points. An AMBIENT CONTEXT enables you to inject custom behavior into any class that uses it, but it's not apparent that this may be so. You can only discover this by reading the documentation or understanding the implementation in far more detail than you might have wanted.

IMPLEMENTATION IS TRICKY

Properly implementing an AMBIENT CONTEXT can be challenging. At the very least, you must guarantee that the context is always in a consistent state—that is, it must not throw any NullReferenceExceptions only because one context implementation was removed without replacing it with another.

To ensure that, you must have a suitable LOCAL DEFAULT which can be used if no other implementation was explicitly defined. In listing 4.11, I used lazy initialization of the Current property, because C# doesn't enable thread-static initializers.

When the AMBIENT CONTEXT represents a truly universal concept, such as time, you can get by with a simple writable Singleton[11]—a single instance that's shared across the entire AppDomain. I'll show you an example of this in section 4.4.4.

An AMBIENT CONTEXT can also represent a context that varies by the call stack's context, such as who initiated the request. We see that often in web application and web services, where the same code executes in context of many different users—each on

---

[10] Evans, *Domain-Driven Design*, 246.
[11] Gamma, *Design Patterns*, 127.

their own thread. In this case, the AMBIENT CONTEXT can have affinity with the currently executing thread and be stored in TLS, as we saw in listing 4.11, but this leads to other issues, particularly with ASP.NET.

CHALLENGES WITH ASP.NET

When an AMBIENT CONTEXT uses TLS, there can be issues with ASP.NET, because it may change threads at certain points in the page lifecycle, and there's no guarantee that anything stored in TLS will be copied from the old to the new thread.

When this is the case, you should use the current `HttpContext` to store request-specific data instead of TLS.

This thread-switching behavior isn't an issue when the AMBIENT CONTEXT is a universally shared instance, because a Singleton is shared across all threads in an `AppDomain`.

4.4.3 *Known use*

The .NET BCL contains a few AMBIENT CONTEXT implementations.

Security is addressed with the `System.Security.Principal.IPrincipal` interface that's associated with every thread. You can get or set the current principal for the thread with the `Thread.CurrentPrincipal` accessor.

Another AMBIENT CONTEXT based on TLS models the current culture of the thread. `Thread.CurrentCulture` and `Thread.CurrentUICulture` allows you to access and modify the cultural context of the current operation. Many formatting APIs, such as parsing and converting value types, implicitly use the current culture if one isn't explicitly provided.

Tracing provides an example of a universal AMBIENT CONTEXT. The `Trace` class isn't associated with a particular thread, but is truly shared across an entire App-Domain. You can write a trace message from anywhere with the `Trace.Write` method and have it written to any number of `TraceListeners` configured by the `Trace.Listeners` property.

4.4.4 *Example: Caching Currency*

The `Currency` ABSTRACTION in the sample commerce application from the previous sections is about as chatty an interface as it can be. Every time you want to convert a currency, you call the `GetExchangeRateFor` method that potentially looks up the exchange rate in some external system. This is a flexible API design because you can look up the rate with close to real-time precision if you need it, but in most cases, this won't be necessary and is more likely to become a performance bottleneck.

The SQL Server–based implementation I exhibited in listing 4.10 certainly performs a database query every single time you ask it about an exchange rate. When the application displays a shopping basket, each item in the basket is being converted, so this leads to a database query for every item in the basket even though the rate is unlikely to change from the first to the last item. It would be better to cache the exchange rate for a little while so that the application doesn't need to hit the database about the same rate several times within the same fraction of a second.

Depending on how important it is to have current currencies, the cache timeout can be short or long: cache for a single second or for hours. The timeout should be configurable.

To determine when to expire a cached currency, you need to know how much time went by since the currency was cached, so you need access to the current time. Date-Time.UtcNow seems like a built-in AMBIENT CONTEXT, but it's not, because you can't assign the time—only query it.

The inability to redefine the current time is rarely an issue in a production application, but can be an issue when unit testing.

> ### Time simulations
> Whereas the average web-based application is unlikely to need the ability to modify the current time, another type of application can benefit greatly from this ability.
>
> I once wrote a rather complex simulation engine that depended on the current time. Because I always use Test-Driven Development (TDD), I had already used an ABSTRACTION of the current time so I could inject DateTime instances that were different from the actual machine time. This turned out to be a huge advantage when I later needed to accelerate time in the simulation by several orders of magnitude. All I had to do was to register a time provider that accelerated time, and the entire simulation immediately sped up.
>
> If you want to see a similar feature in effect, you can take a look at the WorldWide Telescope[12] client application that allows you to simulate the night sky in accelerated time. The figure below shows a screen shot of the control that allows you to run time forward and backward at different speeds. I have no idea whether the developers behind that particular feature implemented it by using an ambient time provider, but that's what I would do.
>
>
>
> **WorldWide Telescope allows you to pause time or move forward or backward in time at different speeds. This simulates how the night sky looks at different times.**

In the case of the sample commerce application, I want to be able to control time when I write unit tests so that I can verify that the cached currencies expire correctly.

---

[12] http://www.worldwidetelescope.org

TimeProvider

Time is a pretty universal concept (even if time moves at different speeds in different parts of the universe), so I can model it as a generally shared resource. Because there's no reason to have separate time providers per thread, the TimeProvider Ambient Context is a writable Singleton, as shown in the following listing.

Listing 4.12 `TimeProvider` Ambient Context

```
public abstract class TimeProvider
{
    private static TimeProvider current;

    static TimeProvider()
    {
        TimeProvider.current =                          ❶ Initialize to default
            new DefaultTimeProvider();                     TimeProvider
    }

    public static TimeProvider Current
    {
        get { return TimeProvider.current; }
        set
        {
            if (value == null)
            {
                throw new ArgumentNullException("value");   ❷ Guard
            }                                                  Clause
            TimeProvider.current = value;
        }
    }

    public abstract DateTime UtcNow { get; }    ◁─┐ The important
                                                 ❸ part
    public static void ResetToDefault()
    {
        TimeProvider.current =
            new DefaultTimeProvider();
    }
}
```

The purpose of the TimeProvider class is to enable you to control how time is communicated to clients. As described in table 4.4, a Local Default is important, so you statically initialize the class to use the DefaultTimeProvider class (I'll show you that shortly) ❶.

Another condition from table 4.4 is that you must guarantee that the TimeProvider can never be in an inconsistent state. The current field must never be allowed to be null, so a Guard Clause guarantees that this isn't possible ❷.

All of this is scaffolding to make the TimeProvider easily accessible from anywhere. Its raison d'être is its ability to serve DateTime instances representing the current time ❸. I purposefully modeled the name and signature of the abstract property after Date-Time.UtcNow. If necessary, I could also have added such abstract properties as Now and Today, but I don't need them for this example.

Having a proper and meaningful LOCAL DEFAULT is important, and luckily it's not hard to think of one in this example because it should simply return the current time. That means that, unless you explicitly go in and assign a different `TimeProvider`, any client using `TimeProvider.Current.UtcNow` will get the real current time.

The implementation of `DefaultTimeProvider` can be seen in the following listing.

Listing 4.13   Default time provider

```
public class DefaultTimeProvider : TimeProvider
{
    public override DateTime UtcNow
    {
        get { return DateTime.UtcNow; }
    }
}
```

The `DefaultTimeProvider` class derives from `TimeProvider` to provide the real time any time a client reads the `UtcNow` property.

When `CachingCurrency` uses the `TimeProvider` AMBIENT CONTEXT to get the current time, it will get the real current time unless you specifically assign a different `TimeProvider` to the application—and I only plan to do this in my unit tests.

CACHING CURRENCIES

To implement cached currencies, you're going to implement a Decorator that modifies a "proper" `Currency` implementation.

> **NOTE** The Decorator[13] design pattern is an important part of INTERCEPTION; I'll discuss it in greater detail in chapter 9.

Instead of modifying the existing SQL Server–backed `Currency` implementation shown in listing 4.10, you'll wrap the cache around it and only invoke the real implementation if the cache has expired or doesn't contain an entry.

As you may recall from section 4.1.4, a `CurrencyProvider` is an abstract class that returns `Currency` instances. A `CachingCurrencyProvider` implements the same base class and wraps the functionality of a contained `CurrencyProvider`. Whenever it's asked for a `Currency`, it returns a `Currency` created by the contained `Currency-Provider`, but wrapped in a `CachingCurrency` (see figure 4.10).

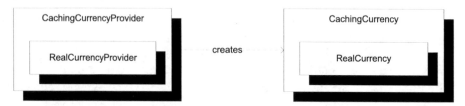

Figure 4.10   A `CachingCurrencyProvider` **wraps a "real"** `CurrencyProvider` **and returns** `CachingCurrency` **instances that wrap "real"** Currency **instances.**

---

[13] Gamma, *Design Patterns*, 175.

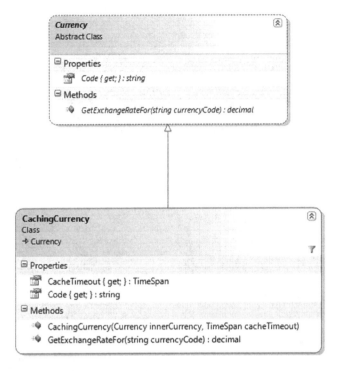

Figure 4.11 Caching-Currency **takes an inner currency and a cache timeout in its constructor and wraps the inner currency's functionality.**

TIP The Decorator pattern is one of the best ways to ensure Separation of Concerns.

This design enables me to cache *any* currency implementation, and not only the SQL Server–based implementation I currently have. Figure 4.12 shows the outline of the CachingCurrency class.

CachingCurrency uses CONSTRUCTOR INJECTION to get the "real" instance whose exchange rates it should cache. For example, CachingCurrency delegates its Code property to the inner Currency's Code property.

The interesting part of the CachingCurrency implementation is its GetExchange-RateFor method exhibited in the following listing.

Listing 4.14 Caching the exchange rate

```
private readonly Dictionary<string, CurrencyCacheEntry> cache;

public override decimal GetExchangeRateFor(string currencyCode)
{
    CurrencyCacheEntry cacheEntry;
    if ((this.cache.TryGetValue(currencyCode,
        out cacheEntry))
        && (!cacheEntry.IsExpired))
    {
        return cacheEntry.ExchangeRate;
    }
```

❶ Return cached exchange rate if appropriate

```
var exchangeRate =
    this.innerCurrency
    .GetExchangeRateFor(currencyCode);

var expiration =
    TimeProvider.Current.UtcNow + this.CacheTimeout;
this.cache[currencyCode] =                                    ❷ Cache
    new CurrencyCacheEntry(exchangeRate, expiration);           exchange rate

return exchangeRate;
}
```

When a client asks for an exchange rate, you first intercept the call to look up the currency code in the cache. If there's an unexpired cache entry for the requested currency code, you return the cached exchange rate and the rest of the method is skipped ❶. I'll get back to the part about evaluating whether the entry has expired a bit later.

Only if there was no unexpired cached exchange rate do you invoke the inner Currency to get the exchange rate. Before you return it, you need to cache it. The first step is to calculate the expiration time, and this is where you use the TimeProvider AMBIENT CONTEXT, instead of the more traditional DateTime.Now. With the expiration time calculated, you can now cache the entry ❷ before returning the result.

Calculating whether a cache entry has expired is also done using the Time-Provider AMBIENT CONTEXT:

```
return TimeProvider.Current.UtcNow >= this.expiration;
```

The CachingCurrency class uses the TimeProvider AMBIENT CONTEXT in all places where it needs the current time, so writing a unit test that precisely controls time is possible.

MODIFYING TIME

When unit testing the CachingCurrency class, you can now accurately control how time seems to pass totally irrespective of the real system clock. That enables you to write deterministic unit tests even though the System Under Test (SUT) depends on the concept of the current time. The next listing shows a test that verifies that even though the SUT is asked for an exchange rate four times, only twice is the inner currency invoked: at the first call, and again when the cache expires.

Listing 4.15   Unit testing that a currency is correctly cached and expired

```
[Fact]
public void InnerCurrencyIsInvokedAgainWhenCacheExpires()
{
    // Fixture setup
    var currencyCode = "CHF";
    var cacheTimeout = TimeSpan.FromHours(1);

    var startTime = new DateTime(2009, 8, 29);
```

```
    var timeProviderStub = new Mock<TimeProvider>();
    timeProviderStub
        .SetupGet(tp => tp.UtcNow)
        .Returns(startTime);                          ❶ Set TimeProvider
    TimeProvider.Current = timeProviderStub.Object;      Ambient Context

    var innerCurrencyMock = new Mock<Currency>();
    innerCurrencyMock
        .Setup(c => c.GetExchangeRateFor(currencyCode))
        .Returns(4.911m)
        .Verifiable();

    var sut =                                         ❷ Should call
        new CachingCurrency(innerCurrencyMock.Object,    inner currency
            cacheTimeout);
    sut.GetExchangeRateFor(currencyCode);
    sut.GetExchangeRateFor(currencyCode);             ❸ Should be      Should call ❺
    sut.GetExchangeRateFor(currencyCode);                cached           inner
                                                                        currency
    timeProviderStub
        .SetupGet(tp => tp.UtcNow)                    ❹ Advance time
        .Returns(startTime + cacheTimeout);              past timeout
    // Exercise system
    sut.GetExchangeRateFor(currencyCode);
    // Verify outcome
    innerCurrencyMock.Verify(                         ❻ Verify that inner
        c => c.GetExchangeRateFor(currencyCode),         currency was
        Times.Exactly(2));                               invoked correctly
    // Teardown (implicit)
}
```

JARGON ALERT   The following text contains some unit testing terminology—I have emphasized it with italics, but because this isn't a book about unit testing, I'll refer you to the book *xUnit Test Patterns*[14] that is the source of all these pattern names.

One of the first things to do in this test is to set up a TimeProvider *Test Double* that will return DateTime instances as defined, instead of based on the system clock. In this test, I use a dynamic mock framework called Moq[15] to define that the UtcNow property should return the same DateTime until told otherwise. When defined, this *Stub* is injected into the AMBIENT CONTEXT ❶.

The first call to GetExchangeRateFor should invoke the CachingCurrency's inner Currency, because nothing has yet been cached ❷, whereas the two next calls should return the cached value ❸, because time is currently not passing at all according to the TimeProvider *Stub*.

With a couple of calls cached, it's now time to let time advance; you modify the TimeProvider *Stub* to return a DateTime instance that's exactly past the cache timeout ❹ and invoke the GetExchangeRateFor method again ❺, expecting it to invoke

---

[14] Gerard Meszaros, *xUnit Test Patterns: Refactoring Test Code* (New York: Addison-Wesley, 2007).
[15] http://code.google.com/p/moq/

the inner `Currency` for the second time because the original cache entry should now have expired.

Because you expect the inner `Currency` to have been invoked twice, you finally verify that this was the case by telling the inner `Currency` *Mock* that the `GetExchange-RateFor` method should have been invoked exactly twice ❻.

One of the many dangers of AMBIENT CONTEXT is that once it's assigned, it stays that way until modified again, but due to its implicit nature, this can be easy to forget. In the unit test, for example, the behavior defined by the test in listing 4.15 stays like that unless explicitly reset (which I do in a *Fixture Teardown*). This could lead to subtle bugs (this time in my test code) because that would spill over and pollute the tests that execute after that test.

AMBIENT CONTEXT looks deceptively simple to implement and use, but can lead to many difficult-to-locate bugs. There's a place for it, but use it only where no better alternative exists. It's like horseradish: great for certain things, but definitely not universally applicable.

4.4.5   *Related patterns*

AMBIENT CONTEXT can be used to model a CROSS-CUTTING CONCERN, although it requires that we have a proper LOCAL DEFAULT.

If it turns out that the DEPENDENCY isn't a CROSS-CUTTING CONCERN after all, you should change the DI strategy. If you still have a LOCAL DEFAULT you can switch to PROPERTY INJECTION, but otherwise, you must change to CONSTRUCTOR INJECTION.

4.5 *Summary*

The patterns presented in this chapter are a central part of DI. Armed with a COMPOSI-TION ROOT and an appropriate mix of the DI patterns, you can implement POOR MAN'S DI. When applying DI, there are many nuances and fine details to learn, but the patterns cover the core mechanics that answer the question, *how do I inject my Dependencies?*

These patterns aren't interchangeable. In most cases, your default choice should be CONSTRUCTOR INJECTION, but there are situations where one of the other patterns affords a better alternative. Figure 4.12 shows a decision process that can help you decide on a proper pattern, but if in doubt, choose CONSTRUCTOR INJECTION—you can never go horribly wrong with that choice.

The first thing to examine is whether the DEPENDENCY is something you need or something you already have but wish to communicate to another collaborator. In most cases, you probably need the DEPENDENCY, but in add-in scenarios, you may wish to convey the current context to an add-in. Every time the DEPENDENCY may vary from operation to operation, METHOD INJECTION is a good candidate for an implementation.

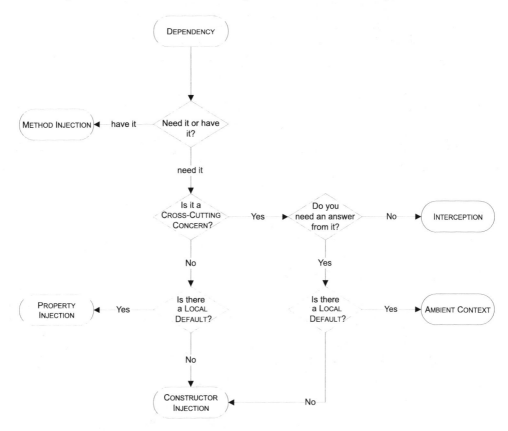

Figure 4.12 In most cases, you should end up choosing CONSTRUCTOR INJECTION, but there are situations where one of the other DI patterns is a better fit.

When the DEPENDENCY represents a CROSS-CUTTING CONCERN, the best pattern fit depends on the direction of communication. If you only need to record something (for example, the length of time an operation took, or what values were being passed in) INTERCEPTION (which I'll discuss in chapter 9) is the best fit. It also works well if the answer you need from it is already included in the interface definition. Caching is an excellent example of this latter use of INTERCEPTION.

  If you need to query the CROSS-CUTTING DEPENDENCY for a response *not* included in the original interface, you can use AMBIENT CONTEXT only if you have a proper LOCAL DEFAULT that enables you to package the context itself with a reasonable default behavior that works for all clients without explicit configuration.

  When the DEPENDENCY doesn't represent a CROSS-CUTTING CONCERN, a LOCAL DEFAULT is once more the deciding factor, as it can make explicitly assigning the DEPENDENCY optional—the default takes over if no overriding implementation is specified. This scenario can be effectively implemented with PROPERTY INJECTION.

  In any other cases, the CONSTRUCTOR INJECTION pattern applies. As illustrated in figure 4.12, it looks as though CONSTRUCTOR INJECTION is a last-ditch pattern that only comes into play when all else fails. This is only partly true, because in most cases the specialized patterns don't apply, and by default CONSTRUCTOR INJECTION is the pattern left on the field. It's easy to understand and much simpler to implement robustly than any of the other DI patterns. You can build entire applications with CONSTRUCTOR INJECTION alone, but knowing about the other patterns can help you choose wisely in the few cases where it doesn't fit perfectly.

  This chapter contained a systematic catalog that explained how you should inject DEPENDENCIES into your classes. The next chapter approaches DI from the opposite direction and takes a look at how not to go about it.

DI anti-patterns

Gastronomically speaking, Denmark was a developing country in the 1970s—I was there, but I never suffered because I didn't know any better. The staple was meat and potatoes, but foreign ideas were slowly being integrated—I think part of the reason was that it was also the dawn of the era of mass tourism.

Danes traveled south to other parts of Europe in increasing numbers, and the most adventurous sampled the local food. Back home, pasta became increasingly popular among the younger generation, but no Italian would have recognized the Danish version of bolognese sauce.

Here's what I imagine happened. Some enterprising Danish tourist liked tagliatelle alla bolognese so much that that she decided to try to make it when she got home. (I'm assuming it was a woman because men didn't cook much back then.) She did her best to remember what went into the sauce, but this wasn't easy on the long bus ride back to Denmark.

As far as ingredients go, the pancetta and red wine were forgotten before she left Italy, the broth and chicken liver were lost from memory somewhere in Austria or Switzerland, and most of the vegetables were one by one dropped during the long haul through (West) Germany. As she crossed the Danish border, what was left of the original recipe were chopped onions and minced meat served with the only type of pasta readily available in Denmark at the time: spaghetti.

We ate the resulting dish for years and liked it. At some time during the 1980s, tomato paste and oregano were added to the recipe to make it more authentic. This was more or less the recipe I used for more than a decade until someone pointed out to me that it might benefit from some carrots, celery, chicken liver, red wine, and so on.

The point of the story is that I thought I was making *ragù alla bolognese* whereas in reality I wasn't even close. It never occurred to me to question the authenticity of the recipe because I grew up with it. Although authenticity isn't the ultimate yardstick, the authentic recipe tastes much better and I'm not going back to my old ways.

In the previous chapter, I briefly compared design patterns to recipes. A pattern provides a common language we can use to succinctly discuss a complex concept—and ragù alla bolognese is such a concept, because we can discuss how it fits with tagliatelle or lasagna. On the other hand, when the concept (or rather, the implementation) becomes warped, we have an *anti-pattern* on our hands.

DEFINITION An anti-pattern is a description of a commonly occurring solution to a problem that generates decidedly negative consequences.[1]

Anti-patterns are often caused by ignorance (as with my bolognese sauce) and are something to avoid, and knowing about these common traps can help you avoid them. They're a more or less formalized way of describing common mistakes that people make again and again, independently of each other.

In this chapter, I'll describe some common anti-patterns related to DI. During my career, I've seen all of them in use in one form or other, and I've been guilty of applying more than one of them myself. In many cases, they represented sincere attempts at DI for an application; but without fully understanding DI fundamentals, the implementations derailed into solutions that did more harm than good.

Learning about these anti-patterns should give you an idea about what traps to be aware of as you venture into your first DI projects. Your mistakes won't look exactly like mine or the examples presented here, but this chapter will show you the danger signs.

Anti-patterns can be fixed by refactoring the code toward one of the DI patterns introduced in chapter 4. Exactly how difficult it is to fix each occurrence depends on the details of the implementation, but for each anti-pattern I'll supply some generalized guidance on how to refactor it toward a pattern.

[1] William J. Brown et al., *AntiPatterns: Refactoring Software, Architectures, and Projects in Crisis* (New York: Wiley Computer Publishing), 1998, 7.

TIP My coverage of refactoring from DI anti-pattern to DI pattern is constrained by the space of this chapter, because it isn't the main topic of this book. If you're interested in learning more about how you can move an existing application in the direction of DI, an entire book discusses refactoring such applications: *Working Effectively with Legacy Code.*[2] Although it doesn't deal exclusively with DI, it covers many of the same concepts I do here.

The anti-patterns covered in this chapter are listed in table 5.1. Figure 5.1 illustrates the structure of the chapter.

WARNING This chapter is different from the other chapters because most of the code I'll show you gives examples of how *not* to implement DI. Don't try this at home!

Just as CONSTRUCTOR INJECTION is the most important DI pattern, CONTROL FREAK is the most dominating of the anti-patterns. It effectively prevents you from applying any kind of proper DI, so you'll need to focus your energy on this anti-pattern before you address the others. On the other hand, SERVICE LOCATOR is the most dangerous because it looks like it's actually solving a problem.

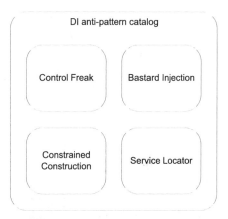

Figure 5.1 This chapter takes the form of a catalog of anti-patterns. Each anti-pattern is written to be read independently of the other anti-patterns.

Table 5.1 DI anti-patterns

Anti-pattern	Description
CONTROL FREAK	DEPENDENCIES are controlled directly, as opposed to INVERSION OF CONTROL.
BASTARD INJECTION	FOREIGN DEFAULTS are used as default values for DEPENDENCIES.
CONSTRAINED CONSTRUCTION	Constructors are assumed to have a particular signature.
SERVICE LOCATOR	An implicit service can serve DEPENDENCIES to consumers but isn't guaranteed to do so.

The rest of this chapter describes each anti-pattern in greater detail. You can read from start to finish or read about only the ones you're interested in—each has a self-contained section. However, if you decide to read about only one anti-pattern, you should focus your attention on CONTROL FREAK.

---

[2] Michael Feathers, *Working Effectively with Legacy Code* (New York: Prentice Hall, 2004).

5.1   *Control Freak*

What is the opposite of INVERSION OF CONTROL? Originally the term INVERSION OF CONTROL was coined to identify the opposite of the normal state of affairs, but we can't very well talk about the *Business as Usual* anti-pattern. Instead, after much deliberation, I named it CONTROL FREAK to describe a class that won't relinquish control of its DEPENDENCIES.

This happens every time we create a new instance of a type by using the new keyword. When we do that, we explicitly state that we're going to control the lifetime of the instance and that no one else will get a chance to intercept that particular object.

> **TIP** The number of times the new keyword is used in code is a *very* rough indication of how tightly coupled that code is.

The CONTROL FREAK anti-pattern occurs every time we get an instance of a DEPENDENCY by directly or indirectly using the new keyword in any place other than a COMPOSITION ROOT.

> **NOTE** Although the new keyword is a code smell when it comes to VOLATILE DEPENDENCIES, you don't need to worry about using it for STABLE DEPENDENCIES. The new keyword isn't suddenly "illegal" in general, but you should refrain from using it to get instances of VOLATILE DEPENDENCIES.

The most blatant example of CONTROL FREAK is when we make no effort to introduce ABSTRACTIONS in our code. You saw several examples of that in chapter 2 when Mary implemented her commerce application (section 2.1.1). Such an approach makes no attempt to introduce DI; but even where developers have heard about DI and composability, the CONTROL FREAK anti-pattern can often be found in some variation.

In the next sections, I'll show you some examples that resemble code I've seen in production use. In every case, the developers had the best intentions of *programming to interfaces* but never really understood the underlying forces and motivations.

5.1.1   *Example: newing up Dependencies*

Many developers have heard about the principle of *programming to interfaces* but don't understand the deeper rationale behind it. In an attempt to do the right thing or follow best practices, they write code that doesn't make much sense.

In chapter 2, you saw an example of a ProductService that uses an instance of the abstract ProductRepository class (listing 2.6) to retrieve a list of featured products. As a reminder, here is the relevant method in essence:

```
public IEnumerable<Product> GetFeaturedProducts(IPrincipal user)
{
    return from p in this.repository.GetFeaturedProducts()
        select p.ApplyDiscountFor(user);
}
```

Compared to listing 2.6, I've omitted a Guard Clause, but the salient point is that the repository member variable represents an abstract class. In chapter 2, you saw how the `repository` field can be populated via CONSTRUCTOR INJECTION, but I've seen other, more naïve attempts, such as the following.

Listing 5.1   newing up a `ProductRepository`

```
private readonly ProductRepository repository;

public ProductService()
{
    string connectionString =
        ConfigurationManager.ConnectionStrings
        ["CommerceObjectContext"].ConnectionString;

    this.repository =
        new SqlProductRepository(connectionString);
}
```

❶ Directly create a new instance

The `repository` field is declared as the abstract `ProductRepository` class so any member in the `ProductService` class (such as `GetFeaturedProducts`) will be programming to an interface. Although this sounds like the right thing to do, not much is gained from doing so, because at runtime, the type will always be a `SqlProduct-Repository` ❶. There is no way you can intercept or change the `repository` variable unless you change the code and recompile.

You don't gain much by defining a variable as an interface or abstract class if you hard-code it to always have a specific concrete type. The only small benefit is that the concrete type is defined in just one or a few places in the code, so replacing one concrete implementation with another need not require major refactoring. In this example, you would only need to new up a different implementation of `ProductRepository` in the constructor ❶ while the rest of the `ProductService` would work without modification.

Directly newing up DEPENDENCIES is just one example of the CONTROL FREAK anti-pattern. Before I get to the analysis and possible ways to fix the problems generated by CONTROL FREAK, let's look at some more examples to give you a better idea of the context and common failed attempts to address some of the resulting issues.

In this particular example, it's apparent that the solution isn't optimal. Most developers will attempt to refine their approach, as you'll see in the next example.

5.1.2   *Example: Factory*

The most common (erroneous) attempt to fix the evident problems from newing up DEPENDENCIES involves a factory of some sort. There are several options when it comes to factories, and I'll quickly cover each of the following:

- Concrete Factory
- Abstract Factory
- Static Factory

If told that she could only deal with the abstract `ProductRepository` class, Mary Rowan (from chapter 2) would introduce a `ProductRepositoryFactory` that would produce the instances she needs to get the job done. Let's listen in as she discusses the approach with her colleague Jens—I predict that their discussion conveniently will cover the factory options I listed:

MARY: *We need an instance of* ProductRepository *in this* ProductService *class. However,* ProductRepository *is abstract, so we can't just create new instances of it, and our consultant says that we shouldn't just create new instances of* SqlProductRepository *either.*

JENS: *What about some sort of factory?*

MARY: *Yes, I was thinking the same thing, but I'm not sure how to proceed. I don't understand how it solves our problem. Look here…*

Mary starts to write some code to demonstrate her problem.

CONCRETE FACTORY

This is the code that Mary writes:

```
public class ProductRepositoryFactory
{
    public ProductRepository Create()
    {
        string connectionString =
            ConfigurationManager.ConnectionStrings
            ["CommerceObjectContext"].ConnectionString;
        return new SqlProductRepository(connectionString);
    }
}
```

MARY: *This* ProductRepositoryFactory *encapsulates knowledge about how to create* ProductRepository *instances, but it doesn't solve the problem because we would have to use it in the* ProductService *like this:*

```
var factory = new ProductRepositoryFactory();
this.repository = factory.Create();
```

See? Now we just have to create a new instance of the ProductRepositoryFactory *class in the* ProductService*, but that still hard-codes the use of* SqlProductRepository*. The only thing we have achieved is moving the problem into another class.*

JENS: *Yes, I see… Couldn't we solve the problem with an Abstract Factory instead?*

Let's pause Mary's and Jens' discussion to evaluate what happened. Mary is entirely correct that a Concrete Factory class doesn't solve the CONTROL FREAK issue but only moves it around. It makes the code more complex without adding any value. The ProductService now directly controls the lifetime of the factory, and the factory directly controls the lifetime of the ProductRepository, so we still can't intercept or replace the repository instance at runtime.

> **NOTE** Don't conclude from this section that I generally oppose the use of Concrete Factory classes. A Concrete Factory can solve other problems, such as code repetition, by encapsulating complex creation logic. It just doesn't provide any value with regard to DI. Use it when it makes sense.

It's fairly evident that a Concrete Factory won't solve any DI problems, and I don't think I've ever seen it used in this fashion. Jens' comment about Abstract Factory sounds more promising.

ABSTRACT FACTORY

Let's resume Mary's and Jens' discussion and hear what Jens has to say about Abstract Factory:

JENS: *What if we made the factory abstract, like this?*

```
public abstract class ProductRepositoryFactory
{
    public abstract ProductRepository Create();
}
```

This means we haven't hard-coded any references to SqlProductRepository, *and we can use the factory in the* ProductService *to get instances of* ProductRepository.

MARY: *But now that the factory is abstract, how do we get a new instance of it?*

JENS: *We create an implementation of it that returns* SqlProductService *instances.*

MARY: *Yes, but how do we create an instance of that?*

JENS: *We just new it up in the* ProductService... *Oh. Wait...*

MARY: *That would just put us back where we started.*

Mary and Jens quickly realize that an Abstract Factory doesn't change their situation. Their original conundrum was that they needed an instance of the abstract Product-Repository class, and now instead they need an instance of the abstract Product-RepositoryFactory.

> ## Abstract Factory
>
> *Abstract Factory* is one of the design patterns from the original *Design Patterns* book.[3] It's useful in relation to DI because it can encapsulate complex logic that creates other DEPENDENCIES.
>
> It offers a good alternative to the complete transfer of control that's involved in full INVERSION OF CONTROL, because it partially allows the consumer to control the lifetime of the DEPENDENCIES created by the factory; the factory still controls what is being created and how creation happens.
>
> The *Abstract Factory* pattern is more common than you may realize—the names of the classes involved often hide this fact. The CurrencyProvider class introduced in section 4.1.4 is actually an *Abstract Factory* with another name: it's an abstract class that creates instances of another abstract class (Currency).
>
> In section 6.1, we'll return to the Abstract Factory pattern to see how it can help address a type of problem that often occurs with DI.

[3] Erich Gamma et al., *Design Patterns: Elements of Reusable Object-Oriented Software* (New York: Addison-Wesley, 1994), 87.

Ironically, Mary and Jens dismiss the only factory implementation that wouldn't be harmful for them. On the other hand, it wouldn't solve their problem either; and because the creation logic for ProductRepository instances isn't expected to be complex, it wouldn't add any value.

Now that Mary and Jens have rejected the only safe factory implementation, just one damaging option is still open.

STATIC FACTORY

Mary and Jens are about to reach a conclusion. Let's listen as they decide on an approach that they think will work:

MARY: *Let's make a Static Factory. Let me show you:*

```
public static class ProductRepositoryFactory
{
    public static ProductRepository Create()
    {
        string connectionString =
            ConfigurationManager.ConnectionStrings
            ["CommerceObjectContext"].ConnectionString;
        return new SqlProductRepository(connectionString);
    }
}
```

Now that the class is static, we don't need to deal with how to create it.

JENS: *But we've still hard-coded that we return SqlProductRepository instances, so does it help us in any way?*

MARY: *We could deal with this via a configuration setting that determines which type of ProductRepository to create. Like this:*

```
public static ProductRepository Create()
{
    var repositoryType =
        ConfigurationManager.AppSettings["productRepository"];
    switch (repositoryType)
    {
        case "sql":
            return ProductRepositoryFactory.CreateSql();
        case "azure":
            return ProductRepositoryFactory.CreateAzure();
        default:
            throw new InvalidOperationException("...");
    }
}
```

See? This way we can determine whether we should use the SQL Server–based implementation or the Windows Azure–based implementation, and we don't even need to recompile the application to change from one to the other.

JENS: *Cool! That's what we'll do. That consultant must be happy now!*

There are several reasons why such a Static Factory doesn't provide a satisfactory solution to the original goal of *programming to interfaces*. Let's look at the dependency graph in figure 5.2.

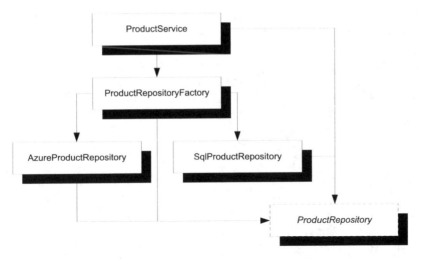

Figure 5.2 Dependency graph for the proposed solution: a static
`ProductRepositoryFactory` **is used to create** `ProductRepository` **instances**

I'm not making this up

If I were the consultant in this example, I wouldn't be at all happy. In fact, such a "solution" was suggested on a project I was involved with, and I ended up writing a 14-page document describing why it wouldn't work and what to do instead.

This was a pretty big project that targeted a central business area of a Fortune 500 company, so proper modularization was important due to the complexity of the application. Unfortunately, I became involved with the project too late, and my suggestions were dismissed because they involved dramatic changes to the already-developed code base.

I moved on to other projects, but I later learned that although the team managed to deliver enough to fulfill the contract, the project was considered a failure and heads rolled.

It would be unreasonable for me to claim that the project failed only because DI wasn't employed, but the approach taken was symptomatic of a lack of proper design. I can't say I was surprised to learn that the project didn't succeed.

All classes need to reference the abstract `ProductRepository` class:

- `ProductService` because it consumes `ProductRepository` instances
- `ProductRepositoryFactory` because it exposes `ProductRepository` instances
- `AzureProductRepository` and `SqlProductRepository` because they implement `ProductRepository`

`ProductRepositoryFactory` depends on both the `AzureProductRepository` and `SqlProductRepository` classes. Because `ProductService` directly depends on `Product-RepositoryFactory`, it also depends on both concrete `ProductRepository` implementations.

> ### Dependency collapse
>
> A degenerate case occurs when the `ProductRepository` ABSTRACTION and the consuming `ProductService` are defined in the same assembly (as is the case in the implementations I've created in the book so far). Let's assume that this is the Domain Model assembly. In that case, the `ProductRepositoryFactory` must also be in the same assembly—otherwise we would have a circular reference, which isn't possible.
>
> However, the factory has references to both implementations, and they have a reference to the Domain Model assembly because they implement the `Product-Repository` class. Once again, the only way to avoid a circular reference is to place the concrete implementations in the same assembly.
>
> Having `AzureProductRepository` and `SqlProductRepository` implemented in the Domain Model assembly totally goes against the principle of Separation of Concerns. We would essentially be left with a monolithic application.
>
> The only way out of this problem is to define the `ProductRepository` ABSTRACTION in a separate assembly. Doing so can be a good idea for many other reasons, but it isn't enough to make a Static Factory a viable DI solution.

Instead of loosely coupled `ProductRepository` implementations, Mary and Jens end up with tightly coupled modules. Even worse, the factory always drags along all implementations—even those that aren't needed.

If Mary and Jens ever need a third type of `ProductRepository`, they'll have to change the factory and recompile their solution. Although their solution may be configurable, it isn't extensible.

It's also impossible to replace the concrete `ProductRepository` implementations with test-specific implementations such as dynamic mocks, because that would require them to define the `ProductRepository` instance at runtime, instead of statically in a configuration file at design time.

> **NOTE**   Dynamic mocks are outside the scope of this book, but I briefly touched on the subject when I described TESTABILITY in chapter 1 (section 1.2.2).

In short, a Static Factory may seem to solve the problem but in reality only compounds it. Even in the best cases, it will force you to reference VOLATILE DEPENDENCIES.

Now that you've seen lots of examples of CONTROL FREAK, I hope you have a pretty good idea what to look for: occurrences of the new keyword next to DEPENDENCIES. This may enable you to avoid the most obvious traps; but if you need to untangle yourself from an existing occurrence of this anti-pattern, the next section discusses how to deal with such a task.

5.1.3 *Analysis*

CONTROL FREAK is the antithesis of INVERSION OF CONTROL. When we directly control the creation of VOLATILE DEPENDENCIES, we end up with tightly coupled code, missing many (if not all) of the benefits of loose coupling outlined in chapter 1.

IMPACT

With the tightly coupled code that's the result of CONTROL FREAK, many benefits of modular design are lost:

- Although we can configure an application to use one of multiple preconfigured DEPENDENCIES, we can't replace them at will. It isn't possible to provide an implementation that was created after the application was compiled, and it certainly isn't possible to provide specific instances as an implementation.
- It becomes harder to reuse the consuming module because it drags with it DEPENDENCIES that may be undesirable in the new context.
- It makes parallel development more difficult because the consuming application is tightly coupled to all implementations of its DEPENDENCIES.
- TESTABILITY suffers because dynamic mocks can't be used as substitutes for the DEPENDENCY.

With careful design, we may still be able to implement tightly coupled applications with clearly defined responsibilities so that maintainability doesn't suffer, but even so, the cost is too high. We need to move away from CONTROL FREAK and toward proper DI.

REFACTORING TOWARD DI

To get rid of CONTROL FREAK, we need to refactor our code toward one of the proper DI design patterns presented in chapter 4. As an initial step, we should use the guidance given to determine which pattern to aim for. In most cases, this will be CONSTRUCTOR INJECTION. The refactoring steps are as follows:

1. Ensure that you're *programming to an interface*. In the examples just presented, this was already the case; but in other situations, you may need to first extract the interface and change variable declarations.
2. If you create a particular implementation of a DEPENDENCY in multiple places, move them all to a single creation method. Make sure this method's return value is expressed as the ABSTRACTION, not the concrete type.
3. Now that you only have a single place where you create the instance, move this creation out of the consuming class by implementing one of the DI patterns, such as CONSTRUCTOR INJECTION.

In the case of the `ProductService` examples in the previous sections, CONSTRUCTOR INJECTION is an excellent solution:

```
private readonly ProductRepository repository;

public ProductService(ProductRepository repository)
{
    if (repository == null)
```

```
    {
        throw new ArgumentNullException("repository");
    }

    this.repository = repository;
}
```

In some cases, the original code uses complex logic to determine how to create instances of the DEPENDENCY. In such cases, this complex logic can be implemented in a factory, and we can then extract an interface of such a factory to create an Abstract Factory. In essence, this means the DEPENDENCY changes so the new Abstract Factory becomes the DEPENDENCY instead of the original ABSTRACTION, and we can apply the same refactoring logic to the factory. In most cases, we'll end up injecting the factory into the consuming class via its constructor.

CONTROL FREAK is the most common DI anti-pattern. It represents the default way of creating instances in most programming languages, so it can be observed even in applications where developers have never considered DI. It's such a natural and deeply rooted way to create new objects that many developers find it difficult to discard. Even when developers begin to think about DI, many have a hard time shaking the mindset that they must somehow control when and where instances are created. Letting go of that control can be a difficult mental leap to make; but even if you make it, there are other, although lesser, pitfalls to avoid.

CONTROL FREAK is by far the most damaging anti-pattern, but even when you have it under control, more subtle issues can arise. The next sections look at these anti-patterns. Although they're less problematic than CONTROL FREAK, they also tend to be easier to resolve, so keep an eye open for them and fix them as you discover them.

5.2   *Bastard Injection*

Constructor overloads are fairly common in many .NET code bases (including the Base Class Library). Often, the many overloads provide reasonable defaults to one or two full-blown constructors that take all relevant parameters as input.

At times, we see other uses when it comes to DI. An all-too-common anti-pattern defines a test-specific constructor overload that allows us to explicitly define a DEPENDENCY while a default constructor is used by the production code.

This can be detrimental when the default implementation of the DEPENDENCY represents a FOREIGN DEFAULT rather than a LOCAL DEFAULT.

When we fully embrace DI, such overloaded constructors become redundant at best. Considering the negative consequences, it's best to avoid them.

5.2.1   *Example: ProductService with Foreign Default*

When Mary originally implemented her ProductService class (in chapter 2), she had only one DEPENDENCY in mind: an implementation based on SQL Server. The Sql-ProductRepository class was originally envisioned as the only implementation of ProductRepository, so it seemed obvious to use it as a default.

FOREIGN DEFAULT

A FOREIGN DEFAULT is the opposite of a LOCAL DEFAULT. It's an implementation of a DEPENDENCY that's used as a default even though it's defined in a different module than its consumer.

As an example, let's consider the `Repository` implementations we have seen in the sample commerce application throughout the previous chapters. A service such as `ProductService` requires an instance of a `ProductRepository` to work. In many cases, when we develop such applications, we have a reasonable implementation in mind: one that implements the desired functionality by reading and writing data to and from a relational database. It would be tempting to use such an implementation as the default.

The problem is that the default implementation we have in mind (`SqlProduct-Repository`) is defined in a different module than `ProductService`. This forces us to take an undesirable DEPENDENCY on the `CommerceSqlDataAccess` module, as shown here.

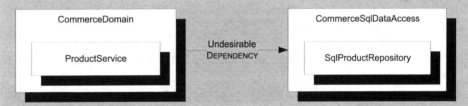

When `ProductService` uses `SqlProductRepository` as a default implementation, it forces us to make a hard reference to the `CommerceSqlDataAccess` module, and we don't want that.

Dragging along unwanted modules robs us of many of the benefits of loose coupling that were discussed in chapter 1. It becomes harder to reuse the `CommerceDomain` module because it drags along the `CommerceSqlDataAccess` module, and we may not wish to use that in a different context. It also makes parallel development more difficult because the `ProductService` class now depends directly on the `Sql-ProductRepository` class.

These are the main reasons you should avoid FOREIGN DEFAULTS if at all possible.

Mary isn't yet comfortable with the idea of CONSTRUCTOR INJECTION because she has trouble figuring out where the object composition will take place. She has yet to grok the concept of a COMPOSITION ROOT.

A visiting consultant told her to use CONSTRUCTOR INJECTION for the `Product-Service`, but she still believes that she must create a new instance of it like this:

```
var productService = new ProductService();
```

To accomplish this, she adds the following code to the `ProductService` class.

Listing 5.2   `ProductService` with BASTARD INJECTION

```
private readonly ProductRepository repository;

public ProductService()
    : this(ProductService.CreateDefaultRepository())    ❶ Default
{                                                          Constructor
}

public ProductService(ProductRepository repository)
{
    if (repository == null)
    {
        throw new ArgumentNullException("repository");   ❷ Injection
    }                                                      Constructor

    this.repository = repository;
}

private static ProductRepository CreateDefaultRepository()
{
    string connectionString =
        ConfigurationManager.ConnectionStrings
        ["CommerceObjectContext"].ConnectionString;

    return new SqlProductRepository(connectionString);
}
```

The `ProductService` class now has a default constructor ❶ that invokes its other constructor using a FOREIGN DEFAULT.

The other constructor correctly implements the CONSTRUCTOR INJECTION pattern by having a Guard Clause and then saving the injected `ProductRepository` in a read-only field ❷. The default constructor calls into this constructor with the FOREIGN DEFAULT created in the private `CreateDefaultRepository` method. The `SqlProduct-Repository` class is a FOREIGN DEFAULT because it's defined in a different assembly than the `ProductService` class. This causes the assembly containing the `ProductService` class to be tightly coupled with the assembly containing the `SqlProductRepository` class.

Although `ProductService` can be reused with different `ProductRepository` types by supplying them via the most flexible constructor overload, Mary won't be able to INTERCEPT the `ProductRepository` instance in her application if she insists on using the default constructor.

5.2.2   *Analysis*

BASTARD INJECTION is most often encountered when developers attempt to make their classes TESTABLE without fully understanding DI. When writing a unit test for a class, it's important that we can replace a VOLATILE DEPENDENCY with a Test Double so we can properly isolate the System Under Test (SUT) from its DEPENDENCIES, and CONSTRUCTOR INJECTION allows us to do just that.

Although it enables TESTABILITY, BASTARD INJECTION has some undesirable consequences.

Case study: ASP.NET MVC

When you create a new ASP.NET MVC project, a few prewritten Controller classes are automatically created. One of these is the AccountController class, which uses BASTARD INJECTION. The source even explains this in the code comments:[4]

```
// This constructor is used by the MVC framework to
// instantiate the controller using the default forms
// authentication and membership providers.
public AccountController()
    : this(null, null)
{
}
// This constructor is not used by the MVC framework but
// is instead provided for ease of unit testing this type.
// See the comments at the end of this file for more
// information.
public AccountController(IFormsAuthentication formsAuth,
    IMembershipService service)
{
    this.FormsAuth =
        formsAuth ?? new FormsAuthenticationService();
    this.MembershipService =
        service ?? new AccountMembershipService();
}
```

How can I say that BASTARD INJECTION is bad when it seems as though Microsoft uses and endorses it? In this case, the motivation seems to be exclusively related to TEST-ABILITY, and BASTARD INJECTION does address that goal adequately—it just doesn't address the other goals of modularity, such as the ability to replace and reuse modules and do parallel development.

Others are of the same mind. Ayende Rahien noted the following in a blog post that reviewed an ASP.NET MVC application:

I mean, if you want to do poor man's IoC, go ahead. But please don't create this bastard child.[5]

This sentence inspired me to name the anti-pattern as I did.

IMPACT

The main problem with BASTARD INJECTION is its use of a FOREIGN DEFAULT. Although TESTABILITY is enabled, we can no longer freely reuse the class because it drags along a DEPENDENCY we may not want. It also becomes more difficult to do parallel development because the class depends strongly on its DEPENDENCY.

---

[4] I had to reformat the code so the line lengths fit in the book. I also added the this keyword to make it more apparent what's going on. Apart from that, I haven't changed anything. You can find this code in the download for this book—I left the default code as it was.

[5] Ayende Rahien, "Reviewing NerdDinner," 2009, http://ayende.com/Blog/archive/2009/07/30/reviewing-nerddinner.aspx

In addition to the consequences of BASTARD INJECTION on the modularity of the application, the existence of multiple constructors also presents a different type of problem. When only one constructor exists, a DI CONTAINER can AUTO-WIRE all dependencies because there is never a question of which constructor to use.

When more than one constructor exists, the choice between constructors becomes ambiguous. A DI CONTAINER must resort to some kind of heuristic to decide between the different constructors—or it may give up. Ironically, this is one of the few scenarios where POOR MAN'S DI is less affected, because we can decide on a case-by-case basis when we manually wire up the dependencies.

Among the different DI anti-patterns, BASTARD INJECTION isn't nearly as damaging as CONTROL FREAK, but it's also much easier to get rid of.

REFACTORING TOWARD DI

BASTARD INJECTION is often the result of a misguided attempt to implement DI. The good thing is that such fundamentals as *programming to interfaces* are already in place, so it's easy to refactor to a proper DI pattern.

> **TIP**   Even if you think the impact of BASTARD INJECTION is of no concern to you, you should still refactor to a proper DI pattern. It's so easy to do that there's no excuse.

The first step is to select which DI pattern is an appropriate goal. Figure 5.3 illustrates a simple decision process. When the default value that has been used so far is a FOREIGN DEFAULT the best choice is CONSTRUCTOR INJECTION. In the other case, PROPERTY INJECTION is a good alternative.

In many cases, the default value used by the default constructor represents a FOREIGN DEFAULT. In these cases, CONSTRUCTOR INJECTION is the best answer, because it's so simple to implement and deals well with any kind of DEPENDENCY. The constructor that takes the DEPENDENCY as a parameter is already in place, so the only change we need to impart on the consuming class is to remove the default constructor.

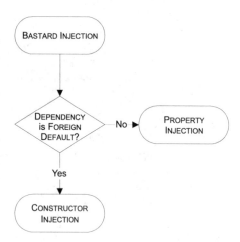

Figure 5.3   When refactoring from BASTARD INJECTION, the deciding factor is whether the DEPENDENCY is a LOCAL or FOREIGN DEFAULT.

This will undoubtedly lead to some compiler errors, but at this point we can *lean on the compiler*[6] and move all code that creates the class in question to a COMPOSITION ROOT.

When the default value represents a LOCAL DEFAULT, the situation closely resembles the core scenario for PROPERTY INJECTION. Although the mechanics are different, the

---

[6]   Feathers, *Working Effectively with Legacy Code*, 315.

structure is the same: in both cases we have a proper LOCAL DEFAULT, but we still wish to open our consuming class for extensibility.

This is a degenerate case of BASTARD INJECTION where the impact is much less severe. Because the default value is a LOCAL DEFAULT, there is no effect on the degree of composability of the class; the only negative consequence is that the constructor ambiguity makes AUTO-WIRING more complex.

In this case, we could implement PROPERTY INJECTION by removing the constructor that takes the DEPENDENCY as a parameter and replacing it with a writable property. If this change results in compiler errors, we can again *lean on the compiler* and move the creating code to a COMPOSITION ROOT.

In a COMPOSITION ROOT there are many different ways to wire up the DEPENDENCIES—including some that are less than ideal, as the next anti-pattern shows.

5.3 *Constrained Construction*

The biggest challenge of properly implementing DI is getting all classes with DEPENDENCIES moved to a COMPOSITION ROOT. When we accomplish this, we've already come a long way.

Even so, there are still some traps to look out for. A common mistake is to require all DEPENDENCIES to have a constructor with a particular signature. This normally originates from the desire to attain late binding so that DEPENDENCIES can be defined in an external configuration file and thereby changed without recompiling the application.

NOTE The so-called Provider pattern[7] used in ASP.NET is an example of CONSTRAINED CONSTRUCTION, because Providers must have default constructors. This is normally exacerbated by the Provider's constructor attempting to read from the application configuration file. Often, the constructor throws an exception if the required configuration section isn't available.

NOTE This section applies only to scenarios where late binding is desired. In scenarios where we directly reference all DEPENDENCIES from the application's root, we don't have this problem—but then again, we don't have the ability to replace DEPENDENCIES without recompiling, either.

In chapter 3, we briefly touched on this issue. This section examines it more carefully.

5.3.1 *Example: late-binding ProductRepository*

In the sample commerce application, some classes depend on the abstract `Product-Repository` class. This means that to create those classes, we first need to create an instance of `ProductRepository`. At this point, you've learned that a COMPOSITION ROOT is

---

[7] Rob Howard, "Provider Model Design Pattern and Specification, Part 1," 2004, http://msdn.microsoft.com/en-us/library/ms972319.aspx

the correct place to do this. In an ASP.NET application, this means Global.asax; the following listing shows the relevant part that creates an instance of ProductRepository.

> **Listing 5.3 Implicitly constraining the ProductRepository constructor**

```
string connectionString =
    ConfigurationManager.ConnectionStrings
    ["CommerceObjectContext"].ConnectionString;

string productRepositoryTypeName =
    ConfigurationManager.AppSettings
    ["ProductRepositoryType"];
var productRepositoryType =
    Type.GetType(productRepositoryTypeName, true);
var repository =
    (ProductRepository)Activator.CreateInstance(          ❶ Create instance of
    productRepositoryType, connectionString);                concrete type
```

The first thing that should trigger suspicion is that a connection string is read from the web.config file. Why do you need a connection string if you plan to treat a ProductRepository as an ABSTRACTION? Although it's perhaps a bit unlikely, you could choose to implement a ProductRepository with an in-memory database or an XML file. A REST-based storage service such as the Windows Azure Table Storage Service offers a more realistic alternative, but once again this year, the most popular choice seems to be a relational database. The ubiquity of databases makes it all too easy to forget that a connection string implicitly represents an implementation choice.

To late-bind a ProductRepository, you also need to determine which type has been chosen as the implementation. This can be done by reading an assembly-qualified type name from web.config and creating a Type instance from that name. This in itself isn't problematic—the difficulty arises only when you need to create an instance of that type.

Given a Type, you can create an instance using the Activator class. The Create-Instance method invokes the type's constructor, so you must supply the correct constructor parameters to prevent an exception from being thrown. In this case, you supply a connection string ❶.

If you didn't know anything else about the application other than the code in listing 5.3, you should by now be wondering why a connection string is passed as a constructor argument to an unknown type. It wouldn't make a lot of sense if the implementation was based on a REST-based web service or an XML file.

Indeed, it doesn't make sense, because this represents an accidental constraint on the DEPENDENCY's constructor. In this case, you have an implicit requirement that any implementation of ProductRepository should have a constructor that takes a single string as input. This is in addition to the explicit constraint that the class must derive from ProductRepository.

> **NOTE** The implicit constraint that the constructor should take a single string still leaves us a great degree of flexibility, because we can encode a lot of

different information in strings to be decoded later. Imagine instead that the constraint was a constructor that takes a `TimeSpan` and a number, and you can begin to imagine how limiting that would be.

You could argue that a `ProductRepository` based on an XML file would also require a string as constructor parameter, although that string would be a file name and not a connection string. However, conceptually it would still be weird, because you would have to define that file name in the `connectionStrings` element in web.config (and in any case, I think such a hypothetical `XmlProductRepository` should take an `Xml-Reader` as constructor argument instead of a file name).

Modeling DEPENDENCY construction exclusively on explicit constraints (interface or base class) is a much better and more flexible option.

5.3.2   *Analysis*

In the previous example, the implicit constraint required implementers to have a constructor with a single string parameter. A more common constraint is that all implementations should have a default constructor so the simplest form of `Activator` `.CreateInstance` will work:

```
var dep = (ISomeDependency)Activator.CreateInstance(type);
```

Although this can be said to be the lowest common denominator, the cost in flexibility is too high.

IMPACT

No matter how we constrain object construction, we lose flexibility. It might be tempting to declare that all DEPENDENCY implementations should have a default constructor—after all, they could perform their initialization internally, like reading configuration data such as configuration strings directly from the .config file. However, this would limit us in other ways, because we might want to be able to compose an application of layers of instances that encapsulate other instances. In some cases, for example, we might wish to *share* an instance between different consumers, as illustrated in figure 5.4.

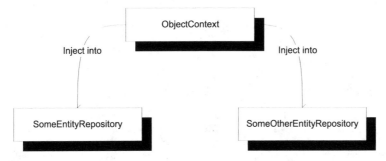

Figure 5.4   In this example, we wish to create a *single* instance of the `ObjectContext` **class and inject the same instance into both Repositories. This is possible only if we can inject the instance from the outside.**

When we have more than one class requiring the same DEPENDENCY, we *may* want to share a single instance among all those classes. This is possible only when we can inject that instance from the outside. Although we could write code inside each of those classes to read type information from a configuration file and use `Activator.CreateInstance` to create the correct type of instance, we could never share a single instance this way—instead, we would have multiple instances of the same class, taking up more memory.

> **NOTE** Just because DI allows us to share a single instance among many consumers doesn't mean we should always do it. Sharing an instance saves memory but may introduce interaction-related problems such as threading issues. Whether we wish to share an instance is closely related to the concept of OBJECT LIFETIME, which is discussed in chapter 8.

Instead of imposing implicit constraints on how objects should be constructed, we should rather implement our COMPOSITION ROOT so that it can deal with any kind of constructor or factory method we may throw at it.

REFACTORING TOWARD DI

How can we deal with having no constraints on components' constructors when we need late binding? It may be tempting to introduce an Abstract Factory that can be used to create instances of the required ABSTRACTION and then require that implementations of such Abstract Factories have default constructors, but doing so is likely to move the underlying problem around without solving it.

> **WARNING** Although we can use Abstract Factories to successfully implement late binding, doing so requires discipline. In general, we're better off with a proper DI CONTAINER; but I'll sketch out how to do it the hard way nonetheless.

Let's briefly examine such an approach. Imagine that you have a service ABSTRACTION imaginatively called `ISomeService`. The Abstract Factory scheme dictates that you also need an `ISomeServiceFactory` interface. Figure 5.5 illustrates this structure.

Now let's assume that you wish to use an implementation of `ISomeService` that requires an instance of `ISomeRepository` to work, as shown in the following listing.

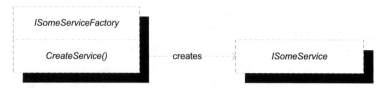

Figure 5.5 `ISomeService` **represents the real** DEPENDENCY. **However, to keep its implementers free of implicit constraints, you attempt to solve the late-binding challenge by introducing the** `ISomeServiceFactory` **that will be used to create instances of** `ISomeService`. **And you** *will* **require of any factories that they have a default constructor.**

Listing 5.4 `SomeService` that requires `ISomeRepository`

```
public class SomeService : ISomeService
{
    public SomeService(ISomeRepository repository)
    {
    }
}
```

The `SomeService` class implements the `ISomeService` interface, but requires an instance of `ISomeRepository`. Because the only constructor isn't the default constructor, the `ISomeServiceFactory` will come in handy.

Currently, you want to use an implementation of `ISomeRepository` that's based on the Entity Framework. You call this implementation `SomeEntityRepository`, and it's defined in a different assembly than `SomeService`.

Because you don't want to drag a reference to the `EntityDataAccess` library along with `SomeService`, the only solution is to implement `SomeServiceFactory` in a different assembly than `SomeService`, as shown in figure 5.6.

Even though `ISomeService` and `ISomeServiceFactory` look like a cohesive pair, it's important to implement them in two different assemblies, because the factory must have references to all DEPENDENCIES to be able wire them together correctly.

By convention, the `ISomeServiceFactory` implementation has a default constructor, so you can write the assembly-qualified type name in a .config file and use `Activator.CreateInstance` to create an instance. Every time you need to wire together a new combination of dependencies, you must implement a new `ISomeServiceFactory` that wires up exactly that combination and then configure the application to use that factory instead of the previous one. This means you can't define arbitrary combinations of DEPENDENCIES without writing and compiling code, but you can do it without recompiling the application itself.

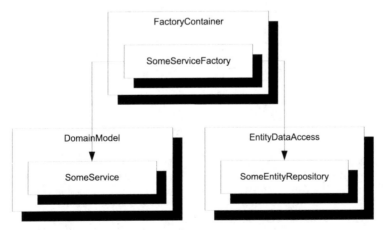

Figure 5.6 The `SomeServiceFactory` class must be implemented in a separate assembly than `SomeService`, to prevent coupling the `DomainModel` library to the `EntityDataAccess` library.

Essentially, such an Abstract Factory becomes an Abstract COMPOSITION ROOT that's defined in an assembly separate from the core application. Although this is certainly a viable approach, it's generally much easier to utilize a general-purpose DI CONTAINER that can do all this for us out of the box based on configuration files.

The CONSTRAINED CONSTRUCTION anti-pattern only really applies when we employ late binding, because when we utilize early binding the compiler ensures that we never introduce implicit constraints on how components are constructed.

The last pattern applies much more generally—some people even consider it a proper pattern instead of an anti-pattern.

5.4   *Service Locator*

It can be difficult to give up on the idea of directly controlling DEPENDENCIES, so many developers take Static Factories (as described in section 5.1.2) to new levels. This leads to the SERVICE LOCATOR anti-pattern.

> **WARNING**   Calling SERVICE LOCATOR an anti-pattern is controversial. Some people consider it a proper design pattern, whereas others (me included) consider it an anti-pattern.[8] In this book, I've decided to describe it as an anti-pattern because I think its disadvantages are greater than its advantages; but don't be surprised if you see it endorsed in other places. The important thing is to understand the benefits and shortcomings enough to be able to make an informed decision for yourself.

SERVICE LOCATOR was introduced as a design pattern by Martin Fowler in 2004,[9] so denouncing it as an anti-pattern is a big step. In short, it introduces a Static Factory with the added detail that it's possible to inject services into this factory.

> **NOTE**   The term *service* in this context is roughly equivalent to a DEPENDENCY.

As it's most commonly implemented, the SERVICE LOCATOR is a Static Factory[10] that can be configured with concrete services before the first consumer begins to use it (see figure 5.7). This could conceivably happen in the COMPOSITION ROOT. Depending on the particular implementation, the SERVICE LOCATOR can be configured with code, by reading a configuration file, or using a combination thereof.

---

[8]   Daniel Cazzulino, "What is all the fuzz about the new common IServiceLocator?" 2008, http://www.clariusconsulting.net/blogs/kzu/archive/2008/10/03/WhatisallthefuzzaboutthenewcommonIServiceLocator.aspx
Nicholas Blumhardt, "Container-Managed Application Design, Prelude: Where does the Container Belong?" 2008, http://blogs.msdn.com/b/nblumhardt/archive/2008/12/27/container-managed-application-design-prelude-where-does-the-container-belong.aspx

[9]   Martin Fowler, "Inversion of Control Containers and the Dependency Injection pattern," 2004, http://martinfowler.com/articles/injection.html

[10]   For more variations, see Mark Seemann, "Service Locator is an Anti-Pattern," 2010, http://blog.ploeh.dk/2010/02/03/ServiceLocatorIsAnAntiPattern.aspx

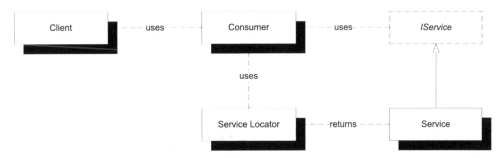

Figure 5.7 A SERVICE LOCATOR's prime responsibility is to serve instances of services when consumers request them. The `Consumer` uses the `IService` interface and requests an instance from the SERVICE LOCATOR, which then returns an instance of whatever concrete implementation it's configured to return.

My personal history with SERVICE LOCATOR

SERVICE LOCATOR and I had an intense relationship for a couple of years before we parted ways. Although I can't remember exactly when I first came across Fowler's article, it provided me with a potential solution to a problem that I had been pondering for some time: how to inject DEPENDENCIES.

As described, the SERVICE LOCATOR pattern seemed like the answer to all my issues, and I quickly set forth to develop a SERVICE LOCATOR for the first version of Microsoft patterns & practices' *Enterprise Library*. It was hosted on the now-defunct GotDotNet site. Although I still have the source code, I lost my release history when GotDotNet shut down; so I can't say for certain, but I seem to have published the first version in mid-2005.

In 2007, I released a complete rewrite targeted at Enterprise Library 2. It's still available on CodePlex, but I've long since abandoned it because I soon thereafter came to the conclusion that it was really an anti-pattern.

As you can see, it took me a couple of years of intense use to realize the shortcomings of SERVICE LOCATOR and that better alternatives existed. For this reason, I find it easy to understand why so many developers find it attractive despite its disadvantages. The patterns described in chapter 4 offer superior alternatives, but it isn't until you learn those that SERVICE LOCATOR starts to look inferior.

WARNING If you look at only the static structure of classes, a DI CONTAINER looks just like a SERVICE LOCATOR. The difference is subtle and lies not in the mechanics of implementation but in how you use it. In essence, asking a container or locator to resolve a complete dependency graph from the COMPOSITION ROOT is proper usage. Asking it for granular services from anywhere else implies the SERVICE LOCATOR anti-pattern.

Let's review an example where it's configured with code.

5.4.1   *Example: ProductService using a Service Locator*

For an example, let's return to our tried-and-true `ProductService` that requires an instance of the abstract `ProductRepository` class. In this case, the `ProductService` can use the static `GetService` method to get the required instance:

```
this.repository = Locator.GetService<ProductRepository>();
```

In this example, I chose to implement the methods using generic type parameters to indicate the type of service being requested, but I could also use a `Type` instance to indicate the type if that's more to my liking.

As the following listing shows, this implementation of the `Locator` class is as minimalistic as possible. I could have added Guard Clauses and error handling, but I wanted to highlight the core behavior. The code could also include a feature that enables it to load its configuration from a .config file, but I'll leave that as an exercise for you.

Listing 5.5   A minimalistic SERVICE LOCATOR implementation

```
public static class Locator
{
    private readonly static Dictionary<Type, object> services
        = new Dictionary<Type, object>();

    public static T GetService<T>()
    {                                                        ❶ Get
        return (T)Locator.services[typeof(T)];                 service
    }

    public static void Register<T>(T service)
    {
        Locator.services[typeof(T)] = service;
    }

    public static void Reset()
    {
        Locator.services.Clear();
    }
}
```

The `Locator` is a class with only static members, so you might as well mark it explicitly as a static class. It holds all the configured services in an internal dictionary that maps the abstract types to each concrete instance.

Clients such as the `ProductService` can use the `GetService` method ❶ to request an instance of the abstract type T. Because this example code contains no Guard Clauses or error handling, this method will throw a rather cryptic `KeyNotFound-Exception` if the requested type has no entry in the dictionary, but you can imagine how to add code to throw a more communicative exception.

The `GetService` method can only return an instance of the requested type if it has previously been inserted in the internal dictionary. This can be done with the `Register` method. Again, this example code contains no Guard Clause, so it would be possible to Register null, but a more robust implementation shouldn't allow that.

In certain cases (particularly when unit testing), it's important to be able to reset the Service Locator. That functionality is provided by the Reset method, which clears the internal dictionary.

Classes like ProductService rely on the service to be available in the Service Locator, so it's important that it has been previously configured. In a unit test, this could be done with a Test Double[11] implemented by a dynamic mock library such as Moq,[12] as used in this example:

```
var stub = new Mock<ProductRepository>().Object;
Locator.Register<ProductRepository>(stub);
```

We first create a Stub of the abstract ProductRepository class and then use the static Register method to configure the Service Locator with that instance. If this is done before ProductService is used for the first time, ProductService will use the configured Stub to work against the ProductRepository. In the full production application, the Service Locator will be configured with the correct ProductRepository implementation in the Composition Root.

This way of locating Dependencies from the ProductService class definitely works if our only success criterion is that the Dependency *can* be used and replaced at will, but it has some other serious shortcomings.

5.4.2 Analysis

Service Locator is a dangerous pattern because it *almost* works. We can locate Dependencies from consuming classes, and we can replace those Dependencies with different implementations—even with Test Doubles from unit tests.

When we apply the analysis model outlined in chapter 1 to evaluate whether Service Locator can match the benefits of modular application design, we find that it fits in most regards:

- We have support for *late binding* by changing the registration.
- We can *develop code in parallel* because we program against interfaces and can replace modules at will.
- We *can* achieve good separation of concerns, so nothing stops us from writing *maintainable* code. But doing so becomes much more difficult.
- We can replace Dependencies with Test Doubles, so Testability is ensured.

There is only one area where Service Locator falls short.

IMPACT

The main problem with Service Locator is that it impacts the reusability of the classes consuming it. This manifests itself in two ways:

- The module drags along a redundant Dependency.
- It isn't apparent that DI is being used.

---

[11] Gerard Meszaros, *xUnit Test Patterns: Refactoring Test Code* (New York: Addison-Wesley, 2007), 522.
[12] http://code.google.com/p/moq/

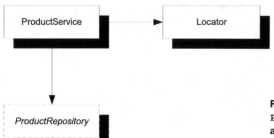

Figure 5.8 Dependency graph for a
`ProductService` **implementation that uses**
a SERVICE LOCATOR to serve instances of the
abstract `ProductRepository` **class**

Let's first look at the dependency graph for the `ProductService` from the example in section 5.4.1, shown in figure 5.8. In addition to the expected reference to the abstract `ProductRepository` class, `ProductService` also depends on the `Locator` class.

This means that to reuse the `ProductService` class, we must redistribute not only it and its relevant DEPENDENCY `ProductRepository`, but also the `Locator` DEPENDENCY that only exists for mechanical reasons. If the `Locator` class is defined in a different module than `ProductService` and `ProductRepository`, new applications wishing to reuse `ProductService` must accept that module as well.

To compound the matter, imagine that a new application reusing `ProductService` is already using a different DI strategy centered on CONSTRUCTOR INJECTION. `Product-Service` doesn't fit into this strategy but instead enforces its own DI strategy that effectively pollutes the DI architecture of the new application. To use it, developers must accept the existence of a SERVICE LOCATOR; and after it's introduced, it may accidentally be used by novice developers for other purposes where better alternatives exist.

Perhaps we could even tolerate that extra DEPENDENCY on `Locator` if it was truly necessary for DI to work—we would accept it as a tax to be paid to gain other benefits. However, there are better options (such as CONSTRUCTOR INJECTION) available, so this DEPENDENCY is redundant.

To add insult to injury, neither this redundant DEPENDENCY nor its relevant counterpart, `Product-Repository`, is explicitly visible to developers wishing to consume the `ProductService` class. Figure 5.9 shows that Visual Studio can offer no guidance on the use of this class.

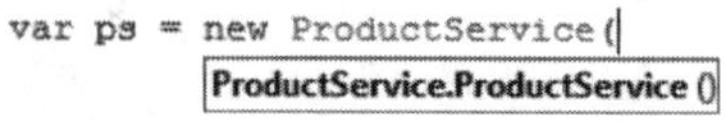

```
var ps = new ProductService (
   ProductService.ProductService ()
```

Figure 5.9 The only thing
IntelliSense can tell us about the
`ProductService` **class is that it has**
a default constructor. Its DEPENDENCIES
are invisible.

When we wish to create a new instance of the `ProductService` class, Visual Studio can only tell us that the class has a default constructor. However, if we subsequently attempt to run the code we just wrote, we get a runtime error if we forgot to register a `ProductRepository` instance with the `Locator` class. This is likely to happen if we don't intimately know the `ProductService` class.

> **TIP** Imagine that the code we write ships in an undocumented, obfuscated .dll. How easy would it be for someone else to use? It's possible to develop

APIs that are close to self-documenting, and although doing so takes practice, it's a worthy goal.

NOTE The problem with Service Locator is that any client using it is being dishonest about its level of complexity. It looks simple as seen through the public API, but it turns out to be complex—and we don't find out about this before we get a runtime exception.

The problem with the `ProductService` class is that it's far from self-documenting: we can't tell which Dependencies must be present before it will work. In fact, the developers of `ProductService` may even decide to *add* more Dependencies in future versions, so code that works on the current version may fail on a future version, and we aren't even going to get a compiler error that warns us. Service Locator makes it easy to inadvertently introduce breaking changes.

WARNING The use of generics may trick you into thinking that a Service Locator is strongly typed. However, even an API like the one shown in listing 5.5 is weakly typed because we can request any type. Being able to compile code invoking the `GetService<T>` method gives us no guarantee that it won't throw exceptions left and right at runtime.

NOTE When unit testing, we have the additional problem that a Test Double registered in one test case will cause Interdependent Tests because it will remain in memory when the next test case is executed. It's therefore necessary to perform Fixture Teardown after each and every test by invoking `Locator.Reset();` This is something that we must manually remember to do, and it's easy to forget.

This is all really bad. Service Locator may seem innocuous, but it can lead to all sorts of nasty runtime errors. How do we avoid those problems?

REFACTORING TOWARD DI

When we decide to get rid of Service Locator, we need to find a way to do it. As always, the default goal should be Constructor Injection unless one of the other DI patterns from chapter 4 provides a better fit.

WARNING When we look at the structure of Service Locator, it's close to Ambient Context. Both are implicitly consumed Singletons,[13] but the difference lies in the availability of Local Defaults. An Ambient Context guarantees that it can always deliver an appropriate instance of the requested service (normally, there's only one). This guarantee can't be made by a Service Locator because it's in essence a weakly-typed container of services about which it has no built-in knowledge.

In many cases, a class that consumes a Service Locator may have calls to it spread throughout its code base. In such cases, it acts as a replacement for the new statement.

---

[13] Gamma, *Design Patterns,* 127.

When this is so, the first refactoring step is to consolidate the creation of each DEPENDENCY in a single method.

If we don't have a member field to hold an instance of the DEPENDENCY, we can introduce such a field and make sure the rest of the code uses this field when it consumes the DEPENDENCY. Mark the field `readonly` to ensure that it can't be modified outside the constructor. Doing so forces us to assign the field from the constructor using the SERVICE LOCATOR. We can now introduce a constructor parameter that assigns the field instead of the SERVICE LOCATOR, which can then be removed. Introducing a DEPENDENCY parameter to a constructor is likely to break existing consumers, so we also need to deal with that and move all wiring of DEPENDENCIES to a COMPOSITION ROOT.

Refactoring a class that uses SERVICE LOCATOR is similar to refactoring a class that uses CONTROL FREAK, because a SERVICE LOCATOR is just a roundabout variant of CONTROL FREAK. Section 5.1.3 contains further notes on refactoring CONTROL FREAK implementations to use DI.

At first glance, SERVICE LOCATOR may look like a proper DI pattern, but don't be fooled: it may explicitly address loose coupling, but it sacrifices other concerns along the way. The DI patterns presented in chapter 4 offer better alternatives with fewer drawbacks. This is true for the SERVICE LOCATOR anti-pattern as well as the other anti-patterns presented in this chapter. Even though they're different, they all share the common trait that they can be resolved by one of the DI patterns from chapter 4.

5.5   *Summary*

Because DI is a set of patterns and techniques, no single tool can mechanically verify whether we've applied it correctly. In chapter 4, we looked at patterns that describe how DI can be used properly, but that's only one side of the coin. It's also important to study how it's possible to fail even with the best of intentions. There are important lessons to be learned from failure, but we don't have to always learn from our own—sometimes we can learn from other people's mistakes.

In this chapter, I've described the most common DI mistakes in the form of anti-patterns. I've seen all these mistakes in real life on more than one occasion, and I confess myself guilty of all of them:

- My name is Mark Seemann, and I've used CONTROL FREAK.
- My name is Mark Seemann, and I've used BASTARD INJECTION.
- My name is Mark Seemann, and I've used CONSTRAINED CONSTRUCTION.
- My name is Mark Seemann, and I've used SERVICE LOCATOR. Worse than that, I not only used it, but I produced it and attempted to get innocent people hooked.

Fortunately, I've long since shed those habits—I've been clean for many years.

The first and most important habit to get rid of is the imaginary need to exert direct control over DEPENDENCIES. It's easy to spot instances of CONTROL FREAK: every place you use the `new` keyword (in C#, at least) to create an instance of a VOLATILE DEPENDENCY, you're a CONTROL FREAK, and it doesn't matter how many layers of factories you use to hide the fact. The only place you're permitted to new up a DEPENDENCY is from a COMPOSITION ROOT.

Getting rid of CONTROL FREAK is by far the most important task. Only when you have succeeded in weeding out instances of CONTROL FREAK should you turn your attention to those other anti-patterns; they're far less damaging.

> **TIP** CONTROL FREAK *prevents* you from using loose coupling; the other DI anti-patterns merely make it awkward, so focus your attention on CONTROL FREAK first.

BASTARD INJECTION enables DI but then spoils the party by dragging along redundant DEPENDENCIES. Fortunately, it's easy to refactor a BASTARD INJECTION implementation toward CONSTRUCTOR INJECTION, so whereas we might have been able to live with the inelegance of BASTARD INJECTION, there's no need to do so. We gain more than we lose by moving to a proper solution—in fact, we only lose the time it takes to perform the refactoring.

CONSTRAINED CONSTRUCTION imposes artificial constraints on the types we use to implement ABSTRACTIONS. In most cases, this takes the form of constraining all implementations to have default constructors, but in other cases constructors may be required to take a particular parameter to initialize the component.

You should lift those constraints and use a DI CONTAINER or manual composition to wire up all objects with their required DEPENDENCIES—whatever they may be. If you have a scenario where you need to initialize certain components with information about the current context, METHOD INJECTION is the proper pattern to apply.

A SERVICE LOCATOR may look compelling, but I consider it an anti-pattern although that's a somewhat controversial opinion. Although it solves some DI challenges, it introduces other problems that outweigh its benefits. There is no reason to accept those disadvantages because the DI patterns presented in chapter 4 offer better alternatives. This is a common theme for all the anti-patterns described in this chapter: the DI patterns from chapter 4 offer solutions to the problems caused by the anti-patterns.

By now, you should know what to avoid and what you should ideally be doing instead, but there may still be issues that look as though they're hard to solve. The next chapter discusses such challenges and how to resolve them.

DI refactorings

You may have noticed that I have a fascination with sauce béarnaise, or sauce hollandaise in general. One reason is that it tastes so good; another is that it's a bit tricky to make. In addition to the challenge of production, sauce hollandaise presents an entirely different problem: it must be served immediately (or so I thought).

This used to be less than ideal when I was having guests. Instead of being able to casually greet my guests and make them feel welcome and relaxed, I was frantically whipping the sauce in the kitchen, leaving them to entertain themselves.

After a couple of repeat performances, my very sociable wife decided to take matters into her own hands. We live just across the street from a restaurant, so one day she chatted up the cooks to find out whether there is a trick that would enable me to prepare a genuine sauce hollandaise well in advance. It turns out that there

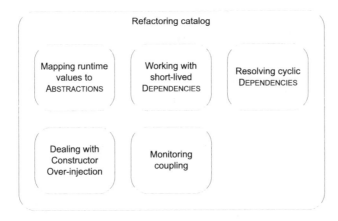

Figure 6.1 The structure of this chapter is a catalog of refactorings or solutions to common DI issues. Each of the sections can be read independently.

is, so now I can serve a delicious sauce for my guests without first subjecting them to an atmosphere of stress and frenzy.

Each craft has its own tricks of the trade. This is also true for software development in general and DI in particular. There are challenges that just keep on popping up, and in many cases there are well-known ways to deal with them.

Over the years, I've seen people struggle when learning DI, and it occurred to me that many of the issues were similar in structure. In this chapter, we'll look at the most common challenges that appear when we apply DI to a code base, and how we can resolve them. When we're finished, you should be able to better recognize and handle these situations when they occur.

Similar to the two previous chapters in this part of the book, this chapter is organized as a catalog—this time of problems and solutions (or, if you will, refactorings). Figure 6.1 shows the structure of the chapter.

In each section, I'll present a common issue and how you can address it, including an example. You can read each section independently or in sequence, as you prefer. The purpose of each section is to familiarize you with a solution to a commonly occurring problem so that you'll be better equipped to deal with it if it occurs.

6.1 *Mapping runtime values to Abstractions*

When you start applying DI, one of the first difficulties you're likely to encounter is when ABSTRACTIONS depend on runtime values. For example, an online map site may offer to calculate a route between two locations. It may give you a choice of how you want the route calculated: Do you want the shortest route? The fastest route based on known traffic patterns? The most scenic route?

Each option represents a different algorithm, and the application may treat each routing algorithm as an ABSTRACTION so it can treat them all equally. To calculate a route, the application needs a routing algorithm, but it doesn't care which one. We must tell it which algorithm it should use, but we don't know this until runtime, because it's based on the user's choice.

This section discusses how we can deal with this type of issue. Before turning to an example, we'll briefly talk about the general problem. When we're finished, your knee-jerk reaction to this challenge should be to introduce an Abstract Factory.

6.1.1   *Abstractions with runtime Dependencies*

When we use CONSTRUCTOR INJECTION, we implicitly state that we expect the DEPENDENCY to be *unambiguous* at runtime. Consider a constructor signature like this one:

```
public RepositoryBasketDiscountPolicy(DiscountRepository repository)
```

Ambiguity not allowed!

This is never going to work if, at *runtime*, it's unclear which implementation of DiscountRepository should be used. At design-time, we can treat the DEPENDENCY as an ABSTRACTION and follow the LISKOV SUBSTITUTION PRINCIPLE; but at runtime, a decision about which DiscountRepository to use *must* be made before the Repository-BasketDiscountPolicy can be created. Because the DEPENDENCY is requested through the constructor, we can't defer the decision past this point.

This only means that, as far as the RepositoryBasketDiscountPolicy class goes, there can be no ambiguity concerning DiscountRepository. Other consumers may also request DiscountRepository instances, and whether they all get the same or different instances is of less importance. Such DEPENDENCIES often represent Services[1] instead of Domain Objects. Conceptually, there is only one instance of a given Service.

> **NOTE**   As you'll see in chapter 9, there may be several implementations of the same ABSTRACTION in play at the same time. However, from the consumer's perspective, there is only one.

Services belong to a common group of DEPENDENCIES, but at times a DEPENDENCY represent a proper Domain Object. This is particularly true when it comes to behavior-changing ABSTRACTIONS such as Strategies.[2] The previous route-calculation algorithm is one such example. Another may be a graphics editor's collection of bitmap effects: each effect performs a transformation of a bitmap, but they may all be exposed to the application as ABSTRACTIONS—this is also an architecture that allows add-ins to be supported.

In such cases, we can't request the DEPENDENCY through the constructor, because a COMPOSER won't know which implementation to pick. There may be zero, one, or many instances in play at different times through an application's lifetime. The DEPENDENCY is ambiguous at design-time.

---

[1] Eric Evans, *Domain-Driven Design: Tackling Complexity in the Heart of Software* (New York: Addison-Wesley, 2004), 104.

[2] Erich Gamma et al, *Design Patterns: Elements of Reusable Object-Oriented Software* (New York: Addison-Wesley, 1994), 315.

As always in software design, the solution is another level of indirection: this time, the Abstract Factory design pattern.

Abstract Factory

The Abstract Factory[3] design pattern addresses the problem when we need to be able to request an instance of an ABSTRACTION at will. It offers a bridge between ABSTRACTIONS and concrete runtime values, allowing us to translate a runtime value to a DEPENDENCY.

The following figure illustrates how it works by introducing a new ABSTRACTION that creates instances of the originally required ABSTRACTION.

If we need to be able to create IFoo instances on request, we need a way to do that. An ABSTRACT FACTORY is another ABSTRACTION that we can use to create such instances as necessary.

An Abstract Factory is itself an ABSTRACTION whose only purpose is to create instances of the originally required ABSTRACTION. If we need to be able to create IFoo instances from concrete Bar instances, the corresponding Abstract Factory might look like this:

```
public interface IFooFactory
{
    IFoo Create(Bar bar);
}
```

In this case, Bar is a concrete class. IFooFactory allows us to translate a concrete Bar instance to an abstract IFoo instance. The IFoo implementation may contain the bar instance or use the input as guidance to pick a particular IFoo instance.

In the degenerate case, an Abstract Factory may take no input parameters:

```
public interface IFooFactory
{
    IFoo Create();
}
```

In that case, the Abstract Factory becomes a pure factory, whereas the translation aspect disappears.

Abstract Factory is one of the most useful design patterns. Keep it in mind, because it can be used to solve many issues with DI.

TIP When one or more of the arguments supplied to an Abstract Factory is in itself an ABSTRACTION, this technique also becomes an example of METHOD INJECTION.

---

[3] Ibid., 87.

An Abstract Factory is the universal solution when we need to create DEPENDENCIES from runtime values.

DESIGN CONSIDERATIONS

As useful as Abstract Factory can be, we must take care to apply it with discrimination. The DEPENDENCIES created by an Abstract Factory should *conceptually* require a runtime value. The translation from a runtime value into an ABSTRACTION should make sense on the conceptual level. If you feel the urge to introduce an Abstract Factory to be able to create instances of a concrete implementation, you may have a LEAKY ABSTRACTION at hand.

LEAKY ABSTRACTIONS

Just as Test-Driven Development (TDD) ensures TESTABILITY, it's safest to define interfaces first and then subsequently program against them. Even so, there are cases where we already have a concrete type and now wish to extract an interface.

When we do this, we must take care that the underlying implementation doesn't leak through. One way this can happen is if we only extract an interface from a given concrete type, but all the parameter and return types are still concrete types defined in the same library.

If we need to extract an interface, we need to do it in a recursive manner, ensuring that all types exposed by the root interface are themselves interfaces. I call this Deep Extraction and the result *Deep Interfaces*.

ASP.NET MVC has some examples of Deep Interface extraction. For example, `HttpContextBase` has a `Request` property of type `HttpRequestBase`, and so on. This ABSTRACTION was recursively extracted from `System.Web.HttpContext`.

Always consider whether a given ABSTRACTION makes sense for other implementations than the one you have in mind. If it doesn't, you should reconsider your design.

Abstract Factories come in many shapes and forms, and it may not always be apparent that you have one.

> **NOTE** Any ABSTRACTION that creates instances of other ABSTRACTIONS is an Abstract Factory. It doesn't need to have a name that ends with *Factory*.

Let's look at a couple of examples: first a simple, idiomatic example and subsequently a more complex example where the Abstract Factory is hidden under a different name.

6.1.2 *Example: selecting a routing algorithm*

The introduction to this section briefly discussed an online map site where the user can choose from different route-calculation algorithms. In this section, we'll walk through how to apply an Abstract Factory to address this requirement.

In a web application, you can only transfer primitive types[4] from the browser to the server, so when the user selects a routing algorithm from a drop-down box, you must

---

[4] To be pedantic, we can only transfer strings, but most web frameworks support type conversion for primitive types.

represent this by a number or a string. An enum is really just a number, so on the server you can represent the selection using this RouteType:

```
public enum RouteType
{
    Shortest = 0,
    Fastest,
    Scenic
}
```

However, what you need is an instance of IRouteAlgorithm that can calculate the route for you. To translate from the runtime RouteType value to IRouteAlgorithm, you can define an Abstract Factory:

```
public interface IRouteAlgorithmFactory
{
    IRouteAlgorithm CreateAlgorithm(RouteType routeType);
}
```

This enables you to implement a GetRoute method for a RouteController by injecting the IRouteAlgorithmFactory and using it to translate the runtime value to the DEPENDENCY you need: IRouteAlgorithm. The following listing demonstrates the interaction.

Listing 6.1 Using an `IRouteAlgorithmFactory`

```
public class RouteController
{
    private readonly IRouteAlgorithmFactory factory;

    public RouteController(IRouteAlgorithmFactory factory)
    {
        if (factory == null)
        {
            throw new ArgumentNullException("factory");
        }

        this.factory = factory;
    }

    public IRoute GetRoute(RouteSpecification spec,
        RouteType routeType)
    {
        IRouteAlgorithm algorithm =                          ❶ Map runtime
            this.factory.CreateAlgorithm(routeType);            value
        return algorithm.CalculateRoute(spec);  ⟵┐
    }                                                        ❷ Use mapped
}                                                              algorithm
```

The RouteController class's responsibility is to handle web requests. The GetRoute method receives the user's specification of origin and destination, as well as a selected RouteType. You need an ABSTRACT FACTORY to map the runtime RouteType value to an IRouteAlgorithm instance, so you request an instance of IRouteAlgorithmFactory using standard CONSTRUCTOR INJECTION.

In the `GetRoute` method, you can use the `factory` to map the `routeType` variable to an `IRouteAlgorithm` ❶. When you have that, you can use it to calculate the route ❷ and return the result.

NOTE   For the sake of conciseness, I omitted a Guard Clause in the `GetRoute` method. However, the supplied `RouteSpecification` may be null, so a more robust implementation should check for that.

The most obvious implementation of `IRouteAlgorithmFactory` would involve a simple switch statement and return three different implementations of `IRouteAlgorithm` based on the input. However, I'll leave this as an exercise for the reader.

This example demonstrated mapping from runtime value to DEPENDENCY using an Abstract Factory in its purest form. The next example shows a more complex variation where at first glance you may not even realize that Abstract Factories are being used.

6.1.3   *Example: using a CurrencyProvider*

In most of chapter 4, you saw how to implement currency conversion in an ASP.NET MVC Controller. The `Currency` type is an abstract class, reproduced here so that you won't have to flip back to section 4.1.4:

```
public abstract partial class Currency
{
    public abstract string Code { get; }

    public abstract decimal GetExchangeRateFor(
        string currencyCode);
}
```

At first glance it seems a little weird to treat a concept like currency as an ABSTRACTION, because it sounds more like a Value Object.[5] However, notice that the `GetExchangeRateFor` method enables us to query it about a virtually unbounded set of conversion rates. If we assume 100 conversion rates, each `Currency` instance would consume more than 2 KB of memory. That doesn't sound like a lot, but it may warrant an optimization like use of the Flyweight[6] design pattern.

Another issue that quickly arises with currency conversion regards the currency (sic!) of the currency: in other words, how up-to-date it is. Applications such as trader software for monetary markets require exchange rates to be updated several times a second, whereas an international commerce site is likely to get by with few updates for stable currencies. Such applications may also include markup or rounding strategies, adding to the potential complexity of implementing a `Currency` type. In that light, an abstract `Currency` class begins to sound reasonable.

[5] Evans, *Domain-Driven Design*, 97.
[6] Gamma, *Design Patterns*, 195.

When a consumer like an ASP.NET MVC Controller needs to convert prices, it requires a Currency as a DEPENDENCY to perform the conversion. In the sample commerce application used in this book, the Money class used to represent prices has this conversion method:

```
public Money ConvertTo(Currency currency)
```

A consumer such as a Controller can supply a Currency instance to all prices to convert them, but the question now arises, which Currency instance?

The choice of target Currency relies on a runtime value: the user's preferred currency. This means we can't request a single Currency object through CONSTRUCTOR INJECTION, because a COMPOSER is unable to know which Currency to use.

As you saw in section 4.1.1, the solution is to inject a CurrencyProvider instead of a single Currency:

```
public abstract class CurrencyProvider
{
    public abstract Currency GetCurrency(string currencyCode);
}
```

Figure 6.2 illustrates how a Controller typically retrieves the user's preferred currency code from the profile and uses the injected CurrencyProvider to create the appropriate Currency instance.

Although it has a different name, CurrencyProvider is an Abstract Factory that helps us bridge the gap between a runtime value and a runtime DEPENDENCY. A Currency *conceptually* depends on a currency code, so we can rest assured that we haven't introduced a LEAKY ABSTRACTION by introducing the CurrencyProvider.

Another example from chapter 4 shows the degenerate case where there is no initial input parameter. In section 4.2.4, you saw how an abstract CurrencyProfile-Service has a GetCurrencyCode method that will return the user's current currency code:

```
public abstract string GetCurrencyCode();
```

Although the GetCurrencyCode method returns a string instead of an ABSTRACTION, you can still view CurrencyProfileService as an Abstract Factory variant.

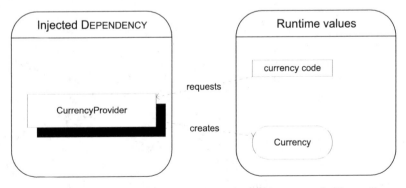

Figure 6.2 The injected CurrencyProvider **is used to map a primitive runtime value (the currency code string) to a runtime** DEPENDENCY **(the** Currency **instance).**

In the `HomeController`, you combine both variations to figure out the user's preferred `Currency`:

```
var currencyCode = this.CurrencyProfileService.GetCurrencyCode();
var currency = this.currencyProvider.GetCurrency(currencyCode);
```

Both `CurrencyProfileService` and `currencyProvider` are injected Abstract Factories that are available to any member of the `HomeController` class. Sections 4.1.4 and 4.2.4 show how they're injected.

Whenever we need to produce a runtime value and we want to be able to vary the means by which we produce this value independently of the consumer, we can inject an Abstract Factory. It's typically a stateless service, so it fits better with how we normally treat DEPENDENCIES, and we can use CONSTRUCTOR INJECTION or PROPERTY INJECTION to supply the consumer with the factory.

There is another, different type of scenario where Abstract Factory also provides a good solution. This happens when we need to deal with short-lived DEPENDENCIES.

6.2   *Working with short-lived Dependencies*

Some DEPENDENCIES seem to be conceptually short-lived. These typically represent connections to external resources such as databases or web services. Such connections must be closed, or resource leaks will occur. In this section, we look at the best way to address such concerns.

Similar to the previous section, we'll start by studying the general case and then proceed to look at an example. When we're finished, you should understand two things:

- You can model such interactions with an Abstract Factory that produces disposable instances.
- You should strive to hide this pattern behind a stateless ABSTRACTION.

Before we turn to an example, let's see what would cause me to say that.

6.2.1   *Closing connections through Abstractions*

The whole point of loose coupling and the LISKOV SUBSTITUTION PRINCIPLE is that a DEPENDENCY can be implemented in any number of ways. Even when you have a particular implementation in mind, a radically different implementation may potentially come along in the future.

Even so, some DEPENDENCIES represent access to external resources, and these tend to drag along issues related to resource usage. I am, of course, talking about connections in many shapes and forms.

Most .NET developers know that they should open an ADO.NET connection just before using it, and close it again as soon as the work is finished. Modern APIs like LINQ to SQL or LINQ to Entities automatically do this for us so we don't have to explicitly deal with it.

Although the correct usage pattern concerning ADO.NET connections should be common knowledge, it's far less known that the same is true for WCF clients. They should be closed as soon as we're finished with a particular set of operations on a service, because they may otherwise leave orphaned resources on the server side.

> ### WCF services and state
>
> A fundamental rule of service orientation is that services should be stateless. If we follow this rule, surely a WCF client should keep no resources alive on the server side, right?
>
> Surprisingly, this may not be true. Even if we design a service to be completely stateless, WCF may not be. It depends on the binding.
>
> One example among many relates to security. Message-based security tends to impact performance. This is true because asymmetric keys are computationally intensive, but it's even more true for Federated security because multiple message exchanges are involved in establishing a security context. WCF's default behavior is to establish a secure conversation based on the asymmetric key exchange. The service and client use the asymmetric security handshake to exchange an ad hoc symmetric key that is used to secure all future messages that are part of that session.
>
> However, that behavior requires that both sides keep the shared secret in memory. The client must sign off with the service when it finishes the session, or it will orphan the symmetric key at the server. It will eventually be cleaned up after a timeout, but it takes up memory until then. To save resources on the server, the client should explicitly close the "connection" when it's finished.
>
> Although this isn't true for all WCF bindings, it's true for so many that we need to ensure that our WCF clients are good citizens.

How can we reconcile the need to close a WCF connection with the desire to avoid a LEAKY ABSTRACTION? This issue can be addressed on two levels:

- Hiding the entire connection management logic behind an ABSTRACTION
- Mimicking opening and closing connections on a more detailed level

The first option is preferred, but sometimes the second is required as well. Both options can be combined to get the best of both worlds.

HIDING CONNECTION MANAGEMENT BEHIND AN ABSTRACTION

DI is no excuse for writing applications with memory leaks, so we must be able to explicitly close connections as soon as possible. On the other hand, any DEPENDENCY may or may not represent out-of-process communication, so it would be a LEAKY ABSTRACTION if we were to model an ABSTRACTION to include a Close method.

Some people resort to letting their DEPENDENCIES derive from IDisposable. However, the Dispose method is just a Close method with another name, so that approach doesn't solve the underlying problem.

Fortunately, database access technologies such as LINQ to SQL and LINQ to Entities show the way. In both cases, we access data through a *context* that contains a connection. Whenever we communicate with the database, the context automatically opens

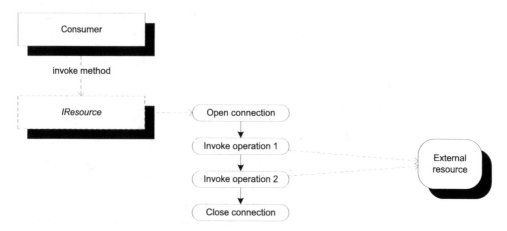

Figure 6.3   We can design an interface so that it's sufficiently coarse-grained that each method encapsulates all interactions with an external resource in a single batch. The Consumer invokes a method on the `IResource` interface. An implementation of that method could open a connection and invoke several methods against the external resource before closing the connection and returning a result to the consumer.

and closes the connection as necessary, entirely freeing us from the burden of dealing with this.

Our first reaction should be to do the same. Figure 6.3 shows how to define the ABSTRACTION at a level that is sufficiently coarse-grained that the implementation can open and close connections as necessary.

The consumer is never aware that some implementations may be opening and closing connections on its behalf.

Whenever possible, we should strive to design a consumer's DEPENDENCIES so that we never need to explicitly deal with the lifetime of the DEPENDENCY at this level. There are, however, instances where we can't do that.

OPENING AND CLOSING DEPENDENCIES
The problem with coarse-grained APIs is that they may not be flexible enough. Sometimes we simply need an ABSTRACTION that lets us explicitly model the lifecycle of DEPENDENCIES that otherwise will cause memory leaks.

> **WARNING**   Stopping one leak creates another. We exchange memory leaks for LEAKY ABSTRACTIONS.

The most common lifecycle we need to model is shown in figure 6.4.

In section 6.1, you saw how to use an Abstract Factory to create DEPENDENCIES at will, so we need to find a coding idiom that fits with closing a connection. As figure 6.4 hints, we can use the `IDisposable` pattern to dispose of connection-using DEPENDENCIES.

> **WARNING**   Disposable DEPENDENCIES are design smells. Use them only when there is no other option. Read more in section 8.2.

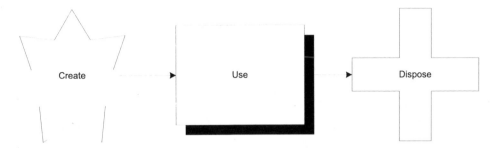

Figure 6.4 The most common lifecycle for a connection is that we create it, use it, and close it when we're finished with it. This is the lifecycle that we should model if we must model such things.

In other words, we can model just about any interaction that fits the lifecycle from figure 6.4 with an Abstract Factory that creates disposable DEPENDENCIES (see figure 6.5).

The usage pattern shown in figure 6.5 is often best implemented by using the C# using keyword (or a similar construct in other languages).

As the following example will show, it makes sense to combine both of the approaches just discussed. The resource access is modeled as a coarse-grained ABSTRACTION that shields the

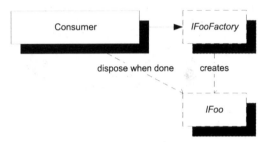

Figure 6.5 We can model connection management and similar lifecycles by taking a DEPENDENCY on an Abstract Factory such as the IFooFactory shown here. Each time the consumer needs an instance of IFoo, it's created by IFooFactory, but the consumer must remember to dispose of it appropriately.

consumer from explicitly dealing with lifecycle management, whereas the implementation uses the described combination of Abstract Factory and disposable DEPENDENCIES. Let's see how that works.

6.2.2 Example: invoking a product-management service

Imagine a Windows Presentation Foundation (WPF) application that provides a rich user interface for managing a product catalog. Such an application could communicate with the backend via a WCF service that exposes the necessary product catalog management operations.

Figure 6.6 shows how an implementation combines both techniques from the previous section.

NOTE We'll return to this WPF application in sections 6.3.2 and 7.4.2.

The consumer is shielded from connection management, which is an implementation detail of WcfProductManagementAgent.

Whenever the MainWindowViewModel class wants to invoke a service operation, it invokes its IProductManagementAgent DEPENDENCY. This is a completely normal

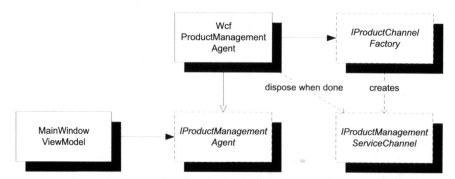

Figure 6.6   The `MainWindowViewModel` class consumes the `IProductManagementAgent`
interface. This is a coarse-grained interface that exposes appropriate methods for the
consumer to call. From `MainWindowViewModel`'s perspective, no connection management
is taking place. When the application is running, the `WcfProductManagementAgent` class
provides the implementation of the coarse-grained interface. It does this by consuming the
Abstract Factory `IProductChannelFactory` that creates disposable instances. The
`IProductManagementServiceChannel` interface derives from `IDisposable`, which
enables `WcfProductManagementAgent` to dispose of the WCF client when the operations
have been successfully invoked.

DEPENDENCY injected via CONSTRUCTOR INJECTION. This, for example, shows how to delete a product:

```
this.agent.DeleteProduct(productId);
```

In this case, `this.agent` is the injected `IProductManagementAgent` DEPENDENCY. As you can see, no explicit connection management is taking place here; but if you look at the implementation in `WcfProductManagementAgent`, you see how Abstract Factory is used in combination with a disposable DEPENDENCY:

```
using (var channel = this.factory.CreateChannel())
{
    channel.DeleteProduct(productId);
}
```

You don't have an injected WCF client you can use to invoke the service operation because you need to close the client as soon as you're finished with it, and it isn't possible to reuse WCF channels. Instead, you have an injected Abstract Factory that you use to create a new channel. Because the operation is enclosed in a `using` scope, leaving the scope disposes the channel.

The `factory` DEPENDENCY is an instance of the `IProductChannelFactory` interface. This is a custom interface created for the occasion:

```
public interface IProductChannelFactory
{
    IProductManagementServiceChannel CreateChannel();
}
```

However, the `IProductManagementServiceChannel` interface is an auto-generated interface created together with all the other WCF proxy types. Every time we create a service reference in Visual Studio or use svcutil.exe, such an interface is created along with the other types. The attractive feature of this auto-generated interface is that it implements IDisposable along with all the service operations.

This type is understood by WCF, making the implementation of IProductChannel-Factory trivial because we can use System.ServiceModel.ChannelFactory<TChannel> to create the instances.

As a dominant principle, I prefer a stateless and coarse-grained interface like IProductManagementAgent to shield the implementation details from consumers. Although we must view disposable Dependencies as Leaky Abstractions, a leak can be contained within a particular implementation; and by doing that we gain Testability without compromising the overall design.

Abstract Factory is an extremely useful design pattern. It helps resolve runtime Dependencies and short-lived Dependencies. We can also include it in an effort to resolve cyclic Dependencies, but it doesn't play a central role in that context.

6.3 *Resolving cyclic Dependencies*

Occasionally, Dependency implementations turn out to be cyclic. An implementation requires another Dependency whose implementation requires the first Abstraction. Such a dependency graph can't be satisfied.

It's important to realize that the Abstractions themselves can be perfectly acyclic, while particular implementation can introduce a cycle. Figure 6.7 shows how this could happen.

As long as the cycle remains, we can't possibly satisfy all Dependencies, and our applications won't be able to run. Clearly, something must be done, but what?

In this section, we look into the issue concerning cyclic Dependencies, including an example. When we're finished, your first reaction should be to try to redesign your Dependencies. If that isn't possible, you can break the cycle by refactoring from

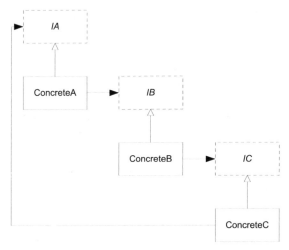

Figure 6.7 Cycles in the dependency graph can occur even if the Abstractions have no relations to each other. In this example, each implementation implements a separate interface but also requires a Dependency. Because ConcreteC requires IA, but the only implementation of IA is ConcreteA with its Dependency on IB and so forth, we have a cycle that can't be resolved as is.

CONSTRUCTOR INJECTION to PROPERTY INJECTION. This represents a loosening of a class's invariants, so it isn't something you should do lightly.

6.3.1 *Addressing Dependency cycles*

Whenever I encounter a DEPENDENCY cycle, my first question is, "Where did I fail?"

> **TIP** A DEPENDENCY cycle is a design smell. If one appears, you should seriously reconsider your design.

A DEPENDENCY cycle should immediately trigger a thorough evaluation of the root cause of the cycle. It's often based on either incorrect assumptions or a serious break of the rule of unidirectional DEPENDENCIES. In a layered application, classes should only talk to other classes in their own layer and the layer immediately below.

If the cycle traverses more than one layer, we know something is fundamentally wrong. As figure 6.8 shows, this would mean that some references go the wrong way.

It's a little less clear what is going on if we have a cycle within a single layer. This may even be the result of valid considerations that just ended up as less-than-optimal implementations.

It's imperative that we break a cycle in some way. As long as the cycle exists, the application won't run.

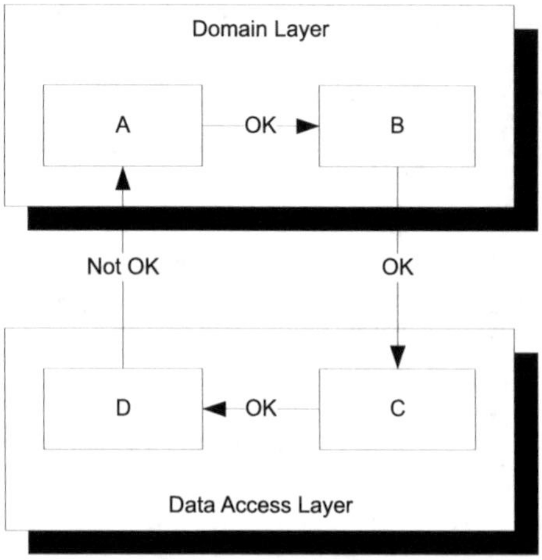

Figure 6.8 When a cycle crosses one or more layer boundaries, at least one reference is architecturally illegal. In this case, the reference from D to A is the culprit. If a situation like this occurs, it should be addressed immediately.

Any cycle is a design smell, so our first reaction should be to redesign the involved part to prevent the cycle from happening in the first place. Table 6.1 shows some general directions we can take.

I don't intend to elaborate upon the first option because the existing literature already provides detailed treatment.

> **TIP** Attempt to address cycles by using events. If that fails, try an Observer. Only if you're still unsuccessful should you consider breaking the cycle by using PROPERTY INJECTION.

Make no mistake: a DEPENDENCY cycle is a design smell. Our first priority should be to analyze the code to understand why the cycle appears. When we understand why, we should change the design.

Still, sometimes we can't change the design. Even if we understand the root cause of the cycle, the offending API may be out of our control.

Table 6.1 Some redesign strategies for breaking DEPENDENCY cycles

Strategy	Description
Events	You can often break a cycle by changing one of the ABSTRACTIONS to raise events instead of having to explicitly invoke a DEPENDENCY to inform the DEPENDENCY that something happened.
	Events are particularly appropriate if one side only invokes void methods on its DEPENDENCY.
	.NET events are an application of the Observer[7] design pattern, and you may occasionally consider implementing it explicitly. This is particularly true if you decide to use Domain Events[8] to break the cycle. This has the potential to enable true asynchronous one-way messaging.
PROPERTY INJECTION	If all else fails, we can break the cycle by refactoring one class from CONSTRUCTOR INJECTION to PROPERTY INJECTION.
	This should be a last-ditch effort because it only treats the symptoms.

BREAKING THE CYCLE WITH PROPERTY INJECTION

In some cases, the design error is out of our control, but we still need to break the cycle. In such cases, we can break the cycle by using PROPERTY INJECTION.

> **WARNING** You should only resort to solving cycles by using PROPERTY INJECTION as a last-ditch effort. It only treats the symptoms instead of curing the illness.

To break the cycle, we must analyze it to figure out where we can make a cut. Because using PROPERTY INJECTION suggests an optional rather than a required DEPENDENCY, it's important that we closely inspect all DEPENDENCIES to determine where cutting hurts the least.

In figure 6.9, B requires an instance of IC (the interface that C implements). We can resolve the cycle by changing B's DEPENDENCY from CONSTRUCTOR INJECTION to PROPERTY INJECTION. This means that we can create B first and inject it into A, and then subsequently assign C to B:

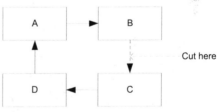

Figure 6.9 Given a cycle, we must first decide where to cut it. In this case, we decide to cut between B and C.

```
var b = new B();
var a = new A(b);
b.C = new C(new D(a));
```

Using PROPERTY INJECTION this way adds extra complexity to B because it must now be able to deal with the case where its DEPENDENCY isn't yet available.

> **TIP** Classes should never perform work involving DEPENDENCIES in their constructors because the injected DEPENDENCY may not yet be fully initialized.

---

[7] Ibid., 293.

[8] Udi Dahan, "Domain Models: Employing the Domain Model Pattern" (*MSDN Magazine*, August 2009), http://msdn.microsoft.com/en-us/magazine/ee236415.aspx

If we don't wish to loosen any of the original classes in this way, we can introduce a Virtual Proxy[9] that leaves B intact:

```
var lb = new LazyB();
var a = new A(lb);
lb.B = new B(new C(new D(a)));
```

LazyB implements IB just like B does. However, it takes its IB DEPENDENCY through PROPERTY INJECTION instead of CONSTRUCTOR INJECTION, allowing us to break the cycle without violating the invariants of any of the original classes.

Although classes with the imaginative names A–D illustrate the structure of a solution, a more realistic example is warranted.

6.3.2   *Example: composing a window*

One of the most common situations where we can't redesign our way out of a DEPENDENCY cycle is when we deal with external APIs. One such example is WPF.

In WPF, we can use the MVVM[10] pattern to implement separation of concerns by splitting the code into Views and underlying models. The models are assigned to the Views through a DataContext property. This is essentially PROPERTY INJECTION at work.

> **TIP** You can read more about composing WPF applications with MVVM in section 7.4.

A DataContext serves as the Window's DEPENDENCY, but the model plays a large part in controlling which Views are activated where. One of the actions a model must be able to perform is to pop up a dialog box. And one way to implement this is by injecting an ABSTRACTION like this into the model:

```
public interface IWindow
{
    void Close();

    IWindow CreateChild(object viewModel);

    void Show();

    bool? ShowDialog();
}
```

With an injected IWindow, any model can create new Windows and display them as modal or modeless windows. However, to implement this interface, we need a reference to the real Window to properly set the Owner property. The following listing shows the implementation of the CreateChild method.

---

[9] Gamma, *Design Patterns*, 208.

[10] Josh Smith, "Patterns: WPF Apps With The Model-View-ViewModel Design Pattern" (*MSDN Magazine*, February 2009), http://msdn.microsoft.com/en-us/magazine/dd419663.aspx

Listing 6.2 Creating a child window

```
public virtual IWindow CreateChild(object viewModel)
{
    var cw = new ContentWindow();
    cw.Owner = this.wpfWindow;
    cw.DataContext = viewModel;
    WindowAdapter.ConfigureBehavior(cw);

    return new WindowAdapter(cw);
}
```

ContentWindow is a WPF Window you can use to show a new window. It's important to set the owner of a Window before showing it, because otherwise weird bugs can occur where a focused or modal window is hidden behind other windows. To prevent such bugs, you set the Owner property to the current Window. The wpfWindow field is another instance of System.Windows.Window.

You also assign the viewModel to the new Window's DataContext before wrapping it in a new IWindow implementation and returning it.

The issue is that with this implementation, you have ViewModels that require IWindow, an IWindow implementation that requires a WPF Window, and WPF Windows that through their DataContext require a ViewModel to work. Figure 6.10 shows this cycle.

There is no reasonable kind of redesign you can apply to get out of the

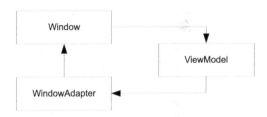

Figure 6.10 A WPF MVVM cycle. In MVVM, a Window **depends on a** ViewModel**, which in turn depends on an** IWindow **instance. The proper implementation of** IWindow **is** WindowAdapter**, which depends on a WPF** Window **to be able to set the owner of each** Window **to avoid focus bugs.**

circular DEPENDENCY. The relationship between Window and ViewModel is fixed because System.Windows.Window is an external API (defined in the Base Class Library [BCL]). Likewise, WindowAdapter depends on a Window to avoid focus bugs, so this relationship is also externally given.

The only relationship you can change is between a ViewModel and its IWindow. Technically, you could redesign this to use events, but that would lead to a rather counter-intuitive API. To show a dialog box, you would have to raise an event and hope someone subscribes by showing a modal window. Furthermore, you would have to return the result of the dialog box by reference via the original event arguments. Raising the event would be a blocking call. This would be technically possible, but strange, so we'll rule that out.

It seems we can't redesign our way out of the cycle, so how do we break it?

BREAKING THE CYCLE

We need to find a relationship where we can cut the cycle to introduce PROPERTY INJEC-TION. In this case it's easy, because the relationship between a WPF `Window` and a View-Model already uses PROPERTY INJECTION. This is where we'll cut.

The simplest solution is to wire up anything else and set the `DataContext` property on the `MainWindow` as the last thing before showing it. This is possible but not particularly DI CONTAINER–friendly, because it would require us to explicitly assign a DEPENDENCY after composition has been performed.

As an alternative, we can encapsulate this deferred assignment in a lazy-loading adapter. This enables us to wire up everything properly with a DI CONTAINER.

> **NOTE** The following example draws on the same project that is also described in section 7.4.2. You can see all the code in the code download for the book.

Let's see how to encapsulate creation of an `IWindow` implementation that correctly bootstraps a `MainWindowViewModel` and assigns it to a WPF `MainWindow` instance. To help do that, you introduce this Abstract Factory:

```
public interface IMainWindowViewModelFactory
{
    MainWindowViewModel Create(IWindow window);
}
```

The `MainWindowViewModel` class has more than one DEPENDENCY, but all the DEPENDEN-CIES other than `IWindow` can be satisfied immediately, so you don't need to supply them as a parameter to the `Create` method. Instead, you can inject them into the concrete implementation of `IMainWindowViewModelFactory`.

You use `IMainWindowViewModelFactory` as a DEPENDENCY in an implementation of `IWindow` derived from the `WindowAdapter` glimpsed in listing 6.2. This enables you to defer initialization of the `IWindow` implementation until the first method is invoked. Here you see how the `CreateChild` method from listing 6.2 is overridden:

```
public override IWindow CreateChild(object viewModel)
{
    this.EnsureInitialized();
    return base.CreateChild(viewModel);
}
```

Before performing any real work, you must make sure that all DEPENDENCIES are fully initialized. When they are, you can safely invoke the base implementation.

The next listing shows how the `EnsureInitialized` method is implemented using the injected `IMainWindowViewModelFactory`.

Listing 6.3   Deferred initialization of DEPENDENCIES

```
private void EnsureInitialized()
{
    if (this.initialized)
    {
```

```
        return;
    }

    var vm = this.vmFactory.Create(this);
    this.WpfWindow.DataContext = vm;
    this.DeclareKeyBindings(vm);

    this.initialized = true;
}
```

❶ Create ViewModel

❷ Inject ViewModel into Window

When initializing the `MainWindowAdapter`, you first invoke the injected Abstract Factory to produce the desired `ViewModel` ❶. This is possible at this point because the `MainWindowAdapter` instance is already created; and because it implements `IWindow`, you can pass the instance to the `Create` method.

When you have the `ViewModel`, you can assign it to the `DataContext` of the encapsulated WPF `Window` ❷. With a bit of further setup, the `Window` is now fully initialized and ready for use.

In the application's COMPOSITION ROOT, you can wire it all up like this:

```
IMainWindowViewModelFactory vmFactory =
    new MainWindowViewModelFactory(agent);

Window mainWindow = new MainWindow();
IWindow w =
    new MainWindowAdapter(mainWindow, vmFactory);
```

The `mainWindow` variable becomes the `WpfWindow` property in listing 6.3, and `vmFactory` matches the field of the same name. When you invoke the `Show` or `Show-Dialog` method on the resulting `IWindow`, the `EnsureInitialize` method is invoked and all DEPENDENCIES are satisfied.

This combination of a deferred initialization with the help of an Abstract Factory can be a nice extra touch, but it's the presence of PROPERTY INJECTION that enables you to break the cycle in the first place. In this case you were "lucky" because a WPF `Window` already uses PROPERTY INJECTION through its `DataContext` property.

Always keep in mind that the best way to address a cycle is to redesign the API so that the cycle disappears. However, in the rare cases where this is impossible or highly undesirable, we must break the cycle by using PROPERTY INJECTION in at least one place. This enables us to compose the rest of the object graph apart from the DEPENDENCY associated with the property. When the rest of the object graph is fully populated, we can inject the appropriate instance via the property. As an optional extra touch, we can encapsulate this property-assignment logic in a class and use an Abstract Factory to assign the property value at the last possible moment.

PROPERTY INJECTION signals that a DEPENDENCY is optional, so we shouldn't make the change lightly. CONSTRUCTOR INJECTION is much preferred in most cases, but it may make some people uneasy. Let's see why.

6.4   *Dealing with Constructor Over-injection*

Unless you have special requirements, CONSTRUCTOR INJECTION should be your preferred injection pattern. However, some people become uncomfortable when the number of DEPENDENCIES grows. They don't like a constructor with too many parameters.

In this section, we'll look at the apparent problem of a growing number of constructor parameters and why this is a good thing rather than a bad thing. As you'll see, it doesn't mean we should accept long parameter lists in constructors, so we'll also review what we can do about too many constructor arguments. An example rounds off the section.

6.4.1   *Recognizing and addressing Constructor Over-injection*

When a constructor's parameter list grows too large, we call the phenomenon *Constructor Over-injection*[11] and consider it a code smell. It's a general code smell unrelated to, but magnified by, DI. Although our initial reaction might be that we don't like CONSTRUCTOR INJECTION because of Constructor Over-injection, we should be thankful that a general design issue is revealed to us.

In this section, we'll first take a moment to appreciate how Constructor Over-injection makes our lives a little easier, and then consider appropriate reactions.

CONSTRUCTOR OVER-INJECTION AS A SIGNAL

Although CONSTRUCTOR INJECTION is easy to implement and use, it makes people uncomfortable when their constructors start looking like this:

```
public MyClass(IUnitOfWorkFactory uowFactory,
    CurrencyProvider currencyProvider,
    IFooPolicy fooPolicy,
    IBarService barService,
    ICoffeeMaker coffeeMaker,
    IKitchenSink kitchenSink)
```

I can't say I blame anyone for disliking such a constructor, but don't blame CONSTRUCTOR INJECTION. We can agree that a constructor with six parameters is a code smell, but it indicates a violation of the SINGLE RESPONSIBILITY PRINCIPLE rather than a problem related to DI.

> **TIP**   CONSTRUCTOR INJECTION makes it easy to spot SINGLE RESPONSIBILITY PRINCIPLE violations.

Instead of feeling uneasy about Constructor Over-injection, we should embrace it as a fortunate side effect of CONSTRUCTOR INJECTION. It's a signal that alerts us whenever a class takes on too much responsibility.

My personal threshold lies at four constructor arguments. Whenever I add a third argument, I begin considering whether I could design things differently, but I can live

---

[11] Jeffrey Palermo, "Constructor over-injection smell—follow up," 2010, http://jeffreypalermo.com/blog/constructor-over-injection-smell-ndash-follow-up/

with four arguments for a few classes. Your limit may be different, but when you cross it, it's time to refactor.

How we refactor a particular class that has grown too big depends on the particular circumstances: the object model already in place, the domain, business logic, and so on. Splitting up a budding God Class[12] into smaller, more focused classes according to well-known design patterns is always a good move.

Still, there are cases where business requirements oblige us to do a lot of different things at the same time. This is often the case at the boundary of an application. Think about a coarse-grained web service operation that triggers many business events. One way to model such operations is by hiding the myriad DEPENDENCIES behind Facade Services.

REFACTORING TO FACADE SERVICES

There are many ways we can design and implement collaborators so that they don't violate the SINGLE RESPONSIBILITY PRINCIPLE. In chapter 9, we'll discuss how the Decorator[13] design pattern can help us stack CROSS-CUTTING CONCERNS instead of injecting them into consumers as services. This can eliminate a lot of constructor arguments.

Still, in some scenarios a single entry point needs to orchestrate many DEPENDENCIES. One example is a web service operation that triggers a complex interaction of many different services. The entry point of a scheduled batch job may face the same issue.

Figure 6.11 shows how we can refactor key relationships into Facade Services.

Refactoring to Facade Services is more than just a party trick to get rid of too many DEPENDENCIES. The key is to identify *natural* clusters of interaction. In figure 6.11, it turns out that DEPENDENCIES A–C form a natural cluster of interaction, and so do D and E.

A beneficial side effect is that discovering these natural clusters draws previously undiscovered relations and domain concepts out in the open. In the process, we turn implicit concepts into explicit concepts.[14] Each Facade becomes a service that captures this interaction on a higher level, and the consumer's single responsibility becomes to orchestrate these high-level services.

NOTE   Facade Services are abstract Facades[15]—hence the name.

Facade Services are related to *Parameter Objects*,[16] but instead of combining and exposing components, a Facade Service exposes only the encapsulated behavior, while hiding the constituents.

---

[12] William J. Brown, et al., *AntiPatterns: Refactoring Software, Architectures, and Projects in Crisis* (New York: Wiley Computer Publishing, 1998), 73.

[13] Gamma, *Design Patterns*, 175.

[14] Evans, *Domain-Driven Design*, 206-223.

[15] Gamma, *Design Patterns*, 185.

[16] Martin Fowler et al., *Refactoring: Improving the Design of Existing Code* (New York: Addison-Wesley, 1999), 295.

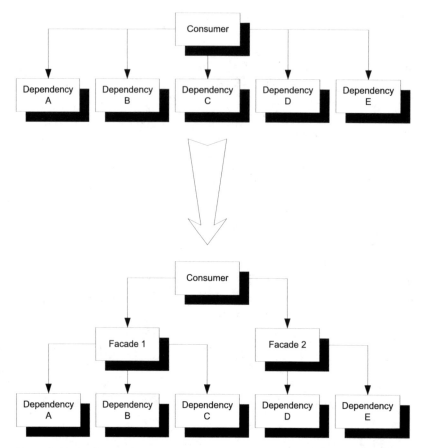

Figure 6.11   In the top diagram, the consumer has five DEPENDENCIES, which is a strong indication that it violates the SINGLE RESPONSIBILITY PRINCIPLE. Still, if the role of the consumer is to orchestrate those five DEPENDENCIES, we can't throw any away. Instead, we can introduce Facade Services that orchestrate parts of the relationship. In the bottom diagram, the consumer has only two DEPENDENCIES, and the Facades have two and three DEPENDENCIES.

Obviously, we can repeat this refactoring if we have such a complex application that the consumer ends up with too many DEPENDENCIES on Facade Services. Creating a Facade for Facade Services is a perfectly sensible thing to do.

Close to the boundary of our application (such as the UI or a web service), we can operate with a set of rather coarse-grained ABSTRACTIONS. As we examine the implementations of DEPENDENCIES, we see that behind coarse-grained services are finer-grained services, which are combinations of even finer-grained services. This enables us to quickly get an overview at the entry level while ensuring that each final implementation adheres to the SINGLE RESPONSIBILITY PRINCIPLE.

Let's look at an example.

6.4.2 *Example: refactoring order reception*

The sample commerce application that we look at from time to time needs to be able to receive orders. This is often best done by a separate application or subsystem because at that point the semantics of the transaction change.

As long as you're looking at a shopping basket, you can dynamically calculate unit prices, exchange rates, and discounts; but when a customer places an order, all those values must be captured and frozen as they were presented when the customer approved the order. Table 6.2 provides an overview of the order-reception process.

Table 6.2   When the order subsystem receives a new order, it must perform a number of different actions.

Action	Required DEPENDENCIES
Save the order	OrderRepository
Send a receipt email to the customer	IMessageService
Notify the accounting system about the invoice amount	IBillingSystem
Select the best warehouses to pick and ship the order based on the items in the order and proximity to the shipping address	ILocationService, IInventoryManagement
Ask the selected warehouses to pick and ship the entire order or parts of it	IInventoryManagement

Five different DEPENDENCIES are required just to receive an order. Imagine which other DEPENDENCIES you would need to handle other order-related operations!

Let's first review how this would look if the consuming OrderService class directly imported all these DEPENDENCIES; subsequently, you'll see how you can refactor the functionality by using Facade Services.

TOO MANY FINE-GRAINED DEPENDENCIES

If you let OrderService directly consume all five DEPENDENCIES, the structure is as shown in figure 6.12.

If you use CONSTRUCTOR INJECTION for the OrderService class (which you should), you have a constructor with five parameters. This is too many and indicates that the OrderService has too many responsibilities. On the other hand, all these DEPENDENCIES are required because the OrderService class must implement all of the desired functionality when it receives a new order.

You can address this issue by redesigning OrderService.

REFACTORING TO FACADE SERVICES

The first thing you need to do is to look for natural clusters of interaction to identify potential Facade Services. The interaction between ILocationService and IInventoryManagement should immediately draw your attention, because you use them to find the closest warehouses that can fulfill the order. This could potentially be a complex algorithm, but after you've selected the warehouses you need to notify them about the order.

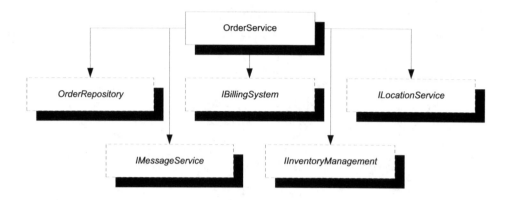

Figure 6.12 `OrderService` **has five direct DEPENDENCIES, indicating that it violates the SINGLE RESPONSIBILITY PRINCIPLE.**

If you think about this a little further, `ILocationService` is an implementation detail of notifying the appropriate warehouses about the order. The entire interaction can be hidden behind an `IOrderFulfillment` interface, as shown in figure 6.13. Interestingly, *order fulfillment* sounds a lot like a domain concept in its own right; chances are that you just discovered an implicit domain concept and made it explicit.

The default implementation of `IOrderFulfillment` consumes the two original DEPENDENCIES, so it has a constructor with two parameters, which is fine. As a further benefit, you've encapsulated the algorithm for finding the best warehouse for a given order into a reusable component.

This refactoring collapses two DEPENDENCIES into one but leaves you with four DEPENDENCIES of the `OrderService` class. You need to look for other opportunities to aggregate DEPENDENCIES into a Facade.

The next thing you may notice is that all the requirements involve notifying other systems about the order. This suggests that you can define a common ABSTRACTION that models notifications—perhaps something like this following code snippet:

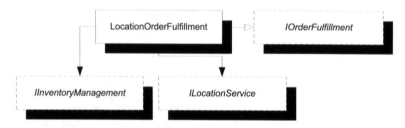

Figure 6.13   **The interaction between** `IInventoryManagement` **and** `ILocationService` **is implemented in the** `LocationOrderFulfillment` **class, which implements the** `IOrderFulfillment` **interface. Consumers of the** `IOrderFulfillment` **interface have no idea that the implementation has two DEPENDENCIES.**

```
public interface INotificationService
{
    void OrderAdded(Order order);
}
```

TIP The Domain Event design pattern is another good alternative in this scenario.

Each notification to an external system can be implemented using this interface. You can even consider wrapping `OrderRepository` in `INotificationService`, but it's likely that the `OrderService` class will need access to other methods on `OrderRepository` to implement other functionality. Figure 6.14 shows how you implement the other notifications using `INotificationService`.

You may wonder how this helps, because you've wrapped each DEPENDENCY in a new interface. The number of DEPENDENCIES didn't decrease, so did you gain anything?

Yes. Because all three notifications implement the same interface, you can wrap them in a Composite.[17] This is another implementation of `INotificationService` that decorates a collection of `INotificationService` instances and invokes the `OrderAdded` method on them all.

From a conceptual perspective, this also makes sense because from a high-level view you don't care about the details of how `OrderService` notifies other systems. However, you do care that it does. Figure 6.15 shows the final DEPENDENCIES of `OrderService`.

This reduces `OrderService` to only two DEPENDENCIES, which is a much more reasonable number. Functionality is unchanged, making this a true refactoring. On the other hand, the conceptual level of `OrderService` changed. Its responsibility is now to receive an order, save it, and notify other systems. The details of which systems are notified and how this is implemented have been pushed down to a more detailed level.

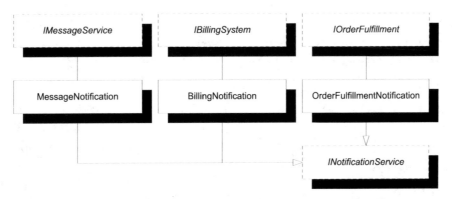

Figure 6.14 Every notification to an external system can be hidden behind the `INotificationService`—**even the new** `IOrderFulfillment` **interface you just introduced.**

---

[17] Gamma, *Design Patterns*, 163.

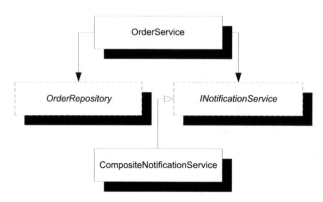

Figure 6.15   The final `OrderService` **with refactored DEPENDENCIES. You keep** `OrderRepository` **as a separate DEPENDENCY because you need its additional methods to implement other functionality of** `OrderService`. **All the other notifications are hidden behind the** `INotificationService` **interface. At runtime, you use a** `CompositeNotification-Service` **that contains the remaining three notifications.**

Even though you consistently use CONSTRUCTOR INJECTION throughout, no single class's constructor ends up requiring more than two parameters (`CompositeNotification-Service` takes an `IEnumerable<INotificationService>` as a single argument).

Constructor Over-injection isn't a problem related to DI in general or CONSTRUCTOR INJECTION specifically. Rather, it's a signal that the class in question has too many responsibilities. The code smell comes from the class, not CONSTRUCTOR INJECTION; and as always, we should regard the smell as an opportunity to improve the code.

There are many ways we can refactor to patterns, but one option is to introduce Facade Services that model concepts at a higher abstraction level. This addresses the violation of the SINGLE RESPONSIBILITY PRINCIPLE and often draws out previously undiscovered domain concepts in the process.

This is one of the many ways DI helps us write better code. Because loose coupling is so valuable, we want to make sure loosely coupled code stays loosely coupled. The next section discusses how to do that.

6.5   *Monitoring coupling*

Loose coupling is valuable, but it's surprisingly easy to introduce tight coupling. All it takes is a novice developer and a moment of inattention, and a hard reference may be introduced. In Visual Studio, it's easy to add new references to an existing project, but this is often what we want to avoid. Discipline must be observed to ensure that each module focuses on its own area of responsibility.

In this section, we'll look at some techniques that can be useful when we want to make sure loosely coupled code stays loosely coupled. Perhaps we want to protect the code against our mistakes, or perhaps junior developers on the team need a bit of help.

Nothing beats human interaction when it comes to transferring knowledge. Pair programming is ideal, but it may still be a good idea to back up manual review with automated tooling. In the next sections, we'll look at how automated testing can be helpful, along with a dedicated tool called NDepend.

6.5.1   Unit-testing coupling

If we have a unit-test suite that we run regularly, we can quickly add a few unit tests that examine DEPENDENCIES and fail if an unwarranted dependency is detected. Using the type system in .NET, we can easily write a unit test that loops through all of an assembly's references and fails if it finds one that shouldn't be there.[18]

The Commerce sample application already has unit tests in place, so you can easily add one more. The following listing shows a unit test that protects the Presentation Logic module from directly referencing the SQL Server–based Data Access module.

Listing 6.4   Enforcing loose coupling with a unit test

```
[Fact]
public void SutShouldNotReferenceSqlDataAccess()
{
    // Fixture setup
    Type sutRepresentative = typeof(HomeController);
    var unwanted = "Ploeh.Samples.Commerce.Data.Sql";
    // Exercise system
    var references =
        sutRepresentative.Assembly
        .GetReferencedAssemblies();
    // Verify outcome
    Assert.False(
        references.Any(a => a.Name == unwanted),
        string.Format(
            "{0} should not be referenced by SUT",
            unwanted));
    // Teardown
}
```

This test looks for DEPENDENCIES of the Presentation Logic module. To get the list of references, you need to query the assembly in question. You can get the assembly from *any* type contained within that assembly, so you can pick one. It's often a good idea to choose a type you expect to stay around for the long haul, because otherwise you'll have to rewrite the test if you ever delete the type you selected. This test chooses Home-Controller because the website will always have a front page.

You also need to identify the assembly you wish to prevent from being referenced. You could use the same technique and pick a representative type from that assembly, but that would mean you need to reference that assembly from the unit test. This isn't quite as bad as referencing the unwanted assembly from the production code, but it would still create an artificial coupling between these two libraries—you could say they become guilty by association. Although type safety is desirable, loose coupling trumps in this case, so instead you identify the unwanted assembly with a string (but see the following discussion for alternatives).

[18] This idea was presented in Glenn Block, "PrismShouldNotReferenceUnity," 2008, http://blogs.msdn.com/b/gblock/archive/2008/05/05/prismshouldnotreferenceunity.aspx

Getting the referenced assemblies from the representative type is as easy as a single method call. You can now use a simple LINQ query to verify that none of the referenced assemblies have the unwanted name. In the assertion, you also print out a message to display if the assertion fails.

TIP This assertion uses a simple LINQ query, but you can replace it with a `foreach` loop if you're developing on .NET 3.0 or earlier versions.

TIP You can also reverse the logic and write the test so that only specific references on a predefined list are allowed and all other references are considered illegal.

Testing coupling with Red/Green/Refactor

If you're using Test-Driven Development (TDD) to implement your code, you're used to the so-called Red/Green/Refactor development cycle where you first write a failing test, then make it pass, and finally modify the code to make it more maintainable.

It turns out that making a tight-coupling-preventing test *fail* is more difficult than you may think. Even if the targeted Visual Studio project has a reference to the undesirable DEPENDENCY, the compiler will only include the reference if it's being used.

Thus, to make such a test fail, we must first add the reference we don't want and then write a line of dummy code that uses a type from the unwanted DEPENDENCY. As soon as we've seen the test fail, we can then reverse the process to make it pass. This is obviously not a problem if the library under test *already* violates the coupling constraint.

The previous example adds the unit test to an existing unit-test suite that targets the Presentation Logic module. Figure 6.16 illustrates the references in action.

Listing 6.4 identifies the unwanted assembly with a simple string, but it would have been more type-safe to identify it using a representative type. However, that would require you to add a reference to the SQL Server–based Data Access module to the unit test, as shown in figure 6.17.

You may think that adding an extra reference to a unit-test project can't be that bad, but doing so has more disadvantages than are immediately apparent.

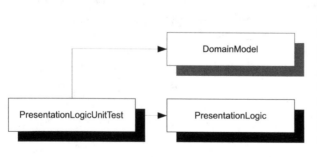

Figure 6.16 The `Presentation-LogicUnitTest` **library is a test suite that targets the** `PresentationLogic` **library. To do that, it needs a reference to its target as well as the shared** ABSTRACTIONS **that are defined in the Domain Model. Because** `PresentationLogicUnitTest` **doesn't target the Domain Model, the** `DomainModel` **module is shown in gray.**

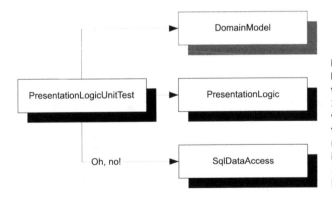

Figure 6.17   **If we want type safety by adding a representative type from the SqlDataAccess library to PresentationLogicUnitTest, we introduce a new DEPENDENCY to the unit-test suite for the sole reason that we want to make sure it's never accidentally added to the PresentationLogic library. Ironic, isn't it?**

Indirect dependencies

A detailed treatment of why a unit-test project should only reference the project it targets is outside the scope of this book, but the overall problem is that it creates an indirect dependency between PresentationModel and SqlDataAccess. Although both of these projects can exist and compile without the other, the unit-test project ties them together.

This indirect dependency can only be broken by throwing away the unit test that originally caused the dependency to exist. However, unit tests are written to be executed, so this is far from desirable.

If we want to keep such tight-coupling-preventing unit tests within an existing unit-test project, the cost of adding a hard reference to all the unwanted assemblies is too great. The best option is to identify the unwelcome DEPENDENCIES using strings, as shown in listing 6.4.

The disadvantage is that if we change the name of the prohibited assembly, the test becomes worthless—or maybe even worse than worthless, because we may think we're protected when we aren't.

This isn't a major issue if we have reason to believe that assembly names are stable. When this isn't the case, we need a different strategy.

6.5.2   *Integration-testing coupling*

There are compelling reasons why unit-test projects should only reference their targets. Yet to stay robust in the face of changing assembly names, we may at times need type-safe references to all the undesirable DEPENDENCIES. These sound like contradictory requirements, but we can solve this conundrum by introducing a new *integration-test* project.

You can add a new test project to the Commerce solution and add all the references you need. Figure 6.18 shows this solution; and although it looks a lot like figure 6.17, the difference is that for the integration test, all the references are legal and equally valid.

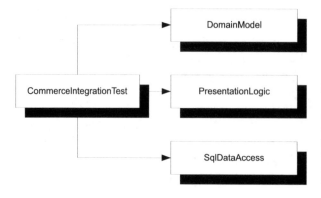

Figure 6.18 The `Commerce-IntegrationTest` **project contains automated tests that verify that the relationships between modules are correct. Unlike unit tests, an integration-test suite can contain as many references as are necessary to perform the test.**

Integration tests

An *integration test* is another type of automated test at the API level. The difference between a unit test and an integration test is that a unit test deals with the unit in isolation, whereas integration tests focus on verifying that several units (often across different libraries) integrate with each other as intended.

Per definition, an integration-test project can reference all the DEPENDENCIES it needs to do its job, so it's well suited to containing tests that enforce architectural constraints.

An integration-test suite is tightly coupled to a particular constellation of modules, so it's much less reusable. It must be constrained to only contain the tests that absolutely only can be defined as integration tests, and tests that protect against unwanted coupling may belong in this category. Listing 6.5 shows a type-safe equivalent to the test in listing 6.4. It follows the same blueprint but varies when it comes to identifying the unwanted DEPENDENCY.

Listing 6.5 Enforcing loose coupling with an integration test

```
[Fact]
public void PresentationModuleShouldNotReferenceSqlDataAccess()
{
    // Fixture setup
    Type presentationRepresentative =
        typeof(HomeController);
    Type sqlRepresentative =
        typeof(SqlProductRepository);
    // Exercise system
    var references =
        presentationRepresentative.Assembly        ❶ Get referenced
        .GetReferencedAssemblies();                   assemblies
    // Verify outcome
    AssemblyName sqlAssemblyName =
        sqlRepresentative.Assembly.GetName();       ❷ Get assembly
    AssemblyName presentationAssemblyName =            names
        presentationRepresentative.Assembly.GetName();
```

```
Assert.False(references.Any(a =>
    AssemblyName.ReferenceMatchesDefinition(
        sqlAssemblyName, a)),
    string.Format(
        "{0} should not be referenced by {1}",
        sqlAssemblyName,
        presentationAssemblyName));
// Teardown
}
```

❸ Look for unwanted Dependency

Now that you have references to all necessary DEPENDENCIES, you can pick a type from each module that you can use to represent their assemblies. In contrast with the previous example, you can identify both in a type-safe way.

Just as you did before, you retrieve a list of all the assemblies the Presentation-Logic library references ❶. Using the AssemblyName of each assembly ❷, you then verify that the references don't contain the SQL Server–based assembly ❸. The built-in static ReferenceMatchesDefinition method compares AssemblyNames.

You may have noticed that the tests in listings 6.4 and 6.5 are similar. You could write new tests like the one in listing 6.5 by varying the two representative types and keep everything else constant.

The next logical step would be to extract the common part of the test into a Parameterized Test.[19] This would allow you to write a simple list of almost declarative tests that define what is and isn't allowed in this particular constellation of modules.

Unit tests and integration tests are great options if you're already using automated API-level tests. If not, you should start doing so today, but there are also other alternatives.

6.5.3 *Using NDepend to monitor coupling*

If for some unfathomable reason you don't wish to use unit tests, you can use a tool called NDepend (http://ndepend.com) to warn you if you or your team members introduce unwanted coupling.

NDepend is a commercial software tool that analyzes projects or solutions and reports a lot of statistics about the code. As an example, it can generate dependency graphs not unlike the ones you've seen throughout this book. If we analyze Mary's original commerce solution from chapter 2, we get the graph shown in figure 6.19.

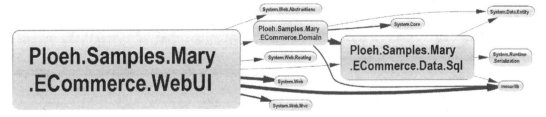

Figure 6.19 Dependency graph generated by NDepend for Mary's commerce solution. By default, NDepend includes all DEPENDENCIES, including modules from the BCL. The size of the boxes reflects the number of code lines in each module, and the thickness of the arrows reflects the number of members used across the references.

---

[19] Gerard Meszaros, *xUnit Test Patterns: Refactoring Test Code* (New York: Addison-Wesley, 2007), 607.

This looks complicated, but we can hide the BCL modules and rearrange the view to arrive at figure 6.20.

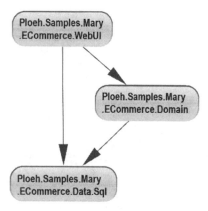

Does figure 6.20 look familiar? If you have eidetic memory, you may recall figure 2.10; but otherwise you can flip back to it. Notice how they share the same structure and illustrate the same relationship.

NDepend can do much more than draw pretty graphs. One of its most powerful features is the Code Query Language (CQL), which lets us query our code about a wide range of information with syntax reminiscent of SQL.

Figure 6.20   Modified NDepend graph for Mary's commerce solution. In this graph, I've manually removed all BCL modules and made the boxes and arrows the same size.

If Mary had written a CQL check before developing her solution, she would have been warned before much damage had been done. Here is a query that could have saved her a lot of trouble:

```
WARN IF Count > 0 IN SELECT ASSEMBLIES WHERE
IsDirectlyUsing "ASSEMBLY:Ploeh.Samples.Mary.ECommerce.Data.Sql" AND
NameIs "Ploeh.Samples.Mary.ECommerce.Domain"
```

When executed, this CQL query issues a warning if the Domain module directly references the SQL Server DataAccess module. In Mary's solution, this query indeed issues a warning.

We can write as many CQL queries for a solution as we like and either run them using a visual editor or automate the process using a command-line tool. In both cases, XML files with analysis results are generated, so we can write our own automation tools that take appropriate action if we want to include such a step in an automated build process.

> **NOTE**   I've only scratched the surface of NDepend's features. It can do many other things, but I wanted to focus on its ability to keep an eye on coupling.

NDepend and automated tests are two ways to automatically monitor code to ensure that illegal DEPENDENCIES don't sneak in by accident. We can use one or both of these methods as part of an automated Build Verification Test (BVT) or Continuous Integration (CI) effort.

In large code bases maintained by big teams, this can protect us from considerable grief. Although we can't keep an eye on everything that goes on and perform manual code reviews of every check-in, automated tools can alert us when suspect things happen.

> **WARNING**   Some tools may produce false positives, so don't blindly believe them when they tell you that you have a problem. Always use your experience and knowledge to evaluate warnings. Discard them if you don't agree.

Review each incident with the appropriate amount of care, and take personal action if it represents a real issue.

Consider using automated tools to monitor coupling in large code bases. Doing so can prevent inadvertent tight coupling from messing up your code base while you concentrate on the other challenges described in this chapter.

6.6   *Summary*

DI isn't particularly difficult when you understand a few basic principles, but as you learn, you're guaranteed to run into issues that may leave you stumped for a while. This chapter attempts to address some of the most common issues people encounter.

One of the most versatile and useful design patterns related to DI is Abstract Factory. We can use it to translate primitive runtime values such as strings or numbers entered by users to instances of complex ABSTRACTIONS. We can also use Abstract Factories in combination with the IDisposable interface to mimic short-lived DEPENDENCIES such as connections to external resources.

> **TIP**   Translate runtime values to DEPENDENCIES with Abstract Factories.

> **TIP**   Mimic connections with ABSTRACT FACTORIES that create disposable DEPENDENCIES.

A problem that sometimes arises is DEPENDENCY cycles. These tend to occur because of APIs that are too demanding. The more APIs are designed around a *query* paradigm, the more likely cycles become. We can avoid cycles by observing the Hollywood Principle (tell, don't ask). Methods with void signatures can be redesigned as events, which can often be used to break cycles. If a redesign is impossible, we can break a cycle by changing a single CONSTRUCTOR INJECTION to PROPERTY INJECTION. However, this shouldn't be done lightly, because it changes the semantics of the consumer.

> **TIP**   Break cycles with PROPERTY INJECTION.

CONSTRUCTOR INJECTION should be your preferred DI pattern; an additional benefit is that it becomes glaringly obvious every time you violate the SINGLE RESPONSIBILITY PRINCIPLE. When a single class has too many DEPENDENCIES, it's a signal that we should redesign it in some way. Perhaps we can split it into several smaller classes, but occasionally we need to keep all the functionality within a single class.

> **TIP**   Resolve Constructor Over-injection by refactoring to Facade Services.

In those cases, we can raise the abstraction level by inserting a layer of Facade Services between the consumer and the original DEPENDENCIES. Performing such a refactoring often results in the positive side effect that some of these Facade Services turn out to be previously undiscovered implicit domain concepts. Drawing implicit concepts out in the open and making them explicit is an improvement of the domain model.

While we perform these nitty-gritty refactorings, we must not lose sight of the big picture. Automated tests or tools can help us monitor whether tight coupling reappears in parts of the code base.

If we write a lot of unit tests (and particularly if we use Test-Driven Development), tight coupling will quickly manifest itself in complex and brittle test code. Or perhaps it's impossible to unit-test large pieces of an application.

TIP   Write automated tests to enforce loose coupling.

If we don't write unit tests, tight coupling may be overlooked, but we may experience many of its symptoms: as the code base evolves, it becomes more and more difficult to maintain. The nice clean design we originally intended slowly erodes into Spaghetti Code.[20] Adding a new feature requires us to touch the code base in many seemingly unrelated areas.

This chapter described solutions for issues commonly encountered with DI. Together with the two preceding chapters, it forms a catalog of patterns, anti-patterns, and refactorings. This catalog constitutes part 2 of the book. In part 3, we'll turn toward the three dimensions of DI: OBJECT COMPOSITION, LIFETIME MANAGEMENT, and INTERCEPTION.

---

[20] Brown, *AntiPatterns*, 119.

Part 3

DIY DI

In chapter 1, I gave a short outline of the three dimensions of DI: Object Composition, Lifetime Management, and Interception. In this part of the book, I expand this viewpoint into three distinct chapters. Many DI Containers have features that directly relate to these dimensions. Some provide features in all three dimensions, whereas others only support some of them.

However, because a DI Container is an optional tool, I feel that it's more important to explain the underlying principles and techniques that containers typically use to implement these features. Part 3 examines how you can *do-it-yourself* instead of using a DI Container. You can potentially use this information to build your own DI Container (but please don't—the world doesn't need yet another container) or apply DI without using a container at all—this is what we call Poor Man's DI. The main purpose of this part of the book, though, is to expose the underlying mechanisms of Object Composition, Lifetime Management, and Interception without having to use a specific DI Container. I think that had I used a specific container, it would have been difficult to distinguish general principles from specific API details.

Chapter 7 explains how to compose objects in various concrete frameworks such as ASP.NET MVC, WPF, WCF, and so on. Not all frameworks support DI equally well, and even among those that do, the ways they do it differ a lot. For each framework, it can be difficult to identify the Seam that enables DI in that framework. However, once that Seam is found, you have a solution for all applications that use this particular framework. In chapter 7, I have done this work for the most common .NET application frameworks. Think of it as a catalog of framework Seams.

Even if your particular framework of choice isn't covered, I've tried to address all the various sorts of framework limitations you may encounter. For instance, from a DI perspective, PowerShell is the most restrictive type of framework I can think of, so I use that as an example. You should be able to extrapolate a solution for similar frameworks, even if they aren't explicitly covered.

Although composing objects isn't particularly hard with POOR MAN'S DI, you should begin to see the benefits of a real DI CONTAINER after reading about LIFETIME MANAGEMENT. It's possible to properly manage the lifetime of various objects in an object graph, but it requires more custom code than OBJECT COMPOSITION, and none of that code adds any particular business value to an application.

In addition to explaining the basics of LIFETIME MANAGEMENT, chapter 8 also contains a catalog of common lifestyles. This catalog serves as a vocabulary for discussing lifestyles throughout part 4, so although you don't have to be able to implement any of these by hand, it's good to know how they work.

In chapter 9, we look at the frequently occurring problem of implementing CROSS-CUTTING CONCERNS in a component-based way. Going from a simple application of the Decorator design pattern all the way to run-time INTERCEPTION, we look at ways to compose loosely coupled applications in a modular way. I consider this chapter the climax of the book—this is where many readers during the early access program said they began to see the contours of a tremendously powerful way to model software.

Although I use POOR MAN'S DI to explore and explain DI, I don't recommend it for professional use. Many good DI CONTAINERS are available on .NET, and they are all free. Thus it's only fitting that part 4 is dedicated to detailed API coverage of specific containers.

Object Composition 7

Cooking a gourmet meal with several courses is a challenging undertaking, particularly if you wish to partake in the consumption. You can't very well eat and cook at the same time, yet many dishes require last-minute cooking to turn out well.

Professional cooks know how to resolve many of these challenges. Amidst many tricks of the trade, they use the general principle of *mise en place*, which can be loosely translated to *everything in place*: everything that can possibly be prepared well in advance is prepared in advance. Vegetables are cleaned and chopped, meats cut, stocks cooked, ovens preheated, tools laid out, and so on.

The *components* of the meal are prepared as much as possible. If ice cream is part of the dessert, it can be made the day before. If the first course contains mussels, they can be cleaned hours before. Even such a fragile component as sauce béarnaise

199

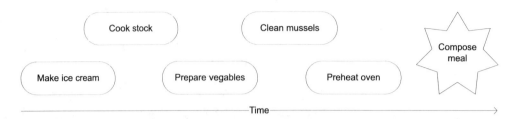

Figure 7.1 *Mise en place* **involves preparing all components of the meal well in advance so that the final composition of the meal can be done as quickly and effortlessly as possible.**

can be prepared up to an hour before. When the guests are ready to eat, only the final preparations are necessary: reheat the sauce while frying the meat, and so on. In many cases, this final *composition* of the meal need not take more than 5 to 10 minutes. Figure 7.1 illustrates the process.

The principle of *mise en place* is similar to developing a loosely coupled application with DI. We can write all the required components well in advance and only compose them when we absolutely must.

> **NOTE** In section 3.3.1, I compared the COMPOSITION ROOT to the concept of the *Last Responsible Moment* from Lean Software Development.[1] Comparing the COMPOSITION ROOT to *mise en place* is a similar analogy, although it highlights a slightly different aspect: composition.

As with all analogies, we can only take them so far. The difference is that in cooking, preparation and composition are separated over time, whereas in application development, this separation occurs across modules and layers. Figure 7.2 shows how we compose the components in the COMPOSITION ROOT (often the UI layer).

At runtime, the first thing that happens is this OBJECT COMPOSITION. As soon as the object graph is wired up, OBJECT COMPOSITION is finished, and the constituent components take over.

Although OBJECT COMPOSITION is the foundation of DI, it's one of the easiest

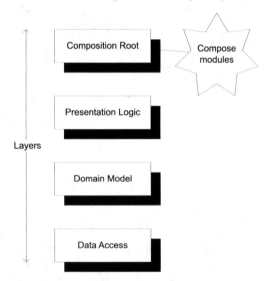

Figure 7.2 The COMPOSITION ROOT composes all the independent modules of the application. In contrast to *mise en place*, this doesn't happen as late as possible, but happens in a place where the integration of the different modules is required.

---

[1] See, for example, Mary Poppendieck and Tom Poppendieck, *Implementing Lean Software Development: From Concept to Cash* (New York: Addison-Wesley, 2007).

parts to understand. You already know how to do it, because you compose objects all the time when you create objects that contain other objects. In section 3.3, we covered the basics of when and how to compose applications. As a consequence, I don't intend to use the next 40 pages telling you how to compose objects.

Instead, I want to help you address some of the difficulties that may arise as you compose objects. Those difficulties stem not from OBJECT COMPOSITION itself, but rather from the application frameworks in which you wish to compose your objects. These issues tend to be specific to each framework, and so do the resolutions. In my experience, these challenges pose some of the greatest obstacles to successfully applying DI, so I'll focus on them. Doing so will make the chapter less theoretical and more practical than the previous chapters.

> **TIP** If you only want to read about applying DI in your framework of choice, you can skip ahead to that section. Each section is intended to stand alone.

It's easy to compose an application's entire dependency hierarchy when we have full control over the application's lifetime (as we do with command-line applications). However, most frameworks (ASP.NET, WCF, and so on) in .NET involve INVERSION OF CONTROL that can sometimes make it difficult to apply DI. Understanding each framework's SEAMS is the key to applying DI for that particular framework. As figure 7.3 illustrates, in this chapter we'll examine how to implement COMPOSITION ROOTS in some common Base Class Library (BCL) frameworks.

> **NOTE** Due to space constraints, I won't cover Windows Forms applications. However, when it comes to OBJECT COMPOSITION, they're similar to WPF applications.

Each section deals with one of these frameworks and can be read more or less independently. I'll begin each section with a general introduction to applying DI in that particular framework, followed by an extensive example that builds on the common Commerce example that runs through most of this book.

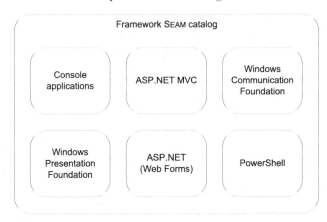

Figure 7.3 The structure of this chapter takes the form of a catalog of various BCL frameworks and the SEAMS they may have for enabling DI. Each section is written so that it can be read independently of the other sections.

We'll start with the easiest framework in which to apply DI and gradually work through more complex frameworks. When we reach ASP.NET, we need to cross an abyss beyond which we can only apply DI by compromising on at least some of our principles. There is no denying that frameworks such as ASP.NET and PowerShell are downright hostile environments in which to apply DI, so we must do the best we can. However, until we reach that point, there is no need to compromise.

A console application is probably the easiest type of application in which to apply DI.

7.1   *Composing console applications*

A console application is hands down the easiest type of application to compose. Contrary to most other BCL application frameworks, a console application involves virtually no INVERSION OF CONTROL. When execution hits the application's entry point (usually the `Main` method), we're on our own. There are no special events to subscribe to, no interfaces to implement, and precious few services we can use.

The `Main` method is a suitable COMPOSITION ROOT. The first thing we should do in the `Main` method is to compose the application's modules and let them take over. There's nothing to it, but let's look at an example.

7.1.1   *Example: updating currencies*

In chapter 4, we looked at how to provide a currency conversion feature for the sample Commerce application. Section 4.3.4 introduced the `Currency` class, which provides exchange rates from one currency to other currencies. Because `Currency` is an abstract class, we could have created many different implementations, but in the example we used a database. The purpose of the example code in chapter 4 was to demonstrate how to retrieve and implement currency conversion, so we never looked at how to update exchange rates in the database.

To continue the example, let's examine how to write a simple console application that allows an administrator or super-user to update the exchange rates without having to interact directly with the database.

THE UPDATECURRENCY PROGRAM

Because the purpose of this program is to update the exchange rates in the database, it's called UpdateCurrency.exe. It will take three command-line arguments:

- The destination currency code
- The source currency code
- The exchange rate

It may sound strange to list the destination before the source, but this way should be most familiar to most people. It tells you how much of the source currency you'll need in order to buy one unit of the destination currency; for example, the exchange rate for USD to EUR is expressed as 1 EUR costing 1.44 USD.[2]

---

[2] January 10, 2010, that is.

At the command line, it looks like this:

```
PS Ploeh:\> .\UpdateCurrency.exe EUR USD "1,44"
Updated: 1 EUR in USD = 1,44.
```

Executing the program updates the database and writes the updated values back to the console.

COMPOSITION ROOT

UpdateCurrency uses the default entry point for a console program: the Main method in the Program class. This is the COMPOSITION ROOT for the application, as shown in the following listing.

Listing 7.1   Console application COMPOSITION ROOT

```
public static void Main(string[] args)
{
    var container = new CurrencyContainer();
    container.ResolveCurrencyParser()
        .Parse(args)
        .Execute();
}
```

The Main method's only responsibility is to compose all relevant modules and let the composed object graph take care of the functionality. In this example, a custom container encapsulates how modules are composed. Because it performs exactly the same function as a DI CONTAINER, I chose to call it a *container*, although it's a custom container with hard-wired DEPENDENCIES. We'll return to it shortly to examine how it's implemented.

With the container in place, you can now ask it to resolve a CurrencyParser that parses the incoming arguments and eventually executes the corresponding command.

> **TIP** The COMPOSITION ROOT should do only two things: set up the container and resolve the type that implements the desired functionality. As soon as it has done that, it should get out of the way and leave the rest to the resolved instance.

> **TIP** Use a proper DI CONTAINER instead of a home-grown custom container for your production applications.

This example uses a custom container explicitly created for this application, but it's straightforward to replace it with a proper DI CONTAINER such as those covered in part 4.

CONTAINER

The CurrencyContainer class is a custom container created for the express purpose of wiring up all DEPENDENCIES for the UpdateCurrency program. The following listing shows the implementation.

Listing 7.2   Custom `CurrencyContainer`

```
public class CurrencyContainer
{
    public CurrencyParser ResolveCurrencyParser()
```

```
    {
        string connectionString =
            ConfigurationManager.ConnectionStrings
            ["CommerceObjectContext"].ConnectionString;

        CurrencyProvider provider =
            new SqlCurrencyProvider(connectionString);
        return new CurrencyParser(provider);
    }
}
```

**Get connection
string from config**

In this example, the dependency graph is rather shallow. The CurrencyParser class requires an instance of the abstract CurrencyProvider class, and in the Currency-Container you decide that the implementation should be the SqlCurrencyProvider that provides the desired communication with the database.

The CurrencyParser class uses CONSTRUCTOR INJECTION, so you pass it the Sql-CurrencyProvider instance that was just created before returning it from the method.

In case you were wondering, here is the constructor signature of CurrencyParser:

```
public CurrencyParser(CurrencyProvider currencyProvider)
```

Recall that CurrencyProvider is an abstract class that is implemented by SqlCurrency-Provider. Although CurrencyContainer contains a hard-coded mapping from CurrencyProvider to SqlCurrencyProvider, the rest of the code is loosely coupled because it consumes only the ABSTRACTION.

This example may seem simple, but it composes types from three different application layers. Let's briefly examine how these layers interact in this particular example.

LAYERING

The COMPOSITION ROOT is the place where components from all layers are wired together. The entry point and the COMPOSITION ROOT constitute the only code of the executable. All implementation is delegated to lower layers, as figure 7.4 illustrates.

The diagram in figure 7.4 may look complicated, but it represents almost the entire code base of the application. Most of the application logic consists of parsing the input arguments and choosing the correct command based on the input. All this takes place in the Application Services layer, which only talks directly with the Domain Model via the abstract CurrencyProvider and Currency classes.

CurrencyProvider is injected into the CurrencyParser by the container and is subsequently used as an Abstract Factory[3] to create a Currency instance used by CurrencyUpdateCommand.

The Data Access layer supplies the SQL Server–based implementations of the Domain Classes. Although none of the other application classes talk directly to these classes, the CurrencyContainer maps the ABSTRACTIONS to the concrete classes.

---

[3] Erich Gamma et al., *Design Patterns: Elements of Reusable Object-Oriented Software* (New York: Addison-Wesley, 1994), 87.

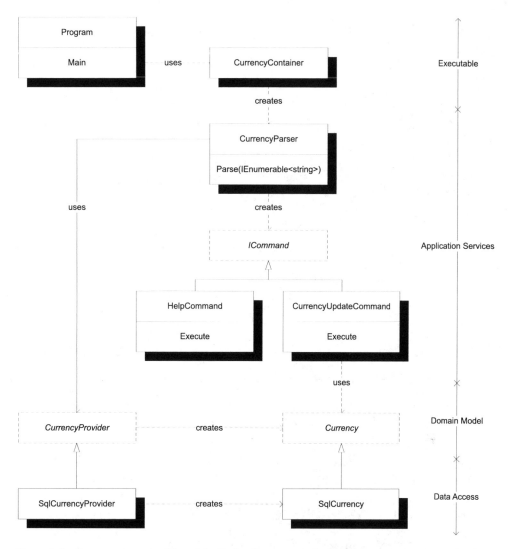

Figure 7.4 Component composition of the UpdateCurrency application. `CurrencyParser` **parses the command-line arguments and returns an appropriate** `ICommand`. **If the arguments were intelligible, it returns a** `CurrencyUpdateCommand` **that uses a** `Currency` **instance to update the exchange rate. The vertical line to the right shows the corresponding application layer. Each layer is implemented in a separate assembly.**

Using DI with a console application is easy because there's virtually no external INVERSION OF CONTROL involved. The .NET Framework simply spins up the process and hands the control to the `Main` method.

In most other BCL frameworks, there is a higher degree of INVERSION OF CONTROL, which means we need to be able to identify the correct extensibility points to wire up the desired object graph. One such framework is ASP.NET MVC.

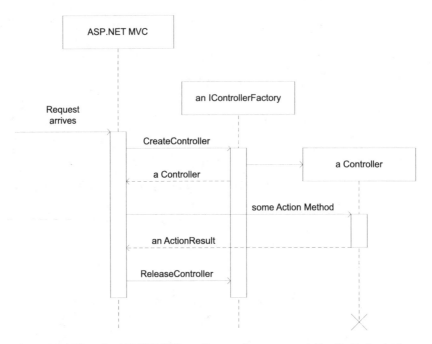

Figure 7.5 **When the ASP.NET MVC runtime receives a request, it asks its Controller Factory to create a Controller for the requested URL. The Controller Factory determines the correct type of Controller to use for the given request and creates and returns a new instance of that type. ASP.NET MVC then invokes the appropriate action method on the Controller instance. When it's finished, ASP.NET MVC gives the Controller Factory a chance to dispose of resources by calling** `ReleaseController`.

7.2   *Composing ASP.NET MVC applications*

ASP.NET MVC was built with the express intent to be DI-friendly, and it is. It doesn't enforce the use of DI, but it easily allows DI without making any assumption about the kind of DI we'll apply. We can use POOR MAN'S DI or whichever DI CONTAINER we like.

7.2.1   *ASP.NET MVC extensibility*

As is always the case with DI, the key to applying it is finding the correct extensibility point. In ASP.NET MVC, this is an interface called `IControllerFactory`. Figure 7.5 illustrates how it fits into the framework.

Controllers are a central concept in ASP.NET MVC. They handle requests and determine how to respond. If we need to query a database, validate and save incoming data, invoke domain logic, and so on, we initiate such actions from a Controller.

A Controller shouldn't do such things itself, but rather delegate the work to appropriate DEPENDENCIES. This is where DI comes in. We want to be able to supply DEPENDENCIES to a given Controller class, ideally by CONSTRUCTOR INJECTION. This is possible with a custom `IControllerFactory`.

IDependencyResolver

When ASP.NET MVC 3 was released in 2011, one of the new features was marketed as "DI support." It turns out that this support revolves around a new interface called IDependencyResolver. This interface and the way it's being used in the ASP.NET MVC framework are problematic.

On a conceptual level, the intended use of IDependencyResolver is as a SERVICE LOCATOR, and that is how the framework uses it.

On a more concrete level, the interface has limited usefulness because it lacks a Release method. In other words, we can't properly manage the lifetime of object graphs using this interface. With some DI CONTAINERS, this guarantees resource leaks.[4]

In its current incarnation, I find it safer and more correct to ignore IDependency-Resolver. The irony of the situation is that true DI has been supported by ASP.NET MVC since the first version through the IControllerFactory interface.

CREATING A CUSTOM CONTROLLER FACTORY

ASP.NET MVC comes with a DefaultControllerFactory that requires Controller classes to have a default constructor. That's a sensible default behavior that doesn't force us to use DI if we don't want to. However, default constructors and CONSTRUCTOR INJECTION are mutually exclusive, so we need to modify this behavior by implementing a custom Controller Factory.

Doing so isn't particularly difficult. It requires you to implement the IController-Factory interface:

```
public interface IControllerFactory
{
    IController CreateController(RequestContext requestContext,
        string controllerName);

    SessionStateBehavior GetControllerSessionBehavior(
        RequestContext requestContext, string controllerName);

    void ReleaseController(IController controller);
}
```

The CreateController method provides a RequestContext that contains such information as the HttpContext, whereas controllerName indicates which Controller is requested.

You may choose to ignore the RequestContext and only use the controllerName to determine which Controller to return. No matter what you do, this is the method where you get the chance to wire up all required DEPENDENCIES and supply them to the Controller before returning the instance. You'll see an example in section 7.2.2.

---

[4] Mike Hadlow, "The MVC 3.0 IDependencyResolver interface is broken. Don't use it with Windsor," 2011, http://mikehadlow.blogspot.com/2011/02/mvc-30-idependencyresolver-interface-is.html

If you created any resources that need to be explicitly disposed of, you can do that when the `ReleaseController` method is called.

> **TIP** `DefaultControllerFactory` implements `IControllerFactory` and has several virtual methods. Instead of implementing `IControllerFactory` from scratch, it's often easier to derive from `DefaultControllerFactory`.

Although implementing a custom Controller Factory is the hard part, it won't be used unless we tell ASP.NET MVC about it.

REGISTERING A CUSTOM CONTROLLER FACTORY

Custom Controller Factories are registered as part of the application startup sequence—usually in Global.asax. They're registered by calling `ControllerBuilder.Current` `.SetControllerFactory`. Here's a snippet from the sample Commerce application:

```
var controllerFactory = new CommerceControllerFactory();

ControllerBuilder.Current.SetControllerFactory(controllerFactory);
```

This example creates and assigns a new instance of the custom `CommerceController-Factory`. ASP.NET MVC will now use the `controllerFactory` instance as its Controller Factory for this application.

If this code looks vaguely familiar, it's because you saw something similar in section 3.3. Back then, I promised to show you how to implement a custom Controller Factory in chapter 7, and what do you know? This *is* chapter 7.

7.2.2   *Example: implementing CommerceControllerFactory*

The Commerce sample application needs a custom Controller Factory to wire up Controllers with the required DEPENDENCIES. Although the entire dependency graph for all Controllers is considerably deeper, from the perspective of the Controllers themselves, the union of all immediate DEPENDENCIES is as small as three items, as shown in figure 7.6.

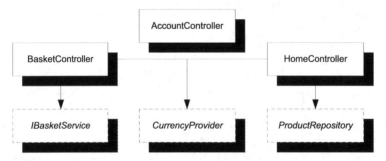

Figure 7.6   **Dependency graph for the three Controllers in the sample Commerce application. The concrete implementations of each of these DEPENDENCIES have other DEPENDENCIES but these aren't shown.**
`BasketController` and `HomeController` **share a DEPENDENCY on**
`CurrencyProvider`. `AccountController` **is inherited unchanged from the default ASP.NET MVC template; because it uses BASTARD INJECTION, it has no unresolved DEPENDENCIES.**

Although you could implement IControllerFactory directly, it's easier to derive from DefaultControllerFactory and override its GetControllerInstance method. This means the DefaultControllerFactory takes care of mapping a Controller name to a Controller type, and all you have to do is return instances of the requested types.

Listing 7.3   Creating Controllers

```
protected override IController GetControllerInstance(          ❶ Override
    RequestContext requestContext, Type controllerType)
{
    string connectionString =
        ConfigurationManager.ConnectionStrings
        ["CommerceObjectContext"].ConnectionString;

    var productRepository =
        new SqlProductRepository(connectionString);
    var basketRepository =
        new SqlBasketRepository(connectionString);
    var discountRepository =
        new SqlDiscountRepository(connectionString);
                                                               ❷ Create
    var discountPolicy =                                         Dependencies
        new RepositoryBasketDiscountPolicy(
            discountRepository);

    var basketService =
        new BasketService(basketRepository,
            discountPolicy);

    var currencyProvider = new CachingCurrencyProvider(
        new SqlCurrencyProvider(connectionString),
        TimeSpan.FromHours(1));

    if (controllerType == typeof(BasketController))
    {
        return new BasketController(
            basketService, currencyProvider);
    }                                                          ❸ Return wired
    if (controllerType == typeof(HomeController))                Controllers
    {
        return new HomeController(
            productRepository, currencyProvider);
    }
    return base.GetControllerInstance(          ❹ Use base for
        requestContext, controllerType);          other Controllers
}
```

This method overrides DefaultControllerFactory.GetControllerInstance ❶ to create instances of the requested Controller types. If the requested type is either BasketController or HomeController, you explicitly wire it up with the required DEPENDENCIES ❷ and return them ❸. Both types use CONSTRUCTOR INJECTION, so you supply the DEPENDENCIES through their constructors.

To keep the code simple, I chose to wire up all the DEPENDENCIES ❷ before checking the controllerType. Obviously, this means some of the created DEPENDENCIES

won't be used, so it's not a particularly efficient implementation. You can refactor listing 7.3 into a more appropriate (but slightly more complex) form.

For those types not explicitly handled, you default to the base behavior ❹, which is
to create the requested Controller using its default constructor. Notice that you aren't
explicitly handling `AccountController`, so you let the base behavior deal with it
instead. `AccountController` is a carryover from the ASP.NET MVC project template
and uses BASTARD INJECTION, which gives it a default constructor.

> **NOTE** I consider BASTARD INJECTION to be an anti-pattern, but I left `Account-`
> `Controller` in that state because I had plenty of other proper DI examples to
> showcase. I did it because this is, after all, sample code, but I would never
> leave it like that in production code.

When a `CommerceControllerFactory` instance is registered in Global.asax, it will correctly create all requested Controllers with the required DEPENDENCIES.

> **TIP** Consider not writing a custom Controller Factory yourself. Instead, use a
> general-purpose Controller Factory that works together with your DI CON-
> TAINER of choice. Look at the MVC Contrib[5] project for inspiration, or use one
> of the reusable implementations available there. Some DI CONTAINERS also
> have "official" ASP.NET MVC integration.

The nice thing about ASP.NET MVC is that it was designed with DI in mind, so we only
need to know and use a single extensibility point to enable DI for an application. In
other frameworks, enabling DI can be a more complex task. Windows Communication
Foundation (WCF), although extensible, is one example.

7.3   *Composing WCF applications*

WCF is one of the most extensible parts of the BCL. Although it's fairly easy to get
started writing WCF services, the myriad of extensibility points can make it difficult to
find exactly the one you need. This is also the case when it comes to DI.

> **NOTE** A joke claims that WCF is an acronym for *Windows Complication Founda-*
> *tion.* There's a certain degree of truth in that claim.

You could easily be led to believe that WCF doesn't support CONSTRUCTOR INJECTION. If
you implement a WCF service with CONSTRUCTOR INJECTION and no default constructor,
the WCF service host will at runtime throw a `ServiceActivationException` with a
message similar to this:

> *The service type provided could not be loaded as a service because it does not have a default*
> *(parameter-less) constructor. To fix the problem, add a default constructor to the type, or*
> *pass an instance of the type to the host.*

This message strongly indicates that a default constructor is required. The only way out seems to be to pass an already-created instance to the WCF host, but doing so raises several issues:

- How can we do this if we host the service in Internet Information Services (IIS)?
- This requires the service to run in the Single `InstanceContextMode`, which is undesirable for a number of other reasons.

The good news is that the exception message is misleading. There are other ways to enable CONSTRUCTOR INJECTION with WCF.

7.3.1   *WCF extensibility*

WCF has lots of extensibility points, but when it comes to DI we only need to know about the `IInstanceProvider` interface and *contract behaviors*. A contract behavior is a SEAM in WCF that allows us to modify how a given contract (that is, a service) behaves.

`IInstanceProvider` is an interface that defines how service instances are created (and released). Here is the interface definition in all its glory:

```
public interface IInstanceProvider
{
    object GetInstance(InstanceContext instanceContext);
    object GetInstance(InstanceContext instanceContext, Message message);
    void ReleaseInstance(InstanceContext instanceContext, object instance);
}
```

The two `GetInstance` overloads are responsible for creating an appropriate service instance, and `ReleaseInstance` provides a hook for cleaning up if necessary.

The default implementation looks for a default constructor on the service type, but we can replace it with one that uses DI. Figure 7.7 illustrates the overall flow when a hosted service receives a message.

When the `ServiceHost` applies behaviors, it picks them up from at least three different places before aggregating them:

- Attributes
- .config file
- In-memory objects

Although we can define behaviors in attributes, it's not a particularly attractive strategy to use when it comes to DI because that means we're compiling into the code a particular creation strategy with particular DEPENDENCIES. The net result is almost the same as if we had hard-coded the DEPENDENCIES directly in the service, just in a much more convoluted way.

A configuration file may sound like the ultimate in flexibility, but it isn't because it doesn't allow us to imperatively configure DEPENDENCIES if we want to do that.

In-memory objects provide the best flexibility because we can choose to create the DEPENDENCIES directly in code or based on configuration settings. If we use a DI CONTAINER, we get both options for free. This means we should create a custom

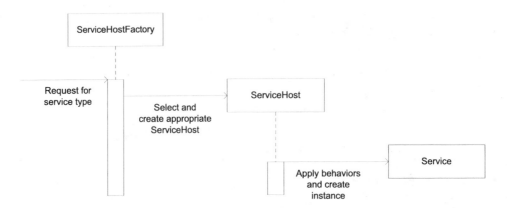

Figure 7.7   When a message (request) arrives for a service operation, WCF determines which CLR type implements the service. It asks a ServiceHostFactory to create an appropriate ServiceHost that can host the requested service. The ServiceHost does its part by applying behaviors and creating the requested instance.

When we host a WCF service in IIS, a ServiceHostFactory is mandatory, although the default implementation will be used if we don't explicitly define an alternative. If we host the service manually, a ServiceHostFactory may still be useful, but it isn't required because we can create the appropriate ServiceHost directly in code.

ServiceHostFactory that creates instances of a custom ServiceHost that again can wire up the desired service with all its DEPENDENCIES.

We can create a set of general-purpose classes that do this based on a DI CONTAINER of choice or use one of the already-implemented reusable container-based Service-HostFactorys. We can also create a specialized ServiceHostFactory for a particular service. Because this provides the best illustration of the process, the following example uses a specialized factory.

7.3.2   *Example: wiring up a product-management service*

As an example, imagine you've been asked to extend the Commerce sample application with a WCF-based service that exposes operations that allow other applications to manage product data. This lets you hook up a rich client (you'll do that in a subsequent section) or a batch job to manage product data.

INTRODUCING THE PRODUCT-MANAGEMENT SERVICE

To keep the example simple, let's assume that you wish to expose simple Create, Read, Update, and Delete (CRUD) operations. Figure 7.8 shows a diagram of the service and associated Data Contracts.

Because you already have an existing Domain Model, you wish to implement this service by extending the Domain Model and expose its operations through this WCF contract. The exact details aren't important; suffice it to say that you expand the abstract ProductRepository class, which you saw in previous chapters.

> **TIP**   Although I won't walk you through all the domain code here, you can review the details in the code download for the book.

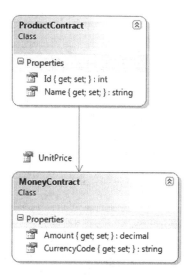

Figure 7.8 `IProductManagementService` **is a WCF service that defines simple CRUD operations on products. It uses the associated** `ProductContract` **and** `MoneyContract` **to expose these operations. Although not shown in this diagram, all three types are decorated with the usual WCF attributes:** `ServiceContract`, `OperationContract`, `DataContract`, **and** `DataMember`.

The Domain Model represents a product as the ENTITY Product, and the service contract exposes its operations in terms of the DATA TRANSFER OBJECT (DTO) Product-Contract. To map between these two different types, you also introduce an interface called `IContractMapper`.

The bottom line is that you end up with a service implementation with two DEPENDENCIES; and because both are mandatory, you wish to use CONSTRUCTOR INJECTION. Here is the service's constructor signature:

```
public ProductManagementService(ProductRepository repository,
    IContractMapper mapper)
```

So far, we've been happily ignoring the elephant in the room: how do we get WCF to correctly wire up an instance of `ProductManagementService`?

WIRING UP PRODUCTMANAGEMENTSERVICE IN WCF

As illustrated in figure 7.7, the COMPOSITION ROOT in WCF is the triplet of Service-HostFactory, ServiceHost, and IInstanceProvider. To wire up a service with CONSTRUCTOR INJECTION, we must supply custom implementations of all three.

> **TIP** You can write completely reusable implementations that wrap your favorite DI CONTAINER in those three types and use them to implement IInstance-Provider. Many people have already done that, so you can probably find a readymade set for your chosen DI CONTAINER.

> **NOTE** This example implements a hard-wired container using POOR MAN'S DI. I chose to encapsulate the hard-coded DEPENDENCIES in a custom container

ENTITY VS. DTO

The previous paragraph threw some more jargon at you, so let's briefly review what is meant by ENTITY and DTO.

An ENTITY is a term from *Domain-Driven Design*[6] that covers a Domain Object that has a long-term identity unrelated to a particular object instance. This may sound abstract and theoretical, but it means that an ENTITY represents an object that lives beyond arbitrary bits in memory. Any .NET object instance has an in-memory address (identity), but an ENTITY has an identity that lives across process lifetimes. We often use databases and primary keys to identify ENTITIES and ensure that we can persist and read them even if the host computer reboots.

The Domain Object `Product` is an ENTITY because the concept of a product has a much longer lifetime than a single process, and we use a product ID to identify it in the `ProductRepository`.

A Data Transfer Object[7] (DTO), on the other hand, exists only for the purpose of being transferred from one application tier to another. Whereas an ENTITY may encapsulate a lot of behavior, a DTO is a structure of data without behavior.

When exposing a Domain Model to external systems, we often do so with services and DTOs because we can never be sure the other system can share our type system (it may not even use .NET). In such situations, we always need to map between the ENTITIES and the DTOs.

class to give you a good idea of how to create a reusable solution based on a particular DI CONTAINER.

Let's start with the custom `ServiceHostFactory`, which is the true entry point to a WCF service. The following listing shows the implementation.

Listing 7.4 Custom `ServiceHostFactory`

```
public class CommerceServiceHostFactory : ServiceHostFactory
{
    private readonly ICommerceServiceContainer container;

    public CommerceServiceHostFactory()
    {
        this.container =                                    ❶ Create container
            new CommerceServiceContainer();                   instance
    }

    protected override ServiceHost CreateServiceHost(
        Type serviceType, Uri[] baseAddresses)
    {
```

---

[6] Eric Evans, *Domain-Driven Design: Tackling Complexity in the Heart of Software* (New York: Addison-Wesley, 2004), 89.

[7] Martin Fowler et al., *Patterns of Enterprise Application Architecture* (New York: Addison-Wesley, 2003), 401.

```
            if (serviceType == typeof(ProductManagementService))
            {
                return new CommerceServiceHost(
                    this.container,                          ❷ Create custom
                    serviceType, baseAddresses);               ServiceHost
            }
            return base.CreateServiceHost(serviceType, baseAddresses);
    }
}
```

The custom `CommerceServiceHostFactory` derives from `ServiceHostFactory` with the single purpose of wiring up `ProductManagementService` instances. It uses a custom `CommerceServiceContainer` to do the actual work, so it creates an instance of the container in its constructor ❶. You can easily expand this example to use a true DI CONTAINER by creating and configuring an instance of that container instead.

When asked to create a `ServiceHost`, it returns a new `CommerceServiceHost` with the configured container ❷ if the requested service type is appropriate. The `Commerce-ServiceHost` is responsible for assigning appropriate behaviors to all the service types it hosts. In this case, you only want to add a single behavior that assigns the desired `IInstanceProvider` to the services. You can accomplish all this work in the constructor shown next, and the base class takes care of the rest.

Listing 7.5 Custom `ServiceHost`

```
public class CommerceServiceHost : ServiceHost
{
    public CommerceServiceHost(ICommerceServiceContainer container,
        Type serviceType, params Uri[] baseAddresses)
        : base(serviceType, baseAddresses)
    {
        if (container == null)
        {
            throw new ArgumentNullException("container");
        }

        var contracts = this.ImplementedContracts.Values;
        foreach (var c in contracts)
        {
            var instanceProvider =
                new CommerceInstanceProvider(          ❶ Create
                    container);                          InstanceProvider
            c.Behaviors.Add(instanceProvider);   ◁┐
        }                                           ❷ Add InstanceProvider
    }                                                 as behavior
}
```

The `CommerceServiceHost` class derives from `ServiceHost`, which is a concrete class that does all the heavy lifting. In most cases, you'll host only a single service type (in this case, `ProductManagementService`), but you're allowed to host multiple services;

this means you must add the `IInstanceProvider` to them all. The `ImplementedContracts` property is a dictionary, so you must loop over its `Values` to target them all.

For each service type, you initialize a new instance of the custom `CommerceInstanceProvider` class with the container ❶. Because it doubles as a behavior, you can add it to the service's `Behaviors` ❷.

The last part of the custom WCF triplet is `CommerceInstanceProvider`, which doubles as both `IInstanceProvider` and `IContractBehavior`. It's a simple implementation, but because it implements two different interfaces with complex signatures, it can look a bit daunting if you see it in one go. Instead, I'll show the code a little at a time; figure 7.9 provides an overview.

Listing 7.6 shows the class declaration and the constructor. Nothing much goes on here apart from the use of CONSTRUCTOR INJECTION to inject the container. Normally, we use CONSTRUCTOR INJECTION to announce to a DI CONTAINER that a class requires some DEPENDENCIES, but here it's backward because you inject the container itself. This is normally a big code smell because it usually indicates intent to use the SERVICE LOCATOR anti-pattern, but it's necessary here because you're implementing the COMPOSITION ROOT.

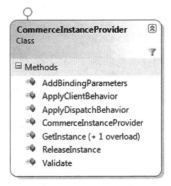

Figure 7.9 `Commerce-InstanceProvider` **implements both** `IInstanceProvider` **and** `IContractBehavior`, **so you're required to implement seven methods. You can leave three empty, and the other four are one-liners.**

Listing 7.6   `CommerceInstanceProvider` **class declaration and constructor**

```
public partial class CommerceInstanceProvider :        ❶  Implement WCF
    IInstanceProvider, IContractBehavior                      interfaces
{
    private readonly ICommerceServiceContainer container;

    public CommerceInstanceProvider(
        ICommerceServiceContainer container)
    {
        if (container == null)                              ❷  Constructor
        {                                                       Injection
            throw new ArgumentNullException("container");
        }

        this.container = container;
    }
}
```

`CommerceInstanceProvider` implements both `IInstanceProvider` and `IContractBehavior` ❶. You supply the container through standard CONSTRUCTOR INJECTION ❷. In this sample, you use the custom `CommerceServiceContainer`, but replacing it with a general-purpose DI CONTAINER is a trivial exercise.

The `IInstanceProvider` implementation in the next listing is used by the WCF runtime to create instances of the `ProductManagementService` class.

Listing 7.7 `IInstanceProvider` implementation

```
public object GetInstance(InstanceContext instanceContext, Message message)
{
    return this.GetInstance(instanceContext);      <-- Delegate to overload
}

public object GetInstance(InstanceContext instanceContext)
{
    return this.container
        .ResolveProductManagementService();                    ① Use container
}                                                                    to resolve

public void ReleaseInstance(InstanceContext instanceContext,
    object instance)
{                                                              ② Ask container
    this.container.Release(instance);                             to release
}
```

The WCF runtime invokes one of the `GetInstance` methods to get an instance of the requested service type, so you ask the container to wire up the `ProductManagement-Service` ① with all its required DEPENDENCIES.

When the service operation has completed, the WCF runtime asks you to release the instance, and again you delegate this work to the container ②.

The other part of `CommerceInstanceProvider` is the `IContractBehavior` implementation. The only reason you implement this interface is to allow you to add it to the list of behaviors as shown in listing 7.5. All the methods on the `IContractBehavior` interface return void, so you can leave most of them empty because you don't need to implement them.

The following listing shows the implementation of the only method you care about.

Listing 7.8 Core implementation of `IContractBehavior`

```
public void ApplyDispatchBehavior(
    ContractDescription contractDescription, ServiceEndpoint endpoint,
    DispatchRuntime dispatchRuntime)
{
    dispatchRuntime.InstanceProvider = this;
}
```

You only need to do one exceedingly simple thing in this method. The WCF runtime calls this method and passes an instance of `DispatchRuntime`, which lets you tell it that it should be using this particular `IInstanceProvider` implementation—recall that `CommerceInstanceProvider` also implements `IInstanceProvider`. The WCF runtime now knows which `IInstanceProvider` to use, and it can subsequently invoke the `Get-Instance` method shown in listing 7.7.

This seems like a lot of code to implement to enable DI for WCF, and I haven't even shown you the implementation of `CommerceServiceContainer`.

TIP Remember that you can easily write reusable versions of these three classes that wrap your favorite DI CONTAINER, and package that implementation into a library. Many developers have done that, so you can probably find a suitable ready-made library on the internet.

The container is the last piece of the WCF DI puzzle.

IMPLEMENTING THE SPECIALIZED CONTAINER

CommerceServiceContainer is a specialized container with the single purpose of wiring up the ProductManagementService class. Recall that this class requires instances of ProductRepository and IContractMapper as DEPENDENCIES.

With the entire WCF infrastructure out of the way, the container is free to concentrate on wiring up the dependency graph.

NOTE In addition to adhering nicely to the SINGLE RESPONSIBILITY PRINCIPLE, this separation of concerns shows that you can replace this specialized container with a general-purpose DI CONTAINER, because there's no WCF-specific code present.

The ResolveProductManagementService method wires up the instance with POOR MAN'S DI, as shown next.

Listing 7.9 Resolving ProductManagementService

```
public IProductManagementService ResolveProductManagementService()
{
    string connectionString =
        ConfigurationManager.ConnectionStrings
        ["CommerceObjectContext"].ConnectionString;

    ProductRepository repository =                      ① Create product
        new SqlProductRepository(connectionString);         repository

    IContractMapper mapper = new ContractMapper();      ② Create contract
                                                            mapper
    return new ProductManagementService(repository,
        mapper);
}
```

In a sense, when it comes to resolving a dependency graph, it often pays to work your way backward. You know you need to return an instance of ProductManagementService with ProductRepository and IContractMapper instances. The IContractMapper instance is easy to create ②, but the ProductRepository requires a bit more work.

You wish to use SqlProductRepository ①, but to do that you need a connection string that you can read from the web.config file.

If you wish to host the service in your own application, you can now do that by creating a new instance of the CommerceServiceHostFactory class and invoking its Create-ServiceHost method with the correct parameters. It will return a CommerceServiceHost instance that you can open, and it will figure out the rest for you and host the Product-ManagementService.

However, if you wish to host the service in IIS, you must take one more step.

HOSTING PRODUCTMANAGEMENTSERVICE IN IIS

In IIS, we don't manually create new instances of `CommerceServiceHostFactory`. Instead, we must tell IIS to do so on our behalf. This can be done in an .svc file by supplying the `Factory` attribute:

```
<%@ ServiceHost
    Factory = "Ploeh.Samples.CommerceService.CommerceServiceHostFactory,
    ➥Ploeh.Samples.CommerceService"
    Service = "Ploeh.Samples.CommerceService.ProductManagementService"
%>
```

This .svc file instructs IIS to use the `CommerceServiceHostFactory` every time it needs to create an instance of the `ProductManagementService` class. It's a requirement that the `ServiceHostFactory` in question has a default constructor, but this is also the case in this example.

Enabling DI in WCF is harder than it should be, but at least it's possible, and the end result is entirely satisfactory. We can use whichever DI CONTAINER we like, and we end up having a proper COMPOSITION ROOT.

Some frameworks don't give us the appropriate SEAMS to allow us that luxury. However, before we look at one such notorious framework, let's relax and look at a much simpler framework.

7.4 *Composing WPF applications*

If you thought that composing a WCF service was difficult (I do), you'll appreciate that composing a Windows Presentation Foundation (WPF) application is almost as easy as composing a console application.

A WPF application's entry point is fairly obvious and uncomplicated, and although it doesn't provide SEAMS explicitly targeted at enabling DI, we can easily compose an application in any way we prefer.

7.4.1 *WPF Composition*

A WPF application's entry point is defined in its `App` class. As with most other classes in WPF, this class is split into two files: App.xaml and App.xaml.cs. We can define what happens at application startup in both files, depending on our need.

When you create a new WPF project in Visual Studio, the App.xaml file defines a `StartupUri` attribute that defines which window is shown when the application starts—in this case, `Window1`:

```
<Application x:Class="MyWpfApplication.App"
    xmlns="http://schemas.microsoft.com/winfx/2006/xaml/presentation"
    xmlns:x="http://schemas.microsoft.com/winfx/2006/xaml"
    StartupUri="Window1.xaml">
</Application>
```

The implication of this declarative style is that the `Window1` object is created and shown without any sort of additional context. When you want to supply DEPENDENCIES to the window, a more explicit approach can be more appropriate. You can remove the `StartupUri` attribute and wire up the window by overriding the `OnStartup` method. This allows you to fully wire up the first window before it's shown, but you pay one tax: you must remember to explicitly invoke the window's `Show` method.

The `OnStartup` method thus becomes the application's COMPOSITION ROOT. You can use a DI CONTAINER or POOR MAN'S DI to compose the window. The next example uses POOR MAN'S DI to illustrate that you don't have to rely on features of any particular DI CONTAINER.

Figure 7.10　The Product Management application's main window is a list of products. You can add new products, edit existing products, or delete them. When adding or editing products, a modal edit dialog is used. All operations are implemented by invoking appropriate operations on the product-management web service from section 7.3.2.

7.4.2　*Example: wiring up a product-management rich client*

The previous example developed a web service we can use to manage the product catalog for the sample Commerce application. In this example, you'll create a WPF application that uses this web service to manage products. Figure 7.10 shows a screen shot of the application.

The entire application is implemented using the Model View ViewModel (MVVM) approach and contains the three layers shown in figure 7.11. As usual, we keep the part with the most logic isolated from the other modules—in this case, `PresentationLogic`. `ProductManagementClient` is a HUMBLE EXECUTABLE that does little apart from defining the UI and delegating implementation to the other modules.

With MVVM, we assign a ViewModel to the main window's `DataContext` property, and data binding and the data-templating engine take care of presenting the data correctly as we spin up new ViewModels or change the data in the existing ViewModels.

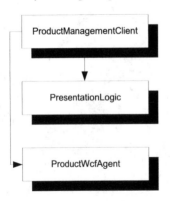

Figure 7.11　The application consists of three distinct assemblies. The `ProductManagementClient` assembly is the executable and contains the UI implemented in XAML with no code-behind. The `PresentationLogic` library contains the `ViewModels` and supporting classes, and the `ProductWcfAgent` library contains an Adapter between the custom `IProductManagementAgent` ABSTRACTION and the concrete WCF proxy that is used to communicate with the product-management web service. The dependency arrows imply that `ProductManagementClient` acts as the COMPOSITION ROOT, because it wires together the other modules.

MVVM

Model View ViewModel (MVVM)[8] is a design pattern for which WPF is particularly well suited. It divides UI code into three distinct responsibilities.

The Model is the underlying model for the application. This is often, but not always, the Domain Model. It often consists of Plain Old CLR Objects (POCOs). In the present example, the Domain Model is implemented in the web service, so you don't have a proper Domain Model in this tier. However, the application operates with an ABSTRACTION on top of the web service proxy, and this is your Model. Notice that the Model is usually expressed in a UI-neutral way. It doesn't assume that it will be exposed directly by a UI, so it doesn't expose any WPF-specific functionality.

The View is the UI we look at. In WPF, we can declaratively express the View in XAML and use data binding and data templating to present the data. It's possible to express the Views without the use of code-behind.

The ViewModel is the bridge between the View and the Model. Each ViewModel is a class that translates and exposes the Model in a technology-specific way. In WPF, this means it may expose lists as `ObservableCollections`, and so on.

INJECTING DEPENDENCIES INTO THE MAIN VIEWMODEL

`MainWindow` contains only XAML markup and no custom code-behind. Instead, it uses data binding to display data and handle user commands. To enable this, we must assign a `MainWindowViewModel` to its `DataContext` property.

`MainWindowViewModel` exposes data such as the list of products as well as commands to create, update, or delete a product. Enabling this functionality depends on a service that provides access to the product catalog: the `IProductManagementAgent` ABSTRACTION.

Apart from `IProductManagementAgent`, `MainWindowViewModel` also needs a service it can use to control its windowing environment, such as showing modal dialog boxes. This other DEPENDENCY is called `IWindow`.

`MainWindowViewModel` uses CONSTRUCTOR INJECTION with this constructor signature:

```
public MainWindowViewModel(IProductManagementAgent agent, IWindow window)
```

To wire up the application, we must create `MainWindowViewModel` and assign it to the `DataContext` property of a `MainWindow` instance.

WIRING UP MAINWINDOW AND MAINWINDOWVIEWMODEL

This example contains the extra spice that to implement `IWindow` correctly, you need a reference to the real WPF window (`MainWindow`); but the ViewModel requires an `IWindow`, and the `MainWindow`'s `DataContext` should be the ViewModel. In other words, you have a circular DEPENDENCY.

In chapter 6, we dealt with circular DEPENDENCIES and walked through the relevant part of this particular example, so I won't repeat it here. Suffice it to say that you

---

[8] Read more about MVVM in Josh Smith, "Patterns: WPF Apps With The Model-View-ViewModel Design Pattern," 2009, http://msdn.microsoft.com/en-us/magazine/dd419663.aspx

introduce a `MainWindowViewModelFactory` responsible for creating instances of `Main-WindowViewModel`.

You use this factory from within an implementation of `IWindow` called `Main-WindowAdapter` to create the `MainWindowViewModel` and assign it to the `MainWindow`'s `DataContext` property:

```
var vm = this.vmFactory.Create(this);
this.WpfWindow.DataContext = vm;
```

The `vmFactory` member variable is an instance of `IMainWindowViewModelFactory`, and you pass its `Create` method an instance of the containing class, which implements `IWindow`. The resulting ViewModel instance is then assigned to the `DataContext` of `WpfWindow`, which is an instance of `MainWindow`.

> **NOTE** I am glossing over the details on purpose because we covered them in chapter 6. Go back and reread the section on circular DEPENDENCIES if you need a refresher about what's going on.

> **TIP** WPF data binding requires us to assign the DEPENDENCY (the ViewModel) to the `DataContext` property. This is, in my opinion, misuse of PROPERTY INJECTION because it signals that the DEPENDENCY is optional, which it isn't. However, WPF 4 introduces something called a `XamlSchemaContext`, which can be used as a SEAM that gives us greater flexibility when it comes to instantiating Views based on markup.[9]

Figure 7.12 shows the complete dependency graph for the application.

Now that you've identified all the building blocks of the application, you can compose it. To keep the POOR MAN'S DI code symmetrical with the use of a DI CONTAINER, I have implemented this as a `Resolve` method on a specialized container class. The following listing shows the implementation.

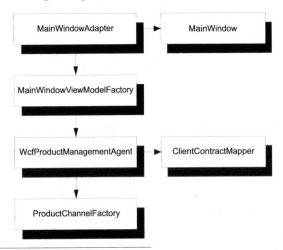

Figure 7.12   Dependency graph for `MainWindowAdapter`, **which ends up being the root object in the application. It uses a** `MainWindowViewModelFactory` **to create the appropriate ViewModel and assign it to the** `MainWindow`. **To create** `MainWindowViewModel`, **the factory needs a** `WcfProductManagementAgent` **to pass to the ViewModel. This agent is an Adapter between** `IProductManagementAgent` **and the WCF proxy. It requires a** `ProductChannelFactory` **to create instances of the WCF proxy, as well as an** `IClientContractMapper` **that can translate between ViewModels and WCF Data Contracts.**

---

[9] For more information, see Simon Ferquel, "[Xaml] IoC-enabled Xaml parser," 2010, www.simonferquel.net/blog/archive/2010/02/19/xaml-ioc-enabled-xaml-parser.aspx

Listing 7.10   Composing the main window

```
public IWindow ResolveWindow()
{
    IProductChannelFactory channelFactory =
        new ProductChannelFactory();
    IClientContractMapper mapper =
        new ClientContractMapper();
    IProductManagementAgent agent =
        new WcfProductManagementAgent(
            channelFactory, mapper);

    IMainWindowViewModelFactory vmFactory =
        new MainWindowViewModelFactory(agent);

    Window mainWindow = new MainWindow();
    IWindow w =
        new MainWindowAdapter(mainWindow, vmFactory);
    return w;
}
```

Ultimately, you return an IWindow instance implemented by MainWindowAdapter, and you need a WPF Window and an IMainWindowViewModelFactory for that. The first window you want to show to users should be a MainWindow, so this is what you pass to MainWindowAdapter.

MainWindowViewModelFactory uses CONSTRUCTOR INJECTION to request an IProduct-ManagementAgent, so you must compose a WcfProductManagementAgent with its two DEPENDENCIES.

The final MainWindowAdapter returned from the method wraps the MainWindow, so when we invoke the Show method, it delegates to the MainWindow's Show method. That is exactly what you'll do from the COMPOSITION ROOT.

IMPLEMENTING THE COMPOSITION ROOT

Now that you know how to wire up the application, you only need to do so in the correct place. As described in the previous section, you first need to open App.xaml and remove the StartupUri attribute because you wish to explicitly compose the startup Window yourself.

After you've done that, you only need to override the OnStartup method in App.xaml.cs and invoke the container.

Listing 7.11   Implementing a WPF COMPOSITION ROOT

```
protected override void OnStartup(StartupEventArgs e)
{
    base.OnStartup(e);

    var container =
        new ProductManagementClientContainer();
    container.ResolveWindow().Show();
}
```

In this example, you use the specialized ProductManagementClientContainer, but you could just as well use a general-purpose DI CONTAINER like Unity or StructureMap. You ask the container to resolve an IWindow instance and subsequently invoke its Show method. The returned IWindow instance is a MainWindowAdapter; when you invoke its Show method, it invokes the Show method on the encapsulated MainWindow, which causes the desired window to be shown to the user.

WPF offers a simple place for a COMPOSITION ROOT. All you need to do is to remove StartupUri from App.xaml, override OnStartup in App.xaml.cs, and compose the application here.

So far, you've seen examples where the frameworks provide a SEAM that allows us to take over the lifetime of key object instances (web pages, service instances, windows, and so on). In many cases, doing so is fairly easy; but even when it gets as difficult as in WCF, we can still prevail and implement pure DI without compromising our principles.

Some frameworks, however, don't give us that luxury.

7.5   Composing ASP.NET applications

Some frameworks insist on creating and managing the lifetime of the classes we write. The most popular framework is ASP.NET (Web Forms, as opposed to MVC).

> **NOTE** Some other frameworks sharing this trait are the Microsoft Management Console (MMC) managed SDK, and such recent inventions as PowerShell.

The most obvious symptom of such frameworks is that to fit in, our classes must have a default constructor. In ASP.NET, for example, any Page class we implement must have a parameterless constructor. We can't use CONSTRUCTOR INJECTION with these frameworks, so let's examine our options.

7.5.1   ASP.NET composition

CONSTRUCTOR INJECTION would be preferable because it would ensure that our Page classes would be properly initialized with their DEPENDENCIES. Because that isn't possible, we must choose from these alternatives:

- Move and duplicate our COMPOSITION ROOTS within each Page class.
- Use a SERVICE LOCATOR to resolve all DEPENDENCIES from within each Page class.

However, remember that SERVICE LOCATOR is an anti-pattern, so that option isn't desirable. A better alternative is to compromise on the location of our COMPOSITION ROOT.

Ideally, we would prefer the scenario in figure 7.13 where we have only one COMPOSITION ROOT per application, but that isn't possible in ASP.NET because we can't compose Page instances from the outside. In other words, the Web Forms framework forces us to compose the application from within each Page.

> **NOTE** So far, I have only talked about Page objects, but ASP.NET requires a default constructor for lots of objects if we want to use the framework. Another example is Object Data Sources. The discussion in this section applies equally well to all other types that must have a default constructor.

Figure 7.13   In a perfect world, we would like to be able to compose `Page`
objects from an application's COMPOSITION ROOT. **When a request arrives, we
should be able to use the defined configuration of** DEPENDENCIES **to compose an
appropriate** `Page` **object. However, this isn't possible because ASP.NET manages
the lifetime of** `Page` **objects on our behalf.**

To address this issue, we must compromise on our ideals, but I find it much safer to
compromise on the location of COMPOSITION ROOTS than to allow a SERVICE LOCATOR to
enter the picture.

In essence, we turn each `Page` into a
COMPOSITION ROOT as shown in figure 7.14.
The SINGLE RESPONSIBILITY PRINCIPLE reminds
us that each class should have only a single responsibility; now that we use the `Page`
to compose all required DEPENDENCIES, we
should delegate the responsibility of implementation to an *implementer.* This effectively
turns the `Page` into a HUMBLE OBJECT, exposing other members such as click-event han-
dlers solely for the purpose of delegating to
the `Page`'s resolved implementer.

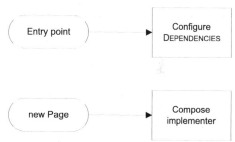

**Figure 7.14   In ASP.NET, we can use the
application entry point (global.asax) to configure
the** DEPENDENCIES, **but we then have to wait until
the framework creates a new** `Page` **object before
we can continue with the composition. From
within each** `Page`, **we can use the configured**
DEPENDENCIES **to compose an implementer that
implements all the behavior of the** `Page` **class.**

The distinction between moving the
COMPOSITION ROOT into each class and
using a SERVICE LOCATOR is subtle. The difference is that with a SERVICE LOCATOR we
resolve each of the `Page` class's DEPENDENCIES individually and use them directly from
within the `Page` class. As always with SERVICE LOCATOR, this tends to blur the focus of the
class. In addition, it becomes tempting to keep the container and use it to resolve
other DEPENDENCIES as necessary.

To counter this tendency, it's important to only use our container to resolve the
implementer and then forget about it. This allows us to follow appropriate DI patterns
(such as CONSTRUCTOR INJECTION) for the rest of the application's code.

Although this is theoretical, you'll be relieved to hear that it's easy to implement.
This is best illustrated with an example.

7.5.2   *Example: wiring up a CampaignPresenter*

The Commerce sample application you know and love supports product discounts and
featured products, but so far you haven't provided business users with an application to
manage these aspects. In this example, we'll examine how to compose the ASP.NET

	Product Id	Product Name	Unit Price	Featured	Discount Price
Edit	1	Criollo Chocolate	34.9500	☑	
Edit	2	Arborio Rice	22.7500	☑	19.5000
Edit	3	White Asparagus	39.8000	☑	
Edit	4	Maldon Sea Salt	19.5000	☐	15.8500
Edit	5	Gruyère	48.5000	☑	
Edit	6	Anchovies	18.7500	☑	
Update Cancel	12	White Truffles	500.0000	☑	

Figure 7.15   The CampaignManagement application allows a business user to edit campaign data (Featured and Discount Price) for a product. It's an ASP.NET application built with the GridView control bound to an ObjectDataSource control.

application (shown in figure 7.15) that allows a business user to update campaign data for a product.

To keep things simple, this application consists of a single GridView control bound to an ObjectDataSource. The data source is an application-specific class that delegates its behavior to the Domain Model and through that ultimately to the data-access library that stores the data in a SQL Server database.

You can still use global.asax to configure DEPENDENCIES, but you must defer composing the application until the Page and its ObjectDataSource have been created. Configuring the DEPENDENCIES is similar to previous examples.

CONFIGURING DEPENDENCIES IN ASP.NET

The application entry point in ASP.NET is the global.asax file, and although you can't compose anything at this point, you can create your *mise en place*, making everything ready for when the application starts:

```
protected void Application_Start(object sender, EventArgs e)
{
    this.Application["container"] =
        new CampaignContainer();
}
```

The only thing you do here is to create your container and save it in the Application Context so you can use it when you need it. This allows you to share the container across separate web requests, which is beneficial if you need to keep some DEPENDENCIES for the duration of the process's lifetime (we'll talk more about lifetimes in chapter 8).

> **NOTE**   As with all the other examples in this chapter, I use POOR MAN's DI to demonstrate the core principles involved. CampaignContainer is a custom class created explicitly for this example, but you can easily replace it with the DI CONTAINER of your choice.

Many different Page and data source objects can share the same container by accessing the Application Context. However, this approach poses a danger of being misused as a SERVICE LOCATOR, because any class can potentially access the Application Context. Thus, it's important to delegate the implementation to classes that can't access the Application Context. In practice, this means delegating to classes implemented in other separate libraries that don't reference ASP.NET.

> **NOTE** We can also get by with a bit of discipline, constraining ourselves from accessing the Application Context unless we're implementing a COMPOSITION ROOT. This can work well when all developers are experienced in writing loosely coupled code; but if we suspect that some team members may not fully understand the issues involved, we can better protect the code by using separate libraries. Section 6.5 described how to do that.

In the current example, you'll delegate all implementation to a separate presentation logic library to ensure that no classes directly access the Application Context. You don't allow the library to reference any of the ASP.NET assemblies (such as System.Web).

Figure 7.16 shows a partial view of the application architecture. The salient point is that you use classes in the root of the application (the Default Page and Campaign-DataSource) as COMPOSITION ROOTS that resolve classes from the Presentation Logic layer together with their DEPENDENCIES.

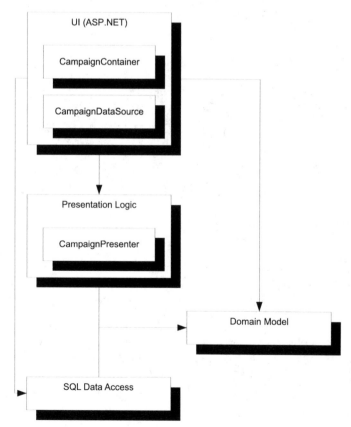

Figure 7.16 The root of the CampaignManagement application is the only part of the application that references ASP.NET. The CampaignDataSource class has a default constructor but acts as a COMPOSITION ROOT and HUMBLE OBJECT that delegates all method calls to a CampaignPresenter. As usual, the arrows denote references, and the root application references all other modules because it wires them together. Both the Presentation Logic and Data Access modules reference the Domain Model library. Not all involved classes are shown.

Armed with the knowledge of the application's dependency graph, you can now implement a COMPOSITION ROOT for the screen shown in figure 7.15.

COMPOSING AN OBJECTDATASOURCE

The Default Page shown in figure 7.15 consists of a `GridView` control and an associated `ObjectDataSource` control. As is the case with `Page` classes, a class used for `ObjectDataSource` must also have a default constructor. To meet that goal, you explicitly create the class shown in the following listing.

Listing 7.12   Composing a Presenter as data source

```csharp
public class CampaignDataSource
{
    private readonly CampaignPresenter presenter;

    public CampaignDataSource()
    {
        var container =
            (CampaignContainer)HttpContext.Current
            .Application["container"];
        this.presenter = container.ResolvePresenter();    // ❶ Compose Presenter
    }

    public IEnumerable<CampaignItemPresenter> SelectAll()
    {
        return this.presenter.SelectAll();
    }
                                                          // ❷ Delegate to Presenter
    public void Update(CampaignItemPresenter item)
    {
        this.presenter.Update(item);
    }
}
```

The `CampaignDataSource` class has a default constructor because this is required by ASP.NET. True to the spirit of *Fail Fast*, it immediately attempts to extract the container from the Application Context and resolve a `CampaignPresenter` instance ❶ that will serve as the real implementation.

All members of the `CampaignDataSource` class delegate the call to the resolved presenter ❷, thus acting as a HUMBLE OBJECT.

> **NOTE**   For design pattern enthusiasts, the `CampaignDataSource` class looks a lot like either a Decorator or an Adapter.[10] It implements no strongly typed interface but wraps a proper implementation in a class that conforms to the requirements put forth by ASP.NET.

You may wonder what we gain from this extra layer of indirection. If you're used to TDD, it should be straightforward: `HttpContext.Current` isn't available during unit

---

[10] Gamma, *Design Patterns*, 139.

testing, so you can't unit-test `CampaignDataSource`. This is an important reason why you must keep it a HUMBLE OBJECT.

Although this construct is awkward at best, it allows you to follow proper DI patterns from the `CampaignPresenter` class and further down through the application's layers.

COMPOSING THE PRESENTER

I won't walk you through the nitty-gritty details of `CampaignPresenter`, but it's worth looking at its constructor signature because it uses CONSTRUCTOR INJECTION:

```
public CampaignPresenter(CampaignRepository repository,
    IPresentationMapper mapper)
```

Its DEPENDENCIES are the abstract `CampaignRepository` class and the `IPresentation-Mapper` interface. Exactly what these ABSTRACTIONS do is less important than how you compose them. This is the job of the `CampaignContainer` in the next listing. You may recall that you configured it in global.asax and registered it in the Application Context.

Listing 7.13 Resolving `CampaignPresenter`

```
public CampaignPresenter ResolvePresenter()
{
    string connectionString =
        ConfigurationManager.ConnectionStrings
        ["CommerceObjectContext"].ConnectionString;
    CampaignRepository repository =                          ❶ Create
        new SqlCampaignRepository(connectionString);            repository

    IPresentationMapper mapper =                      ❷ Create
        new PresentationMapper();                        mapper
                                                              ❸ Compose
    return new CampaignPresenter(repository, mapper);        Presenter
}
```

The `ResolvePresenter` method's responsibility is to compose a `CampaignPresenter` instance. From the constructor, you know it needs a `CampaignRepository`, so you map that to a `SqlCampaignRepository` instance ❶. The other DEPENDENCY is `IPresentation-Mapper`, and you map that to the concrete `PresentationMapper` class ❷.

Armed with all required DEPENDENCIES, you can subsequently ❸ return a new `CampaignPresenter` instance.

Using DI with ASP.NET isn't impossible, but it's more work than we would like. The main drawback with using each `Page` and object data source as a combined COMPOSITION ROOT and HUMBLE OBJECT is that it requires us to duplicate a lot of class members.

Did you notice how every member of `CampaignDataSource` delegates its implementation to a similarly named method on `CampaignPresenter`? You have to repeat this coding idiom throughout an entire ASP.NET application. For every button-click handler, you need to define and maintain an associated method on a Presenter class, and so on.

As we discussed in chapter 3, I liken the concept of a COMPOSITION ROOT to Lean Software Development's idea of the *Last Responsible Moment*. With frameworks such as ASP.NET MVC and WCF, we can defer the composition of the application all the way to the application's entry point, but this isn't the case with ASP.NET. No matter how hard we try, we can only defer decisions about OBJECT COMPOSITION until we meet a requirement for a default constructor.

That, then, becomes the "highest possible place" in which we can compose objects. Although we feel that we're compromising, we still follow the overall spirit of COMPOSITION ROOT. We compose object hierarchies as close to the architectural top as possible and enable correct DI patterns from there on down.

ASP.NET still allows us a small luxury: we can share one container instance through the Application Context. Some frameworks don't even grant us that.

7.6   *Composing PowerShell cmdlets*

Some frameworks offer absolutely no SEAMS that allow us to manage the lifetime of the core elements of the framework. Windows PowerShell is such a framework.

> **NOTE**   Read on even if you have no particular interest in PowerShell. I mainly chose it as an example of the ultimate DI challenge. I could also have chosen the Managed MMC SDK, but it's unpleasant in so many other ways that I found PowerShell preferable as an example.

An important element in PowerShell is a *cmdlet*. (I suppose it's pronounced *command-let*, but I have only seen it spelled *cmdlet*.) You can think of a cmdlet as an advanced command-line utility.

A cmdlet is a class that derives from `Cmdlet`,[11] and it must have a default constructor. As with ASP.NET, that requirement effectively bars any use of CONSTRUCTOR INJECTION. The solution is similar: we move the COMPOSITION ROOT into the constructor of each cmdlet. The only difference is that there is no built-in Application Context so we must instead resort to the lowest common denominator: a static class.

> **NOTE**   I consider any use of the `static` keyword a code smell, but in contrast with anti-patterns, code smells only indicate a *potential* design flaw. In some special cases, the smelly idiom is warranted, and this is such a case.

You may wonder how this is different from the SERVICE LOCATOR anti-pattern. Just as with ASP.NET, the main difference is not in the structure of the code, but in the usage pattern. Instead of trying to use a static SERVICE LOCATOR as a virtual new keyword, we use it only once per cmdlet. To further protect ourselves from misuse, we can make the COMPOSER internal and use it only to resolve types from different assemblies, as shown in figure 7.17.

The result of resolving the dependency graph is a class defined in a different assembly, and that class can't access the static container because it's internal to the application's root assembly. The cmdlet implementer needs to use proper DI patterns

---

[11] `System.Management.Automation.Cmdlet` to be exact, although it can also derive from `System.Management.Automation.PSCmdlet`.

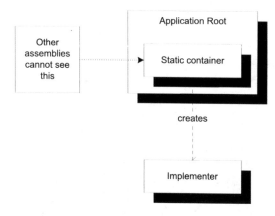

Figure 7.17 When there is no way around a static container, we can make it internal and place it in the application's root assembly. All `Resolve` methods return classes defined in other assemblies. Thus as soon as the container has resolved the implementer, no classes in the resolved dependency hierarchy have access to the static container because they're all outside the application's root assembly and the container is internal.

such as CONSTRUCTOR INJECTION to consume any DEPENDENCIES, and we've effectively shielded ourselves from the dangers of SERVICE LOCATOR.

Let's look at an example that illustrates this principle.

7.6.1 *Example: composing basket-management cmdlets*

This example returns to the commerce sample application. Like all other commerce applications, this one has shopping basket functionality. It's common for users to put items in their shopping basket but then leave the site, never to return.

Although storage is cheap these days, project stakeholders have requested that you provide them with a flexible ability to clean up orphaned baskets based on different criteria. They want to be able to select orphaned baskets based on when they were last updated. If the basket represents a significant amount, it shouldn't be deleted (or perhaps it should be given a longer grace period), but the total should be calculated according to all current business rules.

It sounds like a scripting API would be a good fit, because an administrator would be able to define and schedule simple cleanup scripts. PowerShell is appropriate here because of its advanced filtering and piping functionality.

You can implement the desired API with two cmdlets: one to retrieve all baskets and one to delete a basket for a given user. The following listing is an example of how this might look in an interactive session.

Listing 7.14 Deleting baskets more than a month old

```
PS C:\> Get-Basket

LastUpdated          Owner                        Total
-----------          -----                        -----
19.03.2010 20:5... ploeh                         89,4000      ❶ Old
22.01.2010 19:5... ndøh                         199,0000   ←    basket
21.03.2010 09:1... fnaah                        171,7500

PS C:\> $now = [System.DateTime]::Now
PS C:\> $month = [System.TimeSpan]::FromDays(30)      ❷ Calculate
PS C:\> $old = $now - $month                             cutoff date
```

```
PS C:\> Get-Basket | ? { $_.LastUpdated -lt $old } |
Remove-Basket
PS C:\> Get-Basket
```

<table>
<tr><td>LastUpdated</td><td>Owner</td><td>Total</td></tr>
<tr><td>-----------</td><td>-----</td><td>-----</td></tr>
<tr><td>19.03.2010 20:5...</td><td>ploeh</td><td>89,4000</td></tr>
<tr><td>21.03.2010 09:1...</td><td>fnaah</td><td>171,7500</td></tr>
</table>

❸ **Delete old baskets**

```
PS C:\>
```

Before you begin deleting baskets, you want to review the current baskets in the system. You can use the custom cmdlet `Get-Basket` to list all baskets. Notice that each basket has three properties that tell you when the basket was last updated, who the owner is, and the total value (including discounts) of the basket.

The current date when this particular session was performed was March 22, 2010. Notice that the second basket ❶ is more than 30 days old. You can now calculate the cutoff date ❷ from the current date and use it in a filter expression ❸. You can delete all old baskets by piping the result of `Get-Basket` to the filter and then piping the result of the filtered baskets to the `Remove-Basket` cmdlet. If you wanted to also filter on the `Total` property, you could do so as well.

Finally, you list all baskets to verify that the old basket was deleted.

NOTE Don't worry if you don't understand all the details of the filter expression. This book isn't about PowerShell, so I won't linger on this subject.

To facilitate this scripting API, you need to implement two custom cmdlets. Because one of the requirements is that the `Total` must take into account all relevant business rules, you need to compose the cmdlets with your Domain Model.

COMPOSING GETBASKETCMDLET

Let's examine how the `Get-Basket` cmdlet is implemented. `Remove-Basket` is implemented in a similar manner, so I won't cover it.

To escape the lure of the static container, you'll implement the entire bridge between the PowerShell cmdlet and the Domain Model in a separate library called `BasketPowerShellLogic`. Figure 7.18 shows how the application is composed across libraries.

NOTE If you think figure 7.18 looks a lot like figure 7.16, you're beginning to see a pattern.

NOTE You may remember `IBasketService` from chapter 2, section 2.3.2.

The `GetBasketCmdlet` class must have a default constructor to satisfy PowerShell, so you use it as a COMPOSITION ROOT and leave it as a HUMBLE OBJECT. The next listing demonstrates just how humble it is.

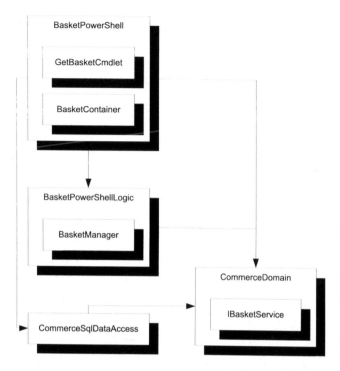

Figure 7.18 The `Basket-PowerShell` library only contains the infrastructure necessary to make PowerShell happy—it's a HUMBLE OBJECT. As soon as the static `BasketContainer` has resolved a `BasketManager`, all further implementation happens in different assemblies. The `BasketManager` class has no access to the internal `BasketContainer` but consumes an `IBasketService` from the Domain Model. As usual, arrows denote references. Not all involved classes are shown.

Listing 7.15   Implementing `GetBasketCmdlet`

```
[Cmdlet(VerbsCommon.Get, "Basket")]
public class GetBasketCmdlet : Cmdlet
{
    private readonly BasketManager basketManager;

    public GetBasketCmdlet()
    {
        this.basketManager =
            BasketContainer.ResolveManager();        ❶ Composition
    }                                                    root

    protected override void ProcessRecord()
    {
        var baskets =
            this.basketManager.GetAllBaskets();      ❷ Delegate to
        this.WriteObject(baskets, true);                 implementer
    }
}
```

In the required default constructor, you use the static container to resolve the `Basket-Manager` ❶ that serves as the implementation ❷. `BasketManager` uses CONSTRUCTOR INJECTION to request an `IBasketService` instance. By now, you should be familiar with this pattern and the implementation of `BasketContainer` shown in the following listing.

Listing 7.16   Resolving `BasketManager`

```
internal static BasketManager ResolveManager()
{                                                        ← ❶  Internal
    BasketRepository basketRepository =                        method
        new SqlBasketRepository(
            BasketContainer.connectionString);
    DiscountRepository discountRepository =
        new SqlDiscountRepository(
            BasketContainer.connectionString);

    BasketDiscountPolicy discountPolicy =
        new RepositoryBasketDiscountPolicy(
            discountRepository);

    IBasketService basketService =
        new BasketService(basketRepository,
            discountPolicy);                             ❷  Return basket
    return new BasketManager(basketService);       ←        manager
}
```

The method, as well as the entire class, is `internal` ❶, which makes it possible to invoke it from the `GetBasketCmdlet` as shown in listing 7.15 but impossible to inadvertently use from `BasketManager` or its DEPENDENCIES.

The implementation of the method should now look familiar to you. Again I find it most straightforward to work backward from the result. The `BasketManager` class requires an `IBasketService` instance ❷, and you use the `BasketService` class (not that you currently have any other implementation to choose from).

`BasketService` requires a `BasketRepository` and a `BasketDiscountPolicy`. For the latter, you use `RepositoryBasketDiscountPolicy`. This class requires another repository ABSTRACTION, and for both repositories, you use the SQL Server–based implementations.

The `BasketManager` implementation is basic, so I won't show it. All it does is express the requested operation in terms of the Domain Model.

The `Remove-Basket` cmdlet follows exactly the same pattern: it uses the static but internal `BasketContainer` to resolve a `BasketManager` instance and then delegates the implementation to the resolved instance. Both cmdlets act as a combination of COMPOSITION ROOT and HUMBLE OBJECT.

The `BasketManager` class is implemented in a different assembly. As soon as the code leaves the cmdlets, there is no risk that any of the underlying implementation will use the static container as a SERVICE LOCATOR because it's internal to the assembly containing the cmdlets.

NOTE   Obviously, the underlying code will never do anything by accident, but the developer writing the code might. We shield the static container from the rest of the code to protect ourselves from making mistakes.

A framework like PowerShell represents the ultimate in DI-unfriendliness. Using the simple technique of making each framework element a COMPOSITION ROOT and a HUMBLE OBJECT gives you an easy way to deal with the issue.

7.7   *Summary*

OBJECT COMPOSITION is one of three important dimensions of DI (the others being LIFETIME MANAGEMENT and INTERCEPTION). In this chapter, I have shown you how to compose applications from loosely coupled modules in a variety of different environments.

Some frameworks make it easy. When we're writing console applications and Windows clients (WPF or Windows Forms), we're more or less in direct control of what is happening at the application's entry point. This provides us with a distinct and easily implemented COMPOSITION ROOT at the entry point.

Other frameworks, such as ASP.NET MVC and WCF, make us work a little harder, but they still provide SEAMS we can use to define how the application should be composed. ASP.NET MVC was designed with DI in mind, so composing an application is as easy as implementing a custom `IControllerFactory` and registering it with the framework. In WCF, the SEAM almost appears to be there accidentally; but although it's more roundabout than implementing a single interface, we can still achieve all the DI goodness we could wish for.

Other frameworks are decidedly DI-unfriendly and require us to use default constructors to fit in. ASP.NET (Web Forms) is the most notorious of these, but other examples include PowerShell and the Managed MMC SDK. These frameworks manage the lifetimes of the classes we provide, so the only option is to treat each class as a separate COMPOSITION ROOT. This is more work, so I personally prefer to use DI-friendly frameworks whenever I have the choice.

Without OBJECT COMPOSITION, there is no DI, but you may not yet have fully realized the implications for OBJECT LIFETIME when we move creation of objects out of the consuming classes. You may find it self-evident that the external caller (often a DI CONTAINER) *creates* new instances of DEPENDENCIES—but when are injected instances deallocated? And what if the external caller decides not to create new instances all the time, but rather hands you an existing instance? These are topics for the next chapter.

Object Lifetime 8

The passing of time has a profound effect on most foods and drinks, but the consequences vary. Personally, I find 12-month-old Gruyère much more interesting than 6-month-old Gruyère, but I prefer my asparagus much fresher than either of those. In many cases, it's easy to assess the proper age of an item; but in certain cases, doing so becomes very complex. This is most notable when it comes to wine (see figure 8.1).

Wines tend to get better with age—until they suddenly become too old and lose most of their flavor. This depends on a lot of factors, including the origin and vintage of the wine. Although wines interest me, I don't expect to ever be able to predict when a wine will peak. For that, I rely on experts: books at home and sommeliers at

Figure 8.1 Wine, cheese, and asparagus. Although the combination may be a bit off, their age greatly affects their overall qualities.

restaurants. They understand wines better than I do because it's their specialty, so whenever I trust them I happily let them take control.

Unless you dove straight into this chapter without reading any of the previous ones, you know that letting go of control is a key concept in DI. This is the INVERSION OF CONTROL aspect, but it implies more than just letting someone else pick an implementation of a required ABSTRACTION. When we accept letting a COMPOSER supply a DEPENDENCY, we must also accept that we can't control its lifetime.

Just as the sommelier intimately knows the contents of the restaurant's wine cellar and can make a far more informed decision than we can, so should we trust the COMPOSER to be able to control the lifetime of DEPENDENCIES more efficiently than the consumer. Composing and managing components is its single responsibility.

DEFINITION COMPOSER—As I use it here, COMPOSER is a unifying term to refer to any object or method that composes DEPENDENCIES. This is often a DI CONTAINER, but may also be any method used in POOR MAN'S DI, such as the `Main` method of a console application.

In this chapter, we'll explore DEPENDENCY LIFETIME MANAGEMENT. Understanding this topic is important because just as you can have a subpar experience if you drink a wine at the wrong age,[1] you may experience degraded performance from configuring DEPENDENCY LIFETIME incorrectly. Even worse, you may get the LIFETIME MANAGEMENT equivalent of spoiled food: resource leaks. Understanding the principles of correctly managing the life cycle scopes of components should enable you to make informed decisions and configure your applications correctly.

> **NOTE**   Throughout this chapter, I use the terms *lifestyle type, life cycle strategy, life cycle scope,* and other unlikely combinations interchangeably.

As figure 8.2 illustrates, we'll start with a general introduction to the concept, followed by a discussion about disposable DEPENDENCIES. This first part of the chapter is meant to provide all the background information and guiding principles you need to make knowledgeable decisions about your own applications' life cycle scope configuration.

After that, we'll use the rest of the chapter to look at different lifetime strategies. This part of the chapter takes the form of a catalog of available lifestyles. In most

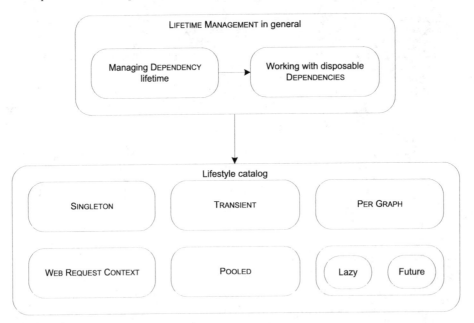

Figure 8.2   The overall structure of this chapter. We'll start with a general discussion about managing DEPENDENCY Lifetime, including a particular discussion of dealing with disposable objects. We need that foundation to efficiently discuss the common patterns of the small lifestyle catalog that follows. We'll start by looking at some common and highly useful patterns and finish with a brief glance at some more exotic lifestyle scopes to give you an impression of the breadth of the topic.

---

[1]   Both your own and the wine's!

cases, one of these stock lifestyle patterns will provide a good match for a given challenge, so understanding them in advance equips you to deal with many difficult situations. When we're finished, you should have a good grasp of LIFETIME MANAGEMENT and common lifetimes.

First, let's look at OBJECT LIFETIME and how it relates to DI in general.

8.1 *Managing Dependency Lifetime*

So far, we've mostly discussed how DI enables us to *compose* DEPENDENCIES. The previous chapter explored this subject in great detail, but as I alluded to in section 1.4, OBJECT COMPOSITION is just one aspect of DI. Managing OBJECT LIFETIME is another.

> **NOTE** In .NET, an object's *life cycle* is simple: the object is created, used, and garbage-collected. The presence of `IDisposable` complicates things a bit, but the life cycle isn't more complicated than that. When we discuss OBJECT LIFETIME, we talk about how we manage objects' life cycles.

The first time I was introduced to the idea that the scope of DI includes LIFETIME MANAGEMENT I failed to understand the deep connection between OBJECT COMPOSITION and OBJECT LIFETIME. I finally got it, and it's simple, so let's take a look!

In this section, I'll introduce LIFETIME MANAGEMENT and how it applies to DEPENDENCIES. We'll start by looking at the general case of composing objects and how it has implications for the lifetimes of DEPENDENCIES. From there, we'll move on to study how DI CONTAINERS can manage DEPENDENCY LIFETIME. Although most of the examples are specialized code that deals with particular configurations, we'll also make a brief detour around a sample DI CONTAINER to get a glimpse at what lifetime configuration might look like.

First, we'll investigate why OBJECT COMPOSITION implies LIFETIME MANAGEMENT.

8.1.1 *Introducing Lifetime Management*

When we accept that we should let go of our psychological need for control over DEPENDENCIES and rather request them through CONSTRUCTOR INJECTION or one of the other DI patterns, we must let go completely. To understand why, we'll examine the issue progressively. Let's begin by reviewing what the standard .NET object life cycle means for DEPENDENCIES. You should already know this, but bear with me for the next half page while I establish the context.

SIMPLE DEPENDENCY LIFE CYCLE

You know that DI means we let a third party (often a DI CONTAINER) serve us the DEPENDENCIES we need. This also means we must let it manage the DEPENDENCIES' lifetimes. This is easiest to understand when it comes to object *creation*. Here is a code fragment from the sample Commerce application's COMPOSITION ROOT (you can see the complete example in listing 7.3):

```
var discountRepository =
    new SqlDiscountRepository(connectionString);
```

```
var discountPolicy =
    new RepositoryBasketDiscountPolicy(discountRepository);
```

I hope that it's evident that the `RepositoryBasketDiscountPolicy` class doesn't control when `discountRepository` is created. In this case, it's likely to happen within the same millisecond; but as a thought experiment, we could insert a call to `Thread.Sleep` between these two lines of code to demonstrate that we can arbitrarily separate them over time. That would be a pretty weird thing to do, but you get the point.

Consumers don't control creation of their DEPENDENCIES, but what about *destruction*? As a general rule, we don't control when objects are destroyed in .NET. The garbage collector collects unused objects, but unless we're dealing with disposable objects, we can't explicitly destroy an object.

> **NOTE** I use the term *disposable object* as shorthand for referring to object instances of types that implement the `IDisposable` interface.

Objects are garbage-collected when they go out of scope. Conversely, they last as long as someone else holds a reference to them. Although a consumer can't explicitly destroy an object, it can keep the object alive by holding on to the reference. This is what we do when we use CONSTRUCTOR INJECTION, because we save the DEPENDENCY in a private field. But as figure 8.3 illustrates, when the consumer goes out of scope, so may the DEPENDENCY.

Even when a consumer goes out of scope, the DEPENDENCY may live on if other objects hold a reference to it. Otherwise, it will be garbage-collected. Because you're an experienced .NET developer, this is old news to you, but now the discussion should begin to get more interesting.

ADDING COMPLEXITY TO THE DEPENDENCY LIFE CYCLE

Until now our analysis of the DEPENDENCY life cycle has been mundane, but we can add some complexity. What happens when more than one consumer requires the same DEPENDENCY? One option is to supply each consumer their own instance, as shown in the following listing.

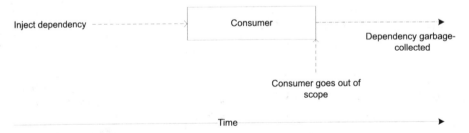

Figure 8.3   Whoever injects the DEPENDENCY into a consumer decides when it's created, but the consumer can keep the DEPENDENCY alive by holding a reference to it. When the consumer goes out of scope, the DEPENDENCY may be eligible for garbage collection.

Listing 8.1 Composing with multiple instances of the same DEPENDENCY

```
var repositoryForPolicy =
    new SqlDiscountRepository(connectionString);
var repositoryForCampaign =
    new SqlDiscountRepository(connectionString);

var discountPolicy =
    new RepositoryBasketDiscountPolicy(
        repositoryForPolicy);

var campaign =
    new DiscountCampaign(repositoryForCampaign);
```

❶ Inject appropriate repository

In this example, two consumers both require a `DiscountRepository` instance, so you wire up two separate instances with the same connection string. You can now pass `repositoryForPolicy` to a new `RepositoryBasketDiscountPolicy` instance and `repositoryForCampaign` to a new `DiscountCampaign` instance ❶.

When it comes to the life cycles of each repository in listing 8.1, nothing has changed compared to the previous example. Each goes out of scope and is garbage-collected when the consumers go out of scope. This may happen at different times, but the situation is only marginally different than before.

It would be a somewhat different situation if both consumers were to *share* the same DEPENDENCY, as shown in this example:

```
var repository =
    new SqlDiscountRepository(connectionString);

var discountPolicy =
    new RepositoryBasketDiscountPolicy(repository);

var campaign = new DiscountCampaign(repository);
```

Instead of creating two different `SqlDiscountRepository` instances, you create a single instance that you inject into both consumers. Both save the reference for later use.

NOTE The consumers are blissfully unaware that the DEPENDENCY is shared. Because they both accept whichever version of the DEPENDENCY they're given, no modification of the source code is necessary to accommodate this change in DEPENDENCY configuration. This is a result of the LISKOV SUBSTITUTION PRINCIPLE.

Liskov Substitution Principle

As originally stated, the LISKOV SUBSTITUTION PRINCIPLE is an academic and abstract concept. But in object-oriented design, we can paraphrase it as follows: *Methods that consume ABSTRACTIONS must be able to use any derived class without knowing it.* In other words, we must be able to substitute the ABSTRACTION for an arbitrary implementation without changing the correctness of the system.

The life cycle situation for the repository DEPENDENCY has changed distinctly compared to the previous example. Both consumers must go out of scope before repository may be eligible for garbage collection, and they may do so at different times. The situation becomes less predictable when the DEPENDENCY reaches the end of its lifetime, and this trait is only reinforced when the number of consumers increases.

Given enough consumers, it's likely that there will always be one around to keep the DEPENDENCY alive. This may sound like a problem, but it rarely is: instead of a multitude of similar instances, we have only one, which saves memory. This is such a desirable quality that we formalize it in a lifestyle pattern called SINGLETON LIFESTYLE. Don't confuse this with the Singleton[2] design pattern, although there are similarities. We'll go into greater detail about this subject in section 8.3.1.

The key point to appreciate is that the COMPOSER has a *greater* degree of influence over the lifetime of DEPENDENCIES than any single consumer. The COMPOSER decides when instances are created, and by its choice of whether to share instances, it determines whether a DEPENDENCY goes out of scope with a single consumer, or whether all consumers must go out of scope before the DEPENDENCY can be released.

This is comparable to visiting a restaurant with a good sommelier. The sommelier spends a large proportion of the day managing and evolving the wine cellar, buying new wines, sampling the available bottles to track how they develop, and working with the chefs to identify optimal matches to the food being served. When we're presented with the wine list, it includes only what the sommelier deems fit to offer for sale. We're free to select a wine according to our personal taste, but we don't presume to know more about the restaurant's selection of wines and how they go with the food than the sommelier does.

The sommelier will often decide to keep lots of bottles in stock for years; and as you'll see in the next section, a COMPOSER may decide to keep instances alive by holding on to their references.

8.1.2   *Managing lifetime with a container*

The previous section explained how we can vary the composition of DEPENDENCIES to influence their lifetimes. In this section, we'll look at how a DI CONTAINER can address these variations.

> **NOTE** This section discusses the *principles* behind managing lifetimes with a DI CONTAINER, so I won't go into great detail about particular containers. As is the case throughout part 3 of this book, I use POOR MAN'S DI to illustrate the concepts.

We'll start by examining how to control the life cycle of DEPENDENCIES using custom containers, and then turn to a quick example of specifying lifestyles in a real DI CONTAINER.

---

[2] Erich Gamma et al., *Design Patterns: Elements of Reusable Object-Oriented Software* (New York: Addison-Wesley, 1994), 127.

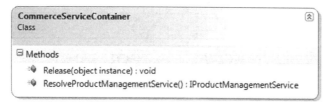

Figure 8.4 All of the `CommerceServiceContainer` **class's implementation currently resides in the** `ResolveProduct-ManagementService` **method. The** `Release` **method does absolutely nothing, and there are no fields or properties on the class. If you're wondering why we have the** `Release` **method, we'll get to it in section 8.2.2.**

MANAGING LIFESTYLES USING A SPECIALIZED CONTAINER

In chapter 7, we created specialized containers to compose applications. One of these was `CommerceServiceContainer`. Listing 7.9 shows the implementation of its `Resolve-ProductManagementService` method; and as figure 8.4 shows, this method is about the only code in the class.

As you may recall from listing 7.9, the `Resolve` method creates the entire dependency graph on the fly each time it's invoked. In other words, each DEPENDENCY is private to the issued `IProductManagementService`, and there is no sharing. When the `IProductManagementService` instance goes out of scope (which it does every time the service has replied to a request), all the DEPENDENCIES go out of scope as well. This is often called a TRANSIENT lifestyle, but we'll talk more about that in section 8.3.2.

Let's analyze the object graph created by `CommerceServiceContainer` and shown in figure 8.5 to see if there is room for improvement.

The `ContractMapper` class is a completely stateless service, so there is no reason to create a new instance every time we need to service a request. The connection string is also unlikely to change, so we may also decide to reuse it across requests.

The `SqlProductRepository` class, on the other hand, relies on an Entity Framework Object Context, and it's considered a best practice to use a new instance per request.

Given this particular configuration, a better implementation of `CommerceService-Container` would reuse the same instances of both `ContractMapper` and the connection string while creating new instances of `SqlProductRepository`. In short, you should configure `ContractMapper` and the connection string to use SINGLETON LIFESTYLE and

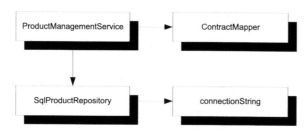

Figure 8.5 Object graph as created by `CommerceServiceContainer`. **Each** `ProductManagementService` **instance created contains its own** `ContractMapper` **and its own** `SqlProductRepository`, **which in turn contains its own connection string. The** DEPENDENCIES **on the right are immutable.**

SqlProductRepository as TRANSIENT. The following listing shows how to implement this change.

Listing 8.2   Managing lifetime with a container

```
public partial class LifetimeManagingCommerceServiceContainer :
    ICommerceServiceContainer
{
    private readonly string connectionString;
    private readonly IContractMapper mapper;

    public LifetimeManagingCommerceServiceContainer()
    {
        this.connectionString =
            ConfigurationManager.ConnectionStrings
            ["CommerceObjectContext"].ConnectionString;       ❶ Create
                                                                Singleton
        this.mapper = new ContractMapper();                    Dependencies
    }

    public IProductManagementService
        ResolveProductManagementService()
    {
        ProductRepository repository =
            new SqlProductRepository(                        ❷ Create Transient
                this.connectionString);                        Dependency
        return new ProductManagementService(
            repository, this.mapper);
    }
}
```

Because you want to reuse the connection string and the ContractMapper across all requests, you save them in private fields and initialize them in the constructor ❶. The readonly keyword provides an extra guarantee that once assigned, these SINGLETON instances are permanent and can't be replaced, but apart from that extra guarantee, readonly is in no way required when implementing the SINGLETON LIFESTYLE.

Each time the container is asked to create a new instance, it creates a TRANSIENT instance of SqlProductRepository using the SINGLETON connection string ❷. It finally uses this TRANSIENT repository together with the SINGLETON mapper to compose and return an instance of ProductManagementService.

NOTE   The code in listing 8.2 is functionally equivalent to the code in listing 7.9—it's just slightly more efficient.

By holding on to the DEPENDENCIES it creates, a container can keep them alive for as long as it wants. In the previous example, it creates both SINGLETON DEPENDENCIES as soon as it's initialized, but it could also have used lazy initialization.

This example should give you an idea of how DI CONTAINERS manage life cycles. Because a DI CONTAINER is a reusable library, we can't modify its source code every time we want to reconfigure a DEPENDENCY's lifestyle. In the next section, we'll take a quick look at how to configure lifestyles for a sample container.

MANAGING LIFESTYLE USING AUTOFAC

Occasionally throughout this book, I take a break from pure POOR MAN'S DI to provide an example of how we can achieve a result using a sample DI CONTAINER. Each DI CONTAINER has its own specific API to express many different features; but although the details differ, the principles remain the same. This is also true for LIFETIME MANAGEMENT.

NOTE Even the term LIFETIME MANAGEMENT isn't ubiquitous. For instance, Autofac[3] calls it *Instance Scope*.

In this section, we'll take a brief glance at configuring lifetimes with Autofac.

NOTE There is no particular reason I chose Autofac over other DI CONTAINERS for this example. I could just as well have chosen a different one.

The next listing shows how to configure Autofac with pure TRANSIENT DEPENDENCIES, equivalent to the example from listing 7.9.

Listing 8.3 Configuring Autofac with TRANSIENT DEPENDENCIES

```
var builder = new ContainerBuilder();
builder.RegisterType<ContractMapper>()
    .As<IContractMapper>();
builder.Register((c, p) =>
    new SqlProductRepository(
        ConfigurationManager
        .ConnectionStrings["CommerceObjectContext"]
        .ConnectionString))
    .As<ProductRepository>();
builder.RegisterType<ProductManagementService>()
    .As<IProductManagementService>();
var container = builder.Build();
```

One peculiarity of Autofac is that you don't configure the container itself, but rather configure a `ContainerBuilder` and use it to create the container when the configuration is completed.

The simplest form of registration is when you only need to define a map between an ABSTRACTION and a concrete type, such as the map from `IContractMapper` to `ContractMapper`. Notice that the concrete type is specified before the ABSTRACTION, which is the reverse order of that used by most other DI CONTAINERS.

Although Autofac supports AUTO-WIRING as well as any other DI CONTAINER, injecting primitive types such as strings always represents a special case because there could potentially be many different strings in play. In this case, you have only a single connection string, but you still need to supply it to the `SqlProductRepository` you now register. You can do that by using a lambda expression[4] that will be executed when the `ProductRepository` type is requested.

---

[3] http://code.google.com/p/autofac/
[4] Technically, it isn't a *lambda expression* but rather a *code block*. Most .NET developers know such code constructs as *lambda expressions*, so I chose the more well-known term over the more correct one.

The use of lambdas is one of Autofac's claims to fame. Although most DI CONTAIN-ERS now have a similar feature, Autofac was among the first to introduce it. You can use the lambda to specify how the `SqlProductRepository` class is created; and, more specifically, you pull the `connectionString` constructor parameter from the application configuration.

The advantage of using a lambda is that it's type-safe, so you get compile-time verification of the construction of the `SqlProductRepository`. The disadvantage is that you don't get AUTO-WIRING, so unless you explicitly need to specify a constructor parameter, the simpler map using the `RegisterType` method is preferable. This is how you map `IProductManagementService` to `ProductManagementService` so it can take advantage of AUTO-WIRING.

You can now use the `container` instance to create new instances of `IProductMan-agementService` like this:

```
var service = container.Resolve<IProductManagementService>();
```

But wait, what about LIFETIME MANAGEMENT? Most DI CONTAINERS have a default lifestyle. In the case of Autofac, the default is called *Per Dependency,* which is the same as the TRANSIENT lifestyle. Because it's the default, you didn't need to specify it, but you could have done it like this if you wanted to:

```
builder.RegisterType<ContractMapper>()
    .As<IContractMapper>()
    .InstancePerDependency();
```

Notice that you use the fluent registration interface to specify the *Instance Scope* (Autofac's term for lifestyle) with the `InstancePerDependency` method.

There is also a *Single Instance Scope* that corresponds to the SINGLETON lifestyle. Armed with that knowledge, you can write the Autofac equivalent of listing 8.2:

```
builder.RegisterType<ContractMapper>()
    .As<IContractMapper>()
    .SingleInstance();
builder.Register((c, p) =>
    new SqlProductRepository(connectionString))
    .As<ProductRepository>();
builder.RegisterType<ProductManagementService>()
    .As<IProductManagementService>();
```

You want `ContractMapper` to have the SINGLETON lifestyle, so you define this by invoking the `SingleInstance` method. When it comes to the `SqlProductRepository`, things become a little more difficult because the `SqlProductRepository` instance should be TRANSIENT, but the injected connection string should be a SINGLETON. You can achieve this by extracting the `connectionString` from the application configuration (not shown, but similar to before) and using this outer variable from within the closure you use to specify the constructor. Because `connectionString` is an outer variable, it remains the same across many invocations of the constructor. Notice how you implicitly scope both `SqlProductRepository` and `ProductManagementService` as TRANSIENTS by not specifying a lifestyle.

Although this example describes how to specify lifestyles with Autofac, other DI CONTAINERS have vaguely similar APIs for the same purpose.

The ability to fine-tune each DEPENDENCY's lifestyle is important for performance reasons but can also be important for functionality. For instance, the Mediator[5] design pattern relies on a shared director through which several components communicate. This only works when the Mediator is shared among the involved collaborators.

So far, we've discussed how INVERSION OF CONTROL implies that consumers can't manage the lifetimes of their DEPENDENCIES because they obviously don't control creation of objects, and because .NET uses garbage collection consumers can't explicitly destroy objects either.

This leaves a question unanswered: what about disposable DEPENDENCIES? We'll now turn our attention to that delicate question.

8.2 *Working with disposable Dependencies*

Although .NET is a managed platform with a garbage collector, it can still interact with unmanaged code. When this happens, .NET code interacts with unmanaged memory that isn't garbage-collected. To prevent memory leaks, we must have a mechanism with which to deterministically release unmanaged memory. This is the key purpose of the IDisposable interface.[6]

It's likely that some DEPENDENCY implementations will contain unmanaged resources. As an example, ADO.NET connections are disposable because they tend to use unmanaged memory, so database-related implementations such as repositories backed by databases are likely to be disposable themselves.

How should we model disposable DEPENDENCIES? Should we also let ABSTRACTIONS be disposable? That might look like this:

```
public interface IMyDependency : IDisposable { }
```

This is technically possible but not a particularly good idea, because it's a design smell that indicates a LEAKY ABSTRACTION:

> *[An] interface [...] generally shouldn't be disposable. There's no way for the one defining an interface to foresee all possible implementations of it - you can always come up with a disposable implementation of practically any interface.*
>
> —Nicholas Blumhardt on the Common Context
> Adapters discussion forum[7]

If you feel the urge to add IDisposable to your interface, it's probably because you have a particular implementation in mind. But you must not let that knowledge leak through to the interface design. Doing so would make it more difficult for other classes to

---

[5] Gamma, *Design Patterns*, 273.

[6] In my opinion, the definitive article about IDisposable is Shawn Farkas's "CLR Inside Out: Digging into IDisposable" (*MSDN Magazine*, July 2007), http://msdn.microsoft.com/en-us/magazine/cc163392.aspx

[7] http://cca.codeplex.com/discussions/82987?ProjectName=cca

implement the interface and would introduce vagueness into the ABSTRACTION. Who is responsible for disposing of a disposable DEPENDENCY? Could it be the consumer?

8.2.1   *Consuming disposable Dependencies*

For the sake of argument, imagine that we have a disposable ABSTRACTION like this abstract OrderRepository class:

```
public abstract class OrderRepository : IDisposable
```

How should an OrderService class deal with such a DEPENDENCY? Most design guidelines (including FxCop and Visual Studio's built-in Code Analysis) would insist that if a class holds a disposable resource as a member, it should itself implement IDisposable and dispose of the resource like this:

```
protected virtual void Dispose(bool disposing)
{
    if (disposing)
    {
        this.repository.Dispose();
    }
}
```

But this turns out to be a spectacularly bad idea because the repository member was originally injected, and it may be shared by other consumers as shown in figure 8.6.

It would be less dangerous not to dispose of the injected repository, but this means we're essentially ignoring the fact that the ABSTRACTION is disposable. In other words, declaring an ABSTRACTION as deriving from IDisposable provides no benefit.

Then again, there can be scenarios where we need to signal the beginning and end of a short-lived scope, and IDisposable is sometimes used for that purpose. Before we examine how a COMPOSER can manage the lifetime of a disposable DEPENDENCY, we should consider how to deal with such ephemeral disposables.

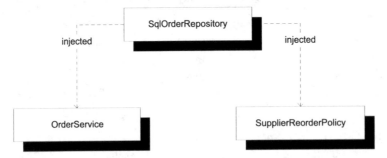

Figure 8.6   A single instance of SqlOrderRepository **is injected into both** OrderService **and** SupplierReorderPolicy. **These two instances share the same DEPENDENCY. If** OrderService **disposes its injected** OrderRepository, **it destroys** SupplierReorderPolicy's **DEPENDENCY, and exceptions will be thrown when** SupplierReorderPolicy **tries to use it.**

CREATING EPHEMERAL DISPOSABLES

Many APIs in the .NET Base Class Library (BCL) use IDisposable to signal that a particular scope has ended. One of the more prominent examples is WCF proxies.

WCF proxies and IDisposable

All auto-generated WCF proxies implement IDisposable, and it's important to remember to invoke the Dispose (or Close) method on a proxy as soon as possible. Many bindings automatically create a session on the service when they submit the first request, and this session lingers in the service until it times out or is explicitly disposed.

If we forget to dispose of our WCF proxies after use, the number of sessions will increase until we hit the limit for concurrent connections from the same source. When we reach the limit, exceptions are thrown. Too many sessions also place an undue burden on the service, so disposing of WCF proxies as soon as possible is important.

To be entirely technically correct, we don't have to invoke the Dispose method on a WCF proxy. Using the Close method achieves the same result.

It's important to remember that the use of IDisposable for such purposes need not indicate a LEAKY ABSTRACTION, because these types aren't always ABSTRACTIONS in the first place. On the other hand, some of them are; and when that is the case, how do we deal with them?

Fortunately, after an object is disposed of, we can't reuse it. This means if we want to invoke the same API again, we must create a new instance. As an example, this fits well with how we use WCF proxies or ADO.NET commands: we create the proxy, invoke its operations, and dispose of it as soon as we're finished. How can we reconcile this with DI if we consider disposable ABSTRACTIONS to be LEAKY ABSTRACTIONS?

As always, hiding the messy details behind an interface can be helpful. If we return to the WPF application from section 7.4, we hid the WCF proxy behind an IProduct-ManagementAgent interface.

> **NOTE** The IProductManagementAgent interface is most notable in listing 7.10, but apart from that, we didn't look at this interface in detail. In essence, such an agent occupies the same spot as a Repository, but many years ago I picked up the habit of naming the data access components of Smart Clients *agent* instead of *repository*.

From the MainViewModel's perspective, this is how you delete a product:

```
this.agent.DeleteProduct(productId);
```

You ask the injected agent to delete the product. MainViewModel can safely hold a reference to the agent because the IProductManagementAgent interface doesn't derive from IDisposable.

Another picture forms when we look at the WCF implementation of that interface. Here is the implementation of the `DeleteProduct` method:

```
public void DeleteProduct(int productId)
{
    using (var channel = this.factory.CreateChannel())
    {
        channel.DeleteProduct(productId);
    }
}
```

The `WcfProductManagementAgent` class has no mutable state but does have an injected Abstract Factory[8] you can use to create a channel. *Channel* is just another word for a WCF proxy, and it's the auto-generated client interface you get for free when you create a service reference with Visual Studio or svcutil.exe. Because this interface derives from `IDisposable`, you can wrap it in a `using` statement.

You use the channel to delete the product. When you exit the `using` scope, the channel is disposed of.

But wait! Didn't I claim that a disposable ABSTRACTION is a LEAKY ABSTRACTION? Yes, I did, but I have to balance pragmatic concerns against principles. In this case, `WcfProduct-ManagementAgent`, the Abstract Factory `IProductChannelFactory`, and `IProduct-ManagementServiceChannel` are all defined in the same, WCF-specific library outlined in figure 8.7.

Every time you invoke a method on the `WcfProductManagementAgent` class, it quickly opens a new channel and disposes it after use. Its lifetime is extremely short, which is why I call such a disposable ABSTRACTION an *ephemeral disposable*.

Notice that the ephemeral disposable is never injected into the consumer. Instead, an Abstract Factory is injected, and you use that factory to control the lifetime of the ephemeral disposable.

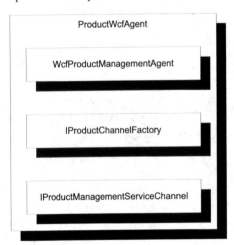

Figure 8.7   **Among other types, the** `Product-WcfAgent` **library contains the implementation of** `IProductManagementAgent` **and its supporting types.** `WcfProductManagementAgent` **uses an** `IProductChannelFactory` **to create instances of** `IProductManagementServiceChannel`**, which is disposable. Although this can be considered a** LEAKY ABSTRACTION**, it doesn't leak very far because all consumers and implementers are contained in the same assembly.**

---

[8] Gamma, *Design Patterns*, 87.

In summary, disposable ABSTRACTIONS are LEAKY ABSTRACTIONS. Sometimes we must accept such a leak to avoid bugs (such as refused WCF connections); but when we do that, we can do our best to contain that leak so it doesn't propagate throughout an entire application.

We've now examined how to *consume* disposable DEPENDENCIES. Let's turn our attention to how we can serve and manage them for consumers.

8.2.2 *Managing disposable Dependencies*

Because I so adamantly insist that disposable ABSTRACTIONS are LEAKY ABSTRACTIONS, the consequence is that ABSTRACTIONS shouldn't be disposable. On the other hand, sometimes implementations are disposable, and if we don't properly dispose of them, we'll have resource leaks in our applications. Someone *must* dispose of them.

> **TIP** Try hard to implement services so they don't hold references to disposables, but rather create and dispose of them on demand as illustrated in figure 6.3. This makes memory management much simpler, because the service can be garbage-collected like other objects.

As always, this responsibility falls on the COMPOSER (such as a DI CONTAINER). It, better than anyone else, *knows* when it creates a disposable instance, so it also knows that the instance needs to be disposed of. It's easy for the COMPOSER to keep a reference to the disposable instance and invoke its `Dispose` method at an appropriate time.

The challenge lies in identifying when the time to dispose is appropriate. How do we know when all consumers have gone out of scope?

Unless someone tells us when that happens, we don't know, but often our code lives inside some sort of context with a well-defined lifetime and events that tell us when a specific scope completes. Table 8.1 shows the scopes for the technologies we looked at in chapter 7.

Table 8.1   Entry and exit points for various .NET Frameworks

Technology	Entry point	Exit point
Console applications	`Main*`	`Main*`
ASP.NET MVC	`IControllerFactory.` `CreateController`	`IControllerFactory.` `ReleaseController`
WCF	`IInstanceProvider.` `GetInstance`	`IInstanceProvider.` `ReleaseInstance`
WPF	`Application.OnStartup`	`Application.OnExit`
ASP.NET	`Constructors**,` `Page_Load`	`IDisposable.Dispose**,` `Page_Unload`
PowerShell	`Constructors**`	`IDisposable.Dispose**`

* The `Main` method is both the entry and exit point because the application starts when it enters `Main` and ends when it exits. Use the beginning of `Main` to resolve DEPENDENCIES and the end to release them.

** We can resolve DEPENDENCIES in constructors, and both ASP.NET and PowerShell at least have the decency to invoke `Dispose` if we implement `IDisposable`.

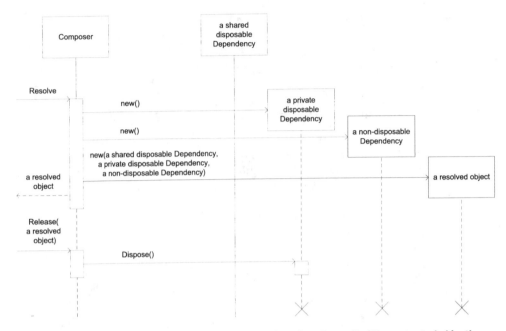

Figure 8.8   When a COMPOSER is asked to resolve an object, it gathers all of the requested object's DEPENDENCIES. In this case, the requested object has three DEPENDENCIES, and two of them are disposable. One of these disposable DEPENDENCIES is shared with other consumers, so it's reused, whereas the other DEPENDENCIES are instantiated on the spot. When the request to release the object comes in, the COMPOSER disposes of the private disposable DEPENDENCY and lets the non-disposable DEPENDENCY and the object itself go out of scope. The only interaction with the shared DEPENDENCY is that it's injected into the requested object; but because it's shared, it isn't disposed of (yet).

We can use the various exit points to tell the COMPOSER that it should release all DEPEN-DENCIES for a given object. It's then up to the COMPOSER to keep track of those DEPEN-DENCIES and their lifestyles and to decide whether anything must be disposed.

RELEASING DEPENDENCIES

Releasing an object graph isn't the same as disposing of it. It's a signal to the COMPOSER that the root of the graph goes out of scope, so if the root itself implements IDisposable, it should be disposed of. But the root's DEPENDENCIES may be shared with other roots, so the COMPOSER may decide to keep some of them around because it knows other objects still rely on them. Figure 8.8 illustrates the sequence of events.

To release DEPENDENCIES, a COMPOSER must track all disposable DEPENDENCIES it has ever served and to which consumers it served them, so it can dispose of them when the last consumer is released.

> **TIP** If you've ever worked with reference counts (or experienced bugs because of bad implementations), you'll appreciate how complex it can be to keep tabs on all DEPENDENCIES and their consumers. This is an area where a DI CONTAINER shines because it takes care of all that for you. Use a DI CONTAINER instead of developing your own lifetime-tracking code. A DI CONTAINER's

implementation of LIFETIME MANAGEMENT is guaranteed to be more thoroughly tested than anything you can produce within a reasonable timeframe.

Let's go back to the WCF service example from section 8.1.2. As it turns out, there is a bug in listing 8.2 because, as figure 8.9 shows, Sql-ProductRepository implements IDisposable.

The code in listing 8.2 creates new instances of SqlProduct-Repository, but it never releases those instances. This will cause

Figure 8.9 `SqlProductRepository` **implements** `IDisposable` **because it encapsulates a disposable resource. It also derives from the abstract** `ProductRepository` **class that** *doesn't* **implement** `IDisposable`**.**

resource leaks, so let's fix that bug with a new version of the specialized container.

First, keep in mind that the container must be able to service many concurrent requests, so it has to associate each SqlProductRepository instance with the IProduct-ManagementService it creates. The container uses a Dictionary<IProductManagement-Service, SqlProductRepository> called repositories to keep track of those associations. The following listing shows how the container resolves requests for IProductManagementService instances.

Listing 8.4 Associating disposable DEPENDENCIES with a resolved root

```
public IProductManagementService ResolveProductManagementService()
{
    var repository = new SqlProductRepository(this.connectionString);
    var srvc = new ProductManagementService(repository, this.mapper);

    lock (this.syncRoot)
    {
        this.repositories.Add(srvc, repository);
    }

    return srvc;
}
```

The method starts by resolving all the DEPENDENCIES. This is similar to the implementation in listing 8.2. But before returning the resolved service, the container must remember the association between the service and the repository.

There is only one instance of the container in the WCF application, and because it's likely that it will receive concurrent requests, you need to lock the dictionary before you add the repository to it. Adding items to a dictionary isn't a thread-safe operation, so you need the lock to ensure that all repositories are saved for later even from within concurrent calls.

If you refer back to listing 7.7, you'll notice that the IInstanceProvider implementation already calls the Release method on the container. So far, you haven't implemented this method, relying on the garbage collector to do the job; but with disposable DEPENDENCIES it's essential that you grasp this opportunity to clean up. Here's the implementation.

Listing 8.5   Releasing disposable DEPENDENCIES

```
public void Release(object instance)
{
    var srvc = instance as IProductManagementService;
    if (srvc == null)
    {
        return;
    }

    lock (this.syncRoot)                                    Dispose of  ❶
    {                                                       repository
        SqlProductRepository repository;
        if (this.repositories.TryGetValue(srvc, out repository))
        {
            repository.Dispose();
            this.repositories.Remove(srvc);    ◁┐  Remove repository
        }                                         ❷  from dictionary
    }
}
```

Because the Release method accepts any type of object, you first need a Guard Clause to make sure that instance is an IProductManagementService.

Concurrent threads may invoke the Release method simultaneously, so once more you must serialize access to the repositories dictionary to ensure that concurrent threads don't corrupt its state. It could lead to memory leaks if repositories aren't removed from the dictionary.

The srvc variable acts as a key to the dictionary, so you can use it to find the disposable DEPENDENCY. When you have it, you can dispose of it ❶ and remove it from the dictionary ❷ to ensure that the container doesn't keep it alive for no good reason.

The examples shown in listings 8.4 and 8.5 are specialized to deal with one particular disposable DEPENDENCY: SqlProductRepository. It would be trivial to expand the code to be able to deal with any sort of disposable DEPENDENCY, but after that it becomes more difficult. Imagine having to deal with multiple disposable DEPENDENCIES for the same object, or nested disposable DEPENDENCIES, where some of them should be SINGLETONS and some of them TRANSIENT—and we haven't even begun to discuss more advanced lifestyles!

TIP   Do yourself a favor and use a DI CONTAINER instead of trying to address all those issues in custom code. The only reason I show this custom code is to explain the principles of LIFETIME MANAGEMENT.

DI CONTAINERS can deal with complex combinations of lifestyles, and they offer opportunities (such as a Release method) to explicitly release components when we're finished with them. We must remember to use these methods to avoid memory leaks, particularly when one or more of the configured DEPENDENCIES are disposable.

We've now discussed LIFETIME MANAGEMENT in some detail. As a consumer, we can't manage the lifetime of injected DEPENDENCIES; that responsibility falls on the COMPOSER, who may decide to share a single instance among many consumers or give each consumer its own private instance. These SINGLETON and TRANSIENT lifestyles are only the most common members of a larger set of lifestyles, and we'll use the rest of the chapter to work our way through a catalog of life cycle strategies.

8.3   Lifestyle catalog

Now that we've covered the principles behind LIFETIME MANAGEMENT in the previous sections, we'll spend the rest of this chapter looking at common lifestyle patterns.

> **NOTE**   I'll use comparable examples throughout this section. But to allow us to focus on the essentials, I'll compose shallow hierarchies, and I'll sometimes ignore the issue with disposable DEPENDENCIES to avoid that added complexity.

Because you've already encountered both SINGLETON and TRANSIENT, we'll begin with them and then expand to other types. As we progress through those lifestyles, we'll move from commonplace lifestyles to more exotic ones, as described in table 8.2.

Table 8.2   Lifestyle patterns covered in this section

Name	Description
SINGLETON	A single instance is perpetually reused.
TRANSIENT	New instances are always served.
PER GRAPH	A single instance is reused within each object graph.
WEB REQUEST CONTEXT	At most one instance of each type is served per web request.
POOLED	Instances are served from a pool of ready objects.
Lazy	An expensive DEPENDENCY is lazily created and served.
Future	A DEPENDENCY becomes available in the future.

Although you may rarely use lifestyles such as POOLED, it's good to know about them, and this list should give you a good indication of the wide range of lifestyles available. Compared to advanced lifestyles, SINGLETON may seem mundane, but it's nevertheless a common and appropriate life cycle strategy.

8.3.1   Singleton

In this book, we have implicitly used the SINGLETON lifetime style from time to time. The name is both clear and somewhat confusing at the same time. It makes a lot of sense because the resulting *behavior* is similar to the Singleton design pattern,[9] but the structure is different.

---

[9]   Ibid., 127.

WARNING Don't confuse the SINGLETON lifestyle with the Singleton design pattern.

Within the scope of a single COMPOSER, a component with SINGLETON lifestyle behaves much like a SINGLETON. Each and every time a consumer requests the component, the same instance is served.

But the similarity ends there. A consumer can't access a SINGLETON-scoped DEPENDENCY through a static member, and if we ask two *different* COMPOSERS to serve us an instance, we'll get two different instances.

TIP Use the SINGLETON lifestyle whenever it's possible.

Because only a single instance is in use, the SINGLETON lifestyle generally consumes a minimal amount of memory. The only time this isn't the case is when the instance is used rarely but consumes inordinate amounts of memory. In such cases, a Lazy lifestyle backed by a TRANSIENT instance may be a better configuration (but I have a hard time coming up with a reasonable example for this).

WHEN TO USE IT

Use the SINGLETON lifestyle when possible. The main issue *preventing* you from using SINGLETON is when a component isn't thread-safe. Because the SINGLETON instance is shared among potentially many consumers, it must be able to handle concurrent access.

All stateless services are by definition thread-safe, as are immutable types and obviously classes specifically designed to be thread-safe. In these cases, there is no reason not to configure them as SINGLETONS.

In addition to the argument for efficiency, some DEPENDENCIES may work as intended only if they're shared. For example, this is the case for implementations of the Circuit Breaker[10] design pattern, as well as in-memory caches. In these cases, it's essential that the implementations are thread-safe.

Let's take a closer look at an in-memory repository.

EXAMPLE: USING A THREAD-SAFE IN-MEMORY REPOSITORY

Let's once more turn our attention to implementing an `ICommerceServiceContainer` like those from sections 7.3.2, 8.1.2, and 8.2.2. Instead of using a SQL Server–based `ProductRepository`, we could decide to use a thread-safe in-memory implementation. For an in-memory data store to make any sense, it must be shared among all requests, so it has to be thread-safe as illustrated in figure 8.10.

Instead of explicitly implementing such a repository as a SINGLETON, we can use a concrete class and scope it appropriately. The only requirement is that it must be thread-safe.

Listing 8.6 shows how a container can return new instances every time it's asked to resolve an `IProductManagementService`, while the `ProductRepository` is shared among all instances.

---

[10] Nygard, *Release It*, 104.

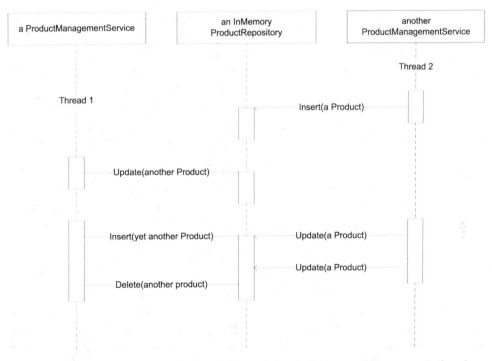

Figure 8.10   When multiple `ProductManagementService` **instances running on separate threads access a shared resource such as an in-memory** `ProductRepository`, **we must ensure that the shared resource is thread-safe.**

Listing 8.6   Managing SINGLETONS

```
public class SingletonContainer : ICommerceServiceContainer
{
    private readonly ProductRepository repository;       ❶ Singleton
    private readonly IContractMapper mapper;                instances

    public SingletonContainer()
    {
        this.repository =                                 Create
            new InMemoryProductRepository();             Singletons
        this.mapper = new ContractMapper();
    }

    public IProductManagementService
        ResolveProductManagementService()
    {
        return new ProductManagementService(             ❷ Create
            this.repository, this.mapper);                   service
    }

    public void Release(object instance) { }        ⬅— Nothing to do
}
```

The SINGLETON lifetime is pretty easy to implement: you keep a reference ❶ to each DEPENDENCY for the duration of the container's lifetime. Notice that you use the readonly keyword to ensure that you can't accidentally change the references at a later date. This isn't strictly necessary to implement the SINGLETON lifestyle but provides a bit of extra safety at the cost of writing eight letters.

Every time the container is asked to resolve an IProductManagementService instance, it creates a TRANSIENT instance with the SINGLETONS injected into it ❷. In this example, both repository and mapper are SINGLETONS, but you can mix lifestyles if you wish.

The SINGLETON lifestyle is one of the easiest lifestyles to implement. All it requires is that you keep a reference to the object and serve the same object every time it's requested. The instance doesn't go out of scope until the COMPOSER goes out of scope. When that happens, the COMPOSER should dispose of the object if it's a disposable type.

Another lifestyle that is trivial to implement is the TRANSIENT lifestyle.

8.3.2   *Transient*

The TRANSIENT lifestyle involves returning a new instance every time it's requested. Unless the instance returned implements IDisposable, there is nothing to keep track of. Conversely, when the instance implements IDisposable, the COMPOSER must keep it in mind and explicitly dispose of it when asked to release the applicable object graph.

It's worth noting that in desktop and similar applications, we tend to resolve the entire object hierarchy only once: at application startup. This means even for TRANSIENT components, only a few instances will be created, and they may be around for a long time. In the degenerate case where there is only one consumer per DEPENDENCY, the end result of resolving a graph of pure TRANSIENT components is equivalent to resolving a graph of pure SINGLETONS, or any mix thereof. This is because the graph is resolved only once, so the difference in behavior never kicks in.

WHEN TO USE IT

The TRANSIENT lifestyle is the safest choice of lifestyles but also one of the least efficient, because it can cause a myriad of instances to be created and garbage-collected even when a single instance would have sufficed. But if you have doubts about the thread-safety of a component, the TRANSIENT lifestyle is safe because each consumer has its own instance of the DEPENDENCY.

In many cases, we can safely exchange the TRANSIENT lifestyle for a context-scoped lifestyle such as WEB REQUEST CONTEXT where access to the DEPENDENCY is also guaranteed to be serialized, but that depends on the runtime environment (WEB REQUEST CONTEXTS make no sense in a desktop application).

EXAMPLE: RESOLVING MULTIPLE REPOSITORIES

You saw several examples of using the TRANSIENT lifestyle earlier in this chapter. In listing 8.2, the repository is created and injected on the spot in the resolving method, and the container keeps no reference to it. In listings 8.4 and 8.5, you subsequently saw how to deal with a TRANSIENT disposable component.

In these examples, you may have noticed that the mapper stays a SINGLETON throughout. This is a purely stateless service, so there is no reason to create a new instance for every ProductManagementService created. The noteworthy point is that you can mix DEPENDENCIES with different lifestyles.

When multiple components require the same DEPENDENCY, each is given a separate instance. The following listing shows a method resolving an ASP.NET MVC Controller.

Listing 8.7 Resolving TRANSIENT DiscountRepositorys

```
public IController ResolveHomeController()
{
    var connStr = ConfigurationManager
        .ConnectionStrings["CommerceObjectContext"]
        .ConnectionString;

    var discountCampaign =
        new DiscountCampaign(                            ❶ New
            new SqlDiscountRepository(connStr));    ⟵      SqlDiscountRepository
    var discountPolicy =                                   instance
        new RepositoryBasketDiscountPolicy(
            new SqlDiscountRepository(connStr));    ⟵   Another
    return new HomeController(                             SqlDiscountRepository
        discountCampaign, discountPolicy);       ❷      instance
}
```

Both the DiscountCampaign and RepositoryBasketDiscountPolicy classes require a DiscountRepository DEPENDENCY. When the DiscountRepository is TRANSIENT, each consumer gets it own private instance, so DiscountCampaign gets one instance ❶ and RepositoryBasketDiscountPolicy gets another ❷.

The TRANSIENT lifestyle implies that every consumer receives a private instance of the DEPENDENCY even when multiple consumers in the same object graph have the same DEPENDENCY (as is the case in listing 8.7). If many consumers share the same DEPENDENCY, this approach can be inefficient; but if the implementation isn't thread-safe, the more efficient SINGLETON lifestyle is inappropriate. In such cases, the PER GRAPH lifestyle may be a better fit.

8.3.3 *Per Graph*

SINGLETON is the most efficient lifestyle and TRANSIENT is the safest, but can we devise a lifestyle that combines the advantages of both? Although we can't get the best of both worlds, in some cases it makes sense to share a single instance across a single resolved graph. We can view this as a sort of locally scoped SINGLETON. We can use a shared instance within a single object graph, but we don't share that instance with other graphs.

Each time we resolve an object graph, we create only a single instance of each DEPENDENCY. If there are multiple consumers of that DEPENDENCY, they share the same instance; but when we resolve a new object graph, we create a new instance.

WHEN TO USE IT

We can use the PER GRAPH lifestyle in most cases where we would otherwise use TRANSIENT. We normally assume that the thread that resolves the object graph is also the only consumer of that object graph. Even when the DEPENDENCY in question isn't thread-safe, we can use the PER GRAPH lifestyle, because the shared instance is only shared by consumers running on the same thread.

In the rare cases where one or more consumers spin up new threads and consume the DEPENDENCY from those threads, TRANSIENT is still the safest lifestyle, but that should be a rare occurrence. There may be other cases when the DEPENDENCY represents a mutable resource and each consumer needs its own private state. In such a case, TRANSIENT is the correct life cycle because it guarantees that the instances are never shared.

Compared to TRANSIENT, there is no additional overhead from using PER GRAPH, so we can often use it as a replacement for TRANSIENT. Although there is no overhead, we also aren't guaranteed any benefit. We only gain a boost in efficiency if a single object graph contains multiple consumers of the same DEPENDENCY. In this case, we can share an instance between those consumers; but if there are no shared DEPENDENCIES, there will be nothing to share and so no benefit.

> **NOTE** PER GRAPH is superior to TRANSIENT in the majority of cases, but not many DI CONTAINERS support it out of the box.

In the cases where the implementation is thread-safe, the SINGLETON lifestyle is still a more efficient choice.

EXAMPLE: SHARING A REPOSITORY WITHIN A GRAPH

In listing 8.7, you saw how each consumer received its own private `SqlDiscountRepository` instance. This class isn't thread-safe, so you shouldn't configure it as a SINGLETON. But you don't expect multiple threads to access individual `HomeController` instances, so it's safe to share a `SqlDiscountRepository` instance between both consumers. The next listing shows how to create a single instance PER GRAPH to the `ResolveHomeController` method.

Listing 8.8 Resolving a single repository per graph

```
public IController ResolveHomeController()
{
    var connStr = ConfigurationManager
        .ConnectionStrings["CommerceObjectContext"]
        .ConnectionString;
    var repository =
        new SqlDiscountRepository(connStr);          ❶ Shared SqlDiscountRepository
                                                         instance
    var discountCampaign =
        new DiscountCampaign(repository);            ❷ Inject
    var discountPolicy =                                shared
        new RepositoryBasketDiscountPolicy(repository);  instance
```

```
        return new HomeController(discountCampaign, discountPolicy);
}
```

Instead of creating separate instances for all consumers, you create a single instance that you can share among all consumers ❶. You inject this single instance into both `DiscountCampaign` and `RepositoryBasketDiscountPolicy` ❷. Notice that compared to Singletons, where the shared instance is a private member of the container, the `repository` instance is local to the `ResolveHomeController` method; the next time the method is invoked, a new instance is created and shared among the two consumers.

The Per Graph lifestyle is a good alternative to Transient when the only reason not to use Singleton is because the implementation isn't thread-safe. Although Per Graph offers a generally usable solution to sharing Dependencies within a well-defined scope, there are other, more specialized alternatives.

8.3.4　Web Request Context

As users of a web application, we would like a response from the application as quickly as possible, even when other users use it at the same time. We don't want our request to be put on a queue together with all the other users' requests. We might have to wait an inordinately long time for a response if there were many requests ahead of ours.

To address this issue, web applications handle requests concurrently. The .NET infrastructure shields us from this by letting each request execute in its own context and with its own instance of Controllers (if you use ASP.NET MVC) or Pages (if you use ASP.NET Web Forms).

Because of concurrency, Dependencies that aren't thread-safe can't be used as Singletons. On the other hand, using them as Transients may be inefficient or even downright problematic if we need to share a Dependency between different consumers within the same request.

Although the ASP.NET engine doesn't guarantee that a single request executes entirely on a single thread, it *does* guarantee that code is executed in a serialized manner. This means that if we can share a Dependency only within a single request, thread-safety isn't an issue.

Figure 8.11 demonstrates how the Web Request Context lifestyle works. Dependencies behave like Singletons within a single request but aren't shared across requests. Each request has its own set of associated Dependencies.

Any disposable components should be disposed of when the request ends.

When to use it
The Web Request Context lifestyle obviously makes sense only in a web application. Even within a web application, it can only be used in requests. Although requests tend to constitute the vast majority of a web application, it's worth noting that if we spin up a background thread for asynchronous processing, this lifestyle doesn't apply because the background thread won't be synchronized with a web request.

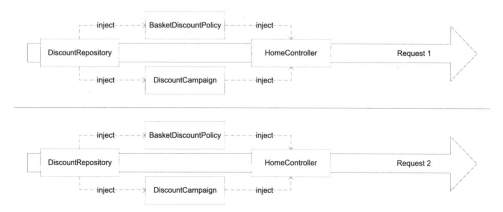

Figure 8.11   The WEB REQUEST CONTEXT lifestyle indicates that we create *at most* one instance per web request. The `DiscountRepository` instance is shared between `BasketDiscountPolicy` and `DiscountCampaign`, but only within Request 1. Request 2 uses the same configuration, but instances are constrained to that request.

The WEB REQUEST CONTEXT lifestyle is preferable to TRANSIENT, but the SINGLETON lifestyle is still more efficient. Use WEB REQUEST CONTEXT only in situations where SINGLETON won't work.

> **NOTE**   If you follow the general advice of only resolving a single object graph per web request, the WEB REQUEST CONTEXT and PER GRAPH lifestyles are functionally equivalent.

> **TIP**   If you ever need to compose an Entity Framework `ObjectContext` in a web request, the WEB REQUEST CONTEXT is an excellent lifestyle. `ObjectContext` instances aren't thread-safe, but there should be only one `ObjectContext` per web request.

Not all DI CONTAINERS support this lifestyle, so obviously we can only use it if it's available.

> **TIP**   Some DI CONTAINERS allow you to write your own lifestyle extension, so this may be an option if your container of choice doesn't support the WEB REQUEST CONTEXT lifestyle out of the box. Still, this may not be a trivial undertaking.

As with other lifestyles, we can mix lifestyles so that, for example, some are configured as SINGLETONS and others are shared per web request.

EXAMPLE: COMPOSING A HOMECONTROLLER WITH A REQUEST-SHARED REPOSITORY

In this example, you'll see how to compose an ASP.NET MVC `HomeController` instance with DEPENDENCIES that both require a `DiscountRepository`. This situation is outlined in figure 8.11: the `HomeController` requires a `BasketDiscountPolicy` and a `Discount-Campaign`, and both of these require a `DiscountRepository`.

> **NOTE**   The example code in this section is more complex than warranted by a one-off solution. I would never expect you to write custom WEB REQUEST

CONTEXT life cycle code like this, but I want to show you how it works. Use a DI CONTAINER that supports this lifestyle instead.

You want to use a shared `SqlDiscountRepository`, but because this class isn't thread-safe you can't share it as a SINGLETON. Instead, you'll share it within each web request. The specialized container composes `HomeController` instances as shown in the following listing.

Listing 8.9   Composing `HomeController`

```
public IController ResolveHomeController()
{
    var discountPolicy =
        new RepositoryBasketDiscountPolicy(
            this.ResolveDiscountRepository());         ◁──┐  ❶ Delegate resolution
    var campaign = new DiscountCampaign(                   │     of repository
        this.ResolveDiscountRepository());         ◁──────┘

    return new HomeController(              │ Return composed
        campaign, discountPolicy);          │ HomeController
}
```

By now, most of the mechanics of this method should be familiar to you. The only noteworthy item is that you delegate resolution of the `DiscountRepository` ❶ to a separate method. This method ensures that at most one instance is resolved per web request.

   When asked to resolve a `DiscountRepository`, the container must check if there is already an instance associated with the web request. If this is the case, that instance is returned; otherwise the instance is created and associated with the web request before it's returned. As the next listing shows, in ASP.NET (both MVC and Web Forms) you can use the current `HttpContext` to maintain this association.

Listing 8.10   Resolving a web request context-scoped DEPENDENCY

```
protected virtual DiscountRepository ResolveDiscountRepository()
{
    var repository = HttpContext.Current            ❶ Look up repository
        .Items["DiscountRepository"]                    in request context
        as DiscountRepository;
    if (repository == null)
    {
        var connStr = ConfigurationManager
            .ConnectionStrings["CommerceObjectContext"]
            .ConnectionString;
        repository = new SqlDiscountRepository(connStr);
        HttpContext.Current                          ❷ Save repository in
            .Items["DiscountRepository"] = repository;    request context
    }

    return repository;
}
```

The point of the WEB REQUEST CONTEXT lifestyle is to reuse instances already associated with the current request, so the first thing to do is check whether the desired instance already exists ❶. If this is the case, you can return it. If the instance isn't found, you must create it and associate it with the current web request ❷ before returning it.

The first time you invoke the ResolveDiscountRepository method, it creates the repository and associates it with the request so that every subsequent call reuses the same instance.

When the request ends, you may have left a disposable DEPENDENCY in the web request, which could lead to memory leaks, so you should also ensure that all DEPENDENCIES are released when the request ends. One way to do this is to register a custom IHttpModule that subscribes to the EndRequest event to properly dispose of all disposable DEPENDENCIES. The following listing shows a sample implementation.

Listing 8.11 Releasing disposable WEB REQUEST CONTEXT–scoped DEPENDENCIES

```
public class DiscountRepositoryLifestyleModule : IHttpModule
{
    public void Init(HttpApplication context)
    {
        context.EndRequest += this.OnEndRequest;
    }

    public void Dispose() { }

    private void OnEndRequest(object sender, EventArgs e)
    {
        var repository = HttpContext.Current        ❶ Look up repository
            .Items["DiscountRepository"];              in request context
        if (repository == null)
        {
            return;
        }

        var disposable = repository as IDisposable;
        if (disposable != null)
        {                                            ❷ Dispose of
            disposable.Dispose();                       repository
        }

        HttpContext.Current                          ❸ Remove repository
            .Items.Remove("DiscountRepository");        from request context
    }
}
```

When a web request ends, you attempt to look up the repository in the request context ❶. If you find it, you can dispose of it if applicable ❷. Whether it's disposable or not, you must remember to remove it ❸ from the request context.

The WEB REQUEST CONTEXT lifestyle associates a DEPENDENCY with the current request by saving and retrieving it via HttpContext.Current. This example demonstrated a specialized solution, but the technique can be generalized so that an arbitrary number of DEPENDENCIES of many different types can be associated with the request context. This is the realm of a proper DI CONTAINER.

VARIATION: SESSION REQUEST CONTEXT

A rarer variation of the WEB REQUEST CONTEXT lifestyle is one where the scope of a DEPENDENCY's lifetime is associated not with a particular web request but rather with a session. This is a much more exotic lifestyle, and you should exercise extreme caution if you decide to use it.

Technically, it may seem similar to the WEB REQUEST CONTEXT, but the most important distinction is that, whereas an HTTP request has a well-defined lifetime, sessions don't. A session rarely ends explicitly but rather expires after a time of inactivity. This means all DEPENDENCIES registered this way are likely to be around for a long time where they aren't being used. All that time they take up memory, which can severely impact an application's capacity.

> **WARNING** Only use the Session Request Context lifestyle if you really need it. It's likely to degrade your system's capacity.[11]

> **TIP** If you need to link certain DEPENDENCIES to a session, you're better off configuring it with a WEB REQUEST CONTEXT and using a factory that wires up each instance based on the appropriate session key. This approach lets you more explicitly manage the lifetime of the DEPENDENCY while still linking it with a session.

Another issue we face is that session state may be saved in an out-of-process store, such as a separate session server or SQL Server session state. In these configurations, all session data must be serializable, and so must the affected DEPENDENCIES. Making a type serializable can be as simple as decorating it with the `[Serializable]` attribute, but it's still something we must remember to do.

Overall, I find Session Request Context unattractive, and I can't recall ever seeing it in use.

VARIATION: THREAD CONTEXT

Another, more applicable, variation is to associate a DEPENDENCY with a particular thread. The concept is the same: the DEPENDENCY is managed as a SINGLETON on each thread, but there is an instance per thread.

This approach is mostly useful in scenarios where we spin up multiple equivalent worker threads and use the start of each thread as a COMPOSITION ROOT. This is the situation illustrated in figure 8.12.

To implement the Thread Context lifestyle, we can look after a requested DEPENDENCY in Thread Local Storage (TLS).[12] If we find the instance, we reuse it; otherwise we create it and store it in TLS.

---

[11] For an in-depth treatment of why session-scoped objects are problematic in general, see Michael T. Nygard, *Release It! Design and Deploy Production-Ready Software* (Raleigh, NC: Pragmatic Bookshelf, 2007), 175.

[12] We also used TLS in section 4.4.1.

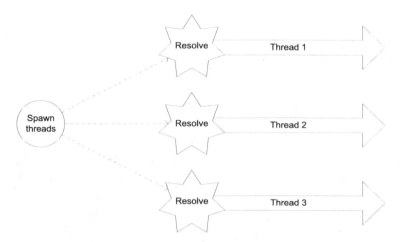

Figure 8.12   When an application immediately spins up a number of parallel tasks and resolves DEPENDENCIES from within each thread, we can use the Thread Context lifestyle to ensure that any DEPENDENCIES that aren't thread-safe can be shared among any number of consumers on the same thread. Each thread has its own instances.

Whereas Session Request Context may be downright dangerous and Thread Context a bit exotic, the WEB REQUEST CONTEXT lifestyle is useful. It enables us to share DEPENDENCIES within a web request without having to worry about whether they're thread-safe. It provides a good middle ground between SINGLETON and TRANSIENT.

It provides a more efficient alternative to the TRANSIENT lifestyle, but we can only use it in web applications. If we have expensive DEPENDENCIES to manage in other types of applications, we can turn to other optimization techniques.

8.3.5   *Pooled*

Sometimes, components are expensive to create. A common solution is to have a pool of already-created components available for easy access. A well-known example is database connections, which are almost always pooled. We automatically use database-connection pooling, and we can use the same technique if we have custom components that are expensive to create.

Although the overall concept of pooled objects should be familiar to you, table 8.3 lists some variation in implementation.

These are all relevant concerns regarding object pools. But as is the case with the WEB REQUEST CONTEXT lifestyle, we shouldn't be custom-developing our own object pools, but rather should use those provided by DI CONTAINERS.

> **NOTE**   Not all DI CONTAINERS provide the POOLED lifestyle, so we can obviously choose this lifestyle only if it's supported by our DI CONTAINER.

When using the POOLED lifestyle provided by a DI CONTAINER, all the options described in table 8.3 may not be available. We have to go with what is available.

Table 8.3 Options for implementing object pools

Option	Description
Pool preparation	How do we prepare the pool? Do we create all the objects in the pool well in advance, or do we fill it gradually as requests arrive? Filling the pool in advance requires that we know at least the starting size of the pool. It may also be an expensive operation, because the purpose of the pool is to make expensive objects readily available. But the advantage of doing this is that the objects are available for fast access. Perhaps it's even possible to prefill the pool from a background thread so it can begin serving objects while it's filling. Alternatively, we can start with an empty pool and gradually fill it as required. This causes access times to be slower in the beginning but may help keep the pool at just the right size.
Minimum size	We can address the issue of pool preparation by introducing a configurable minimum size. If we set the minimum size to anything other than zero, the pool must first fill itself to this point before it can start serving objects. At a minimum size of zero, on the other hand, it can begin serving objects immediately while filling the pool.
Maximum size	What is the maximum size of the pool?
Boundary behavior	What happens when we hit the maximum size of the pool? Do we allow the pool to grow? If so, we run the risk of running out of memory. If not, how do we treat additional requests for objects? One option is to block the call until an object becomes available. But if we do that, we should at least provide the caller with an opportunity to specify a timeout.[12] Another option is to immediately throw an exception.
Pool cleanup	Do we keep the pool filled until the application shuts down, or do we begin to drain it if we notice that it has excess capacity?

WHEN TO USE IT

The POOLED life cycle comes into play when we have specific components that are often used but expensive to create. Even if the component is expensive to create, we should still prefer the SINGLETON lifestyle if possible because that allows us to get by with a single instance and only pay the tax of creating the object once.

From this, it follows that pooling is applicable only when the component in question must not be shared, which is often the case when it isn't thread-safe. If we're running in a web application, the WEB REQUEST CONTEXT lifestyle may be a reasonable alternative; we should mostly expect to see the POOLED lifestyle used outside web applications.

Note that it's a requirement that the component in question can be reused. If it has a natural life cycle that precludes reuse, we can't pool it. One example is WCF's `ICommunicationObject` interface, which has a clearly defined life cycle. When an `ICommunicationObject` is either `Closed` or `Faulted`, it can by definition never leave that state. Such a type of object isn't eligible for pooling. We must be able to return the object back to the pool in pristine state.

---

[13] Read more about the Blocked Threads anti-pattern and the Timeout pattern in Nygard, *Release It*, 70 and 100.

EXAMPLE: REUSING EXPENSIVE REPOSITORIES

I once was involved in a project that required us to communicate with a mainframe from .NET code. Earlier consultants had created an unmanaged COM library that could talk to some endpoint on the mainframe, and we decided to wrap that library in a managed assembly.

The COM library communicated with the mainframe via a proprietary protocol over network sockets. To use it, we had to open the connection and go through a handshake. When the connection was open, we could transfer messages at a reasonable speed, but opening the connection took time.

Let's see how to create a pool of `ProductRepository` instances that can communicate via such a protocol. In the project I was involved with, we called the COM library for Xfer (very generic), so let's create a pool of `XferProductRepository` instances.

> **NOTE**   As was the case with the WEB REQUEST CONTEXT lifestyle example, I don't expect you to write custom object-pooling lifetime managers. Although you should use an appropriate DI CONTAINER to manage object pools, I want to show you a simplified example to give you an idea of how it works.

> **WARNING**   The following example isn't thread-safe. I left out the synchronization code to keep the example at a reasonable level of complexity, and I leave a thread-safe implementation as an exercise to the reader (I have always wanted to write this).

This example is yet another variation of the `ICommerceServiceContainer`, of which you've seen several variations in this chapter. The following listing shows the foundation of the container.

Listing 8.12   Laying out a foundation for a pooling container

```
public partial class PooledContainer : ICommerceServiceContainer
{
    private readonly IContractMapper mapper;
    private readonly List<XferProductRepository> free;
    private readonly List<XferProductRepository> used;
    public PooledContainer()
    {
        this.mapper = new ContractMapper();
        this.free = new List<XferProductRepository>();
        this.used = new List<XferProductRepository>();
    }

    public int MaxSize { get; set; }

    public bool HasExcessCapacity
    {
        get
        {
            return this.free.Count + this.used.Count < this.MaxSize;
```

```
        }
    }
}
```

Although you plan to pool instances of XferProductRepository, you still configure ContractMapper as a SINGLETON because it's a stateless service.

To keep track of the pool, you use two collections: one that holds available repositories and one that contains the repositories that are currently in use. When you create and release components, you'll move repositories between these two collections.

The MaxSize property lets you define the maximum size of the pool, and the HasExcessCapacity property is essentially an encapsulated calculation you can use in a conditional expression to determine whether you still have excess capacity.

In this pool variation, you'll fill the pool gradually as requests arrive, until you reach the maximum. As the next listing shows, you throw an exception if you reach capacity and get more requests.

Listing 8.13 Resolving repositories from a pool

```
public IProductManagementService ResolveProductManagementService()
{
    XferProductRepository repository = null;
    if (this.free.Count > 0)
    {
        repository = this.free[0];                      ❶ Pick from pool
        this.used.Add(repository);                        if available
        this.free.Remove(repository);
    }
    if (repository != null)
    {
        return this.ResolveWith(repository);            ❷ Return from
    }                                                       pool

    if (!this.HasExcessCapacity)
    {
        throw new InvalidOperationException(
            "The pool is full.");
    }

    repository = new XferProductRepository();           ❸ Add new
    this.used.Add(repository);                              repository

    return this.ResolveWith(repository);
}

private IProductManagementService ResolveWith(
    ProductRepository repository)
{
    return new ProductManagementService(repository,
        this.mapper);
}
```

To resolve an `IProductManagementService` instance, you begin by checking whether a reusable repository is available. If this is the case, you pick one from the collection of free repositories and move it to the list of repositories in use ❶. If you succeed in finding a reusable repository, you can return the service ❷ immediately.

If you can't find an available repository in the pool, there are two possible reasons: the pool is full and all repositories are in use, or you have yet to fill the pool. If you can get past the Guard Clause that checks for the first case, you create a new instance of the expensive repository and add it to the collection of repositories in use ❸ before you return the composed service.

`ResolveProductManagementService` only moves repositories from the `free` to the used collection, so it's important to release the services after use. The following listing shows how to do this.

Listing 8.14 Returning repositories to the pool

```
public void Release(object instance)
{
    var service = instance as ProductManagementService;
    if (service == null)
    {
        return;
    }
    var repository = service.Repository
        as XferProductRepository;              Guard
    if (repository == null)                    Clauses
    {
        return;
    }
    this.used.Remove(repository);          ❶  Return repository
    this.free.Add(repository);                 to pool
}
```

Returning the repository to the pool is easy: you move it ❶ from the collection of repositories in use to the collection of available repositories.

Note that even though this example may seem complex, I didn't address a few issues:

- The example definitely isn't thread-safe. A production implementation should allow several threads to resolve and release instances concurrently.

- Because the `XferProductRepository` class encapsulates unmanaged code, it implements `IDisposable`. As long as you keep reusing instances, you need not dispose of them, but you should certainly do so when the container goes out of scope. Thus, the container itself must implement `IDisposable` and dispose of all repositories from its `Dispose` method.

Object pooling is a well-known design pattern, but it's often encapsulated in existing APIs; for example, ADO.NET uses connection pools, but this isn't something we have to explicitly deal with. Only when we explicitly need to optimize access to expensive resources does the POOLED lifestyle begin to make sense.

The POOLED lifestyle helps address the situation where we need to optimize the use of expensive resources. This is the last of the common DEPENDENCY lifestyle types.

8.3.6 *Other lifestyles*

The lifestyle types examined in this chapter represent the most common types, but you may have more exotic needs that aren't satisfactorily addressed. When I find myself in such a situation, my first reaction is to feel immensely proud that I have discovered a rare and precious corner case that requires me to use an exotic item from my programming toolbox.

My next reaction is to realize that my approach is all wrong, and if I change my design a bit, everything will fit nicely into standard patterns. This realization is often a letdown, but it leads to better and more maintainable code. The point is that if you feel a need to implement a custom lifestyle, you should first seriously reconsider your design.

That said, some DI CONTAINERS provide extensibility points that let you develop custom lifestyles. Let's briefly look at two technically possible, but rather exotic, lifestyles. In both cases, I provide only a brief sketch of how the lifetime would work. I don't provide full sections because I'm having a hard time coming up with a reasonable scenario in which they should be applied.

LAZY

The Lazy or Delayed lifestyle is a Virtual Proxy[14] of a more expensive DEPENDENCY. The idea is that if we have an expensive DEPENDENCY that we don't expect to use often, we can defer creation of the expensive DEPENDENCY until it's needed. Figure 8.13 illustrates how a consumer can be injected with a lightweight stand-in for the actual, more expensive implementation.

It only makes sense to use such a lifetime style if the consumer only uses the expensive DEPENDENCY in a small fraction of its own lifetime, or if we can realistically expect that it will take a noticeable amount of time before the DEPENDENCY is invoked. If the DEPENDENCY is invoked immediately or often, the Lazy Decorator buys us nothing, but uses extra resources.

If at all possible, an expensive DEPENDENCY should be registered as a SINGLETON so we only need to pay the tax of creating it once. If this isn't possible for thread-safety reasons, we can often better resolve this conundrum by pooling the expensive component. Even if we can only have a single instance, a pool of one combined with a time-out on access will effectively give us serialized access to the DEPENDENCY.

The Lazy lifetime style is more of a technical curiosity than a practically useful lifecycle strategy; if you're curious, I refer you to the suggested literature associated with this book.[15]

---

[14] Gamma, *Design Patterns*, 208.
[15] Mark Seemann, "Rebuttal: Constructor over-injection anti-pattern," 2010, http://blog.ploeh.dk/2010/01/20/RebuttalConstructorOverinjectionAntipattern.aspx

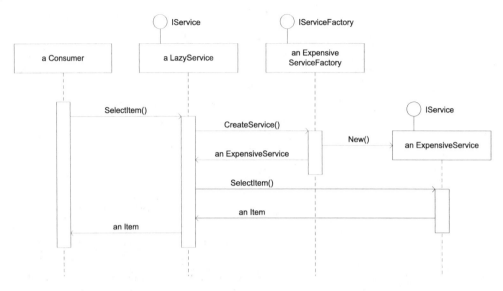

Figure 8.13   A consumer requires an `IService` DEPENDENCY, but if it only uses this DEPENDENCY in a small fraction of the time, it can live for a long time before requiring the services of `IService`. When it finally invokes `IService.SelectItem()`, `LazyService` uses its injected `IServiceFactory` to create an instance of another `IService`. It isn't until this point that the `ExpensiveService` instance is created. After `ExpensiveService` is created, all subsequent calls can be delegated to it.

FUTURE

The Future lifestyle is even more exotic. The idea is that we may want to use a DEPENDENCY that isn't available at the moment but that we'll use as it becomes available.

The best way to implement such a lifestyle is similar to the Lazy lifestyle: we can use a Decorator that delegates to an initial implementation until the desired DEPENDENCY becomes available. Figure 8.14 illustrates the conceptual interaction between components. The initial implementation used as a stand-in while the Future Decorator waits for the desired DEPENDENCY is often an application of the Null Object[16] design pattern.

I must admit that I'm hard pressed to come up with a reasonable example of when a DEPENDENCY may become available after we've wired up the entire object graph. This might sound a bit like the case where we rely on an external resource such as a database or web service, but keep in mind that even if the actual resource is unavailable, the programmatic DEPENDENCY still exists; for example, a web service may be down, but the WCF proxy we use to communicate with it is still available.

We can better deal with the issue of unavailable out-of-process resources using the Circuit Breaker pattern that we'll look at in the next chapter. Until someone presents me with a reasonable scenario, I regard the Future life cycle strategy as a technical curiosity.

---

[16] Robert C. Martin et al., *Pattern Languages of Program Design* (New York: Addison-Wesley, 1998), 5.

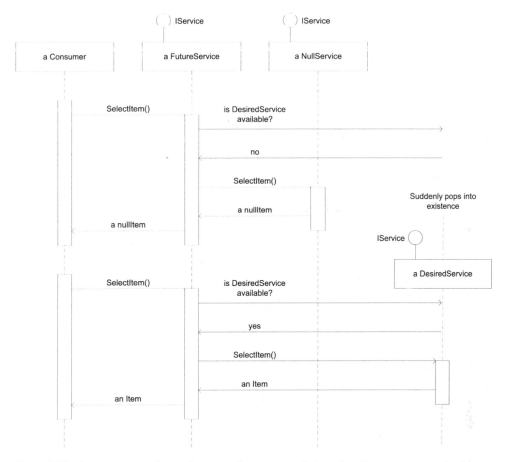

Figure 8.14 **A consumer requires an instance of** `IService`, **but** `DesiredService` **may not yet be available. In this case, we can encapsulate a** `NullService` **as a stand-in to be used while we wait for Godot.** `FutureService` **is a state machine that polls to see if** `DesiredService` **has become available. As long as it isn't, the** `FutureService` **Decorator has no choice but to use the fallback implementation provided by** `NullService`. **When** `DesiredService` **finally becomes available, all future requests are directed to it.**

We've now looked at a wide range of available DEPENDENCY lifestyles, from the commonplace to the truly exotic.

8.4 Summary

When we apply INVERSION OF CONTROL to DEPENDENCIES, we invert control not only over type selection but also over LIFETIME MANAGEMENT. When a consumer no longer creates its own instances of DEPENDENCIES, it can't decide when the DEPENDENCY was created or whether it's shared with other consumers.

COMPOSERS may decide to let many consumers share a single instance, or they may decide to let each consumer have their own instance. More advanced strategies may also come into play.

Although COMPOSERS have a great deal of control over when objects are created, the managed memory model of .NET means that in many cases they have little influence over when objects are destroyed. DEPENDENCIES may go out of scope and be reclaimed by the garbage collector. But a special place is reserved for components that also implement IDisposable because we must ensure that all unmanaged resources are cleaned up—otherwise our applications will soon begin to experience memory leaks.

Equivalent to invoking a Resolve method (or whatever its name is), we must always remember to invoke a Release method when the resolved object graph goes out of scope. This gives the COMPOSER a chance to dispose of any disposable components that become unused.

Each dependency graph may have a mix of many different lifestyles, and we also need to keep track of whether the components are disposable. Add thread-safety to this mix, and it becomes complicated to keep track of all these things. This is an area where a full-blown DI CONTAINER shines, and it's one of the many reasons we should use a DI CONTAINER instead of POOR MAN'S DI.

Each of the many available DI CONTAINERS offers its own mix of available lifestyles. Some support only a few, others support most or all of them, but many also offer extensibility points that allow us to implement our own lifestyles.

The safest lifestyle is TRANSIENT because instances aren't shared with anyone else. It's also the most inefficient because many instances of the same type are likely to be in memory.

The most efficient lifestyle is SINGLETON because only a single instance is in memory (per container, that is). But it requires that the component be thread-safe, so it isn't always possible to use this lifestyle.

The WEB REQUEST CONTEXT and POOLED lifestyles provide good alternatives to SINGLETON and TRANSIENT, but in more limited scenarios.

More exotic lifestyles are possible. The Future lifestyle may at first glance look like a good way to handle unavailable resources, but as you'll see in the next chapter, we can better address such issues with INTERCEPTION.

Interception 9

One of the most interesting things about cooking is the way we can combine many ingredients, some of them not particularly savory in themselves, into a whole that is greater than the parts. Often, we start with a simple ingredient that provides the basis for the meal, and then modify and embellish it until the end result is a delicious dish.

Consider a veal cutlet. If we were desperate, we could eat it raw, but in most cases we'd prefer to fry it. However, if we simply slap it on a hot pan, the result will be less than stellar. Apart from the burned flavor, it won't taste of much.

Fortunately, there are lots of steps we can take to enhance the experience:

- Frying the cutlet in butter prevents burning the meat, but the taste is likely to remain bland.
- Adding salt enhances the taste of the meat.
- Adding other spices, such as pepper, makes the taste more complex.

- Breading it with a mixture that includes salt and spices not only adds to the taste, but also envelops the original ingredient in a new texture. At this point, we're getting close to having a Cotoletta.
- Slitting open a pocket in the cutlet and adding ham, cheese, and garlic into the pocket before breading the cutlet takes us over the top. Now we have Cordon Bleu, which is a most excellent dish.

The difference between a burned cutlet and Cordon Bleu is significant, but the basic ingredient is the same. The variation is caused by the things we add to it. Given a veal cutlet, we can embellish it without changing the main ingredient to create a different dish.

With loose coupling, we can perform a similar feat when developing software. When we program to an interface, we can transform or enhance a core implementation by wrapping it in other implementations of that interface. You already saw a bit of this technique in action in section 8.3.6, where we used it to modify an expensive DEPENDENCY's lifetime by wrapping it in a Proxy.[1]

This approach can be generalized, providing us with the ability to INTERCEPT a call from a consumer to a service; this is what we'll cover in this chapter. Like the veal cutlet, we start out with a basic ingredient and add more ingredients to make it better, but without changing the core of what it was originally. INTERCEPTION is one of the most powerful abilities that we gain from loose coupling. It enables us to apply the SINGLE RESPONSIBILITY PRINCIPLE and Separation of Concerns with ease.

In the previous chapters, we expended a lot of energy maneuvering our code into a position where it's truly loosely coupled. In this chapter, we'll start harvesting the benefits of that investment.

Figure 9.1 shows an outline of the chapter's structure. When you're done with the chapter, you should be able to use INTERCEPTION to develop loosely coupled code according to established object-oriented design principles. In particular, you should gain the ability to successfully observe Separation of Concerns and apply CROSS-CUTTING CONCERNS, all while keeping your code in good condition.

Figure 9.1   The overall structure of this chapter is pretty linear. We'll start with an introduction to INTERCEPTION, including an example. From there we move on to talk about CROSS-CUTTING CONCERNS. This section of the chapter is light on theory and heavy on examples, so if you're already familiar with this subject, you can consider moving directly to the last section, about aspects. This section serves as the climax of the chapter as it introduces the advanced yet versatile concept of dynamic INTERCEPTION.

---

[1]   Erich Gamma et al., *Design Patterns: Elements of Reusable Object-Oriented Software* (New York: Addison-Wesley, 1994), 207.

Because understanding how INTERCEPTION works isn't difficult, we'll start with a quick example to establish the context. To fully appreciate the potential, we must study some related concepts, such as ASPECT-ORIENTED PROGRAMMING (AOP) and SOLID and relate them to INTERCEPTION with examples. Finally, you'll see how a DI CONTAINER can be used to generalize INTERCEPTION and make it easier to apply.

Because the concepts behind INTERCEPTION are well-known design patterns and object-oriented principles, this chapter is rather heavy on examples. The flow of the chapter is fairly linear, beginning with an introductory example and building to increasingly more complex notions and examples. The final, and most advanced, concept can be quickly explained in the abstract, but, because it will probably only click for you with a solid example, the chapter culminates with a multipage example that demonstrates how it works.

Before we get to that point, we must start at the beginning.

9.1   *Introducing Interception*

The concept of INTERCEPTION is simple: we wish to be able to intercept the call between a consumer and a service and execute some code before or after the actual service is invoked. In figure 9.2, a normal call from consumer to service is being intercepted by an intermediary that can execute its own code before or after passing the call on to the real service.

In this section, we're going to get acquainted with INTERCEPTION and learn how, at its core, it's an application of the Decorator design pattern. If you aren't familiar with the Decorator pattern, we'll review it as part of the discussion, and when we're done, you should have a good understanding of how it works. We'll begin by looking at a simple example that showcases the pattern, and follow up with a discussion of how INTERCEPTION relates to the Decorator pattern.

9.1.1   *Example: implementing auditing*

In this example, we'll be implementing auditing for `ProductRepository`. Auditing is a common example of a CROSS-CUTTING CONCERN: it may be required, but the core functionality of reading and editing products should not be affected by auditing. Because

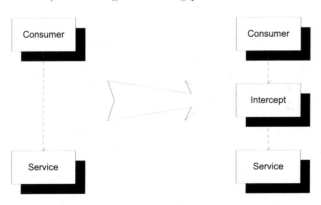

Figure 9.2   INTERCEPTION in a nutshell. We can convert a simple call from consumer to service to a more complex interaction by slotting in a piece of intermediate code. It receives the original call and passes it on to the actual implementation, while also acting on the call by doing whatever it needs to do.

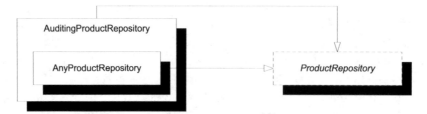

Figure 9.3 The `AuditingProductRepository` **derives from the abstract** `ProductRepository` **class and wraps an instance of any other** `ProductRepository` **implementation. It delegates all work to the decorated** `ProductRepository`, **but adds auditing in appropriate places. Can you spot the breading?**

the SINGLE RESPONSIBILITY PRINCIPLE suggests that we should not let `ProductRepository` itself implement auditing, using a Decorator is an excellent choice.

IMPLEMENTING AUDITINGPRODUCTREPOSITORY

We can do this by introducing a new `AuditingProductRepository` class that wraps another `ProductRepository` and implements auditing. Figure 9.3 illustrates how the types relate to each other.

In addition to a decorated `ProductRepository`, `AuditingProductRepository` also needs a service that implements auditing. In the following listing, this is the role of the `IAuditor` interface.

Listing 9.1   Declaring an `AuditingProductRepository`

```
public partial class AuditingProductRepository :
    ProductRepository
{
    private readonly ProductRepository
        innerRepository;
    private readonly IAuditor auditor;

    public AuditingProductRepository(
        ProductRepository repository,
        IAuditor auditor)
    {
        if (repository == null)
        {
            throw new ArgumentNullException("repository");
        }
        if (auditor == null)
        {
            throw new ArgumentNullException("auditor");
        }

        this.innerRepository = repository;
        this.auditor = auditor;
    }
}
```

❶ Derive from and wrap ProductRepository

❷ Audit service

`AuditingProductRepository` derives from the same ABSTRACTION that it decorates ❶. It uses standard CONSTRUCTOR INJECTION to request a `ProductRepository` that it can wrap and to which it can delegate its core implementation. In addition to the decorated repository, it also requests an `IAuditor` ❷ it can use to audit the operations implemented by the decorated repository.

The following listing shows sample implementations of two methods on `Auditing-ProductRepository`.

Listing 9.2 Implementing `AuditingProductRepository`

```
public override Product SelectProduct(int id)
{
    return this.innerRepository.SelectProduct(id);
}

public override void UpdateProduct(Product product)
{
    this.innerRepository.UpdateProduct(product);
    this.auditor.Record(
        new AuditEvent("ProductUpdated", product));
}
```

Not all operations need auditing. A common requirement is to audit all Create, Update, and Delete operations while ignoring Read operations. Because the `Select-Product` method is a pure Read operation, you delegate the call to the decorated repository and immediately return the result.

The `UpdateProduct` method, on the other hand, must be audited. You still delegate the implementation to the decorated repository, but after the delegated method returns, you use the injected `IAuditor` to audit the operation.

A Decorator, like `AuditingProductRepository`, is like the breading around the veal cutlet: it embellishes the basic ingredient without modifying it. The breading itself isn't just an empty shell, but comes with its own list of ingredients. Real breading is made from breadcrumbs and spices; similarly, the `AuditingProductRepository` contains an `IAuditor`.

Note that the injected `IAuditor` is itself an ABSTRACTION, which means that you can vary the implementation independently of `AuditingProductRepository`. All the `AuditingProductRepository` class does is coordinate the actions of the decorated `ProductRepository` and the `IAuditor`.

You can write any implementation of `IAuditor` you like, but one based on SQL Server is a common choice. Let's see how you can wire up all relevant DEPENDENCIES to make this work.

COMPOSING AUDITINGPRODUCTREPOSITORY

Although many applications use the `ProductRepository` class to retrieve product information, because the CommerceService WCF web service from section 7.3.2 exposes CRUD operations for Products, this is an appropriate place to start.

In chapter 8, you saw several examples of how to compose a ProductManagement-Service instance. Listings 8.4 and 8.5 provided the most correct implementation, but, in the following listing, we'll ignore that SqlProductRepository is disposable in order to focus on composing Decorators.

Listing 9.3   Composing a Decorator

```
public IProductManagementService ResolveProductManagementService()
{
    string connectionString =
        ConfigurationManager.ConnectionStrings
        ["CommerceObjectContext"].ConnectionString;

    ProductRepository sqlRepository =                      ❶ Inner
        new SqlProductRepository(connectionString);           ProductRepository

    IAuditor sqlAuditor =
        new SqlAuditor(connectionString);

    ProductRepository auditingRepository =
        new AuditingProductRepository(                     ❷ Decorator
            sqlRepository, sqlAuditor);

    IContractMapper mapper = new ContractMapper();

    return new ProductManagementService(                   ❸ Inject
        auditingRepository, mapper);                          Decorator
}
```

As in listing 7.9, because you wish to use a SQL Server–based ProductRepository, you create a new instance of SqlProductRepository ❶. But, instead of injecting it directly into a ProductManagementService instance, you'll wrap it in an AuditingProduct-Repository.

You inject both the SqlProductRepository ❶ and a SQL Server–based IAuditor implementation into an AuditingProductRepository instance ❷. Notice how sqlRepository and auditingRepository are both declared as ProductRepository instances.

You can now inject auditingRepository into a new instance of ProductManagement-Service ❸ and return it. The ProductManagementServices sees only the auditing-Repository and knows nothing about the sqlRepository.

WARNING Listing 9.3 is a simplified example that ignores lifetime issues. Because SqlProductRepository and SqlAuditor are disposable types, the code will cause resource leaks. A more correct implementation would be an interpolation of listing 9.3 with listings 8.4 and 8.5—but I'm sure you'll appreciate that it starts to get rather complex at that point.

TIP Use a DI CONTAINER instead of manually dealing with the permutations of OBJECT COMPOSITION, LIFETIME MANAGEMENT, and INTERCEPTION.

Notice that you were able to add behavior to `ProductRepository` without changing the source code of existing classes. We didn't have to change `SqlProductRepository` to add auditing. This is a desirable trait, known as the OPEN/CLOSED PRINCIPLE.

> **OBLIGATORY FOOD ANALOGY**   I think this corresponds to covering a veal cutlet in breading. Although we change the cutlet, we keep it in one size instead of chopping it up and making stew out of it.

Now that you've seen an example of INTERCEPTING the concrete `SqlProductRepository` with a decorating `AuditingProductRepository`, let's take a step back and study the patterns and principles behind it.

9.1.2   *Patterns and principles for Interception*

As is the case with many other DI patterns, the Decorator pattern is an old and well-described design pattern that predates DI by several years. It's such a fundamental part of INTERCEPTION that, whether or not you're intimately familiar with it, it warrants a refresher.

You may have noticed a denser-than-usual usage of terms such as SINGLE RESPONSIBILITY PRINCIPLE and OPEN/CLOSED PRINCIPLE. These are items on the SOLID five-course menu.

All these patterns and principles are recognized as valuable guidance about clean code. The general purpose of this section is to relate this established guidance to DI to showcase that DI is only a means to an end. We use DI as an enabler of maintainable code.

All consumers of DEPENDENCIES should observe the LISKOV SUBSTITUTION PRINCIPLE when they invoke their DEPENDENCIES. This allows us to replace the originally intended implementation with another implementation of the same ABSTRACTION. Because a Decorator implements the same ABSTRACTION as the class it wraps, we can replace the original with a Decorator.

This was exactly what you did in listing 9.3 when you substituted the original `SqlProductRepository` with an `AuditingProductRepository`. You could do this without changing the code of the consuming `ProductManagementService` because it adheres to the LISKOV SUBSTITUTION PRINCIPLE: it requires an instance of `ProductRepository`, and any implementation will do.

Being able to extend a class's behavior without modifying its code is known as the OPEN/CLOSED PRINCIPLE, and this is another of five principles codified as a concept known as SOLID.

> **SOLID**   Who doesn't want to write *solid* software? Software that can withstand the test of time and provide value to its users sounds like a worthy goal; introducing SOLID[2] as an acronym for building quality software makes sense.

---

[2]   Robert C Martin, *The Principles of OOD*, http://butunclebob.com/ArticleS.UncleBob.PrinciplesOfOod

Decorator

The Decorator pattern was first described in the book *Design Patterns*.[3] Its intent is to "attach additional responsibilities to an object dynamically. Decorators provide a flexible alternative to subclassing for extending functionality."[4]

A Decorator works by wrapping one implementation of an ABSTRACTION in another implementation. The wrapper delegates operations to the contained implementation, while adding behavior before or after invoking the wrapped object.

A Decorator can wrap another Decorator, which wraps another Decorator, and so on. The following figure shows how Decorators can wrap each other. At the core, there must be a self-contained implementation that performs the desired work.

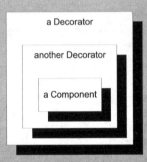

A Decorator wraps another Decorator that wraps a self-contained Component. When a member is invoked on the outmost Decorator, it delegates the call to its wrapped component. Because the wrapped component is itself a Decorator, it delegates the call to its contained component. For each call, a Decorator has the opportunity to use the input or the return value from the contained component to perform additional work.

When a Decorator receives a call to one of the members of the ABSTRACTION it implements, it may choose to simply delegate the call without doing anything at all:

```
public string Greet(string name)
{
    return this.innerComponent.Greet(name);
}
```

It may also choose to modify the input before delegating the call:

```
public string Greet(string name)
{
    var reversed = this.Reverse(name);
    return this.innerComponent.Greet(reversed);
}
```

In a similar move, it may decide to modify the return value before returning it:

```
public string Greet(string name)
{
    var returnValue = this.innerComponent.Greet(name);
    return this.Reverse(returnValue);
}
```

---

[3] Erich Gamma et al., *Design Patterns: Elements of Reusable Object-Oriented Software* (New York: Addison-Wesley, 1994).

[4] Ibid. p. 175.

Given the two previous examples, we can wrap the latter around the former to compose a combination that modifies both input and output.

A Decorator may also decide not to invoke the underlying implementation:

```
public string Greet(string name)
{
    if (name == null)
    {
        return "Hello world!";
    }

    return this.innerComponent.Greet(name);
}
```

In this example, a Guard Clause provides a default behavior for null input, in which case the wrapped component isn't invoked at all.

What differentiates a Decorator from any class containing DEPENDENCIES is that the decorated object implements the same ABSTRACTION as the Decorator. This enables a COMPOSER to replace the original component with a Decorator without changing the consumer. The decorated object is often injected into the Decorator declared as the abstract type, in which case the Decorator must adhere to the LISKOV SUBSTITUTION PRINCIPLE and treat all decorated objects equally.

You've already seen Decorators in action several places in the book. The example in section 9.1.1 used a Decorator, as did section 4.4.4.

Behind the acronym SOLID, we find five principles for object-oriented design that have all turned out to be helpful in writing maintainable code. Table 9.1 lists those principles.

> **NOTE** None of the principles encapsulated by SOLID represent absolutes. They're guidelines that can help you write clean code. To me, they represent goals that help me decide which direction I should take my APIs. I'm always happy when I succeed, but sometimes I don't.

Decorator (and design patterns in general) and guidelines such as the SOLID principles have been around now for many years and are generally viewed as being beneficial when applied. In this section I've attempted to provide you with a hint of how they relate to DI.

The SOLID principles have been relevant throughout the book's chapters, and you may have noticed that I've mentioned some of them here and there. But it is when we start talking about INTERCEPTION and how it relates to Decorators that the connection with SOLID starts to stand out. Some are more subtle than others, but adding behavior (such as auditing) by using a Decorator is a clear application of the OPEN/CLOSED PRINCIPLE with the SINGLE RESPONSIBILITY PRINCIPLE not far behind, because the first allows us to create implementations that have specifically-defined scopes.

In this section, we took a detour around patterns and principles to understand the relationship DI has with other established guidelines. Armed with this extra

Table 9.1   The five principles of SOLID

Principle	Description	Relation to DI
SINGLE RESPONSIBILITY PRINCIPLE (SRP)	A class should only have a single responsibility. It should do one thing only, but do it well. The opposite of this principle is an anti-pattern known as God Class,[5] where a single class can do everything, including making coffee.	It can be difficult to stick to this principle, but one of the many benefits of CONSTRUCTOR INJECTION is that it makes it obvious every time we violate it. In the auditing example in section 9.1.1, you were able to adhere to the SRP by separating responsibilities into separate types: `SqlProductRepository` deals only with storing and retrieving product data, whereas `SqlAuditor` concentrates on persisting the audit trail in the database. The `AuditingProductRepository` class's single responsibility is to coordinate the actions of `ProductRepository` and `IAuditor`.
OPEN/CLOSED PRINCIPLE (OCP)	A class should be open for extensibility, but closed for modification. That is, it should be possible to add behavior to an existing class without modifying its code. This isn't always easy to achieve, but the SRP at least makes it easier, because the simpler the code is, the easier it is to spot potential SEAMS.	There are many ways you can make a class extensible, including virtual methods, injection of Strategies,[6] and application of Decorators—but no matter the details, DI makes this possible by enabling us to compose objects.
LISKOV SUBSTITUTION PRINCIPLE (LSP)	A client should treat all implementations of an ABSTRACTION equally. We should be able to replace any implementation with a different implementation without breaking the consumer.	The LSP is a foundation of DI. When consumers don't observe it, you can't replace DEPENDENCIES at will, and we lose any (if not all) benefits of DI.
INTERFACE SEGREGATION PRINCIPLE (ISP)	Interfaces should be designed to be fine-grained. We don't want to lump too many responsibilities together into one interface, because it becomes too cumbersome to implement. I consider the ISP to be the conceptual underpinning of the SRP. The ISP states that interfaces should model only a single concept, whereas the SRP states that implementations should have only one responsibility.	The ISP may at first seem to be only distantly related to DI. But it's important because an interface that models everything, including the kitchen sink, pulls you in the direction of a particular implementation. It's often a smell of a LEAKY ABSTRACTION and makes it much harder to replace DEPENDENCIES because some of the interface members may make no sense in a context which is different from what originally drove the design.[7]

[5] William J Brown et al., *AntiPatterns: Refactoring Software, Architectures, and Projects in Crisis* (Wiley Computer Publishing, 1998), 73.

[6] Erich Gamma et al., *Design Patterns: Elements of Reusable Object-Oriented Software* (Addison-Wesley, 1994), 315.

[7] Mark Seemann, *Interfaces are not abstractions*, 2010, http://blog.ploeh.dk/2010/12/02/InterfacesAreNotAbstractions.aspx

Table 9.1   The five principles of SOLID *(continued)*

Principle	Description	Relation to DI
DEPENDENCY INVERSION PRINCIPLE (DIP)	Another term for the catch-phrase of *programming to an interface instead of a concrete implementation.*	DIP is the principle that guides DI.

knowledge, let's now turn our attention back to the goal of the chapter, which is to write clean and maintainable code in the face of inconsistent or changing requirements, and the need to address CROSS-CUTTING CONCERNS.

9.2   *Implementing Cross-Cutting Concerns*

Most applications must address aspects that don't directly relate to any particular feature, but, rather, addresses a wider matter. These concerns tend to touch many otherwise unrelated areas of code, even in different modules or layers. Because they cut across a wide area of the code base, we call them CROSS-CUTTING CONCERNS. The following table lists some examples. This table isn't an all-inclusive list of every aspect available; rather, it's an illustrative sample.

Table 9.2   Common examples of CROSS-CUTTING CONCERNS

Aspect	Description
Auditing	Any data-altering operation should leave an audit trail including timestamp, the identity of the user who performed the change, and information about what changed. You saw an example of this in section 9.1.1.
Logging	Slightly different than auditing, logging tends to focus on recording events that reflect the state of the application. This could be events of interest to IT operations staff, but might also be business events.
Performance monitoring	Slightly different than logging, because this deals more with recording performance than specific events. If you have specific Service Level Agreements (SLAs) that can't be monitored via standard infrastructure, you must implement custom performance monitoring. Custom Windows Performance Counters are a good choice for this, but you must still add some code that captures the data.
Security	Some operations should only be allowed for certain users, and you must enforce this.
Caching	You can often increase performance by implementing caches, but there's no reason why a specific data access component should deal with this aspect. You may want to be able to enable or disable caching for different data access implementations. We already saw a glimpse of implementing caching with Decorators in section 4.4.4.
Error handling	We may want to handle certain exceptions and either log them or show a message to the user. We can use an error-handling Decorator to deal with errors in a proper way.
Fault tolerance	Out-of-process resources are guaranteed to be unavailable from time to time. You can implement fault tolerance patterns, such as Circuit Breaker, using a Decorator.

When we draw diagrams of layered application architecture, CROSS-CUTTING CONCERNS are often represented as vertical blocks placed beside the layers, as shown in figure 9.4.

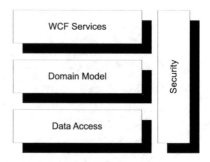

In this section, we'll look at some examples that illustrate how we can use INTERCEPTION in the form of Decorators to implement CROSS-CUTTING CONCERNS. We'll pick a few aspects from table 9.2 to get a feeling for implementing those using SOLID principles, but we'll only look at a small subset. As is the case with many other concepts, INTERCEPTION may be easy to understand in the abstract, but the devil is in the details. It takes exposure to properly absorb the technique, and I'd rather provide you

Figure 9.4 We often represent a CROSS-CUTTING CONCERN in application architecture diagrams with vertical blocks that span all layers. In this case, security is a CROSS-CUTTING CONCERN.

with one too many examples than too few. When we're done with these examples, you should have a clearer picture of what INTERCEPTION is, and how you can apply it.

Because we already saw an introductory example in section 9.1.1, we'll take a look at a more complex example to illustrate how INTERCEPTION can be used with arbitrarily complex logic. Once we've done this, we'll study an example that leads us towards a more declarative approach.

9.2.1 *Intercepting with a Circuit Breaker*

Any application that communicates with out-of-process resources will occasionally experience that the resource is unavailable. Network connections go down, databases go offline, and web services get swamped by Distributed Denial of Service (DDOS) attacks. In such cases, the calling application must be able to recover and appropriately deal with the issue.

Most .NET APIs have default timeouts that ensure that an out-of-process call doesn't block the consuming thread forever. Still, in a situation where you just received a timeout exception, how do you treat the next call to the faulting resource? Do you attempt to call the resource again? Because a timeout often indicates that the other end is either offline or swamped by requests, making a new blocking call may not be a good idea. It would be better to assume the worst and throw an exception immediately. This is the rationale behind the Circuit Breaker pattern.

Circuit Breaker is a *stability pattern* because it adds robustness to an application by failing fast, instead of hanging and consuming resources while it hangs. This is a good example of a nonfunctional requirement and a true CROSS-CUTTING CONCERN, because it has little to do with the feature implemented with the out-of-process call.

The Circuit Breaker pattern itself is a bit complex and can be intricate to implement, but we only need to make that investment once. We could even implement it in a reusable library if we would like. Once we have a reusable Circuit Breaker, we can easily apply it to multiple components by employing the Decorator pattern.

Circuit Breaker

The Circuit Breaker[8] design pattern takes its name from the electric switch of the same name. It's designed to cut the connection when a fault occurs, in order to prevent the fault from propagating.

In software applications, once a timeout or similar communications error occurs, it can often make a bad situation worse if you keep hammering on a downed system. If the remote system is swamped, multiple retries may take it over the edge—a pause might give it a chance to recover. On the calling tier, threads blocked waiting for timeouts may make the consuming application unresponsive. It's better to detect that communications are down and fail fast for a while.

The Circuit Breaker design addresses this by tripping the switch when an error occurs. It usually includes a timeout that makes it retry the connection after a while; this way, it can automatically recover when the remote system comes back up.

The following figure illustrates a simplified view of the state transitions in a Circuit Breaker.

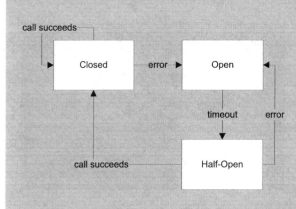

Simplified state transition diagram of the Circuit Breaker pattern. It starts in the Closed state, indicating that the circuit's closed and messages can flow. When an error occurs, the breaker is tripped and the state switches to Open. In this state, the breaker lets no calls through to the remote system; instead, it throws an exception immediately. After a timeout, the state switches to Half-Open, where a single remote call is allowed to go through. If it succeeds, the state goes back to Closed, but if it fails, the breaker goes back to Open, starting a new timeout.

You may want to make a Circuit Breaker more complex than described here. First, you may not want to trip the breaker every time a sporadic error occurs, but, rather, use a threshold. Second, you should only trip the breaker on certain types of errors. Timeouts and communication exceptions are fine, but a `NullReferenceException` is likely to indicate a bug instead of an intermittent error.

Let's look at an example that shows how the Decorator pattern can be used to add Circuit Breaker behavior to an existing out-of-process component. In this example, we'll focus on applying the reusable Circuit Breaker, but not on how it's implemented.

---

[8] Michael T. Nygard, *Release It! Design and Deploy Production-Ready Software* (Cambridge, Massachusetts: Pragmatic Bookshelf, 2007), 104.

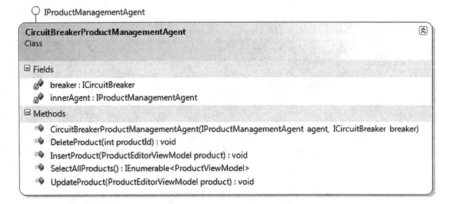

Figure 9.5   The `CircuitBreakerProductManagementAgent` **is a Decorator of**
`IProductManagementAgent`: **notice how it implements the interface and also contains
an instance injected through the constructor. The other** DEPENDENCY **is an**
`ICircuitBreaker` **that we can use to implement the Circuit Breaker pattern.**

EXAMPLE: IMPLEMENTING A CIRCUIT BREAKER

In section 7.4.2, we created a WPF application that communicates with a WCF service
using an `IProductManagementAgent` interface. Although we briefly returned to it in
section 8.2.1, we never studied this interface in detail.

In the previous examples, you used a `WcfProductManagementAgent` that implements
the interface by invoking the WCF service operations. Because this implementation has
no explicit error handling, any communication error will bubble up to the caller.

This is an excellent case for a Circuit Breaker. You would like to fail fast once
exceptions start occurring; this way, you won't block the calling thread and swamp the
service. As figure 9.5 shows, you start by declaring a Decorator for `IProductManagement-`
`Agent` and requesting the necessary DEPENDENCIES via CONSTRUCTOR INJECTION.

You can now wrap any call to the decorated `IProductManagementAgent` like the
example shown in the following listing.

Listing 9.4   Decorating with a Circuit Breaker

```
public void InsertProduct(ProductEditorViewModel product)
{
    this.breaker.Guard();
    try
    {
        this.innerAgent.InsertProduct(product);
        this.breaker.Succeed();
    }
    catch (Exception e)
    {
        this.breaker.Trip(e);
        throw;
    }
}
```

The first thing you need to do before you try to invoke the decorated agent is to check the state of the Circuit Breaker. The Guard method will let you through when the state is either Closed or Half-Open, whereas it will throw an exception when the state is Open. This ensures that you fail fast when you have reason to believe that the call isn't going to succeed.

If you make it past the Guard method, you can attempt to invoke the decorated agent. Notice that the call is wrapped in a try block: if the call fails, you trip the breaker. In this sample, you're keeping things simple, but in a proper implementation, you should only catch and trip the breaker from a selection of exception types. Because NullReferenceExceptions or similar types of exceptions rarely indicate intermittent errors, there'd be no reason to trip the breaker in such cases.

From both the Closed and Half-Open states, tripping the breaker puts us back in the Open state. From the Open state, a timeout determines when we move back to the Half-Open state.

Conversely, you signal the Circuit Breaker if the call succeeds. If you're already in the Closed state, you stay in the Closed state. If you're in the Half-Open state, you transition back to Closed. It's impossible to signal success when the Circuit Breaker is in the Open state, because the Guard method will ensure that you never get that far.

All other methods of IProductManagementAgent look similar, with the only difference being the method they invoke on innerAgent and an extra line of code for methods that return a value. You can see this variation inside the try block for the SelectAllProducts method:

```
var products = this.innerAgent.SelectAllProducts();
this.breaker.Succeed();
return products;
```

Because you must indicate success to the Circuit Breaker, you have to save the return value of the decorated agent before returning it; but that's the only difference between methods that return a value and methods that don't.

At this point, you've left the implementation of ICircuitBreaker open, but the real implementation is a completely reusable complex of classes that employ the State[9] design pattern. Figure 9.6 shows the involved classes.

Although we aren't going to dive deeper into the implementation of Circuit-Breaker here in the book, the important message is that you can INTERCEPT with arbitrarily complex code.

TIP If you're curious about the implementation of the CircuitBreaker class, it's available in the code that accompanies this book.

---

[9] Erich Gamma et al., *Design Patterns: Elements of Reusable Object-Oriented Software* (New York: Addison-Wesley, 1994), 305.

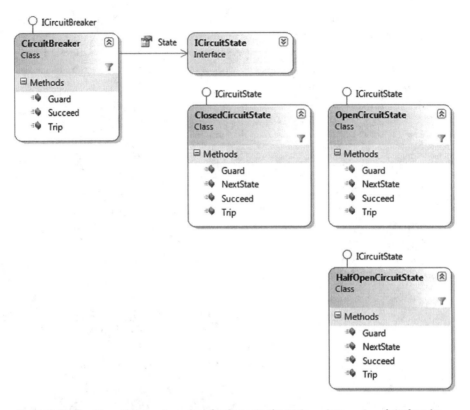

Figure 9.6 The `CircuitBreaker` class implements the `ICircuitBreaker` interface by utilizing the State pattern. All three methods are implemented by delegating to a polymorphic State member that changes as the states transition between each other.

To compose a `ProductManagementAgent` with the Circuit Breaker functionality added, you can wrap it around another implementation:

```
var timeout = TimeSpan.FromMinutes(1);
ICircuitBreaker breaker = new CircuitBreaker(timeout);
IProductManagementAgent circuitBreakerAgent =
    new CircuitBreakerProductManagementAgent(wcfAgent, breaker);
```

In listing 7.10, you composed a WPF application from several DEPENDENCIES, including a `WcfProductManagementAgent` instance. You can decorate this `wcfAgent` variable by injecting it into a `CircuitBreakerProductManagementAgent` instance that implements the same interface. In this particular example, you create a new instance of the `CircuitBreaker` class every time you resolve DEPENDENCIES, and that corresponds to the TRANSIENT lifestyle.

In a WPF application where you only resolve the DEPENDENCIES once, using a TRANSIENT Circuit Breaker isn't an issue, but, in general, this isn't the optimal lifestyle for such functionality. There will only be a single web service at the other end. If this service becomes unavailable, the Circuit Breaker should disconnect all attempts to

A more compact `ICircuitBreaker`

As presented here, the `ICircuitBreaker` interface contains three members: `Guard`, `Succeed`, and `Trip`. An alternative interface definition could use continuation passing[10] to reduce the footprint to a few single-use methods:

```
public interface ICircuitBreaker
{
    void Execute(Action action);

    T Execute<T>(Func<T> action);
}
```

This would allow us to more succinctly use `ICircuitBreaker` in each method, like this:

```
public void InsertProduct(ProductEditorViewModel product)
{
    this.breaker.Execute(() =>
        this.innerAgent.InsertProduct(product));
}
```

I chose to use the more explicit and old-fashioned version of `ICircuitBreaker` because I want you to be able to focus on the current topic of INTERCEPTION. Although I personally like continuation passing, I consider lambdas and generics "advanced" topics in their own right, and I think they might be more distracting than helpful in this context.

Whether we ultimately choose one interface definition over the other doesn't change the conclusion of the current chapter.

connect to it. If several instances of `CircuitBreakerProductManagementAgent` are in use, this should happen for them all.

This is an obvious case for setting up `CircuitBreaker` with the SINGLETON lifetime, but this also means that it must be thread-safe. Due to its very nature, the `Circuit-Breaker` maintains state; thread-safety must be explicitly implemented. This makes the implementation even more complex.

Despite its complexity, you can easily INTERCEPT an `IProductManagementAgent` instance with a Circuit Breaker. Although the first INTERCEPTION example in section 9.1.1 was fairly simple, the Circuit Breaker example demonstrates that you can INTERCEPT a class with a CROSS-CUTTING CONCERN whose implementation is easily more complex than the original implementation.

The Circuit Breaker pattern ensures that an application fails fast instead of tying up precious resources; but, ideally, the application wouldn't crash at all. To address this issue, you can implement some kinds of error handling with INTERCEPTION.

---

[10] For a good introduction to continuation passing style, see Jeremy Miller, *Patterns in practice: Functional Programming for Everyday .NET Development*, MSDN Magazine, October 2009. Also available online at http://msdn .microsoft.com/en-us/magazine/ee309512.aspx

9.2.2 *Handling exceptions*

DEPENDENCIES are likely to throw exceptions from time to time. Even the best-written code will (and should) throw exceptions if it encounters situations it can't deal with. Clients that consume out-of-process resources fall into that category. A class like the WcfProductManagementAgent class from the sample WPF application is one example. When the web service is unavailable, the agent will start throwing exceptions.

A Circuit Breaker doesn't change this fundamental trait. Although it INTERCEPTS the WCF client, it still throws exceptions.

Instead of a crashing application, you might prefer a message box that tells you that the operation didn't succeed and that you should try again later.

You can use INTERCEPTION to add error handling in a SOLID manner. You don't want to burden a DEPENDENCY with error handling. Because a DEPENDENCY should be viewed as a reusable component that can be consumed in a lot of different scenarios, it wouldn't be possible to add an exception-handling strategy into the DEPENDENCY itself that would fit all scenarios. It would also be a violation of the SINGLE RESPONSIBILITY PRINCIPLE if you did this.

By using INTERCEPTION to deal with exceptions, you follow the OPEN/CLOSED PRINCIPLE. It allows you to implement the best error-handling strategy for any given situation. Let's look at an example.

EXAMPLE: HANDLING EXCEPTIONS

In the previous example, you wrapped a WcfProductManagementAgent in a Circuit Breaker for use with the Product Management client application originally introduced in section 7.4.2. A Circuit Breaker only deals with errors by making certain that the client fails fast, but it still throws exceptions. If left unhandled, they'll cause the application to crash, so you should implement a Decorator that knows how to handle some of those errors. When an exception is thrown, it should pop up a message as shown in figure 9.7.

Implementing this behavior is easy to do. The same way you did in section 9.2.1, you add a new ErrorHandlingProductManagement-Agent class that decorates the IProduct-ManagementAgent interface. The following listing shows a sample of one of the methods of that interface, but they're all similar.

Figure 9.7 The Product Management application handles communication exceptions by showing a message to the user. Notice that in this case the error message originates from the Circuit Breaker instead of the underlying communication failure.

Listing 9.5 Handling exceptions

```
public void InsertProduct(ProductEditorViewModel product)
{
    try
    {
        this.innerAgent.InsertProduct(product);          ❶ Delegate to
    }                                                       decorated agent
    catch (CommunicationException e)
    {
        this.AlertUser(e.Message);
    }                                                     ❷ Alert
    catch (InvalidOperationException e)                     the user
    {
        this.AlertUser(e.Message);
    }
}
```

The `InsertProduct` method is representative of the entire implementation of the `ErrorHandlingProductManagementAgent` class. You attempt to invoke the decorated agent ❶ and alert the user with the exception message ❷ if an exception is thrown. Notice that you only handle a particular set of known exceptions, because it can be dangerous to suppress all exceptions.

Alerting the user involves formatting a string and showing it to the user using the `MessageBox.Show` method.

Once again, you added functionality to the original implementation (`WcfProduct-ManagementAgent`) by implementing a Decorator. You're solidly following both the SINGLE RESPONSIBILITY PRINCIPLE and the OPEN/CLOSED PRINCIPLE by continually adding new types instead of modifying existing code. By now, you should already begin to see a pattern that suggests a more general arrangement than Decorator.

For a given CROSS-CUTTING CONCERN, the implementation based on a Decorator tends to be repetitive. Implementing a Circuit Breaker involves applying the same code template to all methods of the `IProductManagementAgent` interface. Had you wanted to add a Circuit Breaker to another ABSTRACTION, you would've had to apply the same code to more methods. Although the template is different, the same is true for the exception handling code we just reviewed.

To drive home this point, let's briefly glance at implementing security. This will suggest a more general approach to composing CROSS-CUTTING CONCERNS that we'll then examine further in section 9.3.

9.2.3 *Adding security*

Security is another common CROSS-CUTTING CONCERN. We wish to secure our applications as much as possible to prevent unauthorized access to sensitive functionality.

NOTE Security is a big topic[11] that addresses many areas, including the disclosure of sensitive information and breaking into networks. In this section, I only touch briefly on the subject of *authorization*—that is, making sure that only authorized people (or systems) can perform certain actions.

Similar to how we used Circuit Breaker, we'd like to INTERCEPT a method call and check whether the call should be allowed. If not, instead of allowing the call to be made, an exception should be thrown. The principle is the same: the difference lies in the criterion we use to determine the validity of the call.

A common approach to implementing authorization logic is to employ role-based security by using `Thread.CurrentPrincipal`. You might start out with a `Secure-ProductRepository` Decorator. Because, as you've seen in the previous sections, all methods look similar, the following listing only shows a sample method implementation.

Listing 9.6 Explicitly checking authorization

```
public override void InsertProduct(Product product)
{
    if (!Thread.CurrentPrincipal.IsInRole("ProductManager"))
    {
        throw new SecurityException();
    }

    this.innerRepository.InsertProduct(product);
}
```

The `InsertProduct` method starts with a Guard Clause that explicitly accesses `Thread.CurrentPrincipal` and asks whether it has the `ProductManager` role. If not, it immediately throws an exception. Only if the calling `IPrincipal` has the required role do you allow it past the Guard Clause to invoke the decorated repository.

NOTE Recall that `Thread.CurrentPrincipal` is an example of the AMBIENT CONTEXT pattern.

This is such a common coding idiom that it's encapsulated in the `System.Security` `.Permissions.PrincipalPermission` class; so you could instead write the previous example a bit more tersely:

```
public override void InsertProduct(Product product)
{
    new PrincipalPermission(null, "ProductManager").Demand();

    this.innerRepository.InsertProduct(product);
}
```

---

[11] For a thorough treatment of security, you may want to read Michael Howard and David LeBlanc, *Writing Secure Code: Second Edition* (Cambridge, Massachusetts: Microsoft Press, 2003).

The `PrincipalPermission` class encapsulates the request for the current `IPrincipal` to have a particular role. Invoking the `Demand` method will throw an exception if `Thread.CurrentPrincipal` doesn't have the `ProductManager` roles. This example is functionally equivalent to listing 9.6.

When the only thing you do is demand that the current `IPrincipal` has a particular role, you can move into a purely declarative style:

```
[PrincipalPermission(SecurityAction.Demand, Role = "ProductManager")]
public override void InsertProduct(Product product)
{
    this.innerRepository.InsertProduct(product);
}
```

The `PrincipalPermission` attribute offers the same functionality as the `PrincipalPermission` class, but exposed as an attribute. Because the .NET Framework understands this attribute, whenever it encounters it, it executes the corresponding `PrincipalPermission` demand.

At this point, having a separate Decorator only to apply an attribute begins to look a little like overkill. Why not apply the attribute directly on the original class itself?

Although this seems attractive, there are several reasons why you might not want to do that:

- The use of attributes precludes more complex logic. What if you wanted to allow most users to update a product's description, but only ProductManagers to update the price? Such logic can be expressed in imperative code, but not easily with an attribute.
- What if you want to make sure that the permission rules are in place no matter which `ProductRepository` implementation you use? Because attributes on concrete classes can't be reused across implementations, that would violate the DRY[12] principle.
- You wouldn't be able to vary the security logic independently of the `ProductRepository`.

Still, the idea of addressing a CROSS-CUTTING CONCERN in a declarative fashion isn't new. Because it's often employed in ASPECT-ORIENTED PROGRAMMING, it's only fitting that we take a closer look at this and how it leads us to loosely coupled INTERCEPTION.

9.3 Declaring aspects

In the previous sections, we looked at patterns for INTERCEPTION and how they can help you address CROSS-CUTTING CONCERNS using SOLID principles. In section 9.2.3 you saw how it was possible to reduce the implementation of a security check to a purely declarative approach.

---

[12] Don't Repeat Yourself.

Applying attributes to declare aspects is a common technique in ASPECT-ORIENTED PROGRAMMING (AOP). But, as alluring it may seem at first, the use of attributes comes with several built-in issues that make it a less-than-ideal solution. I'll use the first part of this section to review this concept and its little known disadvantages.

> **NOTE** I occasionally use the term *aspect attribute* to denote a custom attribute that implements or signifies an aspect.

Once we've properly dismissed the idea of using attributes to declare aspects, we'll spend the rest of this chapter looking at dynamic INTERCEPTION using a DI CONTAINER, which offers a better alternative.

9.3.1   *Using attributes to declare aspects*

Attributes share a trait with Decorators: although they may add or imply a modification of behavior of a member, they leave the signature unchanged. As you saw in section 9.2.3, you can replace explicit, imperative authorization code with an attribute. Instead of writing one or more lines of explicit code, you could achieve the same result by applying the [PrincipalPermission] attribute.

It sounds attractive to extrapolate this concept to other CROSS-CUTTING CONCERNS. Wouldn't it be nice if you could decorate a method or class with a [HandleError] attribute, or even a custom [CircuitBreaker] attribute, and, in this way, apply the aspect with a single line of declarative code?

It might be, but there are several issues with this approach that you need to understand and address.

First and foremost is the challenge that arises from the fact that attributes are inherently passive. Although defining a custom attribute and applying it is as easy as deriving a class from System.Attribute and adorning other classes with the custom attribute, it sits there doing nothing.

But wait! Didn't the [PrincipalPermission] attribute change the behavior of a method? Yes, but this attribute (and some other attributes available in the Base Class Library) is special. The .NET Framework understands and acts upon this attribute, but it won't do so for any custom attribute you'd like to introduce.

You have two options if you want to enable custom attributes to modify behavior of an application:

- Modify the compilation step
- Introduce a custom runtime host

Let's briefly investigate each option.

MODIFYING COMPILATION

One of the most popular AOP frameworks, PostSharp,[13] works exactly by enabling you to add custom attributes to your code. These attributes must derive from a special

---

[13] www.sharpcrafters.com/postsharp

Figure 9.8 PostSharp works by adding a post-compilation step after normal compilation has completed. Because the custom PostSharp attributes on your code are treated no differently than any other attribute by the normal compiler (for example, csc.exe), the output is a normal assembly with passive attributes. PostSharp includes a post-compilation step where PostSharp picks up the compiled assembly and interleaves the code from your custom attributes directly into the attributed code. The result is a new .NET assembly with the aspects embedded.

attribute defined in the PostSharp SDK which supplies virtual methods you can override to define the behavior of the aspect you wish to apply. You can then apply these attributes to your classes or class members. Figure 9.8 shows what happens next.

PostSharp relies on post-compilation to turn passive attributes into active code. The PostSharp processor looks after attributes that derive from the PostSharp attributes and interleaves the code from those attributes with the code adorned by these attributes. The result is a new assembly with the proper aspect code interleaved with the original code.

This assembly is a perfectly normal assembly that runs wherever all other .NET code runs. It requires no special runtime to work.

Among the advantages of this approach is that it doesn't require any special design effort on your part. DI isn't necessary, although not precluded, either. I'm sure that there are other advantages as well.

One disadvantage of this approach is that the code that runs is different from the code you wrote. If you want to debug the code, you'll need to take special steps, and, although the vendor happily supplies tools that allow you to do just that, it also pulls you towards the Vendor Lock-In[14] anti-pattern.

But the greatest disadvantage lies in the use of attributes itself. This disadvantage is shared with using a custom host for activating attributes. Let's review this option before we examine the disadvantages of attributes.

USING A CUSTOM HOST

Another option for activating attributes is to require all code to be activated or initialized by a custom host or factory. Such a factory will be able to inspect all attributes on the classes it initializes and act accordingly.

We know this technique from numerous .NET technologies that rely on attributes. Examples include the following:

---

[14] William J. Brown et al., *AntiPatterns: Refactoring Software, Architectures, and Projects in Crisis* (New York: Wiley Computer Publishing, 1998), 167.

- WCF includes many attributes such as `[ServiceContract]`, `[OperationContract]`, and so on. These attributes only take on behavior when you host a service in a `ServiceHost` instance (this is also what IIS does for you).
- ASP.NET MVC gives you the option to specify which HTTP verbs you'll accept with the `[AcceptVerbs]` attribute, as well as handle exceptions with the `[HandleError]` attribute, and several others. This works because ASP.NET MVC is one big custom host and it controls the lifetime of your controllers.
- All .NET unit testing frameworks that I'm aware of use attributes to identify test cases. A unit test framework initializes test classes and interprets the attributes to figure out which tests to execute.

Composing objects with a DI CONTAINER is similar to these examples. Because a DI CONTAINER initializes instances of the involved classes, it has the opportunity to inspect each class to look for custom attributes.

It should come as no surprise, then, that many DI CONTAINERS come with features that allow you to do just that. If you've already decided to use a DI CONTAINER, shouldn't you go all the way and define and apply custom attributes?

I can only think of one advantage this gives us over dynamic INTERCEPTION: because an attribute is fairly easy to spot, even though it offers a pretty advanced level of indirection, you still get a valuable hint that something else is going on than the method body you're looking at.

But there are disadvantages to applying CROSS-CUTTING CONCERNS with attributes. These disadvantages are common for post-compilation and custom hosts.

DISADVANTAGES OF ASPECT ATTRIBUTES

As attractive as it sounds to implement aspects as custom attributes, there are disadvantages.

First, attributes are compiled together with the code they adorn. This means that you can't easily change your mind. Consider error handling as an example. In section 9.2.2, you saw how you can use the Decorator design pattern to implement error handling for any `IProductManagementAgent`. One interesting point is that the underlying `WcfProductManagementAgent` knows nothing of the `ErrorHandling-ProductManagementAgent`. As figure 9.9 illustrates, they're even implemented in two different libraries.

The core implementation offered by `WcfProductManagementAgent` explicitly doesn't include error handling because proper exception handling is context-dependent. In a GUI application like the WPF application we've been using as an example so far, a dialog message may be a good strategy, but in a console application you might instead prefer writing to the error output stream, and an automated service could move the operation to a retry queue and move on to do something else.

To stay open and flexible, the `ProductWcfAgent` library must not include error handling. But, if you apply an aspect attribute to `WcfProductManagementAgent` (or, even worse, `IProductManagementAgent`), you tightly couple this aspect to the implementation

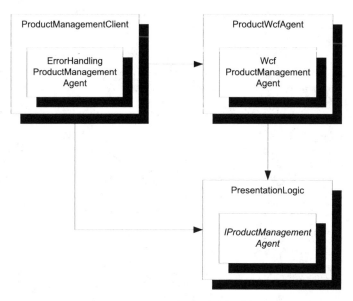

Figure 9.9 `ErrorHandlingProductManagementAgent` and `WcfProductManagementAgent` **both implement** `IProductManagementAgent,` **but are defined in two different libraries. Because the** `ProductManagementClient` **assembly contains the COMPOSITION ROOT, it has a DEPENDENCY on** `ProductWcfAgent` **and** `PresentationLogic.`

(or even the ABSTRACTION). If you do that, you force a particular error-handling strategy on `WcfProductManagementAgent` and you lose the ability to vary the aspect independently of the implementation.

A second problem with aspect attributes is that you have limited options when it comes to applying attributes, which can only be used at the following levels:

- Parameters, including return values
- Members, such as methods, properties and fields
- Types, such as classes and interfaces
- Libraries

Although this provides you with a wide range of options, you can't easily express more convention-based configurations such as "I want to apply the Circuit Breaker aspect to all types whose name starts with Wcf." Instead, you would have to apply a hypothetical `[CircuitBreaker]` attribute to all appropriate classes, violating the DRY principle.

The last drawback of aspect attributes is that attributes must have a simple constructor. If you need to consume DEPENDENCIES from the aspect, you can only do so using an AMBIENT CONTEXT. You already saw an example of that in section 9.2.3, where `Thread.CurrentPrincipal` is an AMBIENT CONTEXT. But, this pattern is rarely the most appropriate, and it makes the LIFETIME MANAGEMENT more difficult. As an example, sharing a single `ICircuitBreaker` instance across multiple WCF clients suddenly becomes much more difficult.

Despite all these shortcomings, the attraction of aspect attributes is that you only have to implement the aspect code in a single place. In the next section, you'll see how you can use INTERCEPTION capabilities of DI CONTAINERS to achieve this goal without the tight coupling of aspect attributes.

9.3.2 *Applying dynamic Interception*

So far you've seen how Decorators can be used to address and implement CROSS-CUTTING CONCERNS. This technique satisfies the SOLID principle but violates the DRY principle. It may not have been apparent from the examples in this chapter, but applying an aspect by manually developing decorating classes involves lots of repetitive code.

REPETITIVENESS OF DECORATORS

The examples in sections 9.1.1 and 9.2.1 show only *representative* methods because every method is implemented in the same way, and I didn't want to dump several pages of near-identical code because it would've detracted from the point I was making. The following listing shows how similar the methods of `CircuitBreaker-ProductmanagementAgent` are. This listing shows only *two* of the methods of the `IProductManagementAgent` interface, but I'm confident that you can extrapolate and imagine how the rest of the implementation looks.

Listing 9.7 Violating the DRY principle

```
public void DeleteProduct(int productId)
{
    this.breaker.Guard();
    try
    {
        this.innerAgent.DeleteProduct(productId);      ◁─┐
        this.breaker.Succeed();
    }
    catch (Exception e)
    {
        this.breaker.Trip(e);
        throw;
    }                                                         ❶ The only
}                                                                 difference
public void InsertProduct(ProductEditorViewModel product)
{
    this.breaker.Guard();
    try
    {
        this.innerAgent.InsertProduct(product);        ◁─┘
        this.breaker.Succeed();
    }
    catch (Exception e)
    {
```

```
            this.breaker.Trip(e);
            throw;
        }
    }
}
```

Because you've already seen the `InsertProduct` method in listing 9.4, the purpose of this code example is to illustrate the repetitive nature of Decorators used as aspects. The only difference ❶ between the `DeleteProduct` and `InsertProduct` methods is that they each invoke their own corresponding method on the decorated agent.

Even though we've successfully delegated the Circuit Breaker implementation to a separate class via the `ICircuitBreaker` interface, this plumbing code clearly violates the DRY principle. It may tend to be reasonably unchanging, but it's still a liability. Every time you want to add a new member to a type you decorate, or when you wish to apply a Circuit Breaker to a new ABSTRACTION, you must apply the same plumbing code.

One way you might consider addressing this issue is by applying code generators like Visual Studio's Text Template Transformation Toolkit (T4), but many DI CONTAIN-ERS offer a better option with dynamic INTERCEPTION.

AUTOMATING DECORATORS

The code in each method in listing 9.7 looks a lot like a template. The hard part of implementing a Decorator as an aspect is to design this template, but from there it's a rather mechanical process:

- Create a new class
- Derive from the desired interface
- Implement each interface member by applying the template

This process is so mechanical that you can use a tool to automate it. Such a tool would use Reflection or similar APIs to discover all the members to implement, and then apply the template to all members. Figure 9.10 shows how this procedure can be applied using a T4 template.[15]

Although code generators allow you to address the symptom of repetitive coding, they still leaves a lot of repetitive code in their trail. If you believe that code is a liability,[16] more code incurs a greater cost, auto-generated or not.

Even if you don't buy this argument, you're still left with a static set of auto-generated Decorators. If you want a new Decorator for a given combination of aspect and ABSTRACTION, you must explicitly add this class. It may be auto-generated, but you still need to remember to create it and wire it up. A more convention-based approach isn't possible in this case.

Some DI CONTAINERS provide you with a better option than automatically generated code: automatically generated classes. This may sound like an esoteric difference, but read on.

---

[15] Read more about Decorators and T4 templates at Oleg Sych, *How to use T4 to generate Decorator classes,* 2007, www.olegsych.com/2007/12/how-to-use-t4-to-generate-decorator-classes/

[16] Tim Ottinger, *Code is a Liability,* 2007, http://blog.objectmentor.com/articles/2007/04/16/code-is-a-liability

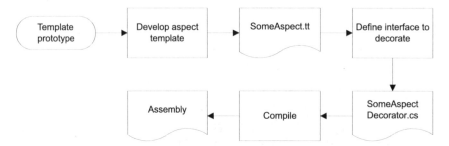

Figure 9.10   T4 makes it possible to auto-generate Decorator code from templates. The starting point is a template prototype that understands the basic concept of Decorator. The template prototype contains the code generation code that will generate the frame of the decorating class, but it doesn't define any aspect code. From the template prototype, an aspect template that describes how a specific aspect (such as Circuit Breaker) should be applied when decorating any interface is developed. The result of that is a specialized template (`SomeAspect.tt`) for that particular aspect, which can be used to generate Decorators for particular interfaces. The result is a normal code file (`SomeAspectDecorator.cs`) that compiles normally together with other code files.

DYNAMIC INTERCEPTION

Among the many powerful features of the .NET Framework is the ability to dynamically emit types. In addition to automatically generating code at design time, it's also possible to write code that emits a fully functional class at runtime. Such a class has no underlying source code file, but is compiled directly from some abstract model.

In the same way that you can automate the generation of Decorators to source code files, you can automate the generation of Decorators to be emitted straight into a running process. As figure 9.11 shows, this is what dynamic INTERCEPTION enables you to do.

> **NOTE**   Not all DI CONTAINERS support runtime INTERCEPTION; if you need this feature, be sure to pick your DI CONTAINER accordingly.

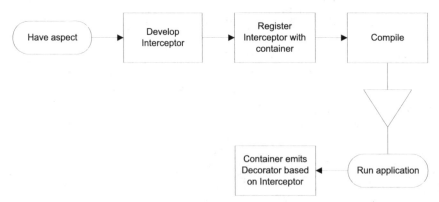

Figure 9.11   Some DI CONTAINERS allow us to define aspects as Interceptors. The Interceptor is a piece of code that implements the aspect and integrates with the container. Registering the Interceptor with the container enables the container to dynamically create and emit Decorators that contain the aspect behavior. These classes only exist at runtime.

To use dynamic INTERCEPTION, you must still write the code that implements the aspect. This could be the plumbing code required for the Circuit Breaker aspect, as shown in listing 9.7. Once you've done this, you must tell the DI CONTAINER about the aspect, and when it should apply it.

At runtime, the DI CONTAINER will dynamically emit new classes into the running `AppDomain` based on the registered aspects. The best part of this approach is that you can use convention-based configuration to define how aspects are applied, and you can decide to use differing conventions in different applications (for example, although you may share a lot of libraries, you may have different error handling strategies in a WPF application and a PowerShell application).

> **NOTE** In AOP, a convention that matches aspects to classes and members is called a *Pointcut*.

Enough with the theory—let's see an example.

9.3.3 *Example: intercepting with Windsor*

With their repetitive code, the Circuit Breaker and error handler aspects from sections 9.2.1 and 9.2.2 are excellent candidates for dynamic INTERCEPTION. As an example, let's see how you can achieve DRY, SOLID code with Castle Windsor's[17] INTERCEPTION capabilities.

> **NOTE** I could've chosen another DI CONTAINER than Castle Windsor, but definitely not just any container. Some support INTERCEPTION while others don't—part 4 covers features of specific DI CONTAINERS.

In this example, you'll implement and register Interceptors for both error handling and Circuit Breaker. Adding an aspect to Windsor is a three-step process, as shown in figure 9.12.

You'll do this for both aspects in this example. Error handling is the simplest to implement because it has no DEPENDENCIES; let's start with that.

IMPLEMENTING THE EXCEPTION HANDLING INTERCEPTOR

Implementing an Interceptor for Windsor requires us to implement the `IInterceptor` interface, which has only a single method. The following listing shows how to implement the exception handling strategy from listing 9.5, but, contrary to listing 9.5, the following listing shows the entire class.

Figure 9.12 The three steps involved in adding an aspect to Windsor

---

[17] www.castleproject.org/

Listing 9.8   Implementing the exception handling Interceptor

```
public class ErrorHandlingInterceptor : IInterceptor          ◁─┐  Implement
{                                                          ❶  IInterceptor
    public void Intercept(IInvocation invocation)
    {
        try
        {                              ❸  Invoke decorated
            invocation.Proceed();   ◁─┘   method
        }
        catch (CommunicationException e)
        {
            this.AlertUser(e.Message);
        }
        catch (InvalidOperationException e)
        {
            this.AlertUser(e.Message);
        }
    }
    private void AlertUser(string message)   ◁─┐  Show
    {                                             dialog box
        var sb = new StringBuilder();
        sb.AppendLine("An error occurred.");
        sb.AppendLine("Your work is likely lost.");
        sb.AppendLine("Please try again later.");
        sb.AppendLine();
        sb.AppendLine(message);

        MessageBox.Show(sb.ToString(), "Error",
            MessageBoxButton.OK, MessageBoxImage.Error);
    }
}
```

❷ Implement aspect

To implement an Interceptor, you must derive from the IInterceptor interface ❶ defined by Windsor. There's only one method to implement, and you implement it by applying the same code ❷ that you used repeatedly when you implemented the ErrorHandlingProductManagementAgent.

The only difference from listing 9.5 is that, instead of delegating the method call to a specific method, you must be more general because you apply this code to potentially any method. You instruct Windsor to let the call proceed to the decorated item by invoking the Proceed method ❸ on the invocation input parameter.

The IInvocation interface passed to the Intercept method as a parameter represents the method call. It might, for example, represent the call to the InsertProduct method. The Proceed method is one of the key members of this interface because it enables us to let the call proceed to the next implementation on the stack.

The IInvocation interface also allows you to assign a return value before letting the call proceed, as well as providing access to detailed information about the method call. From the invocation parameter, you can get information about the name and parameter values of the method, as well as a lot of other information about the current method call.

Implementing the Interceptor is the hard part. The next step is easy.

REGISTERING THE EXCEPTION HANDLING INTERCEPTOR

The interceptor must be registered with the container before it can be used. This step doesn't configure the rules governing how and when the Interceptor is activated (the Pointcut), but only makes it available as a component.

> **NOTE** You may consider this step as ceremony to satisfy Windsor. One of Windsor's quirks is that every component must be explicitly registered, even when it's a concrete type with a default constructor. Not all DI CONTAINERS work the same way, but in Windsor, this behavior is *by design*.

Registering the `ErrorHandlingInterceptor` class is easy (`container` is an instance of `IWindsorContainer`):

```
container.Register(Component.For<ErrorHandlingInterceptor>());
```

This is no different from registering any other component with Windsor, and you could even choose to use a convention-based approach to register all implementations of `IInterceptor` found in a particular assembly. This might look similar to the example code in section 3.2.

The last step in activating the Interceptor is to define the rules for when and how it applies, but because this rule should also address the Circuit Breaker Interceptor, we'll postpone this step until the other Interceptor is ready as well.

IMPLEMENTING THE CIRCUIT BREAKER INTERCEPTOR

The Circuit Breaker Interceptor is a bit more complex because it requires the `ICircuitBreaker` DEPENDENCY, but, as the following listing shows, you address this by applying standard CONSTRUCTOR INJECTION. When it comes to composing the class, Windsor treats it like any other component: as long as it can resolve the DEPENDENCY, all is well.

Listing 9.9 Implementing the Circuit Breaker Interceptor

```
public class CircuitBreakerInterceptor : IInterceptor
{
    private readonly ICircuitBreaker breaker;

    public CircuitBreakerInterceptor(
        ICircuitBreaker breaker)
    {
        if (breaker == null)
        {                                       ❶ Constructor
            throw new ArgumentNullException(       Injection
                "breaker");
        }

        this.breaker = breaker;
    }

    public void Intercept(IInvocation invocation)
    {
```

```
    this.breaker.Guard();
    try
    {
        invocation.Proceed();
        this.breaker.Succeed();
    }
    catch (Exception e)
    {
        this.breaker.Trip(e);
        throw;
    }
}
}
```

❸ Invoke decorated method

❷ Implement aspect

The `CircuitBreakerInterceptor` requires the `ICircuitBreaker` DEPENDENCY, and injecting DEPENDENCIES into an `IInterceptor` is done with CONSTRUCTOR INJECTION ❶, just like in any other service.

As you saw in listing 9.8, you implement the `IInterceptor` interface by applying the template ❷ suggested by the previous, repetitive implementation from listing 9.4. Once more, instead of invoking a specific method, you invoke the `Proceed` method ❸ to instruct the Interceptor to let processing continue to the next component in the Decorator stack.

By now you should begin to see a pattern forming. Instead of repeating the Circuit Breaker plumbing code for each and every method of an ABSTRACTION, you can state it exactly once, in an Interceptor.

You also need to register the `CircuitBreakerInterceptor` class with the container; because it has a DEPENDENCY, this requires not one, but two lines of code.

REGISTERING THE CIRCUIT BREAKER INTERCEPTOR

The exception-handling Interceptor required only a single line of registration code, but, because `CircuitBreakerInterceptor` depends on `ICircuitBreaker`, you must also register this DEPENDENCY:

```
container.Register(Component
    .For<ICircuitBreaker>()
    .ImplementedBy<CircuitBreaker>()
    .DependsOn(new
    {
        timeout = TimeSpan.FromMinutes(1)
    }));
container.Register(Component.For<CircuitBreakerInterceptor>());
```

You map the `ICircuitBreaker` interface to the concrete `CircuitBreaker` class, that itself requires a timeout constructor parameter.

With both Interceptors in place, the only thing you still need to do is to define the rules for when they're activated.

ACTIVATING THE INTERCEPTORS

So far, the Interceptors are implemented and registered with the Windsor container, but you have yet to define when they're activated. If you don't do this, they'll just be passive registrations in the container, without ever getting invoked.

You can think of this step as the equivalent to applying aspect attributes. If we apply a hypothetical [CircuitBreaker] attribute to a method, we connect the Circuit Breaker aspect to that method. Defining and applying custom attributes is one of the ways we can activate Windsor Interceptors, but we also have several other, and better, options available.

The most flexible is to implement and register the IModelInterceptorsSelector interface. This allows us to write imperative code that decides which Interceptor to apply to which types or members. Because we can write arbitrarily complex code, we have the option to apply our aspects in a much more convention-based manner.

In the following listing, you use a simple implementation of such a Pointcut.

Listing 9.10 Implementing a Pointcut

```
public class ProductManagementClientInterceptorSelector :
    IModelInterceptorsSelector
{
    public bool HasInterceptors(ComponentModel model)
    {
        return typeof(IProductManagementAgent)              ❶ Apply Interceptors to
            .IsAssignableFrom(model.Service);                 IProductManagementAgent
    }

    public InterceptorReference[]
        SelectInterceptors(ComponentModel model,
            InterceptorReference[] interceptors)
    {
        return new[]
        {
            InterceptorReference
                .ForType<ErrorHandlingInterceptor>(),       ❷ Return
            InterceptorReference                               Interceptors
                .ForType<CircuitBreakerInterceptor>()
        };
    }
}
```

The IModelInterceptorsSelector interface follows the Tester-Doer[18] pattern. Windsor will first call the HasInterceptors method to ask whether the given component it is about to initialize has any Interceptors. In this case, you answer in the affirmative when the component implements the IProductManagementAgent interface ❶, but you could've written arbitrarily complex code here if you'd wanted to implement a more heuristic approach.

When the HasInterceptors method returns true, the SelectInterceptors method will be called. From this method you return references to the Interceptors you already registered ❷. Notice that you don't return instances of the Interceptors, but, rather, references to the Interceptors you already implemented and registered.

---

[18] Krzysztof Cwalina and Brad Abrams, *Framework Design Guidelines: Conventions, Idioms, and Patterns for Reusable .NET Libraries* (New York, Addison-Wesley 2006), 203.

This enables Windsor to AUTO-WIRE any Interceptors that may have DEPENDENCIES on their own (such as the `CircuitBreakerInterceptor` from listing 9.9).

Guess what! You also need to register the `ProductManagementClientInterceptor-Selector` class with the container. This is done a little differently, but is still a single line of code:

```
container.Kernel.ProxyFactory.AddInterceptorSelector(
    new ProductManagementClientInterceptorSelector());
```

This finally activates the Interceptors so that when you resolve the application using Windsor, they automatically kick in whenever they should.

You may think that this multipage walkthrough of Windsor Interceptors seems pretty complex, but you should keep a few things in mind:

- You implemented two, not one, Interceptors.
- I repeated some code from previous examples to show how it fits in. No matter whether you elect to write manual Decorators, use an AOP framework, or use dynamic INTERCEPTION, you'll always need to write the code that implements the aspect.

Dynamic INTERCEPTION offers a lot of benefits. It enables us to address CROSS-CUTTING CONCERNS following both the SOLID and DRY principles. It gives us truly loosely coupled aspects and an option to apply conventions or complex heuristics to determine when and where to apply which aspects. It's the ultimate level of freedom and flexibility.

You may be concerned about the performance implications of compiling and emitting custom types on the fly, but as far as I've been able to determine, Windsor only does this once and reuses the type for all subsequent invocations. I did a few informal benchmarks without registering any noticeable performance degradation.

Another concern is the added level of indirection. You could argue that, by applying aspect attributes, we still leave a visible trace on the core method that behavior-changing aspects are in place. With Decorators, and dynamic INTERCEPTION in particular, there's no such clue. Novice developers could potentially run afoul in this semi-magical behavior, ending up stuck for days before someone helps them out by explaining the concept to them.

This is a real concern in some organizations. Consider how you would like to address it if you choose to apply dynamic INTERCEPTION.

9.4   *Summary*

DI really shines when it comes to applying recognized object-oriented principles such as SOLID. In particular, the loosely coupled nature of DI lets us use the Decorator pattern to follow the OPEN/CLOSED PRINCIPLE as well as the SINGLE RESPONSIBILITY PRINCIPLE. This is valuable in a wide range of situations, because it enables us to keep our code clean and well-organized, but applies especially well when it comes to addressing CROSS-CUTTING CONCERNS.

CROSS-CUTTING CONCERNS traditionally belong in the realm of ASPECT-ORIENTED PROGRAMMING, but can also be addressed with great success using DI. The Decorator design pattern is the central pattern that enables us to wrap existing functionality in additional layers of behavior without changing the original code.

But, despite its many virtues, the main problem with implementing Decorators is that they tend to be verbose and repetitive. Even though we can follow SOLID design principles, we end up violating the DRY principle because we must write the same plumbing code over and over again—for each member of each interface that we wish to decorate with a particular aspect.

Attributes seem like an appealing alternative to Decorators because they allow us to add aspects in a much terser way. But, because attributes are compiled into the code they decorate, they lead to tight coupling and are better avoided.

Some DI CONTAINERS offer a more attractive alternative, with the ability to dynamically emit Decorators at runtime. These dynamic Decorators provide INTERCEPTION that follow both the SOLID and DRY principles.

It's interesting to note that dynamic INTERCEPTION is the only feature of DI CONTAINERS that have no direct equivalent in POOR MAN'S DI. At this point in part 3, you've seen how to address OBJECT COMPOSITION and LIFETIME MANAGEMENT by judicious application of patterns, but when it comes to INTERCEPTION, the closest we get is a lot of Decorators.

Although the concept of a Decorator is comparable to INTERCEPTION, the leap from many hand-coded Decorators to a single, DRY Interceptor is considerable. The first may lead to an explosion of repetitive plumbing code, whereas the other offers to address CROSS-CUTTING CONCERNS in as few lines of code as possible, and with the option to use convention-based application of aspects as an added bonus.

It's only fitting that here, at the conclusion of part 3, we finally arrive at an area where DI CONTAINERS indisputably leave POOR MAN'S DI behind. Even without INTERCEPTION, a DI CONTAINER can much better manage the complexity involved in mapping ABSTRACTIONS to concrete types and manage their lifetimes; but when we add INTERCEPTION to the mix, we can't beat the combination.

On that note, we can now happily leave POOR MAN'S DI behind in part 3 and move on to read about specific DI CONTAINERS in part 4.

Part 4

DI Containers

The previous parts of the book have been about the various principles and patterns that together define DI. As chapter 3 explained, a DI CONTAINER is an *optional* tool that you can use to implement a lot of the general-purpose infrastructure that you would otherwise have to implement if you were using POOR MAN'S DI.

Throughout the book, I've strived to keep it as container-agnostic as possible. Don't interpret this as a recommendation of POOR MAN'S DI; rather, I wanted you to see DI in its pure form, untainted by any particular container's (possibly quirky) API.

There is little reason to waste your time with POOR MAN'S DI because many excellent DI CONTAINERS are available for .NET. Here in part 4 is a selection of six specific free containers. In each chapter I provide detailed coverage of that particular container's API as it relates to the dimensions covered in part 3, as well as various other issues that traditionally cause beginners grief.

The containers covered in part 4 are Castle Windsor, StructureMap, Spring.NET, Autofac, Unity, and MEF. There are other container frameworks that I didn't include for one reason or another: Ninject, Hiro, Funq, LinFu, OCInject, and so on. Please note that inclusion in this book isn't in itself a seal of approval. Although many of the containers included here are of excellent quality, that wasn't the only selection criterion. There are certain containers I simply couldn't exclude because of their market share, whereas I chose to include others because they provide good contrast due to their different design philosophies or purposes. This also means I had to leave out some excellent containers. Given unlimited space, I would have loved to include them all, but alas, that wasn't possible.

Each chapter follows a common template. This may give you a certain sense of déjà vu as you read the same sentence for the sixth time, but I consider it an advantage because it should enable you to quickly find similar sections across different chapters if you want to compare how a specific feature is addressed across two or more containers. For a quick comparison, refer to this table:

DI CONTAINER	Advantages	Disadvantages
Castle Windsor	Complete Understands Decorator Typed factories Commercial support available	Quirky API in places
StructureMap	Just works in many cases	No INTERCEPTION
Spring.NET	INTERCEPTION Comprehensive documentation Commercial support available	Very XML-centric No convention-based API No custom lifetimes Limited AUTO-WIRING
Autofac	Easy to learn API Commercial support available	No INTERCEPTION Partial support for custom lifetimes
Unity	INTERCEPTION Good documentation Consistent API	Poor lifetime management No convention-based API
MEF	Available in the .NET 4/Silverlight 4 BCL Commercially supported	Not a real DI CONTAINER Configuration based on static attributes No XML support No CODE AS CONFIGURATION No convention-based API No custom lifetimes No INTERCEPTION

Many of the containers described here are open source projects with fast release cycles. The information presented in part 4 was accurate at the time of writing, but always be sure to also consult more up-to-date sources as well.

These chapters are meant as inspiration. If you have yet to pick a favorite DI CONTAINER you can read through all six chapters to compare them all, but you can also just read one or two that particularly interest you.

Castle Windsor

10

In the previous nine chapters, we discussed patterns and principles that apply to DI in general, but, apart from a few examples, we have yet to take a detailed look at how to apply them using any particular DI CONTAINER. In this chapter, you'll see how these overall patterns map to Castle Windsor; you'll need to be familiar with the material from the previous chapters to fully benefit from this.

Castle Windsor is the second-oldest DI CONTAINER for .NET. It's part of a larger open source project known as the *Castle Project*[1] that provides reusable libraries for many purposes. Windsor is the DI CONTAINER part of the Castle Project, but it can be used independently of any other Castle component. In this chapter, we'll review it as a stand-alone component.

---

[1] www.castleproject.org/

313

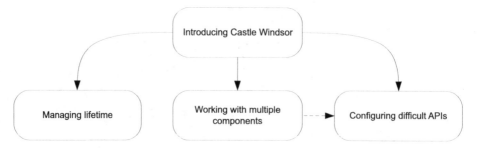

Figure 10.1   The structure of this chapter resembles a tree. The first section introduces the Castle Windsor container and explains how to configure and resolve components. Based on the introduction, the rest of the sections can be read sequentially or more or less independently. The last section uses syntax and a few methods that initially appear in the section about multiple components, so if you decide to skip the penultimate section, you may still want to occasionally refer back to it.

In addition to being one of the oldest DI CONTAINERS, Castle Windsor is one of the most mature and, if we're to believe several totally unscientific internet polls, most popular containers. Although it's fairly easy to get started with Windsor, it offers a rich and extensible API.

In this chapter, we'll take a tour of Castle Windsor. When we're done, you should know enough about it to be able to start using it immediately. We aren't going to cover advanced extensibility scenarios but will instead focus on mainstream usage patterns. Figure 10.1 shows the structure of the chapter.

The first section provides an overall introduction to Castle Windsor and demonstrates how to configure and resolve components. The next three sections deal with usage patterns that require a bit of extra attention; you can read them all in order, or you can skip some and read only the ones that interest you.

This chapter should enable you to get started as well as deal with the most common issues that may come up as you use Castle Windsor on a day-to-day basis. It isn't a complete treatment of Castle Windsor—that would take a whole book in its own right.

You can read the chapter in isolation from the rest of part 4 to learn specifically about Castle Windsor, or you can read it together with the other chapters in part 4 to compare DI CONTAINERS. The focus of this chapter is to show how Castle Windsor relates to and implements the patterns and principles described in the previous nine chapters.

10.1   *Introducing Castle Windsor*

In this section, you'll learn where you get Castle Windsor, what you get, and how you start using it. We'll also look at common configuration options, as well as how we package configuration settings into reusable components. Table 10.1 provides fundamental information that you're likely to need to get started.

As figure 10.2 shows, there's a simple rhythm to Castle Windsor: configure the container by adding components, and subsequently resolve the required components.

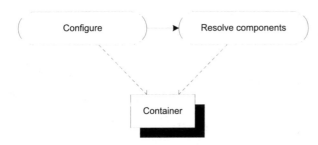

Figure 10.2 The overall usage pattern of Castle Windsor is simple: first we configure the container; then we resolve components from it. In the vast majority of cases, we create an instance of `WindsorContainer` **and completely configure it before we start resolving components from it. We resolve components from the same instance that we configure.**

Table 10.1 Castle Windsor at a glance

Question	Answer
Where do I get it?	Go to www.castleproject.org/castle/projects.html and click the appropriate link under *Stable release*. From Visual Studio 2010 you can also get it via NuGet. The package name is *Castle.Windsor*.
What's in the download?	You can download a .zip file with precompiled binaries. You can also get the current source code and compile it yourself. The binaries are .dll files that you can place wherever you like and reference from your own code.
Which platforms are supported?	.NET 3.5 SP1, .NET 4 Client Profile, .NET 4, Silverlight 3, Silverlight 4.
How much does it cost?	Nothing. It's open source software with a benign (non-viral) license.
Where can I get help?	You can get commercial support from Castle Stronghold. Read more at www.castlestronghold.com/services/support. Other than commercial support, Castle Windsor is still open source software with a thriving ecosystem, so you're likely (but not guaranteed) to get help in the official forum at http://groups.google.com/group/castle-project-users. Stack Overflow (http://stackoverflow.com/) is another good place to ask questions.
On which version is this chapter based?	2.5.2.

When you're done with this section, you should be familiar with the overall usage pattern of Castle Windsor, and you should be able to start using it in scenarios where all components follow proper DI patterns, such as CONSTRUCTOR INJECTION. We'll start with the simplest scenario and see how you can resolve objects using the Windsor container.

10.1.1 *Resolving objects*

Every DI CONTAINER's core purpose is to resolve objects by wiring them up with all their DEPENDENCIES. Castle Windsor offers a simple API to resolve services; but before you can resolve a service, it must be *registered* with the container. Here's the simplest possible use of Windsor:

```
var container = new WindsorContainer();
container.Register(Component.For<SauceBéarnaise>());
SauceBéarnaise sauce = container.Resolve<SauceBéarnaise>();
```

Before you can ask a `WindsorContainer` to resolve *anything*, you must explicitly register the appropriate components. In this case, you can get by registering a single concrete type. However, as you'll see next, you'll more frequently register a map from an ABSTRACTION to a concrete type.

Once you have the container properly configured, you can resolve the Sauce-Béarnaise type to get an instance of it. You don't have to check for null because `WindsorContainer` will throw an exception if it can't AUTO-WIRE and return an instance of the requested type.

> **NOTE** Windsor requires that all required components are registered, even if they're concrete types. This is by design,[2] but not a design shared by all other DI CONTAINERS.

This first example is functionally equivalent to directly creating an instance of the `SauceBéarnaise` class with the new keyword: nothing is yet gained. Recall that DI is a means to an end, and that end is loose coupling. To achieve loose coupling, you must map ABSTRACTIONS to concrete types.

MAPPING ABSTRACTIONS TO CONCRETE TYPES

Although it's sometimes necessary to register a concrete class as itself, a much more common requirement is to map an ABSTRACTION to a concrete type. This is, after all, the core service offered by DI CONTAINERS.

Here you map the `IIngredient` interface to the concrete `SauceBéarnaise` class, which allows you to successfully resolve `IIngredient`:

```
var container = new WindsorContainer();
container.Register(Component
    .For<IIngredient>()
    .ImplementedBy<SauceBéarnaise>());
IIngredient ingredient = container.Resolve<IIngredient>();
```

Instead of registering a concrete type, you map an ABSTRACTION to a concrete type. When you later request an instance of `IIngredient`, the container will return an instance of `SauceBéarnaise`.

The strongly typed fluent API available through the `Component` class (that's `Castle.MicroKernel.Registration.Component`, not `System.ComponentModel.Component`) helps preven configuration mistakes because the `ImplementedBy` method has a generic constraint that makes sure the type specified in the type argument implements the ABSTRACTION type argument specified in the `For` method. That is, the previous example code compiles because `SauceBéarnaise` implements `IIngredient`.

---

[2] See http://docs.castleproject.org/Default.aspx?Page=FAQ&NS=Windsor&AspxAutoDetectCookieSupport=1 for a complete explanation.

In many cases, the strongly typed API is all that you need, and, because it provides desirable compile-time checking, you should use it whenever you can. Still, there are situations where you need a more weakly typed way to resolve services. This is also possible.

RESOLVING WEAKLY TYPED SERVICES

In some cases, we can't write generic code to resolve a type because we might not even know the exact type of the ABSTRACTION at design time. A good example of this is the ASP.NET MVC `DefaultControllerFactory` that we discussed in section 7.2. The relevant part of that class is the virtual `GetControllerInstance` method:

```
protected internal virtual IController GetControllerInstance(
    RequestContext requestContext, Type controllerType);
```

There aren't strongly typed generics in this API. Instead, we're given a `Type` and asked to return an `IController` instance. The `WindsorContainer` class also has a weakly typed version of the `Resolve` method; you can use this method to implement `Get-ControllerInstance`:

```
return (IController)this.container.Resolve(controllerType);
```

Notice that, in this case, you pass the `controllerType` argument to the `Resolve` method. Because the weakly typed version of `Resolve` returns an instance of `System .Object`, you must explicitly cast to `IController` before returning the result.

No matter which overload of `Resolve` you use, Windsor guarantees that it will return an instance of the requested type or throw an exception if there are DEPENDENCIES that can't be satisfied. When all required DEPENDENCIES have been properly registered, Windsor will AUTO-WIRE the requested type based on its configuration.

In the previous example, `this.container` is an instance of `IWindsorContainer`. To be able to resolve the requested types, all types and their DEPENDENCIES must previously have been registered. There are many ways to configure a Windsor container, and the next section reviews the most common ones.

10.1.2 *Configuring the container*

As we discussed in section 3.2, there are several conceptually different ways we can configure a DI CONTAINER. Figure 10.3 reviews the options.

Like other DI CONTAINERS with a long history, Castle Windsor started out with XML as the main configuration source. But it didn't take long for many teams to learn that defining type registrations in XML is extraordinarily brittle; today, we prefer strongly typed configuration. This can be done with CODE AS CONFIGURATION, but it's often more effectively done with more convention-based AUTO-REGISTRATION.

Castle Windsor supports all three approaches and even allows us to mix them all within the same container; in this regard, it gives us all we could ask for. In this section, you'll see how you can use each of these three types of configuration sources.

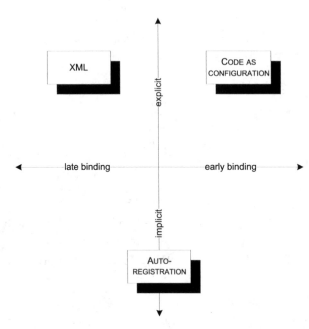

Figure 10.3   Conceptually different configuration options. CODE AS CONFIGURATION **is strongly typed and tends to be explicit. XML, on the other hand, is late bound, but still explicit.** AUTO-REGISTRATION **instead relies on conventions that can be both strongly typed and more loosely defined.**

CODE AS CONFIGURATION

In chapter 3, you saw examples of Castle Windsor's CODE AS CONFIGURATION API. Each registration is initiated with the `Register` method and usually specified using a Fluent API.

We configure a `WindsorContainer` with the `Register` method that takes an array of `IRegistration` as input. At first glance that looks pretty abstract, but, instead of leaving us to figure out which `IRegistration` implementations to use, Castle Windsor also provides a Fluent Registration API that enables us to build `IRegistration` instances with a more intuitive syntax.

To use the Fluent Registration API, we use the static `Component` class as an entry point.

> **WARNING**   Don't confuse `Castle.MicroKernel.Registration.Component` with `System.ComponentModel.Component` from the Base Class Library.

As you saw previously, the simplest possible registration is one for a concrete type:

```
container.Register(Component.For<SauceBéarnaise>());
```

This registers the `SauceBéarnaise` class with the container but provides no mapping. Even though `SauceBéarnaise` implements `IIngredient`, the container will throw an exception if you ask it to resolve `IIngredient`:

```
container.Resolve<IIngredient>()
```

To enable this more relevant scenario, you must map the concrete type to an ABSTRACTION:

```
container.Register(Component
    .For<IIngredient>()
    .ImplementedBy<SauceBéarnaise>());
```

Note how you now register the IIngredient interface instead of the SauceBéarnaise class. This will allow you to resolve IIngredient, but, perhaps a bit surprisingly, you lose the ability to resolve the concrete SauceBéarnaise class. This is rarely an issue when all your code is loosely coupled, but in the rare cases where you need to be able to resolve both types, you can specify this with an overload of the For method:

```
container.Register(Component
    .For<SauceBéarnaise, IIngredient>());
```

This registers the SauceBéarnaise component, while at the same time forwarding the registration to the IIngredient interface. This means that both SauceBéarnaise and IIngredient are registered as resolvable types. In both cases, the implementation is provided by SauceBéarnaise. Notice that when this overload is used, you don't need to implicitly use the ImplementedBy method.

Obviously, you can register multiple types with successive calls to the Register method:

```
container.Register(Component
    .For<IIngredient>()
    .ImplementedBy<SauceBéarnaise>());
container.Register(Component
    .For<ICourse>()
    .ImplementedBy<Course>());
```

This registers both the IIngredient and ICourse interfaces and maps them to concrete types. However, registering the same ABSTRACTION several times has some interesting results:

```
container.Register(Component
    .For<IIngredient>()
    .ImplementedBy<Steak>());
container.Register(Component
    .For<IIngredient>()
    .ImplementedBy<SauceBéarnaise>());
```

In this example, you register IIngredient twice. If you resolve IIngredient, you get an instance of Steak. The first registration wins, but subsequent registrations aren't forgotten. Castle Windsor has a sophisticated model for dealing with multiple registrations; we'll get back to this in section 10.3.

There are more advanced options available in the Fluent Registration API, but we can configure an entire application in this way. However, to save us from too much explicit maintenance of container configuration, we can instead consider a more convention-based approach, using AUTO-REGISTRATION.

AUTO-REGISTRATION

In many cases, a lot of registrations will be similar. Such registrations are tedious to maintain and explicitly registering each and every component is often counterproductive.

Consider a library that contains a lot of IIngredient implementations. You can register each class individually, but it will result in numerous similar-looking calls to the `Register` method. What's worse, every time you add a new `IIngredient` implementation, you must also explicitly register it with the container if you want it to be available. It would be more productive to state that all implementations of `IIngredient` found in a given assembly should be registered.

This is possible using the static `AllTypes` class, which fills a role similar to the `Component` class. We can use one of its methods to scan an assembly for types that fit a certain criterion. This registers all `IIngredient` implementations in one go:

```
container.Register(AllTypes
    .FromAssemblyContaining<Steak>()
    .BasedOn<IIngredient>());
```

The `AllTypes` class provides many methods that enable us to point to a particular assembly, but I find the `FromAssemblyContaining` generic method to be particularly concise: provide a representative type as the type parameter, and it will use the assembly containing that type. There are also other methods that enable us to provide an `Assembly` by other means.

In the previous example, you unconditionally register all implementations of the `IIngredient` interface, but you can specify other selection criteria to either narrow the selection or select on other criteria than interfaces or base classes. Here's a convention-based registration where you add all classes whose names start with *Sauce* and register them against all the interfaces they implement:

```
container.Register(AllTypes
    .FromAssemblyContaining<SauceBéarnaise>()
    .Where(t => t.Name.StartsWith("Sauce"))
    .WithService.AllInterfaces());
```

Notice that you supply a predicate to the `Where` method that filters on the type name. Any type whose name starts with *Sauce* will be selected from the assembly that contains the `SauceBéarnaise` class. The `WithService` property allows you to specify a rule for registering the type; in this case, you register all types against all the interfaces they implement.

With convention-based registration, you can move from strong typing into an area where type safety seems to disappear. An example like the previous one compiles, but you aren't guaranteed that any types will get registered at all. It depends on whether there are any types that satisfy the selection criterion. You could rename all sauce classes to something else, and you'd be left with no sauces.

There's even a method on `AllTypes` that takes the name of an assembly as input. It will use Fusion (the .NET Framework's assembly loading engine) to find the corresponding assembly. By combining a late-bound assembly with an untyped predicate, you can move far into late-bound territory. This can be a useful technique to implement add-ins because Castle Windsor can also scan all assemblies in a directory.

Another way to register add-ins and other late-bound services is by employing Castle Windsor's XML configuration feature.

XML CONFIGURATION

When you need to be able to change a configuration without recompiling the application, XML configuration is a good option.

> **TIP** Use XML configuration only for those types you need to change without recompiling the application. Use AUTO-REGISTRATION or CODE AS CONFIGURATION for the rest.

We can embed XML configuration in normal .NET configuration files, or import XML from specialized files. Like everything else in Castle Windsor, nothing happens unless we explicitly ask for it, so we must also specify if we want to load configuration from XML.

There are several ways to do this, but the recommended way is to use the `Install` method (we'll talk more about Installers in section 10.1.3):

```
container.Install(Configuration.FromAppConfig());
```

The `FromAppConfig` method returns an instance of `ConfigurationInstaller` that reads Castle Windsor's XML configuration from the application's configuration file and translates it to objects understood by the container.

To enable Castle Windsor configuration in a configuration file, you must first add a configuration section:

```
<configSections>
  <section name="castle"
           type="Castle.Windsor.Configuration.AppDomain
         ➥.CastleSectionHandler, Castle.Windsor" />
</configSections>
```

This enables you to add a `castle` configuration section in the configuration file. Here's a simple example that maps the `IIngredient` interface to the `Steak` class:

```
<castle>
  <components>
    <component id="ingredient.sauceBéarnaise"
               service="IIngredient"
               type="Steak"/>
  </components>
</castle>
```

Notice that you don't have to supply the assembly qualified type name for either service or class. As long as the names are unique across all loaded assemblies, they'll be correctly resolved—but, should you have name conflicts, you can still use assembly qualified type names.

Obviously, you can add as many components as you need. The `Configuration-Installer` translates this XML configuration to the registration objects that configure the container, and you can subsequently resolve the types configured.

XML configuration is a good option when you need to change the configuration of one or more components without recompiling the application. However, because it tends to be quite brittle, you should reserve it for those occasions and use either AUTO-REGISTRATION or CODE AS CONFIGURATION for the main part of the container's configuration.

TIP Remember how the first configuration of a type wins? You can use this behavior to overwrite hard-coded configuration with XML configuration. To do this, you must remember to install the `ConfigurationInstaller` before any other components.

In this section, we mainly looked at various configuration APIs for Castle Windsor. Although it's certainly possible to write one big block of unstructured configuration code, it's better to modularize configuration. We have Windsor Installers for this purpose.

10.1.3 *Packaging configuration*

It's sometimes desirable to package configuration logic into reusable groups, and even when reuse itself isn't our top priority, we may want to provide a bit of structure if we have a big and complex application to configure.

With Castle Windsor, we can package configuration into Installers. An Installer is a class that implements the `IWindsorInstaller` interface:

```
public interface IWindsorInstaller
{
    void Install(IWindsorContainer container, IConfigurationStore store);
}
```

Everything you've done so far you can do from inside an Installer as well. The following listing shows an Installer that registers all `IIngredient` implementations.

Listing 10.1   Implementing a Windsor Installer

```
public class IngredientInstaller : IWindsorInstaller
{
    public void Install(IWindsorContainer container,
        IConfigurationStore store)
    {
        container.Register(AllTypes
            .FromAssemblyContaining<Steak>()
            .BasedOn<IIngredient>());
    }
}
```

The `IngredientInstaller` implements the `IWindsorInstaller` interface by using the exact same API you saw earlier to register all `IIngredient` implementations.

To register an Installer, invoke the `Install` method:

```
container.Install(new IngredientInstaller());
```

Although it's possible to invoke the `Install` method multiple times, the Castle Windsor documentation recommends that you perform all configuration in a single call to the `Install` method.[3] The `Install` method takes an array of `IWindsorInstaller` instances:

```
public IWindsorContainer Install(params IWindsorInstaller[] installers);
```

---

[3] http://stw.castleproject.org/Windsor.Installers.ashx

TIP Windsor Installers let you package and structure your container configuration code. Use them instead of inline configuration: it will make your COMPOSITION ROOT more readable.

TIP Besides the benefits that Installers offer for your own code, Castle Windsor is moving in the direction of optimizing much of its API around Installers. It's the idiomatic and recommended way of configuring Castle Windsor to a greater degree than for other containers.

You can also specify one or more Installers in XML and load the configuration file as previously described:

```
<installers>
  <install type="IngredientInstaller" />
</installers>
```

Using Installers, you can configure a `WindsorContainer` in any way you like: CODE AS CONFIGURATION, AUTO-REGISTRATION, or with XML; or, you can mix all three approaches. Once a container is configured, you can ask it to resolve services.

This section introduced the Castle Windsor DI CONTAINER and demonstrated the fundamental mechanics: how to configure the container and subsequently use it to resolve services. Resolving services is easily done with a single call to the `Resolve` method, so the complexity involves configuring the container. This can be done in several different ways, including imperative code and XML. Until now, we've only looked at the most basic API; there are more advanced areas we have yet to cover. One of the most important topics is how to manage component lifetime.

10.2 *Managing lifetime*

In chapter 8, we discussed LIFETIME MANAGEMENT, including the most common conceptual lifetime styles, such as SINGLETON and TRANSIENT. Castle Windsor supports many different lifestyles and enables you to configure the lifetime of all services. The lifestyles shown in table 10.2 are available as part of the API.

Table 10.2 Castle Windsor lifestyles

Name	Comments
Singleton	This is Castle Windsor's default lifestyle.
Transient	A new instance is created each time, but the instance is still tracked by the container.
PerThread	One instance is created per thread.
PerWebRequest	Requires registration in web.config (see section 10.2.2).
Pooled	Configuration of pool size will often be advisable (see section 10.2.2).
Custom	Write your own custom lifestyle (see section 10.2.3).

Some of the built-in lifestyles are entirely equivalent to the general lifestyle patterns described in chapter 8. This is particularly true for the SINGLETON and TRANSIENT lifestyle, so I won't use any dedicated space on them in this chapter.

NOTE   The default lifestyle in Castle Windsor is SINGLETON. This is different from many other containers. As we discussed in chapter 8, SINGLETON is the most efficient, although not always the safest, of all lifestyles; Castle Windsor's default prioritizes efficiency over safety.

In this section, you'll see how we can configure lifestyles for components and how to use some of the more special lifestyles like PerWebRequest and POOLED. We'll also look at implementing a custom lifestyle to showcase that we aren't constrained to use only the built-in lifestyles. At the end of this section, you should be able to use Castle Windsor's lifestyles in your own application.

Let's start by reviewing how to configure lifestyles for components.

10.2.1   Configuring lifestyle

In this section, we'll review how to manage component lifestyles with Castle Windsor. Lifestyle is configured as part of component registration, so the same options are available to us as with configuration in general: code or XML. We'll look at each in turn.

CONFIGURING LIFESTYLE WITH CODE

Lifestyle is configured using the Fluent Registration API with which we register components. It's as easy as this:

```
container.Register(Component
    .For<SauceBéarnaise>()
    .LifeStyle.Transient);
```

Notice that you specify the lifestyle using the `Lifestyle` property. In this example, you set the lifestyle to TRANSIENT so that each time SauceBéarnaise is resolved, a new instance is returned.

You can still explicitly specify the SINGLETON lifestyle even though it's the default. These two examples are entirely equivalent:

```
container.Register(Component          container.Register(Component
    .For<SauceBéarnaise>()                .For<SauceBéarnaise>());
    .LifeStyle.Singleton);
```

Because SINGLETON is the default lifestyle, you don't have to explicitly specify it, but you can do so if you'd like.

In the same way that we can configure components from both code and XML, we can also configure lifestyles in both places.

CONFIGURING LIFESTYLE WITH XML

In section 10.1.2, you saw how to configure components using XML, but you didn't supply any lifestyle. As is the case when configuring a component using the Fluent

Registration API, the SINGLETON lifestyle is default, but you can explicitly specify a different lifestyle if you need to:

```
<component id="ingredient.sauceBéarnaise"
        service="IIngredient"
        type="Steak"
        lifestyle="transient" />
```

Compared to the example in section 10.1.2, the only difference is the added `lifestyle` attribute. As you can see, specifying a lifestyle is easy in both code and XML.

RELEASING COMPONENTS

As we discussed in section 8.2.2, it's important to release objects when we're done with them. This is as easy as calling the `Release` method:

```
container.Release(ingredient);
```

This will release the instance provided to the `Release` method (the `ingredient` variable in the previous example) as well as all those DEPENDENCIES of the instance whose lifetime is up. That is, if the instance has a TRANSIENT DEPENDENCY, this DEPENDENCY will be released (and potentially disposed of), whereas a SINGLETON will remain in the container.

> **TIP** Castle Windsor tracks all, even TRANSIENT, components, so it's important to remember to release all resolved instances to avoid memory leaks.

> **TIP** Release explicitly what you resolve explicitly.

> **TIP** Remember to dispose of the container itself when the application shuts down. This will dispose of SINGLETON components and ensure that the application cleans up properly after itself.

Let's now turn our attention to some of those lifestyles that require a bit more configuration than a simple statement.

10.2.2 *Using advanced lifestyles*

In this section, we'll look at two of Castle Windsor's lifestyles that require more configuration than just a simple declaration: POOLED and `PerWebRequest`.

USING THE POOLED LIFESTYLE

In section 8.3.5, we looked at the general concept of a POOLED lifestyle; in this section, you'll see how to use Windsor's implementation. Castle Windsor's POOLED lifestyle comes with a default pool size, but because the optimal pool size is entirely dependent on the circumstances, you should prefer to explicitly configure the size of the pool. You can specify a POOLED lifestyle with default sizes the same way that you configure any other lifestyle:

```
container.Register(Component
    .For<IIngredient>()
    .ImplementedBy<SauceBéarnaise>()
    .LifeStyle.Pooled);
```

However, this doesn't communicate the size of the pool. Although I haven't been able to find any *documentation* that states what the default pool values are, Castle Windsor 2.1.1's source code reveals that the default initial size is 5 and the max size is 15. To me, these values seem rather arbitrary, which is another reason to explicitly decide the size.

To explicitly configure the pool sizes, you can use the `PooledWithSize` method:

```
container.Register(Component
    .For<IIngredient>()
    .ImplementedBy<SauceBéarnaise>()
    .LifeStyle.PooledWithSize(10, 50));
```

This example sets the initial size to 10 and the maximum size to 50. Castle Windsor pools have two configuration values: initial size and max size. The initial size obviously controls the initial size of the pool and the max size the maximum size of the pool, but the behavior at edge cases may be surprising to some. Figure 10.4 demonstrates how the pool size evolves during the lifetime of a container.

When an instance is resolved from a pool, it's marked as being *in use*. Because it stays in that state until explicitly released from the container, it's important to remember to release instances when you're done with them. This enables the container to recycle the instances:

```
container.Release(ingredient);
```

> **NOTE**   The behavior when the pool is fully utilized is surprising. Instead of throwing an exception or blocking the call, *surplus* instances are created. These are thrown away after use instead of being recycled.

Although slightly more advanced than SINGLETON or TRANSIENT, the POOLED lifestyle is still easy to use. The only extra effort you need to do is to supply two extra numbers to

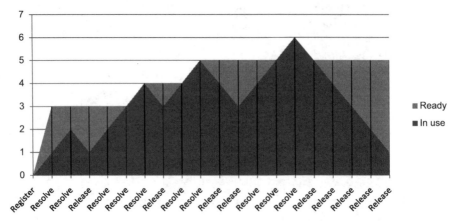

Figure 10.4   Size progression of a pool with an initial size of 3 and maximum size of 5. Even though the initial size of the pool is 3, the pool stays empty until the first instance is resolved. At that point, all 3 instances for the initial size are created and one is immediately put to use. When an instance is released, it's returned to the pool. The pool increases in size if more instances than the minimum size are necessary. Notice that it's possible to exceed the maximum size, but that the surplus instances aren't recycled when released.

configure the pool sizes. The `PerWebRequest` lifestyle is a bit different but a little more complex to configure.

USING THE PERWEBREQUEST LIFESTYLE

As the name implies, the `PerWebRequest` lifestyle works by creating an instance per web request. Declaring it is as easy as declaring the TRANSIENT lifestyle:

```
container.Register(Component
    .For<IIngredient>()
    .ImplementedBy<SauceBéarnaise>()
    .LifeStyle.PerWebRequest);
```

However, if we attempt to use it without further configuration, we receive this exception:

> *Looks like you forgot to register the HTTP module Castle.MicroKernel.Lifestyle.PerWeb-RequestLifestyleModule*

> *Add '<add name="PerRequestLifestyle" type="Castle.MicroKernel.Lifestyle.PerWebRequest-LifestyleModule, Castle.Windsor" />' to the <httpModules> section on your web.config. If you're running IIS7 in Integrated Mode you will need to add it to <modules> section under <system.webServer>*

As far as error messages go, this one is exemplary. It tells you exactly what you need to do.

In any case, it's relevant to notice that the `PerWebRequest` lifestyle uses an HTTP module to figure out which web request is currently executing. One consequence of that is that we need to register the HTTP module as I described; another is that this particular lifestyle *only* works within web requests. If we try to use it in another type of application, we'll get the same exception as in the previous example.

Both the POOLED and `PerWebRequest` lifestyles require a tiny bit more work to use than just a simple declaration, but they're still easy to configure and use. Castle Windsor's built-in lifestyles provide a comprehensive and useful suite of lifestyles that fit most scenarios. Still, if none of them fit a specialized need, we can write a custom lifestyle.

10.2.3 *Developing a custom lifestyle*

In most cases, Castle Windsor's built-in lifestyles should suffice, but if we need something special, we can write a custom lifestyle.

In this section, you'll see how to do this. First, we'll briefly look at the relevant SEAM that makes this possible, but we'll quickly proceed to look at an example.

UNDERSTANDING THE LIFESTYLE API

You can create a custom lifestyle by implementing the `ILifestyleManager` interface:

```
public interface ILifestyleManager : IDisposable
{
    void Init(IComponentActivator componentActivator,
        IKernel kernel, ComponentModel model);
    bool Release(object instance);
    object Resolve(CreationContext context);
}
```

Figure 10.5   An `ILifestyleManager` **acts as a sort of interceptor that's called instead of the underlying** `IComponetActivator`**. An** `ILifestyleManager` **implementation is expected to use the supplied** `IComponentActivator` **to create object instances. Because the** `ILifestyleManager` **sits in the middle, it gets a chance to intercept each call and perform its own lifestyle logic. It's free to reuse instances instead of calling through to the** `IComponentActivator` **each time.**

One of the slightly odd requirements of an `ILifestyleManager` implementation is that it has a default constructor. That is, CONSTRUCTOR INJECTION is prohibited here, of all places. Instead, we're provided with one of the relatively rare cases of METHOD INJECTION. The `Init` method will be invoked, providing among other parameters an `IKernel` instance that we can use as a SERVICE LOCATOR. This is definitely not my cup of tea, and when we look at some example code, you'll also see how this makes the implementation more complicated than it would have been if CONSTRUCTOR INJECTION had been possible.

The other methods of the `ILifestyleManager` interface are `Resolve` and `Release`, but we should use them as hooks more than to provide our own implementations of `Resolve` and `Release`—that's the responsibility of the `IComponentActivator` passed to us in the `Init` method. Figure 10.5 shows that we should only use these methods to intercept calls to `Resolve` and `Release` so that we can control the lifetime of each component.

Castle Windsor provides a default implementation of `ILifestyleManager` in the form of the `AbstractLifestyleManager` class. It implements the interface and provides a reasonable default implementation for most methods. This is the class you'll use to implement a sample lifestyle.

DEVELOPING A CACHING LIFESTYLE

Because Castle Windsor offers a comprehensive set of standard lifestyles, it's difficult to come up with a great example. However, imagine that you'd like to develop a *caching* lifestyle that would keep an instance around for a certain amount of time, and then release it. This is a good example because it's complex enough to demonstrate different aspects of implementing a custom lifestyle, but not so complex that it doesn't fit on a few pages.

> **NOTE** A *caching* lifestyle is a contrived example. There are better ways to implement caching functionality, because normally you don't wish to cache Services,[4] but rather the data those Services manage.

---

[4] Eric Evans, *Domain-Driven Design: Tackling Complexity in the Heart of Software* (New York: Addison-Wesley, 2004), 104.

WARNING   The sample code shown here ignores thread-safety, but a real production implementation of `ILifestyleManager` must be thread-safe.

The easiest way to implement a custom lifestyle is to derive from `AbstractLifestyleManager` as shown in the following listing.

Listing 10.2   Defining a custom lifestyle

```
public partial class CacheLifestyleManager :
    AbstractLifestyleManager                        ◁─┐  Derive from
{                                                   ❶  AbstractLifestyleManager
    private ILease lease;

    public ILease Lease
    {
        get
        {
            if (this.lease == null)
            {
                this.lease = this.ResolveLease();      ❷  Lazy
            }                                              load
            return this.lease;
        }
    }

    private ILease ResolveLease()
    {
        var defaultLease = new SlidingLease(TimeSpan.FromMinutes(1));
        if (this.Kernel == null)
        {
            return defaultLease;
        }
        if (this.Kernel.HasComponent(typeof(ILease)))
        {                                                  ❸  Attempt to
            return this.Kernel.Resolve<ILease>();              locate ILease
        }
        return defaultLease;
    }
}
```

One of the things you get from deriving from `AbstractLifestyleManager` ❶ is that the `Init` method is implemented for you. You can override it, but it isn't necessary in this case. All it does is save the injected services so that you can later access them via protected properties.

To implement the functionality that decides when a cached object times out, you need an instance of `ILease`. If you had been able to use CONSTRUCTOR INJECTION you could have requested an `ILease` through the constructor in three lines of code (including a Guard Clause). Now you need 12 lines of code because you need to deal with the many potential states of the `CacheLifestyleManager`: was the `Init` method invoked yet? Does the `Kernel` have an `ILease`?

You deal with this by exposing a lazy-loaded Lease property ❷. The first time you read it, it invokes the ResolveLease method to figure out what the lease should be. It uses a default lease but attempts to look up an alternative through the Kernel ❸—if there's a Kernel at all. I think this is a pretty good illustration of the demerits of METHOD INJECTION. Notice that if anyone reads the Lease property before the Init method is called, the default lease will be used even if the Kernel contains an ILease component. However, because Castle Windsor knows nothing of the Lease property, this doesn't happen in normal use.

> **NOTE** The ILease interface used in this example is a custom interface defined for this particular purpose. It isn't System.Runtime.Remoting.Lifetime.ILease, which has a similar, but much more complex API.

Compared to all the hoops you must jump through to inject a DEPENDENCY into your custom lifestyle, implementing the Resolve method is simpler, as you can see in the following listing.

Listing 10.3   Implementing the `Resolve` method

```
private object obj;

public override object Resolve(CreationContext context)
{
    if (this.Lease.IsExpired)
    {
        base.Release(this.obj);          ❶ Expire
        this.obj = null;                     object
    }
    if (this.obj == null)
    {
        this.Lease.Renew();              ❷ Renew
        this.obj = base.Resolve(context);    lease
    }
    return this.obj;
}
```

Every time CacheLifestyleManager is asked to resolve the component, it starts by checking whether the current lease is expired. If this is the case, it Releases the current cached instance and nulls it out ❶. The Release method is explicitly invoked on the base class and through it to the IComponentActivator, as shown in figure 10.5. This is important to do because it gives the underlying implementation a chance to dispose of the instance if it implements IDisposable.

The next thing to do is to check whether the cached instance is null. This can be the case if it was released just previously but will also be the case the first time the Resolve method is invoked. In both cases, you renew the lease ❷ and ask the base implementation to Resolve the component for you. This is where the base class invokes the appropriate method on IComponentActivator.

In this custom lifestyle, you override the Release method to do nothing:

```
public override bool Release(object instance)
{
    return false;
}
```

This may seem strange but is a fairly normal thing to do. You should consider that the Release method is a Hook Method[5] that is part of Castle Windsor's lifestyle SEAM. You're being informed that the component can be released, but it doesn't mean that you have to do it. As an example, the SINGLETON lifestyle per definition *never* releases its instance, so it has the same implementation of the Release method as the one shown previously.

In the case of the CacheLifestyleManager, you do release the cached instance from time to time, but, as is shown in listing 10.3, you do it from within the Resolve method, when it's appropriate.

The CacheLifestyleManager caches the resolved instance until the lease expires, and then resolves a new instance and renews the lease. There are several ways we could implement the lease logic, but we'll only look at one.

IMPLEMENTING A LEASE

You need at least one implementation of ILease to go with the CacheLifestyle-Manager. The SlidingLease class expires after a fixed time span, but you could create other implementations that expire on fixed times of the day, or after they have resolved the component a preset number of times.

> **NOTE** The ILease interface and the SlidingLease class shown here have nothing to do with Castle Windsor, but I wanted to show them for completeness' sake. You can skip ahead and read about how to register the custom lifetime if you don't care about SlidingLease.

The following listing shows the SlidingLease implementation.

Listing 10.4 Implementing an ILease

```
public class SlidingLease : ILease
{
    private readonly TimeSpan timeout;
    private DateTime renewed;

    public SlidingLease(TimeSpan timeout)
    {
        this.timeout = timeout;
        this.renewed = DateTime.Now;
    }

    public TimeSpan Timeout
    {
        get { return this.timeout; }
    }
```

---

[5] Erich Gamma et al., *Design Patterns: Elements of Reusable Object-Oriented Software* (New York: Addison-Wesley, 1994), 328.

```
public bool IsExpired
{
    get { return DateTime.Now >
        this.renewed + this.timeout; }        ❶  Expire if past
}                                                 timeout

public void Renew()
{                                              ❷  Renew
    this.renewed = DateTime.Now;
}
}
```

The `SlidingLease` class implements `ILease` by keeping track of when the lease was renewed. Every time you ask it whether it's expired, it compares the current time against the renewal time and the timeout ❶. When you renew the lease, it sets the renewal time to the current time ❷. I could've used the `TimeProvider` AMBIENT CONTEXT from section 4.4.4 instead of `DateTime.Now`, but I chose to keep things as simple as possible.

Now that you know how to implement a custom lifestyle and any custom DEPENDENCIES it might have, you only need to learn how to use them.

CONFIGURING COMPONENTS WITH A CUSTOM LIFESTYLE

Using the `CacheLifestyleManager` with a component is easy and works in the same way as specifying any other lifestyle:

```
container.Register(Component
    .For<IIngredient>()
    .ImplementedBy<SauceBéarnaise>()
    .LifeStyle.Custom<CacheLifestyleManager>());
```

You use a generic overload of the `Custom` method to specify which `ILifestyleManager` type to use, but there's also an overload that takes a `Type` instance.

Unless you remember to also register an `ILease`, the `CacheLifestyleManager` will use the default lease of a `SlidingLease` with a one-minute timeout. Here's one way you can register a custom `ILease`:

```
container.Register(Component
    .For<ILease>()
    .Instance(new SlidingLease(TimeSpan.FromHours(1))));
```

This will register an instance of `SlidingLease` with a one-hour time span. You must remember to register the `ILease` before using the custom lifestyle, because otherwise the default lease will be used instead.

Developing a custom lifestyle for Castle Windsor isn't particularly difficult. In many cases, the `AbstractLifestyleManager` class provides a good starting point, and we only need to override the methods that we particularly care about. Often, this will be the `Resolve` method, although we can leave the few other methods at their default implementations. It will only be in rare cases that we need to create a custom lifestyle, because Castle Windsor's standard set of lifestyles is quite comprehensive.

This completes our tour of LIFETIME MANAGEMENT with Castle Windsor. Components can be configured with mixed lifestyles, and this is even true when we register multiple implementations of the same ABSTRACTION. We have yet to look at how to work with multiple components, so let's now turn our attention in that direction.

10.3 Working with multiple components

DI CONTAINERS thrive on distinctness but have a hard time with ambiguity. When using CONSTRUCTOR INJECTION, a single constructor is preferred over overloaded constructors because it's clear which constructor to use when there's no choice. This is also the case when mapping from ABSTRACTIONS to concrete types. If we attempt to map multiple concrete types to the same ABSTRACTION, we introduce ambiguity.

Despite the undesirable qualities of ambiguity, we often need to work with multiple implementations of a single interface. This can be the case in these situations:

- Different concrete types should be used for different consumers.
- DEPENDENCIES are sequences.
- Decorators[6] are in use.

In this section, we'll look at each of these cases and see how Castle Windsor addresses each one in turn. When we're done, you should be able to register and resolve components even when multiple implementations of the same ABSTRACTION are in play.

Let's first take a look at how we can provide more fine-grained control than what AUTO-WIRING provides.

10.3.1 Selecting among multiple candidates

AUTO-WIRING is convenient and powerful but provides us with less control. As long as all ABSTRACTIONS are distinctly mapped to concrete types we have no problems, but as soon as we introduce more implementations of the same interface, ambiguity rears its ugly head.

Let's first recap how Castle Windsor deals with multiple registrations of the same ABSTRACTION.

REGISTERING MULTIPLE IMPLEMENTATIONS OF THE SAME SERVICE

As you saw in section 10.1.2, you can register multiple components for the same service:

```
container.Register(Component
    .For<IIngredient>()
    .ImplementedBy<Steak>());
container.Register(Component
    .For<IIngredient>()
    .ImplementedBy<SauceBéarnaise>());
```

This example registers both the Steak and SauceBéarnaise classes with the IIngredient service. The first registration wins, so if you resolve IIngredient with container .Resolve<IIngredient>() you'll get a Steak instance. However, a call to container .ResolveAll<IIngredient>() returns an array of IIngredient that contains both

---

[6] Gamma, *Design Patterns*, 175.

Steak and SauceBéarnaise. That is, subsequent registrations aren't forgotten, but are harder to get at.

TIP The first registration for a given type wins. It defines the default registration for that type.

WARNING If there are registrations of a given type that can't be resolved because of missing DEPENDENCIES, ResolveAll silently ignores them and only returns those it can resolve. Because no exception is thrown, this can sometimes lead to some hard-to-understand bugs.[7]

The following listing shows one way you can provide hints that can later be used to select among multiple candidates.

Listing 10.5   Naming components

```
container.Register(Component
    .For<IIngredient>()
    .ImplementedBy<Steak>()
    .Named("meat"));
container.Register(Component
    .For<IIngredient>()
    .ImplementedBy<SauceBéarnaise>()
    .Named("sauce"));
```

You can give each registration a unique name that can later be used to distinguish this particular component from other components.

Given the named components in listing 10.5, you can resolve both Steak and SauceBéarnaise like this:

```
var meat = container.Resolve<IIngredient>("meat");
var sauce = container.Resolve<IIngredient>("sauce");
```

Notice that you supply the same key that you used to name the component during registration.

Given that you should always resolve services in a single COMPOSITION ROOT, you should normally not expect to deal with such ambiguity on this level.

TIP If you find yourself invoking the Resolve method with a specific key, consider if you can change your approach to be less ambiguous.

However, you can use named components to select among multiple alternatives when configuring DEPENDENCIES for a given service.

---

[7] As I'm completing the book, this has changed in the Castle Windsor code base, although no release yet includes this change. However, when you're reading this book, the current version of Castle Windsor most likely has a different behavior than described here.

REGISTERING NAMED DEPENDENCIES

As useful as AUTO-WIRING is, sometimes you need to override the normal behavior to provide fine-grained control over which DEPENDENCIES go where; but it may also be that you need to address an ambiguous API. As an example, consider this constructor:

```
public ThreeCourseMeal(ICourse entrée,
    ICourse mainCourse, ICourse dessert)
```

In this case, you have three identically typed DEPENDENCIES that each represents a *different* concept. In most cases, you want to map each of the DEPENDENCIES to a separate type. The following listing shows how you could choose to register the ICourse mappings.

Listing 10.6   Registering named courses

```
container.Register(Component
    .For<ICourse>()
    .ImplementedBy<Rillettes>()
    .Named("entrée"));
container.Register(Component
    .For<ICourse>()
    .ImplementedBy<CordonBleu>()
    .Named("mainCourse"));
container.Register(Component
    .For<ICourse>()
    .ImplementedBy<MousseAuChocolat>()
    .Named("dessert"));
```

Like listing 10.6, you register three named components, mapping the Rillettes to a registration named "entrée" (American readers are reminded that this is the proper word for *starter* or *appetizer*), CordonBleu to a registration named "mainCourse," and the MousseAuChocolat to a registration named "dessert."

Given this configuration, you can now register the ThreeCourseMeal class, as shown in the following listing.

Listing 10.7   Overriding AUTO-WIRING

```
container.Register(Component
    .For<IMeal>()
    .ImplementedBy<ThreeCourseMeal>()
    .ServiceOverrides(new
        {
            entrée = "entrée",
            mainCourse = "mainCourse",
            dessert = "dessert"
        }));
```

You can explicitly provide overrides for those parameters (or properties) that you wish to explicitly address. In the case of the ThreeCourseMeal class, you need to address all three constructor parameters. However, in other cases, you may only want to override one of several parameters; that's also possible. The ServiceOverrides method enables you to supply an anonymously typed object that specifies which parameters to

override. If you don't want to use anonymous types, other overloads of the Service-
Overrides methods allow us to supply an array of specialized ServiceOverride
instances, or an IDictionary.

Using an anonymous type, you match the parameters that you want to override
with a named registration. In the first case, you match the entrée *parameter name* with
a registration named "entrée." In this case, the parameter names are identical to the
registration names, but this need not be so. The other parameters are mapped in a
similar fashion.

> **WARNING**   Although an anonymous type may look like strong typing, used in
> this fashion it's another group of magic strings. In the end it's converted to a
> dictionary of names and values. The property names of the anonymous type
> must match the parameter names of the corresponding constructor. If you
> change the parameter name in the constructor the ServiceOverride will
> stop working until you correct it, so don't rely on this feature more than
> absolutely necessary.

Because the ServiceOverrides method depends on a text-based match between
parameter names and configured overrides, it's best not to rely on it too much. If you
feel compelled to use it only to deal with ambiguity, a better solution is to design the
API to get rid of that ambiguity. It often leads to a better overall design.

In the next section, you'll see how to refactor the current ThreeCourseMeal class to
a more general implementation and, at the same time, get rid of the inherent ambiguity. You can do that by allowing an arbitrary number of courses in a meal—but that
compels you to understand how Castle Windsor wires lists and sequences.

10.3.2 *Wiring sequences*

In section 6.4.1, we discussed how CONSTRUCTOR INJECTION acts as a warning system for
SINGLE RESPONSIBILITY PRINCIPLE violations. The lesson then was that, instead of viewing
constructor over-injection as a weakness of the CONSTRUCTOR INJECTION pattern, we
should rather rejoice that it makes problematic design so obvious.

When it comes to DI CONTAINERS and ambiguity, we see a similar relationship. DI
CONTAINERS generally don't deal with ambiguity in a graceful manner. Although we can
make a good DI CONTAINER like Castle Windsor deal with it, it often feels awkward. This
is often an indication that we could improve upon the design of our own code.

> **TIP**   If configuring a certain part of your API is difficult with Castle Windsor,
> consider whether you can make your API more explicit and distinct. Not only
> will it make it easier to configure with Castle Windsor, but it's also likely to
> make the overall design better.

Instead of feeling constrained by Castle Windsor, we should embrace its conventions
and let it guide us toward a better and more consistent design. In this section, we'll
look at an example that will demonstrate how we can refactor away from ambiguity, as
well as show how Castle Windsor deals with sequences, arrays, and lists.

REFACTORING TO A BETTER COURSE

In section 10.3.1, you saw how the ThreeCourseMeal and its inherent ambiguity forced us to abandon AUTO-WIRING and, instead, use an explicit ServiceOverride. This should prompt you to reconsider the API design.

A simple generalization moves us toward an implementation of IMeal that takes an arbitrary number of ICourse instances instead of exactly three, as was the case with the ThreeCourseMeal class:

```
public Meal(IEnumerable<ICourse> courses)
```

Notice that, instead of requiring three distinct ICourse instances in the constructor, the single DEPENDENCY on an IEnumerable<ICourse> instance allows you to provide any number of courses to the Meal class—from zero to ... a lot! This solves the issue with ambiguity because there's now only a single DEPENDENCY. In addition, it also improves the API and implementation by providing a single, general-purpose class that can model many different types of meal, from a simple meal with a single course to an elaborate, 12-course dinner.

Given the registration of courses shown in listing 10.6, you might expect to be able to automatically resolve IMeal if you register it like this:

```
container.Register(Component
    .For<IMeal>()
    .ImplementedBy<Meal>());
```

However, when you try to resolve IMeal, the container throws an exception. Although the exception is far from self-explanatory, the reason is that you haven't told the container how it should resolve IEnumerable<ICourse>. Let's review some different options that are available.

CONFIGURING ARRAYS

Castle Windsor understands arrays pretty well. Because arrays implement IEnumerable<T>, you can explicitly configure an array for the courses constructor parameter. This can be done in a way that's similar to the syntax you saw in listing 10.7. In the following listing, you see the same courses specified as services.

Listing 10.8   Explicitly defining an array of services

```
container.Register(Component
    .For<IMeal>()
    .ImplementedBy<Meal>()
    .ServiceOverrides(new
        {
            courses = new[]
                {
                    "entrée",
                    "mainCourse",
                    "dessert"
                }
        }));
```

❶ Override courses parameter

Similar to listing 10.7, you use the `ServiceOverrides` method when you want to override AUTO-WIRING for specific parameters. In this case, you want to explicitly configure the `courses` constructor parameter ❶ of the `Meal` class. Because this parameter is an `IEnumerable<ICourse>` you must now specify a sequence of `ICourse` services.

Because arrays implement `IEnumerable<T>`, you can define an array of named services. You do this by creating an array of service *names*. These names are identical to the names assigned to each registration in listing 10.6, and Castle Windsor is so kind as to translate this array of service names to an array of `ICourse` instances at runtime. This is analogous to listing 10.7, with the only difference being that the fluent registration API natively understands and translates arrays of service names to arrays of services.

Although the refactoring from `ThreeCourseMeal` to `Meal` looked like a step in the right direction, you seem to have gained nothing in the area of configuration awkwardness. Is it possible to do better?

It's certainly possible to make the configuration simpler, but at the expense of loss of control. As figure 10.6 illustrates, sometimes we need to be able to pick from the list of all configured services of a given type, but at other times, we want them all.

The example you saw corresponds to the situation on the left, where we hand-pick an explicit list of named services form the conceptually larger list of all configured services of the given type. In other cases, we might prefer a simpler convention where we use *all* available services of the required type. Let's see how this can be accomplished.

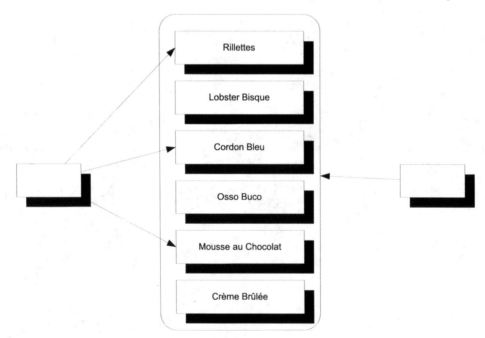

Figure 10.6   There is more than one way to deal with enumerable DEPENDENCIES. In the situation to the right, we want to resolve *all* services configured in the container. In the situation to the left, we only want a subset.

RESOLVING SEQUENCES

Castle Windsor doesn't resolve arrays or `IEnumerable<T>` by default. This may seem a little surprising, because invoking `ResolveAll` returns an array:

```
IIngredient[] ingredients = container.ResolveAll<IIngredient>();
```

However, if you try to let the container resolve a component that depends on an array of services, you'll get an exception. The correct way to deal with this issue is to register the built-in `CollectionResolver` with the container, like this:

```
container.Kernel.Resolver.AddSubResolver(
    new CollectionResolver(container.Kernel));
```

The `CollectionResolver` will enable the container to resolve sequences of DEPENDEN-CIES such as `IEnumerable<T>`. With that, you can now resolve the `Meal` class without using explicit `ServiceOverrides`. Given this registration

```
container.Register(Component
    .For<IMeal>()
    .ImplementedBy<Meal>());
```

you can resolve `IMeal` with the help of the `CollectionResolver`:

```
var meal = container.Resolve<IMeal>();
```

This will create an instance of `Meal` with all `ICourse` services from the container.

Consumers that rely on lists of DEPENDENCIES may be the most intuitive use of multiple registrations of the same ABSTRACTION, but before we leave this subject completely, we need to look at one last, and perhaps a bit surprising, case: a case where multiple registrations come into play.

10.3.3 *Wiring Decorators*

In section 9.1.2, we discussed how the Decorator design pattern is useful when implementing CROSS-CUTTING CONCERNS. By definition, Decorators introduce multiple types of the same ABSTRACTION. At the very least, we have two implementations of an ABSTRAC-TION: the Decorator itself and the decorated type. If we stack the Decorators, we might have even more.

This is another example of having multiple registrations of the same service. Unlike the previous sections, these registrations aren't conceptually equal, but, rather, DEPENDENCIES of each other. In this section, you'll see how to configure Castle Windsor to deal with this pattern.

EXPLICITLY WIRING DECORATORS

Castle Windsor requires us to register all components that we wish to use. When it comes to Decorators, we must register both the Decorator and the decorated types. Because both types implement the same interface, we introduce ambiguity that can be addressed. As the following listing shows, we can do this explicitly.

Listing 10.9   Explicitly configuring a Decorator

```
container.Register(Component
    .For<IIngredient>()
    .ImplementedBy<Breading>()
    .ServiceOverrides(new
        {
            ingredient = "cutlet"
        }));
container.Register(Component
    .For<IIngredient>()
    .ImplementedBy<VealCutlet>()
    .Named("cutlet"));
```

As we discussed in the introduction to chapter 9, you can view breading as a decoration of a veal cutlet; register a Cotoletta. When you resolve the Cotoletta, you want a reference to the breading which should contain the veal cutlet. You first register the Breading. Recall that, in Castle Windsor, the first registration always wins. You explicitly use the ServiceOverrides method to configure which named service should be used for the ingredient constructor parameter. Notice that you reference a component named *cutlet*, although that component hasn't yet been registered at that point. This is possible because the order of registration matters less. You can register components *before* you register their DEPENDENCIES and it will all work, as long as everything is properly registered when you attempt to resolve the services.

This means that you must still register the veal cutlet before resolving IIngredient. You subsequently register it with the *cutlet* name. This name matches the service name supplied to the ingredient constructor parameter in the previous configuration.

Although such explicit configuration of Decorators is possible and sometimes necessary, Castle Windsor natively understands the Decorator pattern and provides a more implicit way to do the same thing.

IMPLICITLY WIRING DECORATORS

Castle Windsor enables us to implicitly configure Decorators by registering them in the correct order. Recall that the first registration wins, in the sense that this is the type returned from a call to the Resolve method; we must register the outermost Decorator first.

By definition, a Decorator has a DEPENDENCY on another instance of the same type. If we don't explicitly define which registration to use, we might expect a circular reference to occur. However, Castle Windsor is smarter than that. Instead, it picks the *next* registration of the appropriate type. This means that instead of listing 10.9, you can write

```
container.Register(Component
    .For<IIngredient>()
    .ImplementedBy<Breading>());
container.Register(Component
    .For<IIngredient>()
    .ImplementedBy<VealCutlet>());
```

There's no need to explicitly name components or use the `ServiceOverrides` method to configure DEPENDENCIES. When you resolve `IIngredient`, Castle Windsor will AUTO-WIRE the `Breading` class with the next available `IIngredient` service, which is the `VealCutlet` class.

> **NOTE** The next logical progression from Decorator is INTERCEPTION. Castle Windsor has excellent INTERCEPTION capabilities, but because section 9.3.3 already contains a comprehensive example, I'll refer you there instead of repeating it here.

Castle Windsor lets us work with multiple components in several different ways. We can register components as alternatives to each other, as peers resolved as sequences, or as hierarchical Decorators. In many cases, Castle Windsor will figure out what to do, but we can always use the `ServiceOverrides` method to explicitly define how services are composed if we need more explicit control.

This may also be the case when we need to deal with APIs that deviate from CONSTRUCTOR INJECTION. So far, you've seen how to configure components in a `WindsorContainer`, including how to specify lifetime styles and how to deal with multiple components; but, until now, we've allowed the container to wire DEPENDENCIES by implicitly assuming that all components use CONSTRUCTOR INJECTION. Because this isn't always the case, in the next section we'll review how we can deal with classes that must be instantiated in special ways.

10.4   Configuring difficult APIs

Until now, we've considered how we can configure components that use CONSTRUCTOR INJECTION. One of the many benefits of CONSTRUCTOR INJECTION is that DI CONTAINERS, such as Castle Windsor, can easily understand how to compose and create all classes in a dependency graph.

This becomes less clear when APIs are less well-behaved. In this section, you'll see how to deal with primitive constructor arguments, static factories, and PROPERTY INJECTION. These all require our special attention. Let's start by looking at classes that take primitive types, such as strings or integers, as constructor arguments.

10.4.1   Configuring primitive Dependencies

As long as we inject ABSTRACTIONS into consumers, all is well. But it becomes more difficult when a constructor depends on a primitive type, such as a string, number, or enum. This is most often the case for data access implementations that take a connection string as a constructor parameter, but is a more general issue that applies to all strings and numbers.

Conceptually, it doesn't make much sense to register a string or number as a component in a container, and, with Castle Windsor, it doesn't even work. If we try to resolve a component with a primitive DEPENDENCY, we'll get an exception even though the primitive type was previously registered.

Consider, as an example, this constructor:

```
public ChiliConCarne(Spiciness spiciness)
```

In this example, `Spiciness` is an enum:

```
public enum Spiciness
{
    Mild = 0,
    Medium,
    Hot
}
```

WARNING As a rule of thumb, enums are code smells and should be refactored to polymorphic classes.[8] However, they serve us well for this example.

You need to explicitly tell Castle Windsor how to resolve the `spiciness` constructor parameter. The following listing shows how it's possible, using syntax very much like the `ServiceOverrides` method, but with a different method.

Listing 10.10 Supplying a primitive constructor argument value

```
container.Register(Component
    .For<ICourse>()
    .ImplementedBy<ChiliConCarne>()
    .DependsOn(new
        {
            spiciness = Spiciness.Hot
        }));
```

Instead of the `ServiceOverrides` method that overrides AUTO-WIRING, you can use the `DependsOn` method that enables you to supply instances for specific DEPENDENCIES. In this case, you supply the value `Spiciness.Hot` for the `spiciness` constructor parameter.

NOTE The difference between `ServiceOverrides` and `DependsOn` is that, with `DependsOn`, we supply *actual instances* that are used for the given parameter or property, whereas with `ServiceOverrides`, we supply *names or types of services* that will be resolved for the given parameter or property.

WARNING As is the case with `ServiceOverrides`, the `DependsOn` method relies on a match between the parameter name and the name of the anonymous property supplied to `DependsOn`. If we rename the parameter we must also edit the `DependsOn` call.

Whenever we need to supply a primitive value, such as a connection string, we can define the value explicitly in code (or pull if from the application configuration) and assign it using the `DependsOn` method. The good thing about the `DependsOn` method is that we don't need to explicitly invoke the constructor or supply any other DEPENDENCIES where AUTO-WIRING is more appropriate. But the disadvantage is that it's more brittle in the face of refactoring.

---

[8] Martin Fowler et al., *Refactoring: Improving the Design of Existing Code* (New York: Addison-Wesley, 1999), 82.

There's a more robust alternative that lets us explicitly invoke the constructor. This can also be used to deal with classes that don't have traditional constructors.

10.4.2 Registering components with code blocks

Some classes can't be instantiated through a public constructor. Instead, you must use some sort of factory to create instances of the type. This is always troublesome for DI CONTAINERS because, by default, they look after public constructors.

Consider this example constructor for the public JunkFood class:

```
internal JunkFood(string name)
```

Even though the JunkFood class is public, the constructor is internal. Obviously, instances of JunkFood should be created through the static JunkFoodFactory class:

```
public static class JunkFoodFactory
{
    public static IMeal Create(string name)
    {
        return new JunkFood(name);
    }
}
```

From Castle Windsor's perspective, this is a problematic API because there are no unambiguous and well-established conventions around static factories. It needs help—and we can provide it with a code block, as shown in the following listing.

Listing 10.11 Configuring a factory method

```
container.Register(Component
    .For<IMeal>()
    .UsingFactoryMethod(() =>
        JunkFoodFactory.Create("chicken meal")));
```

You can use the UsingFactoryMethod method to define a code block that creates the appropriate instance—in this case, by calling the Create method on JunkFood-Factory with the desired parameter.

This code block will be invoked at the appropriate time according to the component's configured lifestyle. In this case, because you didn't explicitly define a lifestyle, SINGLETON is the default and the Create method will be called only once, no matter how many times you resolve IMeal. Had you instead configured the component to use the TRANSIENT lifestyle, the Create method would be invoked each time we resolve IMeal.

Apart from enabling more exotic object initialization than normal public constructors, using a code block also gives you a more type-safe alternative to supplying primitives than the DependsOn method you saw in section 10.4.1:

```
container.Register(Component
    .For<ICourse>()
    .UsingFactoryMethod(() =>
        new ChiliConCarne(Spiciness.Hot)));
```

In this case, you use the code block to explicitly create a new instance of the Chili-ConCarne class with the desired Spiciness. This adds type-safety, but totally disables AUTO-WIRING for the type in question.

> **TIP** There are more advanced overloads of UsingFactoryMethod that enable you to resolve DEPENDENCIES from the container. This is useful when you want to use the UsingFactoryMethod to explicitly assign only a single of several parameters, but must supply all the other parameters in order to compile.

The UsingFactoryMethod is a good tool when you must deal with classes that can't be created through a public constructor. As long as there's some public API you can invoke to create the desired instance of the class, you can use the UsingFactoryMethod method to explicitly define the code block that will create the requested instance.

The last common deviation from CONSTRUCTOR INJECTION we'll examine here is PROPERTY INJECTION.

10.4.3 *Wiring with Property Injection*

PROPERTY INJECTION is a less well-defined form of DI because you aren't forced by the compiler to assign a value to a writable property. Even so, Castle Windsor natively understands PROPERTY INJECTION and assigns values to writable properties, if it can.

Consider this CaesarSalad class:

```
public class CaesarSalad : ICourse
{
    public IIngredient Extra { get; set; }
}
```

It's a common misconception that a Caesar Salad includes chicken. At its core, a Caesar Salad is a *salad*, but, because it tastes great with chicken, many restaurants offer the option to add chicken as an extra ingredient. The CaesarSalad class models this by exposing a writable property named Extra.

If you register *only* the CaesarSalad class without any Chicken, the Extra property will not be assigned:

```
container.Register(Component
    .For<ICourse>()
    .ImplementedBy<CaesarSalad>());
```

Given this registration, resolving ICourse will return an instance of CaesarSalad without any Extra ingredient. However, you can change the outcome by adding Chicken to the container:

```
container.Register(Component
    .For<IIngredient>()
    .ImplementedBy<Chicken>());
container.Register(Component
    .For<ICourse>()
    .ImplementedBy<CaesarSalad>());
```

Now, when you resolve ICourse, the resulting CaesarSalad instance's Extra property will be an instance of the Chicken class. That is, Castle Windsor scans a new instance for writable properties and assigns a value if it can provide a component that matches the type of the property.

> **TIP** In cases where you need to explicitly control how properties are assigned, you can use the ServiceOverrides method.

In this section, you've seen how to deal with APIs that deviate from plain vanilla CON-STRUCTOR INJECTION. You can address primitive constructor arguments with the DependsOn method or with UsingFactoryMethod that also supports factory methods and other alternatives to public constructors. PROPERTY INJECTION is natively supported by Castle Windsor.

10.5 *Summary*

The overview of Castle Windsor provided in this chapter only scratches the surface of what is possible with one of the most mature and comprehensive DI CONTAINERS available. Because SEAMS are everywhere, we can customize it to our heart's content, and many extra features are available.

In this chapter we focused on the most common pieces of Windsor's API. The material presented here covers mainstream usage of the container as well as hints of more advanced parts. It's all you need to know if your code base follows proper DI patterns and conventions; armed with this knowledge, you should be able to wire up entire applications with Castle Windsor.

Even as a bare-bones DI CONTAINER, Castle Windsor is formidable. It supports almost any feature we could ask for. As one of the oldest .NET DI CONTAINERS around, it benefits greatly from years of development. Yet it doesn't show its age; rather, it supports many new ideas and modern language constructs. Still, perhaps the greatest disadvantage of Castle Windsor is that the big feature set is realized at the expense of a somewhat heterogeneous API. Although it's easy to get started with the Windsor-Container class, more advanced scenarios can be harder to implement unless you truly master the entire API. Luckily, because the Castle Windsor support forum is active and monitored by skilled and helpful developers, you're likely to get a quick response if you have a question.

Although the advanced API may seem daunting, it's as easy to get started with Castle Windsor as with any other DI CONTAINER: create an instance of WindsorContainer, configure it, and resolve components with it.

There are several ways to configure the container: CODE AS CONFIGURATION, XML, and convention-based configuration are all possible, and we can even mix and match all three to arrive at an optimal solution.

A broad range of lifetime styles are available, including SINGLETON, TRANSIENT, and WEB REQUEST CONTEXT. If the included lifestyles aren't sufficient, we can also implement custom lifestyles—but this should be a rare occurrence.

Support for multiple components for the same ABSTRACTION seems to be one of Castle Windsor's weaker points. It seems to understand arrays better than other types of sequences or lists, but we can address this shortcoming relatively easily. The exact way this is done depends on whether we want to resolve all or only a subset of components of the same service.

Although we should prefer to rely on AUTO-WIRING, the `ServiceOverrides` method enables us to explicitly configure how DEPENDENCIES are assigned to components.

Sometimes components don't use CONSTRUCTOR INJECTION, but may instead use PROPERTY INJECTION or require use of separate factory classes. Such scenarios are also supported through various methods.

As one of the most versatile DI CONTAINERS available, there's little reason *not* to use Castle Windsor, but that doesn't preclude alternatives that are just as good. In the next chapter, we'll look at another mature and advanced DI CONTAINER: StructureMap.

StructureMap

In the previous chapter, we looked at the Castle Windsor DI CONTAINER to see how the principles and patterns described in parts 1–3 can be applied. In this chapter, we'll do exactly the same with another DI CONTAINER: StructureMap.

StructureMap is the oldest DI CONTAINER for .NET—it has been around longer than the others. Despite its age, it's still being actively developed and has many modern features, so we should view its age mostly as a testament to its maturity. It's also one of the most commonly used DI CONTAINERS.[1]

In this chapter, we'll examine how StructureMap can be used to apply the principles and patterns laid forth in parts 1–3. Figure 11.1 shows the structure of the chapter.

---

[1] Once more I need to stress that there are no scientifically sound statistics about DI CONTAINER usage, so all such claims are based on ad hoc internet polls, and so on. Take it for what it is.

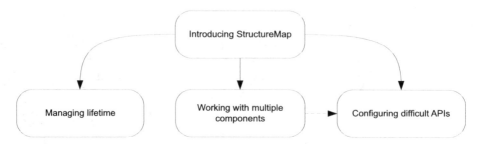

Figure 11.1   This chapter is divided into four sections. The first section introduces the StructureMap API and should be considered a prerequisite for the next three sections. Each of these can be read independently of each other, although the fourth section uses some methods that are introduced in the third section. These methods have relatively self-explanatory names, so you may be able to read the fourth section without reading the third, but on the other hand you may also find that you need to refer back to that section occasionally.

The first section provides an overall introduction to StructureMap and demonstrates how to configure and resolve components. The next three sections each deal with usage patterns that require a bit of extra attention; you can read them all in order, or you can skip some and read only the ones that interest you.

This chapter should enable you to get started, as well as deal with the most common issues that may come up as you use StructureMap on a day-to-day basis. It isn't a complete treatment of StructureMap—that would take several more chapters, or perhaps a whole book in itself.

You can read the chapter in isolation from the rest of part 4 specifically to learn about StructureMap, or you can read it together with the other chapters in part 4 to compare DI CONTAINERS. The focus of this chapter is to show how StructureMap relates to and implements the patterns and principles described in parts 1–3.

11.1   *Introducing StructureMap*

In this section, you'll learn where to get StructureMap, what you get, and how you start using it. We'll also look at common configuration options, as well as how to package configuration settings into reusable components. Table 11.1 provides fundamental information that you're likely to need to get started.

Table 11.1   StructureMap at a glance

Question	Answer
Where do I get it?	Go to http://structuremap.github.com/structuremap/index.html, and click the Download the Latest Release link. From Visual Studio 2010 you can also get it via NuGet. The package name is *structuremap*.
What's in the download?	You can download a .zip file with precompiled binaries. You can also get the source code and compile it yourself. The binaries are .dll files that you can place wherever you like and reference from your own code.

Table 11.1 **StructureMap at a glance** *(continued)*

Question	Answer
Which platforms are supported?	.NET 3.5 SP1, .NET 4.
How much does it cost?	Nothing. It's open source software.
Where can I get help?	There's no guaranteed support, but you're likely to get help in the official forum at http://groups.google.com/group/structuremap-users.
On which version is the chapter based?	2.6.1.

As is also the case with Castle Windsor, using StructureMap follows a simple rhythm, illustrated by figure 11.2.

Container or `ObjectFactory`?

Earlier versions of StructureMap used a static `ObjectFactory` class as a single, application-wide container. It was used like this:

```
SauceBéarnaise sauce =
    ObjectFactory.GetInstance<SauceBéarnaise>();
```

Among several problems with using a static factory is that it encourages us to misuse it as a SERVICE LOCATOR; use of the `ObjectFactory` class is now discouraged in favor of container instances. There are still many examples on the StructureMap site (and elsewhere) that use `ObjectFactory` code samples to demonstrate various StructureMap features, but we should consider these as rudiments of an earlier age.

In the rest of this chapter, we'll ignore that `ObjectFactory` exists and focus exclusively on container instances.

WARNING The StructureMap API has changed a lot recently. It's often the case that we find a code example on the internet that uses a method or class that isn't available in the current version; most likely, it was renamed or otherwise refactored. Although all code examples compiled and worked when this

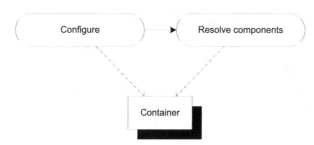

Figure 11.2 **The overall usage pattern of StructureMap is simple: First we configure the container, and then we resolve components from it. In the vast majority of cases, we create an instance of the** `Container` **class and completely configure it before we start resolving components from it. We resolve components from the same instance that we configure.**

chapter was written, some parts of the API might have changed between then and when you're reading this.

When you're done with this section, you should have a good feeling for the overall usage pattern of StructureMap, and you should be able to start using it in well-behaved scenarios where all components follow proper DI patterns such as CONSTRUC-TOR INJECTION. Let's start with the simplest scenario and see how we can resolve objects using a StructureMap container.

11.1.1 *Resolving objects*

The core service of any DI CONTAINER is to resolve components. In this section, we'll look at the API that enables us to resolve components with StructureMap.

If you remember the discussion about resolving components with Castle Windsor, you may recall that Windsor requires you to register *all* relevant components before you can resolve them. This isn't the case with StructureMap; if you request a concrete type with a default constructor, no configuration is necessary. The simplest possible use of StructureMap is this:

```
var container = new Container();
SauceBéarnaise sauce = container.GetInstance<SauceBéarnaise>();
```

Given an instance of `StructureMap.Container`, you can use the generic `GetInstance` method to get an instance of the concrete `SauceBéarnaise` class. Because this class has a default constructor, StructureMap automatically figures out how to create an instance of it. No explicit configuration of the container is necessary.

> **NOTE** The `GetInstance<T>` method is equivalent to Windsor's `Resolve<T>` method.

Because StructureMap supports AUTO-WIRING, even in the absence of a default constructor, it will be able to create instances without configuration as long as the involved constructor parameters are all concrete types and the entire tree of parameters have leaf types with default constructors.

As an example, consider this `Mayonnaise` constructor:

```
public Mayonnaise(EggYolk eggYolk, OliveOil oil)
```

Whereas the mayonnaise recipe is a bit simplified, both `EggYolk` and `OliveOil` are concrete classes with default constructors. Although `Mayonnaise` itself has no default constructor, StructureMap can still create it without any configuration:

```
var container = new Container();
var mayo = container.GetInstance<Mayonnaise>();
```

This works because StructureMap is able to figure out how to create all required constructor parameters. However, as soon as we introduce loose coupling, we must configure StructureMap by mapping ABSTRACTIONS to concrete types.

MAPPING ABSTRACTIONS TO CONCRETE TYPES

Whereas StructureMap's ability to AUTO-WIRE concrete types certainly can come in handy from time to time, loose coupling normally requires you to map ABSTRACTIONS to concrete types. Creating instances based on such maps is the core service offered by any DI CONTAINER, but you must still define the map.

In this example, you map the IIngredient interface to the concrete Sauce-Béarnaise class, which allows you to successfully resolve IIngredient:

```
var container = new Container();
container.Configure(r => r
    .For<IIngredient>()
    .Use<SauceBéarnaise>());
IIngredient ingredient = container.GetInstance<IIngredient>();
```

The Configure method provides the opportunity to configure a Configuration-Expression using a code block (see the following sidebar "Nested Closures" for an explanation). The configuration statement reads almost like a sentence (or like instructions from a cookbook): *for IIngredient use SauceBéarnaise.* The For method enables you to define the ABSTRACTION while the Use method lets you define the concrete type that implements the ABSTRACTION.

The strongly typed API provided by the ConfigurationExpression class helps prevent configuration mistakes because the Use method has a generic constraint that enforces that the type specified in the type argument must derive from the abstraction type argument specified in the For method. The previous example code compiles because SauceBéarnaise implements IIngredient.

In many cases, the strongly typed API is all we need, and, because it provides desirable compile-time checking, we should use it whenever we can. Still, there are situations where we need a more weakly typed way to resolve services. This is also possible.

RESOLVING WEAKLY TYPED SERVICES

Sometimes we can't use a generic API because we don't know the appropriate type at design time. All we have is a Type instance, but we'd still like to get an instance of that type. You saw an example of that in section 7.2, where we discussed ASP.NET MVC's DefaultControllerFactory class. The relevant method is this one:

```
protected internal virtual IController GetControllerInstance(
    RequestContext requestContext, Type controllerType);
```

Because you only have a Type instance, you can't use generics, but must resort to a weakly typed API. Fortunately, StructureMap offers a weakly typed overload of the GetInstance method, which allows you to implement the GetControllerInstance method, like this:

```
return (IController)this.container.GetInstance(controllerType);
```

The weakly typed overload of `GetInstance` enables you to pass the `controllerType` argument directly to StructureMap, but also requires you to explicitly cast the return value to `IController`.

No matter which overload of `GetInstance` you use, StructureMap guarantees that it will return an instance of the requested type or throw an exception if there are DEPENDENCIES that can't be satisfied. When all required DEPENDENCIES have been properly configured, StructureMap can AUTO-WIRE the requested type.

In the previous example, `this.container` is an instance of `StructureMap.IContainer`. To be able to resolve the requested type, all loosely coupled DEPENDENCIES must previously have been configured. There are many ways to configure StructureMap; the next section reviews the most common ones.

11.1.2 *Configuring the container*

As we discussed in section 3.2, there are several conceptually different ways to configure a DI CONTAINER. Figure 11.3 reviews the options.

Like other DI CONTAINERS with a long history, StructureMap started out with XML as the main configuration source. However, many teams soon learned that defining type registrations in XML is extraordinarily brittle, so today we prefer strongly typed configuration. This can be done with CODE AS CONFIGURATION, but is often more effectively done with more convention-based AUTO-REGISTRATION.

StructureMap supports all three approaches and even allows us to mix them all within the same container; in this regard, it gives us all we could ask for. In this section, you'll see how you can use each of these three types of configuration sources.

CODE AS CONFIGURATION

In section 11.1.1, you already saw a brief glimpse of StructureMap's strongly typed configuration API. Here we'll examine it in greater detail.

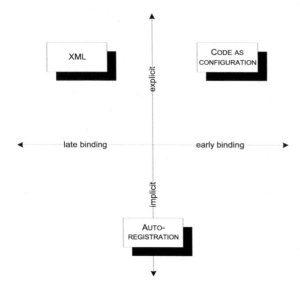

Figure 11.3 **Conceptually different configuration options. CODE AS CONFIGURATION is strongly typed and tends to be explicit. XML, on the other hand, is late bound, but still explicit. AUTO-REGISTRATION instead relies on conventions that can be both strongly typed and more loosely defined.**

There are several entry points into the configuration API. You've seen it invoked through explicit use of the `Configure` method:

```
var container = new Container();
container.Configure(r => r
    .For<IIngredient>()
    .Use<SauceBéarnaise>());
```

Another alternative is to specify the exact same code block directly when creating the `Container` instance:

```
var container = new Container(r => r
    .For<IIngredient>()
    .Use<SauceBéarnaise>());
```

The result is exactly the same; however, in this chapter, I'll follow a consistent convention and prefer the `Configure` method over the constructor.

Nested Closures

StructureMap makes extensive use of the Nested Closure pattern,[2] where configuration is defined by code blocks (popularly known as *lambda expressions*). As an example, this is the `Configure` method's signature:

```
public void Configure(Action<ConfigurationExpression> configure);
```

The `configure` parameter is a delegate that takes a `ConfigurationExpression` as input. In the code examples in this chapter, this parameter is usually denoted by `r`, and I normally supply the delegate as a code block expressed using the `r` parameter.

As a side note: looking through the code samples on the StructureMap site and Jeremy Miller's blog, sometimes the parameter name used in the code block is `x`, and sometimes it is `registry`. Because there's no consistent precedent, I have chosen `r` (for *registry*) as the convention in this chapter; although `r` isn't a particularly self-explanatory variable name, the tiny scope of the code blocks in question makes it more appropriate than a longer, less succinct name.[3]

The `ConfigurationExpression` class contains many methods we can use to configure StructureMap; one of them is the `For` method we've already seen. As you'll see later in this section, another is the `Scan` method with this signature:

```
public void Scan(Action<IAssemblyScanner> action);
```

Notice that the `Scan` method itself takes a delegate as input. When you supply a code block for the `Scan` method, you have a code block within a code block—hence the name *Nested Closure*.

---

[2] For a good introduction to Nested Closures, see Jeremy Miller, "Patterns in Practice: Internal Domain Specific Languages," *MSDN Magazine* (January 2010). Also available online at http://msdn.microsoft.com/en-us/magazine/ee291514.aspx

This article is written by one of the main authors of StructureMap and uses examples from the StructureMap API to illustrate the thinking behind the API design.

[3] Robert C. Martin, *Clean Code: A Handbook of Agile Software Craftsmanship* (Upper Saddle River, NJ: Prentice Hall, 2008), 312 (N5).

Unlike Castle Windsor, mapping IIngredient to SauceBéarnaise in the same way as previously shown doesn't preclude you from resolving SauceBéarnaise itself. That is, both sauce and ingredient will be appropriately resolved here:

```
container.Configure(r =>
    r.For<IIngredient>().Use<SauceBéarnaise>());
var sauce = container.GetInstance<SauceBéarnaise>();
var ingredient = container.GetInstance<IIngredient>();
```

If you recall the discussion in section 10.1.2, mapping IIngredient to Sauce-Béarnaise with Castle Windsor causes the concrete class (SauceBéarnaise) to "disappear," and you have to use *Type Forwarding* to be able to resolve both. Such extra steps aren't necessary with StructureMap, where you can resolve both IIngredient and SauceBéarnaise. In both cases, the returned objects are Sauce-Béarnaise instances.

In real applications, we always have more than one ABSTRACTION to map, so we must configure multiple mappings. We can do so in a single call to the Configure method, or using multiple successive calls. These two examples are equivalent:

```
container.Configure(r =>               container.Configure(r => r
{                                          .For<IIngredient>()
    r.For<IIngredient>()                   .Use<SauceBéarnaise>());
        .Use<SauceBéarnaise>();         container.Configure(r => r
    r.For<ICourse>()                       .For<ICourse>()
        .Use<Course>();                    .Use<Course>());
});
```

Although the example to the right uses two successive calls to configure, the example to the left passes a code block with more statements to a single Configure method call. Both code examples end up registering correct mappings for both ICourse and IIngredient interfaces. However, configuring the same ABSTRACTION multiple times has some interesting results:

```
container.Configure(r =>
    r.For<IIngredient>().Use<SauceBéarnaise>());
container.Configure(r =>
    r.For<IIngredient>().Use<Steak>());
```

In this example, you register IIngredient twice. If you resolve IIngredient you get an instance of Steak. The last configuration wins, but previous configurations aren't forgotten. StructureMap handles multiple configurations for the same ABSTRACTION well, but we'll return to this topic in section 11.3.1.

There are more advanced options available for configuring StructureMap, but we can configure an entire application with the methods shown here. To save ourselves from too much explicit maintenance of container configuration, we could instead consider a more convention-based approach, using AUTO-REGISTRATION.

AUTO-REGISTRATION

In many cases, registrations will be similar. Such registrations are tedious to maintain and explicitly registering each and every component may not be the most productive approach.

Consider a library that contains a lot of IIngredient implementations. We can configure each class individually, but it will result in numerous similar-looking calls to the Configure method. What's worse, every time we add a new IIngredient implementation, we must also explicitly configure it in the container if we want it to be available. It would be more productive to state that all implementations of IIngredient found in a given assembly should be registered.

This is possible with the Scan method, which is another example of StructureMap's extensive use of delegates. The Scan method is available on the Configuration-Expression class, which is already accessed via a code block. This is where we see the Nested Closure pattern in effect. This example configures all IIngredient implementations in a single swoop:

```
container.Configure(r =>
    r.Scan(s =>
    {
        s.AssemblyContainingType<Steak>();
        s.AddAllTypesOf<IIngredient>();
    }));
```

The Scan method is nested within the Configure code block. The s variable represents an IAssemblyScanner instance, which we can use to define how an assembly should be scanned and types configured.

The IAssemblyScanner instance provides several methods we can use to define which assemblies to scan and how to configure types from those assemblies. We can use the generic AssemblyContainingType method to identify an assembly from a representative type, but there are several other methods that enable us to provide an Assembly instance or even add all assemblies from a given file path.

A different set of methods gives us the ability to define which types to add and how to map them. The AddAllTypesOf method provides an easy shortcut to add all types that implement a given interface, but there are several other methods that enable us to accurately control how types are configured.

The previous example unconditionally configures all implementations of the IIngredient interface, but we can provide filters that enable us to select only a subset. Here's a convention-based scan where you add only classes whose name starts with *Sauce:*

```
container.Configure(r =>
    r.Scan(s =>
    {
        s.AssemblyContainingType<Steak>();
        s.AddAllTypesOf<IIngredient>();
        s.Include(t => t.Name.StartsWith("Sauce"));
    }));
```

The only difference from the previous example is the addition of the `Include` method call, which introduces a third level of Nested Closure. The `Include` method takes a predicate that's used to determine whether a given `Type` should be included or not. In this case, the answer is `true` whenever the `Type`'s `Name` starts with *Sauce*.

If we want full control over convention-based configuration, we can define a custom convention by implementing the `IRegistrationConvention` interface. The following listing shows the *Sauce* convention implemented as a custom convention.

Listing 11.1   Implementing a custom convention

```
public class SauceConvention : IRegistrationConvention
{
    public void Process(Type type, Registry registry)
    {
        var interfaceType = typeof(IIngredient);
        if (!interfaceType.IsAssignableFrom(type))
        {
            return;
        }
        if (!type.Name.StartsWith("Sauce"))
        {
            return;
        }

        registry.For(interfaceType).Use(type);
    }
}
```

The `SauceConvention` class implements `IRegistrationConvention`, which defines a single member. The `Process` method will be invoked by StructureMap for each type in the assembly defined in the `Scan` method, so you must explicitly provide a set of Guard Clauses that filters out all those types you don't care about.

The Guard Clauses guarantee that any type that makes it past them is an `IIngredient` whose name starts with *Sauce*, so you can now register it with the registry. Notice, by the way, that the `Registry` is provided through METHOD INJECTION, which makes a lot of sense because `IRegistrationConvention` defines an add-in for StructureMap.

You can use the `SauceConvention` class in the `Scan` method like this:

```
container.Configure(r =>
    r.Scan(s =>
    {
        s.AssemblyContainingType<Steak>();
        s.Convention<SauceConvention>();
    }));
```

Notice that you still define the assembly outside of the convention. This lets you vary the source of the types to process independently of the convention itself. The `Sauce-Convention` is specified using the `Convention` method. This method requires that the `IRegistrationConvention` specified as the type argument has a default constructor, but there's also a `With` method that takes an `IRegistrationConvention` instance that you can manually create any way you want.

Because you can use the `Scan` method to scan all assemblies in a specified folder, you can use it to implement add-in functionality where add-ins can be added without recompiling a core application. This is one way to implement late binding; another is to use the XML-based configuration API.

XML CONFIGURATION

When we need to be able to change a configuration without recompiling the application, XML configuration is a good option.

> **TIP** Use XML configuration only for those types you need to change without recompiling the application. Use AUTO-REGISTRATION or CODE AS CONFIGURATION for the rest.

We can use specialized XML files to configure StructureMap, or we can embed the configuration in the standard application configuration file. However, surprisingly, the last option isn't directly supported, so let's first look at how to use a specialized XML file.

Configuration can be defined in XML and read using the `AddConfiguration-FromXmlFile` method:

```
container.Configure(r =>
    r.AddConfigurationFromXmlFile(configName));
```

In this example, `configName` is a string which contains the name of the appropriate XML file. If you wish to use the standard application configuration file, you need to use the AppDomain API to figure out the path for the current configuration file:

```
var configName =
    AppDomain.CurrentDomain.SetupInformation.ConfigurationFile;
```

> **NOTE** Although the static `ObjectFactory` class directly supports reading configuration from App.config, this isn't supported for Container instances. Using the AppDomain API to get the file name is the recommended workaround.[4]

In addition to pointing StructureMap to a file, you can supply XML configuration as an `XmlNode`:

```
container.Configure(r =>
    r.AddConfigurationFromNode(xmlNode));
```

This enables you to pull XML configuration from arbitrary places besides files, such as databases or embedded resources.

No matter the source of the XML, the schema remains the same. Here's a simple configuration that maps `IIngredient` to `Steak`:

---

[4] This was confirmed in a Twitter conversation between Jeremy Miller and me: http://twitter.com/jeremyd-miller/statuses/18134210141

```
<StructureMap MementoStyle="Attribute">
  <DefaultInstance PluginType="Ploeh.Samples.MenuModel.IIngredient,
                   ➥Ploeh.Samples.MenuModel"
                   PluggedType="Ploeh.Samples.MenuModel.Steak,
                   ➥Ploeh.Samples.MenuModel" />
</StructureMap>
```

Notice that you must supply the assembly qualified type name for both the ABSTRAC-
TION and the implementation—StructureMap calls these *Plugins* and *Plugged types.*

If you want to embed this XML in the application's configuration file, you must
also register the StructureMap element as a configuration section:

```
<configSections>
  <section name="StructureMap"
           type="StructureMap.Configuration.
           ➥StructureMapConfigurationSection, StructureMap"/>
</configSections>
```

XML configuration is a good option when you need to change the configuration of
one or more components without recompiling the application; however, because it
tends to be quite brittle, you should reserve it for only those occasions and use
either AUTO-REGISTRATION or CODE AS CONFIGURATION for the main part of the container's configuration.

> **TIP** Remember that the last configuration of a type wins? You can use this
> behavior to overwrite hard-coded configuration with XML configuration. To
> do this, you must remember to read in the XML configuration after any other
> components have been configured.

In this section, we mainly looked at various configuration APIs for StructureMap.
Although it's certainly possible to write one big block of unstructured configuration code, it's better to modularize configuration. StructureMap supports this
through Registries.

11.1.3 Packaging configuration

It's sometimes desirable to package configuration logic into reusable groups, and
even when reuse itself isn't your top priority, you may want to provide a bit of structure
if you have a big and complex application to configure.

With StructureMap, we can package configuration into Registries, which are
classes deriving from the concrete Registry class. Figure 11.4 shows the relationship
between the Registry class and the Configure method used in section 11.1.2.

Whenever you use the Configure method in this chapter, you represent the
ConfigurationExpression instance with the variable name r. Most of the methods we
invoke on r (such as the For and Scan methods) are defined on the Registry class.

To implement a Registry, we implement a class that derives from Registry. The following listing shows an example that configures a default ICourse and also adds

Figure 11.4 The `Configure` **method of the** `Container` **class takes as input a delegate that operates on a** `ConfigurationExpression`—**in this chapter, we represent this** `ConfigurationExpression` **instance with the variable name** `r`. **The** `ConfigurationExpression` **class is a child class of the concrete** `Registry` **class.**

Registry or ConfigurationExpression?

Whereas most of the configuration API (such as the `For` and `Scan` methods) are still available when we derive directly from `Registry`, we can't use the methods defined directly on the `ConfigurationExpression` class. What functionality do we lose?

There are only five methods defined directly on `ConfigurationExpression`, and they fall into two categories:

- Reading configuration from XML
- Adding Registries

It isn't likely that we'd want to add a Registry from within a Registry, so this doesn't seem like that big of a deal.

Configuration defined in XML is a completely different way to express configuration. We express a certain part of an application's configuration either in XML or by using the configuration API, but not both. In that light, the inability to define XML sources from a Registry isn't much of a limitation.

Even so, wouldn't it be possible to derive a Registry from `Configuration-Expression` instead of directly from `Registry`? Unfortunately, we can't, because the `ConfigurationExpression` constructor is internal.

The bottom line is that a Registry can't derive from `ConfigurationExpression`, but must derive from `Registry` itself.

`IIngredient` types from an assembly. It uses the same API that we already used in section 11.1.2, but now packaged within a separate class.

Listing 11.2 Implementing a Registry

```
public class MenuRegistry : Registry
{
    public MenuRegistry()
    {
        this.For<ICourse>().Use<Course>();
        this.Scan(s =>
        {
```

❶ **Use Registry API**

```
            s.AssemblyContainingType<Steak>();
            s.AddAllTypesOf<IIngredient>();
        });
    }
}
```

❶ Use Registry API

The `MenuRegistry` class derives from `Registry` and defines the entire configuration in the constructor. From within the class you can access the entire public API of the `Registry` class, so you can use the `For` and `Scan` methods in the same way you did in section 11.1.2 ❶—the only difference is that, in this case, you're not implementing an anonymous delegate, but rather a constructor. Instead of the code block and the ubiquitous `r` variable you may have grown accustomed to by now, you access the API through the `this` variable.

With the `MenuRegistry` in place, you can now add it to the container with the `Configure` method:

```
container.Configure(r =>
    r.AddRegistry<MenuRegistry>());
```

This generic version of the `AddRegistry` method requires that the `Registry` implementation has a default constructor, but there's also a non-generic overload available that takes a `Registry` instance as input, giving us full control over how it's created.

NOTE The `AddRegistry` methods are two of the five methods defined directly on `ConfigurationExpression`, and not available from within a `Registry`.

You can also supply a `Registry` directly through a Container's constructor:

```
var container = new Container(new MenuRegistry());
```

I prefer the `Configure` method because it lets me add more than one Registry in a sequence.

TIP Registries let you package and structure your container configuration code. Use them instead of inline configuration, because it will make your COMPOSITION ROOT more readable.

With Registries, we can configure StructureMap with CODE AS CONFIGURATION or AUTO-REGISTRATION, whereas XML configuration must be imported directly via the `Configure` method. We can still mix both approaches, pulling some configuration from XML and other from one or more Registries:

```
container.Configure(r =>
{
    r.AddConfigurationFromXmlFile(configName);
    r.AddRegistry<MenuRegistry>();
});
```

Once the container is configured, you can start resolving services with it as described in section 11.1.1.

This section introduced the StructureMap DI CONTAINER and demonstrated the fundamental mechanics: how to configure the container and subsequently use it to resolve services. Resolving services is easily done with a single call to the `GetInstance` method, so the complexity involves configuring the container. This can be done in several different ways, including imperative code and XML. Until now, we've only looked at the most basic API so there are more advanced areas we have yet to cover. One of the most important topics is how to manage component lifetime.

11.2 *Managing lifetime*

In chapter 8, we discussed LIFETIME MANAGEMENT, including the most common conceptual lifetime styles, such as SINGLETON and TRANSIENT. StructureMap supports many different lifestyles and enables us to configure the lifetime of all services. The lifestyles shown in table 11.2 are available as part of the API.

Table 11.2 StructureMap lifestyles

Name	Comments
PerRequest	StructureMap's name for PER GRAPH. This is the default lifestyle. Instances aren't tracked by the container.
Singleton	Standard SINGLETON.
HttpContext	StructureMap's name for WEB REQUEST CONTEXT.
ThreadLocal	One instance is created per thread.
Hybrid	A combination of HttpContext and ThreadLocal. HttpContext is used when available (for example, when the container is hosted in a web application), but ThreadLocal is used as a fallback scope.
HttpSession	One instance is created per HTTP session. Use with caution.
HybridHttpSession	A combination of HttpSession and ThreadLocal. HttpSession is used when available (for example, when the container is hosted in a web application), but ThreadLocal is used as a fallback scope.
Unique	StructureMap's name for TRANSIENT.

StructureMap's implementations of the different lifestyles are equivalent to the general lifestyles described in chapter 8, so I won't spend much time on them in this chapter.

> **TIP** The default lifestyle is PER GRAPH. As we discussed in section 8.3.3, this offers a good balance between efficiency and safety. Still, when you have thread-safe services, SINGLETON is a more efficient lifestyle, but you must explicitly remember to configure those services like that.

In this section, you'll see how to define lifestyles for components in both code and XML. As a more advanced scenario, you'll also see how to implement a custom lifestyle to showcase that you're not limited to the built-in lifestyles supplied by StructureMap.

At the end of this section, you should be able to use StructureMap's lifestyles in your own application.

Let's start by reviewing how to configure lifestyles for components.

11.2.1 Configuring lifestyles

In this section, we'll review how to manage component lifestyles with StructureMap. Lifestyles are configured as part of configuring components, and you can define them in both code and XML. We'll look at each in turn.

CONFIGURING LIFESTYLES WITH CODE

Lifestyles are configured as part of the Configure API you use to configure components in general. It's as easy as this:

```
container.Configure(r =>
    r.For<SauceBéarnaise>().Singleton());
```

This configures the concrete SauceBéarnaise class as a SINGLETON so that the same instance is returned each time SauceBéarnaise is requested. If you want to map an ABSTRACTION to a concrete class with a specific lifetime, the lifestyle declaration comes between the For and the Use method calls:

```
container.Configure(r =>
    r.For<IIngredient>().Singleton().Use<SauceBéarnaise>());
```

This maps IIngredient to SauceBéarnaise and also configures it as a SINGLETON. There are other methods, similar to the Singleton method, which enable you to declare many of the other lifestyles; but not all lifestyles have a dedicated method. All lifestyles can be configured using the general-purpose LifecycleIs method. As an example, the Unique lifestyle has no dedicated method, but can be configured like this:

```
container.Configure(r => r
    .For<SauceBéarnaise>()
    .LifecycleIs(new UniquePerRequestLifecycle()));
```

The LifecycleIs method takes an instance of ILifecycle, so you can pass in any class that implements that interface. As you'll see in section 11.2.2, this is also how we configure a component with a custom lifetime.

All built-in StructureMap lifestyles have a corresponding ILifecycle implementation except the PER GRAPH lifestyle, which is the default. This lifestyle is normally implicitly configured by omitting an explicit lifestyle. All the configurations you saw in section 11.1 used the PER GRAPH lifestyle.

> **TIP** Omitting the lifestyle declaration implies PER GRAPH, which is the default. But null in place of an ILifecycle instance also implies PER GRAPH.

If we're writing some general-purpose code that takes an ILifecycle instance and passes it to the LifecycleIs method, we can still use it to configure a component with the PER GRAPH lifestyle; null implies PER GRAPH, so these two examples are functionally equivalent:

```
container.Configure(r => r              container.Configure(r => r
   .For<IIngredient>()                     .For<IIngredient>()
   .LifecycleIs(null)                      .Use<SauceBéarnaise>());
   .Use<SauceBéarnaise>());
```

TIP Although you can use `null` to imply the PER GRAPH lifestyle, you should prefer omitting the lifestyle declaration completely.

Whereas the API exposed by the `Configure` method and the `ConfigurationExpression` enables us to declare lifestyles explicitly, the convention-based Scan API doesn't in itself. There's no method on the `IAssemblyScanner` interface that gives us the option of broadly declaring a lifestyle for a set of components in one go.

However, we can implement a simple `IRegistrationConvention` that can do that. Here's how you'd use one called `SingletonConvention`:

```
container.Configure(r =>
   r.Scan(s =>
   {
       s.AssemblyContainingType<Steak>();
       s.AddAllTypesOf<IIngredient>();
       s.Convention<SingletonConvention>();
   }));
```

Notice how this is the same configuration as the first AUTO-REGISTRATION example in section 11.1.2, only you added a line of code that adds the `SingletonConvention` shown in the listing that follows.

Listing 11.3 Implementing a lifestyle-declaring convention

```
public class SingletonConvention : IRegistrationConvention
{
    public void Process(Type type, Registry registry)
    {
        registry.For(type).Singleton();
    }
}
```

If you recall from the previous discussion about `IRegistrationConvention` in listing 11.1, the `Process` method is invoked for each included type in the assembly `Scan` operation. In this case, the only thing you need to do is to declare the lifestyle for each using the `Singleton` method. This configures each type as a SINGLETON.

Using CODE AS CONFIGURATION, we can configure components with various lifestyles in any way we want. Whereas this is by far the most flexible way to configure components, we sometimes need to resort to XML for late binding purposes. In that case, we can also declare lifestyles.

CONFIGURING LIFESTYLES WITH XML

When we need to define components in XML, we'll also want to be able to configure their lifestyles in the same place. This is easily done as part of the XML schema introduced in section 11.1.2. You can use the optional `Scope` attribute to declare the lifestyle:

```
<DefaultInstance PluginType="Ploeh.Samples.MenuModel.IIngredient,
                 ➥Ploeh.Samples.MenuModel"
                 PluggedType="Ploeh.Samples.MenuModel.Steak,
                 ➥Ploeh.Samples.MenuModel"
                 Scope="Singleton" />
```

Compared to the example in section 11.1.2, the only difference is the added `Scope` attribute that configures the instance as a SINGLETON. When you previously omitted the `Scope` attribute, StructureMap's PER GRAPH default was automatically used.

In both code and XML, it's easy to configure lifestyles for components. In all cases it's done in a rather declarative fashion. Although configuration is easy, you must not forget that some lifestyles involve long-lived objects that use memory as long as they're around.

PREVENTING MEMORY LEAKS

Like any other DI CONTAINER, StructureMap creates object graphs for us. But it doesn't track the created objects for us. It may keep track of those objects for its own purposes, but that depends on the object lifetime. As an example, to implement the SINGLETON scope, it must keep a reference to the created instance. This is also the case for the `HttpContext` lifestyle where all instances are stored in `HttpContext.Current.Items`; however, when the HTTP request finishes, all these instances go out of scope and are eligible for garbage collection.

On the other hand, the PER GRAPH and TRANSIENT lifestyles don't keep track of the objects that StructureMap creates. As you saw in listings 8.7 and 8.8, object instances are created and returned with no internal tracking. This has some advantages and disadvantages.

Because StructureMap doesn't hold on to instances unnecessarily, the risk of inadvertent memory leaks is much smaller. With a container like Castle Windsor, memory leaks are guaranteed if we forget to call the `Release` method for all resolved object graphs. This isn't the case with StructureMap because objects will automatically be garbage-collected as they go out of scope.

The disadvantage is that disposable objects can't be deterministically disposed of. Because we can't explicitly release an object graph, we can't dispose of any disposable objects. This means that it becomes even more important to wrap disposable APIs in non-disposable services, as discussed in section 6.2.1.

In short, StructureMap is well behaved and allows objects to be garbage-collected when they go out of scope in our code, but the requirement is that our own classes must be just as well behaved. We can't rely on the container or the calling code to dispose of any services, so we must keep usage of disposable objects within single methods.

The built-in lifestyles of StructureMap are a rather comprehensive collection that should meet most daily needs. Still, in the rare cases where we need a specialized lifestyle, we still have the option to create one ourselves.

11.2.2 *Developing a custom lifestyle*

In most cases, we should be able to get by with the comprehensive selection of lifestyles already offered by StructureMap, but if we have special needs, it's possible to implement a custom lifestyle. In this section, you'll see how to do this. After a brief review of the SEAM that makes this possible, we'll spend most of the time going through an example.

UNDERSTANDING THE LIFESTYLE API

In section 11.2.1, you already got a glimpse of StructureMap's lifestyle API. The `Life-cycleIs` method takes an instance of the `ILifecycle` interface, which models how lifestyles interact with the rest of StructureMap:

```
public interface ILifecycle
{
    string Scope { get; }
    void EjectAll();
    IObjectCache FindCache();
}
```

Of those three methods, the `FindCache` method is the fulcrum. It returns a cache that StructureMap uses to look up and insert objects with that particular lifestyle. The `ILifecycle` interface mostly serves as an Abstract Factory[5] for `IObjectCache` instances that contain the implementation of the lifestyle. This interface is far more complex, but not terribly difficult to implement:

```
public interface IObjectCache
{
    object Locker { get; }
    int Count { get; }
    bool Has(Type pluginType, Instance instance);
    void Eject(Type pluginType, Instance instance);
    object Get(Type pluginType, Instance instance);
    void Set(Type pluginType, Instance instance, object value);
    void DisposeAndClear();
}
```

Most of the methods in this interface deal with looking up, supplying, or evicting an instance based on a `Type` and an `Instance`. Figure 11.5 illustrates how StructureMap interacts with an `IObjectCache` implementation.

> **NOTE** The mechanism illustrated in figure 11.5 is similar to the interaction between Unity and `ILifetimePolicy` as shown in figure 14.6.

StructureMap first attempts to get the requested instance from the `Get` method. If this method returns `null` for the provided `Type` and `Instance`, StructureMap creates the requested instance and adds it to the cache through the `Set` method before returning it.

Let's see how this works in an example.

---

[5] Erich Gamma et al., *Design Patterns: Elements of Reusable Object-Oriented Software* (New York: Addison-Wesley, 1994), 87.

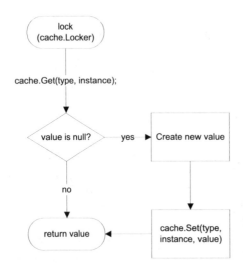

Figure 11.5   StructureMap interacts with the IObjectCache interface by first invoking the Get method on a cache object. If the cache returns a value, this value is used immediately. If not, StructureMap creates the new value and adds it to the cache before returning it.

DEVELOPING A CACHING LIFESTYLE

In this example, you'll develop the same caching lifestyle that you also created for Castle Windsor in section 10.2.3. In short, this lifestyle caches and reuses instances for a time before releasing them.

> **WARNING**   This sample code isn't thread-safe, but a proper production implementation should be, because it's likely that several threads would simultaneously attempt to resolve objects from the container.

Let's start with the easy part: the following listing shows the implementation of the ILifecycle interface.

Listing 11.4   Implementing ILifecycle

```
public partial class CacheLifecycle : ILifecycle
{
    private readonly LeasedObjectCache cache;

    public CacheLifecycle(ILease lease)
    {
        if (lease == null)
        {
            throw new ArgumentNullException("lease");
        }

        this.cache = new LeasedObjectCache(lease);          ❶ Save lease in
    }                                                            custom cache

    public void EjectAll()
    {
        this.FindCache().DisposeAndClear();                 ILifecycle
    }                                                        members

    public IObjectCache FindCache()
    {
```

```
        return this.cache;
    }
                                    ◁─┐  **Return custom**
                                    ❷    **cache**
    public string Scope                            │ **ILifecycle**
    {                                          ◁─┘ **members**
        get { return "Cache"; }
    }
}
```

The CacheLifecycle class implements the ILifecycle interface as required. It uses CONSTRUCTOR INJECTION to receive an ILease instance. The ILease interface is a local helper interface that you introduce to implement the CacheLifestyle. It was initially introduced in section 10.2.3 and has nothing to do with StructureMap or any other particular DI CONTAINER.

NOTE For an example of an ILease implementation, see section 10.2.3.

Instead of saving the ILease instance directly in a private field, you immediately wrap it ❶ in a custom implementation of the IObjectCache interface called Leased-ObjectCache. This is the cache you return ❷ from the FindCache method.

NOTE Contrast the constructor in listing 11.4 with the much more complicated code from listing 10.2. This clearly illustrates the superiority of CONSTRUCTOR INJECTION over METHOD INJECTION.

Although the CacheLifecycle provides the root ILifecycle interface, the real implementation is provided by the custom LeasedObjectCache class, which implements the IObjectCache interface.

StructureMap already provides an implementation of IObjectCache called MainObjectCache. Unfortunately, MainObjectCache doesn't have any virtual members that we can override to implement our caching lifestyle. Instead, we can decorate MainObjectCache with the custom LeasedObjectCache. The following listing shows the constructor.

Listing 11.5 Constructing LeasedObjectCache

```
private readonly IObjectCache objectCache;
private readonly ILease lease;

public LeasedObjectCache(ILease lease)
{
    if (lease == null)
    {
        throw new ArgumentNullException("lease");
    }

    this.lease = lease;
    this.objectCache = new MainObjectCache();
}
```

In the LeasedObjectCache constructor, you use standard CONSTRUCTOR INJECTION to inject an ILease instance. The LeasedObjectCache is a Decorator[6] of MainObjectCache so you create an instance and assign it to a private field. Notice that the objectCache field is declared as IObjectCache, so you could easily extend the LeasedObjectCache class with an overloaded constructor that enabled you to inject any IObjectCache implementation from the outside.

The combination of a decorated IObjectCache and an ILease member makes it close to trivial to implement the LeasedObjectCache class. The following listing shows the implementation of the significant Get and Set methods, but the rest of the implementation follows the same blueprint.

> **Listing 11.6   Implementing Get and Set**

```
public object Get(Type pluginType, Instance instance)
{
    this.CheckLease();
    return this.objectCache.Get(pluginType, instance);
}

public void Set(Type pluginType, Instance instance, object value)
{
    this.objectCache.Set(pluginType, instance, value);
    this.lease.Renew();
}

private void CheckLease()
{
    if (this.lease.IsExpired)
    {
        this.objectCache.DisposeAndClear();
    }
}
```

When StructureMap invokes the Set method, you first ensure that the cache doesn't hold any stale instances. When that method returns, you can be certain that if the decorated cache holds the requested instance, you can safely return it.

Conversely, when the Set method is invoked, you immediately delegate the method to the decorated object cache. Because you understand that StructureMap uses IObjectCache as shown in figure 11.5, you know that the Set method is only invoked when the container has created a new instance because no cached instance was available. This means that the instance supplied by the value parameter represents a newly created instance, so you can safely renew the lease.

---

[6] Erich Gamma et al., *Design Patterns: Elements of Reusable Object-Oriented Software* (New York: Addison-Wesley, 1994), 175.

The `CheckLease` helper method is invoked by many of the `IObjectCache` member implementations in ways similar to the `Get` method. It flushes the decorated cache if the lease has expired.

Now that you know how to implement a custom lifestyle and any custom DEPENDENCIES it might have, you only need to learn how to use it.

CONFIGURING COMPONENTS WITH A CUSTOM LIFESTYLE

Using the `CacheLifecycle` when configuring a component is easy and is done the same way you'd configure any other lifestyle:

```
var lease = new SlidingLease(TimeSpan.FromMinutes(1));
var cache = new CacheLifecycle(lease);
container.Configure(r => r
    .For<IIngredient>()
    .LifecycleIs(cache)
    .Use<SauceBéarnaise>());
```

This configures the container to use a `CacheLifecycle` with a one-minute timeout for the `IIngredient` interface. Within a one-minute time span, you can request as many object graphs as you want, and you'll always get the same `SauceBéarnaise` back whenever the graph contains an `IIngredient` instance. When that minute is up, subsequent requests will get a new `SauceBéarnaise` instance.

It's worth noting that the way `CacheLifecycle` is implemented, it can be used to bundle together several instances with the same lease, like this:

```
container.Configure(r =>
{
    r.For<IIngredient>().LifecycleIs(cache).Use<Steak>();
    r.For<ICourse>().LifecycleIs(cache).Use<Course>();
});
```

This will cause the `ICourse` and `IIngredient` instances to expire and renew at the same time. This may sometimes be desirable and sometimes not. An alternative is to use two separate instances of `CacheLifecycle`. As the following listing shows, this also enables you to use two different timeouts.

Listing 11.7 Using different cache lifestyles for each `Instance`

```
container.Configure(r => r
    .For<IIngredient>()
    .LifecycleIs(
        new CacheLifecycle(
            new SlidingLease(
                TimeSpan.FromHours(1))))
    .Use<Steak>());
container.Configure(r => r
    .For<ICourse>()
    .LifecycleIs(
        new CacheLifecycle(
            new SlidingLease(
                TimeSpan.FromMinutes(15))))
    .Use<Course>());
```

The first cache is defined with a one-hour timeout. No matter how many or few times you need an `IIngredient`, you'll get the same instance within a time span of one hour. When that hour is up, the old instance is discarded and a new instance is used indiscriminately for the next hour.

The cache for `ICourse` is a different instance configured with a 15-minute timeout. Within those 15 minutes, you'll get the same instance, but when they're up, a new instance is used. It's worth noting that even when the `ICourse` times out, the `IIngredient` chugs along on its longer lease. Although they both use the same life-style *type*, they're on different schedules.

In listing 11.7 you used different timeouts, but the `SlidingLease` type in both cases. This isn't a requirement—you could've used two widely different `ILease` implementations for each instance.

Implementing a custom lifestyle for StructureMap isn't particularly difficult. It may look complex on paper, but if you were to look at it in an IDE, you would quickly realize that it consists of only two classes where the *most* complex method (`CheckLease`) has a single `if` statement and two lines of code.

Even so, it should be a rare occurrence when we need to implement a custom life-style for StructureMap. The comprehensive set of built-in lifestyles should meet our everyday needs.

This completes our tour of LIFETIME MANAGEMENT with StructureMap. Components can be configured with mixed lifestyles and this is even true when we register multiple implementations of the same ABSTRACTION. We have yet to look at how to work with multiple components, so let's now turn our attention in that direction.

11.3 *Working with multiple components*

DI CONTAINERS thrive on distinctness but have a hard time with ambiguity. When using CONSTRUCTOR INJECTION, a single constructor is preferred over overloaded constructors because it's evident which constructor to use when there's no choice. This is also the case when mapping from ABSTRACTIONS to concrete types. If we attempt to map multiple concrete types to the same ABSTRACTION, we introduce ambiguity.

Despite the undesirable qualities of ambiguity, we often need to work with multiple implementations of a single interface. This can be the case in these situations:

- Different concrete types should be used for different consumers.
- DEPENDENCIES are sequences.
- Decorators are in use.

In this section, we'll look at each of these cases and see how StructureMap addresses each one in turn. When we're done, you should be able to register and resolve components even when multiple implementations of the same ABSTRACTION are in play.

Let's first see how we can provide more fine-grained control than what AUTO-WIRING provides.

11.3.1 *Selecting among multiple candidates*

Auto-Wiring is convenient and powerful but provides us with little control. As long as all Abstractions are distinctly mapped to concrete types we have no problems, but as soon as we introduce more implementations of the same interface, ambiguity rears its ugly head.

Let's first recap how StructureMap deals with multiple registrations of the same Abstraction.

CONFIGURING MULTIPLE IMPLEMENTATIONS OF THE SAME PLUG-IN

As you saw in section 11.1.2, you can configure multiple plug-ins for the same service:

```
container.Configure(r =>
{
    r.For<IIngredient>().Use<SauceBéarnaise>();
    r.For<IIngredient>().Use<Steak>();
});
```

This example registers both the `Steak` and `SauceBéarnaise` classes with the `IIngredient` plug-in. The last registration wins, so if you resolve `IIngredient` with `container.GetInstance<IIngredient>()` you'll get a `Steak` instance. However, a call to `container.GetAllInstances<IIngredient>()` returns an `IList<IIngredient>` that contains both `Steak` and `SauceBéarnaise`. That is, subsequent configurations aren't forgotten but are harder to get at.

> **TIP** The last configuration for a given type wins. It defines the default instance for that type.

If there are configured instances of a plug-in that can't be resolved when `GetAllInstances` is invoked, StructureMap throws an exception explaining that there are Dependencies which can't be satisfied. This is consistent with the behavior of the `GetInstance` method, but different from the way that Castle Windsor or MEF behaves.

The following listing shows how you can provide hints that can later be used to select among different configured instances.

Listing 11.8 Naming Instances

```
container.Configure(r =>
{
    r.For<IIngredient>()
        .Use<SauceBéarnaise>()
        .Named("sauce");
    r.For<IIngredient>()
        .Use<Steak>()
        .Named("meat");
});
```

You can give each configured instance a unique name that you can later use to distinguish each from other similar instances.

Given the named instances in listing 11.8, you can resolve both `Steak` and `Sauce-Béarnaise` like this:

```
var meat = container.GetInstance<IIngredient>("meat");
var sauce = container.GetInstance<IIngredient>("sauce");
```

Notice that you supply the same key you used to name the instance during configuration.

Given that you should always resolve services in a single COMPOSITION ROOT, you should normally not expect to deal with such ambiguity on this level.

TIP If you find yourself invoking the GetInstance method with a specific key, consider whether you can change your approach so it's less ambiguous.

You can use named instances to select among multiple alternatives when configuring DEPENDENCIES for a given plug-in.

CONFIGURING NAMED DEPENDENCIES

As useful as AUTO-WIRING is, sometimes we need to override the normal behavior to provide fine-grained control over which DEPENDENCIES go where. It may also be that we need to address an ambiguous API. As an example, consider this constructor:

```
public ThreeCourseMeal(ICourse entrée,
    ICourse mainCourse, ICourse dessert)
```

In this case, you have three identically typed DEPENDENCIES that each represents a *different* concept. In most cases, you want to map each of the DEPENDENCIES to a separate type. The following listing shows how you could choose to configure the ICourse mappings.

Listing 11.9   Configuring named courses

```
container.Configure(r => r
    .For<ICourse>()
    .Use<Rillettes>()
    .Named("entrée"));
container.Configure(r => r
    .For<ICourse>()
    .Use<CordonBleu>()
    .Named("mainCourse"));
container.Configure(r => r
    .For<ICourse>()
    .Use<MousseAuChocolat>()
    .Named("dessert"));
```

Like listing 11.8, you register three named components, mapping the Rillettes to an instance named "entrée," CordonBleu to an instance named "mainCourse," and the MousseAuChocolat to an instance named "dessert."

Given this configuration, you can now register the ThreeCourseMeal class, as shown in the following listing.

Listing 11.10   Overriding AUTO-WIRING

```
container.Configure(r => r
    .For<IMeal>()
    .Use<ThreeCourseMeal>()
```

```
.Ctor<ICourse>("entrée").Is(i =>
    i.TheInstanceNamed("entrée"))
.Ctor<ICourse>("mainCourse").Is(i =>
    i.TheInstanceNamed("mainCourse"))
.Ctor<ICourse>("dessert").Is(i =>
    i.TheInstanceNamed("dessert")));
```

You start the configuration expression as usual, by mapping the IMeal interface to the concrete ThreeCourseMeal. But then you extend the expression with the Ctor method. The Ctor (short for *constructor*) method enables you to express how a constructor parameter of a given type should be mapped. In the cases where there's only a single parameter of a given type, you can use an overload where you don't have to supply the parameter name. However, because the ThreeCourseMeal has three ICourse parameters, you need to identify the parameter by its name, "entrée."

The Ctor method returns an object that enables you to define how the constructor parameter will be populated. The Is method allows you to use an IInstance-Expression<ICourse> to pick a named instance—yet another example of the Nested Closure pattern. You can then repeat this coding idiom for the next two parameters.

> **NOTE** In this example, I gave the configuration instances the same names as the parameters, but that isn't required. I could've named the instances whatever I liked, whereas the parameter names are obviously bound by the names of the real constructor parameters.

> **WARNING** Identifying parameters by their names is convenient but not refactoring-safe. If we rename a parameter, we may break the configuration (depending on your refactoring tool).

Overriding AUTO-WIRING by explicitly mapping parameters to named instances is a universally applicable solution. We can do this even if we configure the named instances in one expression and the constructor in a completely different expression because the only identification that ties a named instance together with a parameter is the name. This is always possible but can be brittle if we have a lot of names to manage.

WIRING INSTANCE REFERENCES

Whenever we have the opportunity to define the instances and the constructor in a single expression, we can do it more elegantly. The listing that follows shows how.

Listing 11.11 Using Instance references to override AUTO-WIRING

```
container.Configure(r =>
{
    var entrée =
        r.For<ICourse>().Use<Rillettes>();           ◁─┐
    var mainCourse =                                    │ ❶ Instance
        r.For<ICourse>().Use<CordonBleu>();        ◁─┤   references
    var dessert =                                       │
        r.For<ICourse>().Use<MousseAuChocolat>();  ◁─┘

    r.For<IMeal>()
        .Use<ThreeCourseMeal>()
```

```
            .Ctor<ICourse>("entrée").Is(entrée)
            .Ctor<ICourse>("mainCourse").Is(mainCourse)
            .Ctor<ICourse>("dessert").Is(dessert);
});
```

Until now, we have been ignoring that the typical For/Use method chain returns a result; we've had no use for it. But the returned values are SmartInstance<T> instances, which you can use as references to the configurations you made ➊. Instead of the instance names you had to use in listing 11.10, you can use these references directly with one of the many overloads of the Is method ➋, matching each local variable with the appropriate named constructor parameter.

Although this feature enables us to get rid of the instance names, we're still left with magic strings that identify the constructor parameters. This API depends on a text-based match between the configuration and the parameter names, so it's fragile and best avoided when possible. If we feel compelled to use it only to deal with ambiguity, a better solution is to design the API to get rid of that ambiguity. It often leads to a better overall design.

In the next section, you'll see how you can use the less ambiguous and more flexible approach where you allow any number of courses in a meal. To this end, you must learn how StructureMap deals with lists and sequences.

11.3.2 *Wiring sequences*

In section 10.3.2, we discussed how to refactor an explicit ThreeCourseMeal class to the more general-purpose Meal class with this constructor:

```
public Meal(IEnumerable<ICourse> courses)
```

In this section, we'll look at how you can configure StructureMap to wire up Meal instances with appropriate ICourse DEPENDENCIES. When we're done, you should have a good idea of the options available to you when you need to configure instances with sequences of DEPENDENCIES.

AUTO-WIRING SEQUENCES

StructureMap has a rather good understanding of sequences. If we want to use all configured instances of a given plug-in, AUTO-WIRING just works. As an example, given the configured ICourse instances in listing 11.9, you can configure the IMeal plug-in like this:

```
container.Configure(r => r.For<IMeal>().Use<Meal>());
```

Notice that this is a completely standard mapping from an ABSTRACTION to a concrete type. StructureMap will automatically understand the Meal constructor and determine that the correct course of action is to resolve all ICourse instances. When you resolve IMeal you get a Meal instance with the ICourse instances from listing 11.9: Rillettes, CordonBleu, and MousseAuChocolat.

> **NOTE** Contrast the ease of AUTO-WIRING sequences in StructureMap with section 10.3.2, which shows how hard it is to enable the same functionality in Castle Windsor.

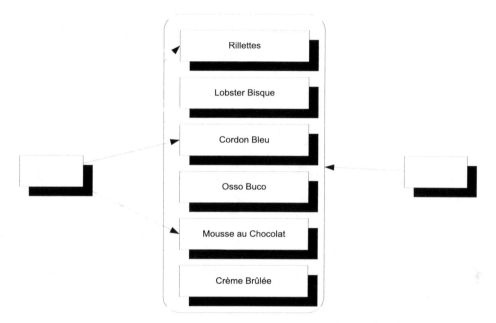

Figure 11.6 In the situation on the left, we wish to explicitly select only certain DEPENDENCIES from the larger list of all configured instances. This is different from the situation to the right, where we indiscriminately want them all.

StructureMap automatically handles sequences, and unless we specify otherwise, it does what we expect it to do: it resolves a sequence of DEPENDENCIES to all registered instances of that type. Only when we need to explicitly pick only some instances from a larger set do we need to do more. Let's see how to do that.

PICKING ONLY SOME INSTANCES FROM A LARGER SET

StructureMap's default strategy of injecting all instances is often the correct policy, but as figure 11.6 shows, there may be cases where we want to pick only some configured instances from the larger set of all configured instances.

When we previously let StructureMap AUTO-WIRE all configured instances, it corresponded to the situation depicted on the right side of figure 11.6. If we want to configure an instance like the left side, we must explicitly define which instances should be used.

When we have the option of configuring the DEPENDENCIES and the consumer in a single invocation of the Configure method, we can use referenced instances as you saw in listing 11.11. The following listing shows the equivalent configuration for the scenario where the constructor expects a sequence of DEPENDENCIES.

Listing 11.12 Using `Instance` references to inject a sequence

```
container.Configure(r =>
{
    var entrée = r.For<ICourse>().Use<Rillettes>();
```

```
var entrée1 = r.For<ICourse>().Use<LobsterBisque>();
var mainCourse = r.For<ICourse>().Use<CordonBleu>();
var dessert = r.For<ICourse>().Use<MousseAuChocolat>();

r.For<IMeal>().Use<Meal>()
    .EnumerableOf<ICourse>()
    .Contains(entrée, mainCourse, dessert);
});
```

Like the code in listing 11.11, you assign a variable to each Instance returned by the Use method. Notice that you configure *four* ICourse instances even though you only use three of them for the IMeal instance. However, you might need the mapping from ICourse to LobsterBisque for some other purpose not shown here. Because you don't use the resulting entrée1 variable, you could've omitted it completely, but I chose to include it to keep the code consistent.

Because the Meal constructor takes an IEnumerable<ICourse> as input, you can use the EnumerableOf method to denote a sequence of ICourse instances, explicitly defined in the Contains method, where you supply the three Instance references you want to use.

This approach works well when we have the opportunity to configure all relevant ICourse instances in the same code block as the IMeal configuration. This isn't always possible—it could be that configuration of ICourse instances are spattered over several different Registries from different assemblies. When that's the case, we can still resort to referring to them by name. The following listing shows one way to do that.

Listing 11.13   Injecting named Instances into a sequence

```
container.Configure(r => r
    .For<IMeal>()
    .Use<Meal>()
    .EnumerableOf<ICourse>().Contains(i =>
    {
        i.TheInstanceNamed("entrée");
        i.TheInstanceNamed("mainCourse");
        i.TheInstanceNamed("dessert");
    }));
```

Given a set of named instances similar to those created in listing 11.9, you can refer to each named instance when configuring the IMeal instance. As you did in listing 11.12, you use the EnumerableOf/Contains method chain to denote a sequence of DEPENDENCIES. This time you don't have Instance variables, so instead you must look them up by name. An overload to the Contains method enables you to supply a Nested Closure that expresses which named instances you wish to be injected into the Meal instance.

StructureMap understands sequences; unless we need to explicitly pick only some instances from all plug-ins of a given type, StructureMap automatically does the right thing. AUTO-WIRING works not only with single instances, but also for sequences, and the container maps a sequence to all configured instances of the corresponding type.

Consumers that rely on sequences of DEPENDENCIES may be the most intuitive users of multiple instances of the same ABSTRACTION, but before we leave this subject completely, we need to look at one last—and perhaps a bit surprising—case, where multiple instances come into play.

11.3.3 *Wiring Decorators*

In section 9.1.2, we discussed how the Decorator design pattern is useful when implementing CROSS-CUTTING CONCERNS. By definition, Decorators introduce multiple types of the same ABSTRACTION. At the very least, we have two implementations of an ABSTRACTION: the Decorator itself and the decorated type. If we stack the Decorators, we may have even more.

This is another example of having multiple registrations of the same service. Unlike the previous sections, these registrations aren't conceptually equal, but rather are DEPENDENCIES of each other. In this section, you'll see how to configure StructureMap to deal with this pattern. There are many ways to configure a Decorator, and we'll look at three different ways of achieving the same result. Each has its own advantages and disadvantages.

DECORATING WITH INSTANCE REFERENCES

Let's see how we can configure the `Breading` class, which is a Decorator of `IIngredient`. It uses CONSTRUCTOR INJECTION to receive the instance it should decorate:

```
public Breading(IIngredient ingredient)
```

To make a Cotoletta, you'd like to decorate a `VealCutlet` (another `IIngredient`) with the `Breading` class. One way to do this is to use `Instance` references within a single `Configure` method:

```
container.Configure(r =>
{
    var cutlet = r.For<IIngredient>().Use<VealCutlet>();
    r.For<IIngredient>().Use<Breading>()
        .Ctor<IIngredient>().Is(cutlet);
});
```

As you already saw in listing 11.11 and 11.12, you can use the return value from the `Use` method to capture a reference to an `Instance`. The `cutlet` variable represents the configured mapping from `IIngredient` to `VealCutlet` and you can use it to express that this is the appropriate `Instance` to use for the `Breading` class's `IIngredient` constructor parameter. Because the last configuration wins, the `Breading` `Instance` is now the default `Instance`.

When you ask the container to resolve `IIngredient`, it will return an object based on the default `Instance`. This is the `Breading` `Instance` where you provided the extra hint that it should resolve the `cutlet` `Instance` for the `Breading` class's `IIngredient` parameter. The end result is a `Breading` instance that contains a `VealCutlet` instance.

Passing objects around is safer than passing strings around, so we should prefer to use this technique whenever we have the option to configure Decorator and the decorated type in a single method call. However, that's not always possible.

DECORATING WITH NAMED INSTANCES

Sometimes we have to resort to `Instance` names because we configure the involved collaborators in different method calls—perhaps even in different Registries implemented in separate assemblies. In such cases, we can't pass objects around, but must rely on strings even though they're easier to mess up.

Let's assume that you have already configured a `VealCutlet` like this:

```
container.Configure(r => r
    .For<IIngredient>()
    .Use<VealCutlet>()
    .Named("cutlet"));
```

Because you know that the name of the instance is *cutlet*, you can use it to configure the `Breading` class:

```
container.Configure(r => r
    .For<IIngredient>()
    .Use<Breading>()
    .Ctor<IIngredient>()
    .Is(i => i.TheInstanceNamed("cutlet")));
```

As you did in listings 11.10 and 11.13, you use the overload of the `Is` method that enables you to provide a code block that identifies a named instance. Once again, you see the Nested Closure pattern in action.

If you compare the two previous examples, you won't notice that they're similar. In both cases you used the `Ctor<T>` method to represent a constructor parameter. The only difference is how you identify the parameter with the `Is` method.

The `Ctor/Is` method chain has the advantage in that we can use it to specify a single constructor parameter even if the constructor in question has more than one parameter. All the parameters we don't configure with the `Ctor` method will be AUTO-WIRED according to StructureMap's default algorithms. This is useful if we only want to explicitly configure a single among several parameters.

However, it isn't a strongly typed solution. There's no guarantee that the constructor in question has a parameter of the identified type. It could have, but then we changed the design, and now it takes parameters of a different type. The compiler doesn't know, because it takes our word when we invoke the `Ctor` method with a particular type argument.

Another alternative offers a more strongly typed approach.

DECORATING WITH DELEGATES

Instead of referring to a constructor parameter by type and name, we can write a strongly typed code block that *uses* the constructor. Although it also has disadvantages we'll return to, the benefit is that it's strongly typed and, by that token, safer from a design-time perspective.

This sounds a bit abstract, so let's see an example of how to configure the Cotoletta in this way:

```
container.Configure(r => r
    .For<IIngredient>().Use<VealCutlet>()
    .EnrichWith(i => new Breading(i)));
```

The EnrichWith method is a member of the generic SmartInstance<T> class returned by the Use method. In this case, you invoke the Use method with the Veal-Cutlet type argument, which returns an instance of SmartInstance<VealCutlet>. The EnrichWith method takes a delegate that takes a VealCutlet as input and returns an object.

You can match this delegate with a code block that takes VealCutlet as input. The compiler infers that the variable i is an instance of VealCutlet, so you can now implement the code block by invoking the Breading constructor with that VealCutlet variable.

When you ask the container to resolve IIngredient, it will first create a Veal-Cutlet instance and then pass that instance as input to the code block you defined with the EnrichWith method. When the code block executes, the VealCutlet instance is passed to the Breading constructor and the Breading instance is returned.

The advantage of this is that in the code block you write code that *uses* the Breading constructor. This is a line of code like any other line of code, so it's checked by the compiler. This provides you with a great deal of confidence that if the Configure method compiles, the VealCutlet will be correctly decorated.

Although strong typing is safer, it also requires more maintenance. If you subsequently decide to add another constructor parameter to the Breading constructor, the code block no longer compiles, and you must manually address the issue. This wouldn't be necessary if you'd used the Ctor<T> method, because StructureMap would've been able to sort out the new parameter for you, with AUTO-WIRING.

As you've seen, there are several different ways to configure Decorators. The strongly typed approach is a bit safer but may require more maintenance. The more weakly typed API is more flexible and enables StructureMap to deal with changes to our API, but at the expense of less type safety.

> **NOTE** In this section we didn't discuss runtime INTERCEPTION. Although StructureMap has SEAMS that enable INTERCEPTION, it has no built-in support for dynamically emitting Proxies. It's possible to use those SEAMS to use another library (such as Castle Dynamic Proxy) to emit such classes, but because this isn't part of StructureMap itself, it's beyond the scope of this chapter.

StructureMap lets us work with multiple instances in several different ways. We can configure instances as alternatives to each other, as peers resolved as sequences, or as hierarchical Decorators. In many cases, StructureMap will figure out what to do, but we can always explicitly define how services are composed if we need more explicit control.

This may also be the case when we need to deal with APIs that deviate from CON-STRUCTOR INJECTION. So far, you've seen how to configure instances, including how to specify lifetime styles and how to deal with multiple components, but until now you've allowed the container to wire DEPENDENCIES by implicitly assuming that all components use CONSTRUCTOR INJECTION. This isn't always the case; in the next section, we'll review how to deal with classes that must be instantiated in special ways.

11.4   *Configuring difficult APIs*

Until now, we've considered how to configure components that use CONSTRUCTOR INJECTION. One of the many benefits of CONSTRUCTOR INJECTION is that DI CONTAINERS such as StructureMap can easily understand how to compose and create all classes in a dependency graph.

This becomes less clear when APIs are less well behaved. In this section, you'll see how to deal with primitive constructor arguments, static factories, and PROPERTY INJECTION. These all require special attention. Let's start by looking at classes that take primitive types, such as strings or integers as constructor arguments.

11.4.1 *Configuring primitive Dependencies*

As long as we inject ABSTRACTIONS into consumers, all is well. It becomes more difficult when a constructor depends on a primitive type, such as a string, number, or enum. Often, this is the case for data access implementations that take a connection string as constructor parameter, but it's also a more general issue that applies to strings and numbers.

Conceptually, it doesn't make much sense to register a string or number as a component in a container, and with StructureMap it doesn't even work. If we try to resolve a component with a primitive DEPENDENCY, we'll get an exception, even though the primitive type was previously registered.

Consider, as an example, this constructor:

```
public ChiliConCarne(Spiciness spiciness)
```

In this example, `Spiciness` is an enum:

```
public enum Spiciness
{
    Mild = 0,
    Medium,
    Hot
}
```

> **WARNING**   As a rule of thumb, enums are code smells and should be refactored to polymorphic classes;[7] here, they serve us well for this example.

You need to explicitly tell StructureMap how to resolve the `spiciness` constructor parameter. This example shows how it's possible to use the `Ctor<T>` method to directly provide a value for a constructor parameter:

---

[7]   Martin Fowler et al., *Refactoring: Improving the Design of Existing Code* (New York: Addison-Wesley, 1999), 82.

```
container.Configure(r => r
    .For<ICourse>()
    .Use<ChiliConCarne>()
    .Ctor<Spiciness>()
    .Is(Spiciness.Hot));
```

In section 11.3, you repeatedly saw how the Ctor<T> method can be used to override AUTO-WIRING for a particular constructor parameter. Here you implicitly state that you expect that the ChiliConCarne constructor only has a single Spiciness parameter—otherwise the Ctor<spiciness>() method call would be ambiguous, and you'd have to supply a parameter name as well.

The Ctor<T> method returns a SmartInstance<T> with various methods. There are five overloads of the Is method, and one of them enables you to provide an instance of the appropriate type. The type argument T is Spiciness in this example, so you provide Spiciness.Hot as a concrete value.

As we discussed in section 11.3, using the Ctor<T> method has advantages and disadvantages. If we want a more strongly typed configuration that invokes the constructor or a static factory, we can do this as well.

11.4.2 *Creating objects with code blocks*

Some classes can't be instantiated through a public constructor. Instead, we must use some sort of factory to create instances of the type. This is always troublesome for DI CONTAINERS because, by default, they look after public constructors.

Consider this example constructor for the public JunkFood class:

```
internal JunkFood(string name)
```

Even though the JunkFood class is public, the constructor is internal. Obviously, instances of JunkFood should be created through the static JunkFoodFactory class:

```
public static class JunkFoodFactory
{
    public static IMeal Create(string name)
    {
        return new JunkFood(name);
    }
}
```

From StructureMap's perspective, this is a problematic API because there are no unambiguous and well-established conventions around static factories. It needs help, and you can provide it by providing a code block it can execute to create the instance:

```
container.Configure(r => r
    .For<IMeal>()
    .Use(() =>
        JunkFoodFactory.Create("chicken meal")));
```

By now, the For/Use method chain should be familiar. However, in this variation, you use a different overload of the Use method than used previously. This overload enables you to supply a Func<IMeal> and you do that by providing a code block that invokes the static Create method on the JunkFoodFactory class.

TIP If you want to resolve the `ChiliConCarne` class from section 11.4.1 in a strongly typed fashion, you can use this `Use` overload to directly invoke the constructor.

When you end up writing the code to create the instance, how is this in any way better than invoking the code directly? By using a code block inside a For/Use statement, you still gain something:

- You map from `IMeal` to `JunkFood`.
- A lifestyle can still be configured. Whereas the code block will be invoked to create the instance, it may not be invoked *every time* the instance is requested—unless you use the `Unique` lifestyle, a cached instance will sometimes be used instead.

In total, there are five different overloads of the `Use` method. We can use the generic version to define a concrete type, but other overloads enable us to supply a concrete instance, or code blocks that create a concrete instance.

The last common deviation from CONSTRUCTOR INJECTION we'll examine here is PROPERTY INJECTION.

11.4.3 *Wiring with Property Injection*

PROPERTY INJECTION is a less well-defined form of DI because you're not forced by the compiler to assign a value to a writable property. This is also the case for Structure-Map, which will leave writable properties alone unless we explicitly ask it to do something about them.

Consider this `CaesarSalad` class:

```
public class CaesarSalad : ICourse
{
    public IIngredient Extra { get; set; }
}
```

It's a common misconception that a Caesar Salad includes chicken. A Caesar Salad is a *salad*, but it tastes great with chicken, so many restaurants offer chicken as an extra ingredient. The `CaesarSalad` class models this by exposing a writable property named `Extra`.

If you configure only the `CaesarSalad` without explicitly addressing the `Extra` property, the property won't be assigned. You can still resolve the instance, but the property will have the default value that the constructor assigns to it (if any).

There are several ways you can configure the `CaesarSalad` so that the `Extra` property will be appropriately populated. One way to do it is to use `Instance` references, as you've seen several times already in this chapter:

```
container.Configure(r =>
{
    var chicken = r.For<IIngredient>().Use<Chicken>();
    r.For<ICourse>().Use<CaesarSalad>()
        .Setter<IIngredient>().Is(chicken);
});
```

You may recall from several previous examples that the Use method returns an Instance you can remember as a variable. In listing 11.10 and many subsequent examples, you used the Ctor<T> method to indicate a constructor parameter of a particular type. The Setter<T> method works in the same way, only for properties. You pass the chicken Instance to the Is method to make StructureMap assign the property when it builds the instance.

When you resolve ICourse based on this configuration, you'll get back a CaesarSalad instance with a Chicken instance assigned to its Extra property. This gives you fine-grained control over specific properties for specific types. A more convention-based API provides the option to state that we want StructureMap to use all properties of a given type for PROPERTY INJECTION. As an example, we could state that all settable IIngredient properties should be injected with the appropriate instance.

For the CaesarSalad, you can express it like this:

```
container.Configure(r =>
    r.For<IIngredient>().Use<Chicken>());
container.Configure(r =>
    r.For<ICourse>().Use<CaesarSalad>());
container.Configure(r =>
    r.FillAllPropertiesOfType<IIngredient>());
```

With the FillAllPropertiesOfType method, you can state that all writable properties of the IIngredient type should be assigned a value. StructureMap will use the default instance configured for IIngredient, so when you resolve ICourse you'll get a CaesarSalad instance with Extra Chicken.

The FillAllPropertiesOfType will fill any writable property of the identified type, so if other concrete classes also have writable properties of that type, they'll also have the configured instances injected. This can be practical if we follow a convention that uses PROPERTY INJECTION for certain types.

In this section, you've seen how you can use StructureMap to deal with more difficult creational APIs. You can use the many overloads of the Use and Is methods to specify concrete instances or code blocks that will be used to create instances. You also saw that PROPERTY INJECTION can be configured explicitly while we configure instances, or as a convention for a specific type.

11.5 *Summary*

This chapter offered a tasting menu of StructureMap and its features, and we related the principles and patterns from the rest of the book to StructureMap's API. StructureMap is the oldest DI CONTAINER available on .NET, but it doesn't show its age, with its pervasive use of Nested Closures, type-safe configuration API, and convention-based type scanning.

The use of Nested Closures may be one of its most distinguishing traits; using it requires familiarity with delegates and code blocks.

Getting started with StructureMap is quite easy. It supports AUTO-WIRING and automatically figures out how to create concrete types, even if they haven't been explicitly configured. This means that you can focus on mapping ABSTRACTIONS to concrete types, and when you're done with that, you're able to resolve object graphs. The type-scanning API even enables you to configure a multitude of services with only a few lines of code, using a convention-based approach to configuration.

Although we don't need to configure concrete services, we may still want to when we want to change the lifestyle. By default, the lifestyle is PER GRAPH, so whenever we have thread-safe services, we can potentially increase efficiency by configuring them as SINGLETONS. This requires an explicit step, although it can be expressed during type-scanning using a custom registration convention.

Instances aren't guaranteed to be tracked by the container, so it offers no API to release a specific object graph. This effectively prevents memory leaks for normal classes, but on the other hand, almost guarantees memory leaks for disposable DEPEN-DENCIES. This makes it important to implement all DEPENDENCIES so that they them-selves manage all use of disposable types internally.

StructureMap handles sequences of DEPENDENCIES well. When a class depends on a sequence of instances of the same type, StructureMap will AUTO-WIRE the instance with all instances of the DEPENDENCY type. Once again, it has intuitive default behavior, so we only need to take explicit action if we have special needs for selecting only a subset of all available instances.

Although we can configure Decorators explicitly, StructureMap has no convention for wiring Decorators, and no dynamic INTERCEPTION capabilities. There are SEAMS that can be used to integrate StructureMap with a dynamic proxy API if we would like to do such a thing.

Because StructureMap relies so heavily on Nested Closures, it should come as no surprise that many of the configuration methods have overloads that enable us to sup-ply a code block that will be invoked upon creation. Although these overloads aren't necessary when the classes we register use CONSTRUCTOR INJECTION, we can use them if one or more of our classes must be created in special ways.

StructureMap is a comprehensive DI CONTAINER that offers a wide range of advanced features. It has excellent default behavior and can be easy to use—particu-larly when it comes to AUTO-WIRING with concrete types or sequences. On the other hand, it has no dynamic INTERCEPTION capabilities and can't dispose of disposable DEPENDENCIES. These apparent shortcomings are mostly the result of a design philoso-phy. If we never implement disposable services and prefer explicit Decorators instead of dynamic INTERCEPTION, StructureMap is an excellent choice because it uses those constraints to make other things simpler for its users.

Spring.NET

12

Menu

- Introducing Spring.NET
- Managing lifetime
- Working with multiple components
- Configuring difficult APIs

In the previous chapters, you saw how to map the principles and patterns from parts 1–3 to Castle Windsor and StructureMap. In this chapter, we'll do the same with the Spring.NET DI CONTAINER.

Together with Castle Windsor and StructureMap, Spring.NET belongs to the set of "first generation" DI CONTAINERS on .NET. It appeared in 2006, and even today it still offers basic support for .NET 1.1. It's a port of the Java version of the Spring Framework, which is a big and comprehensive application framework that addresses many different aspects of software—not only OBJECT COMPOSITION. The DI CONTAINER is one of the many components available in the framework, but it can perfectly well be used as a stand-alone component without the need to reference any of the other Spring.NET components.

In this chapter, we'll focus on the Spring.NET DI CONTAINER while ignoring the rest of the application framework. As in the previous chapters and in those to

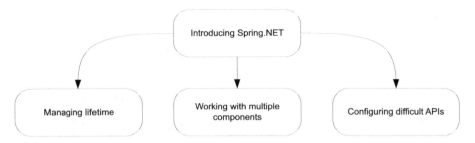

Figure 12.1 This chapter is divided into four sections. The first section introduces the Spring.NET container API and should be considered a prerequisite for the next three sections. Each of these can be read independently of each other.

follow, we'll examine how Spring.NET can be used to apply the principles and patterns set out in parts 1–3. Figure 12.1 shows the structure of the chapter.

The first section provides an overall introduction to Spring.NET and demonstrates how to configure and resolve objects. The next three sections each deal with usage patterns that require a bit of extra attention; you can read them all in order, or you can skip some and read only the ones that interest you.

This chapter should enable you to get started, as well as deal with the most common issues that may come up as you use Spring.NET on a daily basis. It isn't a complete treatment of Spring.NET—that would take several more chapters or perhaps a whole book in itself. In any case, the entire Spring.NET framework is beyond the scope of this book—only the Spring.NET DI CONTAINER pertains to the topic at hand, so when I use the name *Spring.NET*, I am specifically referring to the container.

You can read the chapter in isolation from the rest of part 4 to learn specifically about Spring.NET, or you can read it together with the other chapters in part 4 to compare DI CONTAINERS. The focus of this chapter is to show how Spring.NET relates to and implements the patterns and principles described in parts 1–3.

12.1 Introducing Spring.NET

In this section, you'll learn where to get Spring.NET, what you get, and how you start using it. You'll also look at common configuration options. Table 12.1 provides fundamental information that you're likely to need to get started.

Table 12.1 Spring.NET at a glance

Question	Answer
Where do I get it?	Go to www.springframework.net/download.html and download the latest release. From Visual Studio 2010 you can also get it via NuGet. The package name is *Spring.Core* unless you also want the INTERCEPTION features—in that case, you need the *Spring.Aop* package.
What's in the download?	A .zip file that contains everything you need: compiled binaries, the source code, example code and documentation.

Table 12.1 Spring.NET at a glance *(continued)*

Question	Answer
Which platforms are supported?	All .NET versions from .NET 1.1 are supported, although future versions will target only .NET 2.0 and above.
How much does it cost?	Nothing. It's open source.
Where can I get help?	You can get commercial support from SpringSource, which is the organization behind Spring.NET. Other than commercial support, Spring.NET is still open source software with a thriving ecosystem, so you're also likely (but not guaranteed) to get help in the official forum at http://forum.springframework.net.
On which version is this chapter based?	1.3.1.

Using the Spring.NET DI CONTAINER is a three-step process, as illustrated by figure 12.2.

When you're done with this section, you should have a good feeling for the overall usage pattern of Spring.NET, and you should be able to start using it in well-behaved scenarios where all components follow proper DI patterns, such as CONSTRUCTOR INJECTION. We'll start with the simplest scenario and see how to resolve objects using a Spring.NET container.

12.1.1 Resolving objects

The core service of any DI CONTAINER is to compose object graphs, and Spring.NET is no exception. Because it's such a central feature, it's the most natural place to start when introducing the API, so this is what I'll do here.

In the previous chapters about Castle Windsor and StructureMap, you saw how those DI CONTAINERS take different approaches to whether it's necessary to configure components before we can resolve them. Castle Windsor requires us to explicitly configure every single component, whereas StructureMap can work with concrete types without configuration. But both of these DI CONTAINERS, as well as all of the DI CONTAINERS we'll cover in the next chapters, operate on types: we ask the container to resolve a type for us.

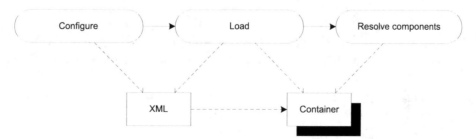

Figure 12.2 The overall usage pattern of Spring.NET involves three steps: first, we define how objects are configured and composed in an XML file. Second, we load that XML configuration into a container instance. In the third and final step, we can resolve objects from the container instance.

Spring.NET is different because its core query mechanism isn't based on types, but on names. Instead of requesting a particular type, we ask Spring.NET for a named object. Similar to Castle Windsor, all objects must be configured before they can be served.

Configuration for Spring.NET is done in XML, so even the simplest scenario involves a piece of XML and some .NET code. As an example, to resolve the concrete SauceBéarnaise class, you must first define the object in XML configuration:

```
<objects xmlns="http://www.springframework.net">
  <object id="Sauce"
          type="Ploeh.Samples.MenuModel.SauceBéarnaise,
          ➥Ploeh.Samples.MenuModel" />
</objects>
```

In Spring.NET, every configured object must appear in an `object` element. The element may have an `id` attribute that names the object, as well as a `type` attribute that defines the .NET type of the object. The name is used when you wish to resolve the object.

To resolve a `SauceBéarnaise` instance, you must load the XML configuration into a container instance. Using an `XmlApplicationContext`, you can load XML from several different sources, including embedded resources and the application configuration file; but this example uses a stand-alone XML file named sauce.xml:

```
var context = new XmlApplicationContext("sauce.xml");
SauceBéarnaise sauce = (SauceBéarnaise)context.GetObject("Sauce");
```

To resolve a `SauceBéarnaise` instance, you invoke the `GetObject` method with the *Sauce* ID you provided for the object in the XML configuration. The ID can be any string, but Spring.NET recommends Pascal casing as a naming convention.

Because the `GetObject` method returns a weakly typed `System.Object` instance, you need to cast the return value to the expected type in order to use it.

Notice how Spring.NET doesn't explicitly distinguish between concrete and abstract types. Whereas other DI CONTAINERS require us to provide a mapping from ABSTRACTIONS to concrete types, Spring.NET is exclusively based on mappings from *names* to concrete types. As this chapter will demonstrate, Spring.NET is still able to resolve requests for ABSTRACTIONS into concrete instances, but the mechanism is more implicit than what other DI CONTAINERS use.

The `GetObject` method is defined by the `IObjectFactory` interface, which is one of the fundamental interfaces defined by Spring.NET. As the name implies, it focuses on *creating* objects, and it contains no methods that enable us to configure the container. Rather, this is the responsibility of higher-level types like the `Xml-ApplicationContext`.

The `GetObject` method is one among several that we can use to resolve objects. However, because all of them are weakly typed, we must always explicitly cast the return value to the type upon which we wish to work. With the `GetObject` method, we can only request objects based on names instead of types, so how do we address situations where a type is all we have?

RESOLVING TYPE REQUESTS

Sometimes we don't have a name, but rather a Type instance that we need to resolve to an instance of that type. You saw an example of that in section 7.2, where we discussed ASP.NET MVC's DefaultControllerFactory class. The relevant method is this one:

```
protected internal virtual IController GetControllerInstance(
    RequestContext requestContext, Type controllerType);
```

Given only a type instead of a name, we might be tempted to define and maintain an explicit map of types to names, but that would be redundant work. A slightly better option would be to use a naming convention that enables us to deterministically derive a name from a Type instance. But the IListableObjectFactory interface, which derives directly from IObjectFactory, defines a method called GetObjectsOf-Type that can be used to get all objects that match a given type. Assuming that the requested controllerType is unique in the Spring.NET configuration, you can implement the GetControllerInstance method like this:

```
IDictionary controllers =
    this.context.GetObjectsOfType(controllerType);
return controllers.Values.OfType<IController>().Single();
```

The context field is an instance of IListableObjectFactory that you can query for all objects that match the controllerType. Although you get back a dictionary, you care only about the values, and you expect that each requested controller will be unique in the underlying XML configuration.

Although Spring.NET doesn't provide any generic APIs, you can easily encapsulate the previous query into an extension method:

```
public static T Resolve<T>(this IListableObjectFactory factory)
{
    return factory.GetObjectsOfType(typeof(T))
        .Values.OfType<T>().Single();
}
```

This would enable you to resolve a type like this:

```
SauceBéarnaise sauce = context.Resolve<SauceBéarnaise>();
```

The GetObjectsOfType method returns all configured objects that match the requested type. Because SauceBéarnaise implements the IIngredient interface, you can also resolve IIngredient from the context:

```
IIngredient ingredient = context.Resolve<IIngredient>();
```

A typical ASP.NET Controller, and any other application code that we're likely to write, will have a complex hierarchy of DEPENDENCIES. To enable Spring.NET to compose objects from loosely coupled services, we must provide proper configuration.

12.1.2 Configuring the container

As we discussed in section 3.2, there are several conceptually different ways you can configure a DI CONTAINER. Figure 12.3 reviews the options and how Spring.NET fits in.

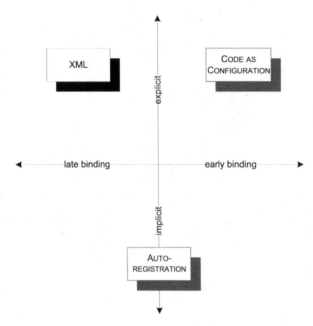

Figure 12.3   **Spring.NET mainly supports XML configuration out of the three possible options outlined in chapter 3. CODE AS CONFIGURATION is only marginally supported and AUTO-REGISTRATION isn't available at all, so these options are shown in grey.**

Like other DI CONTAINERS with a long history, Spring.NET started out with XML as the major configuration source, but contrary to the evolution of both Castle Windsor and StructureMap, Spring.NET has remained focused on XML—perhaps because of its strong ties to the Java Spring framework.

CODE AS CONFIGURATION with Spring.NET

When I wrote this chapter, Spring.NET didn't have support for CODE AS CONFIGURATION. However, literally days before I turned in the final manuscript for the book, SpringSource released Spring CodeConfig, which provides CODE AS CONFIGURATION support for Spring.NET.

Unfortunately, this happened so late that I didn't have time to rewrite the chapter.

In this chapter, the focus will be exclusively on XML configuration.

WORKING WITH .NET TYPES IN XML

Spring.NET works on configuration based on XML. That XML can come from a variety of sources. Most of the time, we'll be loading XML from a file.

In section 12.1.1, you already saw a simple example of Spring.NET's XML configuration:

```
<objects xmlns="http://www.springframework.net">
  <object id="Sauce"
          type="Ploeh.Samples.MenuModel.SauceBéarnaise,
          ➥Ploeh.Samples.MenuModel" />
</objects>
```

It's no secret that XML is a verbose language in itself, but when it comes to identifying .NET types, it becomes extra verbose. To properly identify a .NET type by a string, we must resort to assembly qualified names. Even in the cases where we can omit `Culture`, `Version`, and `PublicKeyToken`, the type will often be identified by a long string with a lot of repeated information. This hurts both readability and maintainability.

Readability is impacted because the relevant part of the type name (`Sauce-Béarnaise`) is buried between a namespace and an assembly name. Maintainability suffers because it becomes harder to rename namespaces or assemblies. Every time we rename anything, we must edit a potentially large set of type definitions.

Granted, these issues apply to all frameworks where types must be defined as XML, but this is also the reason why all other DI CONTAINERS have moved on to other ways of configuring the container. This is also the reason why I generally recommend against XML configuration unless it's mandated by the usage scenario. However, when it comes to Spring.NET, XML is the most prevalent option.

To make it easier to work with .NET types in XML, SpringSource provides tools such as XML schemas and a Visual Studio add-in with type and property completion. The framework itself also enables us to define a set of *type aliases*, which are shorthand names that we can define for types. This is also done in XML. The type alias for the `SauceBéarnaise` class might look like this:

```
<alias name="SauceBéarnaise"
       type="Ploeh.Samples.MenuModel.SauceBéarnaise,
       ➥Ploeh.Samples.MenuModel" />
```

The name can be anything, but I find it most intuitive and easy to remember to pick the simple name of the type as the name of the alias.

This type alias enables us to rewrite the previous example, like this:

```
<object id="Sauce" type="SauceBéarnaise" />
```

This feature can be particularly helpful when we need to refer to the same type multiple times in the same XML file; in any case, it makes the configuration much more readable. In the rest of this chapter, I'll use type aliases. With this notation, the object element begins to look like what it is: a map from a name to a concrete type.

In this simple form, this is all the `object` element does. When the objects have DEPENDENCIES, you must tell Spring.NET how to resolve them.

EXPLICITLY CONFIGURING DEPENDENCIES

The `SauceBéarnaise` class is easy to create because it has a default constructor; no DI CONTAINERS need a lot of help to create such types. This changes when there's no default constructor. As an example, consider this `Mayonnaise` constructor:

```
public Mayonnaise(EggYolk eggYolk, OliveOil oil)
```

Although the mayonnaise recipe is a bit simplified, both `EggYolk` and `OliveOil` are concrete classes with default constructors. However, because the `Mayonnaise` class has no default constructor, you must tell Spring.NET how to resolve it. One option is to explicitly wire the types together:

```
<object id="EggYolk" type="EggYolk" />
<object id="OliveOil" type="OliveOil" />
<object id="Mayonnaise" type="Mayonnaise">
  <constructor-arg ref="EggYolk" />
  <constructor-arg ref="OliveOil" />
</object>
```

The `EggYolk` and `OliveOil` types are configured the way you saw previously, but the `Mayonnaise` element now contains two `constructor-arg` elements. Each of those elements references a named object in order to define the parameters for the `Mayonnaise` constructor. The `ref` attribute identifies another configured object by name, so the `EggYolk` reference refers to the EggYolk *name*—not directly to the `EggYolk` type.

In the previous example, the order of the `constructor-arg` elements is important because you didn't explicitly refer to the parameter names; that's also possible.

Whereas we can always explicitly configure DEPENDENCIES in this way, we don't gain the benefits that AUTO-WIRING can provide. Contrary to other DI CONTAINERS, with Spring.NET we must explicitly ask it to use AUTO-WIRING, and even so it only works in certain cases.

AUTO-WIRING DEPENDENCIES

Spring.NET supports limited AUTO-WIRING, but we must explicitly turn it on using an XML attribute. Instead of the explicitly wired `Mayonnaise` specified previously, you could've configured it like this:

```
<object id="EggYolk" type="EggYolk" />
<object id="OliveOil" type="OliveOil" />
<object id="Mayonnaise" type="Mayonnaise"
        autowire="autodetect" />
```

The optional `autowire` attribute can be used to turn on AUTO-WIRING for a given object. In this example, we use the `autodetect` value which tells Spring.NET to figure out exactly how matching objects are found. Other available options enable us to indicate that matching objects should be found by name, type, or other means.

If we expect to use AUTO-WIRING for all objects, we can enable it for an entire block of configured objects instead of writing out the `autowire` attribute for each and every object element:

```
<objects xmlns="http://www.springframework.net"
         default-autowire="autodetect">
  <object id="EggYolk" type="EggYolk" />
  <object id="OliveOil" type="OliveOil" />
  <object id="Mayonnaise" type="Mayonnaise" />
</objects>
```

The `default-autowire` attribute defines a default AUTO-WIRING strategy for all objects within the `objects` element. This is a much easier way to turn on AUTO-WIRING once and for all—but you should be aware that it won't always work.

The support for AUTO-WIRING in Spring.NET relies on uniqueness. For the `Mayonnaise` class, Spring.NET examines the constructor and determines that it needs instances of `EggYolk` and `OliveOil`. To satisfy the `EggYolk` DEPENDENCY, it searches through all other configured elements to find one that can satisfy that requirement (and it does the same for the OliveOil DEPENDENCY).

In the previous example, there's only one object that satisfies the EggYolk DEPENDENCY, so there's no ambiguity. However, had there been more than one object that could satisfy the requirement, an exception would have been thrown. That goes for both concrete EggYolk elements, but also any derived types.

NOTE In Spring.NET, AUTO-WIRING only works when the DEPENDENCIES can be uniquely resolved. This is different from other DI CONTAINERS.

The advantage of requiring distinctness to support AUTO-WIRING is that the contract with the container is clear and explicit. AUTO-WIRING is only possible when there's no ambiguity regarding resolved types, so the risk of misconfiguration is much smaller. On the other hand, this design makes it harder to work with multiple objects that implement the same ABSTRACTION.

We've looked at some basic configuration options for Spring.NET. Although it's certainly possible to write one big block of unstructured XML, it's better to modularize configuration. Spring.NET supports this by enabling XML to be loaded from more than one source.

12.1.3 Loading XML

It's sometimes desirable to package configuration into reusable groups; and even when reuse itself isn't our top priority, we may want to provide a bit of structure if we have a big and complex application to configure.

With Spring.NET, we can package configuration into separate XML elements that are defined in different resources. Table 12.2 lists the supported resource types. They're easy to use, but I'll briefly discuss each of them to give you an impression.

Table 12.2 XML resource types

Resource type	Uri syntax	Description
FileSystemResource	`file://<filename>` The `file://` moniker is optional.	XML configuration is defined in files.
ConfigSectionResource	`config://<path to section>`	XML configuration is defined in the application configuration file.
UriResource	Standard .NET URI syntax is supported.	XML configuration is read from standard System.Uri protocols, such as HTTP and HTTPS.
AssemblyResource	`assembly://<AssemblyName>/` ➡`<NameSpace>/<ResourceName>`	XML configuration is embedded in an assembly.
InputStreamResource	Not supported.	XML configuration is read from a `System.IO.Stream`.

Some of the resource types support URI syntax, where we can use a moniker to indicate the resource type as part of a string-encoded address. If no moniker is supplied, the resource is assumed to be a file.

USING XML FILES

So far, you've only seen examples of loading XML configuration from a single file. This example loads the entire configuration from the file sauce.xml:

```
var context = new XmlApplicationContext("sauce.xml");
```

Because no explicit path information is given, the sauce.xml file is assumed to be located in the working folder of the running process. A full path can also be used.

In this example, no moniker was supplied so Spring.NET defaults to the File-SystemResource. Alternatively, you could've chosen to explicitly use the file:// moniker like this:

```
var context = new XmlApplicationContext("file://sauce.xml");
```

This is equivalent to the previous example. It's often intuitive to work with XML as files, so in most cases it makes sense to dispense with the file:// moniker and instead write the file path directly.

In addition to defining XML configuration in text files, we can also integrate it in the standard application configuration file.

USING APPLICATION CONFIGURATION FILES

If we prefer to integrate Spring.NET configuration with the rest of the application's configuration, we can also use the standard .NET application .config file.

Because the .NET application configuration system expects custom configuration sections to be explicitly registered, we must also register Spring.NET's configuration sections when we wish to use the .config file. There are various configuration sections that you can register, but to use the objects element you've been using so far, it's necessary to register Spring.NET's default section handler:

```
<configSections>
  <sectionGroup name="spring">
    <section name="objects"
             type="Spring.Context.Support.DefaultSectionHandler,
             ➥Spring.Core" />
  </sectionGroup>
</configSections>
```

This enables you to define objects directly in the .config file, as you've previously been doing in stand-alone XML files:

```
<spring>
  <objects xmlns="http://www.springframework.net">
    <object id="Sauce" type="SauceBéarnaise" />
  </objects>
</spring>
```

Using the `config://` moniker, you can now load the Spring.NET configuration from the .config file into an `XmlApplicationContext` instance, like this:

```
var context = new XmlApplicationContext("config://spring/objects");
```

The `context` instance can now safely resolve the *Sauce* name.

In many ways, integrating Spring.NET configuration into the standard .NET application configuration file format is a special case of using an XML file, because .config files are also XML files; but we can also view files as a special case of XML loaded from any URI.

LOADING XML FROM URIs

When we load XML from files, we use the `file://` moniker as we would a URI scheme delimiter. Spring.NET can download XML files from other URIs than files, such as HTTP, HTTPS, and FTP. It's a simple as this:

```
var context = new XmlApplicationContext("http://localhost/sauce.xml");
```

In this example, the sauce.xml file is hosted by the local machine's web server, but any publicly available resource can be used.

In all the previous cases we can change the configuration without recompiling the application. This isn't possible with the next option.

USING EMBEDDED RESOURCES

In .NET, we can compile resources into assemblies. If we embed XML configuration in an assembly, Spring.NET can load it.

The advantage of embedded XML files is that operations staff can't accidentally change configuration values when they're compiled into the assembly. Only files with parameters that might need to be adjusted by operations staff should be exposed outside the assembly on the file system where they can be edited on a deployment-by-deployment basis.

If you embed the sauce.xml file into an assembly, you can load it into an `Xml-ApplicationContext`, like this:

```
var context = new XmlApplicationContext(
    "assembly://Ploeh.Samples.Menu.SpringNet/
    ➥Ploeh.Samples.Menu.SpringNet/sauce.xml");
```

To load from an embedded resource, we can construct the resource string from the `assembly://` moniker, followed by the assembly name, the namespace, and the name of the embedded resource itself. Table 12.2 shows the required format for referencing an embedded resource.

`AssemblyResources` enable us to load Spring.NET configuration from embedded resources in addition to the externally defined XML files and URIs. If we keep XML configuration in other places, we might need to resort to reading from streams.

USING STREAMS

Until now, we've looked at loading XML from static resources such as files, application configuration, web resources, and embedded resources. At times, we need to load

XML from other sources, or perhaps we need to dynamically build the XML configuration. One way to do that is to load the configuration directly from a stream.

Because a stream isn't a static resource, Spring.NET doesn't support identifying it by a string. We can't use the `XmlApplicationContext` class at all but must instead resort to one of Spring.NET's many other context classes:

```
var resource = new InputStreamResource(stream, "");
var context = new XmlObjectFactory(resource);
```

The `InputStreamResource` serves as an Adapter[1] around a `System.IO.Stream` object. The `stream` object contains the XML configuration that you wish to load. We can load the XML into the stream from many different sources, including a string, or by building up the XML model using LINQ to XML. The empty string supplied to the `Input-StreamResource` constructor is a description. We can supply a proper description, but it isn't required.

Given the `resource` (or any implementation of `IResource`), we can now create an instance of `XmlObjectFactory`. This class offers functionality equivalent to `Xml-ApplicationContext` but loads configuration directly from an `IResource` instance, instead of from strings representing static resources.

The `IResource` interface is a common interface for all the XML resources we reviewed. We can also provide a custom implementation of `IResource` and use it in the same way we used the `InputStreamResource`, or we can register it with its own moniker—but that's beyond the scope of this chapter.

So far, you've seen how to load a single XML configuration from a single resource, but to achieve modularity, we'd often prefer to organize parts of a big application's configuration in different modules.

COMBINING XML RESOURCES

A big application will require a lot of XML configuration code. To keep the configuration more maintainable, we might want to split it into several smaller documents. Perhaps we even want to keep these in separate places; some in XML files, some in the .config file, and some as embedded resources.

The `XmlApplicationContext` makes it possible to combine several different resources because it receives each of the resource strings as part of a parameter array. Here's the signature of the constructor you've been using all along:

```
public XmlApplicationContext(params string[] configurationLocations)
```

Notice that the `configurationLocations` parameter is defined as a parameter array. So far, you've only been supplying a single resource at a time, like this:

```
var context = new XmlApplicationContext("sauce.xml");
```

However, you can supply an arbitrary number of strings to the constructor to combine several resources into a single context:

---

[1]   Erich Gamma et al., *Design Patterns: Elements of Reusable Object-Oriented Software* (New York: Addison-Wesley, 1994), 139.

```
var context = new XmlApplicationContext(
    "config://spring/objects",
    "meat.xml",
    "file://course.xml");
```

This example combines three different resources that each defines a piece of the greater whole. Part of the configuration is defined and loaded from the application's configuration file, while the two other parts are loaded from XML files—one using the implicit syntax for file names and the other explicitly using the file:// moniker. Together, they form a complete set of configuration that defines the Xml-ApplicationContext.

Another way to combine multiple resources is via the import element in an XML file:

```
<objects xmlns="http://www.springframework.net">
  <import resource="config://spring/objects" />
  <import resource="meat.xml" />
  <import resource="file://course.xml" />
</objects>
```

This configuration is identical to the previous example.

As you've seen, there are several different ways in which we can load XML configuration into Spring.NET. Because we can load and combine configuration from more than one resource, this gives us a degree of modularity, which we sorely need for maintainability reasons.

But we shouldn't forget that, overall, XML configuration isn't the most attractive way to configure a DI CONTAINER. It's brittle, verbose, and hard to troubleshoot. Until CodeConfig came along, Spring.NET offered few other options.

This section introduced the Spring.NET DI CONTAINER and demonstrated the fundamental mechanics: how to configure the container with XML and subsequently use it to resolve objects. Resolving objects is done with a single call to the GetObject method, so the complexity involves configuring the container. Until now, we've only looked at the most basic API; there are more advanced areas we have yet to cover. One of the most important topics is how to manage component lifetime.

12.2 *Managing lifetime*

In chapter 8, we discussed LIFETIME MANAGEMENT, including the most common conceptual lifetime styles, such as SINGLETON and TRANSIENT. Spring.NET supports a few different lifestyles and enables us to configure the lifetime of all objects. The lifestyles shown in table 12.3 are available as part of the package.

NOTE The Spring.Net documentation refers to lifestyles as *object scopes*.

Spring.NET's implementations of SINGLETON and TRANSIENT are equivalent to the general lifestyles described in chapter 8, so I won't spend much time on them in this chapter.

Table 12.3 Spring.NET lifestyles

Name	Comments
Singleton	This is the default lifestyle.
Prototype	Spring.NET's name for TRANSIENT. Instances aren't tracked by the container.
Request	Spring.NET's name for WEB REQUEST CONTEXT. Only valid in the context of a web-aware `IApplicationContext`.
Session	One instance is created per HTTP session. Use with caution. Only valid in the context of a web-aware `IApplicationContext`.
Application	Scopes a single object definition to the lifecycle of a web application. Only valid in the context of a web-aware `IApplicationContext`.

> **NOTE** The default lifestyle in Spring.NET is SINGLETON. This is different from many other containers. As discussed in chapter 8, SINGLETON is the most efficient, although not always the safest, of all object scopes; Spring.NET prioritizes efficiency over safety.

The three web-aware scopes (Request, Session, and Application) are all closely coupled with particular `IApplicationContexts` and don't work with the `XmlApplicationContext` or the `XmlObjectFactory` we've been looking at so far. The currently available implementations are so closely coupled to ASP.NET Web Forms that even getting them to work with ASP.NET MVC is difficult. To be frank, it's a mess and not usable, so we won't cover the web-aware scopes in this chapter. Expect future versions of Spring.NET to have a more streamlined story in this space.

Here, I'll show you how to configure object scopes with the SINGLETON and TRANSIENT object scopes. Because Spring.NET doesn't support custom object scopes, this is going to be a short section. When we're done, you should be able to use object scopes with Spring.NET.

12.2.1 Configuring object scopes

Object scopes are configured as part of configuring objects in XML.

To configure an object as TRANSIENT you set the `singleton` attribute to *false*:

```
<object id="Sauce" type="SauceBéarnaise" singleton="false" />
```

Changing the value to *true* instead configures the object as a SINGLETON:

```
<object id="Sauce" type="SauceBéarnaise" singleton="true" />
```

The `singleton` attribute is optional, and because SINGLETON is the default, omitting it implicitly configures a SINGLETON. This is what you've been doing so far in this chapter.

PREVENTING MEMORY LEAKS

Like any other DI CONTAINER, Spring.NET creates object graphs. However, it doesn't track the created objects for us. It may keep track of those objects for its own purposes, but that depends on the object lifetime. As an example, to implement the

SINGLETON scope, it must keep a reference to the created instance. On the other hand, the TRANSIENT object scope doesn't keep track of the objects that Spring.NET creates. As you saw in listings 8.7 and 8.8, object instances are created and returned with no internal tracking. This has some advantages and disadvantages.

Because Spring.NET doesn't hold on to instances, the risk of inadvertent memory leaks is much smaller. With a container like Castle Windsor, memory leaks are guaranteed if you forget to call the `Release` method for all resolved object graphs. This isn't the case with Spring.NET, because objects will automatically be garbage-collected as they go out of scope.

The disadvantage is that disposable objects can't be deterministically disposed of. Because we can't explicitly release an object graph, we can't dispose of any disposable objects. This means that it becomes even more important to wrap disposable APIs in non-disposable services, as discussed in section 6.2.1.

In short, Spring.NET is well behaved and allows objects to be garbage-collected when they go out of scope in our own code—but the requirement is that our own classes must also be as well behaved. Because we can't rely on the container or the calling code to dispose of any services, we must keep usage of disposable objects within single methods.

This chapter has provided a remarkably short tour of object scopes in Spring.NET; there isn't a lot to say. The only universally available object scopes are SINGLETON and TRANSIENT, whereas a couple of other scopes rely on particular implementations of `IApplicationContext`. When we configure objects, we can configure some as SINGLE-TONS and some as TRANSIENTS, and this is even true if we configure multiple implementations of the same ABSTRACTION. We have yet to look at how to work with multiple components, so let's now turn our attention in that direction.

12.3 *Working with multiple components*

DI CONTAINERS thrive on distinctness but have a hard time with ambiguity. When using CONSTRUCTOR INJECTION, a single constructor is preferred over overloaded constructors because it's evident which constructor to use when there's no choice. This is also the case when mapping from ABSTRACTIONS to concrete types. If we attempt to map multiple concrete types to the same ABSTRACTION, we introduce ambiguity.

Despite the undesirable qualities of ambiguity, we often need to work with multiple implementations of a single interface. This can be the case in these situations:

- Different concrete types should be used for different consumers.
- DEPENDENCIES are sequences.
- Decorators are in use.

We'll look at each of these cases and see how Spring.NET addresses each one in turn. When we're done, you should be able to configure and resolve components even when multiple implementations of the same ABSTRACTION are in play.

As you saw in section 12.1.2, contrary to most other DI CONTAINERS, AUTO-WIRING isn't the default behavior for Spring.NET. Fine-grained control of wiring is an equally valid option and can be used to select among multiple candidates.

12.3.1 *Selecting among multiple candidates*

AUTO-WIRING in Spring.NET is convenient, but requires that services are distinct. As long as we have only one object that matches a particular ABSTRACTION we have no problems, but as soon as we introduce more implementations of the same interface, ambiguity rears its ugly head.

To deal with that ambiguity, we can use the explicit wiring of DEPENDENCIES that you've already seen in several examples.

CONFIGURING MULTIPLE IMPLEMENTATIONS OF THE SAME ABSTRACTION

Until now, you've been configuring named objects—but objects don't have to have names. You can configure multiple objects without providing a name:

```
<objects xmlns="http://www.springframework.net">
  <object type="SauceBéarnaise" />
  <object type="Steak" />
</objects>
```

The SauceBéarnaise and Steak classes are both configured without a name. Because you haven't explicitly provided names for the SauceBéarnaise and Steak objects, Spring.NET assigns an automatically generated name for each. If you knew the algorithm that Spring.NET uses to generate a name, you could request the objects using the GetObject method; but it might turn out to be a somewhat brittle solution. Instead, you can use the GetObjectsOfType method which was also introduced in section 12.1.1. As soon as we configure a type in Spring.NET, we can retrieve it using any of the types from which it derives.

To get an instance of the concrete Steak class, for example, you can mix the Get-ObjectsOfType method with a couple of LINQ extension methods:

```
var meat = context.GetObjectsOfType(typeof(Steak))
    .Values
    .OfType<Steak>()
    .FirstOrDefault();
```

You request the Steak type from the GetObjectsOfType method. Spring.NET will find all configured objects that match the requested type (whether they're named or not) and return them as a dictionary. The keys in this dictionary are the object names, but because you don't know the names, you're only interested in the values.

The Values property is an instance of the non-generic ICollection interface, so, to use LINQ, we must somehow cast it to a generic sequence. One possibility is to use the Cast<T> method, but a slightly safer option is to use the OfType<T> filter. Although the Cast method might throw an exception if there's an element that can't be cast to the desired type, the OfType method filters the sequence. Finally, we get the object from the sequence. In this case, we used FirstOrDefault, but a stronger constraint can be introduced by using the Single extension method.

The SauceBéarnaise and Steak classes both implement the IIngredient interface. When we configure objects, Spring.NET places no restrictions on how many objects we can configure of a given interface, but it still enables us to resolve them using the GetObjectsOfType method:

```
var ingredients = context.GetObjectsOfType(typeof(IIngredient));
```

Given the previous configuration, the returned ingredients dictionary will contain instances of both SauceBéarnaise and Steak, and we can use LINQ queries like we did in the previous example to retrieve particular elements that might interest us.

Although we can configure several IIngredient objects without names, we can still give them names if we want to:

```
<objects xmlns="http://www.springframework.net">
  <object id="Sauce" type="SauceBéarnaise" />
  <object id="Meat" type="Steak" />
</objects>
```

This enables us to resolve each of the objects by their names:

```
var meat = context.GetObject("Meat");
var sauce = context.GetObject("Sauce");
```

This doesn't preclude us from using the GetObjectsOfType method, so all of the previous examples would still apply.

Given that we should always resolve services in a single COMPOSITION ROOT, we should normally not expect to deal with such ambiguity on this level—but we can use named objects to select among multiple alternatives when configuring DEPENDENCIES for a given consumer.

CONFIGURING NAMED DEPENDENCIES

Wiring objects with named objects is a central feature in Spring.NET, although we also get limited AUTO-WIRING. Even though we should prefer AUTO-WIRING when possible, there are times when we need to address an ambiguous API. As an example, consider this constructor:

```
public ThreeCourseMeal(ICourse entrée,
    ICourse mainCourse, ICourse dessert)
```

In this case, we have three identically typed DEPENDENCIES that each represents a *different* concept. In most cases, we want to map each of the DEPENDENCIES to a separate type. The following listing shows how we could choose to configure the ICourse and the ThreeCourseMeal objects.

> **Listing 12.1   Wiring a list of dependencies**

```
<object id="Entrée" type="Rillettes" />
<object id="MainCourse" type="CordonBleu" />
<object id="Dessert" type="MousseAuChocolat" />
<object id="Meal" type="ThreeCourseMeal">
  <constructor-arg ref="Entrée" />
  <constructor-arg ref="MainCourse" />
  <constructor-arg ref="Dessert" />
</object>
```

The three `ICourse` implementations are configured as named objects. When we configure the `ThreeCourseMeal` object, we can refer to the names when wiring the constructor arguments. The `constructor-arg` element also takes optional `name` or `index` attributes that we can use to identify exactly which parameter we're referring to; but in this example we're listing them all in the appropriate order.

Explicitly mapping constructor arguments to named objects is a universally applicable solution. We can do this even if we configure the named objects in one XML resource and the constructor in a completely different resource, because the only identification that ties a named object together with an argument is the name. This is always possible but can be brittle if we have a lot of names to manage.

When the original reason prompting us to abandon AUTO-WIRING is to deal with ambiguity, a better solution is to design the API to get rid of that ambiguity. This often leads to a better overall design.

In the next section, you'll see how you can use the less ambiguous and more flexible approach, where you allow any number of courses in a meal. To this end, you must learn how Spring.NET deals with lists and sequences.

12.3.2 *Wiring sequences*

In section 10.3.2, we discussed how to refactor an explicit `ThreeCourseMeal` class to the more general-purpose `Meal` class with this constructor:

```
public Meal(IEnumerable<ICourse> courses)
```

You can configure Spring.NET to wire up `Meal` instances with appropriate `ICourse` DEPENDENCIES, and I'll show you how. When we're done, you should have a good idea of the options available to you when you need to configure instances with sequences of DEPENDENCIES.

AUTO-WIRING SEQUENCES

Spring.NET understands arrays well, but not other types of sequences. If we need an array of a particular ABSTRACTION and want to use all those configured, AUTO-WIRING just works. As an example, imagine that the `Meal` class offers this constructor overload:

```
public Meal(params ICourse[] courses)
```

If we want all configured `ICourse` objects to be injected into `Meal`, we can provide this configuration:

```
<object id="Entrée" type="Rillettes" />
<object id="MainCourse" type="CordonBleu" />
<object id="Dessert" type="MousseAuChocolat" />
<object id="Meal" type="Meal" autowire="autodetect" />
```

The `Meal` object is configured to AUTO-WIRE, and, because Spring.NET inherently understands arrays, it finds all objects that implement the `ICourse` interface and provides them to the `Meal` constructor. Array-based DEPENDENCIES are AUTO-WIRED out of the box.

Now, imagine that the constructor overload that takes an array of `ICourse` doesn't exist; you have only the constructor that takes an `IEnumerable<ICourse>`. Although

AUTO-WIRING doesn't work in this case, you can take advantage of the built-in understanding of arrays by defining a simple Decorator[2] that must be initialized with an array. The following listing shows a generic implementation. Recall that taking `IEnumerable<T>` in a constructor indicates a statically typed request for that particular DEPENDENCY. What you must do is as simple as translating this request into a request for an array of the same type.

Listing 12.2 Translating requests for a sequence into requests for arrays

```
public class ArrayEnumerable<T> : IEnumerable<T>        ◁─┐  Define
{                                                        ❶  sequence
    private readonly IEnumerable<T> sequence;

    public ArrayEnumerable(params T[] items)            ◁─┐  Require
    {                                                    ❷  array
        if (items == null)
        {
            throw new ArgumentNullException("items");
        }

        this.sequence = items;
    }

    public IEnumerator<T> GetEnumerator()
    {
        return this.sequence.GetEnumerator();
    }
}
```

The `ArrayEnumerable<T>` implements `IEnumerable<T>` ❶ so that it satisfies every constructor that requires such a sequence. On the other hand, it requires an array of the same type ❷. Because Spring.NET inherently knows how to deal with arrays, it can satisfy a closed `ArrayEnumerable` by providing it with all the objects that match the item type T.

To properly wire up the `Meal` class with all `ICourse` objects, you can now configure the context like this:

```
<object id="Entrée" type="Rillettes" />
<object id="MainCourse" type="CordonBleu" />
<object id="Dessert" type="MousseAuChocolat" />
<object id="Courses"
        type="ArrayEnumerable&lt;ICourse>"
        autowire="autodetect" />
<object id="Meal" type="Meal" autowire="autodetect" />
```

You define `Courses` as an `ArrayEnumerable<ICourse>` with AUTO-WIRING turned on. Because its only constructor requires an array of `ICourse`, Spring.NET automatically AUTO-WIRES it with all the `ICourse` implementations it can find: `Rillettes`, `CordonBleu`, and `MousseAuChocolat`.

---

[2] Erich Gamma et al, *Design Patterns: Elements of Reusable Object-Oriented Software* (New York: Addison-Wesley, 1994), 175.

The `Meal` class requires an `IEnumerable<ICourse>` and is also configured to be AUTO-WIRED. When you ask Spring.NET to resolve the `Meal` object, it will search for a configured object that implements `IEnumerable<ICourse>` and find the `Courses` object. All three `ICourse` objects will be injected into the `Meal` object via the `Courses` object.

The `ArrayEnumerable<T>` class is a little hack that fills in a small gap in Spring.NET. It's a pure infrastructure component which could be packaged into a reusable library.

Spring.NET automatically handles arrays, and, with a little help from `Array-Enumerable<T>`, it also handles other requests for sequences by resolving them to sequences of objects that implement the requested type. The only thing you need is to configure an `ArrayEnumerable` of the appropriate item type. Only when you need to explicitly pick only some components from a larger set do you need to do more than that. This is possible with more explicit configuration.

PICKING ONLY SOME OBJECTS FROM A LARGER SET

When we use Spring.NET's ability to resolve arrays, all objects are injected into consumers. This is often the correct policy. However, as figure 12.4 shows, there may be cases where we want to pick only some components from the larger set of all registered components.

When we previously let Spring.NET AUTO-WIRE all configured objects, it corresponded to the situation depicted on the right side of figure 12.4. If we want to

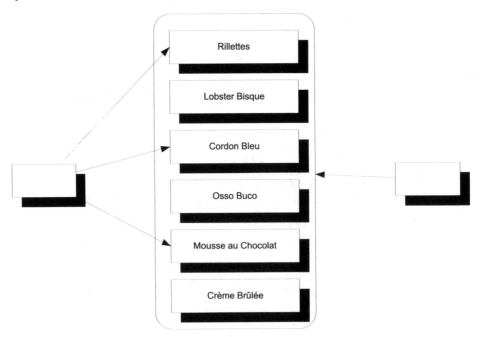

Figure 12.4 In the situation on the left, we wish to explicitly select only certain DEPENDENCIES from the larger list of all configured objects. This is different from the situation to the right, where we indiscriminately want them all.

configure an instance like the left side, we must explicitly define which objects should be used.

This is easy to do with named objects, because it's more or less the idiomatic way to configure Spring.NET, which provides a special `list` XML element to address this particular scenario. The following listing shows an example.

Listing 12.3 Injecting named objects into a sequence

```
<object id="Entrée" type="Rillettes" />
<object id="Entrée1" type="LobsterBisque" />
<object id="MainCourse" type="CordonBleu" />
<object id="Dessert" type="MousseAuChocolat" />
<object id="Meal" type="Meal">
  <constructor-arg>
    <list element-type="ICourse">                    ❶ Indicate
      <ref object="Entrée" />                            list
      <ref object="MainCourse" />       ❷ Named
      <ref object="Dessert" />            objects
    </list>
  </constructor-arg>
</object>
```

The `list` element ❶ can be used to indicate that the following elements are items in a list. When Spring.NET wires up the list, it creates an array of the type indicated by the `element-type` attribute. The `list` element can contain many different child elements; the `ref` element ❷ is used to refer to other named objects.

When you resolve the `Meal` object, you'll get a `Meal` instance with `Rillettes`, `CordonBleu`, and `MousseAuChocolat` as the contained courses, while the `LobsterBisque` won't be used.

Once more, you see that Spring.NET natively works with arrays. Although support for other sequence types is missing, you can work around this limitation by wrapping sequences in a class like `ArrayEnumerable<T>`.

Consumers that rely on sequences of DEPENDENCIES may be the most intuitive use of multiple instances of the same ABSTRACTION, but before we leave this subject, we need to look at yet another case where multiple instances come into play.

12.3.3 *Wiring Decorators*

In section 9.1.2, we discussed how the Decorator design pattern is extremely useful when implementing CROSS-CUTTING CONCERNS. By definition, Decorators introduce multiple types of the same ABSTRACTION. At the very least, we have two implementations of an ABSTRACTION: the Decorator itself and the decorated type. If we stack the Decorators, we may have even more.

This is another example of having multiple objects that implement the same ABSTRACTION. Unlike the previous sections, these objects aren't conceptually equal, but rather DEPENDENCIES of each other. I'll show you two different ways to configure Spring.NET to deal with this pattern.

Decorating with named objects

Throughout this chapter, you've seen plenty of examples of how to reference named objects as constructor arguments. You can also use this idiomatic approach to configure Decorators.

The `Breading` class is a Decorator of `IIngredient`; it uses Constructor Injection to receive the instance it should decorate:

```
public Breading(IIngredient ingredient)
```

To make a Cotoletta, you would like to decorate a `VealCutlet` (another `IIngredient`) with the `Breading` class. Because you already know how to connect named objects with constructor arguments, it should feel natural to do something similar to this:

```
<object id="Breading" type="Breading">
  <constructor-arg ref="Cutlet" />
</object>
<object id="Cutlet" type="VealCutlet" />
```

❶ Reference named object

By now, this approach should be familiar to you. You use a reference to a named object ❶ to wire the `Breading` object with the `Cutlet` object. Because Spring.NET doesn't explicitly deal with mappings from Abstractions to concrete type, each of these two elements represents an object like any other `object` element would. That they both implement the `IIngredient` interface does in no way impact how you configure them.

When you resolve the *Breading* name, you get a `Breading` instance that decorates a `VealCutlet`.

This is a universally applicable way to decorate a component, but when you don't otherwise care about the decorated component, you can use a more implicit method.

Decorating with inline objects

If you never need to resolve the decorated component directly, you can use a more implicit way to decorate it. Imagine that you never expect having to resolve the `Veal-Cutlet` directly as an `IIngredient`; when you want an `IIngredient`, you always want to get the Cotoletta.

In such cases, there's no need to explicitly configure the `VealCutlet` as an independent object. Instead, you can take advantage of Spring.NET's inline object syntax:

```
<object id="Breading" type="Breading">
  <constructor-arg>
    <object type="VealCutlet" />
  </constructor-arg>
</object>
```

Spring.NET enables you to define objects as nested elements. Instead of referring to a named object, the `constructor-arg` element can contain full object configurations. Because you don't expect to have to refer to a `VealCutlet` object from anywhere else in the configuration, you can provide an unnamed `object` element with the correct `type` attribute. When nested within the `constructor-arg` element, the `VealCutlet` type will be resolved as the first constructor argument to the `Breading` class.

Implement the aspect by developing an interceptor	▶	Add the interceptor to the configuration

Figure 12.5 The simple overall process of adding an aspect in Spring.NET.

There are a few variations available to us when configuring Decorators. Unlike Castle Windsor, Spring.NET has no implicit understanding of Decorators, which may be a bit surprising because, like Windsor, it offers the ultimate support for the Decorator pattern: INTERCEPTION.

12.3.4 Creating Interceptors

In section 9.3.3, you saw an example of how to add error handling and a Circuit Breaker[3] to a WCF client with Castle Windsor's dynamic INTERCEPTION capability. To demonstrate Spring.NET's INTERCEPTION capability and compare it to Castle Windsor and Unity, I'll walk you through the same familiar example, but now implemented with Spring.NET.

As figure 12.5 shows, adding an aspect to Spring.NET is a pretty simple process.

The bulk of the work involves developing the interceptor itself, but once we've done that, we must add it to the container. This is done in XML configuration, like everything else.

However, we can't configure the interceptors before we implement them, so the first step is to write some code for the error handling and Circuit Breaker interceptors. Once they're completed, we can configure the container with both.

IMPLEMENTING AN EXCEPTION HANDLING INTERCEPTOR

Implementing an interceptor for Spring.NET requires us to implement the IMethod-Interceptor interface. The following listing shows how to implement the exception handling strategy from chapter 9. This particular implementation for Spring.NET corresponds to listing 9.8 for Castle Windsor and listing 14.13 for Unity.

Listing 12.4 Implementing an exception handling IMethodInterceptor

```
public class ErrorHandlingInterceptor : IMethodInterceptor
{
    public object Invoke(IMethodInvocation invocation)    ◁── ❶ Implement interception logic
    {
        try
        {
            return invocation.Proceed();    ❷ Attempt to return result
        }
        catch (CommunicationException e)
        {
            this.AlertUser(e.Message);    ❸ Handle exceptions
        }
```

---

[3] Michael T Nygard, *Release It! Design and Deploy Production-Ready Software* (Raleigh, NC: Pragmatic Bookshelf, 2007), 104.

```
        catch (InvalidOperationException e)
        {
            this.AlertUser(e.Message);
        }
        return null;
    }
    private void AlertUser(string message)
    {
        var sb = new StringBuilder();
        sb.AppendLine("An error occurred.");
        sb.AppendLine("Your work is likely lost.");
        sb.AppendLine("Please try again later.");
        sb.AppendLine();
        sb.AppendLine(message);

        MessageBox.Show(sb.ToString(), "Error",
            MessageBoxButton.OK, MessageBoxImage.Error);
    }
}
```

❸ Handle exceptions

The ErrorHandlingInterceptor class implements the IMethodInterceptor inter-face, which only defines the single Invoke method ❶. This is where you must define the INTERCEPTION logic. The only argument to the method is an instance of the IMethodInvocation interface; with its Proceed method, you attempt to invoke the decorated method and return the result ❷. However, because the purpose of this interceptor is to handle known exceptions, the call to the Proceed method is wrapped in a try block.

If the Proceed method (or rather the decorated method that Proceed invokes) throws one of the known exceptions, the interceptor catches it and alerts the user about the error ❸. In this example, the set of known exceptions is hard-coded into the interceptor itself, but a more general-purpose implementation could decide to suppress or rethrow exceptions based on an injected Specification.[4]

Because the Invoke method must return an object, it returns null in the cases where an exception was caught and suppressed. This is already the correct value to return in all the cases where the decorated method returns void, but for a method with real return values, this can be problematic because it can easily lead to NullReference-Exceptions. However, we can create another interceptor that assigns appropriate default values for different return types. This would be more correct than trying to guess the correct default value from within the ErrorHandlingInterceptor, which is a general-purpose interceptor that can be used to intercept any interface; it would also be true to the spirit of the SINGLE RESPONSIBILITY PRINCIPLE.

The ErrorHandlingInterceptor takes care of handling certain exceptions from a decorated component. This component can itself be another interceptor in the form of a Circuit Breaker.

---

[4] Eric Evans, *Domain-Driven Design: Tackling Complexity in the Heart of Software* (New York: Addison-Wesley, 2004), 224.

IMPLEMENTING A CIRCUIT BREAKER INTERCEPTOR

The Circuit Breaker interceptor is a bit more complex because it requires the ICircuit-Breaker DEPENDENCY, but as the following listing shows, we address this by applying standard CONSTRUCTOR INJECTION. When it comes to composing the class, Spring.NET treats it like any other object, so as long as it can resolve the DEPENDENCY, all is well.

> **Listing 12.5   Implementing a Circuit Breaker IMethodInterceptor**

```
public class CircuitBreakerInterceptor :            Implement
    IMethodInterceptor                              IMethodInterceptor
{
    private readonly ICircuitBreaker breaker;
    public CircuitBreakerInterceptor(
        ICircuitBreaker breaker)
    {
        if (breaker == null)
        {                                           ❶ Constructor
            throw new ArgumentNullException("breaker");    Injection
        }

        this.breaker = breaker;
    }

    public object Invoke(IMethodInvocation invocation)
    {
        this.breaker.Guard();
        try
        {                                           ❷ Get result from
            var result = invocation.Proceed();         decorated method
            this.breaker.Succeed();
            return result;                          ❸ Record
        }                                              success
        catch (Exception e)
        {
            this.breaker.Trip(e);                   ❹ Trip
            throw;                                     breaker
        }
    }
}
```

The CircuitBreakerInterceptor needs to delegate its actual implementation to an ICircuitBreaker instance. Because Spring.NET can AUTO-WIRE an interceptor like it does any other object, you can use standard CONSTRUCTOR INJECTION ❶ to inject the ICircuitBreaker.

In the Invoke method, you need to implement the Guard-Succeed/Trip idiom you already saw in listings 9.4 and 9.9. As in listing 12.4, you invoke the decorated method by calling the Proceed method ❷, but instead of returning the value right away, you need to assign it to the local result variable so that you can indicate success to the Circuit Breaker ❸. Recall that this can close an otherwise open breaker.

Any exception which might be thrown by the decorated method is rethrown unmodified by the Proceed method, so you can catch it and Trip the breaker ❹ as you would normally do.

With both `ErrorHandlingInterceptor` and `CircuitBreakerInterceptor` imple-mented, it's time to configure the container to make them decorate an `IProduct-ManagementAgent` object.

CONFIGURING INTERCEPTION

What we really want to do is to intercept an `IProductManagementAgent` object with both Circuit Breaker and error handling so that when an exception happens during communication with the web service, the Circuit Breaker is opened and the exception is handled, giving the application a chance to recover once the web service or the net-work is back online.

Configuring INTERCEPTION in Spring.NET is easy. The first thing you need to do is to configure the interceptors themselves:

```
<objects xmlns="http://www.springframework.net"
        default-autowire="constructor">

  <object id="ErrorHandlingInterceptor"
        type="ErrorHandlingInterceptor" />
  <object id="CircuitBreakerInterceptor"
        type="CircuitBreakerInterceptor" />

</objects>
```

Being particularly unimaginative, I gave the objects the same id as their type. Notice that CONSTRUCTOR INJECTION–based AUTO-WIRING is switched on by default. Whereas the `ErrorHandlingInterceptor` has a default constructor, the `Circuit-BreakerInterceptor` uses CONSTRUCTOR INJECTION to request an `ICircuit-Breaker`. AUTO-WIRING works for both, as well as most other objects in the configu-ration, so switching it on by default is the easiest thing to do.

Now that you have the interceptors in place, the only thing left is to configure the `IProductManagementAgent` object with the desired interceptors. Figure 12.6 shows the configuration you're aiming for.

Figure 12.6   The `IProductManagementAgent` should be decorated by the Circuit Breaker interceptor so that when an exception is thrown by the agent, the circuit's opened for a while. Because the Circuit Breaker only registers exceptions, but doesn't handle them, this is the responsibility of the error handling interceptor, which must be outermost to be able to handle exceptions from both the agent as well as the Circuit Breaker.

As the following listing demonstrates, this is done with the configuration XML syn-tax and a special namespace and classes that Spring.NET provides for this purpose. The general concept of configuring INTERCEPTION involves decoupling what to do from where to do it. We must still answer both of these questions, but we do it separately and then tie them together.

Listing 12.6   Configuring interceptors

```
<object type="WcfProductManagementAgent" />
<object id="AgentPointCut"
        type="RegularExpressionMethodPointcut">
  <property name="patterns">
    <list>
      <value>.*WcfProductManagementAgent.*</value>
    </list>
  </property>
</object>
<aop:config>
  <aop:advisor pointcut-ref="AgentPointCut"
               advice-ref="ErrorHandlingInterceptor"
               order="1" />
  <aop:advisor pointcut-ref="AgentPointCut"
               advice-ref="CircuitBreakerInterceptor"
               order="2" />
</aop:config>
```

❶ Object to intercept

❷ Specify where to apply interception

❸ Bind interceptors with specification

In the previous code, you registered the interceptors—but you also need to register the classes to be intercepted ❶. In this example it's a single class, but you could intercept many different classes with the same set of interceptors if you'd like.

To specify which classes or methods to intercept, you must define something called a *Pointcut*, which is a fancy name for a rule that defines what to intercept. If you recall the original introduction of INTERCEPTION back in chapter 9, this corresponds to the Castle Windsor `IModelInterceptorsSelector` implemented in listing 9.10. Like Castle Windsor, Spring.NET allows you to write imperative code that defines a Pointcut, but in addition to that it also provides some declarative Pointcuts. One such *static Pointcut* is the `RegularExpressionMethodPointcut` ❷, which you can use to define the matching rule with a regular expression. For each method call it will attempt to match the full name of the method with the regular expression. In this particular case you only want to match members on the `WcfProductManagement-Agent` class.

Finally, you need to bind the Pointcut to the interceptors you previously registered. This is done with a series of `advisor` elements ❸ that declare the interceptors and the order in which they're composed. Notice that because you list `ErrorHandling-Interceptor` first, it becomes the outermost interceptor, itself intercepting the `CircuitBreakerInteceptor`.

The final thing you need to do to configure the application with robust out-of-process communication management is to make sure that all DEPENDENCIES can be satisfied. Because `CircuitBreakerInteceptor` requires an `ICircuitBreaker`, you must also configure this object:

```
<object type="CircuitBreaker" autowire="no">
  <constructor-arg value="00:01:00" />
</object>
```

The `CircuitBreaker` constructor requires a timeout in the form of a `TimeSpan` instance, and you prefer to define this primitive value inline. To do that, you must disable the default AUTO-WIRING setting to explicitly set the timeout to one minute.

To be effective at all it's important that there's only one Circuit Breaker instance (at least per out-of-process resource), but because the default object scope is SINGLETON, you don't need to explicitly express that.

The example demonstrated how to utilize dynamic INTERCEPTION with Spring.NET. In my personal opinion, I find the complexity comparable with Castle Windsor's and Unity's INTERCEPTION support. While not entirely trivial, the potential benefit is great.

INTERCEPTION is a dynamic implementation of the Decorator pattern, and the Decorator pattern is itself a combined application of multiple objects of the same type. Spring.NET lets us work with multiple components in several different ways. We can configure them as alternatives to each other, as peers resolved as sequences, as hierarchical Decorators, or even as interceptors. When it comes to arrays, Spring.NET will figure out what to do, but we can often map other sequence types into arrays using an adapter such as the `ArrayEnumerable<T>` class. This also enables us to explicitly define how services are composed if we need more explicit control.

This may also be the case when we need to deal with APIs that deviate from CONSTRUCTOR INJECTION. So far, you've seen how to configure objects, including how to specify object scopes and how to deal with multiple objects, but until now we've allowed the container to wire DEPENDENCIES by implicitly assuming that all components use CONSTRUCTOR INJECTION. This isn't always the case, so in the next section we'll review how to deal with classes that must be instantiated in special ways.

12.4   *Configuring difficult APIs*

Until now, we've considered how to configure components that use CONSTRUCTOR INJECTION. One of the many benefits of CONSTRUCTOR INJECTION is that DI CONTAINERS such as Spring.NET can easily understand how to compose and create all classes in a dependency graph.

However, this becomes less clear when APIs are less well behaved. Here I'll show you how to deal with primitive constructor arguments, static factories, and PROPERTY INJECTION. These all require special attention. We'll start by looking at classes that take primitive types, such as strings or integers as constructor arguments.

12.4.1   *Configuring primitive Dependencies*

As long as we inject ABSTRACTIONS into consumers, all is well. But it becomes more difficult when a constructor depends on a primitive type, such as a string, number, or enum. This is often the case for data access implementations that take a connection string as a constructor parameter, but it's a more general issue that applies to all strings and numbers.

Conceptually, it doesn't make much sense to register a string or number as a component in a container, and with Spring.NET, it isn't possible to register the value of a primitive type as an object.

Consider, as an example, this constructor:

```
public ChiliConCarne(Spiciness spiciness)
```

In this example, `Spiciness` is an enum:

```
public enum Spiciness
{
    Mild = 0,
    Medium,
    Hot
}
```

> **WARNING** As a rule of thumb, enums are code smells and should be refactored to polymorphic classes.[5] However, they serve us well for this example.

You need to explicitly supply the value of the `spiciness` constructor parameter as part of configuring the `ChiliConCarne` object:

```
<object id="Course" type="ChiliConCarne">
  <constructor-arg value="Hot" />
</object>
```

① Supply value

Spring.NET comes with several type converters that convert text representations into instances of the desired types. One of the built-in type converters converts text to enums, which enables us to supply the text *Hot* as the value of the `constructor-arg` element ①. Spring.NET looks at the type of the constructor parameter for the `Chili-ConCarne` class, determines that it's an enum, and uses the appropriate type converter to convert the text *Hot* into the value `Spiciness.Hot`.

This feature of Spring.NET addresses situations where we need to supply primitive values as arguments. The `ChiliConCarne` example supplied the argument to a constructor, but sometimes a class has no public constructor.

12.4.2 *Configuring static factories*

Some classes can't be instantiated through a public constructor. Instead, we must use some sort of factory to create instances of the type. This is always troublesome for DI CONTAINERS because, by default, they look after public constructors.

Consider this example constructor for the public `JunkFood` class:

```
internal JunkFood(string name)
```

Even though the `JunkFood` class is public, the constructor is internal. Obviously, instances of `JunkFood` should be created through the static `JunkFoodFactory` class:

```
public static class JunkFoodFactory
{
    public static IMeal Create(string name)
    {
```

---

[5] Martin Fowler et al., *Refactoring: Improving the Design of Existing Code* (New York: Addison-Wesley, 1999), 82.

```
        return new JunkFood(name);
    }
}
```

From Spring.NET's perspective, this is a problematic API because there are no unambiguous and well-established conventions around static factories. It needs help—and you can provide this when you configure the object:

```
<object id="Meal"
        type="JunkFoodFactory"
        factory-method="Create">
  <constructor-arg value="chicken meal" />
</object>
```

As always, the configuration of the object is expressed within an `object` element, but rather than defining the type of the object itself, you define the type of the factory. You must also configure that the name of the `factory-method` is `Create`. Notice that even though the `Create` method isn't a constructor per se, you still use the `constructor-arg` element to define the value of the `name` argument for the `Create` method.

Even though the `type` attribute is defined as the factory type instead of the resulting type, Spring.NET is clever enough to understand that the return type of the `Create` method is `JunkFood`. This means that you can dispense with the `id` attribute and create an unnamed object, as you did in section 12.3.1, and you would still be able to resolve a `JunkFood` object with the `GetObjectsOfType` method.

The last common deviation from CONSTRUCTOR INJECTION we'll examine is PROPERTY INJECTION.

12.4.3   *Wiring with Property Injection*

PROPERTY INJECTION is a less well-defined form of DI because we're not forced by the compiler to assign a value to a writable property. Even so, Spring.NET understands and works with PROPERTY INJECTION in an intuitive way. If we enable AUTO-WIRING it tends to just work, but it will also work with explicit wiring.

Consider this `CaesarSalad` class:

```
public class CaesarSalad : ICourse
{
    public IIngredient Extra { get; set; }
}
```

It's a common misconception that a Caesar Salad includes chicken; this isn't true. A Caesar Salad is a *salad*, but it tastes great with chicken, so chicken is often offered as an extra ingredient. The `CaesarSalad` class models this by exposing a writable property named `Extra`.

If you configure only the `CaesarSalad` without explicitly addressing the `Extra` property, the property won't be assigned. You can still resolve the instance, but the property will have the default value that the constructor assigns to it (if any).

EXPLICITLY WIRING PROPERTIES

There are several ways you can configure the CaesarSalad so that the Extra property will be appropriately populated. One is to explicitly wire the property to a named object:

```
<object id="Course" type="CaesarSalad">
  <property name="Extra" ref="Chicken" />
</object>
<object id="Chicken" type="Chicken" />
```

The property element identifies that the name of the property is *Extra* and that it should be assigned with the named object *Chicken*. Instead of using a reference to a named object, you can also use an inline object:

```
<object id="Course" type="CaesarSalad">
  <property name="Extra">
    <object type="Chicken" />
  </property>
</object>
```

You can always explicitly wire properties with the property element, but because the property is identified by its name, this approach tends to be brittle. If you later rename the property, most refactoring tools won't identify and change the value of a name attribute in various XML files. This may cause runtime errors.

A better option is to AUTO-WIRE objects.

AUTO-WIRING PROPERTIES

As you may recall from section 12.1.2, you must explicitly enable AUTO-WIRING in Spring.NET, but once you do that, PROPERTY INJECTION just works. If the DEPENDENCY can't be satisfied, the property is ignored:

```
<objects xmlns="http://www.springframework.net">
  <object id="Course" type="CaesarSalad"
          autowire="autodetect" />
</objects>
```

In this example, the *Course* object is the only object configured for the container. Although it's configured to be AUTO-WIRED, the Extra property will never be assigned because there's no available IIngredient object. An exception isn't thrown; the property is simply ignored.

This changes as soon as an IIngredient object becomes available:

```
<object id="Course" type="CaesarSalad"
        autowire="autodetect" />
<object type="Chicken" />
```

Now, when you resolve the *Course* object, you'll receive an instance of CaesarSalad with Extra Chicken.

Using AUTO-WIRING is more robust because we can rename properties without fearing that the Spring.NET configuration will break at runtime.

You saw how to use Spring.NET to deal with more difficult creational APIs. In general you can always explicitly configure wiring using the XML configuration, but you also saw that PROPERTY INJECTION can be configured with AUTO-WIRING.

12.5 *Summary*

Among the DI CONTAINERS covered in this book, Spring.NET is unique in the sense that it's the only container which is implemented as a port from Java. Nowhere is this more apparent than in Spring.NET's strong reliance on XML configuration.

Most of the older .NET DI CONTAINERS started out with a strong focus on XML, but while others have moved on, Spring.NET has not.

Although future versions of Spring.NET may get stronger support for CODE AS CONFIGURATION and perhaps even CONVENTION-BASED CONFIGURATION, the current idiomatic usage involves lots of XML.

Perhaps the weakest area is the limited support for LIFETIME MANAGEMENT. One thing is that, like StructureMap, Spring.NET has no explicit support for releasing object graphs—this can be viewed as much as a design decision as a lack of a feature. Another thing is that there's no support for custom object scopes.

Whereas the LIFETIME MANAGEMENT features are weak, Spring.NET is one of the few DI CONTAINERS to offer built-in INTERCEPTION.

Spring.NET is still based on .NET 1.1, which may be a benefit for some people. We get comprehensive documentation and the option of purchasing commercial support, so although the overall impression may be slightly outmoded, it's also one of a professional package.

We may regard Spring.NET as an old-but-trusted framework. In contrast, the next chapter presents one of the most modern DI CONTAINERS: Autofac.

13

Autofac

In the previous chapters, you saw how to map the principles and patterns from parts 1–3 to specific DI CONTAINERS. In this chapter, we'll do the same with the Autofac DI CONTAINER.

Autofac is an example of what we could call second-generation DI CONTAINERS.

NOTE Examples of other second-generation DI CONTAINERS are Ninject[1] and Unity.[2]

The second-generation DI CONTAINERS are based directly on .NET 3.5, so their architectures are often directly based on the language and platform features that became available at that time. Not only do they have an intimate understanding of

---

[1] http://ninject.org/
[2] http://unity.codeplex.com/

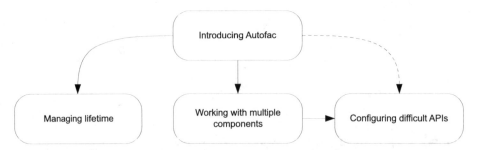

Figure 13.1 **This chapter is divided into four sections. The first section introduces the Autofac API and should be considered a prerequisite for the next three sections. Most of these can be read independently of each other, although the fourth section uses some methods and classes that are introduced in the third section. The subject of the fourth section is sufficiently different from the third, so you may be able to read them independently—but even so, you may want to refer back for an explanation of parts of the API.**

generics, but many also employ lambda expressions as central API elements. Although the majority of the mature DI CONTAINERS also support these more modern language constructs, their core engines are typically based on earlier .NET versions. Because the second-generation containers have no such baggage, they're typically designed around these features from the ground up.

Autofac is a fairly comprehensive DI CONTAINER that offers a carefully designed and consistent API. It has been around since late 2007 and seems to have a fair-sized user base.[3]

In this chapter, we'll examine how Autofac can be used to apply the principles and patterns laid forth in parts 1–3. Figure 13.1 shows the structure of the chapter.

This chapter should enable you to get started, as well as deal with the most common issues that may come up as you use Autofac on a daily basis. It's not a complete treatment of Autofac—that would take several more chapters or perhaps a whole book in itself, but if you want to know more about Autofac, the best place to start is at the Autofac home page at to http://autofac.org.

You can read the chapter in isolation from the rest of part 4 specifically to learn about Autofac, or you can read it together with the other chapters in part 4 to compare DI CONTAINERS. The focus of this chapter is to show how Autofac relates to and implements the patterns and principles described in parts 1–3.

13.1 *Introducing Autofac*

In this section, you'll learn where to get Autofac, what you get, and how you start using it. We'll also look at common configuration options, as well as how to package configuration settings into reusable components. Table 13.1 provides fundamental information that you're likely to need to get started.

---

[3] No official statistics exist on DI CONTAINER usage, so this is my subjective assessment.

Table 13.1 Autofac at a glance

Question	Answer
Where do I get it?	Go to http://autofac.org and click the appropriate link under Featured Download. From Visual Studio 2010 you can also get it via NuGet. The package name is *Autofac*.
What's in the download?	You can download a .zip file with precompiled binaries. You can also download the source code and compile it yourself, although it can be difficult to figure out which change set corresponds to a particular release. The last part of the build number (for example, 724 in this chapter) corresponds to the source code revision, but to find that you'll need the Mercurial source control tools.
Which platforms are supported?	.NET 3.5 SP1, .NET 4, Silverlight 3, Silverlight 4. Older versions are available that support .NET 2.0, 3.0 and Silverlight 2 (select All Releases on the Download tab).
How much does it cost?	Nothing. It's open source.
Where can I get help?	You can get commercial support from companies associated with the Autofac developers. Read more about the options at http://code.google.com/p/autofac/wiki/CommercialSupport. Other than commercial support, Autofac is still open source software with a thriving ecosystem, so you're also likely (but not guaranteed) to get help in the official forum at http://groups.google.com/group/autofac.
On which version is the chapter based?	2.4.5.724.

Using Autofac is a little different from using other DI CONTAINERS. As figure 13.2 illustrates, it's a more explicit two-step process: first we configure a `ContainerBuilder`, and when we're done with that, we use it to build a container that can be used to resolve components.

When you're done with this section, you should have a good feeling for the overall usage pattern of Autofac, and you should be able to start using it in well-behaved scenarios where all components follow proper DI patterns such as CONSTRUCTOR INJECTION. Let's start with

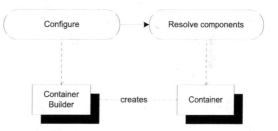

Figure 13.2 With Autofac, we first create and configure a `ContainerBuilder` instance. When we're done configuring the `ContainerBuilder`, we use it to create a Container that we can subsequently use to resolve components. Notice that the rhythm is pretty much similar to Castle Windsor or StructureMap: configure, then resolve. However, here the separation of concerns is much clearer. A `ContainerBuilder` can't resolve components, and we can't configure a `Container`.

the simplest scenario and see how we can resolve objects using an Autofac container.

13.1.1 *Resolving objects*

The core service of any DI CONTAINER is to resolve components. In this section, we'll look at the API that enables us to resolve components with Autofac.

If you recall the discussion about resolving components with Castle Windsor and StructureMap, you may remember that Windsor requires us to register *all* relevant components before we can resolve them, whereas StructureMap makes a best effort to figure it out for us if we're requesting concrete types with public constructors. Autofac can behave in both ways, but by default, it behaves like Windsor. We must register all relevant components before resolving them, so one of the simplest possible uses of Autofac is this:

```
var builder = new ContainerBuilder();
builder.RegisterType<SauceBéarnaise>();
var container = builder.Build();
SauceBéarnaise sauce = container.Resolve<SauceBéarnaise>();
```

As was already foreshadowed by figure 13.2, you need a `ContainerBuilder` instance to configure components. Here you register the concrete `SauceBéarnaise` class with the `builder` so that when you ask it to build a container, the resulting `container` is configured with the `SauceBéarnaise` class. This again enables you to resolve the `Sauce-Béarnaise` class from the container.

If you hadn't registered the `SauceBéarnaise` component, the attempt to resolve it would have thrown a `ComponentNotRegisteredException`.

Comparing this, the simplest of all scenarios, with similar code snippets for Castle Windsor or StructureMap, Autofac seems somewhat verbose. However, the verbosity mostly stems from having to take the extra step of creating a container from a `ContainerBuilder`, so in larger and more complex configurations, Autofac will be completely comparable with other DI CONTAINERS.

By default, Autofac requires us to explicitly register all relevant components; this is the behavior we also get from Castle Windsor. If you'd prefer a behavior more like StructureMap, you can enable it like this:

```
var builder = new ContainerBuilder();
builder.RegisterSource(
    new AnyConcreteTypeNotAlreadyRegisteredSource());
var container = builder.Build();
SauceBéarnaise sauce = container.Resolve<SauceBéarnaise>();
```

The only difference from the previous code example is that you don't explicitly register the `SauceBéarnaise` class. Instead, you register an `IRegistrationSource` called `AnyConcreteTypeNotAlreadyRegisteredSource`. That's quite a mouthful, but it does more or less what it says: it acts as a source for registrations of any concrete type that hasn't already previously been registered. When you add the `AnyConcreteTypeNot-AlreadyRegisteredSource` you don't need to explicitly add the `SauceBéarnaise` type because it's a concrete class with a public constructor, and the registration source can automatically provide a registration for it.

Registration Sources

An advanced feature of Autofac is the ability to provide more advanced sources for registration than by directly using the API exposed by `ContainerBuilder`. It's an extensibility mechanism that Autofac uses internally to implement various features, but because it's based on a public interface called `IRegistrationSource`, we can also use it as an extensibility mechanism.

The only public implementation of `IRegistrationSource` shipping with Autofac is the `AnyConcreteTypeNotAlreadyRegisteredSource` you've already seen, but Autofac has other, internal implementations of the interface.

The idea behind `IRegistrationSource` is that implementations can provide fallback mechanisms or more heuristically-based sources for component registrations than what the normal API allows. Apart from the aforementioned source of concrete types, we could also use it to turn Autofac into an auto-mocking container. This is well beyond the scope of this book,[4] and we don't need to talk more about `IRegistrationSource` to use Autofac effectively.

Registering the `AnyConcreteTypeNotAlreadyRegisteredSource` effectively changes the container's behavior from Castle Windsor style to StructureMap style. Not only can the container resolve concrete types with default constructors—it can also AUTO-WIRE a type with other concrete DEPENDENCIES without the need for explicit registrations. Still, as soon as we introduce loose coupling, we must configure Autofac by mapping ABSTRACTIONS to concrete types.

MAPPING ABSTRACTIONS TO CONCRETE TYPES

Whereas Autofac's optional ability to AUTO-WIRE concrete types can certainly come in handy from time to time, loose coupling normally requires us to map ABSTRACTIONS to concrete types. Creating instances based upon such maps is the core service offered by any DI CONTAINER, but we must still define the map.

In this example, you map the `IIngredient` interface to the concrete `Sauce-Béarnaise` class, which allows you to successfully resolve `IIngredient`:

```
var builder = new ContainerBuilder();
builder.RegisterType<SauceBéarnaise>().As<IIngredient>();
var container = builder.Build();
IIngredient ingredient = container.Resolve<IIngredient>();
```

You use the `ContainerBuilder` instance to register types and define maps. The `RegisterType` method enables you to register a concrete type. As you saw in the first Autofac code example in this chapter, you can stop right there if you only wish to register the `SauceBéarnaise` class. You can also continue with the `As` method to define how the concrete type should be registered.

---

[4] However, for an outline on how to do this, see http://stackoverflow.com/questions/2462340/automockcontainer-with-support-for-automocking-class-instances

NOTE   With Autofac, we start with the concrete type and map it to an ABSTRAC-TION. This is the reverse of most other DI CONTAINERS that start with the ABSTRACTION and map it to a concrete type.

WARNING   Contrary to Castle Windsor and StructureMap, there are no generic type constraints in effect between the types defined by the `Register-Type` and `As` methods. This means that it's possible to map incompatible types. The code will compile, but we'll get an exception at runtime when the `ContainerBuilder` builds the container.

In many cases, the generic API is all we need. Although it doesn't offer the same degree of type safety as some other DI CONTAINERS, it's still a readable way to configure the container. Still, there are situations where we need a more weakly typed way to resolve services. This is also possible.

RESOLVING WEAKLY TYPED SERVICES

Sometimes we can't use a generic API because we don't know the appropriate type at design time. All we have is a `Type` instance, but we'd still like to get an instance of that type. You saw an example of that in section 7.2, where we discussed ASP.NET MVC's `DefaultControllerFactory` class. The relevant method is this one:

```
protected internal virtual IController GetControllerInstance(
    RequestContext requestContext, Type controllerType);
```

Because you only have a `Type` instance, you can't use generics but must resort to a weakly typed API. Fortunately, Autofac offers a weakly typed overload of the `Resolve` method which allows you to implement the `GetControllerInstance` method like this:

```
return (IController)this.container.Resolve(controllerType);
```

The weakly typed overload of `Resolve` enables you to pass the `controllerType` argument directly to Autofac, but also requires you to explicitly cast the return value to `IController`.

No matter which overload of `Resolve` we use, Autofac guarantees that it will return an instance of the requested type or throw an exception if there are DEPENDENCIES that can't be satisfied. When all required DEPENDENCIES have been properly configured, Autofac can AUTO-WIRE the requested type.

In the previous example, `this.container` is an instance of `Autofac.IContainer`. To be able to resolve the requested type, all loosely coupled DEPENDENCIES must previously have been configured. There are many ways to configure Autofac, and the next section reviews the most common ones.

13.1.2   *Configuring the ContainerBuilder*

As we discussed in section 3.2, there are several conceptually different ways we can configure a DI CONTAINER. Figure 13.3 reviews the options.

As a second-generation DI CONTAINER, Autofac wasn't originally designed around XML configuration and later retrofitted with a programmatic configuration API like

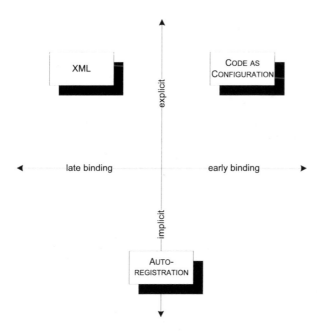

Figure 13.3 Conceptually different configuration options. CODE AS CONFIGURATION is strongly typed and tends to be explicit. XML, on the other hand, is late bound, but still explicit. AUTO-REGISTRATION instead relies on conventions that can be both strongly typed and more loosely defined.

some of the more mature containers. Rather, it's designed to be able to leverage many different sources of configuration, and XML is an optional module we can choose to use.

The core configuration API is centered on code and supports both CODE AS CONFIGURATION and convention-based AUTO-REGISTRATION while XML remains an option.

Autofac supports all three approaches and even allows us to mix them all within the same container, so in this regard it gives us all we could ask for. In this section, you'll see how to use each of these three types of configuration sources.

CODE AS CONFIGURATION

In section 13.1.1, you already saw a brief glimpse of Autofac's strongly typed configuration API. Here, we'll examine it in greater detail.

All configuration in Autofac uses the API exposed by the ContainerBuilder class, although most of the methods we use are extension methods. One of the most commonly used methods is the RegisterType method that you've already seen:

```
builder.RegisterType<SauceBéarnaise>().As<IIngredient>();
```

Like Castle Windsor, registering SauceBéarnaise as IIngredient hides the concrete class so that you can no longer resolve SauceBéarnaise with this registration. However, you can easily fix this by using an overload of the As method that enables you to specify that the concrete type maps to more than one registered type:

```
builder.RegisterType<SauceBéarnaise>()
    .As<SauceBéarnaise, IIngredient>();
```

Instead of registering the class only as IIngredient, you can register it as both itself and the interface it implements. This enables the container to resolve requests for both SauceBéarnaise and IIngredient.

As an alternative, you can also chain calls to the As method:

```
builder.RegisterType<SauceBéarnaise>()
    .As<SauceBéarnaise>().As<IIngredient>();
```

This produces the same result as in the example just given.

There are three generic overloads of the As method that enable us to specify one, two, or three types. If we need to specify more, there's also a non-generic overload we can use to specify as many types as we'd like.

> **TIP** If you need to specify more than three types with the As method, you should consider it a design smell of the class you're registering. If it implements that many interfaces, it probably violates the SINGLE RESPONSIBILITY PRINCIPLE.

In real applications, we always have more than one ABSTRACTION to map, so we must configure multiple mappings. This is done with multiple calls to RegisterType:

```
builder.RegisterType<SauceBéarnaise>().As<IIngredient>();
builder.RegisterType<Course>().As<ICourse>();
```

This maps IIngredient to SauceBéarnaise and ICourse to Course. There's no overlap of types, so it should be pretty evident what's going on. However, you can also register the same ABSTRACTION several times:

```
builder.RegisterType<SauceBéarnaise>().As<IIngredient>();
builder.RegisterType<Steak>().As<IIngredient>();
```

Here you register IIngredient twice. If you resolve IIngredient, you get an instance of Steak. The last registration wins, but previous registrations aren't forgotten. Autofac handles multiple configurations for the same ABSTRACTION well, but we'll get back to this topic in section 13.3.

There are more advanced options available for configuring Autofac, but you can configure an entire application with the methods shown here. However, to save yourself from too much explicit maintenance of container configuration, you could instead consider a more convention-based approach, using AUTO-REGISTRATION.

AUTO-REGISTRATION

In many cases, a lot of registrations will be similar. Such registrations are tedious to maintain, and explicitly registering each and every component might not be the most productive approach.

Consider a library that contains a lot of IIngredient implementations. We can configure each class individually, but it will result in numerous similar-looking calls to the RegisterType method. What's worse is that, every time we add a new IIngredient implementation, we must also explicitly register it with the ContainerBuilder if we want it to be available. It would be more productive to state that all implementations of IIngredient found in a given assembly should be registered.

This is possible using the RegisterAssemblyTypes extension method. This method enables us to specify an assembly and to configure all selected classes from this assembly in a single statement. To get the Assembly instance we can use a representative class—in this case, Steak:

```
builder.RegisterAssemblyTypes(typeof(Steak).Assembly)
    .As<IIngredient>();
```

The RegisterAssemblyTypes method returns the same interface as the RegisterType method, so many of the same configuration options are available. This is really a strong feature because it means that we don't have to learn a new API to use AUTO-REGISTRATION. In the previous example, we used the As method to register all types in the assembly as IIngredient services.

> **NOTE** Although the return type is the same, it's a complex generic interface; and because most of the API we use is implemented as extension methods, not all methods are available in all situations. It depends on the type arguments of the returned generic interface.

The previous example unconditionally configures all implementations of the IIngredient interface, but we can provide filters that enable us to select only a subset. Here is a convention-based scan where we add only classes whose name starts with *Sauce:*

```
builder.RegisterAssemblyTypes(typeof(Steak).Assembly)
    .Where(t => t.Name.StartsWith("Sauce"))
    .As<IIngredient>();
```

When we register all types in an assembly, we can use a predicate to define a selection criterion. The only difference from the previous code example is the inclusion of the Where method, where we select only those types whose names start with *Sauce*. Notice how this is the exact same syntax we used to filter types with both Castle Windsor and StructureMap.

There are many other methods that enable us to provide various selection criteria. The Where method gives us a filter that only lets those types through that match the predicate, but there's also an Except method that works the other way around.

Apart from selecting the correct types from an assembly, another part of AUTO-REGISTRATION is defining the correct mapping. In the previous examples, we used the As method with a specific interface to register all selected types against that interface.

However, sometimes we want to use different conventions. Let's say that instead of interfaces, we use abstract base classes, and we wish to register all types in an assembly where the name ends with *Policy*. For this purpose, there are several other overloads of the As method, including one that takes a Func<Type, Type> as input:

```
builder.RegisterAssemblyTypes(typeof(DiscountPolicy).Assembly)
    .Where(t => t.Name.EndsWith("Policy"))
    .As(t => t.BaseType);
```

The code block provided to the `As` method will be used for every single type whose name ends with *Policy*. This ensures that all classes with the *Policy* suffix will be registered against their base class so that when the base class is requested, the container will resolve it to the type mapped by this convention.

Convention-based registration with Autofac is surprisingly easy and uses an API that closely mirrors the API exposed by the singular `RegisterType` method.

TIP Think of `RegisterAssemblyTypes` as the plural of `RegisterType`.

The `RegisterAssemblyTypes` method takes a `params` array of `Assembly` instances, so we can supply as many assemblies as we'd like to a single convention. It's not a far-fetched thought to scan a folder for assemblies and supply them all to implement add-in functionality where add-ins can be added without recompiling a core application. This is one way to implement late binding; another is to use XML configuration.

XML CONFIGURATION

When we need to be able to change a configuration without recompiling the application, XML configuration is a good option.

TIP Use XML configuration only for those types you need to change without recompiling the application. Use AUTO-REGISTRATION or CODE AS CONFIGURATION for the rest.

The most natural way to use XML configuration is to embed it into the standard .NET application configuration file. This is possible, but we can also use a stand-alone XML file if we need to be able to vary the Autofac configuration independently of the standard .config file. Whether we want to do one or the other, the API is almost the same.

NOTE Autofac's XML configuration support is implemented in a separate assembly, so to use this feature we must add a reference to the `Autofac.Configuration` assembly.

Once we have a reference to `Autofac.Configuration`, we can ask the `Container-Builder` to read component registrations from the standard .config file, like this:

```
builder.RegisterModule(new ConfigurationSettingsReader());
```

We'll discuss Autofac modules in more details in section 13.1.3, but for now all you need to know is that the `ConfigurationSettingsReader` is the class that's responsible for merging XML configuration with the rest of the registrations applied to the `ContainerBuilder`. When we use the default constructor, it automatically reads from a configuration section in the standard application configuration file, but we can use another overload to specify a different XML file.

NOTE Unfortunately, there's no API that enables us to read XML from other sources such as streams or nodes.

To enable Autofac configuration in a configuration file, we must first add the configuration section, using the standard .NET API for defining custom configuration sections:

```
<configSections>
  <section name="autofac"
           type="Autofac.Configuration.SectionHandler,
           ➡Autofac.Configuration"/>
</configSections>
```

This enables you to add an `autofac` configuration section in the configuration file. Here is a simple example that maps the `IIngredient` interface to the `Steak` class:

```
<autofac defaultAssembly="Ploeh.Samples.MenuModel">
  <components>
    <component type="Ploeh.Samples.MenuModel.Steak"
               service="Ploeh.Samples.MenuModel.IIngredient" />
  </components>
</autofac>
```

In the `components` element, you can add as many `component` elements as you'd like. In each element you must specify a concrete type with the `type` attribute. This is the only required attribute, but to map the `Steak` class to `IIngredient` you can use the optional `service` attribute. Specifying a type is done using a fully qualified type name, but you can omit the assembly name if the type is defined in the default assembly. The `defaultAssembly` attribute is optional, but a really nice feature that can save you from a lot of typing if you have many types defined in the same assembly.

XML configuration is a good option when we need to change the configuration of one or more components without recompiling the application, but because it tends to be quite brittle, we should reserve it for only those occasions and use either AUTO-REGISTRATION or CODE AS CONFIGURATION for the main part of the container's configuration.

TIP Remember that the last configuration of a type wins? You can use this behavior to overwrite hard-coded configuration with XML configuration. To do this, you must remember to read in the XML configuration after any other components have been configured.

In this section, we mainly looked at various configuration APIs for Autofac. Although it's certainly possible to write one big block of unstructured configuration code, it's better to modularize configuration. Autofac supports this through Modules.

13.1.3 *Packaging configuration*

It's sometimes desirable to package configuration logic into reusable groups, and even when reuse itself isn't our top priority, we may simply want to provide a bit of structure if we have a big and complex application to configure.

With Autofac, we can package configuration into Modules. A Module is a class that implements the `IModule` interface, but in most cases it's easier to derive from the abstract `Module` class. Figure 13.4 shows the type hierarchy.

Everything you've done so far, you can do from inside a Module as well. The following listing shows a Module that registers all `IIngredient` implementations.

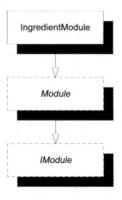

Figure 13.4 Reusable configurations can be packaged into `IModule` implementations. The easiest way to implement `IModule` is to derive from the abstract `Module` class—just as the `IngredientModule` does.

Listing 13.1   Implementing an Autofac Module

```
public class IngredientModule : Module
{
    protected override void Load(ContainerBuilder builder)
    {
        var a = typeof(Steak).Assembly;
        builder.RegisterAssemblyTypes(a).As<IIngredient>();
    }
}
```

The `IngredientModule` derives from the abstract `Module` class and overrides its `Load` method. The `Load` method is a convenience method defined by the `Module` class to make it easier to implement `IModule`. Through the `Load` method, you receive a `ContainerBuilder` instance that you can use to register components in exactly the same way as you would do outside a Module. This makes it easy to implement a Module when you already know how to use the `ContainerBuilder` API.

To use a Module, you can invoke one of the `RegisterModule` overloads. When the Module has a default constructor, you can use a generic shorthand version:

```
builder.RegisterModule<IngredientModule>();
```

There's also an overload that lets you provide an instance to enable situations where you need to create the Module manually:

```
builder.RegisterModule(new IngredientModule());
```

You can also configure Modules in XML:

```
<modules>
  <module
    type="Ploeh.Samples.Menu.Autofac.IngredientModule,
    ➥Ploeh.Samples.Menu.Autofac" />
</modules>
```

These three examples are functionally equivalent.

TIP Autofac Modules let you package and structure your container configuration code. Use them instead of inline configuration; it will make your COMPOSITION ROOT more readable.

Using Modules, we can configure an Autofac container in any way we like: CODE AS CONFIGURATION, AUTO-REGISTRATION, or with XML; or we can mix all three approaches. Once a container is configured, we can ask it to resolve services.

This section introduced the Autofac DI CONTAINER and demonstrated the fundamental mechanics: how to configure a `ContainerBuilder` and subsequently use the constructed container to resolve services. Resolving services is easily done with a single call to the `Resolve` method, so the complexity involves configuring the container. This can be done in several different ways, including imperative code and XML. Until now, we've only looked at the most basic API so there are more advanced areas we've yet to cover. One of the most important topics is how to manage component lifetime.

13.2 *Managing lifetime*

In chapter 8, we discussed LIFETIME MANAGEMENT, including the most common conceptual lifetime styles such as SINGLETON and TRANSIENT. Autofac supports several different lifestyles and enables you to configure the lifetime of all services. The lifestyles shown in table 13.2 are available as part of the API.

NOTE In Autofac, lifestyles are called *instance scopes*.

Table 13.2 Autofac lifestyles

Name	Comments
Per Dependency	Standard TRANSIENT. This is the default instance scope. Instances are tracked by the container.
Single Instance	Standard SINGLETON.
Per Lifetime Scope	Ties the lifetime of components together with a container scope (see section 13.2.1).
Contextual	A finer-grained version of Per Lifetime Scope.

Autofac's implementation of TRANSIENT and SINGLETON are equivalent to the general lifestyles described in chapter 8, so I won't spend much time on them in this chapter.

TIP The default TRANSIENT lifestyle is the safest, but not always the most efficient, choice. SINGLETON is a more efficient choice for thread-safe services, but you must remember to explicitly register those services like that.

In this section, you'll see how we can define lifestyles for components in both code and XML. We'll also look at Autofac's concept of *lifetime scopes* and how they can be used to implement WEB REQUEST CONTEXT and similar lifestyles. At the end of this section, you should be able to use Autofac's lifestyles in your own application.

Let's start by reviewing how to configure instance scopes for components.

13.2.1 *Configuring instance scope*

In this section, we'll review how to manage component instance scopes with Autofac. Instance scope is configured as part of registering components, and we can define it in both code and XML. We'll look at each in turn.

CONFIGURING INSTANCE SCOPE WITH CODE

Instance scope is defined as part of the registrations we make on a `ContainerBuilder` instance. It's as easy as this:

```
builder.RegisterType<SauceBéarnaise>().SingleInstance();
```

This configures the concrete `SauceBéarnaise` class as a SINGLETON so that the same instance is returned each time `SauceBéarnaise` is requested. If we want to map an ABSTRACTION to a concrete class with a specific lifetime, we can use the usual `As` method and place the `SingleInstance` method call wherever we like. These two registrations are functionally equivalent:

```
builder                              builder
    .RegisterType<SauceBéarnaise>()      .RegisterType<SauceBéarnaise>()
    .As<IIngredient>()                   .SingleInstance()
    .SingleInstance();                   .As<IIngredient>();
```

Notice that the only difference is that we've swapped the `As` and `SingleInstance` method calls. Personally, I prefer the sequence on the left because the `RegisterType` and `As` method calls form a mapping between concrete class and ABSTRACTION; keeping them close together makes the registration more readable, and we can then state the instance scope as a modification to the mapping.

Although TRANSIENT is the default instance scope we can still explicitly state it. These two examples are equivalent:

```
builder                              builder
    .RegisterType<SauceBéarnaise>();     .RegisterType<SauceBéarnaise>()
                                         .InstancePerDependency();
```

Configuring instance scope for convention-based registrations is done using the same method as for singular registrations:

```
builder.RegisterAssemblyTypes(typeof(Steak).Assembly)
    .As<IIngredient>()
    .SingleInstance();
```

We can use `SingleInstance` and the other related methods to define the instance scope for all registrations in a convention. In the previous example, we define all `IIngredient`s as SINGLETONS.

In the same way that we can register components from both code and XML, we can also configure instance scope in both places.

CONFIGURING INSTANCE SCOPE WITH XML

When you need to define components in XML, you'll also want to be able to configure their instance scopes in the same place. This is easily done as part of the XML schema you already saw in section 13.1.2. You can use the optional `instance-scope` attribute to declare the lifestyle:

```
<component type="Ploeh.Samples.MenuModel.Steak"
           service="Ploeh.Samples.MenuModel.IIngredient"
           instance-scope="single-instance" />
```

Compared to the example in section 13.1.2, the only difference is the added `instance-scope` attribute that configures the instance as a SINGLETON. When you previously omitted the instance-scope attribute, Autofac's TRANSIENT default was automatically used.

In both code and XML, it's easy to configure instance scopes for components. In all cases it's done in a rather declarative fashion. Although configuration is easy, you must not forget that some lifestyles involve long-lived objects that use resources as long as they're around.

RELEASING COMPONENTS

As discussed in section 8.2.2, it's important to release objects when we're done with them. Autofac has no explicit `Release` method but instead uses a concept called *lifetime scopes*. A *lifetime scope* can be regarded as a throw-away copy of the container. As figure 13.5 illustrates, it defines a boundary where components can be reused.

A *lifetime scope* defines a derived container that we can use for a particular duration or purpose; the most obvious example is a web request. We spawn a scope from a container so that the scope inherits all the SINGLETONS tracked by the parent container, but the scope also acts as a container of "local SINGLETONS." When a lifetime scoped component is requested from a lifetime scope, we always receive the same instance. The difference from true SINGLETONS is that if we query a second scope, we'll get another instance.

TRANSIENT components still act as they should, whether we resolve them from the root container or a lifetime scope.

> **TIP** We can use lifetime scopes to implement context-based lifestyles such as the WEB REQUEST CONTEXT lifestyle: create a new lifetime scope at the start of each context and use it to resolve components. Then dispose of the scope when the request ends. However, for web request scope, Autofac has built-in integration to both Web Forms and ASP.NET MVC, so we don't need to do much of this work ourselves.

One of the important features of lifetime scopes is that they allow us to properly release components when the scope completes. We create a new scope with the `BeginLifetimeScope` method and release all appropriate components by invoking its `Dispose` method:

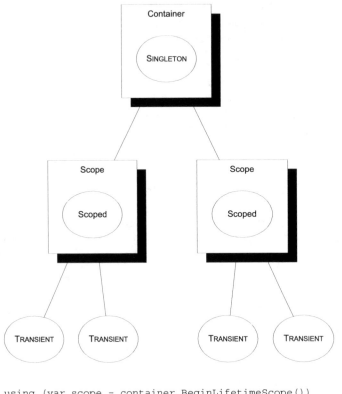

Figure 13.5   Autofac *lifetime scopes* act as containers that can share components for a limited duration or purpose. A lifetime scoped component is a Singleton within that scope. No matter how many times we ask a scope for such a component, we get the same instance. Another scope will have its own instance, and the parent container manages the truly shared Singletons. Transient components are never shared, but will be decommissioned when the scope is disposed of.

```
using (var scope = container.BeginLifetimeScope())
{
    var meal = scope.Resolve<IMeal>();                    Consume
                                                          meal
}
```

A new scope is created from the container by invoking the BeginLifetimeScope method. The return value implements IDisposable, so you can wrap it in a using scope. Because it also implements the same interface that the container itself implements, you can use the scope to resolve components in exactly the same way as with the container itself.

When we're done with the lifetime scope, we can dispose of it. When using a using scope this happens automatically when we exit the scope, but we can obviously also choose to explicitly dispose of it by invoking the Dispose method. When we dispose of scope, we also release all the components that were created by the lifetime scope; here it means that you release the meal object graph.

NOTE   Remember that releasing a disposable component isn't the same as disposing of it. It's a signal to the container that the component is eligible for decommissioning. If the component is Transient or lifetime scoped, it will be disposed of; it will remain active if it's a Singleton.

Earlier in this section, you already saw how to configure components as SINGLETONS or TRANSIENTS. Configuring a component to have its instance scope tied to a lifetime scope is done in a similar way:

```
builder.RegisterType<SauceBéarnaise>()
    .As<IIngredient>()
    .InstancePerLifetimeScope();
```

Similar to the `SingleInstance` and `InstancePerDependency` methods, you can use the `InstancePerLifetimeScope` method to state that the component's lifetime should follow the lifetime scope that created the instance.

> **TIP** Autofac tracks most, even disposable TRANSIENT, components, so it's important to remember to resolve all components from a lifetime scope and dispose of the scope after use.

Due to their very nature, SINGLETONS are never released for the lifetime of the container itself. Still, we can release even those components if we don't need the container any longer. This is done by disposing the container itself:

```
container.Dispose();
```

In practice this isn't nearly as important because the lifetime of a container tends to correlate closely with the lifetime of the application it supports. We normally keep the container around as long as the application runs, so we'd only dispose of it when the application shuts down, in which case memory would be reclaimed by the operating system in any case.

Lifetime scopes enable us to address many of the scenarios where we'd normally want to use a WEB REQUEST CONTEXT or another contextual lifestyle. This is the idiomatic way to implement custom lifetimes with Autofac.

This completes our tour of LIFETIME MANAGEMENT with Autofac. Components can be configured with mixed instance scopes, and this is even true when we register multiple implementations of the same ABSTRACTION. We have yet to look at how to work with multiple components, so let's now turn our attention in that direction.

13.3 *Working with multiple components*

DI CONTAINERS thrive on distinctness but have a hard time with ambiguity. When using CONSTRUCTOR INJECTION, a single constructor is preferred over overloaded constructors because it's evident which constructor to use when there's no choice. This is also the case when mapping from ABSTRACTIONS to concrete types. If we attempt to map multiple concrete types to the same ABSTRACTION, we introduce ambiguity.

Despite the undesirable qualities of ambiguity, we often need to work with multiple implementations of a single interface. This can be the case in these situations:

- Different concrete types should be used for different consumers.
- DEPENDENCIES are sequences.
- Decorators are in use.

In this section, we'll look at each of these cases and see how Autofac addresses each one in turn. When we're done, you should be able to register and resolve components even when multiple implementations of the same ABSTRACTION are in play.

Let's first see how we can provide more fine-grained control than AUTO-WIRING provides.

13.3.1 *Selecting among multiple candidates*

AUTO-WIRING is convenient and powerful but provides us with little control. As long as all ABSTRACTIONS are distinctly mapped to concrete types we have no problems, but as soon as we introduce more implementations of the same interface, ambiguity rears its ugly head.

Let's first recap how Autofac deals with multiple registrations of the same ABSTRACTION.

CONFIGURING MULTIPLE IMPLEMENTATIONS OF THE SAME SERVICE

As you saw in section 13.1.2, you can register multiple implementations of the same interface:

```
builder.RegisterType<SauceBéarnaise>().As<IIngredient>();
builder.RegisterType<Steak>().As<IIngredient>();
```

This example registers both the `Steak` and `SauceBéarnaise` classes as the `IIngredient` service. The last registration wins, so if we resolve `IIngredient` with `container.Resolve<IIngredient>()`, we'll get a `Steak` instance.

TIP The last registration of a given service wins. It defines the default instance for that type.

We can also ask the container to resolve all `IIngredient` components. Autofac has no dedicated method to do that, but instead relies on *relationship types*.[5] A *relationship type* is a type that indicates a relationship that the container can interpret. As an example, we can use `IEnumerable<T>` to indicate that we want all services of a given type:

```
var ingredients = container.Resolve<IEnumerable<IIngredient>>();
```

Notice that we use the normal `Resolve` method, but that we request `IEnumerable<IIngredient>`. Autofac interprets this as a convention and gives us all the `IIngredient` components it has.

TIP As an alternative to `IEnumerable<T>`, we can also request an array. The results are equivalent: in both cases we get all the components of the requested type.

If there are registrations that can't be resolved when we request all services of a type, Autofac throws an exception explaining that there are DEPENDENCIES that can't be satisfied. This is consistent with the behavior when we resolve a single component, but different from the way that Castle Windsor or MEF behaves.

---

[5] Nicholas Blumhardt, *The Relationship Zoo*, 2010, http://nblumhardt.com/2010/01/the-relationship-zoo/

When we register components, we can give each registration a name that we can later use to select among the different components:

```
builder.RegisterType<Steak>()
    .Named<IIngredient>("meat");
builder.RegisterType<SauceBéarnaise>()
    .Named<IIngredient>("sauce");
```

As always, we start out with the `RegisterType` method, but instead of following up with the `As` method, we use the `Named` method to specify a service type as well as a name. This enables us to resolve named services by supplying the same name to the `ResolveNamed` method:

```
var meat = container.ResolveNamed<IIngredient>("meat");
var sauce = container.ResolveNamed<IIngredient>("sauce");
```

> **NOTE** A named component doesn't count as a default component. If we only register named components, we can't resolve a default instance of the service. However, nothing prevents us from also registering a default (unnamed) component with the `As` method, and we can even do it in the same statement by method chaining.

Naming components with strings is a fairly common feature of DI CONTAINERS, but Autofac also enables us to identify components with arbitrary keys:

```
var meatKey = new object();
builder.RegisterType<Steak>().Keyed<IIngredient>(meatKey);
```

The key can be any object, and we can subsequently use it to resolve the component:

```
var meat = container.ResolveKeyed<IIngredient>(meatKey);
```

Given that we should always resolve services in a single COMPOSITION ROOT, we should normally not expect to deal with such ambiguity on this level.

> **TIP** If you find yourself invoking the `Resolve` method with a specific name or key, consider if you can change your approach to be less ambiguous.

However, we can use named or keyed instances to select among multiple alternatives when configuring DEPENDENCIES for a given service.

REGISTERING NAMED DEPENDENCIES

As useful as AUTO-WIRING is, sometimes we need to override the normal behavior to provide fine-grained control over which DEPENDENCIES go where, but it may also be that we need to address an ambiguous API. As an example, consider this constructor:

```
public ThreeCourseMeal(ICourse entrée,
    ICourse mainCourse, ICourse dessert)
```

In this case, you have three identically typed DEPENDENCIES, each of which represents a *different* concept. In most cases, you want to map each of the DEPENDENCIES to a separate type. The following listing shows how you could choose to register the `ICourse` mappings.

Listing 13.2   Registering named courses

```
builder.RegisterType<Rillettes>()
    .Named<ICourse>("entrée");
builder.RegisterType<CordonBleu>()
    .Named<ICourse>("mainCourse");
builder.RegisterType<MousseAuChocolat>()
    .Named<ICourse>("dessert");
```

Here, you register three named components, mapping the Rillettes to an instance named "entrée," CordonBleu to an instance named "mainCourse," and the MousseAuChocolat to an instance named "dessert."

Given this configuration, you can now register the ThreeCourseMeal class with the named registrations. This turns out to be surprisingly complex. In the following listing, I'll first show you what it looks like, and then we'll subsequently pick the example apart to understand what's going on.

Listing 13.3   Overriding AUTO-WIRING

```
builder.RegisterType<ThreeCourseMeal>()
    .As<IMeal>()                              ❶ Defines
    .WithParameter(                             parameter      ❷ Filters
        (p, c) => p.Name == "entrée",
        (p, c) =>                             ❸ Defines value
            c.ResolveNamed<ICourse>("entrée"))
    .WithParameter(
        (p, c) => p.Name == "mainCourse",
        (p, c) =>
            c.ResolveNamed<ICourse>("mainCourse"))
    .WithParameter(
        (p, c) => p.Name == "dessert",
        (p, c) =>
            c.ResolveNamed<ICourse>("dessert"));
```

The WithParameter method ❶ enables you to provide parameter values for the ThreeCourseMeal constructor. One of its overloads takes two arguments. The first one is a predicate that determines whether a parameter is targeted by this particular invocation of the method. For the first parameter you state that it only deals with the parameter called *entrée* ❷. If that expression is true, the second code block is executed to provide the value for the *entrée* parameter. The c parameter is an instance of IComponentContext that you can use to resolve the *entrée* named component ❸.

> **TIP**   The WithParameter method arguments represent a variation of the Tester-Doer pattern.[6]

Let's take a closer look at what's going on here. The WithParameter method really wraps around the ResolvedParameter class that has this constructor:

---

[6] Krzysztof Cwalina and Brad Abrams, *Framework Design Guidelines: Conventions, Idioms, and Patterns for Reusable .NET Libraries* (New York: Addison-Wesley, 2006), 203.

```
public ResolvedParameter(
    Func<ParameterInfo, IComponentContext, bool> predicate,
    Func<ParameterInfo, IComponentContext, object> valueAccessor);
```

The predicate parameter is a test that determines whether the valueAccessor delegate will be invoked: when predicate returns true, valueAccessor is invoked to provide the value for the parameter. Both delegates take the same input: information about the parameter in the form of a ParameterInfo object, and an IComponentContext that can be used to resolve other components. When Autofac uses the ResolvedParameter instances, it provides both of these values when it invokes the delegates.

Sometimes there's no other way than to painstakingly use the WithParameter method for each and every constructor parameter; but in other cases we can take advantage of conventions.

RESOLVING NAMED COMPONENTS BY CONVENTION

If you examine listing 13.3 closely, you may notice a repetitive pattern. Each call to WithParameter addresses only a single constructor parameter, but each valueAccessor does the same thing: it uses the IComponentContext to resolve an ICourse component with the same name as the parameter.

There's no requirement that says we must name the component after the constructor parameter, but whenever this is the case, we can take advantage of this convention and rewrite listing 13.3 in a much simpler way; the following listing demonstrates how.

Listing 13.4 Overriding AUTO-WIRING with a convention

```
builder.RegisterType<ThreeCourseMeal>()
    .As<IMeal>()
    .WithParameter(
        (p, c) => true,
        (p, c) => c.ResolveNamed(p.Name, p.ParameterType));
```

It may be a little surprising, but you can address all three constructor parameters of the ThreeCourseMeal class with the same WithParameter call. You do that by stating that this instance will handle any parameter Autofac might throw at it. Because you only use this method to configure the ThreeCourseMeal class, the convention only applies within this limited scope.

As the predicate always returns true, the second code block will be invoked for all three constructor parameters. In all three cases it will ask the IComponentContext to resolve a component that has the same name and type as the parameter. This is functionally the same as you did in listing 13.3.

> **WARNING** Identifying parameters by their names is convenient but not refactoring-safe. If you rename a parameter, you may break the configuration (depending on your refactoring tool).

Overriding AUTO-WIRING by explicitly mapping parameters to named components is a universally applicable solution. We can do this even if we configure the named components in one Module and the consumer in a completely different Module because the only identification that ties a named component together with a parameter is the name. This is always possible, but can be brittle if we have a lot of names to manage. When the original reason prompting us to use named components is to deal with ambiguity, a better solution is to design our own API to get rid of that ambiguity. It often leads to a better overall design.

In the next section, you'll see how to use the less ambiguous and more flexible approach where you allow any number of courses in a meal. To this end, you must learn how Autofac deals with lists and sequences.

13.3.2 *Wiring sequences*

In section 10.3.2, we discussed how to refactor an explicit `ThreeCourseMeal` class to the more general-purpose `Meal` class with this constructor:

```
public Meal(IEnumerable<ICourse> courses)
```

In this section, we'll look at how we can configure Autofac to wire up `Meal` instances with appropriate `ICourse` DEPENDENCIES. When we're done, you should have a good idea of the options available when you need to configure instances with sequences of DEPENDENCIES.

AUTO-WIRING SEQUENCES

Autofac has a rather good understanding of sequences, so if we want to use all registered components of a given service, AUTO-WIRING just works. As an example, given the configured `ICourse` instances in listing 13.2, you can configure the `IMeal` service like this:

```
builder.RegisterType<Meal>().As<IMeal>();
```

Notice that this is a completely standard mapping from a concrete type to an ABSTRACTION. Autofac will automatically understand the `Meal` constructor and determine that the correct course of action is to resolve all `ICourse` components. When you resolve `IMeal`, you get a `Meal` instance with the `ICourse` components from listing 13.2: `Rillettes`, `CordonBleu`, and `MousseAuChocolat`.

Autofac automatically handles sequences, and unless we specify otherwise, it does what we'd expect it to do: it resolves a sequence of DEPENDENCIES to all registered components of that type. Only when we need to explicitly pick only some components from a larger set do we need to do more. Let's see how we can do that.

PICKING ONLY SOME COMPONENTS FROM A LARGER SET

Autofac's default strategy of injecting all components is often the correct policy, but as figure 13.6 shows, there may be cases where we want to pick only some registered components from the larger set of all registered components.

When we previously let Autofac AUTO-WIRE all configured instances, it corresponded to the situation depicted on the right side of figure 13.6. If we want to register a component as is shown on the left side, we must explicitly define which components should be used.

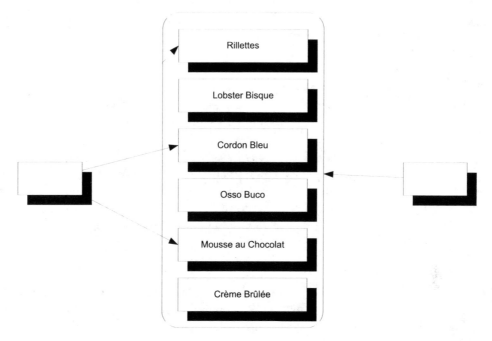

Figure 13.6 In the situation on the left, we wish to explicitly select only certain DEPENDENCIES from the larger list of all registered components. This is different from the situation on the right, where we indiscriminately want them all.

In order to achieve this, you can once more utilize the `WithParameter` method the way you did in listings 13.3 and 13.4. This time around, you're dealing with the `Meal` constructor that only takes a single parameter. The following listing demonstrates how you can implement the value-providing part of `WithParameter` to explicitly pick named components off the `IComponentContext`.

Listing 13.5 Injecting named components into a sequence

```
builder.RegisterType<Meal>()
    .As<IMeal>()
    .WithParameter(
        (p, c) => true,
        (p, c) => new[]
        {
            c.ResolveNamed<ICourse>("entrée"),
            c.ResolveNamed<ICourse>("mainCourse"),
            c.ResolveNamed<ICourse>("dessert")
        });
```

As you saw in section 13.3.1, the `WithParameter` method takes two delegates as input parameters. The first is a predicate that's used to determine if the second delegate should be invoked. In this case, I decided to be a bit lazy and return true. You know that the `Meal` class has only a single constructor parameter, so this will turn out to work. However, if you later refactor the `Meal` class to take a second constructor parameter, this may not work correctly anymore, so it might be safer to define an explicit check for the parameter name.

The second delegate provides the value for the parameter. You use the `IComponent-Context` to resolve three named components into an array. The result is an array of `ICourse`, which is compatible with `IEnumerable<ICourse>`.

Autofac natively understands sequences; unless we need to explicitly pick only some components from all services of a given type, Autofac automatically does the right thing. AUTO-WIRING works not only with single instances, but also for sequences, and the container maps a sequence to all configured instances of the corresponding type.

Consumers that rely on sequences of DEPENDENCIES may be the most intuitive use of multiple instances of the same ABSTRACTION, but before we leave this subject completely, we need to look at one last, and perhaps a bit surprising, case where multiple instances come into play.

13.3.3 *Wiring Decorators*

In section 9.1.2, we discussed how the Decorator design pattern is useful when implementing CROSS-CUTTING CONCERNS. By definition, Decorators introduce multiple types of the same ABSTRACTION. At the very least we have two implementations of an ABSTRACTION: the Decorator itself and the decorated type. If we stack the Decorators, we may have even more.

This is another example of having multiple registrations of the same service. Unlike the previous sections, these registrations aren't conceptually equal, but rather DEPENDENCIES of each other. In this section, you'll see two different ways to configure Autofac to deal with this pattern.

DECORATING WITH WITHPARAMETER

The `WithParameter` method offers a versatile way to define how components are created and injected. In sections 13.3.1 and 13.3.2, you saw how you could use it to select specific components for constructor parameters. It's also a good option to provide parameters for Decorators.

Let's see how you can use it to configure the `Breading` class, which is a Decorator of `IIngredient`. It uses CONSTRUCTOR INJECTION to receive the instance it should decorate:

```
public Breading(IIngredient ingredient)
```

To make a Cotoletta, you'd like to decorate a `VealCutlet` (another `IIngredient`) with the `Breading` class. Another way to look at this is that you want to inject a `VealCutlet` into `Breading`; the following listing demonstrates how you can use the `WithParameter` method to do that.

Listing 13.6 Decorating with `WithParameter`

```
builder.RegisterType<VealCutlet>().Named<IIngredient>("cutlet");
builder.RegisterType<Breading>()
    .As<IIngredient>()
```

```
.WithParameter(
    (p, c) => p.ParameterType == typeof(IIngredient),
    (p, c) => c.ResolveNamed<IIngredient>("cutlet"));
```

Breading is the Decorator, but you also need something to decorate, so you register VealCutlet as a named component. In this example, you register VealCutlet before Breading, but you could also have done it the other way around; the order doesn't matter.

For the Breading registration, you use the WithParameter method to define the *ingredient* parameter of the Breading constructor. You implement the predicate by testing that the parameter type is IIngredient, and provide the value for the parameter by resolving the *cutlet* named component from the provided IComponentContext.

In this example, you used a named registration of IIngredient to register the VealCutlet component. This makes the Breading component the default IIngredient component. Another alternative is to register VealCutlet as both IIngredient and VealCutlet itself. The next example demonstrates that approach and combines it with a strongly typed delegate.

DECORATING WITH DELEGATES

Instead of referring to a constructor parameter by type or name, we can write a strongly typed code block that *uses* the constructor:

```
builder.RegisterType<VealCutlet>()
    .As<IIngredient, VealCutlet>();
builder.Register(c => new Breading(c.Resolve<VealCutlet>()))
    .As<IIngredient>();
```

As an alternative to registering VealCutlet as a named component, you can also register it as both IIngredient and VealCutlet itself. When you do that, it's important that you do it before registering Breading, because otherwise VealCutlet would become the default IIngredient component.

Instead of the RegisterType method that you've mostly been using so far, you can also register a service with a method called Register. There are two overloads of this method, and they both take as input a delegate that creates the service in question. To register the IIngredient service, you implement a code block that creates a new Breading instance by directly invoking the constructor. To supply a value for the constructor's *ingredient* parameter you resolve the VealCutlet type from the supplied IComponentContext. This is possible because you registered VealCutlet as a concrete type as well as IIngredient.

> **NOTE** You could also have resolved the VealCutlet by name if you had registered it as a named component as you did in the previous example.

When you ask the container to resolve IIngredient, it will pass an IComponent-Context as input to the code block you defined in the Register method. When the code block executes, the VealCutlet instance is resolved from the context and passed to the Breading constructor, where the Breading instance is returned.

The advantage of this is that in the code block you write code that *uses* the `Breading` constructor. This is a line of code like any other line of code, so it's checked by the compiler. This provides you with a great deal of confidence that if the `Register` method compiles, the `VealCutlet` will be correctly decorated.

Although strong typing is safer, it also requires more maintenance. If you subsequently decide to add another constructor parameter to the `Breading` constructor, the code block no longer compiles and you must manually address the issue. This wouldn't be necessary if you had used the `WithParameter` method because Autofac would have been able to sort out the new parameter for you with AUTO-WIRING.

As you've seen in this section, there are different ways you can configure Decorators. The strongly typed approach is a bit safer but may require more maintenance. The more weakly typed API is more flexible and enables Autofac to deal with changes to your API, but at the expense of less type safety.

> **NOTE**   In this section, we didn't discuss runtime INTERCEPTION. Although Autofac has SEAMS that enable INTERCEPTION, it has no built-in support for dynamically emitting Proxies. It's possible to use those SEAMS to use another library (such as Castle Dynamic Proxy) to emit such classes, but because this isn't part of Autofac itself, it's beyond the scope of this chapter.[7]

Autofac lets us work with multiple instances in several different ways. We can register components as alternatives to each other, as peers resolved as sequences, or as hierarchical Decorators. In many cases, Autofac will figure out what to do, but we can always explicitly define how services are composed if we need more explicit control.

This may also be the case when we need to deal with APIs that deviate from CONSTRUCTOR INJECTION. So far, you've seen how to register components, including how to specify instance scopes and how to deal with multiple components; however, until now, you've allowed the container to wire DEPENDENCIES by implicitly assuming that all components use CONSTRUCTOR INJECTION. This isn't always the case, so in the next section, we'll review how to deal with classes that must be instantiated in special ways.

13.4   *Registering difficult APIs*

Until now, we've considered how we can configure components that use CONSTRUCTOR INJECTION. One of the many benefits of CONSTRUCTOR INJECTION is that DI CONTAINERS such as Autofac can easily understand how to compose and create all classes in a dependency graph.

But this becomes less clear when APIs are less well behaved. In this section, you'll see how to deal with primitive constructor arguments, static factories, and PROPERTY INJECTION. These all require our special attention. Let's start by looking at classes that take primitive types, such as strings or integers as constructor arguments.

---

[7] However, see http://code.google.com/p/autofac/wiki/DynamicProxy2 for more information.

13.4.1 *Configuring primitive Dependencies*

As long as we inject ABSTRACTIONS into consumers, all is well, but it becomes more difficult when a constructor depends on a primitive type, such as a string, a number, or an enum. This is particularly the case for data access implementations that take a connection string as constructor parameter, but is a more general issue that applies to all strings and numbers.

Conceptually, it doesn't always make much sense to register a string or number as a component in a container. But with Autofac, this is at least possible.

Consider, as an example, this constructor:

```
public ChiliConCarne(Spiciness spiciness)
```

In this example, Spiciness is an enum:

```
public enum Spiciness
{
    Mild = 0,
    Medium,
    Hot
}
```

WARNING As a rule of thumb, enums are code smells and should be refactored to polymorphic classes.[8] But they serve us well for this example.

If you want all consumers of Spiciness to use the same value, you can register Spiciness and ChiliConCarne independently of each other:

```
builder.Register<Spiciness>(c => Spiciness.Medium);
builder.RegisterType<ChiliConCarne>().As<ICourse>();
```

When you subsequently resolve ChiliConCarne, it will have a Medium Spiciness, as will all other components with a DEPENDENCY on Spiciness.

If you'd rather control the relationship between ChiliConCarne and Spiciness on a finer level, you can use the WithParameter method that same way you did in listings 13.4, 13.5, and 13.6:

```
builder.RegisterType<ChiliConCarne>()
    .As<ICourse>()
    .WithParameter("spiciness", Spiciness.Hot);
```

Because you want to supply a concrete value for the *spiciness* parameter, you can use another overload of the WithParameter method that takes a parameter name and a value. This overload delegates to the other WithParameter by creating a NamedParameter instance from the parameter name and value; NamedParameter also derives from Parameter like ResolvedParameter does.

Both of the options described here leverage AUTO-WIRING to provide a concrete value to a component. As we discussed in section 13.3, this has advantages and disadvantages. If you want a more strongly typed configuration that invokes the constructor or a static factory, you can do this as well.

---

[8] Martin Fowler et al, *Refactoring: Improving the Design of Existing Code* (New York: Addison-Wesley, 1999), 82.

13.4.2 *Registering objects with code blocks*

Another option for creating a component with a primitive value is to use the `Register` method that enables you to supply a delegate that creates the component:

```
builder.Register<ICourse>(c =>
    new ChiliConCarne(Spiciness.Hot));
```

You already saw the `Register` method when we discussed Decorators in section 13.3.3. The `ChiliConCarne` constructor will be invoked with `Hot` Spiciness every time the `ICourse` component is resolved.

NOTE The `Register` method is type-safe but disables AUTO-WIRING.

When it comes to the `ChiliConCarne` class, you have a choice between AUTO-WIRING and using a code block. But other classes are more restrictive: they can't be instantiated through a public constructor. Instead, you must use some sort of factory to create instances of the type. This is always troublesome for DI CONTAINERS because, by default, they look after public constructors.

Consider this example constructor for the public `JunkFood` class:

```
internal JunkFood(string name)
```

Even though the `JunkFood` class is public, the constructor is internal. Obviously, instances of `JunkFood` should be created through the static `JunkFoodFactory` class:

```
public static class JunkFoodFactory
{
    public static IMeal Create(string name)
    {
        return new JunkFood(name);
    }
}
```

From Autofac's perspective, this is a problematic API because there are no unambiguous and well-established conventions around static factories. It needs help—and you can give it to it by providing a code block it can execute to create the instance:

```
builder.Register(c =>
    JunkFoodFactory.Create("chicken meal"));
```

This time, you use the `Register` method to create the component by invoking a static factory within the code block. `JunkFoodFactory.Create` will be invoked every time `IMeal` is resolved and the result will be returned.

When we end up writing the code to create the instance, how is this in any way better than invoking the code directly? By using a code block inside a `Register` method call, we still gain something:

- We map from `IMeal` to `JunkFood`.
- Instance scope can still be configured. Although the code block will be invoked to create the instance, it may not be invoked *every time* the instance is requested—by default it does, but if we change it to a SINGLETON, the code block will only be invoked once and the result cached and reused thereafter.

The last common deviation from CONSTRUCTOR INJECTION we'll examine here is PROPERTY INJECTION.

13.4.3 *Wiring with Property Injection*

PROPERTY INJECTION is a less well-defined form of DI because we aren't forced by the compiler to assign a value to a writable property. This is also the case for Autofac, which will leave writable properties alone unless we explicitly ask it to do something about them.

Consider this `CaesarSalad` class:

```
public class CaesarSalad : ICourse
{
    public IIngredient Extra { get; set; }
}
```

It's a common misconception that a Caesar Salad includes chicken; this isn't true. Fundamentally, a Caesar Salad is a *salad*, but it tastes great with chicken, so many restaurants allow customers to order chicken as an extra ingredient in their salad. The `CaesarSalad` class models this by exposing a writable property named `Extra`.

If you configure only the `CaesarSalad` without explicitly addressing the `Extra` property, the property won't be assigned. You can still resolve the instance, but the property will have the default value that the constructor assigns to it (if any).

There are several ways you can configure the `CaesarSalad` so that the `Extra` property will be appropriately populated. The easiest is to use the `PropertiesAutowired` method:

```
builder.RegisterType<CaesarSalad>()
    .As<ICourse>()
    .PropertiesAutowired();
builder.RegisterType<Chicken>().As<IIngredient>();
```

As part of the ordinary fluent Registration API, you can invoke the `Properties-Autowired` method to tell Autofac that it should AUTO-WIRE the writable properties of the `CaesarSalad` class. Autofac will only AUTO-WIRE those properties that it knows how to fill so you also register `Chicken` as an `IIngredient`—if you hadn't done that, the `Extra` property would've been ignored.

When you resolve `ICourse` based on this registration, you'll get back a `Caesar-Salad` instance with a `Chicken` instance assigned to its `Extra` property.

If you want more granular control that the sweeping statement expressed by the `PropertiesAutowired` method, you can use the `WithProperty` method that's similar to the `WithParameter` method you've used so many times already:

```
builder.RegisterType<Chicken>().As<IIngredient>();
builder.RegisterType<CaesarSalad>()
    .As<ICourse>(
    .WithProperty(new ResolvedParameter(
        (p, c) => p.Member.Name == "set_Extra",
        (p, c) => c.Resolve<IIngredient>())));
```

The `WithProperty` method mirrors the `WithParameter` method you already know and love: it takes a single `Parameter` argument and also has an overload that takes a property name and value.

To properly resolve the `Extra` method, we can use the trusted `ResolvedParameter` class. When it comes to properties, the predicate we supply has a little twist because Autofac invokes the code block with a `ParameterInfo`, not a `PropertyInfo`; the p parameter represents the *value* parameter that's always implicitly available when implementing a property,[9] so we need to navigate to the `Member` that defines this parameter. This is a `MethodInfo` instance, so we need to know a little bit about how C# properties are implemented at the IL level: the `Extra` property is really a method named `set_Extra`.

With the predicate in place, it's a breeze to implement the value provider by resolving `IIngredient` from the supplied `IComponentContext`.

Using the `WithProperty` method gives us more fine-grained control over PROPERTY INJECTION while we retain loose coupling. If we want a strongly typed alternative, this is also possible.

Autofac enables us to supply code blocks that will be invoked when certain events occur during a component's lifetime. We can hook into these events to fill properties while a component is being built.

One of these events is the `OnActivating` event that Autofac raises whenever it creates a new component instance. You can use this event to populate the `Extra` property before Autofac returns the `CaesarSalad` instance:

```
builder.RegisterType<Chicken>().As<IIngredient>();
builder.RegisterType<CaesarSalad>()
    .As<ICourse>()
    .OnActivating(e =>
        e.Instance.Extra = e.Context.Resolve<IIngredient>());
```

The `OnActivating` method gives you an opportunity to do something to the component before `Autofac` returns it to whoever requested it. As a single parameter, it takes an `Action<IActivatingEventArgs<CaesarSalad>>` that you can use to implement the post-processing logic of your choice. The e parameter represents the event args and it has an `Instance` property of the `CaesarSalad` type and a `Context` property you can use to resolve other components. You use this combination to resolve `IIngredient` and assign the result to the `Extra` property. When you resolve `ICourse` you'll get a `CaesarSalad` instance with `Extra` `Chicken`.

Because the `Instance` property is tied to the generic type argument of the `IActivatingEventArgs<T>` interface, this approach is strongly typed with the advantages and disadvantages this entails.

In this section, you've seen how you can use Autofac to deal with more difficult creational APIs. You can use various derivations of the abstract `Parameter` class to wire constructors and properties with services to maintain a semblance of AUTO-WIRING, or

---

[9] I assume this must be confusing to VB.NET developers.

you can use the `Register` method with a code block for a more type-safe approach. PROPERTY INJECTION is generally well-supported both for AUTO-WIRING and for strongly typed assignment.

13.5 Summary

In this chapter, you got a taste of the Autofac DI CONTAINER; although it's a second-generation container, it's still fairly comprehensive and addresses many of the more tricky situations we typically encounter when we use DI CONTAINERS. Its architecture is built directly on the features of .NET 3.5 and C# 3.0, but even though it internally utilizes delegates and code blocks, the general API is fairly easy to use.

An important overall theme for Autofac seems to be one of explicitness. It doesn't attempt to guess what we mean, but rather offers an easy-to-use API that provides us with options to explicitly enable features.

One example of this explicitness is that, contrary to many other DI CONTAINERS, Autofac enforces more strict separation of concerns between configuring and consuming a container. We configure components using a `ContainerBuilder` instance, but a `ContainerBuilder` can't resolve components. When we're done configuring a `ContainerBuilder`, we use it to build an `IContainer` that we can use to resolve components.

We can configure a `ContainerBuilder` in every conceivable way: through imperative code, through XML, or by defining conventions, and we can package configurations into Modules.

The way Autofac addresses LIFETIME MANAGEMENT is a bit different than other DI CONTAINERS. Standard lifestyles such as TRANSIENT and SINGLETON are built-in, but other contextual lifestyles such as WEB REQUEST CONTEXT are addressed by *lifetime scopes* where we explicitly interact with the container to define a context within which components are resolved and released. This effectively addresses contextual lifestyles such as WEB REQUEST CONTEXT. On the other hand, this model doesn't enable us to custom implement a POOLED or cached lifestyle, and there's no other easy way to implement custom lifestyles with Autofac. According to Nicholas Blumhardt (the Autofac author), this has never come up in any discussion forum, so it's unlikely to be a real issue.[10] In most cases, the LIFETIME MANAGEMENT offered by Autofac is more than sufficient.

In closing, Autofac is a modern DI CONTAINER that offers a fairly comprehensive feature set. In the next chapter, we'll turn our attention to another second-generation DI CONTAINER: Unity.

---

[10] Private correspondence, 2011.

14

Unity

In the previous chapter, we looked at Autofac, which is one of the more recent DI CONTAINERS to enter the game. Another contemporary DI CONTAINER is Unity, which we'll examine in this chapter.

Autofac can be labeled as a *second-generation* DI CONTAINER because it was conceived and developed directly on .NET 3.5 without any legacy baggage from earlier versions of .NET. Although Unity appeared in roughly the same time frame, it took a more conservative approach. Unity 1.0 was released in May 2008, but targeted .NET 2.0, acknowledging that many development organizations would take their time before upgrading to .NET 3.5.

Unity is an *application block* from Microsoft's *patterns* & *practices* (p&p) group, but don't be fooled by the name: an *application block* is just a reusable library with associated documentation and samples.

448

> ### Unity and Enterprise Library
>
> Some people tend to mix up Unity and Enterprise Library (another p&p offering), or at least how they relate to each other. Let there be no doubt.
>
> Unity is a stand-alone library. It doesn't require Enterprise Library.
>
> Enterprise Library, on the other hand, ships with Unity included in the bundle, although even here it simply acts as the default container for Enterprise Library. Other DI CONTAINERS can replace Unity in Enterprise Library if necessary.

According to one completely unscientific internet poll,[1] Unity is the most widely used DI CONTAINER. This is surprising given its relatively late entry on the scene, but is likely to be related to the fact that Microsoft is behind it. The existing contenders, like Castle Windsor or StructureMap, haven't noticed any drop in interest, so it seems likely that Unity has introduced the concept of DI CONTAINERS to a completely new segment of users who weren't aware of it before.

In this chapter, we give Unity the exact same treatment that we give the other DI CONTAINERS. You'll see how Unity can be used to apply the principles and patterns laid forth in parts 1–3. Figure 14.1 shows the structure of the chapter.

The first section introduces the Unity API and should be considered a prerequisite for the next three sections. Each of these can be read independently of each other, although the fourth section uses some classes that are introduced in the third section. These classes have relatively self-explanatory names, so you may be able to read the fourth section without reading the third, but on the other hand, you may also find that you need to refer back to that section occasionally.

Like Castle Windsor, Unity supports several advanced features, such as custom lifetimes and INTERCEPTION.[2] This chapter provides examples of both, as well as many of

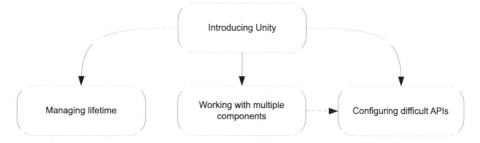

Figure 14.1   This chapter is divided into four sections. The first section provides an overall introduction to Unity and demonstrates how to configure and resolve components. The next three sections each deal with usage patterns that require a bit of extra attention; you can read them all in order, or you can skip some and read only the ones that interest you.

---

[1] Oliver Sturm, *Poll Results: IoC containers for .NET.* 2010, www.sturmnet.org/blog/2010/03/04/poll-results-ioc-containers-for-net

[2] We already covered INTERCEPTION with Castle Windsor in chapter 9, which kept the page count of chapter 10 down.

the more common DI CONTAINER features. This all adds up, which is why this is one of the longest chapters in the entire book.

This chapter should enable you to get started, as well as deal with the most common issues that may come up as you use Unity on a daily basis. It isn't a complete treatment of Unity, but you can get more information online.[3] Unity is perhaps the best-documented DI CONTAINER currently available.

You can read the chapter in isolation from the rest of part 4 specifically to learn about Unity, or you can read it together with the other chapters in part 4 to compare DI CONTAINERS. The focus of this chapter is to show how Unity relates to and implements the general DI patterns and principles described in the rest of the book.

14.1   *Introducing Unity*

In this section, you'll learn where to get Unity, what you get, and how you start using it. We'll also look at common configuration options, as well as how you package configuration settings into reusable components. Table 14.1 provides fundamental information that you're likely to need to get started.

Table 14.1   Unity at a glance

Question	Answer
Where do I get it?	http://unity.codeplex.com/ is a good place to start. Links to the latest release are available on the front page and will typically take you to the Microsoft Download Center. From Visual Studio 2010, you can also get it via NuGet. The package name is *Unity*.
What's in the download?	Contrary to other containers, the Unity download is an .msi file. When installed, it creates Start Menu shortcuts and places the binaries and source code in the Program Files folder. But once you have the binaries, you can Xcopy deploy them if you prefer that.
Which platforms are supported?	.NET 3.5 SP1 and 4.0. Silverlight 3 and 4.
How much does it cost?	Nothing. In a sense, Unity is open source software, although the p&p team doesn't accept patches.
Where can I get help?	Unity isn't a Microsoft *product*, but rather an offering from p&p. As such, it doesn't come with Microsoft's usual support, but there's a lively discussion forum at http://unity.codeplex.com/discussions.
On which version is the chapter based?	2.0.

As is also the case with Castle Windsor and StructureMap, using Unity follows a simple rhythm, illustrated by figure 14.2.

---

[3] http://msdn.microsoft.com/unity is a good place to start.

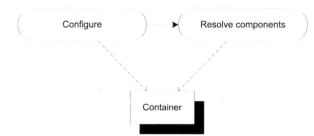

Figure 14.2 First, configure the container, and then resolve components from it. In the vast majority of cases, we create an instance of the `UnityContainer` class and completely configure it before we start resolving components from it. We resolve components from the same instance that we configure.

When you're done with this section, you should have a good feeling for the overall usage pattern of Unity, and you should be able to start using it in well-behaved scenarios where all components follow proper DI patterns such as CONSTRUCTOR INJECTION. We'll start with the simplest scenario to see how to resolve objects using a Unity container.

14.1.1 Resolving objects

The core service of any DI CONTAINER is to resolve components. In this section, we'll look at the API that enables us to resolve components with Unity.

In previous chapters, you learned that some containers (such as Castle Windsor) require you to explicitly configure *all* components with the container before you can resolve them, whereas other containers (such as StructureMap) implicitly figure out how to AUTO-WIRE requested components as long as they're concrete types with public constructors. In a sense you could say that Unity *defined* the latter category by being the first DI CONTAINER to include this feature, so the simplest possible use of it is this:

```
var container = new UnityContainer();
SauceBéarnaise sauce = container.Resolve<SauceBéarnaise>();
```

Given an instance of `UnityContainer`, you can use the generic `Resolve` method to get an instance of the concrete `SauceBéarnaise` class. Because this class has a default constructor, Unity automatically figures out how to create an instance of it. No explicit configuration of the container is necessary.

Unity supports AUTO-WIRING, so even in the absence of a default constructor, it will be able to create instances without configuration, as long as the involved constructor parameters are all concrete types and the entire tree of parameters have leaf types with default constructors.

As an example, consider this `Mayonnaise` constructor:

```
public Mayonnaise(EggYolk eggYolk, OliveOil oil)
```

Although the mayonnaise recipe is a bit simplified, both `EggYolk` and `OliveOil` are concrete classes with default constructors. `Mayonnaise` itself has no default constructor, but Unity can still create it without any configuration:

```
var container = new UnityContainer();
var mayo = container.Resolve<Mayonnaise>();
```

This works because Unity is able to figure out how to create all required constructor parameters. But as soon as we introduce loose coupling, we must configure Unity by mapping ABSTRACTIONS to concrete types.

MAPPING ABSTRACTIONS TO CONCRETE TYPES

While Unity's ability to AUTO-WIRE concrete types certainly can come in handy from time to time, loose coupling normally requires you to map ABSTRACTIONS to concrete types. Creating instances based upon such maps is the core service offered by any DI CONTAINER, but you must still define the map.

In this example, you map the `IIngredient` interface to the concrete `Sauce-Béarnaise` class, which allows you to successfully resolve `IIngredient`:

```
var container = new UnityContainer();
container.RegisterType<IIngredient, SauceBéarnaise>();
IIngredient ingredient = container.Resolve<IIngredient>();
```

The generic `RegisterType` method is one of several extension methods that all invoke a weakly typed `RegisterType` method defined on `IUnityContainer`. In the previous example, you use an overload where you define the ABSTRACTION as well as the concrete type as two generic type arguments. Here you map from `IIngredient` to `SauceBéarnaise` so that when you subsequently resolve `IIngredient`, you get a `Sauce-Béarnaise` instance.

The generic `RegisterType` extension method helps prevent configuration mistakes because the destination type has a generic constraint that states that it must derive from the source type. The previous example code compiles because `Sauce-Béarnaise` implements `IIngredient`.

In many cases the strongly typed API is all that you need, and because it provides desirable compile-time checking, you should use it whenever you can. Still, there are situations where you need a more weakly typed way to resolve services. This is also possible.

RESOLVING WEAKLY TYPED SERVICES

Sometimes you can't use a generic API because you don't know the appropriate type at design time. All you have is a `Type` instance, but you would still like to get an instance of that type. You saw an example of that in section 7.2, where we discussed ASP.NET MVC's `DefaultControllerFactory` class. The relevant method is this one:

```
protected internal virtual IController GetControllerInstance(
    RequestContext requestContext, Type controllerType);
```

Because you only have a `Type` instance, you can't use generics, but must resort to a weakly typed API. Fortunately, Unity offers a weakly typed overload of the `Resolve` method which allows you to implement the `GetControllerInstance` method like this:

```
return (IController)this.container.Resolve(controllerType);
```

The weakly typed overload of `Resolve` enables you to pass the `controllerType` argument directly to Unity, but also requires you to explicitly cast the return value to `IController`.

No matter which overload of `Resolve` you use, Unity guarantees that it will return an instance of the requested type or throw an exception if there are DEPENDENCIES that can't be satisfied. When all required DEPENDENCIES have been properly configured, Unity can AUTO-WIRE the requested type.

In the previous example, `this.container` is an instance of `IUnityContainer`. To be able to resolve the requested type, all loosely coupled DEPENDENCIES must previously have been configured. There are many ways to configure Unity, and the next section reviews the most common ones.

14.1.2 *Configuring the container*

As discussed in section 3.2, there are several conceptually different ways we can configure a DI CONTAINER. Figure 14.3 reviews the options.

Despite having a comprehensive XML configuration schema, Unity is built around imperative configuration. XML configuration is well supported, but implemented in an optional library that we must explicitly reference if we want to use it.

Although Unity supports both CODE AS CONFIGURATION and XML configuration, there's no built-in support for convention-based AUTO-REGISTRATION. Still, as we'll briefly cover, we can always implement a convention by writing custom imperative code. In this section, you'll see how you can use the various configuration options.

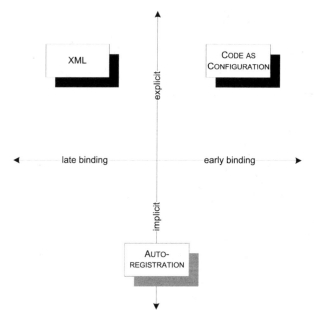

Figure 14.3 **Conceptually different configuration options. CODE AS CONFIGURATION is strongly typed and tends to be explicit. XML, on the other hand, is late bound, but still explicit. AUTO-REGISTRATION instead relies on conventions that can be both strongly typed and more loosely defined, but Unity has no built-in support for that.**

CODE AS CONFIGURATION

In section 14.1.1, you already saw a brief glimpse of Unity's strongly typed configuration API. Here we'll examine it in greater detail.

With a few exceptions, all configuration of Unity goes through the weakly typed `RegisterType` method defined on `IUnityContainer`:

```
IUnityContainer RegisterType(Type from, Type to, string name,
    LifetimeManager lifetimeManager,
    params InjectionMember[] injectionMembers);
```

In addition to this method, Unity also includes many extension methods; some of those are strongly typed generic methods, and some are weakly typed convenience methods. In this chapter, we'll concentrate on the strongly typed API. One of the most commonly used methods is this overload that you've already seen:

```
container.RegisterType<IIngredient, SauceBéarnaise>();
```

Unlike Castle Windsor or Autofac, mapping `IIngredient` to `SauceBéarnaise` like the previous example doesn't preclude you from resolving `SauceBéarnaise` itself. Both sauce and ingredient will be appropriately resolved here:

```
container.RegisterType<IIngredient, SauceBéarnaise>();
var sauce = container.Resolve<SauceBéarnaise>();
var ingredient = container.Resolve<IIngredient>();
```

As you may recall from the discussion in sections 10.1.2 and 13.1.2, mapping `IIngredient` to `SauceBéarnaise` with Castle Windsor or Autofac causes the concrete class (`SauceBéarnaise`) to "disappear," unless you take extra steps. This isn't necessary with Unity, where you can resolve both `IIngredient` and `SauceBéarnaise`. In both cases, the returned objects are `SauceBéarnaise` instances.

In real applications we always have more than one ABSTRACTION to map, so we must configure multiple mappings. This is done with multiple calls to `RegisterType`:

```
container.RegisterType<IIngredient, SauceBéarnaise>();
container.RegisterType<ICourse, Course>();
```

This maps `IIngredient` to `SauceBéarnaise` and `ICourse` to `Course`. There's no overlap of types so it should be pretty evident what's going on. You can also try to register the same ABSTRACTION several times, but if you do it like this, something surprising happens:

```
container.RegisterType<IIngredient, Steak>();
container.RegisterType<IIngredient, SauceBéarnaise>();
```

Registering a type without a name defines the default for the type, but *the previous default is overwritten*. The end result here is that if you resolve `IIngredient` you'll get an instance of `SauceBéarnaise`, but the `Steak` registration is no longer available. There can be only one default for a type, but you can register as many named components as you want. To keep `Steak` as the default `IIngredient`, you can register `SauceBéarnaise` with a name:

```
container.RegisterType<IIngredient, Steak>();
container.RegisterType<IIngredient, SauceBéarnaise>("sauce");
```

Steak remains the default IIngredient, but now you can also resolve IIngredient to SauceBéarnaise by requesting the named *sauce* IIngredient. You can use named components to fine-tune how DEPENDENCIES are wired; we'll return to this subject in section 14.3.1.

There are more advanced options available for configuring Unity, but we can configure an entire application with the methods shown here. To save ourselves from too much explicit maintenance of container configuration, it would be nice if we could instead use a more convention-based approach, using AUTO-REGISTRATION.

AUTO-REGISTRATION

In many cases, many registrations will be similar. Such registrations are tedious to maintain and explicitly registering each and every component may not be the most productive approach.

Consider a library that contains a lot of IIngredient implementations. You can register each class individually, but it will result in numerous similar-looking calls to the RegisterType method. What's worse is that every time you add a new IIngredient implementation, you must also explicitly register it with the container if you want it to be available. It would be more productive to state that all implementations of IIngredient found in a given assembly should be registered.

Unfortunately, Unity has no built-in support for AUTO-REGISTRATION, but because it has a comprehensive imperative API, we can write custom code to achieve the same effect. In the following listing we'll review a simple example that demonstrates how this can be achieved. This is in no way meant to be a comprehensive treatment of the subject, but more as a sketch of the options available to us.

To scan an assembly and register all IIngredient implementations we can combine .NET's Reflection API with the weakly typed RegisterType method, as demonstrated in the following listing.

Listing 14.1   Registering all IIngredients in an assembly

```
foreach (var t in typeof(Steak).Assembly.GetExportedTypes())
{
    if (typeof(IIngredient).IsAssignableFrom(t))
    {
        container.RegisterType(typeof(IIngredient), t, t.FullName);
    }
}
```

From a given assembly, you can pull a list of all public types and select only those that directly or indirectly implement the IIngredient interface. After having applied the filter, you can use the weakly typed Register method to register each IIngredient type against the interface. For each registration, you must remember to supply a unique name to prevent them from overwriting each other—here you use the full name of each concrete class, but anything that ensures the uniqueness of the name will do.

Although Unity offers no API that addresses convention-based Auto-registration, we can write our own code to achieve the same effect. It would have been preferable to have built-in support for this, but at least the Unity API doesn't preclude us from defining conventions manually.

TIP The *Unity Auto Registration* open source project[4] is one attempt to define a reusable API to enable Auto-registration for Unity.

If we were to be generous, we could say that the lack of an Auto-registration API puts us in a position with no constraints. If we can code it, we can have it. If we want to scan a folder for assemblies and scan each assembly for types we could even implement add-in functionality where add-ins can be added without recompiling a core application. This would be one way to implement late binding; another is to use XML configuration.

XML CONFIGURATION

When we need to be able to change a configuration without recompiling the application, XML configuration is a good option.

TIP Use XML configuration only for those types you need to change without recompiling the application. Use Code as Configuration for the rest.

Unity assumes that we place the XML configuration in an application configuration file. It uses the standard .NET configuration API to load and interpret the XML configuration.

TIP Unity's support for XML configuration is quite comprehensive compared to many other DI Containers; there's even an XSD file that can be used to get IntelliSense support in Visual Studio.

NOTE Because Unity's XML configuration support is implemented in a separate assembly, to use this feature, we must add a reference to the `Microsoft`
`.Practices.Unity.Configuration` assembly.

Once we have a reference to `Microsoft.Practices.Unity.Configuration`, we must also add a *using* directive for the `Microsoft.Practices.Unity.Configuration` namespace to make the `LoadConfiguration` extension method available. This enables us to load XML configuration with a single method call:

```
container.LoadConfiguration();
```

The `LoadConfiguration` method loads XML configuration from the standard application configuration file into the container.

NOTE Unfortunately, there's no API that enables us to read XML from other sources, such as streams or XML nodes.

TIP Although we can't read XML from arbitrary sources, we can read from any configuration file using the `ConfigurationManager` API.

---

[4] http://autoregistration.codeplex.com/

To enable Unity configuration in a configuration file, we must first add the configuration section, using the standard .NET API for defining custom configuration sections:

```
<configSections>
  <section name="unity"
           type="Microsoft.Practices.Unity.Configuration.
           ➥UnityConfigurationSection,
           ➥Microsoft.Practices.Unity.Configuration"/>
</configSections>
```

This enables us to add a `unity` configuration section in the configuration file. Here is a simple example that maps the `IIngredient` interface to the `Steak` class:

```
<unity>
  <namespace name="Ploeh.Samples.MenuModel" />
  <assembly name="Ploeh.Samples.MenuModel" />
  <container>
    <register type="IIngredient" mapTo="Steak" />
  </container>
</unity>
```

The Unity XML schema provides us with options for defining sensible defaults that can help reduce the verbosity that often occurs when we work with assembly qualified type names in XML. Although not required, we can add as many `namespace` elements as we would like. They're equivalent to `using` directives in C# code. Here, we add the `Ploeh.Samples.MenuModel` namespace as the only namespace, but we could've added more, or omitted this element altogether. If we omit a namespace element, we can still explicitly supply the fully qualified type name as part of a registration.

The `assembly` element works in the same way as the `namespace` element. We can add as many as we want—or none at all. Here we add the `Ploeh.Samples.MenuModel` assembly where the `IIngredient` interface and `Steak` class are defined.

This enables us to define the map between `IIngredient` and `Steak` in a concise manner using the `register` element. Because we added namespaces and assemblies to the context, we can refer to `IIngredient` and `Steak` by their short-form names. As long as the names are unambiguous within the context, Unity figures it out for us, much like the C# compiler does.

XML configuration is a good option when we need to change the configuration of one or more components without recompiling the application, but because it tends to be quite brittle, we should reserve it for only those occasions and use CODE AS CONFIGURATION for the main part of the container's configuration.

> **TIP** Remember that the last configuration of a type wins? You can use this behavior to overwrite hard-coded configuration with XML configuration. To do this, you must remember to load XML configuration after any other components have been configured. Conversely, if you have configuration that must never be overwritten by XML, apply that configuration after loading the XML configuration.

In this section, we mainly looked at various registration APIs for Unity. While it's certainly possible to write one big block of unstructured configuration code, it's better to modularize configuration. Although Unity doesn't have any explicit support for this, it turns out we can achieve that goal nevertheless.

14.1.3 *Packaging configuration*

It's sometimes desirable to package configuration logic into reusable groups, and even when reuse itself isn't our top priority, we may want to provide a bit of structure if we have a big and complex application to configure.

Castle Windsor has Installers, StructureMap Registries, and Autofac Modules, but Unity doesn't have anything quite equivalent. There's no interface defined with the main purpose of packaging configuration into reusable components. It does have something else that's a more-than-adequate substitute: Container Extensions.

The purpose of a Unity Container Extension is much broader than packaging configuration into reusable packages; as the name implies, it can be used to extend the behavior of Unity in various different ways. Unity's INTERCEPTION feature, for instance, is implemented as a Container Extension (we'll cover that particular extension in section 14.3.4).

Although they can be used for many other things, Container Extensions can also be used to modularize configuration. To implement a Container Extension, all we have to do is to derive from the abstract `UnityContainerExtension` class and implement its `Initialize` method. The following listing demonstrates how the code from listing 14.1 is easily moved into a Container Extension.

Listing 14.2 Implementing a Container Extension

```
public class IngredientExtension : UnityContainerExtension
{
    protected override void Initialize()
    {
        var a = typeof(Steak).Assembly;
        foreach (var t in a.GetExportedTypes())
        {
            if (typeof(IIngredient).IsAssignableFrom(t))
            {
                this.Container.RegisterType(
                    typeof(IIngredient), t, t.FullName);
            }
        }
    }
}
```

The `IngredientExtension` class derives from the abstract `UnityContainerExtension` class to package the convention-based configuration from listing 14.1 into a reusable class. When you derive from that class, you must implement the abstract `Initialize` method, which is also where you can perform all the work you need to do.

The only functional difference from listing 14.1 is that you now invoke the `Register-Type` method on the inherited `Container` property instead of a local variable.

To use a Container Extension, you can invoke the `AddExtension` method or a related extension method. When the Extension has a default constructor, you can use the generic shorthand extension method:

```
container.AddNewExtension<IngredientExtension>();
```

The `AddNewExtension` method invokes the `AddExtension` method which you can also use in situations where you need to create the Module manually:

```
container.AddExtension(new IngredientExtension());
```

These two examples are functionally equivalent.

> **TIP** Unity Container Extensions let you package and structure your container configuration code. Even though they aren't particularly designed for this exact purpose, you may prefer using them instead of inline configuration—it will make your COMPOSITION ROOT more readable.

Using Container Extensions, we can configure a Unity container with both CODE AS CONFIGURATION and XML—even with custom implemented AUTO-REGISTRATION, although this is a bit of a stretch. Once the container is configured, we can start resolving services with it, as described in section 14.1.1.

This section introduced the Unity DI CONTAINER and demonstrated the fundamental mechanics: how to configure the container and subsequently use it to resolve services. Resolving services is easily done with a single call to the `Resolve` method, so the complexity involves configuring the container. This can be done in several different ways, including imperative code and XML. Until now, we've only looked at the most basic API; there are more advanced areas we have yet to cover. One of the most important topics is how to manage component lifetime.

14.2 *Managing lifetime*

In chapter 8, we discussed LIFETIME MANAGEMENT, including the most common conceptual lifetime styles, such as SINGLETON and TRANSIENT. Unity supports many different lifestyles and enables you to configure the lifetime of all services. The lifestyles shown in table 14.2 are available as part of the API.

Unity's implementation of TRANSIENT, PER GRAPH, and SINGLETON are equivalent to the general lifestyles described in chapter 8, so I won't spend much time on them in this chapter.

> **WARNING** Although the *Per Resolve* lifetime matches the description from section 8.3.3, it has a known bug[5] that makes it less desirable to use.

---

[5] http://unity.codeplex.com/workitem/8777

Table 14.2   Unity lifetimes

Name	Comments
Transient	This is the default lifestyle. Instances aren't tracked by the container.
Container Controlled	Unity's name for SINGLETON.
Per Resolve	Unity's name for PER GRAPH. Instances aren't tracked by the container.
Hierarchical	Ties the lifetime of components together with a child container (see section 14.2.1).
Per Thread	One instance is created per thread. Instances aren't tracked by the container.
Externally Controlled	A variation of SINGLETON where the container itself holds only a weak reference to the instance, allowing it to be garbage-collected if not used.

TIP   The default TRANSIENT lifestyle is the safest, but not always the most efficient, choice. SINGLETON is a more efficient choice for thread-safe services, but you must remember to explicitly register those services like that.

In this section, you'll see how to define lifetimes for components in both code and XML. As a more advanced scenario, you'll also see how to implement a custom lifestyle to showcase that we aren't limited to the built-in lifetimes supplied by Unity. At the end of this section, you should be able to use Unity's lifetimes in your own application.

Before we go into the advanced topic of developing a custom lifetime, we need to review how to configure and use lifetimes.

14.2.1 Configuring lifetime

In this section, we'll review how to manage component lifetimes with Unity. Lifetime is configured as part of registering components, and we can define it in both code and XML. We'll look at each in turn.

CONFIGURING LIFETIME WITH CODE

Lifetime is configured with an overload of the `RegisterType` method that we use to register components in general. It's as easy as this:

```
container.RegisterType<SauceBéarnaise>(
    new ContainerControlledLifetimeManager());
```

This configures the concrete `SauceBéarnaise` class as a SINGLETON so that the same instance is returned each time `SauceBéarnaise` is requested. If we want to map an ABSTRACTION to a concrete class with a specific lifetime, we can use another, familiar `RegisterType` overload:

```
container.RegisterType<IIngredient, SauceBéarnaise>(
    new ContainerControlledLifetimeManager());
```

This maps `IIngredient` to `SauceBéarnaise` and also configures it as a SINGLETON. In both the previous examples you used `RegisterType` overloads that take a `Lifetime-Manager` instance as an argument. Besides `ContainerControlledLifetimeManager` you can use any other class that derives from the abstract `LifetimeManager` class. Unity has a `LifetimeManager` for every lifetime in table 14.2, but as you'll see in section 14.2.2, you can also create your own.

Although TRANSIENT is the default instance scope, we can still explicitly state it. These two examples are equivalent:

```
container.RegisterType<SauceBéarnaise>();
```

```
container.RegisterType<SauceBéarnaise>(
    new TransientLifetimeManager());
```

Using CODE AS CONFIGURATION, we can register components with various lifetimes in any way we want. Although this is by far the most flexible way to configure components, we sometimes need to resort to XML for late binding purposes. In that case, we can also declare lifetimes.

CONFIGURING LIFETIME WITH XML

When we need to define components in XML, we'll also want to be able to configure their lifetimes in the same place. This is easily done as part of the XML schema you already saw in section 14.1.2. You can use the optional `lifetime` element to declare the lifetime:

```
<register type="IIngredient" mapTo="Steak">
  <lifetime type="ContainerControlledLifetimeManager" />
</register>
```

Compared to the example in section 14.1.2, the difference is that you have now added the optional `lifetime` element to define which `LifetimeManager` should be used for the registration. To configure the component as a SINGLETON you set the type attribute to the `ContainerControlledLifetimeManager` *alias*, but you could also have used an assembly qualified type name or a custom *alias* if you wanted to assign a custom `LifetimeManager`.

In both code and XML it's easy to configure lifetimes for components. In all cases it's done in a rather declarative fashion. Although configuration is easy, you must not forget that some lifetimes involve long-lived objects that use resources as long as they're around.

RELEASING COMPONENTS

As discussed in section 8.2.2, it's important to release objects when we're done with them so that any disposable instances can be disposed of if their lifetime is up. This is possible, but surprisingly difficult to do with Unity.

> **WARNING** Unity doesn't dispose of disposable DEPENDENCIES unless very explicitly told to do so.

`IUnityContainer` defines a `Teardown` method that at first glance looks like a direct equivalent of Castle Windsor's `Release` method. We can attempt to use it in the same manner:

```
container.Teardown(ingredient);
```

However, no matter which of the built-in lifetimes we choose, no components are disposed of. This certainly violates the Principle of Least Surprise.

WARNING   The `Teardown` method doesn't dispose of disposable DEPENDENCIES.

Although the `Teardown` method doesn't (by default) do what we'd like it to do, there are still a few other options available to us. One is to implement a custom lifetime (which you'll do in the next section); another is to use a combination of child containers and the Hierarchical lifestyle.

The concept of a Hierarchical lifetime is that it acts like a SINGLETON within a child container, but that each child container has its own local SINGLETON.

NOTE   The combination of child containers and Hierarchical lifetime is similar to Autofac's lifetime scopes described in section 13.2.1.

A child container is a copy of the parent container. When we create a child container from a parent container, the child inherits its entire configuration from the parent, but we can subsequently change the child without affecting the parent. This can be useful if we wish to override only a small part of the parent's configuration. A child container is normally intended to have a more limited scope. As figure 14.4 illustrates, it also defines a boundary within which components can be reused.

When we create a new child container, it inherits all the SINGLETONS tracked by the parent container, but it also acts as a container of "local SINGLETONS." When a

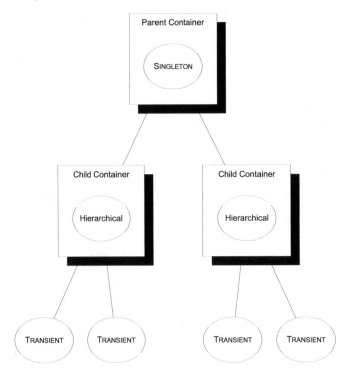

Figure 14.4   Child containers can share components for a limited duration or purpose. A Hierarchical component is essentially a SINGLETON within that container. No matter how many times we ask a child container for such a component, we get the same instance. Another child container will have its own instance, and the parent container manages the truly shared SINGLETONS. TRANSIENT components are never shared.

Hierarchical component is requested from a child container, we always receive the same instance. The difference from true SINGLETONS is that if we query a second child container, we'll get another instance.

TRANSIENT components still act as they should, whether or not we resolve them from the parent or a child container.

> **TIP** You can use child containers and the Hierarchical lifetime as an alternative to the missing WEB REQUEST CONTEXT lifestyle: create a new child container at the beginning of each web request, and use it to resolve components. Then dispose of the child container when the request ends.

One of the important features of child containers is that they allow us to properly release components when the usage scope completes. We create a new child container with the `CreateChildContainer` method and release all appropriate components by invoking its `Dispose` method:

```
using (var child = container.CreateChildContainer()
{
    var meal = child.Resolve<IMeal>();          Consume
                                                 meal
}
```

A new child container is created from the `container` by invoking the `CreateChild-Container` method. The return value implements `IDisposable` so you can wrap it in a `using` scope. It's a new instance of `IUnityContainer`, so you can use the `child` to resolve components in exactly the same way as with the parent container.

When you're done with the child container, you can dispose of it. When using a `using` scope this happens automatically when you exit the scope, but you can obviously also choose to explicitly dispose of it by invoking the `Dispose` method. When you dispose of `child` you also release all the components that were created by the child container; here it means that you release the `meal` object graph.

> **NOTE** Remember that releasing a disposable component isn't the same as disposing of it. It's a signal to the container that the component is eligible for decommissioning. If the component is Hierarchical it will be disposed of, whereas it will remain active if it's a SINGLETON.

> **WARNING** Disposable objects with TRANSIENT or PER GRAPH lifetimes aren't disposed of when a child container is disposed of. This can lead to memory leaks.

Earlier in this section, you already saw how to configure components as SINGLETONS or TRANSIENTS. Configuring a component with a Hierarchical lifetime is done in the same way:

```
container.RegisterType<IIngredient, SauceBéarnaise>(
    new HierarchicalLifetimeManager());
```

Registering a component with a lifetime always uses an overload of the `RegisterType` method that takes a `LifetimeManager` as an argument. To use the Hierarchical lifetime, you supply a `HierarchicalLifetimeManager` instance.

Due to their nature, SINGLETONS are never released for the lifetime of the container itself. Still, we can release even those components if we don't need the container any longer. This is done by disposing of the container itself:

```
container.Dispose();
```

In practice, this isn't nearly as important because the lifetime of a container tends to correlate closely with the lifetime of the application it supports. We normally keep the container around as long as the application runs, so we would only dispose of it when the application shuts down, in which case memory would be reclaimed by the operating system.

The built-in lifetimes of Unity may seem like a rather comprehensive set that could meet many of your daily needs. But there are issues in the form of bugs as well as inconsistencies when it comes to releasing components. On the other hand, Unity has enough SEAMS to enable us to address these issues by developing custom lifetimes.

14.2.2 *Developing a custom lifetime*

In many cases, we should be able to get by with the selection of lifetimes already offered by Unity, but if we have special needs or need to address the decommissioning issues, it's possible to implement a custom lifetime. In this section, you'll see how to do this. We'll both review the SEAMS that make this possible and spend some time going through an example, alternating back and forth between theory and example.

UNDERSTANDING THE LIFETIMEMANAGER API

In section 14.2.1, you already got your first glimpse of Unity's lifetime API. Several overloads of the `RegisterType` method take an instance of the abstract `Lifetime-Manager` class, which models how lifetimes interact with the rest of Unity. Figure 14.5 shows the small type hierarchy related to the `LifetimeManager` class.

When implementing a custom lifetime, the important type is the abstract `Lifetime-Manager` class. Even though `LifetimeManager` implements `ILifetimePolicy`, it's of no direct concern to us because the `RegisterType` overloads only accept `LifetimeManager` instances, and not `ILifetimePolicy` or `IBuilderPolicy` instances.

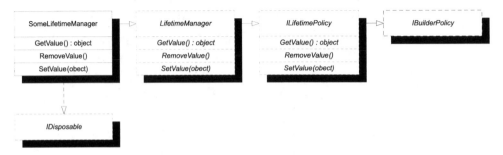

Figure 14.5 The `SomeLifetimeManager` implements a custom lifetime by deriving from the abstract `LifetimeManager` class which itself implements the `ILifetimePolicy` interface that derives from the `IBuilderPolicy` marker interface. A custom lifetime can optionally implement `IDisposable` to implement cleanup functionality when a container is being disposed of.

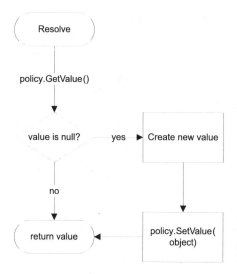

Figure 14.6 Unity interacts with the
`ILifetimePolicy` interface by first invoking the
`GetValue` method. If the policy returns a value, this
value is used immediately. If not, Unity creates the
new value and sets the value on the policy before
returning it.

We can optionally implement `IDisposable` to implement cleanup functionality, but by default it doesn't work exactly as we'd expect; the `Dispose` method isn't always invoked. We'll get back to this subject a little later in this section.

> **WARNING** Implementing `IDisposable` doesn't guarantee that the `Dispose` method will be invoked.

When Unity resolves a component, it interacts with its `LifetimeManager` as illustrated in figure 14.6.

> **NOTE** The mechanism illustrated in figure 14.6 is similar to the interaction between StructureMap and `IObjectCache`, as shown in figure 11.5.

Unity first attempts to get the requested instance from the `GetValue` method. If this method returns null, Unity creates the requested instance and adds it to the policy through the `SetValue` method before returning it. In this way, a single `ILifetime-Policy` instance manages a single component.

> **WARNING** The `RemoveValue` method is *never* invoked by Unity.

Although the `GetValue` and `SetValue` methods take part when Unity resolves a request, the `RemoveValue` method is never invoked by Unity. This goes a long way toward explaining why the `Teardown` method doesn't do what you'd expect it to do. We could leave the implementation blank, but it turns out we can repurpose the method. Before we go into details about that, an example covering the basics should make it all clearer.

DEVELOPING A CACHING LIFESTYLE
In this example, you'll develop the same caching lifestyle that you also created for Castle Windsor and StructureMap in sections 10.2.3 and 11.2.2. In short, this lifestyle caches and reuses instances for a time before releasing them.

Although you can add extra behavior by implementing IDisposable and doing other tricks, at minimum you need to implement the three abstract methods defined by LifetimeManager; this is shown in the following listing.

Listing 14.3   Implementing a custom LifetimeManager

```
public partial class CacheLifetimeManager :
    LifetimeManager, IDisposable
{
    private object value;
    private readonly ILease lease;

    public CacheLifetimeManager(ILease lease)
    {
        if (lease == null)
        {
            throw new ArgumentNullException("lease");
        }

        this.lease = lease;
    }

    public override object GetValue()
    {
        this.RemoveValue();                        ❶ Provide
        return this.value;                            value
    }

    public override void RemoveValue()
    {
        if (this.lease.IsExpired)
        {                                          ❷ Remove
            this.Dispose();                           value
        }
    }

    public override void SetValue(object newValue)
    {
        this.value = newValue;                     ❸ Set
        this.lease.Renew();                           value
    }
}
```

The CacheLifetimeManager class derives from the abstract LifetimeManager class to implement the caching lifetime. It also implements IDisposable, but we'll wait a little before we look at the implementation so the Dispose method is omitted from listing 14.3.

CacheLifetimeManager uses CONSTRUCTOR INJECTION to receive an ILease instance. The ILease interface is a local helper interface that you introduce to implement the desired functionality. It was initially introduced in section 10.2.3 and has nothing to do with Unity or any other particular DI CONTAINER.

NOTE   For an example of an ILease implementation, see section 10.2.3.

The GetValue method ❶ returns the value field after first invoking the RemoveValue method to guard against an expired lease. The value field may be null, but as figure 14.6 illustrates, this is an expected scenario. On the other hand, the field may also have a value if the SetValue method was initially invoked and the lease didn't expire in the meantime.

Although the RemoveValue method ❷ is never invoked by Unity itself, it's still a good place to implement code for releasing the component. Because the purpose of the CacheLifetimeManager is to cache the value for a time, you only dispose of the component when the lease has expired; otherwise, you hold on to it a little longer. The Dispose method isn't included in listing 14.3, but we'll get back to it shortly.

The SetValue method ❸ saves the value to the value field and renews the lease. According to the diagram in figure 14.6, the SetValue method is only invoked when Unity creates a new value for the component in question, in which case it's appropriate to renew the lease.

> **NOTE** Contrast the constructor in listing 14.3 with the much more complicated code from listing 10.2. This clearly illustrates the superiority of CONSTRUCTOR INJECTION over METHOD INJECTION.

This implements the core functionality required by a LifetimeManager. Although we still need to discuss the implementation of IDisposable and what this means, we should briefly look up from the implementation itself to see how the CacheLifetime-Manager fits together with a UnityContainer instance.

REGISTERING COMPONENTS WITH A CUSTOM LIFETIME

Using the CacheLifetimeManager with a component is easy and works like specifying any other lifestyle:

```
var lease = new SlidingLease(TimeSpan.FromMinutes(1));
var cache = new CacheLifetimeManager(lease);
container.RegisterType<IIngredient, SauceBéarnaise>(cache);
```

This configures the container to use a CacheLifetimeManager with a one-minute timeout for the IIngredient interface. Within a one-minute time span, you can request as many object graphs as you want, and you'll always get the same SacueBéarnaise back whenever the graph contains an IIngredient instance. When that minute is up, subsequent requests will get a new SauceBéarnaise instance.

Resolving components with a custom lifetime works as expected. The surprises only begin when we attempt to release the resolved object graphs.

RELEASING COMPONENTS WITH A CUSTOM LIFETIME

As I mentioned, the RemoveValue method is never invoked by Unity. However, if we want to add clean-up functionality to a custom LifetimeManager, we can make it implement IDisposable. This will cause it to be disposed of when the owning container is disposed of.

There are still some surprises left for you, but let's take a closer look. In listing 14.3 you already saw that CacheLifetimeManager implements IDisposable, but the following listing is the first time you see the implementation.

Listing 14.4   Disposing a `LifetimeManager`

```
public void Dispose()
{
    GC.SuppressFinalize(this);
    this.Dispose(true);
}

protected virtual void Dispose(bool disposing)
{
    if (disposing)
    {
        var d = this.value as IDisposable;
        if (d != null)
        {
            d.Dispose();
        }
        this.value = null;
    }
}
```

❶ Dispose disposable

The `CacheLifetimeManager` class implements `IDisposable` by following the standard Dispose pattern.[6] If the managed value implements `IDisposable`, you dispose of it ❶, but in any case you set the `value` field to null to allow the component to be garbage-collected.

According to theory, if you register and resolve a disposable component with the `CacheLifetimeManager`, the component should be disposed of together with the container like this:

```
var lease = new SlidingLease(TimeSpan.FromMinutes(1));
var cache = new CacheLifetimeManager(lease);
container.RegisterType<IIngredient, Parsley>(cache);

var ingredient = container.Resolve<IIngredient>();

container.Dispose();
```

As you'd expect from the Unity documentation, disposing of the container also releases `ingredient`. As we all know, we must never re-heat parsley, so the `Parsley` class is obviously disposable. Disposing of the container also disposes of the `Parsley` instance. So far, so good.

However, if you create and dispose of a child container, you'd expect the disposable `LifetimeManager` to act in the same manner as `HierarchicalLifetimeManager`:

```
IIngredient ingredient;
using (var child = container.CreateChildContainer())
{
    ingredient = child.Resolve<IIngredient>()
}
```

❶ Doesn't dispose of ingredient!

---

[6]   Krzysztof Cwalina and Brad Abrams, *Framework Design Guidelines: Conventions, Idioms, and Patterns for Reusable .NET Libraries* (New York: Addison-Wesley, 2006), 248.

Given the same configuration of the Parsley component as in the previous example, you'd expect that the ingredient is disposed of when the child container is disposed of ❶. Alas, this doesn't happen; CacheLifetimeManager.Dispose is never invoked.

WARNING Even when a LifetimeManager implements IDisposable, the Dispose method is only invoked when the owning container is disposed of.

How can this be the case when similar code worked with HierarchicalLifetime-Manager as you saw in section 14.2.1? It turns out that Unity has an associated Builder-Strategy that contains special logic for HierarchicalLifetimeManager that enables this functionality. The good news is that we can do the same.

IMPLEMENTING A CUSTOM LIFETIMESTRATEGY

The reason that HierarchicalLifetimeManager works as it does is that Unity has a BuilderStrategy that makes a copy of the parent container's Hierarchical-LifetimeManager and associates it with the child container. This enables the child container to dispose of the LifetimeManager when it is itself disposed of. We can do the same by implementing a custom BuilderStrategy, as shown in the following listing.

Listing 14.5 Implementing a custom LifetimeStrategy

```
public class CacheLifetimeStrategy : BuilderStrategy
{
    public override void PreBuildUp(              ❶ Override
        IBuilderContext context)                    PreBuildUp
    {
        if (context == null)
        {
            throw new ArgumentNullException("context");
        }

        IPolicyList policySource;
        var lifetimePolicy = context                ❷ Get lifetime
            .PersistentPolicies                       policy
            .Get<ILifetimePolicy>(context.BuildKey,
                out policySource);

        if (object.ReferenceEquals(policySource,
            context.PersistentPolicies))            ❸ Check
        {                                             ownership
            return;
        }

        var cacheLifetime =
            lifetimePolicy as CacheLifetimeManager;
        if (cacheLifetime == null)                  ❹ Check
        {                                             type
            return;
        }
        var childLifetime = cacheLifetime.Clone();  ❺ Make
                                                      copy
```

```
    context
        .PersistentPolicies
        .Set<ILifetimePolicy>(childLifetime,
            context.BuildKey);
    context.Lifetime.Add(childLifetime);
    }
}
```

⑥ **Replace lifetime policy**

`CacheLifetimeStrategy` derives from the abstract `BuilderStrategy` class and implements the `PreBuildUp` method ❶, which is invoked every time Unity creates an instance. This gives you the chance to modify the context before the object is created.

The first thing you want to do is to get the current `ILifetimePolicy` for the component ❷. The context can provide this information, as well as information about the source of the policy. The `policySource` instance indirectly tells you where the lifetime was defined. If the source is a parent container, but you're currently building within a child container, you expect the source of the lifetime to be different from the current context if the lifetime was originally defined on the parent container. This is the scenario we're targeting, so you return prematurely from the method if this isn't the case ❸.

This particular implementation only cares about `CacheLifetimeManager`, so you also return if the lifetime is something else ❹. On the other hand, if the lifetime *is* a `CacheLifetimeManager`, you make a copy ❺ to be used in the child container.

Now that you know that you are, indeed, building within a child container, you add the cloned `CacheLifetimeManager` back to the context ❻, effectively overwriting the inherited lifetime from the parent container with a lifetime specific for this child container.

That's a bit of a mouthful, and then you're even not quite done yet. Although you've implemented a custom `BuilderStrategy`, you haven't yet told Unity about it. Fortunately, as the following listing demonstrates, that's a lot easier than implementing the `CacheLifetimeStrategy`.

Listing 14.6   Extending Unity with `CacheLifetimeStrategy`

```
public class CacheLifetimeStrategyExtension : UnityContainerExtension
{
    protected override void Initialize()
    {
        this.Context.Strategies
            .AddNew<CacheLifetimeStrategy>(
                UnityBuildStage.Lifetime);
    }
}
```

To add the `CacheLifetimeStrategy` to Unity, you create a new Container Extension. Remember how you used you used Container Extensions to package configuration in section 14.1.3? Here is another, perhaps more idiomatic, usage of a Container Extension.

In the `Initialize` method, you add the `CacheLifetimeStrategy` to the context, with the added information that this particular `BuilderStrategy` deals with lifetime management.

Finally, with all this in place, you can extend Unity so that `CacheLifetimeManager` now works exactly like `HierarchicalLifetimeManager`:

```
container.AddNewExtension<CacheLifetimeStrategyExtension>();
```

After adding this Container Extension, the scenario that didn't work at first finally works: you can use child containers to release objects with a `CachedLifetimeManager`.

Now that you've learned about BuilderStrategies, we can now complete the circle and implement support for the `Teardown` method.

IMPLEMENTING SUPPORT FOR TEARDOWN

When we started the discussion about releasing components in section 14.2.1, we quickly dismissed the `Teardown` method because it doesn't properly release components. On the other hand, this shouldn't lead you to believe that the `Teardown` method does nothing; on the contrary, it invokes various methods on registered BuilderStrategies. This implies that we can implement a custom `BuilderStrategy` that properly releases components during Teardown.

Teardown support for the `CacheLifetimeManager` would be desirable. Fortunately, although this involves creating another `BuilderStrategy` (or extending the one we already created), listing 14.7 shows that this is a lot easier than implementing the `CacheLifetimeStrategy` displayed in listing 14.5.

Listing 14.7 Implementing a releasing strategy

```
public class CacheReleasingLifetimeStrategy : BuilderStrategy
{
    public override void PostTearDown(        ❶ Implement
        IBuilderContext context)                PostTearDown
    {
        if (context == null)
        {                                         Guard
            throw new ArgumentNullException("context");   clause
        }
        var lifetimes = context
            .Lifetime.OfType<CacheLifetimeManager>();
        foreach (var lifetimePolicy in lifetimes)   ❷ Release
        {                                               value
            lifetimePolicy.RemoveValue();
        }
    }
}
```

Instead of overriding the `PreBuildUp` method as you did in listing 14.5, you override the `PostTearDown` method ❶ which is invoked from the `Teardown` method after most other resources have been decommissioned for the component in question.

The context has a list of lifetime objects, but in most cases you expect that it only contains a single `CacheLifetimeManager` instance. Even so, for good measure, you pretend that there can be any number of them and invoke `RemoveValue` on each one ❷. If you recall the implementation of `CacheLifetimeManager` from listing 14.3, the `RemoveValue` method only removes and disposes of the tracked value if the lease has expired.

Now you're close to closing the loop. You can add `CacheReleasingLifetimeStrategy` to the `CacheLifetimeStrategyExtension` from listing 14.6:

```
this.Context.Strategies
    .AddNew<CacheLifetimeStrategy>(
        UnityBuildStage.Lifetime);
this.Context.Strategies
    .AddNew<CacheReleasingLifetimeStrategy>(
        UnityBuildStage.Lifetime);
```

This finally enables you to release cached components with the `Teardown` method:

```
container.AddNewExtension<CacheLifetimeStrategyExtension>();

var lease = new SlidingLease(TimeSpan.FromTicks(1));
var cache = new CacheLifetimeManager(lease);
container.RegisterType<IIngredient, Parsley>(cache);

var ingredient = container.Resolve<IIngredient>();

container.Teardown(ingredient);
```

With all this infrastructure in place, the `ingredient` variable, which is really an instance of the disposable `Parsley` class, is properly released when the `Teardown` method is invoked. When the lease is expired the instance is disposed of, whereas nothing happens if it isn't expired.

After we have added all these `LifetimeManagers`, `BuilderStrategies`, and Container Extensions, Unity finally behaves like we want it to behave—for the cache lifetime, that is. Recall that TRANSIENT and PER GRAPH still don't behave as we would like them to do.

> **TIP** Although neither `TransientLifetimeManager` nor `PerResolveLifetimeManager` implements `IDisposable` or performs any logic in their `RemoveValue` methods, they're at least unsealed. If we need them to properly release components, we can derive from them and also remember to implement associated `BuilderStrategies`.

In conclusion, we must recognize that while Unity provides us with all the SEAMS necessary to implement custom lifetimes exactly how we would like them, it's more work than it ought to be. On the other hand, at least it's possible, which is more than we can say about some other DI CONTAINERS.

It would be possible to package such a custom lifetime into a reusable library so that at least we wouldn't have to re-implement them for every new application we were to build. This is also necessary, because Unity's LIFETIME MANAGEMENT model leaves something to be desired, despite its apparent comprehensive support for different lifetimes.

This completes our tour of LIFETIME MANAGEMENT with Unity. Compared to other chapters about specific DI CONTAINERS, this was a long section. In part, this is because we have a lot of options available to us when we implement custom lifetimes, and in part it's also because Unity presents some unique pitfalls in this area that I wanted to point out. Components can be configured with mixed lifestyles, and this is even true when we register multiple implementations of the same ABSTRACTION. We have yet to look at how to work with multiple components, but the next section dives into this subject. Unity enables us to go deep here, because it's one of the few containers that support INTERCEPTION. This fits naturally as an extension to a discussion about Decorators.

14.3 *Working with multiple components*

DI CONTAINERS thrive on distinctness, but have a hard time with ambiguity. When using CONSTRUCTOR INJECTION, a single constructor is preferred over overloaded constructors because it's evident which constructor to use when there's no choice. This is also the case when mapping from ABSTRACTIONS to concrete types. If we attempt to map multiple concrete types to the same ABSTRACTION we introduce ambiguity.

Despite the undesirable qualities of ambiguity, we often need to work with multiple implementations of a single interface. This can be the case in these situations:

- Different concrete types should be used for different consumers.
- DEPENDENCIES are sequences.
- Decorators are in use.

In this section, we'll look at each of these cases and see how Unity addresses each one in turn. When we're done, you should be able to register and resolve components even when multiple implementations of the same ABSTRACTION are in play.

First, let's see how we can provide more fine-grained control than AUTO-WIRING provides.

14.3.1 *Selecting among multiple candidates*

AUTO-WIRING is convenient and powerful, but provides us with little control. As long as all ABSTRACTIONS are distinctly mapped to concrete types we have no problems, but as soon as we introduce more implementations of the same interface, ambiguity rears its ugly head.

Unity's way of dealing with multiple registrations of the same ABSTRACTION is slightly different than most other DI CONTAINERS. This is a good place for us to start, because it establishes some ground rules we'll need in the rest of this section.

REGISTERING MULTIPLE IMPLEMENTATIONS OF THE SAME COMPONENT

As you saw in section 14.1.2, you can register multiple components for the same service:

```
container.RegisterType<IIngredient, Steak>();
container.RegisterType<IIngredient, SauceBéarnaise>("sauce");
```

There can be only one unnamed registration. This is called the *default registration*. If you subsequently invoke the `RegisterType` method for `IIngredient` without a name, the `Steak` registration will be overwritten by the new component.

> **NOTE**   There can be only one *default registration* for a type, but as many named registrations as we need.

When we invoke the `Resolve` method without a name, we get back an object based on the default registration. Given the previous configuration, this returns a `Steak` instance:

```
var ingredient = container.Resolve<IIngredient>();
```

The named *sauce* registration isn't forgotten. You can resolve multiple `IIngredients` like this:

```
IEnumerable<IIngredient> ingredients =
    container.ResolveAll<IIngredient>();
```

Based on the configuration in the previous example, you'd get back a sequence that includes a `SauceBéarnaise` instance, but not a `Steak`.

> **WARNING**   `ResolveAll` returns all named registrations, but not the default registration.

If there are configured instances of a plug-in that can't be resolved when `ResolveAll` is invoked, Unity throws an exception explaining that there are DEPENDENCIES that can't be satisfied. This is consistent with the behavior of the `Resolve` method but different from the way that Castle Windsor or MEF behaves.

The following listing shows how you can use named registrations to provide hints that can later be used to select among different configured components.

Listing 14.8   Naming registrations

```
container.RegisterType<IIngredient, Steak>("meat");
container.RegisterType<IIngredient, SauceBéarnaise>("sauce");
```

You can give each registration a unique name that you can later use to distinguish each from other similar components.

> **NOTE**   It's possible to register only named components for a type. If we do that, there will be no default registration.

Given the named registrations in listing 14.8, you can resolve both `Steak` and `Sauce-Béarnaise` like this:

```
var meat = container.Resolve<IIngredient>("meat");
var sauce = container.Resolve<IIngredient>("sauce");
```

Notice that you supply the same key that you used to name the component during registration.

Given that we should always resolve services in a single Composition Root we should normally not expect to deal with such ambiguity on this level.

TIP If you find yourself invoking the `Resolve` method with a specific key, consider if you can change your approach to be less ambiguous.

We can use named registrations to select among multiple alternatives when configuring Dependencies for a given service.

Configuring named dependencies

As useful as Auto-wiring is, sometimes we need to override the normal behavior to provide fine-grained control over which Dependencies go where; but it may also be that we need to address an ambiguous API. As an example, consider this constructor:

```
public ThreeCourseMeal(ICourse entrée,
    ICourse mainCourse, ICourse dessert)
```

In this case, you have three identically typed Dependencies, each of which represents a *different* concept. In most cases, you want to map each of the Dependencies to a separate type. The following listing shows how you could choose to configure the `ICourse` mappings.

Listing 14.9 Registering named courses

```
container.RegisterType<ICourse, Rillettes>("entrée");
container.RegisterType<ICourse, CordonBleu>("mainCourse");
container.RegisterType<ICourse, MousseAuChocolat>("dessert");
```

As you did in listing 14.8, you register three named components, mapping the `Rillettes` to an instance named "entrée," `CordonBleu` to an instance named "mainCourse," and the `MousseAuChocolat` to an instance named "dessert."

Given these registrations, you can now register the `ThreeCourseMeal` class, as shown in the following listing.

Listing 14.10 Overriding Auto-Wiring

```
container.RegisterType<IMeal, ThreeCourseMeal>(
    new InjectionConstructor(
        new ResolvedParameter<ICourse>("entrée"),
        new ResolvedParameter<ICourse>("mainCourse"),
        new ResolvedParameter<ICourse>("dessert")));
```

Something that we haven't yet discussed in detail is that all `RegisterType` overloads take a params array of an abstract class called `InjectionMember`. An `InjectionMember` is a Strategy[7] that Unity uses as a guide when composing types with each other. The `InjectionConstructor`, for example, enables you to define parameters used for Constructor Injection.

---

[7] Erich Gamma et al., *Design Patterns: Elements of Reusable Object-Oriented Software* (New York: Addison-Wesley, 1994), 315.

One of the ways you can do that is by defining it with an array of Resolved-Parameter instances. Each ResolvedParameter defines a type to be resolved, as well as an optional name—this isn't the name of the constructor argument, but rather of a named registration. The *entrée* ResolvedParameter refers to the named *entrée* registration. Constructor parameters are filled in a positional manner, so that the first ResolvedParameter is matched with the first constructor argument, and so on.

> **NOTE** Compared to most other DI CONTAINERS, the positional strategy makes Unity more robust when faced with refactorings in the form of the constructor argument name changes. On the other hand, it breaks down if we reorder the constructor arguments—something that other DI CONTAINERS can handle.

Overriding AUTO-WIRING by explicitly mapping parameters to named components is a universally applicable solution. We can do this even if we configure the named components in one Container Extension and the consumer in a completely different Container Extension, because the only identification that ties a named component together with a parameter is the name. This is always possible, but can be brittle if we have a lot of names to manage. When the original reason prompting us to use named components is to deal with ambiguity, a better solution is to design our own API to get rid of that ambiguity. It often leads to a better overall design.

In the next section, you'll see how to use the less ambiguous and more flexible approach where you allow any number of courses in a meal. To this end, you must learn how Unity deals with lists and sequences.

14.3.2 *Wiring sequences*

In section 10.3.2, we discussed how to refactor an explicit ThreeCourseMeal class to the more general-purpose Meal class with this constructor:

```
public Meal(IEnumerable<ICourse> courses)
```

In this section, we'll look at how we can configure Unity to wire up Meal instances with appropriate ICourse DEPENDENCIES. When we're done, you should have a good idea of the options available to you when you need to configure instances with sequences of DEPENDENCIES.

AUTO-WIRING SEQUENCES

Unity understands arrays well, but not other types of sequences, such as IEnumerable<T> or IList<T>. To effectively work with sequences, we must define or transform them into arrays to enable Unity to deal appropriately with them.

If you try to register Meal without telling the container how it should deal with the IEnumerable<ICourse> DEPENDENCY, an exception will be thrown when you try to resolve IMeal:

```
container.RegisterType<IMeal, Meal>();
var meal = container.Resolve<IMeal>();
```

Resolving `IMeal` throws an exception because Unity doesn't know how to resolve `IEnumerable<ICourse>`. This is true even if you have previously registered several `ICourse` components, as you did in listing 14.9.

To map all named `ICourse` registrations to `IEnumerable<ICourse>`, we can take advantage of Unity's built-in knowledge of arrays. The easiest way to do this is by mapping those two types:

```
container.RegisterType<IEnumerable<ICourse>, ICourse[]>();
```

That may look a little weird, but it works well. Whenever Unity encounters an `IEnumerable<ICourse>` DEPENDENCY, it converts it to a request for an array of `ICourse` instances, which gives us the same result that a call to `container.ResolveAll <ICourse>()` would.

> **NOTE** Unity resolves arrays like it returns a result from `ResolveAll`. All named components of the requested type are returned, but the default component isn't.

With this translation in place, resolving `IMeal` now gives us the correct result: a `Meal` instance with the `ICourse` instances from listing 14.9: `Rillettes`, `CordonBleu`, and `MousseAuChocolat`.

Unity handles arrays consistently with the way it implements `ResolveAll`. But other types of sequences aren't natively understood, so we must map them into arrays to make Unity understand them. This will give us all registered components of a given type, which is often sufficient. Only when we need to explicitly pick only some components from a larger set do we need to do more than that. This is possible with more explicit configuration.

PICKING ONLY SOME COMPONENTS FROM A LARGER SET

When we use Unity's ability to resolve arrays, all named components are injected into consumers. This is often the correct policy, but as figure 14.7 shows, there may be cases where we want to pick only some components from the larger set of all registered components.

When we previously let Unity AUTO-WIRE all configured instances, it corresponded to the situation depicted on the right side of figure 14.7. If we want to configure an instance like the left side, we must explicitly define which instances should be used.

In listing 14.10, you used the InjectionConstructor class to define an alternative strategy to the default AUTO-WIRING strategy. When it comes to the `Meal` class, you can do the same, with the only difference that the injected DEPENDENCY is now an `IEnumerable <ICourse>` instead of three separate `ICourse` arguments. The following listing shows how to configure an explicit array with an InjectionConstructor.

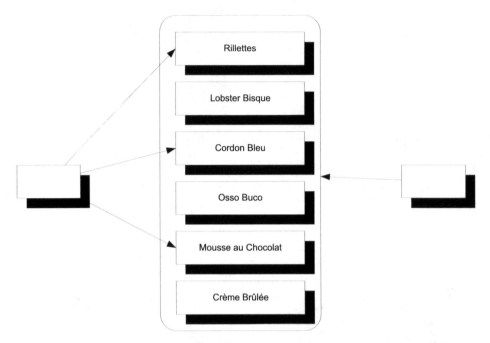

Figure 14.7   In the situation on the left, we wish to explicitly select only certain DEPENDENCIES from the larger list of all registered components. This is different from the situation on the right, where we indiscriminately want them all.

Listing 14.11   Injecting named components into a sequence

```
container.RegisterType<IMeal, Meal>(
    new InjectionConstructor(
        new ResolvedArrayParameter<ICourse>(
            new ResolvedParameter<ICourse>("entrée"),
            new ResolvedParameter<ICourse>("mainCourse"),
            new ResolvedParameter<ICourse>("dessert"))));
```

To override AUTO-WIRING and explicitly define a strategy for injecting DEPENDENCIES into the Meal constructor, you once more look toward the InjectionConstructor class. Because the Meal constructor requires an IEnumerable<ICourse>, you can use a ResolvedArrayParameter<ICourse> instance to define an array that will be evaluated when the container resolves the Meal class. The ResolvedArrayParameter<ICourse> class defines a Strategy where resolution of the array of ICourse instances is deferred until Meal itself is being resolved.

To define the values that will be used when Meal is resolved, you use three named instances of ResolvedParameter<ICourse>, as you did in listing 14.10; the only difference is that they're now used as arguments for the ResolvedArrayParameter<ICourse> constructor instead of directly in the InjectionConstructor. When IMeal is resolved, the ResolvedArrayParameter<ICourse> resolves the three named registrations *entrée*, *mainCourse*, and *dessert* and creates an array of ICourse from those three components. Because ICourse[] implements IEnumerable<ICourse>, the constructor for Meal can be satisfied.

Once more, you see that Unity has good support for arrays. Although support for other sequence types is missing, we can work around this limitation by mapping our DEPENDENCIES into arrays.

Consumers that rely on sequences of DEPENDENCIES may be the most intuitive use of multiple instances of the same ABSTRACTION, but before we leave this subject, we need to look at one more, and perhaps a bit surprising, case where multiple instances come into play.

14.3.3 *Wiring Decorators*

In section 9.1.2, we discussed how the Decorator design pattern is useful when implementing CROSS-CUTTING CONCERNS. By definition, Decorators introduce multiple types of the same ABSTRACTION. At the very least, we have two implementations of an ABSTRACTION: the Decorator itself and the decorated type. If we stack the Decorators, we may have even more.

This is another example of having multiple registrations of the same service. Unlike the previous sections, these registrations aren't conceptually equal, but rather DEPENDENCIES of each other. In this section, you'll see two slightly different ways to configure Unity to deal with this pattern.

DECORATING A NAMED COMPONENT

The Breading class is a Decorator of IIngredient; it uses CONSTRUCTOR INJECTION to receive the instance it should decorate:

```
public Breading(IIngredient ingredient)
```

To make a Cotoletta, you'd like to decorate a VealCutlet (another IIngredient) with the Breading class. Because you already know how to connect named components with constructor arguments, it should feel natural to do something similar with the following listing.

Listing 14.12 Decorating with a named component

```
container.RegisterType<IIngredient, VealCutlet>("cutlet");
container.RegisterType<IIngredient, Breading>(
    new InjectionConstructor(
        new ResolvedParameter<IIngredient>("cutlet")));
```

The Breading component should be the default IIngredient, so you need the VealCutlet to be a named IIngredient because there can be only one default IIngredient. When you register the Breading component, you once more use an InjectionConstructor to define how Unity should wire the Breading class's *ingredient* constructor argument. A ResolvedParameter<IIngredient> enables you to define that the first (and only) constructor parameter should be resolved and wired with the named *cutlet* component.

When you resolve IIngredient, you get a Breading instance that decorates a VealCutlet.

This is a universally applicable way to decorate a component, but when we don't otherwise care about the decorated component, we can use a more implicit method.

DECORATING A CONCRETE COMPONENT

If we never need to resolve the decorated component directly, we can use a more implicit way to decorate it. Imagine that you never expect having to resolve the Veal-Cutlet directly as an IIngredient; when you want an IIngredient, you always want to get the Cotoletta.

In such a case, there's no need to configure the VealCutlet at all. Instead, you can take advantage of the fact that Unity automatically resolves concrete types, even if they aren't registered:

```
container.RegisterType<IIngredient, Breading>(
    new InjectionConstructor(
        new ResolvedParameter<VealCutlet>()));
```

You already know that what you want to inject into the Breading instance is a Veal-Cutlet, so there's no particular reason why you need to take the indirect route of defining a ResolvedParameter<IIngredient> when you can directly supply a ResolvedParameter<VealCutlet>. When you ask the container to resolve IIngredient, the ResolvedParameter<VealCutlet> will automatically resolve into a VealCutlet instance because it's a concrete class. Because VealCutlet implements IIngredient, the Breading constructor is satisfied.

Although you didn't register the VealCutlet component at all, you can still do that if you need to configure other aspects, such as its lifetime:

```
container.RegisterType<VealCutlet>(
    new ContainerControlledLifetimeManager());
container.RegisterType<IIngredient, Breading>(
    new InjectionConstructor(
        new ResolvedParameter<VealCutlet>()));
```

Here you configure the concrete VealCutlet as a SINGLETON, but because you never expect to have a need for resolving it as an IIngredient, you don't map it to the interface. This makes it the default VealCutlet; the ResolvedParameter<VealCutlet> can then correctly resolve it.

As you've seen in this section, there are a few variations available to us when configuring Decorators—both involve the InjectionConstructor class. Unlike Castle Windsor, Unity has no implicit understanding of Decorators, which may be a bit surprising because, like Windsor, it offers the ultimate support for the Decorator pattern: INTERCEPTION.

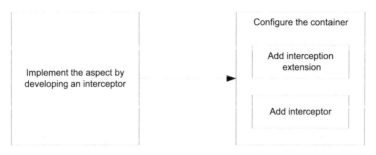

Figure 14.8   The steps involved in adding an aspect to Unity

14.3.4 *Creating Interceptors*

In section 9.3.3, you saw an example of how to add error handling and a Circuit Breaker[8] to a WCF client with Castle Windsor's dynamic INTERCEPTION capability. In this section, we'll do the same with Unity.

Adding an aspect to Unity is a process involving a few steps, as illustrated in figure 14.8.

The bulk of the work involves developing the interceptor itself, but once we have done that, we must add it to the container. INTERCEPTION is an extension to Unity, so we must also add the extension to the container to make it all work.

In this section, we'll first create interceptors for error handling and Circuit Breaker, and finally configure the container with both.

IMPLEMENTING AN EXCEPTION HANDLING INTERCEPTOR

Implementing an interceptor for Unity requires us to implement the IInterception-Behavior interface. Listing 14.13 shows how to implement the exception handling strategy from chapter 9. This particular implementation for Unity corresponds to listing 9.8 for Castle Windsor and listing 12.4 for Spring.NET.

Listing 14.13   Implementing an exception handling IInterceptionBehavior

```
public class ErrorHandlingInterceptionBehavior :
    IInterceptionBehavior
{
    public IEnumerable<Type> GetRequiredInterfaces()
    {                                                   ❶ Supply
        return Type.EmptyTypes;                            interfaces
    }

    public bool WillExecute
    {
        get { return true; }          ❷ Enable
    }                                     interceptor

    public IMethodReturn Invoke(
        IMethodInvocation input,                        ❸ Implement
        GetNextInterceptionBehaviorDelegate getNext)       interception logic
```

---

[8] Michael T Nygard, *Release It! Design and Deploy Production-Ready Software* (Raleigh, NC: Pragmatic Bookshelf, 2007), 104.

```
    {
        var result = getNext()(input, getNext);
        if (result.Exception is CommunicationException
            || result.Exception is
                InvalidOperationException)
        {
            this.AlertUser(result.Exception.Message);
            return input.CreateMethodReturn(null);
        }
        return result;
    }

    private void AlertUser(string message)
    {
        var sb = new StringBuilder();
        sb.AppendLine("An error occurred.");
        sb.AppendLine("Your work is likely lost.");
        sb.AppendLine("Please try again later.");
        sb.AppendLine();
        sb.AppendLine(message);

        MessageBox.Show(sb.ToString(), "Error",
            MessageBoxButton.OK,
            MessageBoxImage.Error);
    }
}
```

⑤ Handle exceptions

Get result from decorated object ④

The ErrorHandlingInterceptionBehavior class implements IInterceptionBehavior which is an interface with three members. Two of those members are mostly concerned with Unity infrastructure and trivial to implement. The GetRequiredInterfaces method ❶ enables you to specify which interfaces this interceptor addresses, but by returning an empty array, you can postpone that decision until the time you configure which components you want intercepted. The WillExecute property ❷ must return true if you want the interceptor to work. This gives you an opportunity to configure whether a particular interceptor should execute or not, but in this case you always want to execute the ErrorHandlingInterceptionBehavior if it's configured for a component.

The core implementation of an IInterceptionBehavior happens in the Invoke method ❸, which is invoked (sic!) by Unity when an intercepted component is invoked. The input parameter provides you with some information about the current method call, while the getNext parameter provides a delegate that you can use to invoke the decorated component. It corresponds roughly to Castle Windsor's Proceed method that you see in listing 9.8.

Invoking the getNext method ❹ gives you an Invoke method that represents the method that this interceptor decorates. It may be another interceptor, or the leaf component itself. Invoking this Invoke method with the original parameters gives you the result from the decorated method.

If the result is one of the exceptions that you've decided to handle, you alert the user by showing a dialog box ❺. In the case of a handled exception, you wish to suppress the exception now that you've alerted the user. Returning the result from the decorated method would allow the exception to propagate, so instead you create a new return value and return it. Conversely, if there were no exceptions, you'd return the `result` from the decorated method.

The `ErrorHandlingInterceptionBehavior` takes care of handling certain exceptions from a decorated component. This component can itself be another interceptor in the form of a Circuit Breaker.

IMPLEMENTING A CIRCUIT BREAKER INTERCEPTOR

The Circuit Breaker interceptor is a bit more complex because it requires the `ICircuit-Breaker` DEPENDENCY, but as the following listing shows, we address this by applying standard CONSTRUCTOR INJECTION. When it comes to composing the class, Unity treats it like any other component: as long as it can resolve the DEPENDENCY, all is well.

Listing 14.14 Implementing a Circuit Breaker `IInterceptionBehavior`

```
public class CircuitBreakerInteceptionBehavior :
    IInterceptionBehavior
{
    private readonly ICircuitBreaker breaker;

    public CircuitBreakerInteceptionBehavior(
        ICircuitBreaker breaker)
    {
        if (breaker == null)
        {
            throw new ArgumentNullException("breaker");
        }

        this.breaker = breaker;
    }

    public IMethodReturn Invoke(IMethodInvocation input,
        GetNextInterceptionBehaviorDelegate getNext)
    {
        try
        {
            this.breaker.Guard();
        }
        catch (InvalidOperationException e)               ❶ Implement
        {                                                    guard
            return
                input.CreateExceptionMethodReturn(e);
        }
        var result = getNext()(input, getNext);           ❷ Get result from
        if (result.Exception != null)                        decorated method
        {
            this.breaker.Trip(result.Exception);          ❸ Handle
        }                                                    exception
        else
        {
            this.breaker.Succeed();                       ❹ Indicate
        }                                                    success
```

❶ Implement guard

❷ Get result from decorated method

❸ Handle exception

❹ Indicate success

```
        return result;
    }

    public IEnumerable<Type> GetRequiredInterfaces()
    {
        return Type.EmptyTypes;
    }

    public bool WillExecute
    {
        get { return true; }
    }
}
```

**Required by
IInterceptionBehavior**

The `CircuitBreakerInteceptionBehavior` needs to delegate its implementation to an `ICircuitBreaker` instance. Because Unity will AUTO-WIRE an interceptor like it does any other component, you can use standard CONSTRUCTOR INJECTION to inject the `ICircuitBreaker`.

In the `Invoke` method you need to implement the Guard-Succeed/Trip idiom you already saw in listings 9.4 and 9.9. First, you need to invoke the `Guard` method and return an exception if the `Guard` method throws an exception ❶. Unity doesn't expect you to communicate exceptions by throwing them, but by encapsulating them in `IMethodReturn` instances, so you must explicitly catch the `InvalidOperation-Exception` and create a return value from the caught exception.

If you make it past the `Guard` method you can proceed to invoke the decorated method ❷. This is done in exactly the same way as you saw in listing 14.13. Now that you have the `result` from the decorated method, you can examine it to see if it returned an exception. If this is the case, you `Trip` the breaker ❸, but notice that you don't change the `result`. Recall that after you `Trip` the breaker you still want the exception to be rethrown, so you can leave the `result` as it is—it already encapsulates the exception.

When there's no exception, you can likewise indicate this to the breaker ❹ by invoking its `Succeed` method. Recall that this can close an otherwise open breaker.

Now that we have both `ErrorHandlingInterceptionBehavior` and `CircuitBreaker-InteceptionBehavior`, it's time to configure the container to make them decorate an `IProductManagementAgent`.

CONFIGURING INTERCEPTION

What we want to do is to intercept an `IProductManagementAgent` component with both Circuit Breaker and error handling so that when an exception happens during communication with the web service, the Circuit Breaker is opened and the exception is handled, giving the application a chance to recover once the web service or the network is back online.

The first thing we need to do is to add the INTERCEPTION feature to Unity. Although INTERCEPTION is part of the Unity Application Block, it's implemented in a separate assembly and must be added explicitly.

NOTE To use INTERCEPTION with Unity, you must add a reference to the `Microsoft.Practices.Unity.InterceptionExtension` assembly.

Once we have a reference to `Microsoft.Practices.Unity.InterceptionExtension`, we must add the `Interception` extension to the container. This is yet another Container Extension, so we can add it with the `AddNewExtension` method:

```
container.AddNewExtension<Interception>();
```

Although this adds general INTERCEPTION capability to the container, we must still configure the `IProductManagementAgent` component with the desired interceptors. Figure 14.9 shows the configuration we're aiming for.

Configuring INTERCEPTION for a component utilizes the fact that all overloads of `RegisterType` accept an array of `InjectionMember`. Until now you've only seen the `InjectionConstructor` class, but a set of other `InjectionMember` classes is used to configure INTERCEPTION:

```
container.RegisterType<IProductManagementAgent,
    ➥WcfProductManagementAgent>(
    new Interceptor<InterfaceInterceptor>(),
    new InterceptionBehavior<ErrorHandlingInterceptionBehavior>(),
    new InterceptionBehavior<CircuitBreakerInteceptionBehavior>());
```

Let's break that down into its constituent parts. First of all, you add an `Interceptor<InterfaceInterceptor>`. This is an `InjectionMember` that signals to Unity that what follows is one or more interception behaviors that intercepts on the interface level (as opposed to intercepting virtual members, for example).

The next two `InjectionMembers` add the `ErrorHandlingInterceptionBehavior` and `CircuitBreakerInteceptionBehavior` interceptors you implemented. Notice that because you list `ErrorHandlingInterceptionBehavior` first, it becomes the outermost interceptor, itself intercepting the `CircuitBreakerInteceptionBehavior`.

The final thing you need to do in this example is to make sure that all DEPENDENCIES can be satisfied. Because `CircuitBreakerInteceptionBehavior` requires an `ICircuitBreaker`, you must also register this component:

```
container.RegisterType<ICircuitBreaker, CircuitBreaker>(
    new ContainerControlledLifetimeManager(),
    new InjectionConstructor(TimeSpan.FromMinutes(1)));
```

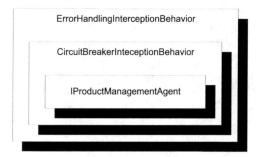

Figure 14.9 The `IProductManagement-Agent` should be decorated by the Circuit Breaker interceptor so that when an exception is thrown by the agent, the circuit's opened for a while. The Circuit Breaker only registers exceptions but doesn't handle them, so this is the responsibility of the error handling interceptor which must be outermost to be able to handle exceptions from both the agent as well as the Circuit Breaker.

To be effective at all it's important that there's only one Circuit Breaker instance (at least per out-of-process resource), so we register the component as a SINGLETON. We also configure the `CircuitBreaker` constructor with a one-minute timeout, ensuring that the application is allowed to retry a failed connection once per minute.

This section demonstrated how to utilize dynamic INTERCEPTION with Unity. In my personal opinion, I find the complexity comparable with Castle Windsor's and Spring.NET's INTERCEPTION support. Although not entirely trivial, the potential benefit is great.

INTERCEPTION is a dynamic implementation of the Decorator pattern,[9] and the Decorator pattern is itself a combined application of multiple components of the same type. Unity lets us work with multiple components in several different ways. We can configure them as alternatives to each other, as peers resolved as sequences, as hierarchical Decorators, or even as interceptors. When it comes to arrays, Unity will figure out what to do, but we can often map other sequence types into arrays. This also enables us to explicitly define how services are composed if we need more explicit control.

This may also be the case when we need to deal with APIs that deviate from CONSTRUCTOR INJECTION. So far you've seen how to configure instances, including how to specify lifetimes and how to deal with multiple components, but until now we have allowed the container to wire DEPENDENCIES by implicitly assuming that all components use CONSTRUCTOR INJECTION. This isn't always the case, so in the next section we'll review how to deal with classes that must be instantiated in special ways.

14.4   *Configuring difficult APIs*

Until now, we've considered how we can configure components that use CONSTRUCTOR INJECTION. One of the many benefits of CONSTRUCTOR INJECTION is that DI CONTAINERS such as Unity can easily understand how to compose and create all classes in a dependency graph.

This becomes less clear when APIs are less well behaved. In this section, you'll see how to deal with primitive constructor arguments, static factories, and PROPERTY INJECTION. These all require your special attention. We'll start by looking at classes that take primitive types such as strings or integers as constructor arguments.

14.4.1   *Configuring primitive Dependencies*

As long as we inject ABSTRACTIONS into consumers all is well. It becomes more difficult when a constructor depends on a primitive type, such as a string, a number, or an enum. This is particularly the case for data access implementations that take a connection string as a constructor parameter, but it's a more general issue that applies to all strings and numbers.

---

[9]   Gamma, *Design Patterns*, 175.

Conceptually, it doesn't always make much sense to register a string or number as a component in a container. However, with Unity this is at least possible.

Consider, as an example, this constructor:

```
public ChiliConCarne(Spiciness spiciness)
```

In this example, Spiciness is an enum:

```
public enum Spiciness
{
    Mild = 0,
    Medium,
    Hot
}
```

> **WARNING** As a rule of thumb, enums are code smells and should be refactored to polymorphic classes.[10] However, they serve us well for this example.

If you want all consumers of Spiciness to use the same value, you can register Spiciness and ChiliConCarne independently of each other:

```
container.RegisterInstance(Spiciness.Medium);
container.RegisterType<ICourse, ChiliConCarne>();
```

When you subsequently resolve ChiliConCarne it will have a Medium Spiciness, as will all other components with a DEPENDENCY on Spiciness.

If you'd rather control the relationship between ChiliConCarne and Spiciness on a finer level, you can do so with the ubiquitous InjectionConstructor, supplying the value to the constructor:

```
container.RegisterType<ICourse, ChiliConCarne>(
    new InjectionConstructor(Spiciness.Hot));
```

Previously in this chapter, you've mostly seen InjectionConstructor used with ResolvedParameter<T>, but another alternative is to supply a value that will then be passed directly to the constructor of the component. Here you supply Spiciness.Hot, which will be passed directly to the ChiliConCarne constructor, resulting in Hot chili.

Both of the options described here leverage AUTO-WIRING to provide a concrete value to a component. If we want a more strongly typed configuration that invokes the constructor or a static factory, we can do this as well.

14.4.2 *Registering components with code blocks*

Another option for creating a component with a primitive value is to use yet another InjectionMember that enables us to supply a delegate that creates the component:

```
container.RegisterType<ICourse, ChiliConCarne>(
    new InjectionFactory(
        c => new ChiliConCarne(Spiciness.Hot)));
```

---

[10] Martin Fowler et al., *Refactoring: Improving the Design of Existing Code* (New York: Addison-Wesley, 1999), 82.

The `InjectionFactory` is another class that derives from the abstract `Injection-Member` class. There are two overloaded constructors, but we use the simplest one that takes a `Func<IUnityContainer, object>` as input. This gives us the opportunity to provide a code block that will create the component. Here the `ChiliConCarne` constructor will be invoked with the `Hot Spiciness` every time the `ICourse` component is resolved.

> **NOTE** The code block in the previous example looks completely identical to the corresponding code block for Autofac in section 13.4.2.

When it comes to the `ChiliConCarne` class, you have a choice between AUTO-WIRING and using a code block, but other classes are more restrictive: they can't be instantiated through a public constructor. Instead, you must use some sort of factory to create instances of the type. This is always troublesome for DI CONTAINERS because, by default, they look after public constructors.

Consider this example constructor for the public `JunkFood` class:

```
internal JunkFood(string name)
```

Even though the `JunkFood` class is public, the constructor is internal. Obviously, instances of `JunkFood` should be created through the static `JunkFoodFactory` class:

```
public static class JunkFoodFactory
{
    public static IMeal Create(string name)
    {
        return new JunkFood(name);
    }
}
```

From Unity's perspective, this is a problematic API because there are no unambiguous and well-established conventions around static factories. It needs help—and you can give it to it by providing a code block it can execute to create the instance:

```
container.RegisterType<IMeal, JunkFood>(
    new InjectionFactory(
        c => JunkFoodFactory.Create("chicken meal")));
```

This time, you use the `InjectionFactory` class to create the component by invoking a static factory within the code block. `JunkFoodFactory.Create` will be invoked every time `IMeal` is resolved and the result will be returned.

When we end up writing the code to create the instance, how is this in any way better than invoking the code directly? By using a code block inside an `InjectionFactory` constructor, we still gain something:

- We map from `IMeal` to `JunkFood`.
- Lifetime can still be configured. Although the code block will be invoked to create the instance, it may not be invoked *every time* the instance is requested—by default it does, but if we change it to a SINGLETON the code block will only be invoked once and the result cached and reused thereafter.

The last common deviation from CONSTRUCTOR INJECTION we'll examine here is PROPERTY INJECTION.

14.4.3 *Wiring with Property Injection*

PROPERTY INJECTION is a less well-defined form of DI because we aren't forced by the compiler to assign a value to a writable property. This is also the case for Unity, which will leave writable properties alone unless we explicitly ask it to do something about them.

Consider this `CaesarSalad` class:

```
public class CaesarSalad : ICourse
{
    public IIngredient Extra { get; set; }
}
```

It's a common misconception that a Caesar Salad always includes chicken. A Caesar Salad is fundamentally a *salad*, but it tastes great with chicken, so many menus offer chicken as an extra ingredient. The `CaesarSalad` class models this by exposing a writable property named `Extra`.

If you configure only the `CaesarSalad` without explicitly addressing the `Extra` property, the property won't be assigned. You can still resolve the instance, but the property will have the default value that the constructor assigns to it (if any).

Once again, you can use an `InjectionMember` to configure a component to populate a property:

```
container.RegisterType<IIngredient, Chicken>();
container.RegisterType<ICourse, CaesarSalad>(
    new InjectionProperty("Extra"));
```

Just as you can use the `InjectionConstructor` class to configure CONSTRUCTOR INJECTION, you can use the `InjectionProperty` class to configure PROPERTY INJECTION. The `InjectionProperty` is yet another class that derives from `InjectionMember`. To use it, you must specify the name of the property to be filled; here you want to populate the `Extra` property. This will cause the property to be AUTO-WIRED so it's important that Unity can resolve the type. The `Extra` property's type is `IIngredient`, so Unity will resolve the property to `Chicken` because you previously registered `Chicken` as `IIngredient`.

> **WARNING** When we configure PROPERTY INJECTION for a property, Unity must be able to resolve the property's type. If it can't, an exception will be thrown when we attempt to resolve the owning type.

When you resolve `ICourse` based on this registration, you'll get back a `CaesarSalad` instance with a `Chicken` instance assigned to its `Extra` property.

The previous example uses the default `IIngredient`, but we can use another overload of the `InjectionProperty` class to provide a value for the property. We can provide a direct value, or we can use the trusted `ResolvedParameter<T>` class to refer to a named component:

```
container.RegisterType<IIngredient, Chicken>("chicken");
container.RegisterType<IIngredient, Steak>("steak");
container.RegisterType<ICourse, CaesarSalad>(
    new InjectionProperty("Extra",
        new ResolvedParameter<IIngredient>("chicken")));
```

The `ResolvedParameter` instance refers to the *chicken* component previously registered, ensuring that when you resolve `ICourse`, you get back a `CaesarSalad` with `Extra Chicken`.

In this section, you've seen how to use Unity to deal with more difficult creational APIs. We can use the many classes that derive from `InjectionMember` to specify concrete instances or code blocks that will be used to create instances, as well as configuring PROPERTY INJECTION. This is a consistent API that I find easy to learn once you get the hang of it.

14.5 *Summary*

Unity is a DI CONTAINER developed and offered by Microsoft *patterns* & *practices*. Although not a Microsoft product as such, many development organizations still view it as a sort of semi-official Microsoft commodity. This can be perceived as an advantage by development organizations that follow a strict policy of using only Microsoft products, because p&p application blocks are often included. The official documentation is also second to none.

Unity offers a consistent API for configuration, but, unlike many other containers, has no fluent API. This can sometimes make discoverability a little more difficult, but once you get the hang of it, you may appreciate the consistency: apart from the optional names and `LifetimeManagers`, all further configuration is done via classes that derive from the abstract `InjectionMember` class. The most commonly used derived class may be `InjectionConstructor`.

In addition to the imperative API, Unity also has a comprehensive XML schema that enables us to define container configuration in XML as well as in code. On the other hand, there's no support for convention-based AUTO-REGISTRATION.

Unity is one of the relatively few DI CONTAINERS to support INTERCEPTION. This support is an extension to the core container, but bundled as part of the Application Block.

One of Unity's relative weaknesses is in the area of LIFETIME MANAGEMENT. Although the built-in lifetimes seem to present an appropriate menu of lifestyles, resource management can become difficult because components aren't properly released after use. Fortunately, not all is lost, because we can implement custom lifetimes that address these issues. It's much harder than it should be, but at least it's possible.

All in all, Unity provides us with a reasonably solid DI CONTAINER. It has weaknesses in some slightly surprising places, but on the other hand offers a near-complete feature set. The only major feature missing is AUTO-REGISTRATION, but because there's an open API, it's possibly to retrofit this if desired.

This chapter provided an introduction to Microsoft's semi-official DI CONTAINER. In the next chapter, we'll look at something a little bit different. Some say that it isn't a DI CONTAINER at all. On the other hand, it's a part of the Base Class Library from .NET 4, and it shares a lot of similarities with DI CONTAINERS, so it's still appropriate to look at the *Managed Extensibility Framework*.

MEF

Menu

- Introducing MEF
- Managing lifetime
- Working with multiple components
- Configuring difficult APIs

In the previous five chapters, you saw how various DI CONTAINERS can be used as tools to implement the patterns and practices laid out in the rest of the book. In this chapter, we're going to do something slightly different, because the Managed Extensibility Framework (MEF) isn't really a DI CONTAINER.

As its name implies, MEF is a framework that addresses extensibility concerns for applications. The focus is on enabling add-in scenarios for standard software. Visual Studio 2010 is probably the first and most prominent application that uses MEF to support plug-ins, but any application built on .NET 4 or Silverlight 4 can use it to expose extensibility features.

If MEF isn't a DI CONTAINER, then why use an entire chapter covering it in this book? The most important reason is that MEF looks *so much* like a DI CONTAINER that you need to spend some time with it to understand the differences between it and real DI CONTAINERS. Because it's part of .NET 4 and Silverlight 4, it may be tempting to use it as a DI CONTAINER if you don't understand the subtle differences. The purpose of this chapter is to exhibit these differences so you can make an informed decision.

NOTE Please keep in mind that you can always skip this chapter if MEF doesn't interest you and you've already decided to use another DI CONTAINER.

Is MEF a DI CONTAINER?

There's a lot of confusion about whether or not MEF is a DI CONTAINER. The short answer is that it isn't, but that it shares so many traits with "proper" DI CONTAINERS that it may become a full-fledged DI CONTAINER in the future.

MEF was built for a different purpose than a DI CONTAINER. Its purpose is to provide a common framework for enabling add-in functionality for standard applications. From the perspective of a standard application, an add-in is an unknown component. Whereas the add-in is most likely required to expose a certain interface, this is about all the application knows about it. There may be zero, one, or a lot of add-ins, depending on the environment. This is different from a DI CONTAINER, where we typically know about all (or most of) the components at compile time.

When we use a DI CONTAINER as a tool to compose an application, we know about the components that make up the application, and we use this knowledge to configure the container in the application's COMPOSITION ROOT.

On the other hand, when it comes to plug-ins, we only know that the plug-ins must implement some sort of ABSTRACTION, but we can't compile the application with a configuration of specific plug-ins, because they are unknown at design time. Instead, we need a discoverability mechanism.

A traditional discoverability mechanism for add-ins is to scan a certain folder for assemblies to find all classes implementing the required ABSTRACTION. However, this doesn't address the issue that may occur when the add-in itself has DEPENDENCIES. MEF, on the other hand, addresses exactly this scenario through its advanced discovery model that uses attributes to define consumers and their services.

A DI CONTAINER favors decoupled composition of services. This provides the greatest degree of flexibility, but comes at a cost: as developers, we must have knowledge about the components we wish to compose at the time we configure the container.

MEF favors *discovery* of components. This successfully addresses the issue when we know little about the add-ins at design time. The tradeoff is that the discovery mechanism is tightly coupled with the components, so we lose some flexibility.

When we consider the internal architecture of MEF, it turns out that discovery and composition are decoupled. This means that it's possible for Microsoft to evolve MEF in the direction of a true DI CONTAINER.[1] On the other hand, some DI CONTAINERS offer such powerful convention-based features that they may encroach on MEF in the future.

Even today, MEF shares so many similarities with DI CONTAINERS that some of its creators already view it as one, while others don't.

---

[1] For more information, see Glenn Block, "Should I use MEF for my general IoC needs?" 2009, http://blogs.msdn.com/b/gblock/archive/2009/08/16/should-i-use-mef-for-my-general-ioc-needs.aspx

TIP If you've already attempted to use MEF as a DI CONTAINER and have been left bewildered and disappointed, this chapter should explain why.

Although being a dedicated DI CONTAINER was not the first priority when MEF was conceived and designed, it turns out that you *can* use it as one. At times it's somewhat awkward, but still possible. There are some scenarios where it makes sense to use MEF as a DI CONTAINER—particularly in applications that already use it to implement extensibility features.

NOTE The whole premise of this chapter is (inadvertently) setting MEF up to fail. This doesn't mean that MEF isn't good at what it does; it means that we're trying to make it do something for which it isn't designed. We're trying to fit a square peg in a round hole.

In this chapter, we'll examine how MEF can be used to apply the principles and patterns covered in parts 1–3. Figure 15.1 shows the structure of the chapter.

The structure of the chapter mirrors the structure of all the other chapters in part 4, because I believe that this makes it easier to compare the different DI CONTAINERS. In the case of MEF, this results in four sections of rather unequal size and importance. We'll spend a lot of time in the introduction to get a feel for MEF and its API, but then cover LIFETIME MANAGEMENT in only a few pages, because MEF doesn't have many options in that area. The topic of multiple components then takes up most of the rest of the chapter, with the last section again being rather short. With the introduction as a prerequisite, each of the three other sections can be read independently of each other.

This chapter should enable you to get started, as well as deal with the most common issues that may come up as you use MEF. However, this is by no way a fair or comprehensive treatment of MEF because we evaluate it in terms of a DI CONTAINER,[2] instead of its real purpose.

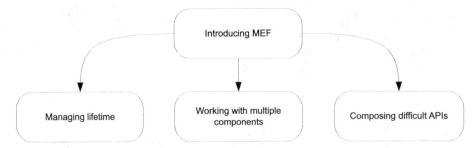

Figure 15.1 This chapter is divided into four sections. The first section provides an overall introduction to MEF and demonstrates how to configure and resolve components. The next three sections each deal with usage patterns that require a bit of extra attention; you can read them all in order, or you can skip some and read only the ones that interest you.

---

[2] For a more idiomatic introduction to MEF, see Glenn Block, "Managed Extensibility Framework: Building Composable Apps in .NET 4 with the Managed Extensibility Framework," *MSDN Magazine* (February 2010). Also available online at http://msdn.microsoft.com/en-us/magazine/ee291628.aspx

You can read the chapter in isolation from the rest of part 4 specifically to learn about MEF, or you can read it together with the other chapters in part 4 to compare it with "real" DI CONTAINERS. The focus of this chapter is to show how MEF relates to and implements the patterns and principles described in parts 1–3.

15.1 Introducing MEF

In this section, you'll learn where to get MEF, what you get, and how you start using it. We'll also look at how components are configured and packaged. Table 15.1 provides fundamental information that you're likely to need to get started.

Table 15.1 MEF at a glance

Question	Answer
Where do I get it?	MEF is part of .NET 4 and Silverlight 4.
What's in the download?	You get MEF when you install .NET 4 or Silverlight 4. It's part of the Base Class Library and packaged in the System .ComponentModel.Composition assembly. If you visit http://mef.codeplex.com/, you can also download the source code to peruse.
Which platforms are supported?	.NET 4 and Silverlight 4. On http://mef.codeplex.com/ you can also find unsupported versions for .NET 3.5 SP1 and Silverlight 3.
How much does it cost?	Nothing. It's part of .NET 4 and Silverlight 4.
Where can I get help?	Because MEF is part of .NET and Silverlight, you can get support from Microsoft.
On which version is this chapter based?	.NET 4.

In contrast with other DI CONTAINERS, MEF has a different rhythm of usage. We never configure a container, but rather annotate the components themselves with attributes. Figure 15.2 shows the relationship between components and the composition engine itself.

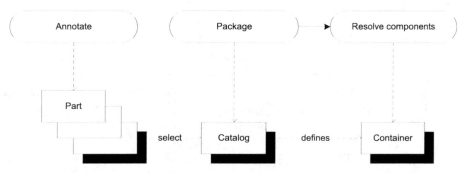

Figure 15.2   With MEF, we annotate parts (for example, classes and members) with attributes in a separate work phase. When we compose an application, we first select the appropriate parts into a catalog and then use the catalog to define a container from which we can resolve components.

> **MEF terminology**
>
> MEF uses terminology that's a bit different than what you're used to when we talk about DI CONTAINERS.
>
> We normally call collaborating classes *components*, but in MEF the nearest term is *part*. A *part* is a class or member that provides or consumes DEPENDENCIES.
>
> When a part consumes a DEPENDENCY, we say that it *imports* it. Conversely, when it provides a service, it *exports* it. In a classic case of jargon-fueled grammatical mayhem, both *import* and *export* can also be used as nouns.
>
> Exports and imports are defined by annotating parts with attributes.
>
> When we compose applications, we match exports with imports according to *contracts*. We often use types (such as interfaces) as *contracts*, but MEF is more flexible than that; a contract is really just a string.

With other DI CONTAINERS, we use a decoupled configuration API to define which components are available, how concrete types map to ABSTRACTIONS, how components are created, and whether instances are shared or not.

Conversely, with MEF, we bundle that information with each part by applying attributes on types and members. This is easy to understand, but tightly couples the configuration of the component to the component itself.

NOTE   Keep in mind that MEF in version 1 uses attributes as the default (and only) method of discovery, but at the core, isn't at all coupled to attributes as a means of discovery.

To compose an application, we select appropriate parts and package them into a *catalog*, and then create a container that can resolve components from that catalog.

When we're done with this section, you should have a good feeling for the overall usage pattern of MEF, and you should be able to start using it in well-behaved scenarios where all parts define simple imports and exports. We'll start with the simplest scenario and see how you can resolve objects using a MEF container.

15.1.1 *Resolving objects*

The core service of any DI CONTAINER is to compose and resolve components. In this section, we'll look at the API that enables us to resolve components with MEF. As with any other container, *resolving* objects is as simple as invoking a simple method, but with MEF, we can't resolve anything until the required exports are available.

If you recall the discussion about resolving components with Castle Windsor, you may remember that Windsor requires us to register *all* relevant components before we can resolve them. MEF has an analogous requirement, although there's no way we can *register* a component; instead, a part must export the desired service.

To resolve the `SauceBéarnaise` service, we must export it. The easiest and most idiomatic way to do that is by annotating the class itself like this:

```
[Export]
public class SauceBéarnaise : IIngredient { }
```

Notice the [Export] attribute annotating the SauceBéarnaise class. This is a MEF attribute that declares that the SauceBéarnaise class exports itself. This means that if you put the class in a catalog, you can now resolve the SauceBéarnaise class, but nothing else, because it's the only export:

```
var catalog = new TypeCatalog(typeof(SauceBéarnaise));
var container = new CompositionContainer(catalog);
SauceBéarnaise sauce =
    container.GetExportedValue<SauceBéarnaise>();
```

You already saw a glimpse of the catalog concept in figure 15.2, and we'll discuss it in greater detail in section 15.1.3. For now, suffice it to say that you package the annotated SauceBéarnaise class into a catalog that you use to define a container. Now that you have the container, you can use it to resolve the SauceBéarnaise service.

NOTE The GetExportedValue method corresponds directly to Windsor's, Autofac's, and Unity's Resolve methods.

Apart from the GetExportedValue method, MEF also supports another style where we first get an export and then later extract the value from the export. In its simplest form, it looks like this:

```
Lazy<SauceBéarnaise> export =
    container.GetExport<SauceBéarnaise>();
SauceBéarnaise sauce = export.Value;
```

The GetExport method is a good example of an *export* being a first-class concept in MEF. It encapsulates the export without necessarily instantiating the part. Creation of the part may be postponed until we query its Value property, but that also depends on the lifetime of the part.

Both the GetExportedValue and GetExport methods have plural counterparts that enable us to resolve sequences of parts. They look like this:

```
IEnumerable<IIngredient> ingredients =
    container.GetExportedValues<IIngredient>();
IEnumerable<Lazy<IIngredient>> exports =
    container.GetExports<IIngredient>();
```

So far, the SauceBéarnaise class exports only its own, concrete type. Even though it also implements IIngredient, it doesn't export that interface unless you explicitly state that it does. Mapping ABSTRACTIONS to concrete types also involves the [Export] attribute.

MAPPING ABSTRACTIONS TO CONCRETE TYPES

The [Export] attribute exports the part it annotates. Sometimes the exported part is already an ABSTRACTION, but when we annotate a class, the concrete class is exported by default, even if it implements one or more interfaces.

Loose coupling normally requires us to map ABSTRACTIONS to concrete types. Creating instances based upon such maps is the core service offered by any DI CONTAINER, but we must still define the map. With MEF, we do that by modifying the export by explicitly stating what it exports.

In this example, you let the concrete SauceBéarnaise class export the IIngredient interface:

```
[Export(typeof(IIngredient))]
public class SauceBéarnaise : IIngredient { }
```

Compared to the previous example, you've now changed the [Export] attribute to use an overload that enables you to specify that IIngredient is the export. Once again, you can package the SauceBéarnaise class into a catalog and create a container out of the catalog.

```
IIngredient ingredient = container.GetExportedValue<IIngredient>();
```

When you resolve IIngredient from the container, the ingredient value now turns out to be a SauceBéarnaise instance, as you would've expected. However, if you attempt to resolve SauceBéarnaise as you did in the first example, you'll now get an exception because there are no parts that export the SauceBéarnaise contract.

You can easily resolve this by applying the Export attribute multiple times:

```
[Export]
[Export(typeof(IIngredient))]
public class SauceBéarnaise : IIngredient { }
```

The [Export] attribute can be applied as many times as needed, so this version exports both the concrete SauceBéarnaise class as well as the IIngredient interface.

So far, we've looked at a strongly typed, generic method that can be used to resolve services. Still, there are situations where we need a more weakly typed way to resolve services. This is also possible, although a bit more involved than we might wish.

RESOLVING WEAKLY TYPED SERVICES

Sometimes we can't use a generic API because we don't know the appropriate type at design time. All we have is a Type instance, but we'd still like to get an instance of that type. You saw an example of that in section 7.2, where we discussed ASP.NET MVC's DefaultControllerFactory class. The relevant method is this one:

```
protected internal virtual IController GetControllerInstance(
    RequestContext requestContext, Type controllerType);
```

Because we only have a Type instance, we can't use generics, but must resort to a weakly typed API. Unfortunately, the only untyped API exposed by Composition-Container is a little unwieldy. There's no untyped version of the GetExportedValue or GetExportedValues methods, so we must resort to the non-generic version of Get-Exports to implement GetControllerInstance:

```
var export = this.container.GetExports(
    controllerType, null, null).Single();
return (IController)export.Value;
```

There are several overloads of the non-generic GetExports method, and here we use one that enables us to pass in the controllerType directly. The two other parameters can be used to provide constraints for the query, but we can pass in null when we don't need to do that. The GetExports method returns a sequence of exports, but we require that there's only a single export that satisfies the query, so we invoke the Single extension method to get the single instance from the sequence.

Because the GetExports method is weakly typed, we must cast the exported value to IController before returning it. In any case, no matter which specific method we use to resolve parts, MEF composes the parts by matching imports with exports. It can only do this when we have explicitly defined these in advance.

15.1.2 *Defining imports and exports*

In section 3.2, we discussed several conceptually different ways we can configure a DI CONTAINER. Figure 15.3 reviews the options and illustrates how MEF doesn't fit into that model at all.

We can't configure the container itself in any way—neither with imperative code nor through XML configuration. MEF only gives us one option to define imports and exports, and that is by applying attributes to parts. Attributes are part of the type they annotate, so we must view this mechanism as more explicit and early bound than even CODE AS CONFIGURATION. Catalogs, on the other hand, provide us with a great deal of flexibility because they enable us to pick the types we wish to include into a composition.

> **WARNING** The use of attributes tightly couples the configuration to the implementation. In section 9.3.1, we discussed the disadvantages of using attributes for aspects, but the discussion applies in general. Keep in mind that MEF may gain alternatives to attributes in the future.

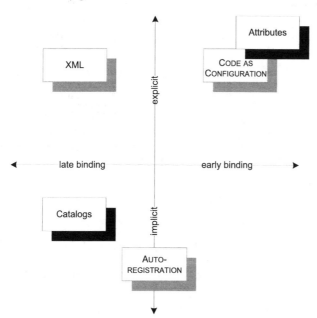

Figure 15.3 **MEF doesn't fit into our standard conceptual model for configuration options, because we can't configure *the container*. All the normal options we're used to reviewing are unavailable and grayed out. Annotating parts with attributes defines the configuration statically together with the type, whereas catalogs provide flexibility.**

In this section, we'll look at options for importing and exporting parts, and then in section 15.1.3, we'll look at catalogs. Although we can't cover our standard options for configuring a container, we can make some approximations to cover different scenarios. In this section, you'll see different ways in which we can export and import parts.

EXPORTING TYPES

In this section, we'll cover the scenario where we control the classes we wish to export. When we have full control over the source code for the classes that we want to export, we can export a class by applying the [Export] attribute:

```
[Export]
[Export(typeof(IIngredient))]
public class SauceBéarnaise : IIngredient { }
```

The [Export] property can be applied as many times as needed, so that the same class can export different contracts. The SauceBéarnaise class shown here exports both itself as a concrete class and the IIngredient interface.

The [Export] overload that enables you to specify an exported type provides no compile-time checking. You can declare an invalid export without compilation errors:

```
[Export(typeof(ICourse))]
public class SauceBéarnaise : IIngredient { }
```

The SauceBéarnaise class doesn't implement the ICourse interface, yet you can still compile the claim that it does. However, when you attempt to resolve ICourse, an exception will be thrown because MEF can't cast SauceBéarnaise to ICourse.

WARNING   It's possible to declare invalid exports.

Obviously, you can let different classes export different contracts without conflict:

```
[Export(typeof(IIngredient))]
public class SauceBéarnaise : IIngredient { }
```

```
[Export(typeof(ICourse))]
public class Course : ICourse { }
```

Because each class exports different contracts, there's no conflict and you can ask the container to resolve both ICourse and IIngredient and receive instances of Course and SauceBéarnaise, respectively.

However, exporting the same ABSTRACTION multiple times changes the picture:

```
[Export(typeof(IIngredient))]
public class SauceBéarnaise : IIngredient { }
```

```
[Export(typeof(IIngredient))]
public class Steak : IIngredient { }
```

In this example, you export IIngredient twice. If you attempt to resolve IIngredient, the container will throw an exception because there are multiple exports; by invoking GetExport or GetExportedValue you imply that you request a ubiquitous part. You can still get both SauceBéarnaise and Steak by invoking the plural methods GetExports and GetExportedValues.

NOTE MEF has no concept of a *default component*. All exports are equally ranked.

This is your first glimpse of an important concept in MEF: *cardinality* of imports and exports. The number of exports must be compatible with the number of imports. Table 15.2 shows how MEF matches imports and exports based on cardinality.

Table 15.2 Import and export cardinality matches

	Export.Single	Export.Many
Import.Single	Match	No match
Import.Many	Match	Match

In this context, the term *many* indicates a sequence of parts, typically an array or IEnumerable<T>. If we explicitly import many parts of the same contract, MEF will always find us a match because zero exports is a special case of multiple exports.

On the other hand, when we explicitly import a single instance we get a cardinality mismatch if there are zero or multiple exports because importing a single instance indicates that we must have exactly one, ubiquitous instance.

NOTE Cardinality is one among several dimensions where imports and exports must match.

As you'll see in section 15.2, LIFETIME MANAGEMENT can also play a role when it comes to matching parts, but cardinality is always active. Later in this section, you'll see how to define single and multiple imports; but before we cover that we should look at exporting parts when we don't control the classes involved.

EXPORTING ADAPTERS
Applying the [Export] attribute to a class is the easiest way to export a part, but this might not always be possible. We may wish to export classes that were already compiled, and we might not have access to the source code. In such cases, we can't apply attributes, yet we would still like to include the class into a composition.

We can still achieve that goal by leveraging MEF's ability to export properties as well as classes. As an example, consider this Mayonnaise constructor:

```
public Mayonnaise(EggYolk eggYolk, OliveOil oil)
```

Imagine that the Mayonnaise class and its constituent EggYolk and OliveOil DEPENDENCIES are outside your control. One option would be to derive from the original class and apply the [Export] attribute to the derived class:

```
[Export(typeof(OliveOil))]
[Export(typeof(IIngredient))]
public class MefOliveOil : OliveOil { }
```

Notice that if you wish to export both the original concrete class as well as the IIngredient interface, you must explicitly state that the base class (which is also a concrete class) is being exported. Had you used the [Export] attribute without a type, you would've exported the MefOliveOil class instead.

However, if the classes in question are sealed, you can't export them in this way. Instead, as the following listing shows, you can create an adapter[3] and export the part via a property.

Listing 15.1   Exporting OliveOil via an adapter

```
public class OliveOilAdapter
{
    private readonly OliveOil oil;

    public OliveOilAdapter()
    {
        this.oil = new OliveOil();
    }

    [Export]
    public OliveOil OliveOil
    {
        get { return this.oil; }
    }
}
```

❶ Export property

The OliveOilAdapter class is a completely new class that wraps the original OliveOil class and exports it through an annotated property ❶. The [Export] attribute can be applied to properties as well as types, but otherwise works in the same way. The type of the OliveOil property is OliveOil, which is also the contract you wish to export, so in this case, you can use the [Export] property without explicitly stating a type.

TIP   It's always possible to export a type by creating an adapter.

When the class that you need to compose has DEPENDENCIES of its own, you need to import these through the adapter. As the following listing demonstrates, this becomes a little more involved, but is still quite manageable.

Listing 15.2   Adapting a class with DEPENDENCIES

```
public class MayonnaiseAdapter
{
    private readonly Mayonnaise mayo;

    [ImportingConstructor]
    public MayonnaiseAdapter(
        EggYolk yolk, OliveOil oil)
    {
        if (yolk == null)
        {
```

❶ Mimic Mayonnaise constructor signature

---

[3] I have chosen the term *adapter* because the purpose of such MEF Adapters corresponds to the purpose, if not all the specifics, of the original Adapter design pattern: Erich Gamma et al., *Design Patterns: Elements of Reusable Object-Oriented Software* (New York: Addison-Wesley, 1994), 139.

```
            throw new ArgumentNullException("yolk");
        }
        if (oil == null)
        {
            throw new ArgumentNullException("oil");
        }

        this.mayo = new Mayonnaise(yolk, oil);
    }

    [Export]
    public Mayonnaise Mayonnaise
    {
        get { return this.mayo; }
    }
}
```

❷ Create Mayonnaise

❸ Export Mayonnaise

To export the Mayonnaise class via an adapter, you must address the fact that it has DEPENDENCIES of its own that you need to import. To be able to provide an instance, you must mimic the signature of the Mayonnaise constructor in the adapter's constructor ❶ so that you can import all the necessary parts. After passing appropriate Guard Clauses, you create a new Mayonnaise instance ❷ from the constructor parameters and save the result in a private field. This is the CONSTRUCTOR INJECTION pattern at work.

To export Mayonnaise, you can expose the mayo field as a property and annotate it with an [Export] attribute ❸.

With an EggYolkAdapter similar to the OliveOilAdapter from listing 15.1, you can create a catalog from the three adapters and successfully resolve a Mayonnaise instance even though you never modified the original classes.

You may have noticed the [ImportingConstructor] attribute that appeared in listing 15.2. This is part of the other side of the equation. So far, we've been looking at how to export parts; now we need to see how to import them.

IMPORTING PARTS

There's symmetry about MEF. Most of the statements we can make about exports we can also make about imports. However, when it comes to CONSTRUCTOR INJECTION, we must resort to the [ImportingConstructor] attribute, which has no equivalent for exports. We saw it applied to the MayonnaiseAdapter in listing 15.2, but it must be applied wherever we wish to use CONSTRUCTOR INJECTION.

In the example we assumed that the Mayonnaise class was out of our control. In a sudden reverse of fortune, we have unexpectedly gotten hold of the source code and can now change the types directly. In this case, we don't have to create adapters, but can apply the [Export] attributes directly to the Mayonnaise, OliveOil, and EggYolk classes.

MEF doesn't recognize the CONSTRUCTOR INJECTION pattern, so even though Mayonnaise has only a single constructor, we'll initially get an exception if we attempt to resolve it. We need to explicitly tell MEF which constructor it should use if there's no default constructor available:

```
[ImportingConstructor]
public Mayonnaise(EggYolk eggYolk, OliveOil oil)
```

The [ImportingConstructor] is a signal to MEF that the constructor it annotates should be used to compose the type.

> **TIP** The [ImportingConstructor] isn't necessary for default constructors. Use it if a class has no default constructor, or if composition should happen through a different constructor than the default.

We can also use an [Import] attribute to support PROPERTY INJECTION, but we'll get back to that in section 15.4.3, which deals explicitly with this pattern. Likewise, there's an [ImportMany] attribute which is used to import sequences of parts, but we'll deal with that in section 15.3.2.

Importing and exporting parts relies on applying attributes, and because attributes are compiled into the type, this is about as inflexible as it gets. MEF instead gets its flexibility from *catalogs*.

15.1.3   *Working with catalogs*

A catalog encapsulates a collection of parts that the container can use to compose an object graph. In this section, we'll review various types of catalogs that MEF makes available.

USING CATALOGS WITH CONTAINERS

In section 15.1.1, you already saw an example of a catalog and a container interacting:

```
var catalog = new
    TypeCatalog(typeof(SauceBéarnaise));
var container = new
    CompositionContainer(catalog);
```

Here you use a TypeCatalog with a single type, but you can create a Composition-Container with any ComposablePartCatalog; TypeCatalog is one child class among several. Figure 15.4 sketches the type hierarchy.

> **DEFINITION** A *catalog* is any class that derives from the abstract Composable-PartCatalog class.

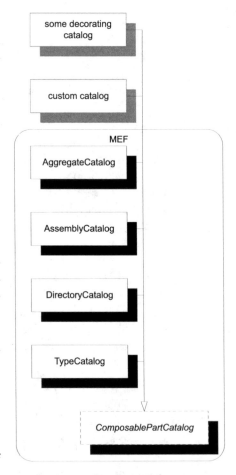

Figure 15.4   MEF include four concrete catalogs, but we can also conceivably define custom catalogs. It may be fairly straightforward to implement a catalog that acts as a Decorator for other catalogs (for example, a filtering catalog), whereas a true custom catalog would be more involved.

As the name implies, a ComposablePartCatalog is a catalog of parts that a Composition-Container uses to match imports with exports. One of the CompositionContainer class's constructor overloads enables us to supply a `ComposablePartCatalog`, and this is the constructor we've been using so far:

```
public CompositionContainer(ComposablePartCatalog catalog,
    params ExportProvider[] providers)
```

In addition to accepting a `ComposablePartCatalog` instance, this constructor also accepts a params array of `ExportProviders`, which is another extensibility mechanism outside the scope of this chapter.

Because `ComposablePartCatalog` is an abstract class and `CompositionContainer` accepts any derived class, we can in theory create custom catalogs from scratch. This is a major SEAM for MEF and can even be used to define alternatives to the MEF's default attributed model for defining imports and exports. Although this is possible, it's also a lot of work, so it isn't something we'll cover in this chapter.

> **TIP** The *MEF Contrib* open source project[4] provides an example of a custom `ComposablePartCatalog` that completely replaces the attributed configuration model with a more open model that looks more like other DI CONTAINERS.

All the catalogs provided with MEF in .NET 4 use `[Import]` and `[Export]` attributes to define imports and exports, but they locate parts in different ways. As an example, `TypeCatalog` locates parts by reading attributes off the types contained in the catalog.

USING TYPE CATALOGS

The `TypeCatalog` class lets us define a catalog from a list of types, with the underlying assumption that these types define imports and exports via attributes. There are two overloaded constructors that both enable us to provide an arbitrary number of `Type` instances:

```
public TypeCatalog(params Type[] types)
public TypeCatalog(IEnumerable<Type> types)
```

As an example, to be able to compose `Mayonnaise` from the adapters you created in listings 15.1 and 15.2, you can create a catalog like this:

```
var catalog = new TypeCatalog(
    typeof(MayonnaiseAdapter),
    typeof(EggYolkAdapter),
    typeof(OliveOilAdapter));
```

This is the minimal catalog that enables you to resolve `Mayonnaise`. If you remove any of the three adapter types, exports would be missing. In addition to letting you resolve `Mayonnaise` itself, this catalog also enables you to resolve `EggYolk` and `OliveOil`, but nothing else.

Obviously you could provide more types to a `TypeCatalog` to offer more exports, but you must explicitly provide the list of types. This makes sense for small scenarios with limited scope. The advantage is that you can pick only those types from which

---

[4] http://mefcontrib.codeplex.com/

you wish to compose. If you have types that export competing parts, you can select only the ones you want.

> **TIP** You can create different adapters that export the same part in mutually exclusive ways, and supply only one of them to a `TypeCatalog`. When writing the sample code for this chapter I used this trick to vary the attributes of `MayonnaiseAdapter` without having to edit the code.

The disadvantage of using a `TypeCatalog` is that you must explicitly supply all the types. When you add a new type to an assembly, you also need to add it to a `TypeCatalog` if you want to include it. This violates the DRY[5] Principle. You could get around that issue by writing code that uses Reflection to scan an assembly for all public types, but you don't have to do that because there's already a catalog that does exactly that.

USING ASSEMBLY CATALOGS

The `AssemblyCatalog` class scans an assembly for all imports and exports defined in that assembly. This enables us to keep adding parts to an assembly without having to remember to also add the part to a catalog.

Using `AssemblyCatalog` is as simple as providing an `Assembly` instance via the constructor:

```
var assembly = typeof(Steak).Assembly;
var catalog = new AssemblyCatalog(assembly);
```

Here you use an indiscriminate representative type (`Steak`) to define the assembly, but any method that creates the appropriate `Assembly` instance will do.

There's also a constructor overload that takes a file name instead of an `Assembly` instance. This enables more loosely coupled scenarios because we can replace the .dll file without recompiling the rest of the application. This moves us even closer toward MEF's raison d'être of enabling add-in scenarios. With the `AssemblyCatalog`, we could write an imperative loop and create a catalog for each file we find in a given directory. However, we don't need to do that because MEF already provides a dedicated catalog that does that.

USING DIRECTORY CATALOGS

The main purpose of MEF is to enable add-in scenarios. A common add-in architecture is to designate a special directory for add-ins; any assembly placed in this directory will be loaded and used by the main application.

MEF supports this scenario through the `DirectoryCatalog` class. We supply a directory path to the constructor, and it automatically scans that directory for .dll files and loads all parts from the assemblies it finds:

```
var catalog = new DirectoryCatalog(directory);
```

An alternative constructor overload also enables us to specify a search pattern using common wildcards.

---

[5] Don't Repeat Yourself.

NOTE When MEF is used in its key role as an extensibility framework you should expect `DirectoryCatalog` to be the most commonly used catalog.

Although we can place any number of assemblies in a directory and use a `Directory-Catalog` to pick them up, we may want to combine catalogs from several different sources. Even if we use a `DirectoryCatalog` to enable extensibility, we may also want to provide some default or internal implementations of the relevant imports and exports. These shouldn't reside in the add-in folder because that would enable users to remove vital functionality from the application. Such default implementations may be better provided by a `TypeCatalog`, but that means that we must combine different catalogs into one.

USING AGGREGATE CATALOGS

To combine catalogs, we can use an `AggregateCatalog`, which is a Composite[6] with another name. It aggregates any number of other catalogs while being a catalog in its own right:

```
var catalog = new AggregateCatalog(catalog1, catalog2);
var container = new CompositionContainer(catalog);
```

The four catalogs included with MEF already provide a good deal of flexibility, and we can also implement custom catalogs for greater control. One example that is fairly easy to implement and use could be a filtering catalog.

IMPLEMENTING A FILTERING CATALOG

Although it can be a rather intricate undertaking to implement a custom catalog completely from scratch, we can fairly easily implement a Decorator[7] that modifies the behavior of another catalog.

The most obvious example is a filtering catalog that filters a decorated catalog. The following listing shows a custom catalog that decorates another catalog and only allows through those parts that export a contract containing the string *Sauce*; you can use it to get only the sauces from a catalog of all ingredients.

Listing 15.3   Implementing a custom catalog

```
public class SauceCatalog : ComposablePartCatalog
{
    private readonly ComposablePartCatalog catalog;

    public SauceCatalog(ComposablePartCatalog cat)
    {
        if (cat == null)
        {
            throw new ArgumentNullException("cat");
        }

        this.catalog = cat;
    }
```

❶ Derive from ComposablePartCatalog

❷ Constructor Injection

---

[6] Gamma, *Design Patterns*, 163.
[7] Ibid., 175.

```
public override
    IQueryable<ComposablePartDefinition> Parts
{
    get
    {
        return this.catalog.Parts.Where(def =>
            def.ExportDefinitions.Any(x =>
                x.ContractName
                    .Contains("Sauce")));
    }
}
}
```

❸ Implement filter

To implement a custom catalog, you derive from the abstract `ComposablePartCatalog` class ❶. Because you wish to decorate another catalog you request it via CONSTRUCTOR INJECTION ❷.

The `Parts` property ❸ is the only abstract member of `ComposablePartCatalog`, so this is the only member you *must* implement; there are other virtual members that you *can* implement if you like, but this isn't necessary for this example. The filter is implemented by a `Where` expression that filters away all `ComposablePartDefinitions` that don't export any contract that contains the word *Sauce*.

The `SauceCatalog` is specific, but you can generalize the concept to create a general-purpose `FilteringCatalog`; the MEF documentation includes an example.[8]

Custom catalogs

Perhaps listing 15.3 made you wonder: if we only need to implement a single property to create a custom catalog, how can it be so difficult? The problem is that `Composable-PartDefinition` is an abstract type without any public implementations. Implementing a derived `ComposablePartCatalog` requires that we also implement a custom `ComposablePartDefinition`. The pattern is now repeated because `Composable-PartDefinition` defines another abstract method with a return type that has no public implementation. Although it's possible to implement a custom catalog, it's outside the scope of this book.

Catalogs are an essential building block of MEF. Whereas attributes are static, catalogs provide a certain flexibility that partially makes up for that. MEF comes with four built-in catalogs that contain parts drawn from explicit types, from a single assembly, or from assemblies found in a folder. When we need to combine parts from multiple catalogs, we can use an `AggregateCatalog`.

MEF only supports configuration of parts via attributes, but if we need to compose parts without attributes we can always create adapters that import and export those parts. Such adapters can be used to bridge the gap between the static attributed model and the container configuration we're used to from other DI CONTAINERS. We

---

[8]　http://mef.codeplex.com/wikipage?title=Filtering%20Catalogs

can subclass the existing catalog types to pre-package a set of parts or adapters that can later be combined with an AggregateCatalog to compose an application.

Until now, we've only looked at how to define imports and exports so that MEF can compose object graphs. There are other dimensions of DI that we have yet to look at. One of the most important topics is how to manage OBJECT LIFETIME.

15.2 Managing lifetime

In chapter 8, we discussed LIFETIME MANAGEMENT, including the most common conceptual lifetime styles such as SINGLETON and TRANSIENT. It's easy to get an overview of the available lifestyles in MEF, because there are only the two shown in table 15.3.

Table 15.3   MEF lifestyles

Name	Comments
Shared	You should consider this the default, although it depends on matching imports and exports. This is MEF's name for the SINGLETON lifestyle.
NonShared	MEF's name for the TRANSIENT lifestyle. Instances are tracked by the container.

NOTE   MEF calls lifestyles *creation policies*.

MEF's implementation of both SINGLETON and TRANSIENT are equivalent to the general lifestyles described in chapter 8, so I won't spend much time on them in this chapter.

TIP   The default lifestyle in MEF is SINGLETON. This is different from many other containers. As we discussed in chapter 8, SINGLETON is the most efficient, although not always the safest, of all lifestyles, so MEF's default prioritizes efficiency over safety.

There are only two creation policies, and it isn't possible to implement custom lifetimes, so compared to the other chapters in part 4, this section will be rather short. You'll see how to declare lifestyles for parts and how to release components. At the end of this section, you should be able to use MEF's creation policies in your own application.

Consistently with the rest of MEF's API, creation policy is defined with attributes.

15.2.1 Declaring creation policy

Declaring the creation policy for a part is as easy as adding the [PartCreationPolicy] attribute to a class:

```
[Export(typeof(IIngredient))]
[PartCreationPolicy(CreationPolicy.NonShared)]
public class SauceBéarnaise : IIngredient { }
```

The [PartCreationPolicy] attribute requires that you specify a CreationPolicy value. Here you specify NonShared to declare SauceBéarnaise as TRANSIENT, but as table 15.4 shows, the CreationPolicy enum has a few other options.

Table 15.4 `CreationPolicy` **values**

Value	Description
Any	This is the default value. The part can be either a SINGLETON or TRANSIENT, but unless NonShared is explicitly requested, the part will behave as `Shared`.
Shared	The part is a SINGLETON.
NonShared	The part is always TRANSIENT.

NOTE The [PartCreationPolicy] attribute can only be applied to classes. This is different than the [Import] and [Export] attributes that can be applied to classes, members, and parameters.

It isn't surprising that we can specify the values Shared and NonShared, but the Any value may come as a surprise. We'll look at the Any value shortly, but before we do that we should first complete the short tour of Shared and NonShared.

EXPORTING WITH CREATION POLICIES

As we just discussed, we specify the creation policy with the [PartCreationPolicy] attribute. If we don't supply this attribute, the default creation policy is Any. However, if we stick with the standard [Import] and [ImportingConstructor] attributes you've seen in this chapter so far, this effectively defaults to SINGLETON behavior.

In that context, the following two examples are equivalent:

```
[Export(typeof(IIngredient))]
public class SauceBéarnaise : IIngredient { }

[Export(typeof(IIngredient))]
[PartCreationPolicy(CreationPolicy.Shared)]
public class SauceBéarnaise : IIngredient { }
```

The only difference between the top two and the bottom three lines of code is that in the lower example you explicitly state that the part is a SINGLETON. As long as the importer doesn't specifically request a particular creation policy, the behavior will be identical.

The difference is that the top example has an implicit creation policy value of Any. Whereas *in most cases* this will default to SINGLETON behavior, it's a little more complex than that.

IMPORTING WITH CREATION POLICY REQUIREMENTS

CreationPolicy.Any explicitly states that the creation policy of the part hasn't been decided, and that matching of imports and export will decide the lifetime.

Among the many options MEF gives us for importing DEPENDENCIES is a feature that enables us to *require* a part with a certain creation policy. This might look like this:

```
[ImportingConstructor]
public Mayonnaise(
```

```
    [Import(RequiredCreationPolicy = CreationPolicy.NonShared)]
    EggYolk eggYolk,
    OliveOil oil)
{ }
```

This `Mayonnaise` constructor explicitly states that only fresh egg yolks are accepted. From a culinary perspective, this might not sound so bad, but when it comes to code, this creates a hard constraint on the importing part. This requirement is compiled into the `Mayonnaise` class via the `[Import]` attribute that annotates the `eggYolk` constructor argument. Notice that only the `eggYolk` parameter is annotated, allowing you to use olive oil from the same bottle to make mayonnaise more than once.

> **WARNING** Specifying a creation policy requirement in a compiled attribute on the consumer is a variation of the CONTROL FREAK anti-pattern. MEF allows it, but you should abstain from it, because it constrains your options for composition.

The `RequiredCreationPolicy` property has the potential of changing the context of matching exports with imports. When we don't use it, we accept anything (`Shared` and `NonShared` alike), but when we do use it, incompatible exports will be rejected.

Do you recall table 15.2 that describes how imports and exports are matched on cardinality? Matching on creation policy is another dimension of MEF's matching algorithm. Table 15.5 shows how creation policies are matched.

Table 15.5   Import and export creation policy matches

	Export.Any	Export.Shared	Export.NonShared
Import.Any	Shared	Shared	NonShared
Import.Shared	Shared	Shared	*No match*
Import.NonShared	NonShared	*No match*	NonShared

Remember that matching on creation policy is only one dimension of matching imports and exports, and all constraints must be satisfied before a match can be made. Keeping imports unspecified with respect to creation policy is by far the preferable option.

In this section, you saw that creation policy is defined with attributes, like imports and exports in general. Specifying creation policies is the first part of LIFETIME MANAGEMENT, but after we resolve object graphs that may contain parts with mixed lifetimes, we should also remember to release them again.

15.2.2 Releasing objects

As discussed in section 8.2.2, it's important to release objects when we're done with them so that any disposable instances can be disposed of if their lifetime is up. With MEF, this is fairly easy to accomplish. We can explicitly release exports, or we can dispose of the entire container when we don't need it any longer.

RELEASING EXPORTS

Releasing an export is easy, but a quirk of MEF is that, although we can release exports, we can't release exported values. What's the difference?

This is an exported value:

```
var ingredient = container.GetExportedValue<IIngredient>();
```

As you saw in section 15.1.1, the GetExportedValue method returns an instance of the requested type, so that ingredient is an instance of IIngredient. As an alternative to requesting the exported value, you can request the export:

```
var x = container.GetExport<IIngredient>();
```

Instead of returning an IIngredient instance, the GetExport method returns a Lazy<IIngredient>. You can still get the exported value from the Value property on the export:

```
var ingredient = x.Value;
```

Whereas x is an instance of Lazy<IIngredient>, ingredient is an instance of IIngredient. When you want to release the resolved components, you must keep the export around because there's only one Release method available on Composition-Container:

```
public void ReleaseExport<T>(Lazy<T> export)
```

The ReleaseExport method requires the export and not the exported value. This means that you can't release the exported value directly by supplying the ingredient variable, but must keep the export around to release it:

```
container.ReleaseExport(x);
```

Because ingredient was created from x, it's released when you release the export like that. Disposable DEPENDENCIES are properly disposed of if their lifetime is up. Releasing parts is as easy as invoking the ReleaseExport method, but you must keep around the original export to be able to do it.

It's important to be able to release exports without disposing of the entire container in scenarios where the same container resolves many instances. This is a typical scenario in web applications and web services where the same container handles multiple requests. On the other hand, in client applications, they should only resolve a single object graph, in which case we can dispose of the container when the application shuts down.

DISPOSING OF THE CONTAINER

Client applications like WPF, Windows Forms, or console applications should follow the pure REGISTER RESOLVE RELEASE pattern, only composing a single object graph for the entire lifetime of the application. This means that we only need to release the object graph at the end of the application's lifetime.

Although we can still release the export with the ReleaseExport method, an easier alternative that doesn't require us to keep a reference to the export is to dispose of the container itself. When the application exits, the container is no longer needed, so we can properly release all parts by disposing of the container:

```
container.Dispose();
```

Disposing of the container releases all parts, disposing of both SINGLETON and TRANSIENT disposables.

This completes our tour of LIFETIME MANAGEMENT with MEF. Parts can be composed from constituents with mixed lifestyles, and this is even true when we define multiple exports of the same ABSTRACTION. We have yet to look at how to work with multiple parts, so we'll now turn our attention in that direction.

15.3 *Working with multiple components*

DI CONTAINERS thrive on distinctness but have a hard time with ambiguity. When using CONSTRUCTOR INJECTION a single constructor is preferred over overloaded constructors because it's evident which constructor to use when there's no choice.[9] This is also the case when mapping from ABSTRACTIONS to concrete types. If we attempt to map multiple concrete types to the same ABSTRACTION, we introduce ambiguity.

Despite the undesirable qualities of ambiguity, we often need to work with multiple implementations of a single interface. This can be the case in these situations:

- Different concrete types should be used for different consumers.
- DEPENDENCIES are sequences.
- Decorators are in use.

In this section, we'll look at each of these cases and see how MEF addresses each one in turn. When we're done, you should be able to annotate and successfully resolve parts even when multiple implementations of the same ABSTRACTION are in play.

> **NOTE** In this section, we don't discuss runtime INTERCEPTION because MEF doesn't support it.

Sometimes we need to provide more fine-grained control than what AUTO-WIRING allows. The next section describes how we can do that with MEF.

15.3.1 *Selecting among multiple candidates*

AUTO-WIRING is convenient and powerful but provides us with little control. As long as all ABSTRACTIONS are distinctly mapped to concrete types we have no problems, but as soon as we introduce more implementations of the same interface, ambiguity rears its ugly head.

First we need a little recap of how MEF deals with multiple exports of the same ABSTRACTION.

---

[9] Even in this case, however, MEF still requires the redundant `[ImportingConstructor]` attribute.

WORKING WITH MULTIPLE IMPLEMENTATIONS OF THE SAME EXPORT

As you saw in section 15.1.2, you can create multiple parts for the same export:

```
[Export(typeof(IIngredient))]
public class SauceBéarnaise : IIngredient { }

[Export(typeof(IIngredient))]
public class Steak : IIngredient { }
```

This example defines both SauceBéarnaise and Steak as IIngredient exports. However, contrary to most other DI CONTAINERS, MEF has no concept of a default component. There's either a single export of a part, or there are multiple exports. This is the concept of cardinality that you saw illustrated by table 15.2. When you export both SauceBéarnaise and Steak as IIngredient you have multiple exports and you can only resolve them by importing multiple instances.

With the two exports, trying to resolve a single IIngredient instance throws an exception:

```
var ingredient = container.GetExportedValue<IIngredient>();
```

This throws an exception because there are multiple exports of IIngredient and MEF refuses to pick one over the other. This makes a lot of sense when we consider the core scenario of MEF: in extensibility scenarios, we'll typically get the exports from assemblies in a folder. Exports are add-ins, so at design time we don't know which exports will be available—if any. In such a context, it doesn't make much sense to pick a single export at the expense of others. Either we must make the exports unambiguous in some other way, or we must be able to deal with a multitude. We'll shortly return to the subject of importing multiple components, but first we'll look at the options we have for making exports more distinct.

One way we can make an export more distinct is by naming it. An overload to the [Export] attribute's constructor allows us to supply a name for the export:

```
[Export("sauce", typeof(IIngredient))]
public class SauceBéarnaise : IIngredient { }

[Export("meat", typeof(IIngredient))]
public class Steak : IIngredient { }
```

Instead of defining two parts that provide the same export (IIngredient), this example defines two different exports: one that exports the combination of IIngredient and the name *sauce*, and one that exports the combination of IIngredient and the name *meat*. Now there's no export of the unnamed IIngredient contract.

NOTE When exporting only named types, there's no export for the unnamed type.

If you attempt to resolve an unnamed IIngredient, an exception will be thrown:

```
var ingredient = container.GetExportedValue<IIngredient>();
```

Although that throws an exception, you can resolve both named IIngredient exports by asking specifically for them:

```
var meat = container.GetExportedValue<IIngredient>("meat");
var sauce = container.GetExportedValue<IIngredient>("sauce");
```

Explicitly resolving a named export by using the appropriate overload for GetExported-Value is a good way to demonstrate how parts are resolved, but when we follow the REGISTER RESOLVE RELEASE pattern, it shouldn't be necessary to request a specifically named component in this way.

> **TIP** If you find yourself invoking the GetExportedValue method with a specific name, consider whether you can change your approach to be less ambiguous.

We can use named exports to select among multiple alternatives when defining parts to be matched with a given consumer.

IMPORTING NAMED EXPORTS

As useful as AUTO-WIRING is, sometimes we need to override the normal behavior to provide fine-grained control over which DEPENDENCIES go where, but it may also be that we need to address an ambiguous API. As an example, consider this constructor:

```
public ThreeCourseMeal(ICourse entrée,
    ICourse mainCourse, ICourse dessert)
```

In this case, you have three identically typed DEPENDENCIES that each represents a *different* concept. In most cases, you want three distinct exports to fill in the appropriate parameters. The following listing shows how you can annotate the desired classes to provide the necessary exports.

Listing 15.4   Defining named exports

```
[Export("entrée", typeof(ICourse))]
public class Rillettes : ICourse { }

[Export("mainCourse", typeof(ICourse))]
public class CordonBleu : ICourse { }

[Export("dessert", typeof(ICourse))]
public class MousseAuChocolat : ICourse { }
```

You annotate the Rillettes with the "entrée" named export, the CordonBleu class with the "mainCourse" named export, and the MousseAuChocolat with the "dessert" named export.

Given these exports, you can annotate the ThreeCourseMeal class's constructor with matching [Import] attributes like this:

```
[ImportingConstructor]
public ThreeCourseMeal(
    [Import("entrée", typeof(ICourse))]ICourse entrée,
    [Import("mainCourse", typeof(ICourse))]ICourse mainCourse,
    [Import("dessert", typeof(ICourse))]ICourse dessert)
```

Notice that you can apply the [Import] attribute to constructor arguments. Normally you don't need to do this explicitly when you already have the [ImportingConstructor] attribute on the constructor, but in this case you need to annotate each parameter to match a different named export. Because you have the matching exports defined in listing 15.4, you can now successfully resolve `ThreeCourseMeal` from these parts.

> **TIP**   If you can't (or don't want to) alter the classes directly, you can create exporting adapters instead.

Metadata

Matching imports with exports using named contracts is a convenient and easy way to address ambiguity. However, using hard-coded strings as we have done in this chapter isn't refactoring-safe. We can attempt to remedy this by defining constants which we use instead of hard-coded strings, but this doesn't ensure that all developers remember to use the constants.

Another alternative is to use MEF's metadata feature. This enables us to define custom export attributes that encapsulate extra metadata we would like to attach to an export. A full treatment is beyond the scope of this book, but a good overview is provided in Glenn Block's MSDN article.[10]

We can always match named imports with similarly named exports to get rid of ambiguity, but a better solution is to design the underlying API to get rid of that ambiguity. It often leads to a better overall design.

In the next section, you'll see how you can use the less ambiguous and more flexible approach where you allow any number of courses in a meal. To this end, you must learn how MEF deals with lists and sequences.

15.3.2   *Wiring sequences*

In section 10.3.2, we discussed how to refactor an explicit `ThreeCourseMeal` class to the more general-purpose `Meal` class with this constructor:

```
public Meal(IEnumerable<ICourse> courses)
```

In this section, we'll look at how we can configure MEF to wire up `Meal` instances with appropriate `ICourse` DEPENDENCIES. When we're done, you should have a good idea of the options available to you when you need to configure parts with sequences of DEPENDENCIES.

AUTO-WIRING SEQUENCES

As we discussed in sections 15.1.2 and 15.3.1, *cardinality* is an explicit concept with MEF. This also means that MEF has an inherent understanding of multiple imports and exports, but that we need to be explicit about it. In section 15.1.2, you saw how you must apply the `[ImportingConstructor]` attribute to explicitly enable

---

[10] Block, *Managed Extensibility Framework.*

CONSTRUCTOR INJECTION. Although it's necessary to apply the [ImportingConstructor] attribute to the Meal constructor, it isn't enough. This instructs MEF that the Meal constructor should be used for composition, but the implied import here is IEnumerable<ICourse>.

You can export ICourse parts in a manner similar to listing 15.4. However, now that you don't want to explicitly distinguish between them, none of them should be named:

```
[Export(typeof(ICourse))]
public class Rillettes : ICourse { }

[Export(typeof(ICourse))]
public class CordonBleu : ICourse { }

[Export(typeof(ICourse))]
public class MousseAuChocolat : ICourse { }
```

Notice that the only difference from listing 15.4 is that none of the exports are named. You now have multiple exports of ICourse, but that doesn't in itself bridge the gap from *multiple* ICourse exports to a *single* import of IEnumerable<ICourse>. The last step is to apply the [ImportMany] attribute:

```
[ImportingConstructor]
public Meal([ImportMany]IEnumerable<ICourse> courses)
```

The [ImportMany] attribute is used to explicitly map multiple exports to a single import of a sequence. The exports can originate from different assemblies but will be composed into a single sequence. When you resolve IMeal, you get a Meal instance with the three ICourse exports: Rillettes, CordonBleu, and MousseAuChocolat.

Using the [ImportMany] attribute, a part can import a sequence of all the exports that match. Only when we need to explicitly pick only some instances from a larger set do we need to do more. Let's see how to do that.

PICKING ONLY SOME EXPORTS FROM A LARGER SET

When we deal with a multitude of exports, the strategy implied by [ImportMany] is often the correct policy. This provides the importer with all the exports of the desired contract, but as figure 15.5 shows, there may be cases where we want to pick only some exports from the larger set of all exports.

When we previously let MEF AUTO-WIRE all exports it corresponded to the situation depicted on the right side of figure 15.5. If we want to compose a part as shown on the left side, we must explicitly define which exports should be used.

The only way we can do that is to once more resort to named exports. However, compared to listing 15.4, the solution is a bit different because now we want to use a named export to mark all those exports we wish to import into the Meal class. As the following listing demonstrates, this doesn't preclude the parts from exporting other contracts, as well as a set-based contract.

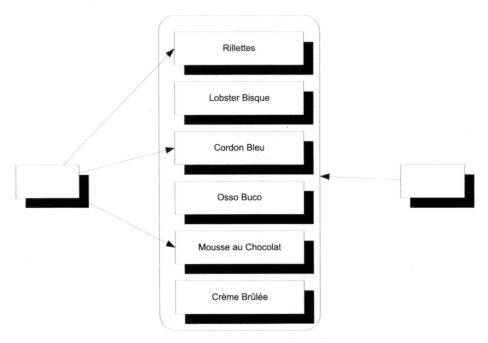

Figure 15.5   In the situation on the left, we wish to explicitly select only certain DEPENDENCIES from the larger list of all exports. This is different from the situation on the right, where we indiscriminately want them all.

Listing 15.5   Targeting exports for a set

```
[Export(typeof(ICourse))]
[Export("meal", typeof(ICourse))]
public class Rillettes : ICourse { }

[Export(typeof(ICourse))]
public class LobsterBisque { }

[Export(typeof(ICourse))]
[Export("meal", typeof(ICourse))]
public class CordonBleu : ICourse { }

[Export(typeof(ICourse))]
[Export("meal", typeof(ICourse))]
public class MousseAuChocolat : ICourse { }
```

❶ Targeted export ❷ Normal export ❸ No targeted export

The three classes Rillettes, CordonBleu, and MousseAuChocolat all export a contract with the name *meal* ❶. This named contract can be used to import only those parts that export this particular contract. However, for other consumers that may want all ICourse exports irrespective of the name, you can also export these three classes as the unnamed ICourse contract ❷; you can add as many [Export] attributes to a part as you'd like.

The LobsterBisque class only exports the unnamed ICourse contract, but not the named *meal* contract ❸. This means that those consumers that wish to import all ICourse exports can do that using the default [ImportMany] attribute as you saw before. However, you can also state that a part only imports those parts that explicitly export the named *meal* contract:

```
[ImportingConstructor]
public Meal(
    [ImportMany("meal", typeof(ICourse))]
    IEnumerable<ICourse> courses)
```

❶ Import a subset

Instead of using the default constructor of the [ImportMany] attribute, you can use a constructor overload that enables you to import only a named contract ❶. The attribute annotates the courses parameter, which means that only those parts that export the named *meal* contract will be composed into the courses sequence. Given the exports from listing 15.5, you'd end up with a Meal with Rillettes, CordonBleu, and MousseAuChocolat, but without the LobsterBisque.

Named exports can be used as markers so that the marked exports can be selectively composed into consumers. Because you can apply as many [Export] attributes as you'd like, you can mark an export for more than a single purpose.

In both of the cases shown in figure 15.5, the [ImportMany] attribute is the key to importing a multitude of exports into a single consumer. Importing sequences is an important way of dealing with ambiguity, and with its concept of cardinality and explicit attributes, MEF makes this clear.

Consumers that rely on sequences of DEPENDENCIES may be the most intuitive example of having multiple exports of the same ABSTRACTION, but before we leave this subject completely, we need to look at one last, and perhaps a bit surprising, case where multiple exports come into play.

15.3.3 *Wiring Decorators*

In section 9.1.2, we discussed how the Decorator design pattern is useful when implementing CROSS-CUTTING CONCERNS. By definition, Decorators introduce multiple types of the same ABSTRACTION. At the very least, we have two implementations of an ABSTRACTION: the Decorator itself and the decorated type. If we stack the Decorators, we may have even more.

This is another example of having multiple exports of the same contract. Unlike the previous sections, these exports aren't conceptually equal, but rather are DEPENDENCIES of each other. In this section, you'll see how to configure parts to deal with this pattern. There are several ways we can compose Decorators with MEF, but because they're all similar, we'll look at only one.

DECORATING WITH CONCRETE CONTRACTS

Consider our trusty Breading class, which is a Decorator of IIngredient. It uses CONSTRUCTOR INJECTION to receive the instance it should decorate:

```
public Breading(IIngredient ingredient)
```

To make a Cotoletta, you'd like to decorate a VealCutlet (another IIngredient) with the Breading class. One way you can accomplish this is to link the VealCutlet together with the Breading class using the concrete VealCutlet class as a contract:

```
[Export(typeof(VealCutlet))]
public class VealCutlet : IIngredient { }
```

Notice that the `VealCutlet` part only exports the concrete type, but not `IIngredient`—even though it implements the interface. The `Breading` constructor can now explicitly state that it imports the concrete `VealCutlet` contract:

```
[ImportingConstructor]
public Breading(
    [Import(typeof(VealCutlet))]
    IIngredient ingredient)
```

MEF matches exports and imports, so as long as there's an unambiguous match, the composition succeeds. `VealCutlet` implements `IIngredient`, so even though the matching algorithm uses the concrete type as a contract, the parts are still compatible. However, note that the compiler doesn't guarantee this.

> **NOTE** This approach is conceptually similar to the approach outlined in section 14.3.3 where we used Unity to compose `Breading` and `VealCutlet` via the concrete `VealCutlet` class.

> **NOTE** Because the attribute is compiled into the class, it would've been even simpler to change the `Breading` constructor to take a `VealCutlet` as a parameter instead of `IIngredient`. In my opinion, this is an excellent demonstration of the shortcomings of using attributes to guide composition.

Although the `VealCutlet` class implements `IIngredient`, it doesn't export it. This is an essential part of this approach. If `VealCutlet` had also exported `IIngredient` it would've introduced ambiguity because `Breading` already exports the interface. This would result in a cardinality mismatch because there would now be two exports of `IIngredient`, and you wouldn't be able to resolve `Breading` by importing `IIngredient`.

> **WARNING** Wiring Decorators isn't possible if the decorated export must also export its ABSTRACTION.

The `Breading` and `VealCutlet` parts are composed together because they have matching contracts. The exact form of the contract is less important. In this example, you used the concrete type of the decorated class, but you also could've used a named contract, or for that matter, any distinct string. The important part is that the match between the two parts is unambiguous.

MEF enables us to work with multiple exports in several different ways. We can configure exports as alternatives to each other, as peers resolved as sequences, or as hierarchical Decorators. In every case we must explicitly specify how MEF should match imports and exports.

This is also the case when we need to deal with APIs that deviate from CONSTRUCTOR INJECTION. So far you've seen how to compose parts, including how to specify creation policies and how to deal with multiple exports, but until now we have only used CONSTRUCTOR INJECTION. Sometimes we must deal with other patterns and APIs, so in the next section, we'll review how we can deal with classes that must be instantiated in special ways.

15.4   Composing difficult APIs

Until now, we've considered how we can compose parts that use CONSTRUCTOR INJECTION. As a general observation, one of the many benefits of CONSTRUCTOR INJECTION is that DI CONTAINERS can easily understand how to compose and create all classes in a dependency graph. MEF, on the other hand, requires explicit use of the `[Importing-Constructor]` attribute, so this is less true for MEF.

In this section, you'll see how to deal with primitive constructor arguments, static factories, and PROPERTY INJECTION. These all require special attention. Let's start by looking at classes that take primitive types, such as strings or integers as constructor arguments.

15.4.1   Compositing primitive parts

As long as we inject ABSTRACTIONS into consumers all is well. However, it becomes more difficult when a constructor depends on a primitive type, such as a string, a number, or an enum. This is particularly the case for data access implementations that take a connection string as a constructor parameter, but is a more general issue that applies to all strings and numbers.

Conceptually, it doesn't always make much sense to register a string or number as a contract. What does it mean to import a string or a number if the type is the only thing we have to go by? Do we really want just any string? Most of the time, we want a specific string, such as a connection string. The same sort of consideration can be applied to any primitive value, including strings, numbers, and enums.

Consider, as an example, this constructor:

```
public ChiliConCarne(Spiciness spiciness)
```

In this example, `Spiciness` is an enum:

```
public enum Spiciness
{
    Mild = 0,
    Medium,
    Hot
}
```

> **WARNING**   As a rule of thumb, enums are code smells and should be refactored to polymorphic classes.[11] But they serve us well for this example.

To properly annotate `ChiliConCarne`, you can add the `[ImportingConstructor]` attribute to the constructor. To export `Spiciness` it makes most sense to do it via an adapter:

```
public class SpicinessAdapter
{
```

---

[11] Martin Fowler et al., *Refactoring: Improving the Design of Existing Code.* (New York: Addison-Wesley, 1999), 82.

```
[Export]
public Spiciness Spiciness
{
    get { return Spiciness.Hot; }
}
}
```

This adapter exports the value `Spiciness.Hot` so that if you compose `ChiliConCarne` from a catalog containing those parts, we'll get a hot Chili con Carne.

> **TIP**   Instead of exporting and importing the `Spiciness` type itself, you can instead choose to use a custom string as a shared contract. That would require you to add an additional `[Import]` attribute to the spiciness constructor argument to specify the contract.

With adapters and contracts, we can properly match primitive types with imports. This still works well when all types and constructors are public, but how do we deal with types without public constructors?

15.4.2 *Composing parts with non-public constructors*

Some classes can't be instantiated through a public constructor. Instead, we must use some sort of factory to create instances of the type. This is always troublesome for DI CONTAINERS because by default they look after public constructors.

Consider this example constructor for the public `JunkFood` class:

```
internal JunkFood(string name)
```

Even though the `JunkFood` class is public, the constructor is internal. Obviously, instances of `JunkFood` should be created through the static `JunkFoodFactory` class:

```
public static class JunkFoodFactory
{
    public static IMeal Create(string name)
    {
        return new JunkFood(name);
    }
}
```

Assuming that you can't change this API, then how do you deal with this situation so that you can properly wire and compose `JunkFood`? The answer is the same as in any other case where you can't change the original exported type: you use an adapter like the one in the following listing.

Listing 15.6   Exporting a type with an internal constructor

```
public class JunkFoodAdapter
{
    private readonly IMeal junk;

    public JunkFoodAdapter()
    {
        this.junk = JunkFoodFactory.Create("chicken meal");
    }
```

```
[Export]
public IMeal JunkFood
{
    get { return this.junk; }
}
}
```

The `JunkFoodAdapter` encapsulates the knowledge that a `JunkFood` instance is created with the `JunkFoodFactory.Create` method. It creates the instance in the constructor and exports it via a property. Because the type of the property is `IMeal`, this is also the exported contract.

With the `JunkFoodAdapter` class available in a catalog, you can successfully resolve `IMeal` and get back a "chicken meal" `JunkFood` instance.

The last common deviation from CONSTRUCTOR INJECTION we'll examine here is PROPERTY INJECTION.

15.4.3 *Wiring with Property Injection*

PROPERTY INJECTION is a less well-defined form of DI because we aren't forced by the compiler to assign a value to a writable property. Ironically, MEF is designed with PROPERTY INJECTION in mind much more than CONSTRUCTOR INJECTION. This explains why we need to explicitly apply attributes to everything we wish to compose: from MEF's perspective, the default composition pattern is PROPERTY INJECTION (which is ambiguous) and CONSTRUCTOR INJECTION is a less idiomatic alternative.

Although I consider this perspective both backwards and wrong, it does make PROPERTY INJECTION easy to apply with MEF. All we have to do is apply the `[Import]` attribute to a property.

Consider this `CaesarSalad` class:

```
public class CaesarSalad : ICourse
{
    public IIngredient Extra { get; set; }
}
```

It is a common misconception that a Caesar Salad includes chicken; this isn't the case. At its core, a Caesar Salad is a *salad*, but it tastes great with chicken, so many restaurants offer chicken as an extra ingredient. The `CaesarSalad` class models this by exposing a writable property named `Extra`.

To enable PROPERTY INJECTION for `CaesarSalad`, all you have to do is to apply the `[Import]` attribute:

```
[Import(AllowDefault = true)]
public IIngredient Extra { get; set; }
```

In this book, I consistently consider PROPERTY INJECTION a pattern that applies when it's optional to supply the DEPENDENCY from the outside. This makes sense because the compiler doesn't force you to assign a value to the property (as opposed to a constructor argument). But this isn't the view taken by MEF. By default, an import *must* be satisfied unless you explicitly state that it's optional, using the `AllowDefault` property. To stay true to the PROPERTY INJECTION pattern as described here, you set the `AllowDefault` property to true. This means that MEF will not throw an exception when it can't satisfy the `IIngredient` import.

You should be aware that with `AllowDefault` set to `true`, MEF will explicitly assign the default value (in this case `null`) to the property instead of ignoring it if it can't satisfy the import. To utilize this feature, you must be ready to deal with null values, but this can wreak havoc with the class's invariants; you should go to great lengths to avoid assigning null to private fields.

One way to deal with null values is to silently swallow such a value, like this:

```
[Import(AllowDefault = true)]
public IIngredient Extra
{
    get { return this.extra; }
    set
    {
        if (value == null)
        {
            return;                  ❶ Silently ignore
        }                                null
        this.extra = value;
    }
}
```

You can explicitly check for null and return if the caller attempts to inject null ❶. This violates the Principle of Least Astonishment, because callers may be surprised to find that assigning a value has no effect, even though no exception is thrown. Once again, you're left with the experience that PROPERTY INJECTION is a more problematic pattern which is best avoided unless absolutely warranted.

On the surface, PROPERTY INJECTION is the idiomatic use case for MEF, but as is so often the case, the devil is in the details. Even with MEF, I'd prefer to use CONSTRUCTOR INJECTION as my default approach.

In this section, you've seen how we can use MEF to deal with more difficult creational APIs. PROPERTY INJECTION is easy to apply, and the rest we can address with exporting adapters. This is always the universal solution if all else fails and we can't change the parts.

15.5 *Summary*

Among all the DI CONTAINERS covered in part 4, MEF is special in more than one way. First, it's the only composition technology officially delivered and supported by Microsoft. Second, it isn't a real DI CONTAINER, but rather an extensibility framework (as the name *Managed Extensibility Framework* implies), so examining it as if it were a DI CONTAINER isn't entirely fair.

There are so many similarities between MEF and real DI CONTAINERS that this chapter isn't only warranted, but necessary. You need to understand in what ways MEF isn't a DI CONTAINER to make an informed decision on when to use it and when not to use it.

This chapter demonstrated that we can squeeze a lot of regular DI CONTAINER functionality out of MEF, but often in rather awkward ways. The most problematic part of MEF is the dependency on attributes because it tightly couples issues such as lifetime and set-based selection of imports to the type. In extensibility scenarios this isn't an issue, but when we work with composition of a full application, this constraint becomes unwieldy.

When we can't, or don't wish to, annotate our types with MEF attributes we can create adapters that import and export the appropriate parts on behalf of the real implementation. In many ways, we can think of such MEF Adapters as MEF's configuration API, but compared to most other DI CONTAINERS' strongly typed fluent interfaces, this is still clunky. However, a MEF Adapter is a universally applicable trick we can use to address particular challenges with MEF. Not only can we use them to compose unattributed types with MEF, but we can also use them to export parts from factory methods, and so on.

Does it make sense to use MEF as a DI CONTAINER in an application? As always, the answer depends on circumstances. One of the strong arguments for using MEF is that it ships as part of .NET 4 and Silverlight 4, so if the application targets these platforms, MEF is already available. This isn't only a question of convenience, but can also be a huge benefit in organizations where policies dictate that only official Microsoft technologies can be used.

Because MEF is an official Microsoft product we also get a different level of support for MEF than we do for other DI CONTAINERS. We get the same support that we get for the rest of .NET and Silverlight, and we can have confidence that MEF is going to be around for a long time.

Still, these benefits may not outweigh the disadvantages of using MEF in a role it was not designed for. MEF was designed for extensibility scenarios, so it makes a lot of sense to use it in applications where extensibility is a major feature. In such applications it may make sense to expand the responsibility of MEF to include composition of the overall application, because it's already in use.

For applications where extensibility isn't a feature it may make more sense to select a dedicated DI CONTAINER for object composition.

No matter which DI CONTAINER you select, or even if you prefer POOR MAN'S DI, I hope that this book has conveyed one important point: DI doesn't rely on a particular technology, such as a particular DI CONTAINER. An application can, and should, be designed using the DI-friendly patterns and practices presented in this book. When we succeed in doing that, selection of a DI CONTAINER becomes of less importance; a DI CONTAINER is a tool that composes our application, but ideally, we should be able to replace one container with another without rewriting any other part of our application than the COMPOSITION ROOT.

resources

All URLs listed here were valid at the time of publication. No doubt some of these will change over time.

In print

Block, Glenn. "Managed Extensibility Framework: Building Composable Apps in .NET 4 with the Managed Extensibility Framework." *MSDN Magazine*, February 2010.

Brown, William J., et al. *AntiPatterns: Refactoring Software, Architectures, and Projects in Crisis.* New York: Wiley Computer Publishing, 1998.

Cwalina, Krzysztof, and Brad Abrams. *Framework Design Guidelines: Conventions, Idioms, and Patterns for Reusable .NET Libraries.* New York: Addison-Wesley, 2006.

Dahan, Udi. "Domain Models: Employing the Domain Model Pattern." *MSDN Magazine*, August 2009.

Evans, Eric. *Domain-Driven Design: Tackling Complexity in the Heart of Software.* New York: Addison-Wesley, 2004.

Farkas, Shawn. "CLR Inside Out: Digging into IDisposable." *MSDN Magazine*, July 2007.

Feathers, Michael. *Working Effectively with Legacy Code.* New York: Prentice Hall, 2004.

Fowler, Martin, et al. *Patterns of Enterprise Application Architecture.* New York: Addison-Wesley, 2003.

————. *Refactoring: Improving the Design of Existing Code.* New York: Addison-Wesley, 1999.

Gamma, Erich, et al. *Design Patterns. Elements of Reusable Object-Oriented Software.* New York: Addison-Wesley, 1994.

Howard, Michael, and David LeBlanc. *Writing Secure Code*, 2nd ed. New York: Microsoft Press, 2003.

Martin, Robert C. *Clean Code: A Handbook of Agile Software Craftmanship.* New York: Prentice Hall, 2008.

Martin, Robert C., et al. *Pattern Languages of Program Design 3*. New York: Addison-Wesley, 1998.

Meszaros, Gerard. *xUnit Test Patterns: Refactoring Test Code*. New York: Addison-Wesley, 2007.

Miller, Jeremy. "Patterns in Practice: Convention Over Configuration." *MSDN Magazine*, February 2009.

———. "Patterns in Practice: Functional Programming for Everyday .NET Development." *MSDN Magazine*, October 2009.

———. "Patterns in Practice: Internal Domain Specific Languages." *MSDN Magazine*, January 2010.

———. "Patterns in Practice: The Open Closed Principle." *MSDN Magazine*, June 2008.

———. "Patterns in Practice: The Unit Of Work Pattern And Persistence Ignorance." *MSDN Magazine*, June 2009.

Nygard, Michael T. *Release It! Design and Deploy Production-Ready Software*. Cambridge, Massachusetts: Pragmatic Bookshelf, 2007.

Osherove, Roy. *The Art of Unit Testing with Examples in .NET*. Shelter Island, New York: Manning Publications, 2009.

Poppendieck, Mary, and Tom Poppendieck. *Implementing Lean Software Development: From Concept to Cash*. New York: Addison-Wesley, 2007.

Seemann, Mark. "Unit Testing: Exploring The Continuum Of Test Doubles." *MSDN Magazine*, September 2007.

Skeet, Jon. *C# in Depth*. Shelter Island, New York: Manning Publications, 2008.

Smith, Josh. "Patterns: WPF Apps With The Model-View-ViewModel Design Pattern." *MSDN Magazine*, February 2009.

Online

Abdullin, Rinat. *CQRS Starting Page*.
http://abdullin.com/cqrs

Block, Glenn. *Managed Extensibility Framework: Building Composable Apps in .NET 4 with the Managed Extensibility Framework*. 2010.
http://msdn.microsoft.com/en-us/magazine/ee291628.aspx

———. *PrismShouldNotReferenceUnity*. 2008.
http://blogs.msdn.com/gblock/archive/2008/05/05/prismshouldnotreference-unity.aspx

———. *Should I use MEF for my general IoC needs?* 2009.
http://blogs.msdn.com/b/gblock/archive/2009/08/16/should-i-use-mef-for-my-general-ioc-needs.aspx

Blumhardt, Nicholas. *Container-Managed Application Design, Prelude: Where does the Container Belong?* 2008.
http://blogs.msdn.com/b/nblumhardt/archive/2008/12/27/container-managed-application-design-prelude-where-does-the-container-belong.aspx

————. *The Relationship Zoo.* 2010.

   http://nblumhardt.com/2010/01/the-relationship-zoo/

Cazzulino, Daniel. *What is all the fuzz about the new common IServiceLocator.* 2008.

   http://www.clariusconsulting.net/blogs/kzu/archive/2008/10/03/Whatisallthe-
   fuzzaboutthenewcommonIServiceLocator.aspx

Dahan, Udi. *Domain Models: Employing the Domain Model Pattern.* 2009.

   http://msdn.microsoft.com/en-us/magazine/ee236415.aspx

Farkas, Shawn. *CLR Inside Out: Digging into IDisposable.* 2007.

   http://msdn.microsoft.com/en-us/magazine/cc163392.aspx

Ferquel, Simon. [Xaml] IoC-enabled Xaml parser. 2010.

   http://www.simonferquel.net/blog/archive/2010/02/19/xaml-ioc-enabled-xaml-
   parser.aspx

Fowler, Martin. *AnemicDomainModel.* 2003.

   http://www.martinfowler.com/bliki/AnemicDomainModel.html

————. *Event Sourcing.* 2005.

   http://www.martinfowler.com/eaaDev/EventSourcing.html

————. *InversionOfControl.* 2005.

   http://martinfowler.com/bliki/InversionOfControl.html

————. *Inversion of Control Containers and the Dependency Injection pattern.* 2004.

   http://martinfowler.com/articles/injection.html

Hadlow, Mike. *The MVC 3.0 IDependencyResolver interface is broken. Don't use it with Windsor.* 2011.

   http://mikehadlow.blogspot.com/2011/02/mvc-30-idependencyresolver-interface-
   is.html

Howard, Rob. *Provider Model Design Pattern and Specification, Part 1.* 2004.

   http://msdn.microsoft.com/en-us/library/ms972319.aspx

Koźmic, Krzysztof. *How I use Inversion of Control containers.* 2010.

   http://kozmic.pl/2010/06/20/how-i-use-inversion-of-control-containers/

Lippert, Eric. *Immutability in C# Part One: Kinds of Immutability.* 2007.

   http://blogs.msdn.com/ericlippert/archive/2007/11/13/immutability-in-c-part-
   one-kinds-of-immutability.aspx

Martin, Robert C. *The Principles of OOD.* 2003.

   http://butunclebob.com/ArticleS.UncleBob.PrinciplesOfOod

Miller, Jeremy. *Patterns in Practice: Convention Over Configuration.* 2009.

   http://msdn.microsoft.com/en-us/magazine/dd419655.aspx

————. *Patterns in Practice: Functional Programming for Everyday .NET Development.* 2009.

   http://msdn.microsoft.com/en-us/magazine/ee309512.aspx

————. *Patterns in Practice: Internal Domain Specific Languages.* 2010.

   http://msdn.microsoft.com/en-us/magazine/ee291514.aspx

————. *Patterns in Practice: The Open Closed Principle.* 2009.

   http://msdn.microsoft.com/en-us/magazine/cc546578.aspx

————. *Patterns in Practice: The Unit Of Work Pattern And Persistence Ignorance.* 2009.
  http://msdn.microsoft.com/en-us/magazine/dd882510.aspx

Munsch, John, et al. *How to explain Dependency Injection to a 5-year old.* 2009.
  http://stackoverflow.com/questions/1638919/how-to-explain-dependency-injection-to-a-5-year-old

Ottinger, Tim. *Code is a Liability.* 2007.
  http://blog.objectmentor.com/articles/2007/04/16/code-is-a-liability

Palermo, Jeffrey. *Constructor over-injection smell—follow up.* 2010.
  http://jeffreypalermo.com/blog/constructor-over-injection-smell-ndash-follow-up/

Pryce, Nat. *"Dependency Injection" Considered Harmful.* 2011.
  http://www.natpryce.com/articles/000783.html

Rahien, Ayende: *Reviewing NerdDinner.* 2009.
  http://ayende.com/Blog/archive/2009/07/30/reviewing-nerddinner.aspx

Seemann, Mark. *Ambient Context.* 2007.
  http://blogs.msdn.com/ploeh/archive/2007/07/23/AmbientContext.aspx

————. *Compose object graphs with confidence.* 2011.
  http://blog.ploeh.dk/2011/03/04/ComposeObjectGraphsWithConfidence.aspx

————. *Interfaces are not abstractions.* 2010.
  http://blog.ploeh.dk/2010/12/02/InterfacesAreNotAbstractions.aspx

————. *Pattern Recognition: Abstract Factory or Service Locator?* 2010.
  http://blog.ploeh.dk/2010/11/01/PatternRecognitionAbstractFactoryOrService-Locator.aspx

————. *Rebuttal: Constructor over-injection anti-pattern.* 2010.
  http://blog.ploeh.dk/2010/01/20/RebuttalConstructorOverinjectionAntipattern.aspx

————. *The Register Resolve Release pattern.* 2010.
  http://blog.ploeh.dk/2010/09/29/TheRegisterResolveReleasePattern.aspx

————. *Service Locator is an Anti-Pattern.* 2010.
  http://blog.ploeh.dk/2010/02/03/ServiceLocatorIsAnAntiPattern.aspx

————. *Unit Testing: Exploring The Continuum Of Test Doubles.* 2007.
  http://msdn.microsoft.com/msdnmag/issues/07/09/MockTesting/default.aspx

Smith, Josh. *Patterns: WPF Apps With The Model-View-ViewModel Design Pattern.* 2009.
  http://msdn.microsoft.com/en-us/magazine/dd419663.aspx

Sturm, Oliver. *Poll Results: IoC containers for .NET.* 2010.
  http://www.sturmnet.org/blog/2010/03/04/poll-results-ioc-containers-for-net

Sych, Oleg. *How to use T4 to generate Decorator classes.* 2007.
  http://www.olegsych.com/2007/12/how-to-use-t4-to-generate-decorator-classes/

Other resources

Autofac
  http://code.google.com/p/autofac/
Castle Windsor
  http://www.castleproject.org/
Common Service Locator
  http://commonservicelocator.codeplex.com/
FxCop
  http://code.msdn.microsoft.com/codeanalysis
MEF Contrib
  http://mefcontrib.codeplex.com/
MVC Contrib
  http://www.codeplex.com/MVCContrib/
Moq
  http://code.google.com/p/moq/
NDepend
  http://ndepend.com
Ninject
  http://ninject.org/
PostSharp
  http://www.sharpcrafters.com/postsharp
Spring.NET
  http://www.springframework.net/
StructureMap
  http://structuremap.github.com/structuremap/
Unity
  http://unity.codeplex.com/
Unity Auto Registration
  http://autoregistration.codeplex.com/
WorldWide Telescope
  http://www.worldwidetelescope.org

glossary

Here are brief definitions of selected terms, patterns, and other concepts discussed in this book. Each definition includes a reference to the chapter where the term is discussed in greater detail.

ABSTRACTION

A unifying term that encompasses both interfaces and (abstract) base classes. See chapter 2.

AMBIENT CONTEXT

A DI pattern that makes a strongly typed DEPENDENCY implicitly available via a context which is always present. See chapter 4.

ASPECT-ORIENTED PROGRAMMING (AOP)

An approach to software that addresses Separation of Concerns by composing CROSS-CUTTING CONCERNS in a declarative manner. See chapter 9.

AUTO-WIRING

The ability to automatically compose an object graph once mappings from ABSTRACTIONS to concrete types are known. See chapter 3.

AUTO-REGISTRATION

Use of conventions to configure a DI CONTAINER instead of using explicit registrations of each component. See chapter 3.

BASTARD INJECTION

A DI anti-pattern. See chapter 5.

CODE AS CONFIGURATION

Use of imperative code to configure a module or application instead of using an external configuration mechanism, such as a configuration file. See chapter 3.

COMPOSER
A unifying term that encompasses any object or method that composes DEPENDEN-CIES. See chapter 8.

COMPOSITION ROOT
A central place in an application where the entire application is composed from its constituent modules. See chapter 3.

CONSTRAINED CONSTRUCTION
A DI anti-pattern. See chapter 5.

CONSTRUCTOR INJECTION
A DI pattern where DEPENDENCIES are injected into the consumer as constructor arguments. See chapter 4.

CONTROL FREAK
The opposite of INVERSION OF CONTROL. A DI anti-pattern. See chapter 5.

CONVENTION-BASED CONFIGURATION
Another term for AUTO-REGISTRATION.

CROSS-CUTTING CONCERN
A concern that spans multiple modules or entire applications. Typical examples include logging, auditing, access control, and validation. See chapter 9.

DEPENDENCY
In principle, any reference that a module holds to another module. When a module references another module, it *depends* on it. Informally, the term *Dependency* is often used instead of the more formal VOLATILE DEPENDENCY. See chapter 1.

DI CONTAINER
A library or framework that provides reusable DI functionality. See chapter 3.

DTO
Data Transfer Object. See chapter 7.

ENTITY
A Domain Object with an inherent, long-term identity. See chapter 7.

FOREIGN DEFAULT
A default implementation of an ABSTRACTION that's defined in a different assembly than the consumer. See chapter 5.

HUMBLE OBJECT
An object that contains little-to-no behavior itself and that instead delegates all its operations to other objects. See chapter 2.

INTERCEPTION
The act of modifying a DEPEDENCY before it's passed to its consumer. See chapter 9.

INVERSION OF CONTROL
Letting a framework control the lifetime of objects instead of directly controlling them. See chapter 2.

LEAKY ABSTRACTION
Even though an ABSTRACTION is defined, the implementation details show through and thus lock the ABSTRACTION to the implementation. See chapter 6.

LIFETIME MANAGEMENT
See OBJECT LIFETIME.

LISKOV SUBSTITUTION PRINCIPLE
A software design principle that states that a consumer should be able to use any implementation of an ABSTRACTION without changing the correctness of the system. The *L* in SOLID. See chapter 8. See also SOLID.

LOCAL DEFAULT
A default implementation of an ABSTRACTION that's defined in the same assembly as the consumer. See chapter 4.

METHOD INJECTION
A DI pattern where DEPENDENCIES are injected into the consumer as method parameters. See chapter 4.

OBJECT COMPOSITION
The concept of composing applications from disparate modules. See chapter 7.

OBJECT LIFETIME
Generally speaking, this term covers how any object is created and deallocated. In DI context, this term covers the lifetime of DEPENDENCIES. See chapter 8.

OPEN/CLOSED PRINCIPLE
This principle states that classes should be open for extensibility, but closed for modification. The *O* in SOLID. See also SOLID.

PER GRAPH LIFESTYLE
A DEPENDENCY lifecycle scope where we reuse a single instance across several different consumers inside the same object graph, but use separate instances in different object graphs. See chapter 8.

POOLED LIFESTYLE
A DEPENDENCY lifecycle scope where we reuse a pool of prepared instances. See chapter 8.

POOR MAN'S DI
DI without the use of a DI CONTAINER. See part 3.

PROPERTY INJECTION
A DI pattern where DEPENDENCIES are injected into the consumer via writable properties. See chapter 4.

REGISTER RESOLVE RELEASE
A pattern that describes how a DI CONTAINER should be used. See chapter 3.

SEAM
A place in application code where ABSTRACTIONS are used to separate modules. See chapter 1.

SERVICE LOCATOR
A DI anti-pattern. See chapter 5.

SINGLE RESPONSIBILITY PRINCIPLE
This principle states that a class should only have a single responsibility. The S in SOLID. See also SOLID.

SINGLETON LIFESTYLE
A DEPENDENCY lifecycle scope where a single instance is reused for all consumers. See chapter 8.

SOLID
An acronym which stands for five fundamental design principles: SINGLE RESPONSIBILITY PRINCIPLE, OPEN/CLOSED PRINCIPLE, LISKOV SUBSTITUTION PRINCIPLE, Interface Segregation Principle, and Dependency Inversion Principle. See chapter 9.

STABLE DEPENDENCY
A DEPENDENCY that can be referenced without any detrimental effects. The opposite of a VOLATILE DEPENDENCY. See chapter 1.

TESTABILITY
The degree to which an application is susceptible to automated unit tests. See chapter 1.

TRANSIENT LIFESTYLE
A DEPENDENCY lifecycle scope where all consumers get their own instance of a DEPENDENCY. See chapter 8.

VOLATILE DEPENDENCY
A DEPENDENCY that involves side effects that may be undesirable at times. This may include modules that don't yet exist, or that have adverse requirements on its runtime environment. These are the DEPENDENCIES that are addressed by DI. See chapter 1.

WEB REQUEST CONTEXT LIFESTYLE
A DEPENDENCY lifecycle scope where a single instance is reused within a single web request. See chapter 8.

index